THE LIBRARY
OF
BIBLICAL STUDIES

Edited by

Harry M. Orlinsky

JACOB BEN CHAJIM IBN ADONIJAH'S

INTRODUCTION

TO

THE RABBINIC BIBLE,

HEBREW AND ENGLISH;

WITH EXPLANATORY NOTES.

BY

CHRISTIAN D. GINSBURG, LL. D.

Second Edition.

WIPF & STOCK · Eugene, Oregon

Wipf and Stock Publishers
199 W 8th Ave, Suite 3
Eugene, OR 97401

Jacob Ben Chajim Ibn Adonijah's Introduction to the Rabbinic Bible
Hebrew and English with Explanatory Notes
By Ginsburg, Christian D.
ISBN 13: 978-1-60608-443-4
Publication date 01/02/2009
Previously published by KTAV, 1867

TABLE OF CONTENTS

Introduction to The Rabbinic Bible

Preface	XXXVI
Jacob B. Chajim Ibn Adonijah (Life and Works)	1
Introduction (of Jacob B. Chajim Ibn Adonijah)	36
Index I. Passages of Scripture Referred to	85
Index II. Topics and Names	88

Massoreth Ha-Massoreth

Preface	VII
Life of Elias Levita	1
Information for the Reader	85
Preface (of Elias Levita)	86
Introduction I. A Song of Praise, Simple, and of Four Feet	89
Introduction II. The Rhythmical Introduction, According to German Rhyme	92
Introduction III. I Shall Now Turn My Face to the Third Introduction	102

MASSORETH HA-MASSORETH

FIRST PART: 144

    SECTION I. treats on *defective* and *plene* in so far as they relate to the *matres lectiones Vav* after *Cholem* and *Shureck*, and *Jod* after *Chirek* and *Tzere*. 145

    SECTION II. treats on the passages wherein the *Vav* is absent after the *Cholem* in verbs and nouns, and the difference between them. 146

    SECTION III. treats on nouns which are *Milra* and have a *Vav plene* after the *Cholem* on the top, and those which are *Milra* and have not the *Vav*; as well as of all the *Cholems* on the participle *Kal*, which are generally defective, and most of the plurals feminine which have a *Vav* at the end. 149

    SECTION IV. treats on the absent *Vav* of the *Shurek*, and on the *Kibutz* being substituted in its place. 153

    SECTION V. treats on all the words which have a long *Chirek*, i. e., *Chiruk* with a *Jod*, having mostly *Jod*; and on those words which have *Cholem*, being mostly defective of *Vav*. 155

    SECTION VI. treats on the quiescent *Jod* after the *Tzere* and *Segol*, as well as on the quiescent *Jod* after the *Kametz* of the third person. 160

SECTION VII. treats on the *plene* and *defective* of monosyllabic words, being small words. ... 163

SECTION VIII. treats on the Massoretic marks, or words, which have two or three quiescents, some being *plene* and some *defective,* or all being *plene* or all *defective.* ... 166

SECTION IX. treats on words which have a quiescent *Aleph,* either expressed or not, and which are called 'with audible Alephs,' or 'without audible Alephs.' ... 170

SECTION X. treats on words, the final *He* of which is either *plene* or *defective,* and are called *Maphkin He,* consisting of four kinds. ... 173

SECOND PART: ... 180

SECTION I. Concerning *Keri* and *Kethiv,* divided into seven classes. 180

SECTION II. Concerning *Kametz* and *Pattach.* ... 195

SECTION III. Concerning *Dagesh, Raphe, Mapik,* and *Sheva.* ... 197

SECTION IV. Concerning *Milel, Milra,* and *Pesakim.* ... 204

SECTION V. Concerning *Registers, Groups, Resemblances,* and *Parallels.* ... 210

SECTION VI. Concerning *Junctions, Severances,* and *Identical.* ... 212

SECTION VII. Concerning *the Presence* or *Absence of Prefixes* or *Serviles.* ... 219

SECTION VIII. Concerning *Conjectural Readings, Misleadings,* and *Exchanges.* ... 225

SECTION IX. Concerning *Letters, Words, Expressions, Short Letters, Accents, Certainties,* and *Transpositions.* ... 228

SECTION X. Concerning *Scripture, Book, Form, Connection,* and *Verse.* ... 234

THIRD PART; OR, THE BROKEN TABLES ... 244

Now Before I Finish to Speak, I Shall Compose A New Song ... 267

That You May Know How Many Times Each Letter Occurs in the Bible, Read all the Words in this Poem. ... 269

Index I. Massoretically Annotated Passages of Scripture Referred to ... 279

Index II. Massoretic Lists Quoted Entire ... 298

Index III. Massoretic Terms and Abbreviations Explained ... 302

Index IV. Massoretic Lists Quoted in this Book, Which Are Also Found in Ochla Ve-Ochla ... 303

Index V. Topics and Names ... 304

PREFACE.

SINCE the publication of the first edition of Jacob b. Chajim Ibn Adonijah's Introduction to the Rabbinic Bible, with an English Translation, I have spent two years of almost uninterrupted study in Massoretic lore. When, therefore, called upon to issue a second edition, I determined to embody in it as much of the results of my researches as was required to elucidate the text and the translation.

The principal alterations in this edition are as follow: i. The present text is a reprint of the *editio princeps* (Venice, 1525), which I did not possess at first — carefully collated with the editions of 1546–48, 1568, 1617–19, 1619, and 1724–27. ii. The text has been carefully punctuated throughout. iii. The translation has been thoroughly revised and improved. iv. The Hebrew and the English are printed in parallel columns, so that the book may now be used as a help by those who are desirous to study Rabbinic Hebrew. v. The Annotations have been augmented from forty-two to upwards of a hundred. And vi. A life of Jacob b. Chajim has been added, with an account of the Massorah, and a description of a newly discovered, and very important, MS. of this ancient critico-exegetical apparatus.

If the Christian literary and scientific public should be inclined to manifest that interest in the criticism of the sacred text of the Old Testament which scholars have always evinced in securing correct texts of profane classics, I shall deem it a privilege to devote some years of my life to the publication and annotation of this newly discovered MS.

For the elaborate Indices, I am to a great extent indebted to a friend, whose name I am not at liberty to mention.

BROOKLEA, AIGBURTH ROAD,
  LIVERPOOL, *October*, 1867.

JACOB B. CHAJIM IBN ADONIJAH.

VERY little is known of the life of JACOB BEN CHAJIM IBN ADONIJAH, who rescued the Massorah from perdition, and for the first time collated, compiled, and gave to the world in a printed form the grand critico-exegetical apparatus, bequeathed to us by the Jews of olden times. Even the date and the place of his birth are matters of conjecture, and can only be approximately guessed from the autobiographical fragments scattered through his writings.

In his celebrated Introduction to the Rabbinic Bible, which we publish with an English translation, he tells us that he was a resident of Tunis; and it is concluded, from this remark, that this ancient city was his native place. Hence he is also called *Tunisi*. Indeed Fürst, who, in his work on Hebrew Bibliography, treats on our author under the name *Jacob b. Chajim*, has also a second notice of him under *Tunisi*.[1] It is, however, to be remarked, that Jacob b. Chajim does not call Tunis his native place, but simply says that he resided in it and prosecuted his studies therein.[2] Nor must we omit to state that he calls himself Jacob Ibn *Adonijah*, and that this, or simply *Ibn Adonijah*, is the surname by which he is quoted in the writings of his learned contemporaries.[3] But though *Ibn Adonijah* is the more correct appellation, we shall not entirely discard the name Jacob b. Chajim, because he is better known by it in modern days.

From the fact that Jacob b. Chajim carried through the press of the celebrated Daniel Bomberg, at Venice, the complete editions of the Babylonian and Jerusalem Talmuds, in 1520–1523, it may reasonably

---

[1] Comp. *Bibliotheca Judaica*, vol. ii., p. 17, with vol iii., p. 451.

[2] שלו הייתי בביתי ורעין בהיכלי שוקד על למודי בטונים המדינה אשר קרוב לקצה גבול קרטגינא הקדומה, *vide infra*, p. 88.

[3] Thus in this Introduction (*vide infra*, p. 36), and in the *Treatise on the Points and Accents* which is printed in the upper and lower margins of the *Massorah finalis*, he calls himself *Jacob b. Chajim b. Isaac Ibn Adonijah* (יעקב בן חיים בן יצדק ן' אדוניהו). Levita, in the poem at the end of the Bible, calls him *Jacob [Ibn] Adonijah* (יעקב אדוניה); whilst De Rossi (1513–1577), simply calls him *Ibn Adonijah* (ן' אדוניהו). Comp. *Meor Enajim*, part iii., cap. lix., p. 471, ed. Cassel, Berlin, 1867.

B

be concluded that he was then at least fifty years of age, and that he was born about 1470. Whether his ancestors were among the first and second masses of emigrants from Spain, who successively fled from that accursed country, to escape the fiery persecution consequent upon the successive inflammatory preachings of the fanatical priests, Fernando Martinez (March 15—August 1391), and Vincente Ferrer (1412–1414), and settled down in the North of Africa by thousands; or whether they were among the three hundred thousand who were expelled from Spain in 1492, is difficult to decide. According to the former view, Ibn Adonijah, though of Spanish descent, was born at Tunis, whilst according to the latter, he emigrated with his parents into this city when about twenty-two years of age.

Among those whom the cruel edict of Ferdinand and Isabella drove from their peaceful homes, and who sought an asylum at Tunis, were Abraham Saccutto, the celebrated astronomer and historian, and Moses b. Isaac Alashkar, the famous Kabbalist and philosopher. These, together with other distinguished literati, established schools at Tunis, and taught hundreds of students the different branches of Biblical and Talmudic literature. It was among these eminent men, and in their schools, that Jacob b. Chajim prosecuted his Hebrew studies, and acquired his extraordinary knowledge of the Massorah, thus preparing himself for the great work which Providence had in store for him elsewhere.

He was, however, not permitted to continue the enjoyment of his quiet home and peaceful studies under the hospitable protection of the Crescent. The bloody persecutors under the Cross, not satisfied with having deprived the whole Jewish population of Spain of all that is precious to men on earth, carried fire and sword, in the name of Christ, among the Jews who had obtained an asylum in Mohamedan countries, and who were diligently employed in the revival of Biblical literature. This time, however, the crusade was not originally organised against the Jews, but against the Moors, since it was believed to be base ingratitude to the goodness of Providence, which had delivered these infidels into the hands of the Church, to allow them any longer to usurp the fair inheritance of the Christians.

Hence no less a person than Cardinal Ximenes, the distinguished Archbishop of Toledo, resorted to Granada, in 1449, to convert the stiff-necked race of Mohamed; seeing that the rational and benevolent measures adopted by Fray Fernando de Talavera, the Archbishop of that province,—who at an advanced age studied Arabic, and caused a vocabulary, grammar, and catechism to be compiled, and a version of the liturgy to be made in the same tongue,—had produced few proselytes. He first employed arguments and presents; if these failed to convince the Mussulman of the error of his ways, imprisonment, with fetters, and a few days' fasting, soon humbled the unbeliever; so much so, that the devout Ferreras was constrained to exclaim, "Thus did Providence avail itself of the darkness of the dungeon to pour on the benighted minds of the infidel the light of the true faith."[4]

Effectually to extirpate heresy, and to preclude the possibility of the converts returning to their former errors, Cardinal Ximenes caused all procurable Arabic manuscripts to be piled together and burned, in one of the great squares of the city, so as to exterminate the very characters in which the teachings of the infidels were recorded. This outrageous burning of most valuable MSS., relating to all branches of science and literature, was effected by the learned Prelate at the very time that he was spending a princely fortune in the publication of the stupendous Complutensian Polyglott, and in the erection and endowment of the university of Alcalá, which was the most learned in Spain. From the thousands of MSS. destined for the conflagration, Ximenes indeed reserved three hundred, relating to medical science, for his university.

As to the Jews, their doom was sealed. In ordinary warfare it mattered very little to them whether the Christians vanquished the infidels, or the infidels the Christians, since the tribute levied by the conqueror upon the conquered was obtained by stripping the Israelites. In the present instance, however, they saw that those who won the day, and forced their religion by means of the sword upon the vanquished, were the very people from whom they themselves had suffered in an unparalleled degree; and that the victors were simply re-enacting the same deeds abroad which they perpetrated at home, upon those who were out of the pale of the Church. They expected again to be dragged from their peaceful homes in the name of Christ, as soon as the Spaniards had a respite from the Mussulman infidels. Hence when they heard that Ximenes, flushed with success at Granada, had instigated Ferdinand, immediately after the death of Isabella, to organise an expedition against the neighbouring Moslems of Africa, and that Mozarquivir, an important port on the Barbary

[4] Prescott, *History of the reign of Ferdinand and Isabella*, part ii., cap. 6.

coast, nearly opposite Carthagena, had actually been captured (Sep. 13, 1505), consternation spread among the numerous Jewish communities in the cities of North Africa.

The consternation became still greater when they heard that Ximenes, mounted upon a mule, had triumphantly entered Oran (May 17, 1509), preceded by a Franciscan friar, and followed by a cavalcade of brethren of the same monastic order, bearing aloft the massive silver cross, the archiepiscopal standard of Toledo, and banners emblazoned with the Primate's arms on one side, and the Cross on the other. All their fears were more than realised when, after the return of Ximenes to Spain, Pedro Navarro, the general of the army, had vanquished Bugia (Jan. 31, 1510), when Tunis had to capitulate, and when they saw the banner of the Cross floating triumphant from the walls of almost every Moslem city on the Mediterranean. It was then that Jacob b. Chajim, Saccutto, and a host of other eminent Jewish scholars were despoiled of their possessions, banished from their homes and families, interrupted in their most important works in the cause of Biblical literature, and driven to wander in exile.

For more than seven years (1510–1517) Ibn Adonijah roamed about homeless in the different towns of Italy, where at that time Hebrew literature was greatly cultivated and patronised by the highest of the land; and where popes and cardinals, princes and statesmen, warriors and recluses of all kinds were in search of Jewish teachers, in order to be instructed in the mysteries of the Kabbalah. Whether it was owing to his conscientious scruples, which would not allow him to initiate Gentiles into this esoteric doctrine, or to his not having been so fortunate in tuition as his contemporary, Elias Levita, he had at first to endure great privations during his sojourn in Rome and Florence. He at last went to Venice, where the celebrated Daniel Bomberg, of Antwerp, had at that very time established his famous Hebrew press (1516), and through the exertions of R. Chajim Alton, whom he honourably mentions in the Introduction, he at once became connected with the printing office.

The connection of so profound and assiduous a scholar with so cultivated and spirited a publisher proved one of the greatest benefits to Biblical literature, at the time of the Church's greatest need. For whilst the followers of the Prince of Peace were arrayed against each other in deadly conflict, to decide by the sword whether the Bible alone, or the infallible vicar of Christ on earth, is to be appealed to for the rule of faith and practice, Jacob Ibn Adonijah was studiously engaged in the collation of Biblical MSS., in compiling the grand critico-exegetical apparatus of the Old Testament, bequeathed to us by the Jews of olden times, and in editing it, together with the Hebrew Scriptures, the ancient Chaldee paraphrases, and valuable Hebrew commentaries, which has contributed more to the advancement of Biblical knowledge than all the bitter controversies of Catholics and Protestants.

Before, however, we describe this gigantic Rabbinic Bible which has immortalised his name, we have to mention other important works edited by him. It has already been remarked, that Ibn Adonijah must have taken up his abode at Venice soon after Bomberg established in it his celebrated printing office (1516). For we find that the *editio princeps* of the entire Babylonian Talmud, published by Bomberg in 1520–1523, was partly edited by Jacob b. Chajim; and as the Talmud consists of twelve volumes folio, the preparations for its printing, and the printing itself, must have commenced a considerable time before 1520, when a portion of it was published. Hence his work and connection with Bomberg must have begun about 1517 or 1518. This conclusion is confirmed by the fact that, simultaneously with the appearance of the Babylonian Talmud, Ibn Adonijah also worked at the *editio princeps* of the Jerusalem Talmud, which he carried through the press in 1522–23, as well as at the *editio princeps* of R. Nathan's Hebrew Concordance, which appeared in 1523, and over which he must have spent a considerable time.

His assiduity was truly marvellous. He not only carried through the press in three years the first editions of these gigantic works, consisting of fourteen volumes folio, closely printed, both in square Hebrew characters and Rabbinic Hebrew, and replete with references, the very sight of which would astound any one who is not acquainted with them; but, within twelve months after the appearance of the Concordance, he edited, conjointly with David de Pizzightone, the stupendous legal and ritual code of Maimonides, entitled, *Mishne Thora* (משנה תורה) = *Deuteronomy, Second Law*, or *Jad Ha-Chezaka*, (יד החזקה) = *The Mighty Hand*, in allusion to Deut. xxxiv. 12; and because the work consists of fourteen books (יד = 14). To this code, which appeared in 1524, in two volumes folio, Ibn Adonijah wrote an Introduction.

It is perfectly amazing, to find that the editing of these works, which would of itself more than occupy the whole time of ordinary mortals in the present day, was simply the recreation of Jacob b. Chajim; and that the real strength of his intellect, and the vast stores of his learning, were employed at that very time in collecting and collating MSS. of the Massorah, and in preparing for the press the Rabbinic Bible, which is still a precious monument to his vast erudition and almost unparalleled industry, and which was the most powerful auxiliary to the then commencing Reformation. This Rabbinic Bible, which was published in 1524–25, consists of four volumes, folio, as follows :—

I. *The first volume*, embracing the Pentateuch (תורה), begins — i. With the elaborate Introduction of Jacob b. Chajim, which we now give for the first time with an English translation;[5] ii. An Index to the sections of the entire Old Testament according to the Massorah; and iii. Ibn Ezra's Preface to the Pentateuch. Then follow the five Books of Moses in Hebrew, with the so-called Chaldee Paraphrases of Onkelos and Jonathan ben Uzziel, and the Commentaries of Rashi and Ibn Ezra, which are given all round the margin; The Massorah parva, which is in the centre between the Hebrew text and the Chaldee paraphrase; and such a portion of the Massorah magna as the space between the end of the text and the beginning of the commentaries on each page would admit; for which reason this portion obtained the name of *Massorah marginalis*.

II. *The second volume*, comprising the Earlier Prophets (נביאים ראשונים), *i. e.*, Joshua, Judges, 1 and 2 Samuel, and 1 and 2 Kings, has the Hebrew text, the Chaldee paraphrases of Jonathan b. Uzziel, the Commentaries of Rashi, David Kimchi, and Levi ben Gershon, the Massorah parva, and that portion of the Massorah magna which constitutes the *Massorah marginalis*.

III. *The third volume*, comprising the Later Prophets (נביאים אחרונים), *i. e.*, Isaiah, Jeremiah, Ezekiel, and the Twelve Minor Prophets, has the Hebrew text, the so-called Chaldee paraphrase of Jonathan ben Uzziel, the Commentaries of Rashi, which extend over all the books in the volume of Ibn Ezra on Isaiah

---

[5] Fürst's assertion (*Bibliotheca Judaica*, iii. 454), that this introduction had been translated into English, and published by Kennicott in his work entitled *The state of the printed Hebrew Text of the Old Testament*, Oxford, 1758, is incorrect. Kennicott simply published an abridged and incorrect *Latin* version, from a MS. which he found in the Bodleian Library.

and the Minor Prophets, the Massorah parva, and the Massorah marginalis.

IV. *The fourth volume*, comprising the Hagiographa (כתובים), *i.e.*, the Psalms, Proverbs, Job, Canticles, Ruth, Lamentations, Ecclesiastes, Esther, Daniel, Ezra, Nehemiah, and Chronicles, has the Hebrew text; the so-called Chaldee paraphrases of Joseph the Blind; the Commentaries of Rashi, which only embrace the Psalms, the Five Megilloth (*i. e.*, Canticles, Ruth, Lamentations, Ecclesiastes, and Esther), Ezra, Nehemiah, and Chronicles; the Commentaries of Ibn Ezra, which only embrace the Psalms, Job, the Five Megilloth, and Daniel; the Commentaries of David Kimchi on the Psalms and Chronicles; the Commentaries of Moses Kimchi on Proverbs, Ezra, and Nehemiah;[6] the Commentaries of Levi ben Gershon on Proverbs and Job; the so-called Commentary of Saadia on Daniel; the Massorah parva, the Massorah marginalis, and the (תרגום שני) Second Targum on Esther. Appended to this volume are — i. The Massorah, for which space could not be found in the margin of the text in alphabetical order, and which is therefore called the Massorah finalis, with Jacob ben Chajim's directions. ii. A Treatise on the Points and Accents of the Hebrew Scriptures, embodying the work (דרכי הניקור והנגינות or כללי הניקוד) of Moses the Punctuator (ר׳ משה הנקדן). iii. The variations between the Western and Eastern Codices, or between the Jerusalem and Babylonian MSS., called חלופין שבין מערבאי ומדנחאי or חלוף המקרא שבין בני ארץ ישראל ובין בני בבל. And iv. The variations between Ben Asher and Ben Naphtali, called חלופי התורה שבין בני אשר ובין בני נפתלי.

It is perfectly impossible for any one, but those students who have seen the MSS. of the Hebrew Bible, with the Massorah round the margin, in a most fantastic manner, who have encountered the difficulties in deciphering the hieroglyphic signs, the conceited abbreviations, the strange forms and ornaments into which the writing of the Massorah is twisted, the confusion of the Massoretic notes, &c.; and who have grappled with the blunders which are to be found in almost every

---

[6] The Commentaries on Proverbs, Ezra, and Nehemiah are ascribed, in all the editions of the Rabbinic Bible, to Ibn Ezra. That this, however, is incorrect, and that they belong to Moses Kimchi, is now established beyond the shadow of a doubt. Comp. Reifmann in *Literaturblatt des Orients*, vol. ii., pp. 750, 751; *Zion*, vol. i., p. 76; vol. ii., pp. 113-117, 129-133, 155-157, 171-174, 185-188: Frankfort-on-the-Maine, 1841, 1842. Geiger, *Ozar Nechmad*, vol. ii., p. 17, &c.; Vienna, 1857; Kitto's *Cyclopædia of Biblical Literature*, *s. v.* KIMCHI, MOSES.

sentence, to form an adequate conception of the extraordinary labour and learning which Jacob Ibn Adonijah must have bestowed, in bringing such beautiful order out of such a chaos. His modesty and humility, in speaking of the toil, are becoming his vast erudition.

"Behold," he says, "I have exerted all my might and strength to collate and arrange the Massorah, with all the possible improvements, in order that it may remain pure and bright, and shew its splendour to the nations and princes; for, indeed, it is beautiful to look at. This was a labour of love, for the benefit of our brethren, the children of Israel, and for the glory of our holy and perfect law; as well as to fulfil, as far as possible, the desire of Don Daniel Bomberg, whose expenses in this matter far exceeded my labours. And as regards the Commentaries, I have exerted my powers to the utmost degree to correct in them all the mistakes as far as possible; and whatsoever my humble endeavours could accomplish was done for the glory of the Lord, and for the benefit of our people. I would not be deterred by the enormous labour, for which cause I did not suffer my eyelids to be closed long, either in the winter or summer, and did not mind rising in the cold of the night, as my aim and desire were to see this holy work finished. Now praised be the Creator, who granted me the privilege to begin and to finish this work." [6*] Such is the touching account which Jacob b. Chajim gives us of his labour of love.

Not less striking is the gratitude which he expresses to Bomberg, for having so cheerfully and liberally embarked upon so expensive a work. "When I explained to Bomberg," he tells us, "the advantage of the Massorah, he did all in his power to send into all the countries in order to search out what may be found of the Massorah; and, praised be the Lord, we obtained as many of the Massoretic books as could possibly be got. He was not backward, and his hand was not closed, nor did he draw back his right hand from producing gold out of his purse, to defray the expenses of the books, and of the messengers who were engaged to make search for them in the most remote corners, and in every place where they might possibly be found." [7*]

With all our abuse of the Roman Catholics for withholding the Bible from the people, and with all our boasted love for the Scriptures, neither will the Bible Society with its annual income of £80,000, nor will any publisher in this Protestant country of ours, undertake a revised edition of that stupendous work which was published in a

[6*] *Vide infra*, p. 83, &c.   [7*] *Vide infra*, p. 77, &c.

Roman Catholic country, when Luther began to make his voice heard in defence of the word of God. Thus it is, that we in the present day are still left to the labours of Jacob b. Chajim, though the results of modern researches, and the discovery of valuable MSS., would enable us to issue a new edition of the critical apparatus of the Old Testament, with important corrections and additions, and in a form more easily accessible to Biblical students.

Bomberg, who took the liveliest interest and the greatest pride in this magnificent edition of the Bible, got Elias Levita, whose fame as a Hebraist was at that time spread not only all over Italy where he resided, but over Germany, both among the most distinguished dignitaries in the Catholic Church and the great leaders of the Reformation, to write an epilogue to the work of his ambition. In this poem, Levita celebrates the praises of the munificent publisher, "who though uncircumcised in the flesh [*i. e.*, a gentile], is circumcised in heart," of "the learned Jacob Ibn Adonijah," who carried it through the press, and of the unparalleled work itself.[7] Levita was then residing at Rome, in the house of his friend and patron, Cardinal Egidio de Viterbo, where he was diligently engaged in printing his works on the grammar and structure of the Hebrew language, teaching the Roman Catholic and Protestant combatants the original of the Old Testament, and enjoying the literary society of popes, cardinals, princes, ambassadors, and warriors, who were bewitched by the mysteries of the Kabbalah, and little thinking of the misfortunes which were soon to befall him.

Within two years of his writing the epilogue to Jacob Ibn Adonijah's Rabbinic Bible, and whilst engaged on an Aramaic grammar, the Imperialists under Charles V. sacked Rome (May 6, 1527), and in the general work of spoliation and destruction, Levita lost all his property and the greater part of his MSS. In a most destitute and deplorable condition, he left the Eternal city, and betook himself to Venice in the same year (1527); and Bomberg, at whose request he had written the epilogue, at once engaged him as joint corrector of the press and as editor. Thus the two learned Hebraists, Jacob b. Chajim and Elias Levita, who were the great teachers of Hebrew to the greatest men of Europe, at the commencement and during the development of the Reformation, now became co-workers in the same printing office.

[7] For the different editions of the Bible, and for the alterations which were afterwards made in it, see Kitto's *Cyclopædia of Biblical Literature*, *s.v.* RABBINIC BIBLES.

It is more than probable that Levita told Jacob Ibn Adonijah of the Aramaic work on which he was engaged, the MS. of which he lost in the sacking of Rome, and that this exercised some influence on the latter in the choice of his next literary undertaking. For we find Jacob Ibn Adonijah, immediately after Levita's arrival, writing " *A Treatise on the Targum*" (מאמר על התרגום). It is a matter of dispute whether this Treatise first appeared in Bomberg's edition of the Pentateuch and the Five Megilloth, published in 1527, or in that published in 1543–44, after Jacob Ibn Adonijah's death.[8] Not possessing the editions in question, I cannot state which opinion is the correct one.

Although no one who is at all acquainted with his assiduity, and who knows what an uncontrollable and inextinguishable passion to continue therein is kindled in the hearts of those who have embarked upon authorship and found their works acceptable, will for a moment doubt that Jacob Ibn Adonijah ever would relinquish his literary pursuits, as long as he possessed his faculties and the use of his limbs; yet, with the exception of one solitary and incidental reference to his work, presently to be mentioned, we henceforth hear nothing more about his productions. Fürst indeed enumerates no less than fifteen important Midrashim and Commentaries on the Bible, which Bomberg published in 1543–47, and which he says may have been prepared for the press by our author.[9] But this is mere conjecture. I myself possess the very editions of some of the works in question, and though Cornelius Adelkind and Elias Levita are distinctly stated as having

---

[8] Comp. the article *Jüdische Typographie*, by Steinschneider and David Cassel, in Ersch and Gruber's *Allgemeine Encyklopädie*, section II., vol. xxviii., p. 44, note 32, and Professor Luzzatto's Letter (reprinted below, p. 11), and with Fürst, *Bibliotheca Judaica*, vol. iii., p. 451.

[9] The works referred to are as follows:— *Midrash Rabboth* (מדרש רבות), Venice, 1545, fol.; *Mechilta* (מכלתא), *ibid*. 1545, fol.; *Siphra* (ספרא), *ibid*. 1545, fol.; *Siphre* (ספרי), *ibid*. 1545, fol.; *Midrash Tanchuma* (מדרש תנחומא), *ibid*. 1545, fol.; *Midrash Tilim* (מדרש תלים), *ibid*. 1546, fol.; *Pisikta Sutratha* (פסקתא וזוטרתא), *ibid*. 1546, fol.; Elias Mishrachi's *Supra Commentary* on Rashi's Comment. on the Pentateuch, called *Sepher Ha-Mizrache* (ספר מזרחי), *ibid*. 1545, fol.; Arama's Commentary on the Pentateuch, called *Akedath*, (עקדה), *ibid*. 1547, fol.; Ralbag's *Commentary on the Pentateuch* (רל"בג על התורה), *ibid*. 1547, fol.; Abraham Sabba's *Kabbalistic Commentary on the Pentateuch*, entitled *Tzeror Ha-Mor* (צרור המור), *ibid*. 1546, fol.; Nachmanides' *Commentary on the Pentateuch* (על רמ"בן התורה), *ibid*. 1548, fol.; Ibn Shemtob's *Homiletical Commentarg on the Pentateuch* (דרשות התורה לבוטמ"ב), *ibid*. 1547, fol.; Jacob Ibn Chibib's *Collection of Hagodas*, called *En Jacob* (עי עקב), *ibid*. 1546, fol.; R. Solomon b. Abraham b. Aderethe's *Theological Answers to Queries* (ש"ות הרש"בא), *ibid*. 1545-6, fol.; R. Moses de Corecy's Homiletical work, entitled, *The Major Book on the Commandments* (סמ"ג), *ibid*. 1547, fol. (Comp. *Bibliotheca Judaica*, vol. iii. p. 452.)

been connected with them, Jacob's name is not even mentioned. This, however, may be owing to the change in Ibn Adonijah's religious sentiments, which, as we shall presently see, is more than probable.

The disappearance of Jacob Ibn Adonijah from the field of active labour in connection with Bomberg, which happened almost simultaneously with the arrival of Levita at Venice, and his appointment as corrector and annotator of the Hebrew works, is most significant, and we believe that it was caused by Ibn Adonijah's relinquishing Judaism.

It is now established beyond the shadow of a doubt, that this eminent Hebraist embraced Christianity about this time. Levita, who had occasion to refer to Adonijah, when writing his exposition of the Massorah (*circa* 1537–38), not only speaks of him as dead, but intimates that he had avowed the Christian faith some considerable time before he departed this life, and hence descends to unworthy vituperations against him. Referring to the Massorah, edited by Ibn Adonijah, in the celebrated Rabbinic Bible, Levita says, "I have not seen anything like it among all the ancient books, for arrangement and correctness, for beauty and excellence, and for good order. The compiler thereof was one of the learned, whose name was formerly, among the Jews, Jacob. Let his soul be bound up in a bag with holes!"[10] This spiteful perversion of a beautiful, charitable, and reverential prayer, which the Jews use when speaking of or writing about any one of their brethren who has departed this life, in allusion to 1 Sam. xxv. 29, justifies us in assuming that Jacob Ibn Adonijah embraced Christianity several years before 1537.

As the statement in question, in Levita's work, was till lately the only reference to Ibn Adonijah's having embraced Christianity towards the end of his life, the fact was generally unknown, and many of the learned Jews doubted whether the passage in Levita really meant to convey the idea. Amongst those who doubted it, was the erudite Frensdorff. He therefore wrote to the late Professor Luzzatto, asking him the meaning of the passage in question, to which he replied as follows:[11] "As to the meaning of Levita's words, which he wrote in

---

[10] אכן המסורת מהארבע ועשרים הנדפסות הנה· לא ראיתי כהנה· בכל ספרי הקדמונים· מסודרים ומתוקנים· ביופי ובהדור· ובטוב הסדור· סדרם אחד מהנבונים· היה שמו לפנים· בישראל נקרא יעקב· תהי נשמתו צרורה בצרור נקוב. Comp. *Massoreth Ha-Massoreth*, p. 94, ed. Ginsburg.

[11] ולענין דברי הבחור שכתב בהקדמתו החרוזית למסורת המסורת "אחד מהנבונים היה שמו לפנים בישראל נקרא יעקב· תהי נשמתו צרורה בצרור נקוב" ששאלת אם אאמין שכוונתו לזכר של יעקב בר חיים ן' אדניהו הנייר דתו—· ודאי כן הוא· והדבר הזה היה סבה שנמנערי מהשיב למהתנך· כי הרבה

the poetical Introduction to the *Massoreth Ha-Massoreth*, 'one of the learned, whose name was formerly, among the Jews, Jacob. Let his soul be bound up in a bag with holes;' and your asking me whether I believe it to imply that R. Jacob b. Chajim Ibn Adonijah changed his religion; it is assuredly so. This was the reason why I delayed replying to your letter, for I was greatly perplexed about this subject; since for a truth, from the import of R. Elias Levita's words in question, it is beyond doubt that R. Jacob changed his religion, and I was unwilling to publish this strange report about such a learned man till I found another witness. Now last year, one of my friends, the erudite R. Moses Soave, of Venice, found an edition of the Mishna, with the Commentaries of Maimonides and Shimshon b. Abraham, printed at Venice (Giustiniani), 1546; at the end of Tractate *Taharoth* was written as follows, which I also saw myself with my own eyes: 'These are the words of the first editor, whose name was formerly, among the Jews, Jacob b. Chajim, and who revised the Tractate *Taharoth*, with the Commentary of R. Shimshon, of blessed memory. Since, however, the sage said, 'Receive the truth by whomsoever it is propounded,' we deemed it proper to print his remarks here.' Now is peradventure the lie to be given also to this testimony, or is the fact to be established from this witness?

"Before this, however, happened, I rejoiced as one that findeth great spoil, for I bought a copy of the Pentateuch, with the Targum, printed by Bomberg in 1543-44, at the end of which are seven pages on the Targum, beginning—'Thus saith Jacob b. Chajim b. Isaac Ibn Adonijah,' &c.; as I thought from this it is evident that in the years 1543-44 he was alive, and was still a Jew; and how then

הייתי נבוך בענין הזה. כי אמנם משמעות דברי ר' אליה הנ"ל היא בלא ספק כי ר' יעקב המיר דתו ולא הייתי רוצה להוציא לעז על חכם כמוהו בטרם אשכיע עד שני. ואולם בשנה שעברה מצא אחד מיודידי המשכיל ר' משה סואבי מעיר ויניציאה משניות עם פירוש הר"מ והר"ש דפוס ויניציאה (יוסטיניאני) שנת ש"ו. ובסוף סדר טהרות כתוב כך (וכן ראיתי גם אני בעיני) "אלה הם דברי המגיה הראשון שהיה שמו לפנים בישראל יעקב בר חיים שהגיה סדר טהרות עם פירוש רבינו שמשון ז"ל. ולפי שאמר החכם קבל האמת ממי שאמרו ראינו להדפיס דבריו פה" — היתכן להכזיב גם העדות הזאת. או להוציא ממשמעות בריה:

ואני קודם לכן ששתי כמוצא שלל רב כי קניתי חומש עם תרגום דפוס בומבירג שנת ש"ג וש"ד ובסופו ז' דפים על התרגום. תחלתם "אמר יעקב בן חיים בן יצחק ן' אדניהו יש"י עמד"ן "ואמרתי הרי מבואר כי בשנת ש"ג וש"ד היה חי והיה יהודי' ואיך בשנת רצ"ח (כשנדפס ס' מסרת המסרת) כבר היתה נשמתו צרורה? — אבל כשראיתי המשניות הנ"ל. אמרתי מה אדבר? ובמה אצידקהו? הלא על פי שנים עדים יומת המת ואז אמרת: אין ספק כי ן' אדניהו כתב מאמרו על התרגום כשהיה יהודי. ואולי כבר נדפס בדייו בחומש אחר שלא בא עדיין לידי. ואולי ג"כ לא נדפס בחייו. אבל נשאר ביד דניאל בומבירג קצת שנים. עד שהדפיס חומש עם תרגום ואז הרפיס המאמר ההוא בסופו. This letter is published in the Hebrew Essays and Reviews, entitled *Ozar Nechanad*, vol iii., p. 112, Vienna, 1860.

could his soul long ago be bound up (*i. e.* have departed) in the year 1538, when the *Massoreth Ha-Massoreth* was printed? But when I saw the edition of the Mishna in question, I thought, what am I now to say? and how am I to reconcile it? Surely upon the testimony of two witnesses the man must be executed. Whereupon I concluded that Ibn Adonijah wrote his Treatise on the Targum when still a Jew, and that it had either been already printed when he was alive, in an edition of the Pentateuch which I have not yet seen, or it was not printed in his life-time, but remained for some years in the possession of Daniel Bomberg, till he printed an edition of the Pentateuch, with the Targum, when he also printed at the end the Treatise in question."

This fact may perhaps give us the clue to Jacob Ibn Adonijah's sudden disappearance from the field of labour in connection with Bomberg's printing office. The apology of the second editor of the edition of the Mishna in question, for printing, in a work intended for the Jews, opinions propounded by one who had ceased to be a member of the community, seems to imply several things which have hitherto been unknown in connection with the life of Ibn Adonijah. We see from it—i. That he still continued to work for Bomberg after he embraced Christianity. For had Ibn Adonijah revised the Tractate of Mishna in question when he was still a Jew, the future editor would not have found it necessary to apologise for reprinting Ibn Adonijah's opinions; just as the future editors of the Rabbinic Bible did not require to explain why they reprinted his compilation of the Massorah, and the Introduction to the Rabbinic Bible, which he wrote when still a Jew. ii. The fact that Bomberg's works were for the Jews, and that an apology was needed to be made to them for printing the corrections and annotations made by a converted Jew, would of itself show the inexpediency of retaining a Jewish Christian on such works. To conciliate, therefore, the prejudice of his Jewish customers, Bomberg was undoubtedly obliged to part with his old friend Jacob Ibn Adonijah. How bitter this prejudice was against those who embraced Christianity, may be seen from the vituperations uttered against Ibn Adonijah, even by so enlightened a man as Elias Levita. If our conclusions are correct, they will also supply us with the clue to the sudden and mysterious disappearance of Ibn Adonijah's name from nearly all the books printed by Bomberg since the year 1527. However much Ibn Adonijah may have done to them by way of correction and annotation, it was the best trade policy to suppress the name of the converted Jew. Hence Fürst may be perfectly correct in his supposition that Jacob b. Chajim had a share in preparing for the press the fifteen important works already alluded to, though the learned bibliographer neither accounts for, nor mentions, the fact that Ibn Adonijah's name is suppressed.

The precise year in which Ibn Adonijah died has not as yet been ascertained, though it is perfectly certain, from the remarks of Levita already alluded to, that he departed this life before 1538. That the Jews did not record anything connected with his life and death is no matter of surprise, when we remember that he had left their community, and that, in their unparalleled sufferings, the converted Israelites of those days, in their blind zeal, were considerable abettors. But that the Christian writers of those days, both Catholics and Protestants, who thought it worth their while to chronicle and perpetuate events which we cannot read now without blushing, should have passed over in total silence the death of one who had done so much for Biblical literature, and suffered the loss of all things to join the ranks of the followers of Christ, will remain an indelible blot on the gratitude of Christian historians. As far as Ibn Adonijah himself is concerned, he has left a monument behind him in his contributions to Biblical literature, which will last as long as the Bible is studied in the original; and the critical student of the Scriptures can never examine the Massorah, nor look at the gigantic Rabbinic Bible, without feelings of reverence for, and gratitude to, Jacob b. Chajim Ibn Adonijah, who, being dead, yet speaketh.

It now remains that we should advert to the materials from which Ibn Adonijah compiled the Massorah, and to the merits of his compilation. Before, however, this is done, it is necessary to give the reader some idea of the origin, development, import, and transmission of the Massorah. The account must necessarily be very succinct.

Owing to the extreme sacredness with which the letter of the text was regarded, and believing that the multifarious legal enactments which were called forth by the ever-shifting circumstances of the commonwealth, the sacred legends which developed themselves in the course of time, and all the ecclesiastical and civil regulations, to which an emergency may at any time give rise, are indicated in the Bible by a superfluous letter, or redundant word, or the repetition of a phrase, or the peculiarity of a construction, the greatest care has been taken, since the beginning of the Christian era, to mark every peculiarity and phenomenon in the spelling and construction of the words in the Scriptures, so that " one jot or one tittle shall in no wise pass from the law."

The duty of noting these peculiarities devolved more especially upon the Scribes, or copyists, who multiplied the Codices of the Bible.[12] As the collation of MSS. for the purpose of producing correct copies was deemed unsafe, inasmuch as the multiplication always gives rise to a multitude of errors ; and as, moreover, the process of collation is not only tedious, but demands a number of MSS. belonging to different families, and various ages, the Scribes found it more practicable to count the number of times a word was spelled in an exceptional way, or a peculiar phrase was used, or any anomaly occurred throughout the Bible. The different peculiarities, thus numbered, were rubricated, and formed into separate registers and lists. These were at first committed to memory by the professional Scribes and doctors of the law, and transmitted orally in the schools; but afterwards, like all other traditions, were written down, and now constitute the *Massorah* (מסורה), = *tradition*.[13]

Like the science of grammar and lexicography, the Massoretic researches were at first limited. They were confined to the rubrication of words and phrases to which some legal enactment was attached, or which had some caligraphical and orthographical peculiarity. But as the Massoretic schools extended over a millennium,[14] and as the

---

[12] Hence the remark, לפיכך נקראי הראשונים סופרים עדהיו סופרים כל האותיות שבתורה שדיו אומרים וא'ו דגחון חציין של אותיות של ספר תורה, דרש דרש חציין של תיבות, והתגלח של פסוקים, יכרסמנה חזיר מיער עי"ן דיער חציים של התלים, וחוא רחום יכפר עון חצוי דפסוקים: "therefore are the ancients called Sopherim, because they counted all the letters in Holy Writ. Thus they said that the *Vav*, in גחון [Levit. xi. 42], is the half of all the letters in the Pentateuch; דרש דרש [*ibid.* x. 16] is the middle word; והתגלח [*ibid.* xiii. 33] the middle verse; that *Ain*, in מיער [Ps. lxxx. 14]. is the middle letter in the Psalms; and Ps. lxxvii. 38 the middle verse." *Kiddushin*, 30 *a*.

[13] The expression מסורה, which now denotes all the labours of the Massorites effected during a millennium, is the post-Talmudic form. In the Talmud it is מָסוֹרֶת and originally denoted *the traditional pronunciation* of the unpointed text. Thus it was transmitted authoritatively that שבעים (Levit. xii. 5) is to be read שְׁבָעַיִם, *two weeks*, and not שִׁבְעִים, *seventy days;* and that בחלב (Exod. xxiii. 19) is to be pronounced בְּחֵלֶב, *in the milk*, and not בְּחָלָב, *in the fat*. Comp. Geiger, *Jüdische Zeitschrift*, vol. i., p. 90, &c.; vol. iii., p. 79.

[14] This has already been pointed out by Levita; comp *Massoreth Ha-Massoreth*, p. 137, ed. Ginsburg.

absence of concordances precluded the possibility of discovering at once all the instances in which certain anomalies were to be found, the continued exertions of the Massorites resulted, not only in supplementing and completing the already existing rubrics, but in adding new registers and lists of words, forms, phrases, and combinations, which exhibited the slightest deviation from the ordinary usage. Hence the Massorah, in its present development, embraces almost everything connected with the external appearance of the text. It gives the number of times each letter of the alphabet occurs throughout the Bible. It states how many verses there are in each separate book. It shows which is the middle letter, which the middle word, and which is the middle verse in every book. It registers the majuscular, the minuscular, the inverted, the suspended, and the peculiarly pointed letters, the anomalous forms and phrases, defective and plene, textual and marginal readings, conjectural readings, lexical features, &c.

When the Massorah began to be written down, it assumed a double form. The first form of it is more like an index, simply stating alongside the margin, against the word which exhibits a certain peculiarity, that the word in question is one of such and such a number, possessing the same peculiarity, without giving the other words of the same rubric. This form assumed the name of *Massorah parva* (מסורה קטנה). The second is the more extensive form. It not only gives all the words which possess the same peculiarity in full, but adds a few words, by which each expression is preceded, or followed, so as to enable the student to recognise, from the connection, in what book the anomaly occurs. This form of it obtained the name of *Massorah magna*, and is written above and below the text.

As, however, the Massorah constantly increased in bulk in the course of time, extending to every phenomenon of the text, and as the large dimensions it assumed precluded the possibility of its being written entirely above and below the margin of the page to which it referred, the different lists, both alphabetical and otherwise, had to be arranged according to alphabetical or other order, and chronicled in separate works. These books are either called by the general name *Massoretic Treatises* (ספרי המסרה), or *Ochla Ve-Ochla* (אכלה ואכלה). The latter appellation the Massoretic Treatises obtained from the first two examples, אָכְלָה (1 Sam. i. 9), וְאָכְלָה (Gen. xxvii. 19), in the alphabetical list of words occurring twice in the Bible, once without and once with *Vav*, with which the Massorah begins.[15] It must be remarked, however, that in copying the *Ochla Ve-Ochla*, or the Massorah, the scribes or students did not always transcribe the whole of it. Some portions were omitted as being unimportant, or not being wanted by the transcriber; some were transposed by the students to facilitate reference; whilst other portions were added by those who devoted themselves to this kind of study. Hence obtained different redactions, some called by the general name *Massoretic Treatises*, and others by the more specific appellation *Ochla Ve-Ochla*; hence the difficulty of ascertaining the particular redaction meant by the different commentators, lexicographers, and grammarians, who quote the *Ochla Ve-Ochla*; and hence too the impossibility of specifying particularly the various nameless fragments and forms of the Massorah, used for collation in the compilation of this critico-exegetical apparatus, as edited by Ibn Adonijah.

This impossibility of specifying the nameless fragments, which Jacob Ibn Adonijah realised in the compilation of the Massorah, has recently been construed into a deliberate suppression of the materials which he used, and the sources whence he drew his information. Thus Geiger, in showing the importance of the Massorah to Biblical criticism, and deploring its neglect by commentators and lexicographers, remarks,[16] "Acquaintance with the Massorah, and with the numerous MSS. which contain it in its various forms, has for centuries become so rare, that people did not at all know any more whether the Massorah actually existed in former times, in the form of a comprehensive view, or whether it has been made into such a form for the first time by Jacob b. Chajim, at the end of his edition of the Bible; and whether this whole compilation which he made from the isolated Massorahs, both parva and magna, to be found connected immediately with the

---

[15] Levita, who made the *Ochla Ve-Ochla* the basis of his Massoretic researches, plainly declared that it is so called from its beginning words, הנקרא כן בעבור התחלהו; *Massoreth Ha-Massoreth*, p. 131. We cannot, therefore, understand why the learned Dr. Steinschneider should be so anxious to claim the originality of this remark. Comp. Geiger's *Jüdische Zeitschrift*, vol. i., pp. 316, 317, note 31, Breslau, 1862.

[16] Die Bekanntschaft mit ihr, mit den zahlreichen Handschriften, welche sie in ihrer verschiedenen Gestalt enthalten, ist schon seit Jahrhunderten so spärlich geworden, daß man gar nicht mehr wußte, ob denn wirklich früher auch die Maßorah in der Gestalt einer umfassenden Uebersicht existirt habe, oder ob sie so erst von Jakob ben Chajim am Ende der Bibelausgabe geordnet worden, diese ganze Zusammenstellung, die er eben aus den vereinzelten unmittelbar neben dem Texte befindlichen kleinen und großen

text, is exclusively his work. From his words, with which he introduces this work, it does not appear whether he had before him one or more such compilations, nay, on the contrary, it seems as if he claimed for himself this compilation. We can scarcely avoid the suspicion, that the man, whose merit is at all events to be acknowledged as permanent, designedly intended to envelope it in darkness, with the artificial words in which he introduces this work, as well as the grammatical Treatise of Moses Ha-Nakden, in order that it might scarcely be guessed what he had originally before him, and that it should be supposed that he had done far more at it than is actually the case; on the contrary, he would surely have increased his merit if he had told very plainly what sources he used, in what form they were, and how he had worked them up. Nevertheless he omitted to give this information, and the most distinguished literati and collators of MSS. could give no information whether there existed any MS. compilation of the Massorah."

That this accusation is unmerited, may be seen both from Jacob Ibn Adonijah's Introduction, and from the various notes which he made in different parts of the Massorah finalis. Thus in the passage already quoted,[17] he not only tells us that Bomberg despatched messengers to different countries to search for copies of the Massorah, but distinctly declares that they succeeded in obtaining as many codices as could possibly be secured. These Massorahs, he moreover says, embraced both kinds: First, the Massorahs written in the margin of

---

Maßorah's vorgenommen, ausschließlich sein Werk sei. Aus seinen Worten, mit denen er diese Arbeit einleitet, geht nicht hervor, ob er eine oder gar mehrere solcher Uebersichten vorliegen gehabt habe, ja es scheint im Gegentheile, als nehme er diese Zusammenstellung für sich allein in Anspruch; wir können uns kaum des Verdachtes erwehren, daß der Mann, dessen Verdienst jedenfalls ein dauernd anzuerkennendes ist, durch die künstlichen Worte, mit denen er dieses Werk, wie das grammatische des Moses Ha-Nakdan, einleitet, absichtlich ein gewisses Halbdunkel darüber verbreiten wollte, so daß man, was ihm ursprünglich vorgelegen, kaum ahnen könne und man auf die Vermuthung kommen solle, er habe weit mehr dabei gethan, als wirklich der Fall ist. Sicher hätte er sein Verdienst im Gegentheile erhöht, wenn er uns recht genau gesagt hätte, welche Quellen er benützt, welche Gestalt dieselben gehabt und wie er sie verarbeitet. Jedoch er unterließ diese Mittheilung, und die bedeutendsten Kenner und Handschriftensammler wußten von der maßorethischen Uebersicht, ob sie handschriftlich vorhanden sei, keine Nachricht zu geben. *Jüdische Zeitschrift für Wissenschaft und Leben*, vol. iii., p. 112, &c. Breslau, 1865.

[17] *Vide supra*, p. 8, &c.

the Bible, thus constituting what is called the Massorah parva and the Massorah marginals; and second, separate Massoretic Treatises, or the different redactions of what is called the *Ochla Ve-Ochla.*

Equally explicit and straightforward are his remarks about the nature of these materials, and the manner in which he elaborated them. We cannot do better than give his own description of the condition of the Massorahs, written in the margins of the Bibles. "After mastering their contents," he says, "I found them in the utmost disorder and confusion, so much so, that there is not a sentence to be found without a blunder: that is to say, the quotations from the Massorites are both incorrect and misplaced; since in those codices in which the Massorah is written in the margin, it is not arranged according to the order of the verses contained in the page. Thus, for instance, if a page has five or six verses, the first of which begins with וַיֹּאמֶר, *and he said;* the second with וַיֻּגַּד, *and it was told;* the third with וַיְהִי, *and it is;* the fourth with וַיִּשְׁלַח, *and he sent;* the fifth with וַתֵּשֶׁב, *and she sat;* the Massorah commences with the fourth verse, "the word וַיִּשְׁלַח, occurs twenty-two times;" then follows verse two, "the word וַיֻּגַּד, occurs twenty-four times;" and then the fifth verse, "the word וַתֵּשֶׁב, occurs fifteen times," without any order or plan. Moreover, most of these [Massoretic remarks] are written in a contracted form, and with ornaments; so much so, that they cannot at all be deciphered, as the desire of the writer was only to embellish his writing, and not to examine or to understand the sense. Thus, for instance, in most of the copies, there are four lines [of the Massorah] on the top of the page, and five at the bottom, as the writer would under no circumstances diminish or increase the number. Hence, whenever there happened to be any of the alphabetical lists, or if the Massoretic remarks were lengthy, he split up the remarks in the middle or at the beginning, and largely introduced abbreviations, so as to obtain even lines." [18]

That this is by no means an exaggerated description of the state in which the Massorah, written in the margins of the Bible, was in the days of Ibn Adonijah, may be seen from the account given by Levita, his contemporary and co-labourer in the same department. Levita, who fourteen years later (1538) had to collate it for his Introduction to the Massorah, says, "as for the Massorah, written round the margin in the Codices, it contains numberless errors. The copyists have perverted it, as they did not care for the Massorah, but

---

[18] *Vide infra,* p. 78, &c.

only thought to ornament their writing, and to make even lines, so as not to alter the appearance, in order that all the pages should be alike. Moreover they ornamented them with illuminations of divers kinds of buds, flowers, &c. Hence they were obliged sometimes to narrow, and sometimes to widen, the margins round the illuminations with words already stated, although they were superfluous, and out of place; whilst the Massoretic registers were entirely omitted from their proper place, because the space did not suffice; and hence they had to break off in the middle of a sentence, thus leaving the whole edifice incomplete, and greatly defective.[18*]

Thus much for the Massorah, which accompanied the Codices of the Bible, prior to, and after, the time of Ibn Adonijah's compilation. As to the means for collating, correcting, and compiling it, and the extent of his labours, he distinctly tells us that he used different separate redactions of the Massorah, which Bomberg procured, and which he himself possessed. Here, again, we must let Ibn Adonijah speak for himself. "Now," says he, "when I observed all this confusion, I bestirred myself in the first place to arrange all the Massoretic notes, according to the verses to which they belonged; and then to investigate the Massoretic treatises in my possession, apart from what was written in the margins of the Bibles. Wherever an omission or contraction occurred, in order to obtain even lines, or four lines at the top and five lines at the bottom, I at once consulted the Massoretic treatises, and corrected it according to order. And whenever I found that the Massoretic treatises differed from each other, I put down the opinions of both sides, as will be found in the margin of our edition of the Bible with the Massorah, the word in dispute being marked to indicate that it is not the language of the Massorah; and whenever I took exception to the statement in a certain Codex of the Massorah, because it did not harmonise with the majority of the Codices of the Massorah, whilst it agreed with a few, or wherever it contradicted itself, I made careful search till I discovered the truth, according to my humble knowledge."[19]

How, in the face of such a plain declaration, that he had used sundry Codices of the Massorah, apart from the Massorah which accompanied the copies of the Bible, an accurate and profound scholar like Geiger could say—"from his words it does not appear

---

[18*] *Massoreth Ha-Massoreth*, p. 94, ed. Ginsburg, Longmans, 1867.
[19] *Vide infra*, p. 79, &c.

whether he had before him one or more such compilations, nay, on the contrary, it seems as if he claimed for himself this compilation," and then charge Ibn Adonijah with designedly concealing his original sources, is to us a matter of the utmost astonishment. Can it be that Geiger has not read through Ibn Adonijah's Introduction to the Rabbinic Bible, in which he gives this detailed description of his labours?

The imputation appears still more unaccountable when it is compared with the correct account which a few pages before Geiger gives of Ibn Adonijah's most assiduous and *conscientious* work. "Jacob b. Chajim," he says,[19*] "has the great merit of having transmitted to us the Massorah, in the second Bomberg Bible, edited by him (1525), after comparing it most carefully with different MSS. He has furnished us with a work of the utmost discernment and indescribable industry. He has used several MSS. for the Massorah parva and magna, endeavoured to reconcile and solve contradictions and difficulties; and has conscientiously given an account of this, as well as of his scruples. He must certainly have had before him a Massoretic survey, but this he has entirely recast in its arrangement. By his not only referring frequently in the large marginal Massorah to articles in the survey, but, *vice versa*, being sometimes satisfied with a reference in the latter to the former, he actually also endeavoured to make it a complete survey, inasmuch as he has tried to work up the whole Massoretic material, in so far as it did not relate to entirely isolated details; and moreover, by arranging it alphabetically, he has

---

[19*] Jakob ben Chajim hat das große Verdienst, uns dieselbe in der von ihm besorgten Ausgabe der zweiten rabbinischen Bomberg'schen Bibel (1525), mit sorgfältiger Vergleichung verschiedener Handschriften, überliefert zu haben. Er hat uns ein Werk einsichtsvoller Kenntniß und unsäglichen Fleißes geliefert; er hat für die kleine und die große Maßorah mehrere Handschriften benützt, Differenzen und Schwierigkeiten auszugleichen und zu lösen gesucht, und gewissenhaft giebt er darüber wie über seine Skrupel Bericht. Auch die maßorethische Uebersicht lag ihm sicherlich vor; diese aber arbeitete er in Betreff der Anordnung vollständig um. Nicht blos daß er in der großen Randmaßorah häufig auf Artikel der Uebersicht verwies, umgekehrt zuweilen in dieser sich mit einer Verweisung auf die große Randmaßorah begnügte, hat er sie auch wirklich zu einer vollständigen Uebersicht zu gestalten versucht, indem er den ganzen maßorethischen Stoff, soweit er nicht ganz vereinzeltes Detail betraf, darin zu verarbeiten suchte, und daß er sie ferner alfabetisch ordnete, sie also zu einem maßorethischen Lexikon umgestaltete, das die Auffindung der maßorethischen Bestimmungen sehr erleichterte. Daß ihm Handschriften zu dieser Arbeit vorlagen,

transformed it into a Massoretic lexicon, so that the finding of the Massoretic definitions is greatly facilitated. That he had MSS. before him for this work is evident from the whole plan, and especially from his frank confession, in separate articles, that the statements are sometimes contrary in themselves, and sometimes contradict other statements, and that he leaves the solution. However, the bringing together of the separate and scattered stones into a well compacted edifice is his work. The arrangement was uncommonly difficult; he had often to hesitate, in the course of his work, in which to put single articles; and this indeed constituted simply a single and subordinate part in the great work of a complete edition of the Bible, with Targum and a number of Commentaries."

From this description, which is irreconcilable with the other, wherein Ibn Adonijah is charged with designed concealment of the original sources, it is almost certain that Geiger could not have read through Jacob b. Chajim's Introduction to the Bible. For here, where Geiger is really anxious to do him justice, and where he alludes to Ibn Adonijah's materials, he simply refers to his remarks in the Massorah finalis, drawing from them his conclusion, and does not at all refer to Ibn Adonijah's Introduction, where he most explicitly states that he had before him separate Codices of the Massorah. That he does not specify these Codices, is owing to the fact that the several redactions of the survey of the Massorah, and the fragmentary nature of many of the Codices, precluded such a bibliographical description. Besides, paleographical and bibliographical descriptions of MSS., used in editing a work, belong to modern days. The editors of the greatest works, after the invention of printing, and in the days of Ibn Adonijah, never thought of giving an account of the materials they used up. Cardinal Ximenes, and his co-workers at the magnificent edition of the Complutensian Polyglott, gave no account whatsoever of the materials and MSS. they used for the texts of the Old and New

ist aus der ganzen Anlage ersichtlich, besonders daraus, daß er unumwunden zu einzelnen Artikeln bekennt, daß die Angaben bald in sich selbst bald mit andern im Widerspruch stehn, und er die Lösung anheimstellt. Allein die Zusammenschichtung der einzelnen zerstreuten Bausteine zu einem wohlgefügten Bau ist sein Werk. Die Anordnung war ungemein schwierig, er mußte oft schwanken, an welcher Stelle er den einzelnen Artikel unterbringen solle, im Laufe der Arbeit selbst — und dieselbe schloß sich ja blos als einzelner untergeordneter Theil an das große Werk einer vollständigen Bibelausgabe mit Thargum und einer Anzahl Commentare an — änderte er zuweilen seinen Plan. *Jüdische Zeitschrift*, vol. iii., p. 105.

Testaments; and Biblical critics have to the present day not succeeded in finding out these materials. Yet who ever thinks of charging the Cardinal, and the editors of the Complutensian Polyglott, with designedly concealing the original sources of their work, in order that it might appear greater than it actually was?

Levita, who, in referring to the extraordinary dimensions of the Massorah magna, tells us that "if all the words of it which he had seen in his life were to be written down, and bound up in a book, it would exceed in bulk the Bible itself," declares that the greater part of Ibn Adonijah's compilation is from the *Ochla Ve-Ochla*.[20] Now Ibn Adonijah does not even mention the name of this Massoretic Compendium; and it would at first sight seem as if we had here one of the original sources, which he had designedly concealed. But the fact that Levita found a copy of this treatise, after great exertions,[21]— though he lived in the very place where Ibn Adonijah sojourned, and was engaged by the very printer who employed Ibn Adonijah, and who collected and possessed all the Codices of the Massorah used in the edition of the Rabbinic Bible, would of itself show that Ibn Adonijah could not have had before him this particular redaction when he compiled the Massorah. Levita's remark, therefore, simply proves that the different redactions of the separate Massorah, or the *Ochla Ve-Ochla*, which Ibn Adonijah worked up in his great compilation, also embodied the greater portion contained in the particular redaction in question.

Had the *Ochla Ve-Ochla* referred to by Levita come to light, we should have been able, by comparing it with the present Massorah, to see how much of it Ibn Adonijah incorporated in his compilation, and in what manner he worked up the materials. But, unfortunately, this Codex, like all other Massoretic compilations, has disappeared. There can, however, be no doubt that Levita's statement is exaggerated, and that, from his known enmity to Ibn Adonijah for having embraced Christianity, he would only too readily seize any plausible opportunity of depreciating his fellow-labourer's work. Yet even he was constrained to bestow the greatest praise upon Ibn Adonijah's compilation, and to account for its deficiencies by adducing the ancient proverb that "every beginning is difficult."[22]

The few independent surveys of the Massorah, which have of late

---

[20] *Massoreth Ha-Massoreth*, p. 138, ed. Ginsburg.
[21] *Ibid*, p. 93.   [22] *Ibid*, p. 95, &c.

years been discovered in public libraries, only show how vast Ibn Adonijah's labours must have been in producing his compilation. For, not only do these MSS. exhibit the greatest diversity in details, but not a single one of them can be compared, in number of rubrics or in point of arrangement, with the present Massorah finalis. About the relationship of the Great Massorah, which the celebrated R. Gershom b. Jehodab (*circa* 960–1028), " the luminary of the dispersed," already copied with his own hands,[23] and which is frequently quoted by Rashi, and by the transcribers of the Leipsig Codex (No. 1), with Ibn Adonijah's compilation, we can say nothing, since no Codex of this particular redaction of the Great Massorah has as yet been found. We can, however, speak positively about the recently discovered and published *Ochla Ve-Ochla*.

The *Ochla Ve-Ochla*, as has already been remarked, is the name which in the course of time was given by some to one or more redactions of the independent survey of the Massorah, to distinguish it from the other *Great Massorah*,[24] which was written above and below the text of the Bible. By this appellation, this particular redaction of the Great Massorah was first quoted, towards the end of the twelfth century, by David Kimchi,[25] and Ibn Aknin.[26] It is then quoted again by Isaac b. Jehudah, in the middle of the thirteenth century;[27] and then again by Levita in 1538, who describes it as the only separate Massorah.[28] Henceforth it entirely disappeared. Even R. Salmon Norzi, the great Biblical critic, and Massoretic authority (*circa* 1560–1630), who wrote his celebrated critical and Massoretic

[23] Comp. Delitzsch, *Catal. Codd. Lips.*, p. 273; and also Zunz, *Additamenta*, to Delitzsch's Catalogue, p. 315, where the passages are given in which Rashi quotes the "Great Massorah."

[24] Hebrew, מסורת הגדולה, מסורה גדולה; Chaldee, מסורתא רבתי, מסורתא רבתא, מסורתא רבתא. *Vide supra*, p. 16, &c.

[25] Kimchi quotes the *Ochla Ve-Ochla* in his grammar, entitled *Michlol*, 35 *b*, col. 2; 51 *a*, col 2; ed. Levita, Bomberg, 1545, fol.; or 112 *b*, 163 *a*, ed. Hechim. Fürth, 1793; and in his Lexicon, *s. v.*, קרב.

[26] For Ibn Aknin's quotations, which are to be found in his ethical work entitled טב אלנפוס, and in his Methology, see Steinschneider, in Geiger's *Jüdische Zeitschrift*, vol. i., p. 316, note 31, Breslau, 1862.

[27] The work in which Isaac b. Jehudah quotes the *Ochla Ve-Ochla* is entitled ספר האשל. Comp. Steinschneider, *Catalogus Libr. Hebr.*, *in Bibliotheca Bodleiana*, col. 1418; the same author in Geiger's *Jüdische Zeitschrift*, vol. i., p. 317, note; Graetz, *Geschichte der Juden*, vol. v., p. 555, note, Magdeburg, 1860; and see also Neubauer, *Notice sur la Lexicographie Hébraiqué*, p. 9. Paris, 1863.

[28] Comp. *Massoreth Ha-Massoreth*, pp. 93, 94, 138.

Commentary on the Hebrew Bible, about half a century later could no longer find it;[29] and such distinguished scholars as Lebrecht and Fürst have pronounced it as lost.[30] Dr. Derenburg, however, whilst preparing the catalogue of Hebrew MSS. in the Imperial Library, at Paris, had the good fortune to discover an independent "Great Massorah," commencing with the words *Ochla Ve-Ochla*.[31] Shortly after, Dr. Frensdorff, who has for years been engaged in Massoretic studies, heard of the discovery (January, 1859), and, with the zeal and disinterested love with which this author prosecutes his Massoretic researches, he went to Paris in 1862, copied the MS., and published it, with learned annotations, in 1864.[32]

The questions which we now purpose to examine are — i. What relationship does this Massoretic work sustain to the Massorah, published by Ibn Adonijah? And, ii. Is this *Ochla Ve-Ochla* the identical work which is quoted by Kimchi, Ibn Aknim, Isaac b. Jehudah, and Elias Levita, or is it simply one of the redactions of the ancient Great Massorah, which, like the several other redactions, obtained the appellation *Ochla Ve-Ochla?*

i. The first great difference between the Ibn Adonijah compilation and the *Ochla Ve-Ochla* is that the former contains upwards of six thousand one hundred rubrics, whilst the latter only contains about four hundred. ii. Though Ibn Adonijah's compilation comprises more than fifteen times the number of rubrics that the *Ochla Ve-Ochla* contains, yet the latter has no less than fifty-three entire rubrics which are not at all to be found in the former. They are as follows, according to the numbers of the *Ochla Ve-Ochla*: — Nos. li., lx., lxviii., lxxiii., lxxiv., lxxviii., clxxv., clxxvi., cxxx., clxxx., clxxxi., clxxxii., clxxxiii., clxxxix., ccii., ccvii., ccxvi., ccxx., ccxxiii., ccxxiv., ccxxv., ccxxvi., ccxxix., ccxxxii., ccxxxiii., ccxlii., cclvii., cclviii., cclxiii., cclxv., cclxvii., cclxxxi., cclxxxii.,

---

[29] See the edition of the Hebrew Scriptures, with his Commentary, entitled, *A Gift Offering*, or *Oblation of Salomon ben Jehudah* (מנחת ש"י), 1 Sam. i. 9, vol. ii. p. 27 b. Mantua, 1742–44.

[30] Thus Lebrech, in the Introductory notes to his edition of Kimchi's Lexicon, remarks, "*sed posquam tota argumentorum ejus summa in Masoram magnam bibliorum rabbinorum transiit, ipse liber periisse videtur*, p. xlix., Berlin, 1847; and Fürst, ספר אכלה ואכלה והוא ספר מסורת וכו' ונראה שנאבד מאתנו.—*Appendices to his Concordance*, p. 1382.

[31] Bibliothèque Impériale, *Ancien Fonds Hébreu*, No. 56.

[32] The complete title of the book is *Das Buch Ochla W'Ochla (Massora) Herausgegeben übersetzt und mit erläuternden Anmerkungen versehen nach einer, soweit bekant, einzigen, in der Kaiserlichen Bibliothek zu Paris befindlichen Handschrift.*— Von Dr. S. Frensdorff, Hanover, 1864.

cclxxxiii., cclxxxiv., cclxxxvi., cclxxxvii., ccxciv., ccci., cccvi., cccvii., cccviii., cccix., cccxvii., cccxxix., cccxxx., cccxxxi., cccxlii., cccxlix., ccclx., ccclxviii., ccclxx., and portions of three rubrics, Nos., xviii., cclxvi., and cccxxvii.[33] iii. Some of the parallel rubrics in the one have occasionally a few instances less than the other, and *vice versa*. iv. The order in which the instances are enumerated in the respective rubrics is more confused, and less in accordance with the sequence of the books in the Bible in Ibn Adonijah's compilation, than in the *Ochla Ve-Ochla*. In the *Ochla Ve-Ochla* the order of the books is as follows: Pentateuch, earlier Prophets as usual, then Jeremiah, Ezekiel, Isaiah, and the Minor Prophets; the Five Megilloth are sometimes placed before the Psalms, and sometimes before Chronicles; sometimes, however, they follow irregularly immediately after the Hagiographa.

With these important differences between the two redactions of the Massorah, we turn to the second question, viz., whether the *Ochla Ve-Ochla* now published by Dr. Frensdorff is the identical redaction referred to by the different lexicographers and expositors, and declared by Levita to have been used by Ibn Adonijah for his compilation. Dr. Frensdorff, the learned editor of the *Ochla Ve-Ochla*, maintains that it is the identical Massoretic work which had been lost for nearly three centuries. Levita, who, as far as can be ascertained, was the last that possessed a copy of the *Ochla Ve-Ochla*, and who had studied it most carefully, distinctly maintains that the greatest part of Ibn Adonijah's compilation, *i. e.*, of the present Massorah finalis, is taken

---

[33] Frensdorff also marks Nos. ccxxxix. and cclix., as wanting in Ibn Adonijah's compilation. But this is a mistake, as Geiger has already pointed out, since rubric ccxxxix., which gives three groups of words, respectively occurring three times in the same section, the first time with *Vav* conjunctive, and the second and third times without it, is also to be found in the Massorah finalis, p. 28 *b*, cols. 1 and 2, ed. Buxtorf or Frankfurter. Only that the Codex from which this rubric of the printed Massorah was taken, had erroneously *four* such groups, and that this error has been transferred into the Massorah finalis. For ואתם ידי which is quoted as occurring twice, once beginning with הגדתי (read והגדתי), and once beginning with אל תפחדו, occurs only once, and the two references are to one and the same verse, Isaiah xlviii. 8. The other rubric, No. cclix., which gives nine instances of two combined words, the first of which occurs once only with the prefix *Mem*, is to be found complete in the Massorah finalis, under the letter *Mem*, p. 43 *b*, col. 4, ed. Buxtorf or Frankfurter, where, however, מחצי חמשה, the reference to Jeremiah xxxix. 14, is erroneously put for מחצר המטרה, as the Paris redaction rightly has it. It is to be added, that in enumerating the rubrics in the Paris redaction, which are wanted in the printed Massorah, Geiger has omitted Nos. li., lx., cxxx., ccxix., and cclxv., marked by Frensdorff in his notes on the respective articles.

from it.[84] Now the most cursory comparison of the two works will show, beyond the shadow of a doubt, that Ibn Adonijah could not have had before him the redaction of the *Ochla Ve-Ochla*, published by Dr. Frensdorff; and that either this *Ochla Ve-Ochla* is not the one which Levita made the principal basis of his Massoretic studies, and which is quoted by Kimchi, Ibn Aknim, &c., or that Levita's statement is not true.

Indeed, Dr. Frensdorff himself admits that the *Ochla Ve-Ochla*, which has recently been found in the Imperial Library at Paris, and which he has published, could not possibly have been used by Jacob Ibn Adonijah. We cannot do better than give Dr. Frensdorff's own proofs for this statement: i. The *Ochla Ve-Ochla* has fifty-six articles which are wanting in Ibn Adonijah's compilation, and which he surely would not have omitted if he had had this redaction before him; and ii. Some of the articles, which are to be found in the two Massorahs alike, are very defective in the printed Massorah finalis, thus showing that Ibn Adonijah did not copy the articles into his compilation from this redaction of the *Ochla Ve-Ochla*, or the articles in the copy would have been as complete as those in the original.

Thus under the alphabetical list of words which begin with *Vav* and *Mem*, and occur only once, Ibn Adonijah remarks, "the above registers, which begin with ומ in alphabetical order, from ומא to ומל, have all been collected from several Massoretic treatises, piece by piece. There is, however, a large alphabetical list of them complete, from ומא to ומת; but he has not been able to procure it complete, except from ומל to ומת. The rest he has had to search out register by register, and he does not know whether it is complete or defective."[35] If Ibn Adonijah had before him the *Ochla Ve-Ochla*, published by Dr. Frensdorff, he would have found this complete list in No. xviii. Moreover, from this list, which occurs in the list in the *Ochla Ve-Ochla*, he would have been able to fill up many a gap which occurs in the list of the Massorah finalis, from וכל to ומת.

Constrained to admit that Ibn Adonijah could not have had this redaction of the *Ochla Ve-Ochla* before him when compiling the

---

[84] גם כל המסורה הנדפסת פה רינ"סייה בעשרים וארבע הגדול רובו אינו אלא מספר ההוא *Massoreth Ha-Massoreth*, p. 138, ed. Ginsburg.

[85] אמר המעתיק כל אלו השמו דשמשין ומה בא"ב מא' ועד ל' כולהין לקטוי מספרי המסר' זעיר שם וזעיר שם' אבל היא כולה א"ב גדולה אחת דמשמשת ומא' עד התי' לא הגיע לידה ממנה ביחד כי אם כ"ל ועד תי"ו וישאר לקטתי שטה שטה שט"ה ולא ידענא אם חסר או מל ע"ל Comp. *Massorah finalis*, p. 44 a, col. 3.

Massorah, and yet anxious to maintain that it is the identical *Ochla Ve-Ochla* which is quoted by Kimchi, Ibn Aknin, and others, which Levita made the basis of his Massoretic labours, and which he positively declares yielded to Jacob b. Chajim *the greatest part of his compilation*, Dr. Frensdorff simply disputes Levita's statement. But so plain a declaration by a contemporary scholar, and the first Massoretic authority of his time, is not to be set aside. Indeed, Dr. Frensdorff would never have resorted to so desperate and hazardous a measure, had he not started from the false hypothesis, that there was only one redaction of the *Ochla Ve-Ochla*, and that his was the unique copy which has survived the ravages of time. The incorrectness of this assumption, however, is now proved beyond the shadow of a doubt, by the discovery of another and much larger redaction of the *Ochla Ve-Ochla* than that published by Dr. Frensdorff. The MS. is in the Library of the University of Halle (Y. *b* 10), and a description of it, by the late Professor Hupfeld, has just appeared in the Journal of the German Oriental Society.[36] This description we recast and condense, so as to adapt it for our purpose, in order to show its relationship both to Ibn Adonijah's compilation, or the Massorah finalis, and to the *Ochla Ve-Ochla*, edited by Dr. Frensdorff.

The Halle MS., which is a small quarto on parchment, beautifully written in square Hebrew characters of the middle ages, consists of 138 numbered leaves, or 276 pages, and contains upwards of 1,000 Massoretic rubrics, in two parts, as follows:—

THE FIRST PART wants six leaves of apparently a grammatical import. On p. 7 *a* stands, after the superscription סימן מלכי ישראל, a table of the accents, with their respective figures and names; and on p. 7 *b*–11, an Index (7 *b*–11), of the Rubrics contained in both parts. The Massorah proper of the first part, which contains one hundred and seventy rubrics, begins on p. 12 and extends to p. 72, thus embracing sixty-one leaves, or one hundred and twenty-two pages. The rubrics of this part, which contain almost exclusively the essence and older portion of the Massorah, viz., lists of words, forms, and constructions of a unique nature or rare occurrence, are divisible into three groups. The first group consists of seventy, nearly all alphabetical lists (1–70) of words, forms of words, and combinations, which occur once only, or a few times, partly alone, and partly with certain prefixes, with this or that vowel or accent. The

---

[36] Comp. *Zeitschrift der deutschen morgenländischen Gesellschaft*, vol. xxi., pp. 201–220. Leipzig, 1867.

second group consists of eighty lists (71—150), giving the various readings, and thus being to a certain extent of a critical nature. Of these, the first two lists only are still alphabetical, the others are incomplete alphabets. The third group consists of twenty lists (151—170), of a similar import to those in the first group. Besides the rubrics, there are a great number of marginal additions throughout this part. They are written both in small square and in Rabbinic characters. Some of these simply continue the statements in the text, or supplement the examples adduced; but most of them contain new lists, so that the total number of lists in the first part amounts to upwards of 260.

THE SECOND PART extends over fol. 73—128, as well as over an unnumbered folio, thus making together fifty-seven leaves, or one hundred and fourteen pages, and contains three hundred and forty-three rubrics, which are again divisible into groups. The first group consists of eighty-eight lists (1—88), of forms of peculiar verbs and nouns, just as a concordance. The second group consists of twenty-one registers (89—109), of textual phenomena, similar to those enumerated in the first part. The third group consists of forty-five rubrics (110—155), of words, which are unique in one book only, which are peculiar in their orthography, vowel points, or terminations. The fourth group consists of a hundred and eighty-eight registers (156—344), giving forms and textual peculiarities of all sorts. Besides these numbered ones, there are two lists, one between Nos. 113 and 114, and the other at the end, which are not numbered, so that the total sum of rubrics in this part is three hundred and forty-five. To this must be added a large unnumbered piece, extending over six pages, designated כללות, and giving one hundred and thirty short rubrics, between Nos. 279 and 280. There are, moreover, in this part, a much larger number of marginal additions than in the first part. They are to be found on almost every page, and the additional rubrics amount to upwards of a hundred and eighty; so that the total number of rubrics in the second part amounts to upwards of five hundred and twenty.

Immediately after the second part, p. 129 *a*, are registers of the numbers of verses in the Old Testament, the chronology of Biblical events, and the respective authors of the sacred books. Whereupon follow, pp. 129 *b*—132 *b*, sundry Massoretic remarks, which, though under the inscription זו ממסרה הקטנה, *this is from the Massorah parva*, consist mostly of lists of peculiar forms, orthography, and phrases strictly connected with the *Massorah magna*. These lists, some of which already occur in the marginal notes, make together about two hundred and fourteen. Then follow, on two unnumbered half leaves, thirty-four rubrics, written in Rabbinic characters, of forms and phrases with peculiar points and orthography, and of verses containing certain words. And, finally, there are other pages (pp. 135 a – 136 a) of lists, written in Rabbinic characters, giving the passages throughout the entire Old Testament where *Pattach (Segol)* is to be found with *Athnach* and *Soph Pasuk*. The Appendix, therefore, contains (214 + 34 =) 248 additional rubrics, thus making the sum total upwards of a thousand rubrics.

It now remains that we should point out the relationship of this redaction of the *Ochla Ve-Ochla*, or the great Massorah, both to Ibn Adonijah's compilation, and to the redaction published by Dr. Frensdorff.

i. The Halle MS., though rich in its Massoretic lore, has incomparably fewer rubrics than Ibn Adonijah's compilation.

ii. In several instances where the arrangement and superscription of the rubrics in Ibn Adonijah's compilation differs to advantage from the Paris redaction, edited by Dr. Frensdorff, the Halle MS. agrees with the printed Massorah. Thus the Massorah marginalis, on Levit. i. 1, in giving the alphabetical lists of words which occur once only with *Kametz*, instead of *Pattach*, adds the important designation, בזקפא with *Zakeph*. The Halle redaction, where this rubric is No. 22, has the same addition, whereas in the Paris redaction, where it is No. 21, this definition is omitted. Again, the rubric of the verses giving the names of the Canaanitish nations, has the inscription in the Massorah finalis, "two groups of three verses each in which the six names, viz., the Canaanites, the Hittites, the Amorites, the Perizzites, the Hivites, and the Jebusites, follow in the same order; in fourteen verses they have a unique order, making together twenty verses,"[87] distinguishing two features, first the order of the Canaanitish nations, and second the absence of the *Vav*. In accordance with this the two groups are first enumerated, whereupon follow the instances, in each one of which the order is peculiar,[88] mostly in pairs. After this follow two other rubrics, with separate inscriptions, giving the variations of *Vav*, &c. The Halle redaction has the same arrangement,

---

[87] חד מן ב' זוגין כן ג' אית בהון מן ר מלין הכנעני החתי האמרי הפרזי החוי והיבוסי י״ד פסוקים דמיחדין כולהון כ' פסוקים. Compare that portion of it entitled *Various Readings* (חלופי קריאה), p. 62 b, ed. Frankfurter, or ed. Buxtorf.

[88] There are properly only twelve instances, Exod. xiii. 5, and Josh. xxiv. 11, being omitted.

with the same examples, only without the inscription of the last rubric; whilst the Paris redaction, edited by Dr. Frensdorff (rubric 274) mixes up both the order of the Canaanitish names and the absence of the *Vav* in one rubric, with the inscription, " twenty verses in which the sequence of the words is irregular; fourteen of them have each a peculiar order, and also those which have *Vav*, and those which have not *Vav*.[89] "

iii. In many instances where Ibn Adonijah's compilation is defective and incorrect, and the Paris redaction is correct, the Halle redaction has the same blunders as the printed Massorah. Thus in the alphabetical list of words which occur once only with the preposition אֶל, and once with the preposition עַל, the Massorah finalis gives three incorrect instances, viz., עַל הַמְּזוּזָה, אֶל מְלֶאכֶת, and אֶל קוֹלְךָ, which do not occur, and which are rightly wanting in the Paris redaction;[40] whilst the Halle redaction has the same errors. In the alphabetical list of words occurring twice, once with the article ה, and once without it, the Massorah finalis erroneously gives הַכֶּבֶשׂ הָאֶחָד, inasmuch as it not only occurs in the passage adduced (Exod. xxix. 29), but also in Levit. xiv. 12. This error, which does not occur in the Paris redaction,[41] is also to be found in the Halle MS. The printed Massorah, in the incomplete alphabetical list of words which respectively occur, once with *Daleth*, and once with *Resh*, erroneously places וַיִּפְרוּ under the letter *Pe*, instead of *Vav*, which is also the case in the Halle redaction; whilst in the Paris redaction it is in its right place.[42] The alphabetical list of words beginning with וּמ, and occurring only once, to which reference has already been made,[43] is exactly as imperfect in the Halle redaction as it is in the Massorah finalis. The other instances, adduced by Eupfeld, which exhibit the agreement in the imperfections between the printed Massorah and the Halle MS., we must omit for want of space.

As to the relation of the Halle MS. to the Paris redaction, the

---

[89] כ' פסוקים דמשתבשין בהון י"ד מנהון מיחדרין וסומן אלין דנסבין וי"ו ואלין בלא נסבין וי'ו. Compare rubric 274, p. 53, &c.; 149, ed. Frensdorff, Hanover, 1864.

[40] Compare *Massorah finalis*, letter *Aleph*, p 7b, with the Paris redaction, rubric 2, p. 3, &c., notes.

[41] Compare *Massorah finalis*, under letter *He*, p. 21a, col. 3, with the Paris redaction, rubric 3, p. 4, notes.

[42] Compare *Massorah finalis*, under letter *Daleth*, p. 19b, col. 1, with Paris redaction, rubric 7, p. 6.

[43] *Vide supra*, p. 27.

following striking points must be adduced. Apart from the fact that the Halle redaction has nearly treble the number of rubrics, the one having upwards of a thousand, the other scarcely four hundred, a comparison of the materials which these two Massorahs contain in common will show that they both proceeded from the same ancient source, and have been so elaborated, curtailed, expanded, and adapted, as to meet the special requirements of the respective redactors. Before, however, we proceed to point out this connection, it is necessary to remark that the essential portion of the Massorah, which treats on the forms of the words, and gives the number of times these forms occur, is divisible into two parts. The one specifies only the exceptional or rare forms, which occur once, twice, thrice, or at most four times, grouping these together according to analogies, or parallels, or alphabetical lists, or in certain numbers. The other part gives the number of times certain words occur, and assumes the form of a concordance. The Paris redaction is devoted more especially to the first part, whilst the Halle redaction embraces both parts. It is by comparing that part of the Halle redaction which rubricates the anomalies catalogued in the Paris redaction, that we can see the affinity of the two.

Now on comparing the first part of the Halle MS. with the Paris Massorah, it will at once be evident that both the redactors had the same materials before them. The first list in both begins with the significant words *Ochla Ve-Ochla*. The first great group of alphabetical lists and pairs of forms which occur once or twice only, contained in the first part of the Halle redaction (Nos. 1–70), is to be found in the Paris Massorah entirely, and in the same order, with the exception that No. 13 of the former stands as No. 70 in the latter. The same is the case with the second group of the Halle MS. (Nos. 71–150). These are almost entirely to be found in the Paris redaction, only that rubrics 71 and 72 in the Halle, are rubrics 80 and 81 in the Paris Massorah; and that the latter contains alphabetical, and a few other lists from 82 to 90, so that the parallel sequence is resumed with rubric 91; rubrics 73–150 of the Halle MS. having their correspondence in rubrics 91–166 of the Paris redaction. In this group, however, the Halle MS. has ten rubrics in the orthography of certain words,[44] which are wanting in the Paris Massorah, whilst the latter has

---

[44] These rubrics are on the orthography of נבוכדנצר, זה, שָׂדַי, כֻּלֹּה, לָכָה, הוּא and הִיא, as well as on יָדֶיךָ, מֵעֲשֵׂי, עֲשֵׂי. To this may also be added the contrast (חֹלוּץ), to rule 151,

about thirteen rubrics (161, 167–170, 176–181, 214, 216–218), which are wanted in the former. Rubric 130, however, of the Paris redaction, is to be found in the marginal additions of the Halle redaction, and rubric 214 stands as rubric 163, second part of the Halle MS. Greater differences between the two redactions occur in the third group of the Halle MS. (151–170), though the bulk of this group is also to be found in the Paris redaction. Thus Nos. 155–161 are in the latter 76–78, 85–89, 348, 350–353. The corresponding portion in the Paris Massorah, however, is much richer, having lists of logical deductions (182–184); textual phenomena (192–194, 268, 273–295); registers of expressions repeated in the same verses (296–365); and of unique forms and combinations (254–267, 366–373), which are not found in the Halle MS. The latter again has two lists of anomalies in the Divine names and their various combinations (152–154); five catalogues of ˙לא and ולא (162–167), and other things which do not exist in the former.

The real difference, however, is to be seen in the second part. Here the Halle MS. is much richer than the Paris redaction. Thus, for instance, the latter wants the whole of the second group (Nos. 89–108), and has only three rubrics of the one hundred and eighty-eight which constitute the fourth group (156–344) in the Halle MS., viz., those which are in the Halle MS. Nos. 163, 277, 327. These are in the Paris redaction Nos. 214, 369, 191. Moreover the one hundred and thirty short rules which stand after No. 279 in the Halle MS., are also wanting in the Paris redaction. Of all the rules which are to be found in the marginal glosses and in the Appendices, with the exception of the marginal notes on the first group of the second part (Nos. 1–88), only about fifteen occur in the Paris redaction. Altogether the Paris redaction has about fifty rubrics which are not to be found in the Halle MS., as well as about fifty lists of words which occur in the same verse. Moreover, of the twenty-four rubrics in the Appendix to the Paris Massorah, the Halle MS. has only two rubrics, viz., 23 and 24. The Halle MS., on the other hand, has at least five hundred rubrics which are not to be found in the Paris redaction.

As to the age of the Paris redaction, this cannot be ascertained even approximately. All that is known for certain is that several hands

which properly begins the third group, giving a list of 154 instances wherein אדֹנָי occurs in contrast to ˙אדֹנִי, and which, too, is wanted in the Paris redaction.

worked at it, and that it could not have been compiled earlier than the twelfth century. This has been shown by Geiger, who refers to No. 216. Here three words are rubricated, which in an exceptional manner have *Chirek* followed by *Jod* before *Dagesh*, viz., לִמְשׁוּסָה (Isa. xlii. 24), בִּיקְרוֹתָיִךְ (Psalm xlv. 10), and לִיקְהַת (Prov. xxx. 17). Now Geiger shows that these readings were not fixed till the tenth century, and that R. Saadia Gaon (892–942), was the first who rubricated them, since Rashi (1040–1105), in his commentary on Psalm xlv. 10, mentions to have seen them in R. Saadia's *Nikkud* (נקוד רב סעדיה). From this, it is evident that this rubric was not in the Massorah in the twelfth century, and that it was inserted afterwards, since this celebrated expositor, who so frequently quotes the Massorah in his explanations of anomalous readings, would surely in this instance not have referred to R. Saadia's *Nikkud*, had the rubric in question then formed part of the Massorah. As the compilers of the Paris redaction made their compilation from Massorahs which already contained this rubric, it must at least have been effected *circa* 1200.

The age of the Halle MS. is not fixed by Hupfeld, and not having as yet had an opportunity of inspecting it, I cannot ascertain it. The fact, however, that both it and the Massorah finalis contain many incomplete lists, and that the order in which the anomalies are enumerated is not according to the sequence of the books, shows that the materials from which they were elaborated were not only the same as but much older than the Paris redaction, and that the latter was made at the time when these Massoretic materials had already been shaped into proper order and form. It is therefore of the utmost importance that the Halle MS. should be published, for it is only by a careful comparison of the three Massorahs, viz., the Paris redaction, the Halle MS., and the Massorah finalis, that the readings of the Hebrew verity can properly be fixed.

Now that two independent Massorahs have been discovered, we are in a better position to judge of the labour which Ibn Adonijah bestowed upon his compilation. Not only have the Paris and Halle redactions incomparably less rubrics than the printed Massorah, but they have neither any fixed plan nor definite order in the disposition and arrangement of the various rubrics. With the exception of sometimes placing together a few lists of similar subjects, they have an arbitrary sequence of the different articles. Jacob b. Chajim Ibn Adonijah, therefore, has not only the merit of having amassed a larger quantity of Massoretic materials than is to be found in the independent Massorahs now discovered, but he was the first who distributed the Massoretic remarks under the proper places to which they belonged, and who arranged the whole mass of the multifarious rubrics constituting this critico-exegetical apparatus into an alphabetical and lexical order, so that any anomaly or Massoretic remark may now easily be found by the student of the Hebrew text.

That Ibn Adonijah's compilation, which involved so much research and labour, and which after all constitutes one portion *only* of his gigantic Rabbinic Bible, should contain many imperfections, is no matter of surprise to any one who understands the nature of the work. Indeed it could not be otherwise, when the state of the materials which he had to work up is considered. But though Elias Levita, his contemporary and co-worker in the same department, had already alluded to these imperfections, and rightly accounted for them by quoting the old adage that "every beginning is difficult,"[45] yet he, as well as Morinus,[46] Michaelis,[47] and others who repeated his strictures, found it a far more easy task categorically to refer to errors and omissions than to collect and correct them. Buxtorf, who alone had the courage to embark upon correcting Jacob b. Chajim Ibn Adonijah, has more generally mistaken the meaning of the Massorah than rectified the errors. Now that the Paris redaction has been published, and that another and more important independent MS. has been discovered, which yield ample materials for amending and completing this ancient critical apparatus, it will be a burning shame if those who love the Bible, and are anxious for a correct text of the Old Testament verity, do not come forward to aid in the publication of the newly discovered MS., and help us in procuring an edition of the Massorah in as complete and accessible a form as the present rich materials enable us to obtain.

[45] *Vide Supra*, p. 28.
[46] *Excercitatt. Biblicæ*, pp. 384, &c., 556, &c.
[47] Preface to the edition of the Hebrew Bible, cap. IV., section v., p. 21, &c., Halle, 1720.

INTRODUCTION.

הקדמה

THUS saith the humble Jacob ben Chajim ben Isaac Ibn Adonijah: "He entereth in peace, where the righteous rest upon their couches, who walked in uprightness."[1]

Praised be the Creator, who exists and yet none can see him, who is hidden and yet found by every one that seeks him, who graciously bestowed language on mankind in order that they might communicate precious things joined together by wisdom, so as to become one, to gather his rain and flame, and learn his words and ways. He endowed his people, his first-born son, with the holy tongue, which is the language of the Law and the Prophets, and is very wonderfully adapted to open the eyes of the blind, and impart light unto them, so that all the nations of the world may know that there is nothing like this holy language in purity of style and charm of diction; it is like a tree of life to those who possess it, and its wisdom imparts life to the owner

אמר הצעיר יעקב בן חיים בן יצחק ן' אדוניהו יש"י עמ"הן.[1]

ישתבח הבורא הנמצא ואין לא תשורנו, הנעלם וכל דרשו ימצאנו, אשר חנן למין האנושי לשון למודים, למלאת ענינים חמודים, ביד השכל צמודים, והיו לאחדים, ללקוט רביביו ושביביו, וללמוד ניביו ונרתיביו, וזרח לעמו, בנו בכורו, לשון הקדש אשר היא לשון התורה והנבואות, היורדה פלאות, לפקוח עינים עורות, והיו למאורות, למען דעת כל עמי הארץ, כי לשון הקדש אין ערוך אליה, בצחות מליה, ונועם משליח, והיא כעץ חיים רפואה לבעליה, והחכמה תחיה בעליה, והאלהים

---

[1] This introductory formula is only to be found in the *editio princeps* of the Rabbinic Bible, edited by Ibn Adonijah himself (1524-25). All the subsequent editions, which were published long after his embracing Christianity and his death, have omitted it, and substituted for it the words אמר המעתיק, *thus saith the author*, thus removing from the very beginning of the Introduction to the Bible the name of the author, who had left the Jewish community. This fully confirms our opinion that his name was also removed from other works which he prepared for the press and annotated, and that his sudden disappearance from the field of literary labour is to be ascribed to the fact of his having renounced Judaism (*vide supra*, p. 13). As to the abbreviation עמ"הן יש"י, it is the accrostic of the second verse in Isaiah lvii., יבוא שלום ינוחו על משכבותם הלך נכחו which the Jews use as a euphemic expression when speaking of the dead, in consequence of the traditional explanation given to this passage. Thus the Talmud not only explains it as referring to a beatified future life, but says that, when a pious man dies, an angel announces his arrival in heaven. Whereupon the Lord says that the righteous are to go to meet and welcome him with the salutation, "He cometh in peace, to where they rest upon their couches, who walked in uprightness." (Isa. lvii. 2.) Indeed we are told that this verse is used by three companies of angels, who go to meet the saint. The first angelic group salute him with the words, "He cometh in peace!" the second with "Who walked in uprightness!" and the third with "May he rest upon his couch!" (Compare *Kethuboth*, 104 a.)

thereof. Now God gave it to his people whom he had chosen for himself — gave it to them only to be concealed under the shadow of His hand; for they alone know its mysteries, its grammar, its rules, and its anomalies. And the men of the Great Synagogue,[2] in whom was heavenly light, bright and powerful, like pure gold, on whose heart every statute of the Law was engraved, have set up marks, and built a wall around it, and made ditches between the walls, and bars, and gates, to preserve the citadel in its splendour and brightness; and they all came to the transparent cloud of its burning doctrine and rising incense; and they sanctified themselves to take the fire from off its altar, so that no other hand might touch it and desecrate it so as to become a bat for every fool; they strung together its golden words from columns of the Word of God — words of purity; and the Spirit alighted upon them, and as if by prophecy they wrote down their labours in books, to which nothing is to be added. The princes of the people gathered together to hear their sublime words; and when they had finished their work, the supernatural vision and its source were sealed, and the glory and splendour departed, and the angel of the Lord appeared no more. For no one rose after them who could do as they did. And now we are here this day gathering the gleanings which they have left; and we capture the faint ones of

אשר נתנה לעם אשר בחר לו, לחם לבדם הביאה, ובצל ידו החביאה, והם ידעו סודיה, דקדוקיה ופרטיה, ומסלולי ארחותיה, ואנשי הכנסיה הגדולה[2] אשר היה בתוכם אור חבזק. הנמרץ החזק, הזהב המזוקק, אשר בלבו כל חק מחוקק, הציבו ציונים, ובני לה חיל וח מח, ומקוה בין החומותים, וישימו בריח ודלתים, לבצר מעוזה ולחשאירה, ברה וטהורה, ויתנגשו כלם לערפל שביב לקחה, וקיטורות רקחה, והתקדשו לחתות אש שיחה, אשר על מזבחה, למען לא ישולה בה יד ולא ירמסנה כף ישימנה ממרה לכל ככל, וקשרו קשרי רצי זהב מלחיה, ממור אמרות יהוה, אמרות טהורות, ותחת עליחם דרוח, והמה בכתובים וירנבאו ולא יסף, ולשמוע נוראות, ניבם נדיבי עמים נאספי, ואחריהם נכתם החזון ומוצא׳, ונכתלק הככוד ההוא ומוראו, ולא יסף עור מלאך יהוה להראה, כי לא קם אחריהם, מי יעשה כמעשיהם, וחנה אנחנו אלה פה היום, מלקטים שכחת

---

[2] The Great Synagogue or Synod (כנסת הגדולה, כנשתא רבתא, Synagoga magna) to which Jacob b. Chajim refers, was instituted by Nehemiah (comp. Neh. x. 1-10; *Midrash Ruth*, cap. iii. fol. 45 *b*; *Jerusalem Shebiith*, v 1, 35 *b*), and continued till the death of Simon the Just (B. C. 300), who was the last member of it. It consisted of one hundred and twenty members, comprising the representatives of the following five classes of the Jewish nation :—i. The chiefs of the Priestly divisions (ראשי בית אב); ii. The chiefs of the Levitical Families (ראשי הלויים); iii. The Heads of the Israelite Families (ראשי העם); iv. Deputies from the different towns; and, v. The distinguished men of all ranks (שבינים). They were all divided into ELDERS (זקנים, πρεσβύτεροι) and SCRIBES (סופרים, γραμματεῖς); and among the many important enactments and institutions which are ascribed to them are—i. The compilation of the Hebrew canon and the various readings; ii. The composition of the Book of Esther; iii. The introduction of fixed formulæ of prayer; and iv. The foundation of colleges. Comp Kitto's *Cyclopædia*, *s. v.* SYNAGOGUE, THE GREAT.

their rear-guard, and run in their path day and night, and toil, but can never come up to them.

Thus says the writer: I was dwelling quietly in my house, and flourishing in my abode, prosecuting diligently my studies, at Tunis, which is on the borders of ancient Carthage, when fate removed me to the West, but did not withdraw its hand from afflicting me, and afterwards brought me to the famous city of Venice. And even here I had nothing to do, for the hand of fate was still lifted up, and exalted over me; and its troubles and cares found me in the city, smote me, wounded me, and crushed me. And after about three months of sufferings, I left for a little while the furnace of my afflictions, for I was in a thirsty land. I said in the thoughts of my heart, I will arise now, and walk about the streets of the city. As I was walking in the streets, wandering quietly, behold God sent a highly distinguished and pious Christian, of the name of Daniel Bomberg, to meet me. May his Rock and Redeemer protect him! This was effected through the exertions of an Israelite, who bestowed great kindness upon me, and whose name is R. Chajim Alton, son of the distinguished Moses Alton. May his Rock and Redeemer protect him! He brought me to his printing-office, and shewed me through his establishment, saying to me, Turn in, abide with me,[3] for here thou shalt find rest for thy soul, and balm for thy wound, as I want thee to revise the books which I print, correct the mistakes, purify the style, and examine the works, till they are as refined silver and as purified gold.

Although I saw that his desire was greater than my ability, yet I thought that we must not refuse a superior. Still I told him that I

---

[3] The expression עמדי, *with me*, is not the *editio princeps*, but there can be no doubt that it has dropped out by mistake. The subsequent editions have, therefore, rightly inserted it.

did not know as much, nor nearly as much [as he supposed], in accordance with that we find at the end of chap. ii. of *Jerusalem Maccoth:* "A man who knows only one book, when he is in a place where he is respected for knowing two books, is in duty bound to say I only know one book."⁴ And as I have no great intellect, how could I, being so low and insignificant, undertake such great things, from which, peradventure, mischief might ensue, seeing that R. Ishmael had already exhorted a Scribe in his days (*Sota,* 20 a, and in other places), "My son, take great care how thou doest thy work, for thy work is the work of heaven, lest thou drop or add a letter, and thereby wilt be a destroyer of the whole world,"⁵ which is still more applicable to the present time, when the distinction between the oral and written law has ceased, as both are now written down, and a mistake may describe the right wrong, and the wrong right. Therefore, I felt that I must not rely upon my own judgment, but examine two or three codices, and follow them wherever they agree; and if they do not agree, must choose from among the readings those which appear to me unobjectionable, and sift them till I am convinced that they are correct and clear, especially as Ramban⁶ and Rashbam⁷ have already counselled, in their Theological Decisions, not to make emendations upon mere conjectures.

אמינא ליה דאנא לא ידענא כולי האי, ולא
קרוב מחאי, כדנדרכינן בירושלמי סוף פרק
אלו הנולין, בר נש דתני חדא מכילא והוא
אזל לאתר דאינון מוקרין ליה בנין תרתי, צריך
למימר לחו חדא מכילא אנא חכים, כלומר
בהדא מסכתא אני חכם,⁴ ולפי דדעתי
קלישא דמה אנא הפעוט השפל לחכנס
בנדולות כאלה, דחס ושלום נפיק מניהו
חרבא כהא דרבי ישמעאל בפרק היה נוטל
ובדוכרני אחרירחי, בני הזהר במלאכתך
שמלאכתך מלאכת שמים, שמא תחסיר או
תותיר אות נמצאת מחריב העולם כלו.⁵ וכל
שכן בזמן הזה, דאין לחלק בין תורה שבכתב
לתורה שבעל פה, שמאז חושמה בספר אין
בין זה לזה, שמוה יבא לאסור המותר ולהחיר
האסור, לפום כן לא סמיכנא על דעתי, עד
דחזינא בספרי דוקני בתרין ותלתא, אי הוו
מכווני מוטב, ואי לא ברירנא מנהון מה דחוי
לן דלא קשה מידי, ומתקנינן ליה עד דאתבריר
לן דנהיר וצחיר, וכבר הזהירו והרביצו אלה
הרמב"ן⁶ והרשב"א⁷ בחידושיחם לבלתי הניה
מסברא:

⁴ The quotation from the Talmud is not literal. It is as follows: בר נש דחכם חדא מיכלה ואזיל לאת' ואינון מייקרין ליה כד הוא חכם תרין מיכלא צריך לומר לון חדא מיכלא אנא חכים' (Comp. *Jerusalem Maccoth,* ii. 7, p. 32 a, ed. Grætz. Krotoshin, 1866). It must be added, that the *editio princeps* rightly reads חכים, at the end of the quotation, and that the future editions have wrongly substituted for it מכיר.

⁵ Neither is this quotation literal. It is as follows in the Talmud: בני הוי זהיר שמלאכתך מלאכת שמים היא שמא תחסיר אות אחת או תתיר אות אחת נמצאת אתה מחריב את כל העולם כולו

⁶ *Ramban* (רמב"ן), is a contraction of the initials of ר' משה בן נחמן, *R. Moses b. Nachman* = Nachmanides. This distinguished Commentator, Talmudist, and Kabbalist was born at Gerona, in Catalonia, about 1195, whence he is also called by Christian writers *Moses Gerundensis.* He died at Ano (Ptolemais), about 1270. For his life and writings, see Kitto's *Cyclopædia, s. v.* NACHMANIDES.

⁷ *Rashbam* רשב"ם is a contraction of the initials of רבי שמואל בן מאיר, *Rabbi Samuel*

| And it came to pass, after I had remained there for some time, doing my work, the work of heaven, the Lord, blessed be his name, stirred up the spirit of the noble master for whom I worked, and encouraged his heart to publish the twenty-four sacred books. Whereupon he said to me, Gird up thy loins now like a man, for I want to publish the twenty-four sacred | ויהי כי ארכו לי שם הימים, לעשות מלאכתי מלאכת שמים, העיר השם יתברך רוח השר אשר עשיתי עמו, ואמץ לבבו, להדפיס עשרים וארבע, ויאמר לי אזור נא כגבר חלציך, כי חפצי להדפיס עשרים וארבע, באופן זה שיהיה עם פירושים ותרגום ומסרה גדולה וקטנה[8] וקריין וכתבן וכתבן ולא קריין[9] ומלאי מוחסרים וכולהו דקרוקי ספרי, ובתר הכי המסרה הגדולה כדרך הערוך[10] |

books, provided they contain the commentaries, the Targums, Massorah magna and the Massorah parva,[8] *the Keri* and *Kethiv*, and *the ethiv Kvelo Keri*,[9] *plene* and *defective*, and all the glosses of the Scribes, with appendices containing the Massorah magna, according to the alphabetical order of *the Aruch*,[10] so that the reader may

---

ben Meier, grandson of Rashi, and a very excellent commentator of the Bible. He was born about A.D. 1085, and died about 1155. Comp. Kitto's *Cyclopædia*, s. v. RASHBAM.

[8] Both the Massorah magna (מסורה הגדולה) and the Massorah parva (מסורה הקטנה) contain the traditional and authoritative glosses on the external form of the Hebrew text. The former, which is generally given in the margin above and below the text, as well as at the end of the Rabbinic Bibles, is more extensive, and quotes in full the passages which come under the same rubric; whilst the latter, which is written in the margin at the side of the text, or in the margin between the columns containing the Hebrew text and the Chaldee paraphrase, simply indicates the number of the passages which come under the same rubric, or hints at other glosses in an abbreviated form, without giving the reference. It was for want of space in the margin of the Hebrew text that the Massorah magna had to be divided into two parts. The divisions thus obtained are respectively denominated—i. מסורה גליונית, MASSORAH MARGINALIS, because this portion of it is given above and below the text; and, ii. מסורה סופית or מסורה מערכית, MASSORAH FINALIS, because this portion is given at the end of the Rabbinic Bibles.

[9] The various readings exhibited in the KERI (*i. e.*, as read in the margin), and THE KETHIV (*i. e.*, as written in the text), are divisible into three general classes—i. The class denominated KERI AND KETHIV and KETHIV AND KERI (כתיב וקרי קרי וכתיב), which comprises words differently read to what they are written, arising from the omission, insertion, exchanging, or transposition of a *single letter*. This class, by far the greater portion of the marginal readings, may properly be called VARIATIONS. ii. The class called KERI VELO KETHIV (קרי ולא כתיב), *marginal insertions of entire words not to be found written in the text*, of which the Massorah gives ten instances, viz., Judges x. 13; Ruth iii. 5, 17; 2 Sam. viii. 3, xvi. 23, xviii. 20; 2 Kings xix. 31, 37; Jer. xxxi. 38, l. 29; and, iii. The class called KETHIV VELO KERI (כתיב ולא קרי) *omissions in the margin of entire words written in the text*, of which the Massorah gives eight instances, viz., Ruth iii. 12; 2 Sam. xiii. 33, xv. 31; 2 Kings v. 18; Jer. xxxviii. 16, xxxix. 12, li. 3; Ezek. xlviii. 16. For a more extensive discussion on this subject, see the article KERI and KETHIV, in Kitto's *Cyclopædia*.

[10] As the glosses which constitute the Massorah magna are too extensive to be given entire in the margin of the text, by far the greater portion of them have been removed

easily find what he wants.[11] Like a bear bereft of its young ones he hastened to this work, for he loved the daughter of Jacob. He summoned the workmen who were skilled in printing, and each one with his tools in his hand at once betook himself to the work. Seeing then that the work was urgent, and that it would redound to the glory of Israel, inasmuch as it will shew the nations and princes the beauty and excellence of our holy law, — for since it was committed to writing nothing has appeared like it, — and seeing, moreover, that its excellency was magnified in the eyes of the publisher, becoming, as it were, the chief corner-stone with him, I set my face to the fulfilling of his desire.

למען ידוץ קורא בה למצוא מבוקשו,[11] ותכף בדוב שכול לא אחר לעשות, כי חפץ בבת יעקב, קרא לאומנים הבקיאים במיב הדפוס, ואיש כלי מפוז בידו לעשות מלאכתו, ובראותי כי הדבר נחוץ, ותועלה ותפארת ישראל, להראות העמים והשרים יפי ומעלת תורתינו הקדושה, כי למן היום אשר נתנה בספר לא נעשת כמתכונתה, וגדלה מעלתה בעיני הבונים היתה לראש פנה, שמתי מגמת פני למלאת כפו:

ובהיות כי ראיהי הרבה מהחמון, ועמם הרבה מכתות חכמינו אשר עמנו היום בדורינו זה, אינם מעריכין בלבם לא מסורת ולא הד מדרכי המסרה, באמרם כי מה תועלת ימשך להם ממנה, וכמעט נשכחה ונאבדה: לכן נערתי הצני משום עת לעשות לי״י, להראות העמים והשרים מעלת המסרה, וכי זולתה אי איפשר לכתוב הספרים ביושר ובתיקון, וכל שכן ספר תורה:

ונם נשיב ונשיג על קצת מגדולי הכמינו

And now, since many of the people, and among them are even some of the different classes of our learned contemporaries, who in their heart value neither Massorah nor any of the methods of the Massorah, say, What profit can be derived from the Massorah? and for this reason it has almost been forgotten and lost, therefore I bestirred myself, as this afforded me the opportunity to do the work of the Lord, to shew the nations and the princes the value of the Massorah; for without it none of the sacred books, and particularly the Pentateuch, can be written with propriety and correctness.

We purpose, in the first place, to reply to and refute some of the

to the end of the Hebrew Scriptures, where all the words on which there are any Massoretic remarks are classified and arranged in alphabetical order. This portion as has been remarked in the preceding note, is called *Massorah finalis*. The *Aruch* (ערוך) is the celebrated Rabbinic and Aramaic Lexicon of R. Nathan B. Jechiel (born about 1030, died about 1106), which was finished A.D. 1101. It was first published sometime before 1480, in square letters, then in Pisauri 1517, then in Venice 1531, by Bomberg, in beautiful square letters, and several times since. The best edition, however, is that of Landau, in five volumes, Prague, 1819-1324. Etheridge's description of the time when this Lexicon was finished, as well as his remarks about the *editio princeps* (*Jerusalem and Tiberias*, Longmans, 1856, pp. 284, &c.), are incorrect. Comp. Steinschneider, *Catalogus Libr. Hebr. in Bibliotheca Bodleiana*, cols. 2040-2043. Zunz, *Notes on Ascher's Edition of the Itinerary of Rabbi Benjamin of Tudela*, London, 1841, vol. ii., p. 18; Kitto's *Cyclopædia*, s.v. NATHAN B. JECHIEL.

[11] A description of this Rabbinic Bible has already been given, *vide supra*, p. 6, &c.

later great sages of blessed memory, who were nearer our time, and who maintained that the *Keri* and the *Kethiv* originated as follows: During the Babylonian captivity, when the sacred books were lost and scattered about, and those wise men who were skilled in the Scriptures were dead, the men of the Great Synagogue found different readings in the sacred books; and in every place where they met with a doubtful and perplexing case they wrote down a word in the text, but did not put the vowels to it, or wrote it in the margin and left it out in the text, not being sure as to what they found. Thus far their words. But I am far from adopting their opinion, as I shall shew in the sequel, and refute them from the Talmud.

I shall, secondly, notice the differences which in many places exist between our Talmud and the Massorites, and everywhere side with the latter, and state what we have learned from them.

I shall, thirdly, refute the heretics who dared to accuse us of wilfully altering and changing passages in our holy law, as in the case of the eighteen passages called the corrections of the Scribes, the removal of the *Vav* by the Scribes,[12] the *Keri* and the *Kethiv*, and the order of the construction.

I shall, fourthly, explain the plan which I have adopted, both in the Massorah parva and the Massorah magna, to facilitate the reader.

Let me then, firstly, do battle with the sages of blessed memory, who lived nearer our time, for they spoke unseemly against our holy law, saying that the *Keri* and the *Kethiv* exhibit the doubts which the men of the Great Synagogue entertained. And these are their names, and these their words.

Ephodi,[13] in chap. vii. of his grammar, writes as follows: "Ezra

---

[12] An explanation of the phrases, '*emendations of the Scribes*,' and '*the removal of Vav* by the Scribes,' will be found below, p. 48, &c.

[13] Ephodi (אפד) is the appellation of R. Isaac b. Moses Ha-Levi, the celebrated grammarian and polemical writer, who flourished A.D. 1360-1412. It is a contraction of אמר אני פרופיט דורן, *thus says*, or *I, Prophiat Duran*; and though it is the same

כתב וזה לשונו: השלם ראש הסופרים עזרא חכהן הסופר נער הצנו ושם כל מאמצי כחו לתקן המעוות, וכן עשו כל הסופרים הבאים אחריו, ותקנו הספרים ההם בתכלית מה שאיפשר, עד שהיה זה מבח להשאירם שלמים במנות הפרשיות והפסוקים והתיבות והאותיות והמלא והחסר והזר והנוהג מנהג הלשון וזולת זה, ול-ח נקראו סופרים, ועשו בזה חבורים והם ספרי המסרה, ובמקומות אשר חשינם ההפסד והבלבול עשו הקרי וכתיב, להיותו מסופק במה שמצא, עד כאן לשונו:

והקמחי זכרונו לברכה[14] תמהני על פה קדוש, שדבר מסכים לוה בהקדמתו לנביאים ראשונים וזה לשונו: ונראה כי המלות האלה נמצאו כן, לפי שבגלות הראשונה אבדו הספרים ונמטלטלו טלטול, והחכמים יודעי המקרא מתו, ואנשי כנסת הגדולה שהחזירו התורה לישנה, מצאו מחלוקת בספרים, ותלכו בהם אחר הרוב לפי דעתם על הבירור, כתבו הא' ולא נקדוהו, או כתבו מבחוץ ולא

the priest, who was the most accomplished and the chief of the Scribes, bestirred himself, and exerted all his powers to rectify what was wrong; and in like manner acted all the Scribes who followed him. They corrected all the sacred books as much as possible, in consequence of which they have been preserved to us perfect in the numbers of chapters, the verses, the words, letters, plene, defective, the abnormal and normal phrases and the like, and for this reason are denominated Scribes. To this effect they have also composed treatises, which are the books of the Massorah, and made *the Keri* and *Kethiv* in every passage in which they met with some obliterations and confusion, not being sure what the precise reading was." Thus far are his words.

But what surprises me still more is, that so holy a man as Kimchi[14] should also utter similar things in his introduction to the earlier Prophets. The following is his language: " It appears that these marginal and textual readings originated because the sacred books were lost and scattered about during the Babylonian captivity, and the sages who were skilled in the Scriptures were dead. Whereupon the men of the Great Synagogue, who restored the law to its former state, found different readings in the books, and adopted those which the majority of copies had, because they, according to their opinion, exhibited the true readings. In some places they wrote down one word in the text but did not punctuate it, or noted it in the margin but omitted it from

---

which he especially assumed after 1391, to conceal his real person from the Christians, who at this period of his life compelled him to abjure Judaism, he is also known by the name *Prophiat Duran*. His grammar, entitled *the Grammar of Ephod* (מעשה אפד), to which Jacob Ibn Adonijah refers, has only recently been published for the first time (Vienna, 1865), and the passage in question is to be found in p. 40.

[14] The Kimchi here referred to is *David* Kimchi, also called *Redak*, רד״ק=ר׳ דוד קמחי (born A.D. 1160, died about 1235), who wrote commentaries on nearly the whole of the Old Testament, and who is the author of the famous Hebrew Grammar called מכלול, and the Lexicon entitled השרשים. He may be regarded as the teacher of Hebrew of both Jews and Christians throughout Europe. Comp. Kitto's *Cyclopædia*, s. v. KIMCHI, where an account is given of his contributions to Hebrew lexicography and Biblical exegesis.

the text, whilst in other places they inserted one reading in the margin and another in the text." [15] Thus far is his language.

Don Isaac Abravanel,[16] the memory of the righteous be blessed, refutes them in his introduction to Jeremiah in this manner, and these are his words:—"The opinion wherein all these wise men agree, and their conclusions, are far from being mine. For how can I believe with my heart, and speak with my lips, that Ezra the scribe found the book of the law of God, and the books of his holy Prophets, in an unsettled state, through obliterations and confusions? Is not the scroll of the law in which one letter is omitted illegal? How much more must it be so through *the Keri* and *the Kethiv*, which are found in the law, since, according to *the Keri*, many letters are wanting in the law," etc.?

Again he says, and these are his words, "Behold, I ask these men if, according to their prevailing opinion, *the Keri* and *the Kethiv* originated because they [Ezra and his associates] found various readings, and Ezra, not being sure which was the right one, put down both readings, one in the margin and the other in the text; if it be so, why should we, in explaining the Scriptures, always follow the *Keri*, and not *the Kethiv?* And why should Ezra, who was himself doubtful, always have put the points in accordance with *the Keri*, and not with *the Kethiv?* And if he meant [to give preference to *the Keri*] he ought to have inserted *the Keri* in the text, as it is the true one and agrees with the points, and put *the Kethiv* in the margin because he did not approve of it.

"Moreover, if the obliterations and confusion to which the books were subject in consequence of the captivity gave rise to it [*i. e., the*

כתבו מבפנים, וכן כתבו בדרך אחד מבחוץ ובדרך אחד מבפנים עד כאן: [15]

והשר דון יצחק אברבנאל זכר צדיק לברכה [16] השיג עליהם בהקדמתו לספר ירמיה וזה לשונו, והדעת הזה אשר הסכימו בו החכמים האלה ועצתם רחקה מני, כי איך אוכל בנפשי לחאמין, ואיך אעלה על שפתי, שמצא עזרא הסופר ספר תורת האלחים וספרי נביאיו מסופקים בהפסד ובלבול, והלא ספר תורה שחסר ממנו אות אחת הוא פסול, כל שכן בקרי וכתיב שבאו בתורה, שכפי הקרי יחסרו בתורה כמה וכמה מהאותיות וכולי:

עוד אמר וזה לשונו, הנה עוד אשאל מאתם כפי הסברה הגוברת, אם היה הקרי וכתיב כפי מה שמצאו בספרים המחולפים, ולא אפשיטא לעזרא הסופר איזה הדרך מהם ישכון אור, ושם שתי הנסחאות אחד מבחוץ ואחד מבפנים, אם כן איפה למה בפירוש הכתובים נסמוך תמיד על הקרי ולא על הכתיב, ולמה עזרא בהיות הרבר אצלו מסופק, עשה הניקוד תמיר מסכים עם הקרי ולא עם הכתיב, ואם היה כן דעתו, היה לו לשום נוסחת הקרי מבפנים, כי היא האמת והמסכמת עם הנקודה, והכתיב ישים מבחוץ כיון שלא הסכים בה דעתו:

שנית אם היתה סבת זה חפסד ובלבול שנפל בספרים מצד הגלות, היה ראוי שיבא

---

[15] The quotation from Kimchi is from *the Introduction to his Commentary on Joshua.*

[16] Abravanel, or Abarbanel, the famous statesman, philosopher, theologian, and commentator of Spain, was born in Lisbon in 1437, and died at Venice in 1508. For a list of his works on Biblical literature, see Kitto's *Cyclopædia, s. v.* ABRAVANEL.

Keri and *the Kethiv*], it ought to occur accidentally in the passage which happened to be obliterated, or in which [a doubtful reading] was found. Whereas thou wilt find in the law of God, in the section *Lech L'Cha* [Gen. xiv. 2],[17] that *Kethiv* is צביים, and *the Keri* is צבאים; and the same thing occurs a second time [*ibid.* verse 8]. Now, could this accidental obliteration always occur in this word צביים? The same is the case with all, *e. g.* נערה, which is written twenty-two times נער,[18] and occurs only once as *plene*, in Deut. xxii. 19; so also בעפולים, which is always *the Keri*, and *the Kethiv* is טחורים, and *the Keri* ישגלנה, whilst *the Kethiv* is always ישכבנה.[19] It is evident, therefore, that the thing is not as these sages thought, and may the Lord forgive them!"

על דרך מקרה, כפי המקום שנ׳ טשטש או נמצא, ואחת תמצא בספרי תורת האלהים בפרשת לך לך[17] שכתוב מלך צביים, והקרי הוא מלך צבאים, יכן כתוב פעם אחרת, האם נפל במקרה הטשטוש והבלבול בצלת צביים תמיד, וכן כולם. כמו נערה שכתוב נער עשרים ושנים פעמ׳ים[18] במקום אחד מלא, שהוא ונתנו לאבי הנערה,[19] וכן בעפולים, בטחורים, ישגלנה, ישככנה, אלא שאין הדבר כאשר חשבו חחכמים דאלה, ושרי להו מריהו:

ותירץ כי אמתת הענין אצלו כי עזרא הסופר וסיעתו מצאו ספרי התורה בשלמותם ותמותם, וקודם שהתעורד לעשות חנקוד והטעמים וסופי פסוקים עיין במקרא, והדברים אשר נראו אליו זרים, כפי טבע הלשון וכוונת

Abravanel, therefore, submits that the true account of the matter is as follows:—"Ezra the Scribe and his associates found the books of the law entire and perfect, but before betaking themselves to make the vowel points, the accents and the division of verses, they examined the text, when they found words which, according to the genius of the language and the design of the narrative, appeared to them irregular.

---

[17] This is the name of one of the Sabbatic lessons, comprising Gen. xii. 1; xvii. 27. According to an ancient custom, the Jews to the present day divide the Pentateuch into *fifty-four* sections, to provide a lesson for each Sabbath of those years which, according to the Jewish chronology, have fifty-four Sabbaths, and thus read through the whole Book of the Law (תרה) in the course of every year. Each of these Sabbath sections, or *sidras* (סידרא), as it is called by the Jews, has a special name, which it derives from the first or second word with which it commences; and Jewish writers, when they quote a passage from the Pentateuch, instead of saying it occurs in such and such a chapter and verse, give, as in the instance before us, the name of the Sabbatic lesson, because this practice obtained prior to the division of the Bible into chapters and verses. A full description of these Sabbatic lessons, as well as of the manners and customs connected therewith, is given in Kitto's *Cyclop.*, art. HAPHTARA.

[18] In the present text we have only twenty-one times נער for נערה, viz., Gen. xxiv. 14, 16, 28, 55, 57; xxxiv. 3 (twice), 12; Deut. xxii. 15 (twice), 16, 20, 21, 23, 24, 25, 26 (twice), 27, 28, 29.

[19] The marginal reading טחורים for the textual בעפולים occurs six times (Deut. xxviii. 27; 1 Sam. v. 6, 9, 12; vi. 4, 5), and ישכבנה for ישגלנה four times (Deut. xxviii. 30; Isa. xiii. 16; Jer. iii. 2; Zech. xiv. 2). The former instances are given in the Massorah marginalis on 1 Sam. v 6, and *Ochla Ve-Ochla*, section 170; and the latter in the Massorah marginalis on Isaiah xiii. 16, and the *Ochla Ve-Ochla*, section 169. Comp. also *Megilla* 25 *b*; *Sopherim* viii. 8; and *infra*, p. 50., &c.

Hence he concludes that this must have originated from one of two causes: (1) Either the writer, according to the degree of inspiration vouchsafed unto him, conveys by these anomalous expressions some of the mysteries of the law, and therefore he [Ezra] did not venture to expunge anything from the sacred books. Having thus perceived that it was written by the highest wisdom, and that there is one reason or another why the words are sometimes defective or plene, and why the phrases are anomalous, he left them in the text as they were written, and put *the Keri* in the margin, which simply explains the said anomaly in accordance with the idiom of the language and the design of the narrative; and of this nature are all *the Keris* and *Kethivs* in the Pentateuch. In like manner, when Ezra found the word בעפולים, which denotes *heights*, and which conveys no meaning to us, he put in the margin the word טחורים *emerods*; and this is also the case with the word ישגלנה, the root of which (שגל) is used with regard to a queen; he therefore put in the margin ישכבנה. (2) Or Ezra may have been of opinion that these anomalous letters and words

חספור, השב בעצמו שהיה זה לאחד משתי סבות, אם שכיון הכותב בדברים הזרים החם סוד מן הסודות מסתרי התורה כפי מעלת נבואתו, ולכן לא מלאה ידו לגנת למחוק דבר מספרי האלהים, כי הבין בדעתו שבחכמה יתירה נכתבו כן, ולסבה מן הסבות נכתבו האותיות החסרות והלשונות הזרים, ולכן הניחם בכתב מבפנים כמו שנכתבו, האמנם שם מבחוץ הקרי, שהוא פירוש הכתוב הזר ההוא כפי טבע הלשון ופשיטות הענין, ומזה המין תמצא כל הקרי וכתיב שבתורה, וככה כשמצא עזרא שכתוב בתורה ובעפולים שהוא לשון גובה, ולא י״ו ענו מה הם הנבוהים ההם, הוצרך לפרש בקרי שהם טחורים. וכן ישגלנה, לפי ששם שגל נאמר על המלכה, הוצרך לפרש בקרי ישכבנה. גם אפשר שהשב עזרא שחיו בספרי הקדש תיבות ומלות שלא נכתבו כן בזרותם, אלא לסבה מן הסבות אם להיות האומר אותם בלתי מרקדק כראוי אם בקצור ידיעת דקדוק הכתיבה, והיה זה מהנביא כשגנגת היוצאת מלפני השלים, ולכן הוצרך לפרש אמתת חמלה ההיא כפי הספור, והוא ענין הקרי אשר שם מבחוץ, כי ירא הסופר הקדוש לשלוח ידו בדברי המדברים ברוח הקדש וכתיבתם, ועשה זה בעצמו, רצוני לומר לפרש התיבה והמלה ההיא, ושמו מבחוץ להיותו פירוש שפירש הוא מעצמו, ואין כפק שכך קבלו מהנביאים וחכמי חדור שקדמוהו, והנה רוב חקרי וחכתיב שבא בספר ירמיה כשתעיין בם

are owing to the carelessness of the sacred speaker or writer; and this carelessness on the part of the prophet was like an error which proceeded from a prince. Ezra had therefore to explain such words in harmony with their connection, and this is the origin of *the Keri* which is found in the margin, as this holy Scribe feared to touch the words which were spoken or written by the Holy Ghost. These remarks he made on his own account, in order that he might explain such letters and words, and on that account he put them in the margin, to indicate that this gloss was his own. And there can be no doubt that they [*i. e.*, Ezra and his associates] received the text in such a state from the prophets and the sages who had preceded them. Hence, if you examine the numerous *Keris* and *Kethivs* which occur in Jeremiah, and look into their connection, you will find that all of them are of this nature, viz., that Jeremiah wrote them through mistakes and carelessness, etc. Abravanel has a great deal more upon this subject in his introduction to Jeremiah: "Hitherto [he says further on] we have shewn that *the Keri* and *the Kethiv*, and *the Keri velo Kethiv*, are simply explanations. This is also the nature of *the Kethiv velo Keri*. When Ezra saw that words were put down in the text which had no meaning according to the simple sense of the words, he did not punctuate them, and therefore they are not to be read. From this you learn that the books, in which there are many such instances, shew that the speaker or writer was deficient in the syntax, or in his knowledge of orthography. Hence you find in Jeremiah alone eighty-one *Keris* and *Kethivs*, and in the books of Samuel, which Jeremiah wrote, the number of *Keris* and *Kethivs* rises to one hundred and thirty-three; . . . whilst in the Pentateuch, which proceeded from the mouth of the Lord, though it is four times as large as the book of Jeremiah, there are comparatively few, only sixty-five *Keris* and *Kethivs*."[20] Thus far his words.

ובעניינם תמצא כולם שהם מזה חכין, שכתבם ירמיהו כן במעות ובשגנה וכולי, והאריך בהקדמתו שם לספר ירמיה, עד הנה התבאר שהקרי וכתיב, והקרי ולא כתיב, כולו ענין הפירוש, וכן הוא הכתיב ולא קרי, שראה עזרא מלות כתובות שאין להם ענין כפי פשט הדברים, ולכן לא עשה בהם נקוד בכלל ולא יקרא, ומזה תדע שהספרים אשר נפל בהם הרבה מזה הוא לחסרון המדבר בידיעת דרכי הלשון או בידיעת דקדוק הכתיבה, ולכן היו בספר ירמיה שמונים ואחד מקרי וכתיב, ובספר שמואל שכתבו ירמיה רבו בו בכמו חקרי וכתיב בכמו מאה ושלשים ושלש וכלוי, עד אבל בחורת האלחים להיותה כולה מפי הגבורה וכמות כתיבתה קרוב לארבע פעמים ספר ירמיהו לא נמצאו בה מקרי יכתיב אלא מעט מוער סך חכל[20] וכולי עד כאן לשונו,

[20] There is a great difference of opinion about the number of these various readings, and the passages in which they occur. As it is impossible to discuss this question in a note of this nature, we subjoin the following table, which is the result of a careful perusal and collation of the Massorah, as printed in the Rabbinic Bible of Jacob b. Chajim, and which exhibits the numbers of *the Keris* and *Kethivs* in each book, according to the order of the Hebrew Bible:—

Genesis	25	Ezekiel	143	Proverbs	70
Exodus	17	Hosea	6	Job	54
Leviticus	6	Joel	1	Song of Songs	5
Numbers	11	Amos	3	Ruth	13
Deuteronomy	23	Obadiah	1	Lamentations	28
Joshua	38	Micah	4	Ecclesiastes	11
Judges	22	Nahum	4	Esther	14
1 Samuel	73	Habakkuk	2	Daniel	129
2 Samuel	99	Zephaniah	1	Ezra	33
1 Kings	49	Haggai	1	Nehemiah	28
2 Kings	80	Zechariah	7	1 Chronicles	41
Isaiah	55	Malachi	1	2 Chronicles	39
Jeremiah	148	Psalms	74	Total	1359

For a further discussion on this subject, we must refer to Kitto's *Cyclopædia*, *s. v.* KERI AND KETHIV.

He, in like manner, counts how many *Keris* and *Kethivs* occur in every book of the Bible, in order to shew which of the prophets was more conversant with the grammar. But all his views on this subject are far from my notions, as I shall presently shew, in refuting him.

The strictures, however, which he made upon Kimchi and Ephodi are good and apposite; and, in refuting his arguments, those of his opponents will be criticised at the same time, since both his decisions and the opinions of Kimchi and Ephodi are mere. conjectures, whereas we rely solely upon the Talmud, which we acknowledge; for the heart of its sages was as large as the door of the temple; they are truth, and their words are truth.

Now I submit that Don Abravanel, of blessed memory, is perfectly right in saying that Ezra the Scribe and his associates found the books of the law entire and perfect, just as they were originally written.

But what he says in his first hypothesis, beginning with the words, "Either the writer, according to the degree of inspiration vouchsafed unto him, conveyed by these anomalous expressions some of the mysteries of the law," etc., till "he put *the Keri* in the margin, which simply explains the said anomaly in accordance with the idiom of the language;"[21] all this is not correct, for in the Talmud we learn most distinctly, "R. Ika b. Abaja said in the name of R. Hannael, who repeated it in the name of Rab, What is meant by "and they read in the book, in the law of God, distinctly, and gave the sense, and caused them to understand the reading" [Neh. viii. 8]? [Reply.] The words "they read in the book, in the Law of God," mean the Hebrew text; the expression "distinctly" denotes the Targum, "and gave the sense" means the division of the verses, whilst "caused them to understand the reading" signifies, according to some the dividing accents, and according to others the Massorah. R. Isaac said the pronunciation of certain words according to the Scribes, the removal of *Vav* by the Scribes, *the Keri*

ובן הולך ומונה כמה מהקרי וכתיב באו בכל ספר, להורות מי מהנביאים היה יותר בקי בדקדוק הלשין, ותשובותיו הִקּוּ מני, כאשר אבאר ואשיג עליו:

אמנם קשיותיו אשר הקשה על הקמחי והאפודי טובים ונכוחים הם, ובהשיגי והשיבי על תשובותיו יושגו גם כן הם, כי כל אלו התרוצים ודעת הקמחי והאפודי כולם הם מסברה, ואנן לית לן כי אם תלמודא דילן אשר קבלנו עלינו, כי לבן של ראשונים כפתחו של אולם, והם אמת ודבריהם אמת:

ואומר במה שאמר השר האברבנאל זכרונו לברכה, שעזרא הסופר וסיעתו מצאו ספרי תורה בשלמותם ותמותם כמו שנכתבו, אמת ויציב דבר:

ואמנם במה שאמר בתירוץ הראשון, אם שכיון הכותב כמו שנכתבו בדברים הזרים ההם וכולי, עד האמנם שם מבחוץ חקרי שהוא פירוש הכתוב הזר ההוא כפי מבע הלשון ליתא לדבריו,[21] דהא בהדיא גרסינן במסכת נדרים פרק אין בין המודר, אמר רב איקא בר אביי אמר רב הננאל אמר רב, מאי דכתיב ויקראו בספר תורת אלהים מפורש ושום שכל ויבינו במקרא, ויקראו בספר תורת אלהים זה מקרא, מפורש זה תרגום, ושום שכל אלו הפסוקים, ויבינו במקרא זה פסק טעמים, ואמרי לה אלו המסורת, אמר רב יצחק מקרא סופרים ועטור

---

[21] *Vide supra*, p. 45, &c.

velo Kethiv, and *the Kethiv velo Keri*, are laws of Moses from Mount Sinai. The pronunciation of the Scribes shews how to read אֶרֶץ, *earth*, שָׁמַיִם, *heaven*, מִצְרַיִם, *Egypt*,[22] the removal of Vau by the Scribes is to be found four times in the case of אַחַר, *afterwards* [Gen. xviii. 5; xxiv. 55; Numb. xxxi. 2; Ps. lxviii. 26], and once by מִשְׁפָּטֶיךָ, *thy judgements* [Ps. xxxvi. 7];[23] *the Keri velo Kethiv* is seen in פְּרָת, *Euphrates* [2 Sam. viii. 3]; אִישׁ, *a man* [Ibid. xvi. 23]; בָּאִים, *they are coming* [Jer. xxxi. 38]; לָהּ, *to her* [Ibid. l. 29]; אֵת, *accusative* [Ruth ii. 11]; אֵלַי, *unto me* [Ibid. iii. 5, 17]; these words are read without being written in the text. *The Kethiv velo Keri* is seen in נָא, *now* [2 Kings v. 18], אֵת, sign of the accusative; יִדְרֹךְ, *he shall bend* [Jerem. li. 3]; חָמֵשׁ, *five* [Ezek. xlviii. 16]; אִם, *if* [Ruth iii. 12]; these words are in the text, but are not read [*Nedarim*, 37 *b*]." Thus far the Talmud. The expression אֵת connected with הַמִּצְוָה, *the commandment*, some say occurs in Deut. v. 31, but it is not true, since it is not found in our copies; nor is it mentioned in the works of the Massorah. The Massorah, indeed, does enumerate all the above-mentioned examples [as given in the Talmud], and even many others, but does not give אֵת connected with הַמִּצְוָה, *the commandment;* it only gives אֵת as connected with הַנֶּפֶשׁ, *the soul*, which is found in

סופרים וקריין ולא כתיבן, ומתיבן ולא קריין הלכה למשה מסיני; מקרא סופרים ארץ, שמים, מצרים,[22] עמור סופרים אחד תעבורו, אחר חלך, אחר תאסף, קדמו שרים אחר נוגנים, צדקתך כהררי אל;[23] קריין ולא כתיבן פרת דבלכרתו, איש רכאשר ישאל איש בדבר האלחים, באים תבנתה, לה דפליטה, את דהנד הוגד לי, אלי דהנודן, אלי דהשעורים, הלין קריין ולא כתבן; וכתבן ולא קריין נא דיסלה, את דהמצוה, ידרוך דהדרוד, המש דפאה נגב, אם דכי נואל, חלין כתיבן ולא קריין, ער כאן לשון הגמרא; את דהמצוה אית דאמרי דבפרשת ואתחנן ולא היא, דלא נמצא בספרים שלנו וגם בספרי המסרה לא מני ליה, ובמסרה חשיב כל הני ומפי עליהו אחריני מיהו לא חשיב את דהמצוה אלא את דהנפש, דכתיב בירמיהו גבי צדקיהו, חי יי אשר עשה לנו את

---

[22] That is to say, since there were no vowel points to indicate when it was pronounced אֶרֶץ and when אָרֶץ (in pause), or to shew that שָׁמַיִם and מִצְרַיִם have simply dual forms without being duals, the Sopherim pointed out how these and other words are to be read.

[23] There is a difference of opinion as to what is meant by עמור סופרים and the examples here adduced to illustrate it. According to Rashi on this passage, it denotes the idiomatic construction fixed by the Sopherim, which necessitates the writing of אחר תעבורו and not תעבורו אחר, and is called עמור because it is an improvement of or ornament to the style. According to others, this ornament of style (עימור סופרים) consists in using the word אחר at all, since it is superfluous in all these instances given in the Talmud, as we could very well say, קדמו שרים נוגנים, תסגר שבעת ימים ותאסף, סערו לבכם ותעבורו, whilst, according to *the Aruch*, as given below, it is the removal of a superfluous ו which has crept into the text in all these instances through a vitiated provincial pronunciation. The latter is the general opinion of critics as to the meaning of עמור סופרים. Compare Geiger, *Urschrift*, p. 251, &c. The instances of the *Itur Sopherim*, quoted from the Talmud (*Nedarim* 37 *b*) are also given in the *Ochlah Ve-Ochlah*, section ccxxvii pp. 46, 128; and in the Massorah marginalis on Psalm xxxvi. 7, which, however, only gives *four* passages, omitting Gen. xxiv. 55.

H

50

Jeremiah in connection with the history of Zedekiah [xxxviii. 16].[24] And Rashi,[25] of blessed memory, also says that אֶת הַמִּצְוָה occurs in Jeremiah. As for the removal of Vav by the Scribes, see below, in my reply to the heretics.

From this, then, it is evident that the whole of it is a law of Moses from Mount Sinai, and that Ezra the Scribe did not put *the Keri* in the margin to explain ungrammatical phrases; nothing appeared anomalous to Ezra, nor did he meet with any uncertainties and confusions, for the whole of it is the law of Moses from Mount Sinai, as stated above.

הנפש הזאת,[24] ורש"י זכרונו לברכה,[25] פירש את דהמצוה כתיב בידמיה עד כאן: ועטור סופרים עיין לקמן בתשובת המינים:
הא נקיטינן דכולהו הלכה למשה מסיני, ולא שם עזרא הסופר מבחוץ הקרי שהוא פירוש הכתוב הור, וגם לא היה זר בעיניו חם ושלום, ולא השיגו לא ספק ולא בלבול, כי כלה הלכה למשה מסיני, כדנרסינא לעיל:
ותו קשה בעיני מה שאמר וזה לשונו, וככה כשמצא עזרא שכתוב בתורה ובעפולים שהוא לשון גובה ולא ידענו מה הם הגבוהים חהם, חוצרך לפרש בקרי שהם טחורים, וכן ישגלנה לפי ששם שגל נאמר על המלכות, הוצרך לפרש בקרי ישכבנה, עד כאן לשונו:[26]

Moreover, I object to Abravanel's assertion, that Ezra, finding the word בַּעֲפוֹלִים, which denotes *heights*, and which conveys no meaning to us, he had to put in the margin the word טְחוֹרִים, *emerods;* and that this is also the case with the word יִשְׁגָּלֶנָּה, the root of which (שָׁגַל) is used with regard to a queen, he therefore put in the margin יִשְׁכָּבֶנָּה."[26]

[24] We have already remarked that the Massorah gives ten instances of *Keri velo Kethiv*, or *marginal insertions of entire words not to be found in the text;* and eight instances of *Kethiv velo Keri*, or *omissions in the margin of entire words written in the text* (vide supra, p. 40). The list of the marginal insertions is as follows:—

בני, sons of	. . . . . Judges xx. 13	צבאות, Sabaoth	. . Isaiah xxxvii. 32
פרת, Euphrates	. . . 2 Sam. viii. 3	באים, they are coming	. Jerem. xxxi. 38
איש, man	. . . . . 2 Sam. xvi. 21	לה, to her	. . . . . Jerem. 1. 29
כן, thus	. . . . . 2 Sam. xviii. 20	אלי, to me	. . . . . . Ruth iii. 5
בניו, his sons	. . . 2 Kings xix. 37	אלי, to me	. . . . . . Ruth iii. 17

This list is to be found in the Massorah marginalis on Deut. i. 1; and on Ruth iii. 17; *Sopherim* vi. 8; *Ochla Ve-Ochla*, section xcvii. The list of the marginal omissions is as follows:—

אם, if	. . . . . . 2 Sam. xiii. 33	אם, if	. . . . . Jerem. xxxix. 12
אם, if	. . . . . . 2 Sam. xv. 21	ידרך, he shall tread	. . . Jerem. li. 3
נא, now	. . . . . . 2 Kings v. 18	חמש, five	. . . . . . Ezek. iii. 12
את, accusative sign	. Jerem. xxxviii. 16	אם, if	. . . . . . Ruth iii. 12

This list is given in the Massorah marginalis on Ruth iii. 12; *Sopherim* vi. 9, where, however, six instances only are enumerated, נא, 2 Kings v. 18, and את, Jerem. xxxviii. 16, being omitted; and in the *Ochla Ve-Ochla*, section xcviii. Comp. also Levita's *Massoreth Ha-Massoreth*, p. 109, &c., ed. Ginsburg.

[25] *Rashi* is that celebrated commentator of the Old Testament and the Talmud, who is commonly but erroneously called *Jarchi*. The name *Rashi* רש"י is a contraction of רבי שלמה יצחקי, *Rabbi Solomon Isaki* or *Itzchaki* = *R. Solomon ben Isaac*. He was born at Troyes, in Champagne, in 1040, where he also died, July 26th, 1105.

[26] *Vide supra*, p. 46.

This statement is not correct, since we are distinctly told in the Talmud: "Our sages submit, All the verses wherein are written indecent expressions, decent expressions are read in their stead, *e. g.*, שָׁכַב instead of יִשְׁגַּל [Deuteronomy xxviii. 30; Isa. xiii. 16; Jer. iii. 2; Zech. xiv. 2]; טְחֹרִים instead of עֳפָלִים [Deut. xxviii. 27; 1 Sam. v. 6. 9. 12.; vi. 4. 5]; דִּבְיוֹנִים instead of חֲרִיוֹנִים [2 Kings vi. 25]; צוֹאָתָם instead of חֲרֵיהֶב [2 Kings xviii. 27; Isa. xxxvi. 12]; רַגְלֵיהֶם instead of שִׁינֵיהֶם [2 Kings xviii. 27; Isa. xxxvi. 12]; לְמוֹצָאוֹת instead of לְמַחֲרָאוֹת [2 Kings x. 27]."[27] And Rashi, of blessed memory, submits that the expression שָׁגַל is used for illegitimate cohabitation like that of dogs, as it is written in Nehemiah [ii. 6], where שֵׁגַל is used in this sense. *The Aruch*, too, explains it in like manner under the words דביון, whereas שָׁכַב denotes the cohabitation of people who are legally married. Hence we see that it is not as Abravanel maintains; that טְחֹרִים did not originate from our ignorance of the word עֳפָלִים, and that שָׁגַל is not used in connection with a queen. Compare *Rosh Ha-Shana*, 4 *a*.

I am not going to reply to the words of Abravanel in his second hypothesis, viz., "that the anomalous expressions are owing to the deficiency of the writer in his knowledge of Hebrew or orthography," for I am amazed that such a thing should have proceeded from a man like him, of blessed memory. How can any one entertain such an idea in his mind, that the prophets were deficient in such matters? If it really were so, then Abravanel, of blessed memory, had a greater knowledge of Hebrew than they; and for the life of me I cannot believe this. And if they really did inadvertently commit an error, as he, of blessed memory, insinuates, how is it that the prophet or the inspired speaker did not correct it himself? Is it possible that

[27] Comp. *Megilla*, 25 *b*.; *Sopherim* ix. 9; *Ochla Ve-Ochla*, sections clxix., clxx., pp. 38, 114; Massorah marginalis on 1 Sam. v. 6, Isaiah xiii. 16; and *supra*. p. 45, note 19.

eighty-one errors should occur in the Book of Jeremiah, and one hundred and thirty-three in the Book of Samuel, which he, of blessed memory, himself has counted, and has shewn was written by Jeremiah? Can we entertain the idea that a prophet, of whom it is said, "Before I formed thee in the belly I knew thee, and I ordained thee a prophet unto the nations" [Jer. i. 5], should have fallen into such errors? In conclusion, it appears that the Don, of blessed memory, had not seen the Talmud on this subject; for, according to the Talmud, there is neither light nor any glimpse of light in what he submits. It may, however, be that the Don, of blessed memory, entertained this strange opinion, not because he was unacquainted with the Talmud, but because he followed in this respect the steps of the great Rabbi, Maimonides,[28] of blessed memory, in the *More Nebuchim,* wishing to shew his ability to account for it without the Talmud.

בספר ירמיה אחד ושמונים פעמים, ובספר שמואל שכחבו ירמיה, כמו שהוכיח הוא זכרונו לברכה, רבו בו הקרי והכתיב בכמו מאה ושלשים ושלש, כמו שמנא הוא זכרונו לברכה, היעלה על לב, נביא שנאמר עליו, בטרם אצרך בבטן ידעתיך, ובטרם תצא מרחם הקדשתיך, נביא לגוים נתתיך, יפול בשגגות כאלה, סוף דבר נראה חם ושלום כאלו השר זכרונו לברכה לא ראה הגמרא, ואליבא דגמרא לא נהיר ולא צחיר מה דתיריץ, ואולי כי השר זכרונו לברכה היתה רוח אחרת עמו, ולא נעלם ממנו ח'ו הגמרא, כי דרך בדרך הרב הגדול הרמב'ם[28] זכרונו לברכה במורה הנבוכים, להראות כחו, כי זולת הגמרא יש דרך לתרץ:

ואם יקשה המקשה, הא לא אשכחנא בגמרא מקריין וכתבן וכתבן ולא קריין ועטור סופרים וכולי, אלא מה דחשיב בגמרא, ובמסרה חשיב כל הני וטפי עליהו כמה וכמה, ולעולם אימא לך דבשאירא בעי לתרוצי בדתיריץ חשר האברבנאל זכרונו לברכה, דכלקא דעתך למימר הני דקחש'ב בגמרא כולהו הלכה למשה מסיני, ובשאר לא:

ואברא דבמסרה חשיב כל הני וטפי עליהו וטפי ממה דמייתי במסכת סופרים, אבל לא קשה מידי, דגרסינן במסכת סופרים פרק ששי, אמר רבי שמעון בן לקיש שלשה

If an objector should urge, "Behold we do not find in the Talmud any more *Keris* and *Kethivs, Kethivs velo Keris,* removal of *Vav* by the Scribes, etc., besides those enumerated above, whereas the Massorah gives those and a great many others, I am therefore compelled to tell thee, that in the last-mentioned cases I am obliged to account for them in the manner of Abravanel, of blessed memory; since I believe that those only which are mentioned in the Talmud are the law of Moses from Mount Sinai, but not the others."

Now though it is true that the Massorah does indeed count all those which are mentioned in the Tract *Sopher'm,* and a great many more, yet this presents no insurmountable difficulty. For we learn, in the Mishna *Sopherim,* vi. 4, " R. Simon b. Lakish says three

---

[28] *Rambam* רמב״ם, is a contraction of the initials of ר׳ משה בן מימון, *R. Moses ben Maimon,* also called *Maimonides,* one of the most extraordinary Jewish philosophers who have lived since the destruction of Jerusalem by Titus. He was born March 30, 1135, in Cordova, and died December 13, 1204. His religio-philosophical work, entitled *More Nebuchim,* has recently been published by Munk, Paris, 1856–1866.

ספרים נמצאו בעזרה,[29] כפר מעון, ספר זעטוטי, codices [of the Pentateuch] were found in the court of the temple,[29] one of which had the reading מָעוֹן, the other זַעֲטוּטֵי, and the third differed in the number of passages wherein היא is read with a *Iod*. Thus in the one codex it was written מְעוֹן, *dwelling* [Deut. xxxiii. 27], whilst the other two codices had מְעוֹנָה; the reading of the two was therefore declared valid, whereas that of the one was invalid.[30] In the second codex, again, זַעֲטוּטֵי was found [in Ex. xxiv. 11], whilst the other two codices had אֲצִילֵי:[31] the reading in which the two codices agreed was declared valid, and that of the one invalid."[32] Now if there

---

[29] In the court of the temple those codices of the Law were kept which were used for reading the lessons for the Sabbaths and festivals.

[30] This variation affects the final ה, the insertion or omission of which was left to the taste of the individual scribes, and depended upon the different localities. This is evident, from the remark in the Talmud אנשי ירושלים היו כותבין ירושלים ירושלימה ולא היו) מקפידין ודכוחה צפון צפונה תימן תימנה), that the inhabitants of Jerusalem omitted it in one word and appended it in another, according to pleasure (*Jerusalem Megilla* i. 11, p. 71 *b*, ed. Graetz), as well as from the omissions and insertions of ה exhibited in the *Keri* and *Kethiv* in the Talmud (*Sopherim* vii. 2); and in the Massorah finalis under letter ה (comp. also Massorah magna on Exod. iv. 19; xix. 22). It was afterwards, when uniformity in orthography was found desirable, that R. Ishmael and R. Nehemiah laid it down as a rule, that *direction to, motion towards*, should be indicated by an appended ה if the word has not the prefix ל (*Jebamoth* 13 *b*). The Samaritans, however, would not submit to this revision and criticism of the text, and retained the old corruptions, for which reason they are upbraided by R. Eliezer, who tells us (נומיתי לסופרי כותים מי גרם לכם לטעות דלית אתון דרשין כרבי נחמיה דתני בשם ר' נחמיה כל דבר שדוא צריך למ"ד מתחילתו ולא ניתן לו ניתן לו ה"א בסופו כגון לחוץ חוצה לשעיר שעירה לסוכות סוכותה), I said to the Samaritan Scribes, What is the use of your error in not adopting the rule of R. Nehemiah? For it is propounded in the name of R. Nehemiah: Every word which ought to have a prefixed ל [to indicate its motion towards] and which has it not, is to have ה at the end; as, for instance, חוצה instead of לחוץ, שעירה instead of לשעיר, סוכותה, instead of לסוכות (*Jerusalem Jebamoth* i. 6, p. 3*a*, ed. Graetz).

[31] There is evidently a mistake in Jacob b. Chajim's quotation, since the variation recorded in the Talmud is not in the reading of ואל אצילי (Exod. xxiv. 11), but of את נערי (Exod. xxiv. 5). The erudite Geiger has no doubt that זעטוטי is the Greek ζητητής, *seeker, enquirer*, as the verb ζητέω is frequently used in the Apocrypha for one *who seeks God, who searches after wisdom;* and that this variation is not owing to an oversight, but is intentional, since it was not thought becoming to say that at this great revelation *boys* or *youths* (נערים) were brought as sacrifices. Hence they substituted זעטוטי, *worthy searchers after wisdom*, which is countenanced by the fact that the Mishna (*Sebachim* xiv. 4), the Gemara (*ibid.*, 115 *b*), and the Chaldee paraphrases, render נערי by *first-born*. (Geiger, *Urschrift und Uebersetzungen der Bibel*. Breslau, 1857, p. 243.)

[32] Jacob b. Chajim does not finish the quotation from the Talmud giving the examples of the third variation found in the third codex, which is as follows: באחד מצאו כתוב תשע היא ובשנים מצאו כתוב אחד עשר היא וקיימו שנים וביטלו אחד, *in the third*

be any foundation in what Don Abravanel said, that the reason why Ezra did not venture to omit anything from the books of God is, that he considered them to be written by Divine wisdom, this cannot escape one of two alternatives: either Ezra knew that they were all the law of Moses from Mount Sinai, or that they were doubtful readings, as Kimchi, of blessed memory, and Ephodi maintained. And if you say that he did not know whether they were the law of Moses from Mount Sinai, why did he not expunge the reading of the one copy, and adopt that of the majority of codices, seeing that, in the case of the three codices found in the court of the temple, they followed the majority of copies? But you will perhaps argue that the MSS. were equally divided, and that he could therefore omit nothing, but was obliged to put *the Keri* in the margin. Then let such an one shew me how it is possible to read the Pentateuch, when [according to the Talmud] we must not read a single letter which is not written in the text. How then can it enter into one's mind that we should read *the Keri*, which, according to the opinion of Abravanel, of blessed memory, Ezra the Scribe put down to explain the anomalous text, and leave out

איתא להא דאמר השר האברבנאל, שלכן לא מלאה ידו דעזרא לגשת למחוק דבר מספרי האלהים, כי חבין בדעתו שבחכמה נכתבו, לא ימנע מחלוקה, אם שהיה יודע שהם הלכה למשה מסני, ואם שהיו ספקות כדפירש הקמחי זכרונו לברכה והאפודי: ואם תאמר שלא היה יודע שהם הלכה למשה מסני, למה לא מחק וחלך אחר הרוב, דהא הוינן דבשלשה ספרים שנמצאו בעזרה הלכו אחר הרוב, ואם תאמר כלם היו שוים ולכן נמנע מלנשת למחוק ועשה הקרי מבחוץ, אם כן יורני כיצר נקרא בספר תורה שאסור לקרות אפילו אות אחת שלא מן הכתב, היעלה על לב שנקרא הקרי שתקן עזרא הסופר שהוא פירוש הכתוב הזר לדעתו זכרונו לברכה, וניח הכתב שהוא

codex, again, there were only nine passages which had היא *written with a* IOD [as it is generally written* הוא *with a* VAV], *whereas the other two had eleven passages; the readings of the two were declared valid, and those of the one invalid.* These eleven instances, which are given in *Abboth de Rabbi Nathan* (cap. xxxiv.) and in the Massorah ma na on Gen. xxxviii. 25, are as follows: Gen. xiv. 2, xx. 5, xxxviii. 25; Lev. ii. 15, xi. 39, xiii. 10, 21, xvi. 31, xxi. 9; Numb. v. 13, 14. It must be borne in mind that in all other instances הוא with *Vav* retains its archaic and epicene character throughout the Pentateuch, and is used for both the masculine and the feminine. When the text of the Hebrew Scriptures was afterwards subjected to a critical revision, according to grammatical rules laid down by the Scribes, הוא was changed into היא throughout the Prophets and the Hagiographa, wherever it referred to the feminine gender; and the few cases in which הוא is still left, or in which the newly introduced היא refers to the masculine gender, are noted by the Massorah as *Keri* and *Kethiv*. Thus the Massorah on Ps. lxxiii. 16, gives *five* instances in which the textual reading is היא with *Iod*, when referring to the masculine gender; whilst the emended marginal reading is הוא (viz., 1 Kings xvii. 15; Ps. lxxiii. 16; Job xxxi. 11; Eccles. v. 9; 1 Chron. xxix. 16), and, *vice versa*, three instances in which the textual reading has הוא, when referring to the feminine gender (viz., 1 Kings xvii. 15; Isa. xxx. 33; Job xxxi. 11), whilst the marginal emendation has היא. These are also marked in the margin of the ordinary editions of the Hebrew Bible, as *Keri* and *Kethiv*, and *Kethiv* and *Keri*.

the textual reading, which was written by the finger of God? We are therefore bound to believe that all of them are a law of Moses from Sinai. Now the same question was put to Rashba of blessed memory, "How can we read בַּמְחוֹרִים instead of בָּעֳפוֹלִים, and יִשְׁכָּבֶנָּה instead of יִשְׁגָּלֶנָּה, which are not in the text?" When Rashba, of blessed memory, answered as follows:—

"As regards thy question, 'Seeing that in reading the law one must not change even a single letter, how can the Prelector read יִשְׁכָּבֶנָּה when the text has יִשְׁגָּלֶנָּה, or substitute another reading in any other passage for what is in the text, seeing that all *the Kethivs* in the law are according to the Massorah, and not according to *the Keri?*'

"The answer is, that it is the law of Moses from Sinai, as it is written in *Tract Nedarim* [37 *b*], 'the pronunciation of certain words according to the Scribes, the removal of *Vav* by the Scribes, *the Kethiv velo Keri*, and *the Keri velo Kethiv*, &c., are all a law of Moses from Sinai.'" Thus far his language. From this it is evident that the interrogator did not know that it

כתוב באצבע אלהים, אלא על כרחין אית לן למימר שכלם חלכה למשה מסיני, ונשאלה שאלה זו להרשב'א זכרונו לברכה, היאך נקרא שלא מן הכתב בעפולים בטחורים, ישגלנה ישכבנה, יתירץ הרשב'א זכרונו לברכה וזה לשונו:

וששאלת כיון שאסור לקרות בתורה אפילו אות אחת שלא מן הכתב, היאך שליח צבור קורא ישכבנה והוא כתוב ישגלנה, וכן בכל תיבה שיש בה קרי וכתיב, שכולם כתובים בתורה כפי המסורת ולא כפי חקרי:

תשובה זו הלכה למשה מסיני, וכמו שכתוב בנדרים פרק אין בין חמודר, מקרא סופרים, ועטור סופרים, כתבן ולא קריין כולן הלכה למשה מסני עכ'ל: מהתשובה איכא למידק דהשואל לא היה ידע דאינון הלכה למשה מסני, מדקחזינן דהרשב'א זכרונו לברכה השיב זו הלכה למשה מסני וכולי: ומאחר דאינון הלכה למשה מסני תו ליכא לאקשויי מידי: וראה שגם הרשב'א זכרונו לברכה נסתייע מההוא דפרק אין בין המודר, ואף על פי שבאו בתורה כמה וכמה קרי וכתיב זולת מה רמיתי בגמרא כדפרכינן לעיל, ואם היו ספקות כדפירש הקמחי זכרונו לברכה והאפודי, היאך לא מני לון בהדי חנך דמסכת סופרים, ומדקחזינן דלא מני ולא קחשיב אלא שלש, אם כן שארא כולהו לא חוו ספיקי, ואם איהא דהוו ספיקי הוה אזל בהו בתר רובא, כדאולי בהנך דמסכת סופרים, ולא הוה חולה מבחוץ כדתרצינן לעיל:

was a law of Moses from Sinai, since Rashba, of blessed memory, informed him that it was so; and now, seeing that it is a law of Moses from Sinai, there can be no more any question about it. See, moreover, that even Rashba, of blessed memory, supported himself therein on the above quotation from *Nedarim*, in spite of there being a great many more *Keris* and *Kethivs* than those enumerated in the Talmud, as already stated before. If these were doubtful readings, as Kimchi, of blessed memory, and Ephodi maintain, why were they not enumerated with the three instances of doubtful readings in *Sopherim* [vi. 4]? Seeing, then, that there are no more than three, it is evident that the others were not doubtful, for if they were doubtful they [the Sopherim] would in these, as in the former instances, have followed the majority of MSS., and not have put them in the margin, as we have stated above.

Thers is then no more difficulty in the Don's, of blessed memory, remark, which is as follows: "there is no doubt that they [*i. e.*, Ezra and his associates] have received [*i. e., the Keri*] from the prophets and sages of by-gone days." Thus far his language. To this I reply; Choose one of two positions. If you say that they received it from the prophets and sages of by-gone days, then this cannot escape one of the two alternatives. Either it [*the Keri*] was a law of Moses from Sinai, and they [the prophets and sages] told him [Ezra] that it [*the Keri*] ought to be so, or they did not tell him that such and such readings were a law of Moses from Sinai. If they have not told him that such and such a reading is a law of Moses from Sinai, then he clearly knew already that it [the marginal reading] ought to be so [is the correct one], since it was received so from the prophets. And if it be so, what then does Abravanel mean by saying that the sacred Scribe was afraid to touch any of the words which were spoken by the Holy Ghost? Moreover, there is another objection [to be urged]. If it be that they have received it from the prophets and sages of by-gone days, why have not the prophets and sages themselves corrected it? We are therefore bound to conclude that *the Keri* and *the Kethiv* are both a law of Moses from Sinai, as we have proved above from the Talmud [*Nedarim* 37, *b.*]

As to what Abravanel said in his first hypothesis, "that the writer, according to the degree of inspiration vouchsafed unto him, conveyed by these anomalous expressions some of the mysteries of the law, and therefore Ezra did not venture to expunge them from the sacred books," this is certainly true; as the great Ramban[33] of blessed memory, the chief of the later Kabbalists, has propounded it, in the Introduction to his Commentary on the Pentateuch *(vide in loco)*. And for this very reason I am all the more astonished at Don Abravanel, of blessed memory, for having left the subject undecided, ascribing in his second hypothesis carelessness to Jeremiah, because of the anoma-

---

[33] For Ramban, or Nachmanides, see above, p. 39.

lous expressions in נַפְשׁוֹ, *his soul* [Jerem. ii. 24], *the Keri* in the margin being נַפְשָׁהּ, *her soul*, fem., as is evident from the usage of the language. Whereas in fact this is one of the mysteries of the law connected with the Levirate law, and the initiated know it.

Thus we learn from these and similar arguments that *the Keri velo Kethiv, the Kethiv velo Keri*, and all the Massoretic statements, are a law of Moses from Sinai, and not as the afore-mentioned sages propound, which is evident from the Talmud [*Nedarim* 37 *b*] quoted above.

We do indeed find that the Talmud differs in many places from the Massorah, as we see in the *Tract Nidda* [33 *a*], where וְחַנּוּשָׂא, *and he that beareth* [Levit. xv.. 10], is written וחנשא, without *Vav*.

Tossafoth [84] thereupon remarks, "It is strange that the reading of the Massorah is *plene;*" and concludes that the Talmud in fact does sometimes differ from the Massorah, as we find in *Sabbath* [55 *b*] on *the sons of Eli*, where מַעֲבָרִים [1 Sam. ii. 24] is quoted. And this is the remark of the Talmud: [query] "Is not the reading מַעֲבָרִים? Whereupon R. Hunnah b. R. Joshua said the reading is מעברם."

Now Rashi of blessed memory remarks on this passage, "I cannot

---

[84] *Tossafoth* תוספות denotes those *additions* or *supplementary glosses* to Rashi's *Commentary on the Talmud* which are found along with the commentary of Rashi in every edition of the Talmud. The disciples of Rashi, finding that the expositions of their master might be extended and improved, set about to continue his work of exposition immediately after his death, filling up every gap, and using up every scrap which their immortal teacher left. Their reverence for him, however, was so great, that they would not put down their opinions in an independent manner, but denominated them תוספות *additions*, and hence they derived the name *Tossafists*. The first Tossafists consisted chiefly of Rashi's own relations, his two sons-in-law, R. Meier b. Samuel and R. Jehudah b. Nathan, called by way of abbreviation *Riban* (רבי יהודה בן נתן=ריב״ן), his three grandsons, R. Isaac, R. Samuel, and R. Jacob Tam, sons of R. Meier, who are respectively called from their initials *Ribam* (רבי יצחק בן מאיר=ריב״ם), *Rashbam* (רבי שמואל בן מאיר=רשב״ם), and *R. Tam*, and lastly R. Isaac ben Asher of Speier, called *Riba* (רבי יצחק בן אשר=ריב״א), also a relative of Rashi's. Comp. Graetz, *Geschichte der Juden*, vol. vi., p. 170, etc., Leipzig, 1861; and vol. vii., p. 129, etc., Leipzig, 1863.

I

understand how this sage is here cited, for I am of opinion that the whole passage is spurious, and that he never said it, since the reading of the most trustworthy Codices is מַעֲבָרִים *plene*, and since it is not mentioned in the great Massorah, where all the words in which the *Jod* is in *the Kethiv* but not in the *Keri* are numbered and rubricated. Besides, the whole question is irrelevant, as the meaning of מַעֲבָרִים is not *to transgress*, but *to circulate a report;* and this is what Eli said, ' *No, my son, it is not a good report which I hear the people of God circulate about you* [1 Sam. ii 24];' מַעֲבָרִים is the plural, and refers to עַם יְהוָֹה, *the people of Jehovah*, and not to the sons of Eli, who were the transgressors themslves, and did make others to transgress." Thus far his language.

Tossafoth again comments thus upon the passage; and this is its language: "Our Talmud differs from our copies of the Bible, which read מַעֲבָרִים, and we find a similar difference in the *Jerusalem Talmud* on Samson, where it has, 'And he judged Israel *forty* years;' and submits it is evident that the Philistines feared him [*i. e.*, Samson] twenty years after his death, as well as twenty years during his life-time," whereas our copies of the Bible read *twenty* years [Judges xvi. 31]. Thus far its language.

בעיני שם החכם הנזכר כאן, כי אומר אני שמעות גדול הוא ולא גלה לחא מלתא, שהרי בספרים מוגהים כתוב מעברים מלא, וגם במסורת הגדולה במקום שמניין שם כל התיבות שכתוב בהן יו'ר דלא קרינן לא נמנה זה והם מניין על פי החשבון וזו אינה קשיא, דהאי מעברים לאו לשון עבירה הוא אלא לשון ויעבירו קול במחנה, והכי קאמר להו עלי, לא טובה השמועה אשר אנכי שומע את עם יי מעבירין ומכריזין וקובלין עליכם, והאי מעברים לשון רבים הוא, ואעם יי קאי ולא אבני עלי, שחרי הם היו עוברים ולא היו מעבירים את אחרים, עד כאן לשונו:

וכתבו התוספות על זה ז'ל, התלמוד שלנו חולק על ספרים שלנו שכתוב בהם מעבירים, וכן מצינו בירושלמי בשמשון והוא שפט את ישראל ארבעים שנה, מלמד שהיו פלשתים יראים ממנו עשרים שנה אחר מותו כמו בחייו, ובכל הספרים שלנו כתוב עשרים שנה, עד כאן לשון התוספות:

ולי נראה דלא קשה מידי חא דשמשון משמע כבדרש, למה נאמר שני פעמים כי שפט את ישראל עשרים שנה, אמר רב אחא מלמד שהיו פלשתים יראים ממנו עשרים שנה אחר מותו ועשרים אחר חייו והיינו ארבעים בתרי זימני, דהתלמוד לא אמר מאי דכתיב וחוא שפט את ישראל ארבעים שנה, אלא והוא שפט את ישראל ארבעים שנה דמשמע כבדרש, והשתא אתי שפיר ודוק, עד כאן:

ותמיהא לי על רש'י זכרונו לברכה, דחא

To me it appears, however, that there is no difficulty in it; for what the Talmud speaks about Samson refers to the Midrashic interpretation, viz., "Why is the verse, that he judged Israel twenty years, repeated twice? R. Acha answered, From this we see that the Philistines feared him [*i. e.*, Samson] twenty years after his death, just as they did twenty years before it, and this makes forty years." Hence the Talmud does not say, Why is it written in the text, "he judged Israel forty years?" but simply, "he judged forty years," that is, according to the Midrash. And now everything comes out right when thou lookest into it. Thus far.

Now I wonder at Rashi,—who was versed in the Massorah and Massoretic conclusions, as we have seen in the above quotation from the *Tract Sabbath* [55 *b*] on the sons of Eli, where he argues from the Massorah against R. Hunna b. Joshua, and concludes that the said passage in the Talmud is spurious, — that he should in various other places entertain opinions contrary to those of the Massorah. Thus, for instance, he writes in his Commentary on Gen. xxv. 6, "The reading is פלגשם without the י, to shew that it was only one concubine *i. e.*, Hagar, who was identical with Keturah, according to the opinion of *Bereshith Rabba*."[35] He also remarks on Numbers vii. 1, that the reading is כלת and not כלוֹת; whereas the Massorah most distinctly remarks פִּילַגְשִׁים is "twice entirely *plene*," viz., in Gen. xxv. 6, and in Esther ii. 9. Thus also the Massorah parva remarks on כַּלּוֹת, Numb. vii. 1, "Not extant, *plene*."

היה בקי במסורה וסבירא ליה כדעת בעלי המסרה, דהא לעיל גבי בני עלי דפרק במה בהמה, הקשה מהמסרה על רב הונא בריה דרב יהושע וכתב, ואומר אני שמעות גדול הוא וכולי, והא אשכחן בכמה דוכתי דסבירא ליה דלא כדעת בעלי חמסרה, גבי ולבני הפילגשים כתב בפירוש החומש פלגשם כתיב חסר יו"ד שלא היתה אלא פלגש אחת, והיא הגר והיא קטורה מלשון בראשית רבה,[35] וכן ויהי ביום כלות משה כלת כתיב עד כאן. ובהדיא במסרה כתיב הפילנשים ב' מלא דמלאים, דין ועל יד חני שומר הפילנשים, וכן ביום כלות משה כתיב במסורת הקטנה לית מלא:

ותו אשכחן דפירש בפירוש החומש בפרשת ואתחנן מזוזות ביתיך מזוזת כתיב, שאין צריך אלא אחת,[36] ותימא דבמסורת הוא כדתיב מלא בוי"ו בין זיי"ן לתי"ו, ורש"י זכרונו לברכה סבר לה כרבי מאיר במנחות פרק הקומץ את המנחה, גבי חא דגרסינן רב פפא איקלע לבי מר שמואל, חזא חחוא פיתחא דלא חוה ליד פציתיא אלא משמאלא ועבידה ליה מוזזה, אמר ליה כמאן, כרבי

And again Rashi remarks, in his Commentary on the Pentateuch, the reading is מְזֻזַת [Deut. vi. 9] in order to shew that even if a door has only one post, it requires *a Mezuzah*.[36] Now I wonder at this, for we find in the Massorah that it is written with a ו between the ז and the ת. Rashi, of blessed memory, however, adopts the opinion of Rabbi Meier in *Menachoth*, 34 *a*, where we learn, "R. Papa, happening to call at the house of Mar Samuel, saw there a door which had only one post on the left side, and yet had *a Mezuzah*, and asked, According to whom is this? According to Rabbi Meier [was the

---

[35] *Bereshith Rabba* is that part of the *Midrash Rabba* which treats on *Bereshith*, or on the Book of Genesis. For an account of this *Midrash*, we must refer to Kitto's *Cyclopædia, s. v.* MIDRASH.

[36] מזוזה with the Jews denotes the piece of parchment on which is written Deut. vi. 4–9; xi. 13–21, which they regard as containing the injunction to inscribe on the doorposts the words of the law. This slip of vellum thus written upon is then enclosed in a cylindrical tube of lead, cane, or wood, and to the present day is nailed to the right door-post of every door. A detailed description of this institution is given by Maimonides, *Jad Ha-Chezaka, Hilchoth Mezuzah*, vol. i., p. 93. etc., ed. Immanuel Athias, Amsterdam, 1702; Joreh Deah, §§ 285–292; and in Kitto's *Cyclopædia, s. v.* MEZUZAH.

reply.] Whereupon it was asked, Where is this remark of Rabbi Meier? [Reply.] We find that a house which has a door with only one post, Rabbi Meier says it ought to have *a Mezuzah*, but the sages say it ought not. [Query.] What is the reason of the sages? [Reply.] Because the text has מְזֻזוֹת in the plural [thus shewing that two posts were required]. [Query.] And what is the reason of Rabbi Meier? [Reply.] For we learn that it is מְזֻזוֹת *plural*, whence I see that it cannot be less than two; and when מְזֻזוֹת is again mentioned in another verse, where it is superfluous, it is to teach us that it comes within the exegetical rule, *inclusion after inclusion*; and every *inclusion after inclusion* is meant for *diminution*; hence we must have *a Mezuzah* when there is only one post to the door.[87]

מאיר, ושיילינן עלה מאי רבי מאיר, דתניא בית שאין לו אלא פצים אחד רבי מאיר מחייב במזוזה וחכמים פוטרים, מאי טעמא דרבנן מזוזות כתיב, מאי טעמא דרבי מאיר, דתניא מזוזות, שומע אני מיעוט מזוזות שתים, כשהוא אומר מזוזות בפרשה שניה, שאין תלמוד לומר רבוי אחר רבוי, ואין רבוי אלא למעט מעטו הכתוב למזוזה אחת[87] דברי רבי ישמעאל וכולי עכ'ל הגמרא שם: ואף על גב דהוה משמע קצת דכתיב מזוזות מלא בשני ווין ולא מזוזה חסר, דהא רבי ישמעאל אית ליה יש אם למסורת, פידוש לדרוש על פי הכתב, כדנרסינן בריש סנהדרין גבי לטטפת, מיהו אין ראיה מזה, דהכי נמי אשכחן רבי עקיבא דאית ליה יש אם למקרא פידוש לדרוש כפי הדבור חקרוי כההיא דלטטפת, ובפרק כל שעה אית ליה יש אם למסרה תוספת עד כאן:

ותו בפרק הבונה הקשו התוספת על רש"י זכרונו לברכה גבי הא דתניא רבי יהודה בן בתידא אומר נאמר בשני ונסביהם, בששי

Thus says Rabbi Ishmael, &c. [upon which Tossafoth remarks]; and accordingly it would appear that the reading is מְזוּזוֹת *plene* with two *Vavs*, and not defective with one *Vav*; and this is the remark of Rabbi Ishmael, who says that the text is of paramount importance, *i. e.*, that we must explain it according to the written text or *the Kethiv*, just as we find in *Sanhedrin*, 4 *b*, in the case of טֹטָפוֹת. But the fact is that we cannot infer anything from this; since we find Rabbi Akiva, who maintains that the marginal reading is of primary consideration, *i. e.*, that we must be guided by *the Keri* as in the case of טֹטָפוֹת, yet he himself admits that text is of paramount importance."

Again, in *Sabbath*, 103 *b*, Tossafoth is at variance with Rashi, of blessed memory, where we find that Rabbi Jehudah b. Bethira says:—"The Scriptures use וְנִסְכֵּיהֶם [Numb. xxix. 19] with regard to the second day of the feast of tabernacles, וּנְסָכֶיהָ [*ibid.*, verse 31] with regard to the sixth day, and כְּמִשְׁפָּטָם [*ibid.*, verse 33] with regard

---

[87] To understand the discussion given in the text, it is necessary to remark that, according to the exegetical rules of the ancient Rabbins, the Bible never repeats a word twice without designing to convey thereby a special meaning. Accordingly, if a thing is repeated twice, and the repetition appears superfluous, it is explained as implying more than one statement would convey. But if the repetition cannot be explained as implying inclusion, it is taken to denote exclusion. This rule is called אין ריבוי אחר ריבוי, ריבוי אלא למעט, *inclusion after inclusion, effecting exclusion*. Comp. Kitto's *Cyclopædia*, *s. v.* MIDRASH, p. 170, rule iv.

to the seventh day,[38] whence we obtain the final ם [of the first], the י [from the second], and the final ם [from the third word]; and have therein an intimation from the law about the ceremony of pouring out water on this festival. Whereas Rashi, of blessed memory, reads [*Succa*, 46 b] כְּמִשְׁפָּטָם in connection with the eighth day of the festival [*i. e.*, at the end of verse 37,] and כְּמִשְׁפָּט in connection with the seventh day [*i. e.*, at the end of verse 33].[39] Now Tassafoth criticises Rashi, and these are the words of Tossafoth: "We read כְּמִשְׁפָּטָם on the seventh day, as is evident from *Taamith*, 4 b, and from the Massorah magna, and not as Rashi, who reads on the eighth day." Thus far the remark of Tossafoth.

ונסכיה, בשביעי כמשפטם, חרי מ׳ם יו׳ד מ׳ם,[38] מכאן רמו לניסוך המים מן התרה וכולי; ודש׳י זכרונו לברכה גרים במקום בשביעי כמשפטם, בשמיני כמשפטם,[39] וזה לשון התוספת בשביעי כמשפטם גרסתן כדסמוכה בפרק קמא דתענית וכן הוא במסודת חנדולח ודלא כרש׳י זכרונו לברכה גרים בשמיני בסוף פרק לולב וערבה, עד כאן לשון התוספת:

ונם בההיא דמנהות רש׳י זכרונו לברכה לא הקשה לחתלמודא דפליג על הספרים המדוייקים, כמו דהקשה גבי בני עלי, וזה לשון הגמרא שם בפרק יקומץ את המנחה, תנו רבנן למטפת למטפת לטוטפת[40] הרי כאן דרש דברי רבי ישמעאל כי׳לי עד כאן לשון הגמרא. ובספרים מדוייקים ובספר תגי[41] שמע כך דינם,

Moreover, in *Menachoth*, 34 b, Rashi, of blessed memory, does not animadvert upon the Talmud, which reads differently from the correct Codices, as he animadverted in connection with the sons of Eli [*vide supra*, p. 20], and yet these are the words of *Menachoth:* "The sages propound, 'Rabbi Ishmael said in לְטֹטָפֹת לְטֹטָפֹת לְטוֹטָפֹת, the four compartments [in the phylactery] are indicated."[40] Thus far the words of the Talmud. In the Correct codices, however, as well as in the Book of the Crowns,[41] the reading is as follows, לְטֹטָפֹת

---

[38] These words also occur in connection with the other days of the feast, but without the letters in question: and as, according to the Talmudic laws of exegesis, no superfluous letter is ever used in the Bible without its having a recondite meaning (compare Ginsburg's *Commentary on Ecclesiastes*, p. 30, &c., Longman, 1861); these three letters have been combined into מים, *water*. This exegetical rule, which is called זורעין ומוספין ודורשין, *letters taken from one word and joined to another, or formed into new words*, will be found in Kitto's *Cyclopædia*, s. v. MIDRASH, p. 172, rule iii.

[39] The passage must have been altered since the day of the Tossafoth, and made conformable to the present text of the Bible, as in my copy of the Talmud there is no difference between Rashi and the Massoretic text.

[40] The word מטפת occurs only three times (Exod. xiii. 16; Deut. vi. 8, xi. 18); in two instances it has no ו (Deut. vi. 8, xi. 18), and in the third (Exod. xiii. 16), there is a ו after the first ט, *i. e.*, טוטפת; hence R. Ishmael regards it as a dual, and makes of the three words *four*, to obtain the four compartments in the phylacteries. As the limits of a note do not permit of a detailed description of these compartments, we must refer to Kitto's *Cyclopædia*, art. PHYLACTERIES, for it.

[41] The Book of Crowns (ספר תגי) to which Jacob b. Chajim refers, is an ancient treatise, containing Massoretical rules on the ornamental letters. It has only just been published, for the first time, by Burges, Paris, 1866. The passage in question is to be

[in Deut. vi. 8; xi. 18] and וּלְטֹטָפֹת [Exod. xiii. 16], but there is no ו between the פ and the ת; yet I myself have seen that in the ancient Book of the Crowns, even לְטוֹטָפֹת, in Deut. xi. 18, is written with a ו after the the first ט. Still we may rely upon the authors of the Tossafoth, since they saw the Book of Crowns, and know more thoroughly about *plene* and *defective* than we know. Tossafoth on *Menachoth* [34 *b*] observes as follows:[42] "In Deut. vi. 8 and xi. 18, the reading is לְטֹטָפֹת, and in Exod. xiii. 16, וּלְטוֹטָפֹת, according to the correct Codices, but there is no ו between the פ and ת," and asks, "How can a dual be made out of it? If we could apply to it the exegetical rule, *letters taken from one word and joined to another, or formed into new words*, it would be all right, but we find it only applied to letters at the end and beginning of words, but not in the middle. Thus, for instance, in *Zebachim*, 24 *b*, the first מ is taken over from מִדַּם, *from the blood*, to הַפָּר, *of the bullock*, making it דַּם מֵהַפָּר, *the blood of the bullock* [Exod. xxxix. 12]. Thus also in *Baba Bathra*, 111, the ו is taken from the end of נַחֲלָתוֹ, *his inheritance*, and the ל from the beginning of לִשְׁאֵרוֹ, *to his kinsmen*, and made into a separate word לוֹ, *i. e.*, וּנְתַתֶּם אֶת נַחֲלַת שְׁאֵרוֹ לוֹ, *and ye shall give the inheritance of his wife to him*, *i. e.*, the husband [Numb. xxvii. 11]. To this, Rabbi Tam[43] replies, that the first ו of וּלְטֹטָפֹת [*i. e.*, the copulative] is taken from the beginning of the word and put between the ת and פ, thus reading לְטוֹטָפוֹת, as we find it done in *Baba Meziah* [54 *b*], on Lev. xxvii. 27, where the ו

והיה אם שמוע כתיב לטטפת, והיה כי יביאך ולטוטפת, אבל בין פ'א לחי'ו לא כתיב וי'ו, ואני ראיתי בספר תגי קדמון שגם והיה אם שמוע כתוב לטוטפת, ומיהו סמכינן אמאי דגרסי התוספות כדלקמן דאינהו חזו ספר תגי, וחוו בקיאי במלא וחסר יתיר מינן; והקשו התוספות שם במנחות[42] גבי תנו רבנן לטטפת וכולי דלעיל על לטוטפות דוהיה כי יביאך דבנמרא מצריך שיהא מלא דמלא, ובספרים מדוייקים כך דינם, שמע והיה אם שמע לטטפת, והיה כי יביאך ולטוטפת, אבל בין פ'א לחי'ו לא כתיב וי'ו, הימה היכי משמע תרי, ואי הוה אמרינן נודעין ומוסיפין, ודורשין ניחא, אבל לא אשכחן אלא בתחלת תיבה ובסוף תיבה, בפרק שני דזבחים גבי ולקחו מדם הפר דדרשינן דם מהפר יקבלנו, וכן ונתתם את נחלתו לשארו, דדרשינן בפרק יש נוחלין ונתתם נחלת שארו לו, ומפרש רבינו תם[43] דוי'ו קמא דולטוטפת מוקמינן בסוף, כאלו כתוב לטמפות, כדאשכחן בפרק הזהב אי שקלת ליה לוי'ו דויסף ושדית ליה על חמישתו הוה ליה חמישיתו, והשתא מוקמינן

---

found on p. 9. It must, however, be remarked that in the present recension it is spelled לטטפות, both in Exod. xiii. 16 and Deut. vi, 8. Comp. also the *Sepher Tagin*, pp. 18, 19.

[42] As Jacob ben Chajim has somewhat abbreviated this quotation from Tossafoth, and thereby made it difficult to translate, I have translated the whole of it as found in the Talmud.

[43] Jacob Tam was born at Remers about 1100, and died about 1171. He was the grandson of the immortal Rashi, and was a very distinguished Talmudist, Tossaphist (*vide supra*, p. 57, note 34), Grammarian, and Commentator, The appellation Tam (תם) = *the pious, the saint*, he obtained in after life because of his great piety, and in allusion to Gen. xxv. 27, where his namesake, the patriarch Jacob, is denominated *Tam*.

is taken from וְיָסַף, *and he shall add*, converted into the allied letter י, and put between the ת and ו of חֲמִשְׁרתוֹ, thus reading "חֲמִישְׁתָיו." But Tossafoth objects to this explanation, on the ground that the Talmud asks further on, "If this can be done, let us apply it also to the things devoted to the sanctuary, where it is likewise written וְיָסַף חֲמִישִׁת [Lev. xxvii. 15]?" And the answer is, "Even if you take away the ו from וְיָסַף, and put it to the end of חֲמִשִׁית, it would only be חֲמִישִׁיתוֹ [making no plural]." But now [if Rabbi Tam's principle of applying this exegetical rule be right] we might put the ו in the middle of the word, so as to obtain חֲמִישִׁיוֹת *plural*. It is therefore evident that we never put the letters except at the end of the word, as is the case with all the instances which I have adduced." Thus far the words of Tossafoth. Rashi, of blessed memory, too, quotes the same principle [in his Commentary, on *Baba Meziah*, 54 *b*], that we only add to the beginning and end of words, but that in the middle the letters must remain as they are [*vide in loco*]. And we cannot urge in such a case that we cut up the Scriptures with too sharp a knife, as it is urged in all other places, because it cannot be called cutting except when the words are displaced, as it is remarked there [*i. e.*, in *Baba Bathra*, 111] in connection with the verse "and ye shall give his inheritance," &c. [Numb. xxvii. 11], against Rabbi Abja, who wanted to do it; and Rabbi said to him, "Thou cuttest the Scriptures with a sharp knife." Thus far his reply.

It appears difficult to me, that when we are distinctly told in the Talmud [Megilla, 24 *b*.], "The sages say that all passages which are written in the law in indelicate expressions are rendered decent by *the Keri*, as, for instance, יִשְׁכָּבֶנָּה instead of יִשְׁגָלֶנָּה [Deut. xxxviii. 30; Isa. xiii. 16; Jer. iii. 2; 1 Sam. v. 6, 9, 12; vi. 4, 5, 17]; טְחֹרִים instead of עֳפָלִים; the Massorah should only give six instances where *the Kethiv* is עֳפָלִים," and *the Keri* טְחֹרִים [Deut. xxviii. 27; 1 Sam. v. 6, 9, 12; vi. 5, 6], and omit the one which occurs in 1 Sam. vi. 12;

ליה באמצע תיבה והוה ליה חמישיתיו, ומוקמינן ליה במקום יו"ד באמצע תיבה; וקשה לפירושו דפריך בתר חכי, אי הכי גבי הקדש נמי דכתיב ויסף חמישית כולי, ומשני דכי שקלת לוי'ו דויסף הוה ליר חמישיתו, והשתא לוקמינן באמצע תיבה דלהוו חמשיות הרבה, הילכך נראה דבשים פעם לא מוקמינן אלא בסוף תיבה ככל הני שחבאתי, עד כאן לשון התוספות; וכך העלה רש"י וכדרונו לברכה שם פירש הזהב דלא מ'סיפין אלא בראש תיבה או בסופה, אבל באמצע כדקאי קאי עיין שם; וליכא למיפרך בכהאי גוונא סכינא חריפא מפסקינהו לקראי, כדפריך בכל דוכתא, משום דלא מיקרא הפסקה אלא דוקא בתיבות להקדים תיבה זו לזו, כדאמרינן התם מעיקרא גבי הך קרא דונתחם את נחלתו דסבר אביי למימר חידק, ואמר ליה רבא סכינא חריפא מפסקינהו לקראי, עד כאן:

יקשה בעיני דבגמרא בחדיא דרסינן בפרק הקורא את המגלה עומד, תני רבנן כל המקראות הכתובים בתורה לגנאי קורין אותן לשבח, כגון ישגלנה ישכבנה. בעפולים בטחורים, ובמסורת לא מני כי אם ששה דכתיב בעפולים קרי בטחורים, ומשמים ההוא דשמואל דפסוק וישימו את ארון יי אל העגלה, כתיב וקרי טחורים, וכן הוא בכל

and, indeed, all our best Codices do the same. Now, I cannot account for this in any other way except in the manner already stated above, viz., that the Talmud is sometimes at variance with the Massorah.

In *Bereshith Rabba*, Rabbi Idia remarks on Psalm cv. 22, that *the Kethiv* is שָׂרָו, *his prince*, without a ' [*i. e.*, in the singular], and that it refers to Potiphera. Now the difficulty is, that we do not find this ' omitted in any Codex; nor is it mentioned in the Massorah magna among the number of fifty-six passages where the ' is omitted in the text and found in *the Keri*;[44] and there is no way of accounting for this again, except as I accounted for the manner of the Talmud, viz., that it disagrees with the Massorah.

הספרים המדויקים שלנו, ולא ידענא מה לתרוצי, אלא כדתריצנא לעיל, דאורחיה דתלמודא לפלוגי על המסורה:

ובבראשית רבה מצאתי על פסוק לאסור שריו בנפשו, אמר רב אידי שרו כתיב חסר יו"ד זה היה פוטיפר, וקשה כי לא נמצא בשום ספר שיהיה חסר, וגם במסרה דבתא לא נמנה בחשבון החמשים ושש חסר יו"ד במצעות תיבות וקריין,[44] ואין דרך לתרוצי כי אם כמה דתרוצנא, דאורחיה דתלמודא לחכחיש המסורה:

ואיכא לתמהויי טובא במה דאשכחית לרש"י זכרונו לברכה ולרבינו סעדיה גאון,[45]

It is very suprising that we find Rashi, of blessed memory, and Saadia Gaon,[45] giving *Keris* and *Kethivs* which are not to be found

---

[44] The fifty-six words which are in the textual reading without *Jod* (mostly indicating the plural) in the middle, but have *Jod* in the marginal reading, are as follows:—

צוארו	Gen. xxxiii. 4	אלמנתו	Jerem. xv. 8	גבורתו	Job xxvi. 14
ועמודו	Exod. xxvii. 11	ומו	Jerem. xvii. 11	בתחבולתו	Job xxxvii. 12
ענו	Numb. xii. 3	מבראהו	Ezek. xvii. 21	ואפרוחיו	Job xxxix. 30
בינו	Joshua viii. 11	פארתו	Ezek. xxxi. 5	פהדו	Job xl. 17
תוצאותו	Joshua xvi. 3	עולתו	Ezek. xl. 26	כנפו	Job xxxix. 26
מריבו	1 Sam. ii. 9	וחלונו	Ezek. xl. 22	חלצו	Job xxxi. 20
עלו	1 Sam. ii. 9	ותכירו	Ezek. xl. 22	ילדו	Job xxxviii. 41
למשפחתו	1 Sam. x. 21	בצאתו	Ezek. xlvii. 11	ברגלו	Prov. vi. 13
ואנשו	1 Sam. xxiii. 5	פדו	Habak. iii. 14	בשפתו	Prov. xxvi. 24
בבגדו	2 Sam. i. 11	שערו	Obad. 11	ארחתו	Prov. xxii. 25
שמלתו	2 Sam. xii. 20	דרשו	Ps. xxiv. 6	אדנו	Prov. xxx. 10
רחמו	2 Sam. xxiv. 14	הצו	Ps. lviii. 8	מרגלותו	Ruth iii. 14
משרתו	1 Kings x. 5	חסדו	Ps. cvi. 45	כנותו	Ezra iv. 7
ברכו	1 Kings xviii. 42	דברו	Ps. cxlvii. 19	דמאו	Lament. iii. 39
בסוסו	2 Kings v. 9	צבאו	Ps. cxlviii. 2	ויתו	1 Sam. xxi. 14
כפו	2 Kings iv. 34	הקו	Job xiv. 5	הסתו	Song of Songs ii. 11
מזבחתו	2 Kings xi. 18	בקדשו	Job xv. 15	שלו	Ps. cv. 40
צפו	Isa. lvi. 10	עלומו	Job xx. 11	השלו	Numb. xi 32
משלו	Isa. lii. 5	ויודעו	Job xxiv. 1		

They are enumerated in the Massorah finalis under the letter *Jod*, p. 34 *a*, cols. 2 and 3; and in the *Ochla Ve-Ochla*, section cxxviii., pp. 33 and 104. It must be remarked, that this list only registers such words as occur *once* as *defective*, and therefore excludes many other words which likewise want the *Jod* plural, but which occur more than once. Comp. also Levita's *Massoreth Ha-Massoreth*, p. 183, ed. Ginsburg.

[45] *Saadia Gaon* (סעדיה גאון) *ben Joseph Ha-Pithomi*, the celebrated philosopher, commentator, and translator of the Bible into Arabic, was born at Fajum, in Upper

in any of the Massoretic work. Thus, for instance, Rashi, of blessed memory, in his commentary on Psalm cxliv. 2, remarks that in his copy *the Keri* was תַּחְתּוֹ, *under him*, and *the Kethiv* תַּחְתָּי, *under me*, and I carefully looked for it, but could not find it in the Massorah magna numbered among the eighteen words in which the ו is omitted at the end of the word.[46] And this, again, is the language of Rabbi Saadia Gaon on Daniel xi. 15, "*The Kethiv* is מִבְחָרָי, *of his choice*, and *the Keri* מִבְצָרָיו, *of his fortresses.*"[47] Now, I carefully examined the Massoretic books in all the places where the letters are changed, but could not find it; and my difficulty is [to understand] how these Gaonim could overlook the Massorah, for, according to the Massorah which we have, their statements are incorrect. However, they [Saadia and Rashi] are much wiser then we, who are as it were blind men in a window compared with them.

שהביאו קרי וכתיב מה שלא נמצא בשום ספר מספרי המסרה, וזה לשון רש״י בפירוש תלים בפסוק חרודש עמים תחתי, כתב שבכספרו היה קרי תחתיו וכתיב תחתי, ובקשתי ולא מצאתיו במסרה גדולה שיהיה נמנד בחשבון השמונה עשרה מלין דחסרים בחו״ ו״י בסוף תיבותא;[46] וזה לשון רבינו סעדיה גאון בסוף דניאל, בפסוק ויבא מלך הצפון וישפוך סוללה ולכד קרי וכתיב זאת המלה, מבחריו כתיב וקרי מבצריו,[47] ובקשתי בספרי המסרה בכל חלופי האותיות ולא מצאתיו, וקשה לי איך נעלם מהגאונים האלה המסרה, דאליבא דמסרה דאית לן הוא טעות, ומיהו בקיאי הוו יתיר מגן בכל טלי, ואגן כסומים בארובה לגביהו:

נתקשה בעיני זה כמה ימים, מאחר דאורחיה דדתלמודא להכחיש המסורת,

For some time I was in great perplexity, seeing that the Talmud generally ignores the Massorah, as we have shewn above in the instance

---

Egypt, A. D. 892, and died in 942. It is somewhat strange that Jacob ben Chajim should name him *after* Rashi, who lived so much later. The title *Gaon*, which denotes *excellency*, was given to those who were the spiritual heads of the Jewish community.

[46] The eighteen words, which according to the Massorah want the suffix *Vav* in the text, are as follows:—

וישתחו	. . Gen. xxvii. 29	וישתחו	. . 1 Kings ix. 9	וחללוה	. . Ezek. vii. 21
וישתחו	. . Gen. xliii. 28	וידבר	. 1 Kings xii. 7	שוי	. . . . Dan. v. 21
ויצו	. . Judg. xxi. 20	יקח	. . 2 Kings xx. 18	ויעל	. . . Ezra iii. 2
ויעלה	. . 1 Sam. vii. 9	ותנה	. 2 Kings xxii. 5	אחרי	. . Nehem. iii. 30
ויאמר	. 1 Sam. xii. 10	ואכול	. Isaiah xxxvii. 30	אחרי	. . Nehem. iii. 30
אמר	. . 1 Sam. xiii. 19	יחד	. Jerem. xlviii. 7	וקבל	. . Esther ix. 27

These instances are enumerated in the Massorah marginalis, on 1 Kings i. 1; in the Massorah finalis under letter *Vav*, p. 27 *a*, col. 4—27 *b*, col. 1; *Ochla Ve-Ochla*, section cxix., and *Tractate Sopherim* vii. 1. It is, however, to be remarked, that *Sopherim* only gives thirteen instances, וישתחו (Gen. xliii. 28); ויצו (Judges xxi. 20); and אחרי (Nehem. iii. 30), being omitted. Comp. also Frensdorff's note on section cxix., *Ochla Ve-Ochla*, p. 32, and Levita's *Massoreth Ha-Massoreth*, p. 117, note 69, ed. Ginsburg.

[47] It is now established beyond doubt, that the commentary on Daniel which Jacob b. Chajim Ibn Adonijah published in the Rabbinic Bible, under the name of Saadia, and which he here quotes is spurious. Comp. the article SAADIA, in Kitto's *Cyclopædia of Biblical Literature*.

of *plene* and *defective*. According to whom [I asked myself] are we then to write the scrolls of the law, since what is lawful according to the one is unlawful according to the other? At the first thought it would seem that we ought to write our scrolls according to the Talmud in the case of *plene* and *defective*, since we have taken it upon ourselves [to follow its authority], and since they [*i. e.*, the authors of the Talmud] were better versed in the Mossorah, as well as in *plene* and *defective*, than we are. Nevertheless, we find that Rashi, of blessed memory, draws objections from the Massorah against our Talmud, as in the case of the sons of Eli [1 Sam. ii. 24], and even declares that the statement in the Talmud that *the Kethiv* מַעֲבִרִים is a mistake, as we have shewn above.[48] The authors of the Tassafoth, too, raise objections from the Massorah against the Talmud, and make the Massorah their basis, as will be seen in the sequel from a quotation in *Tract Jebamoth* [106 b] Now if the Massorah were not their basis, they would not have argued from it against the Talmud. But since we see that though they were later than the Talmudists, and yet made the Massorah their basis to argue from it against the Talmud, it is evident that we too must act according to the Massorah. And, indeed, this is the reason why the Codices and the corrections of the scrolls are all according to the Massorah; and of a truth the men of the Great Synagogue [*i. e.*, the authors of the Massorah] are of great authority, and fully worthy that we should rely upon them. And though Rashi, of blessed memory, as we have seen, sides with Rabbi Meier in the Talmud, in the case of מְזוּזוֹת, against the Massorah, taking *the Kethiv* to be מְזוּזֹת, as we have stated above,[49] and in many other cases, yet we also see that in other places he argues from the Massorah against the Talmud, as I have shewn in this section.

As to the heretics, there is no foundation in the charge which they prefer against us, that we have wilfully altered and changed the text of the Scriptures, which they derive from the removal of *Vav* by

---

[48] *Vide supra*, p. 57, &c.   [49] *Vide supra*, p. 59, &c.

the Scribes, the alterations of the Scribes, *Keri* and *Kethiv*, &c.,[50] because by *Itur Sopherim* is not meant that they [*i. e.*, the Scribes] have removed the ו, but as it is explained in the *Aruch* under עטור; where it is remarked *Itur Sopherim* denotes *removal*, as the Chaldee renders סוּר, *to remove* [1 Kings xxii. 44], by עֲטַר; and so we find in *Gittin*, 86, the nature of the bill of divorce is "absolved and (וְעָטִיר), *discharged*." Now it appears that the villagers were at first not particular in reading the Scriptures, and read וְאַחַר, AND *afterward* [Gen. xviii. 5, Ps. lxviii. 26]; וּמִשְׁפָּטֶיךָ, AND *thy judgments* [Ps. xxxvi. 7]: they committed a blunder at that time [by inserting *Vav* conjunctive in these passages], thinking that these were the correct readings because they seemed to be so. Whereupon the Sopherim came and removed the *Vav*, and the reading became again, as it originally was, אַחַר, *afterwards*, מִשְׁפָּטֶיךָ, *thy judgments;* and when it was seen that the Sopherim had removed the *Vav*, the words thus corrected were denominated *Itur Sopherim*. Rabbi Isaac, therefore, came and propounded that they [*i. e.*, these restored readings] are those received by Moses on Sinai [*i. e.*, are the original readings]. And even up to the generations nearer that time they blundered and read וְלֹא, *and not*, with *Vav* [Exod. xxiii. 13], when the Sopherim decreed that it should be read without a *Vav*." Thus far his argument.

Thus it is evident that they [*i. e.*, the Sopherim] made no wilful changes. But if they [*i. e.*, the heretics] will persist in it in spite of what the Gaon [*i. e.*, the author of the *Aruch*], of blessed memory says, we can repel them with the power of argument as follows. Can any man believe that if one intends to make wilful alterations and changes he would say, See what wilful changes I have made, espe-

---

[50] The heretics or Christians to whom Jacob b. Chajim refers, have taken their inspiration from Raymond Martin, the celebrated Spanish Dominican, who was born about 1220, and died about 1287. It was this distinguished orientalist, the oracle of the church on Rabbinical lore during the middle ages, who boldly declared that these variations in question were wilful corruptions and perversions introduced by the Jews into the sacred text. Comp. Levita's *Massoreth Ha-Massoreth*, p. 45, &c., ed. Ginsburg.

סופרים, ותיקון סופרים,[50] וקרי וכריב וזולחם, דהא בעטור סופרים חם ושלום לא סליקו להנהו וי"ו, אלא כדפירש בערוך בערך עטר דאמר וזה לשון עטור סופרים פידושו לשון עטירה הוא, תרגומא דק הבמות לא סרו לא עטרו; וכן חא דנרסינן בפרק המנרש בגמ"א גופו של גט פמיר ועטיר, כלומר פטור ומסולק, ונראים הדברים שבתחלה אנשי כפרים לא הוו דייקי במקרא, והוו קרי וסערו לבכם ואחר העבורו, קרמו שרים ואחר נוגנים, צדקתך כהררי אל ומשפטיך תהום רבה, והוו משח"ש באילין מילי בההוא זמן, וסברי דהכי דקדוק משום דהכי מסתבר, ואתו סופרים וסלק להני וי"ו, והוו קרי אחר תעבורו, אחר נוגנים, משפטיך תהום רבה, וכד חזו סופרים קא עטרו להו להלין וי"ו, והוו קרו להו להלין מלי עטור סופרים, ואתא רבי יצחק ואורי דקבלה אינון הלכה למשה מסני, ועד דורות קרובים להשתא הוו משחבשי וקראו ולא ישמע על פיך, וסופרי מנמרי דלא מקרי בוי"ו, עד כאן לשונו,

הנך דואה כי לא שנו כלל חם ושלום, ואם יקשו דליתא לדברי הגאון זכרונו לברכה, נשיב עליהם מכח הסברה, היעלה על לב אדם שרוצה לשנות ולהחליף דבר יאמר,

cially in the Prophets? Yet we find the Massorah declares "In five passages the *Vav* has been removed by the Scribes," &c. Again "eighteen words are emendations of the Scribes," &c.⁵¹ Now if they had intended to make wilful changes,

ראו מה החלפתי, וכל שכן ברברי הנבואות, והנה לשון המסרה חמש מלין עטור סופרים כולי, וכן שמונה עשר מלין תקון סופרים, אם היה דעתם לשנות,⁵¹ לא היו מגלים מה ששינו

---

⁵¹ The eighteen *Tikun Sopherim* (תיקון סופרים) = *Emendations of the Scribes*, refer to eighteen alterations which the Scribes decreed should be introduced into the text, in order to remove anthropomorphisms and other indelicate expressions. These eighteen emendations (י״ח מלין) are as follows according to the order of the Hebrew Bible:— i. Gen. xviii. 22, where, for the original reading ויהוה עודני עמד לפני אברהם, *and Jehovah still stood before Abraham*, is now substituted by the decree of the Scribes = *Tikun Sopherim*, ואברהם עודנו עמד לפני יהוה, *and Abraham still stood before Jehovah*, because it appeared offensive to say that the Deity stood before Abraham. ii. Numb. xi. 15, where Moses addresses God, "*Kill me, I pray thee . . . . that I may not see* (ברעתך) THY EVIL," *i. e.*, the punishment wherewith thou visitest Israel, is altered into "*that I may not see* (ברעתי) MY EVIL," because it might seem as if evil were ascribed to the Deity. iii. and iv. Numb. xii. 12, where the original reading, "*let her not be as one dead, who proceeded from the womb of* (אמנו) OUR MOTHER, *and half of* (בשרנו) OUR FLESH *be consumed*," is altered into "*let her not be as one dead born, which when it proceeds from the womb of* (אמו) ITS MOTHER *has half of* ITS FLESH (בשרו) *consumed*;" here are two Sopheric emendations. v. 1 Sam. iii. 13, where the original "*for his sons cursed* (אלהים) GOD" (as the Sept. still has it Θεόν), is altered into "*for his sons cursed* (להם) THEMSELVES," because it was too offensive to say that the sons of Eli cursed God, and that Eli knew it and did not reprimand them for it. vi. 2 Sam. xvi. 12, where "*will God see* (בעיי) WITH HIS EYE," is altered into "*will God look* (בעוני) AT MY AFFLICTION," because it was too anthropomorphic. vii. 1 Kings xii. 16, where "TO HIS GOD (לאלהיו) *O Israel . . . . and Israel went* (לאלהיו) TO THEIR GOD," is altered into "TO YOUR TENTS (לאהליך) *O Israel . . . . and Israel departed* (לאהליו) TO THEIR TENTS," because the separation of Israel from the house of David was regarded as a necessary transition to idolatry; it was looked upon as leaving God and the sanctuary for the worship of idolatry in tents. viii. 2 Chron. x. 16, where the parallel passage is similarly altered, for the same reason. ix. Jer. ii. 11, where "*my people have changed* (כבודי) MY GLORY *for an idol*," is altered into "*have changed* (כבודו) THEIR GLORY *into an idol*," because it was too offensive to say such a thing. x. Ezek. viii. 17, where "*they have put the rod to* (אפי) MY NOSE," is altered into "*they have put the rod to* (אפם) THEIR NOSE," because of its offensiveness, and to avoid too gross an anthropomorphism. xi. Hos. iv. 7, where "*they have changed* (כבודי) MY GLORY *into shame*," is altered into "*I will change their glory into shame*" (כבודם בקלון אמיר), for the same reason which dictated the ninth alteration. xii. Hab. i. 12, where the address of the prophet to God, "THOU DIEST NOT" (תמות), is altered into "WE shall not die" (נמות), because it was deemed improper. xiii. Zech. ii. 12, where "*the apple of* (עיני) MINE EYE," is altered into "*the apple of* (עינו) HIS EYE," for the reason which called forth the tenth emendation. xiv. Mal. i. 13, where "*ye make* (אותי) ME *expire*," is altered into "*ye weary* (אותו) IT," because of its being too gross an anthropomorphism. xv. Ps. cvi. 20, where "*they have changed* (כבודי) MY GLORY *into the similitude of an ox.*' is altered into "*they have changed* (כבודם) THEIR GLORY *into the similitude of an ox,*" as in Jer. ii. 11 and Hos. iv. 7. xvi. Job. vii. 20, where Job's address to God, "*am I a*

they would surely not have proclaimed what they have changed, and said, "Eighteen words are *Tikun Sopherim*, as given in the *Mechiltha*" [on Exod. xv. 7].⁵² Moreover, the Sopherim made no changes nor corrections, they only submitted that the text ought originally to have been so and so, but is veiled in other expressions, out of respect to *the Shechina*, as you will find out by examining the subject. The same is the case with *the Keri* and *the Kethiv;* they [*i. e.*, the *Sopherim*] point out what they have altered, if peradventure you choose to characterise them as alterations; we of the class of believers, however, believe that they all are a law of Moses from Sinai [*i. e.*, the original readings], including the emendations of the Scribes. But even if you still insist that the Sopherim did make alterations, the alterations in question neither raise nor lower the points upon which the heretics rest. Consult, also, the work done for Ptolemy the king, and you will see that in the thirteen instances where they made changes, they state the reason why they have made these alterations, and what these alterations are in what they did for him.⁵³ In conclusion, the heretics can have nothing to say in this matter.

ולומר, י'ח מלין תיקון סופרים כדנרסינן במכילתא; ⁵² ועוד דלא שינו חס ושלום הסופרים ולא תקנו, אלא שכך היה לו לומר אלא מפני שכנה הכתוב מפני כבוד השכינה ודוק ותשכח: וכן בקרי וכתיב הא מראים מה דשינו, אם תמצא לומר דחס ושלום שינו, אבל אנו כת המאמינים נאמין דכולהון דלכה למשה מסני, וכן בתיקון סופרים, אפילו אם תמצא לומר שתקנו הסופרים, לא מעלה ולא מוריד במה שהמינים פוקרים, וראה גם ראה בעובדא דתלמי המלך בשלשה עשר דבר ששינו, שבפירש נאמר למה שינו ומה שינו במה שכתבו לו,⁵³ סוף דבר בזה אין להם פה להשיב:

burden (עליך) TO THEE,' is altered into "*so that I am a burden* (אלי) TO MYSELF," to remove its offensiveness. xvii. Job xxxii. 3, where the original, "*they condemned* (את אלהים, or את הדין) GOD or THE DIVINE JUSTICE," is altered into "*they condemned* (את איוב) JOB," for the same reason as the foregoing. And xviii. Lam. iii. 19, where the inspired writer calls on God to remember his sufferings, and then expresses his conviction, "*yea thou wilt remember, and* THY SOUL WILL MOURN OVER ME (וְתָשִׁיחַ עָלַי נַפְשֶׁךָ), this is altered into "*and my soul is humbled within me* (וְתָשׁוּחַ עָלַי נַפְשִׁי), because of the remark that God will mourn. These eighteen *Decrees of the Scribes* are enumerated in the Massorah magna on Numb. i. 1, and on Ps. cvi. 20, and in the Massoretic work *Ochla Ve-Ochlah*, p. 113. The whole question of the *Tikun Sopherim* is most elaborately discussed by Pinsker, in the *Hebrew Annual* called *Kerem Chemed*, vol. ix., pp. 52, etc., Berlin, 1856, and Geiger *Urschrift und Uebersetzungen der Bibel*, p. 308, etc., Breslau, 1857.

⁵² *The Mechiltha* מכילתא is a Midrashic exposition of Exodus xii.—xxxv. 3, attributed to R. Ishmael ben Elisha, who flourished in the first century of the Christian era. For a description of the Mechiltha, as well as for R. Ishmael b. Elisha's rules of interpretation and influence on Biblical exegesis, see Alexander's edition of Kitto's *Cyclopædia*, *s. v.* ISHMAEL BEN ELISHA, and MIDRASH. The passage referred to, is to be found in Exod. xv. 7, section vi., p. 47, &c., ed. Weiss, Vienna, 1865.

⁵³ The work for King Ptolemy, referred to in the text, is the Septuagint, in which the translators, according to ancient tradition, designedly made thirteen alterations, in order

But for the men of the Great ואלולי אנשי כנסת הגדולה שהחזירו Synagogue who restored the crown העטרה ליושנה כרכתיב, ויקראו בספר תורת to its ancient state, as it is written, "They read in the law of God," &c. [Nehem. viii. 8], see *Nedarim*

to remove certain offensive expressions, and to prevent misunderstanding the text. They are as follows according to the order of *Jerusalem Talmud*, to which Jacob Ibn Adonijah evidently refers.—i. Gen. i. 1-3, according to the structure of the language, and the most ancient traditions still preserved by Rashi and Ibn Ezra, is to be rendered "*In the beginning when* God created heaven and earth [*i. e.*, the universe, comp. ii. 1, 4], and the earth was still desolate and void, and darkness was upon the face of the earth, and the spirit of God hovered upon the face of the earth, then God said let there be light," &c. But as this presupposes the existence of primordial waters, and of a chaotic mass, which by the draining of the waters on the second day became the formed earth, it was thought necessary in translating the Bible into Greek, and in opposition to the Greek cosmogony and polytheism, to lay great stress on the absolute unity of God, and on the absolute creation from nothing. Hence the word בראשית, had to be made independent of the following verses, and to be rendered *in the beginning* ἐν ἀρχῇ ἐποίησεν ὁ θεὸς, instead of in the beginning WHEN. This change the Talmud indicates by the pregnant construction אלהים ברא בראשית, thus placing בראשית last, and precluding every other translation than *God created in the beginning.* (Geiger, *Urschrift*, p. 344, &c). ii. Gen. i. 26, where "let *us* make man in *our* image, after *our* likeness," has been altered into "*I* will make man in the image, and in the likeness," to remove the appearance of polytheism. iii. Gen. ii. 2, where "and he ended on *the seventh* (השביעי) day," has been changed into (השש׳) *the sixth* day, to avoid the apparent contradiction, since God did not work on the seventh day. iv. Gen. v. 2 (i. 27), where "male and female created he *them*" (ברא אתם ברא), has been altered into *created he him* (בְּרָאוֹ), to remove the apparent contradiction in the passage where the man and woman are spoken of as having been created together, or simultaneously, and ii. 21-23, where the woman is described as having been made out of the man ; as well as to introduce into the version the notion which obtained among the Jews, that man was created an hermaphrodite, thus showing the Greeks, that the Hebrew, like their philosopher, believed man to have been originally androgynous (comp. *Midrash Rabba*, on Gen. i. 26, section viii., p. 10 *a*, ed. Stettin, 1863, with Plato, *Synposion*, p. 84, &c., ed. Engelmann). v. Gen. xi. 7, "let *us* go down, and let *us* confound" (נרדה ונבלה), has been changed into "*I* will go down, and *I* will confound" (ארדה ואבלה), to remove the apparent polytheism. vi. Gen. xviii. 12, "after my decay, I had again pleasure," has been altered into אחרי בְּלֹתִי היתה לי עֶדְנָה, οὔπω μέν μοι γέγονεν ἕως τοῦ νῦν, *after it had been thus with me hitherto*, to avoid the offensive application to the distinguished mother of Israel of the expression בְּלָה, which is used for rotten old garments (comp. Geiger, *Urschrift*, p. 415, &c). vii. Gen. xlix. 6, "in their anger they slew a man, and in their self-will they hamstrung an ox," has been altered into "in their anger they slew an ox (שׁור), and in their self-will they hamstrung a fatted bull (אָבוּס), to do away with the wholesale slaughter of men. viii. Exod. iv. 20, חמור, *ass*, is altered into ὑποζύγια, *beasts of burden*, because of the reluctance which the translator had to mention the name of this beast. ix. In Exod. xii 40, *and all other lands, i. e.*, "the land of Canaan" has been added, in order to remove the apparent contradiction, since the Israelites did not sojourn four hundred and thirty years in Egypt. x. In Levit. xi. 6, and Deut. xiv. 7, ארנבת = λαγός, *a hare*, has been altered into χοιρογρούλλος, *porcupine*, or *hedgehog*, to avoid giving offence to the Ptolemy family, whose name was *Lagos*. xi. In Numb. xvi. 15, חמר, *ass*, has been altered into

[87 b],⁵⁴ as quoted above, we should have walked about as blind men, and as those who are smitten with blindness, and could not have found any correct Codex, nor any scroll of the Law on which we could rely. Thus we could not have known whether a word has the ו conjunctive or not but for the Massorah, as Tossafoth remarks on this subject in connection with the Levirate law (*Jebamoth*, 106 b), where "Rabbi Abaja says the one who sends a letter of divorce must not pause after the לא, *not*, and thus read אָבָה יַבְּמִי, *he wants to per- form the duty of levir* [Deut. xxv. 7], since this might convey the idea that he wants to marry her, &c. Now R. Ashai found R. Kahana, who, being perplexed about it, read וְלֹא אָבָה יַבְּמִי with ו conjunctive; where the former said to him, Have you not heard what Rabe said upon

אלחים וכולי, ודרשינן בנדרים פרק אין בין המודר וכולי עיין לעיל,⁵⁴ היינו הולכים כסומים וכמוכים בסתרים, ולא היה נמצא לנו ספר שיהיה מוגה ילא ספר תורה שנוכל להסמך עליו ; דמיון זה אם מלה אחת היא בו״י או בלא וי״ו, כגון ולא בו״י או לא בלא וי״ו, לא הוינן ידעין לאוכוחי כמאן, אלולי המכרה, כהא דכתבו התוספות ב־במות סוף פרק מצות חליצה, גבי אמר אבי״ האי מאן דמקרי גם חליצה לא ליקרי לרידה לא לחודיה, ואבה יבמי לחודיה, דכשמע אבה יבמי כולי. עד רב אשי אשכחיה לרב כהנא דקמצטער ומקרי לה, ולא אבה יבמי אמר

ἐπιθύμημα = חמד, *a desirable thing*, by changing *Resh* into *Daleth*, in order not to mention the ass as already stated. xii. Deut. iv. 19, where the sun, moon, and the stars, are said to have been apportioned to the nation as objects of worship, the word להאיר = διακοσμέω, *to shine*, has been inserted, so as to avoid the idolatry of the heathen being ascribed to God. xiii. Deut. xvii. 3, where we have the statement that God had not commanded *the Israelites* to worship other Gods, in accordance with Deut. iv. 19; it has been altered אשר לא צויתי לאומות לעבדם, *which I have forbidden the nations to worship*, to preclude the possibility of ascribing the origin of idolatry to the God of Israel.

It only remains to be added, that these alterations are also enumerated in the *Mechilta*, on Exod. xii. 40, p. 19, &c., ed. Weiss, Vienna, 1865; and in the Babylonian Talmud, *Megilla* 9 a, where, however, the following variations occur. i. The *Mechilta*, which contains the original account, says nothing about these alterations being restricted to thirteen. ii. It erroneously makes alteration ii. to consist in ונקוביו, and not in בראו. iii. It restricts alteration vii. to אבוס only; and iv. It does not give the reason for alteration x., which is given in the Jerusalem Talmud. The variations in the Babylonian Talmud again, are as follows: i. It gives *fifteen* instead of thirteen alterations, adding the substitution of זאטוטי = ζητητής, for נערי, Exod. xxiv. 5, and for אצילי, *ibid.* xxiv. 11. The substitution of this Greek word in both these passages, shows that I was wrong in my strictures on Jacob b. Chajim's quotation (*vide supra*, p. 53, note 31). ii. It rightly gives בראו, as alteration iii., Gen. i. 2 (v. 2). iii. It states that these alterations were made in the Pentateuch, and by seventy-two elders, which is not mentioned in the other records. Of these thirteen alterations so minutely described in these documents, there are only eight to be found in the present recensions of the Septuagint, viz., Gen. i. 1, ii. 2, xviii. 12, xlix. 6; Exod. iv. 20, xii. 40; Levit. xi. 16 (Deut. xiv. 7); Numb. xvi. 15. Comp. Frankel, *Vorstudien zu der Septuaginta*, p. 25, &c.; Geiger, *Urschrift und Uebersetzungen der Bibel*, p. 439, &c., Breslau, 1857; Weiss, *Commentary on the Mechilta*, p. 19, &c., Vienna, 1865.

⁵⁴ *Vide supra*, p. 48, &c.

this subject ? R. Kahana answered him, In this case Rabe himself yields."[55] Thus far.

Tossafoth remarks thereupon, and this is its language, "In the correct Codices it is לֹא without the *Vav*, and this is also evident from the Massorah [which says], 'לֹא occurs three times, in conjunction with אָבָה, viz., Deut. x. 10, xxv. 7, and Ps. lxxxi. 12; and in two other passages it commences the verse, and is with *Vav* conjunctive, viz., Deut. xi. 30. and xxiii. 6.' It also occurs in two other passages of the same kind, not mentioned in the Massorah, viz., 1 Sam. xxxi. 4, and Judges xi. 17." Thus far the language of Tossafoth. You can see now that if it had not been for the Massorah we should not have known whether to read לֹא, *not*, or וְלֹא, *and not* [in Deut. xxv. 7]. But finding in the Massorah that לֹא אָבָה occurs three times, and that the passage in question is counted among them, it is evident that the reading was not וְלֹא, *and not*, with *Vav*. Indeed innumerable examples might be adduced which are like it. Again, when the Massorah enumerates a certain word which is in so many instances preceded by לֹא, but in none of them by וְלֹא, saying that this construction occurs so many times, we know positively that in all other places it is וְלֹא. Thus, for instance, it tells us that in fourteen verses occur לֹא, לֹא, and וְלֹא, וְלֹא, and *vice versa*; and so all the rest. The same is also the case with אֶת and וְאֶת, in Numb. xxxi. 22, upon which the Massorites remark: "And the sign is, *the gold belongs to the king*," and the meaning is, that this passage ought to be so, for there are two passages which take this ו before the second and the last nouns, whilst the remaining ones have no copulative, viz., the passages before us, and Joshua ix. 1. Now the meaning of this [Massoretic sign] is that *the gold*, which indicates the passage beginning with *but the gold* [Numb. xxxi. 22], is similar in construction, and belongs to *the king*, which indicates

---

[55] The allusion to Rabe arises from the circumstance that he laid no weight on a pause. Compare *Jebamoth*, 106, *b*.

ליה לא סבר ליה מר להא דרבא, אמר ליה מודה רבא בלא אבה יבמי,[55] עד כאן:

וכתבו התוכפת וזה לשונם, לא אבה כתוב בספרים מדוייקים, וכן מוכח במסרת לא אבה ג' דכתיכי, לא אבה יי השחיתך, לא אבה יבמי, וישראל לא אבה לי, ויש שנים ריש פרשה במשנה תורה ולא אבה כיהון, ולא אבה יי לשמוע אל בלעם, ויש פסוק דלא שייכי לאותו מסורת ולא אבה נושא כליו דשאול, וגם אל מלך מואב שלח ולא אבה דיפתח, עד כאן לשון התוכפת; הנך רואה בעיניך שאלולי המסורת היינו מסופקים אי הוה קרינן לא אבה או ולא אבה, ומדקאחזינן דבמסורת אמר דאינון ג' לא אבה, ומני דין חד מנהון, ידעינן בבירור דלא קרינן ולא אבה, ודכוותיה טובא לאין מספר; וחו במסרה מני לא ומלה אחרא ולית חד מנהון ולא, ואמר אינון כך וכך, בבירור ידעינן דשארא כתבין וקריין ולא, וכן המשל ארבע עשרה פסוקים אית בהון לא לא ולא ולא או החפך וכן כולם, וכן את את ואת ואת, כהא דאמרינן אך את הזהב ואת הכסף את הנחשת את הברזל את הבדיל ואת העופרת, כתב עליו בעל המסורת וסימניך דהבא למלכיא, ופידש כי כך דינו, ואינון שני פסוקים דנסבין הלין ווי"ן חניגא ואת ובתרא ואת ושארא את דין ופסוק ויהי כשמוע' כל המלכים ריהושע החתי והאמורי הבנעני חפריזי החוי והיבוסי,

the passage, "*and it came to pass, when all the kings heard*" [wherewith the verse in Joshua ix. 1 begins]. From this you can see the beautiful and laconic style of the Massorites, for thereby they make known to us how the passage is to be read and written. If it had not been for the Massorites, how could we tell, when we find it written, *the Hittites*, AND *the Amorites*, AND *the Canaanites*, AND *the Perizzites*, whether the order is right or wrong?[56] The same is the case with *plene* and *defective*, since with us the *Keri* and *Kethiv* are of paramount importance, although there is a dispute as to which of them should be made the basis in expounding the text]; *e. g.*, in *Pessachim*, 16 *b*, where the question is about the word יאכל

ופירש דהבא אך את הזהב למלכיא ויהי כשמוע כל המלכים, הנך רואה צחות לשון בעל המסורת וקוצר לשונו, ובזה הודיענו כיצד קריאת וכתיבת הפסוק, ואלולי בעל המסורת היכא היינן ידעין אם הוה מצינן כתוב החתי והאמורי והכנעני ורפרייז, לא היינן ידעין לחוכחא אם אמת או שקר,[56] וכן במלאים וחסרים, דיש לנו אם למקרא ואם למסורות, ומיהו פלוגתא היא במה עבדינן עיקר, כגון בפרק כיצד צולין גבי בבית אחד

[56] To understand the remark in the text, it is necessary to add to what we have already said upon this subject (*vide supra*, p. 30, &c.), that Ibn Adonijah alludes to those six verses out of the twenty, containing the names of the Canaanitish nations, which are divisible into two groups, of three verses each (זוגין מן ג'), and which with the other fourteen form one rubric. They are as follows:—

Exod. iii. 8	הכנעני והחתי והאמרי והפרזי והחוי והיבוסי
Exod. iii. 17	הכנעני והחתי והאמרי והפרזי והחוי והיבוסי
Judges iii. 5	הכנעני החתי והאמרי והפרזי והחוי והיבוסי
Deut. xx. 17 . . .	החתי והאמרי הכנעני והפרזי החוי והיבוסי
Joshua ix. 1	החתי והאמרי הכנעני הפרזי החוי והיבוסי
Joshua xii. 8	החתי האמרי והכנעני הפרזי החוי והיבוסי

These are the only six instances out of the twenty passages which follow in definite order; of the other fourteen, there are not only some which do not give all the names, but each has an arbitrary sequence in the enumeration. They are as follows:—

Exod. xiii. 5	הכנעני והחתי והאמרי והחוי והיבוסי
Exod. xxiii. 23	האמרי והחתי והפרזי והכנעני החוי והיבוסי
Exod. xxiii. 28	את החוי את הכנעני ואת החתי
Exod. xxxiii. 2	את הכנעני האמרי והחתי והפרזי החוי והיבוסי
Exod. xxxiv. 11	את האמרי והכנעני והחתי הפרזי והחוי והיבוסי
Numb. xiii. 29	והחתי והיבוסי והאמרי . . . והכנעני
Deut. vii. 1	החתי והגרגשי והאמרי והכנעני והפרזי והחוי והיבוסי
Josh. iii. 10	את הכנעני ואת החתי ואת החוי ואת הפרזי ואת הגרגשי והאמרי והיבוסי
Josh. xi. 3	הכנעני והאמרי והחתי והפרזי והיבוסי והחוי
Josh. xxiv. 11	האמרי והפרזי והכנעני והחתי והגרגשי החוי והיבוסי
1 Kings ix. 20	האמרי החתי הפרזי החוי והיבוסי
Ezra ix. 1	לכנעני החתי הפרזי היבוסי והאמרי
Nehem. ix. 8	הכנעני החתי האמרי והפרזי והיבוסי והגרגשי
2 Chron. viii. 7	החתי והאמרי והפרזי והחור והיבוסי

It will be seen that even in those instances where the order is the same, the use of the *Vav* conjunctive is so arbitrary, that were it not for the Massorah, which most minutely marks both its presence and absence; it would be very difficult to ascertain the correct orthography.

[Exod. xii. 46];[57] and the similar case in connection with the feast of tabernacles, where we have בַּסֻּכֹּת בַּסֻּכֹּת [*Succa*, 6 *b*];[58] and many other examples might be adduced on this subject (*vide* Tossafoth on *Succa*). This also obtains by the marginal readings which are not in the text, the *Kametz* and *Pattach*, and other things of a similar kind, which alter the sense, and of which there are numerous examples. Again, also, in the point of the numbers of passages which the Massorah gives,

יאכל,[57] ודכוורתיה בפרק קמא דסוכה סוכות סוכת,[58] ואיכא לקהוי ולאקושי טובא בהא ועיין בתוספת פרק קמא דסוכה; והוא הדין בקריין ולא כתיבין, וקמצין ופתחין, והמקומות שהם משתנין בטעמא, ודכוותיה טובא לאין מספר; ותו ג'כ במניינא, דמני חמסורת באמרו ג' או ד' או זולתו, מכולהו ילפינן כמה וכמה דינין ודרשות, כהא דאמרינן במסורת בראשית ג' ר'פ וסימן בראשית ברא, בראשית ממלכות יהויקים, בראשית ממלכת צדקיה, היינו דאמרינן במסכת ערכין ס'פ יש בערכין, בקש הקב'ה להחזיר את העולם לתוהו ובהו בשביל יהויקים, כיון שנסתכל

saying, "There are three or four more," &c.; from all this we learn many different laws and explanations. Thus, for instance, when it is said in the Massorah on the word בְּרֵאשִׁית, *in the beginning*, that it begins the verse three times, viz., Gen. i. 1; Jerem. xxvi. 1, xxviii. 1; it throws light upon what is said in the Talmud, where it is declared "God wanted to reduce the world again to void and emptiness, because of the wicked Jehojakim, but when He looked upon the people of his

---

[57] As *the Kethiv* is יֵאָכֵל *passive*, and *the Keri* יֹאכַל *active*, two inferences are deduced therefrom in the Talmud. R. Jehudah maintains that the man who partakes of the passover, HE must eat it (יֹאכַל) in one place (בבית אחד), but that the passover itself may be divided, and a part of it may be eaten by another company in another place; basing his argument upon *the Keri* יֹאכַל *he must eat it at one place*. Whereas R. Simeon maintains that the passover itself IT must be eaten (יֵאָכֵל) in one place (בבית אחד), and cannot be divided between two different companies in different places, though the man himself, after having eaten his passover at home, may go to another place and partake of another company's passover; basing his argument upon *the Kethiv* יֵאָכֵל *it must be eaten in one place*.

[58] The word בסכות occurs three times in the Pentateuch (twice in Lev. xxiii. 42, and once in ver. 43); in two cases (Lev. xxiii. 42) it is defective, *i. e.*, without the ו, and in the third instance it is plene, *i. e.*, with the ו. Now, upon the saying of the Rabbins that a tabernacle must have two whole walls, and the third may be a partial one, to be a legal tabernacle, R. Simeon remarks that it must have *three* entire walls, and that the fourth may be a partial one, to constitute it a tabernacle according to the law. This difference of opinion the Talmud explains by saying that the sages follow the spelling בסכת בסכת בסכות, which makes *four* (since two are in the singular and one in the plural); one of these four represents the commandment itself, shewing that we must have a סכה, and the remaining three indicate the three walls, one of which is allowed by the Halacha to be partial. Whereas R. Simeon follows the pronunciation, which is alike plural in all the three instances, and hence obtains *six*. He then takes one of these three (*i. e.*, of the plurals) to indicate the commandment respecting the feast itself, and the remaining two plurals, being four in number, he refers to the four walls of the סכה, one of which may, according to the Halacha, be partial.

time, His mind was appeased: God again wanted to reduce the world to void and emptiness, because of the people of Zedekiah's time, but when He looked upon Zedekiah, His mind was appeased" [*Erachin*, 17 *a*].⁵⁹ Again we read in the Massorah, "וַיַּבְדֵּל, *and he separated*, occurs three times, viz., Gen. i. 4, 7; 1 Chron. xxv. 1."⁶⁰ Now it is said in the Talmud, "Whoso [in the *Havdalah*]⁶¹ mentions the separations [of God] must not mention less than three, nor more than seven. [Query.] To say not more than seven is right, because seven separations are instanced, and there are no more; but why should there be not less than three? [Reply]. Because וַיַּבְדֵּל occurs three times; and as the first separation was between the Sabbath and the week days, therefore must the three separations be mentioned at the close of the Sabbath, viz., "between holy and profane," "between light and darkness," and "between Israel and the Gentiles;"⁶² the fourth separation which is mentioned on this occasion, viz., "between the seventh day and

בדורו נתישבה דעתו, בקש הקב"ה להחזיר את העולם לתהו ובוהו מבני דורו של צדקיהו, כיון שנסתכל בצדקיה⁰ נתיישבה דעתו, עד כאן; ⁵⁹ ותו גרסינן במסורת ויבדל ג׳, ויבדל אלהים בין האור, ויבדל בין המים, ויבדל דוד ושרי הצבא בדברי הימים כ"ה,⁶⁰ כדאמר בערבי פסחים כל הפוחת לא יפחות משלשה הבדלות,⁶¹ ולא יוסיף על שבע, בשלמה אין מוסיפין על שבע, דהתם קא חשיב שבע הבדלות ולא אשכחן טפי, אלא שלשה אמאי, משום דשלש פעמים כתיב ויבדל, והבדלה ראשונה היתה במוצאי שבת, לפיכך עושים שלשה הבדלות במוצאי שבת, בין קדש לחול, בין אור לחשך בין ישראל לגוים,⁶² ובין יום השביעי לששת ימי

---

⁵⁹ The Massoretic enumeration of these three passages suggests an explanation of the passage in the Talmud, where Jer. xxvi. 1 and xxviii. 1, are connected with Gen. i. 1, shewing that God wished, in those cases where בראשית is used, to destroy the work of the first בראשית. May not this striking illustration also suggest the design of the Massorah in its first origin?

⁶⁰ The *editio princeps* differs from the succeeding editions in the quotations. Thus, for instance, the first, second, and third editions of Jacob b. Chajim's Bible indicate the reference to Genesis i. 7, by quoting simply ויבדל בן המים, whereas the later editions add אשר מתחת לרקיע; whilst the third reference in the *editio princeps* is to ויבדל אהרן קדש קדשים, which does not occur in the Hebrew Scriptures, and has therefore rightly been altered in the second, third, and the other editions into ויבדל דוד ושרי הצבא בד"ה כ"ח.

⁶¹ *Havdalah* הבדלה is the name of the prayer which the Jews to this day offer on Sabbath evening, at the going out of the Sabbath and coming in of the week day. The last benediction in this prayer, in which occur the passages referred to in the Talmud, is as follows: ברוך אתה יי אלהינו מלך העולם המבדיל בין קדש לחול בין אור לחשך בין ישראל לעמים בין יום השביעי לששת ימי המעשה ברוך אתה יי המבדיל בין קדש לחול. *Blessed be the Lord our God, king of the universe, who hast made a distinction between the holy and the common, between light and darkness, between Israel and the other nations, between the seventh day and the other six days of work; blessed be thou, O God, who hast made a distinction between the holy and the common!*

⁶² This is the reading of the *editio princeps*, as well as of the second and third editions, of the Rabbinic Bibles; later editions have substituted לעמים for לגוים, because of the fear of Christians, who took it to refer to themselves.

the six days of creation," is included in "between holy and profane," and is simply repeated in order to make it agree in sense with the concluding benediction [63] [*Pessachim*, 103 *b*, 104 *a*]. Again we read in the Massorah, "פָּתוּחַ, *opened*, occurs four times, and the passages are Numb. xix. 15, Job xxix. 19, Psalm v. 10, and Jerem. v. 16;" and these four correspond to the four laws which obtain with regard to an earthen vessel, viz., when it has a hole through which the water runs into it, the law is that it must not be used for consecrating therein the water of sin-offering, thus answering to "and every open vessel" [Numb. xix. 15]; yet it is still a vessel with respect to the growing of plants. But if the hole is so large that a small root can be put through it, then it is clean for growing therein plants, for when a plant grows in a vessel which has a hole, it is no longer subject to defilement, thus answering to "my root is opened" [Job xxix. 19]; yet it is still a vessel with respect to olives. If the hole, however, is so large that an olive can pass through it, then it is clean [or not subject to defilement], thus answering to "an open sepulchre is their throat" [Ps. v. 10], for what amounts to eating is the size of an olive; yet it is still a vessel with respect to pomegranates. But if the hole is so large that a pomegranate can pass through it, then it is no longer subject to any defilement, and thus answers to "his heap is as an open sepulchre" [Jerem. v. 16]; that is to say, when the vessel has a hole through which a pomegranate can pass, it is like a heap of rubbish, for it is no longer regarded as a vessel.[64] Many of the Massoretic signs are used for such explanations in innumerable cases; some of them are dispersed through *the book Mordecai*,[65] and in the

המעשה, בכלל בין קדש לחול, ואומרים אותו כדי לסמוך לחתימה מעין חתימה,[63] ותו גרסינן במסורת פתוח ד', וסימנו וכל כלי פתוח, שרשי פתוח אלי מים, קבר פתוח גרונם, אשפתו כקבר פתוח, ואינון כנגד ארבע מדות שחם בכלי חרס, נקב בכונס משקה, נפסל מלקדש בו מי חטאת, היינו וכל כלי פתוח ונומר, ועדיין כלי הוא לזרעים, נקב בשורש קטן, טהור הוא לזרעים, אם היה בעציץ נקוב אינו מקבל טומאה, היינו שרשי פתוח דאיוב, ועדיין כלי הוא לקבל בו זיתים, נקב במוציא זית, טהור העשוי לאוכלין, היינו קבר פתוח גרונם דתלים, דסתם אכילה כזית, ועדיין כלי הוא לרמונים, נקב במוציא רמון, טהור חוא לגמרי, וחיינו אשפתו פתוח, כלומר כשהכלי במוציא רמון, נדמה לאשפה דשוב אין תורת כלי עליו;[64] והרבה מסימנים אלו נדרשים בכהאי גוונא לאין מספר, ומהם מפוזרים במרדכי,[65] וברשובות

---

[63] חתימה is the reading of the first, second, and third editions of the Rabbinic Bibles, in accordance with the Talmud (*Pessachim*, 103 *a*), whence it is quoted. Later editions have erroneously פתיחה.

[64] Things in a vessel are, according to the Talmud, subject to defilement. If the vessel, however, happens to have a hole, then it all depends upon the size of this hole, the definition of which is the subject of discussion. Compare Maimonides, *Iad Ha-Chesaka, Hilchoth Kelim*, section xiv., vol. iii., p. 350; ed. Amsterdam, 1702.

[65] מרדכי, *Mordecai*, also called ספר המורדכי, *the Book of Mordecai*, is a treatise on the Legal Code (ספר הלכות), embodying all the laws of the Talmud, which was compiled, revised, corrected, annotated, and supplemented by Isaac Alphasi. This *Sepher*

Theological Decisions of Maharam,[66] where the latter defines what is meant by the word הִכּוּנִי, *he smote me*, which the Massorah says occurs twice, viz., Song of Songs v. 7, Proverbs xxiii. 35 (by a comparison of these two passages), *vide in loco*. In fact, there can be no doubt that whenever the Massorites state an expression occurs 7 or 4 or 10 or 3 times, they are designed for some great purpose, and are not useless. All this shews the great sanctity of our holy law, and that the parallels are marked with a design. Moreover, when the Massorah makes the remark in Chaldee, there is a reason for it, which will be found upon examination. For this reason I have collected all that I could find of their remarks in the Massoretic books which I possess, collated it, and put it in these twenty-four sacred books, arranging everything in its proper place, and I have repeated it again in the Massorah finalis, so that it can easily be found. Were I inclined to write more largely upon this subject, and to show the use of all the Massorah, and support it by proofs, it would occupy too much space, and the perusal of it would be a weariness to the flesh.

When I saw the great benefit which is to be derived from the Massorah magna, the Massorah parva, and the Massorah finalis, I apprised Seignior Daniel Bomberg of it, may his Rock and Redeemer protect him! and shewed him the advantage of the Massorah. Where-

---

Mordecai has been printed with the *Sepher Ha-Halachoth*, Constantinople, 1509; Venice, 1521–22; Sabionetta, 1524, &c. It has also appeared separately, Venice, 1558; Cracow, 1598, &c. Compare Fürst, *Bibliotheca Judaica*, ii., 324, &c.; Steinschneider, *Catalogus Libr. Hebr. in Bibliotheca Bodleiana*, 1659, &c. The work derives its appellation from the author, whose name was Mordecai b. Hillel, and who was martyred at Nürnberg, 1310.

[66] מה׳רמ, *Maharam*, is the acrostic of מורנו הרב מאיר, *our teacher the Rabbi Meier*. This R. Meier b. Baruch, who was born 1230, and died 1293, was one of the most distinguished Jewish literati during the middle ages, and the first official chief Rabbi in the German empire, to which dignity he was nominated by the Emperor Rodolph I., of Hapsburg. He had his seat and college at Rottenburg-an-der-Tauber, whence he is also called Meier of Rottenburg, or Meier Rottenburg. His *Theological Decisions*, or *Questions and Answers* (שאלות ותשובות), have been published at Cremona, 1557; Prague, 1603. He also wrote *Commentaries on the Massorah* (באורי מסרת), which are still in MS. in the public libraries. Compare Fürst, *Bibliotheca Judaica*, iii., 176, &c., Graetz, *Geschichte der Juden*, vol. vii., p. 183, &c.; Leipzig, 1863.

upon he did all in his power to send into all the countries in order to search what may be found of the Massorah; and, praised be the Lord, we obtained as many of the Massoretic books as could possibly be got. The said gentleman was not backward, and his hand was not closed, nor did he draw back his right hand from producing gold out of his purse to defray the expenses of the books, and of the messengers who were engaged to make search for them in the most remote corners, and in every place where they might possibly be found.

And when I examined these Massoretic books, and mastered their contents, I found them in the utmost disorder and confusion, so much so that there was not a sentence to be found without a blunder, that is to say, the quotations from the Massorites are both incorrect and misplaced; since in those copies [of the Bible] in which the Massorah is written in the margin, it is not arranged according to the order of the verses contained in the page. Thus, for instance, if a page has five or six verses, the first of which begins with וַיֹּאמֶר, *and he said*, the second with וַיֻּגַּד, *and it was told*, the third with וְזֶה, *and this*, the fourth with וַיִּשְׁלַח, *and he sent*, the fifth with וַתֵּשֶׁב, *and she sat*, the Massorah begins with וַיִּשְׁלַח, *the fourth* verse, "the word וַיִּשְׁלַח occurs twenty-two times;"[67] then follows verse two, "the word וַיֻּגַּד occurs twenty-four times;"[68] and

מאמצי כחו לשלוח בכל אלו הגלילות, לחפש כל מה שימצא מהמסרה, ותהלה לאל נתגלגלו לידינו מספרי המסרה מה שאיפשר להתגלגל, והשר חנזכר לא נתעצל, וידו לא קפץ, וימינו לא השיב אחור, מלהוציל זהב מכיסו בהוצאת קניית הספרים, והשלוחים אשר נשתדלו לחפשם בחורים ובסדקים ובכל מקום שהיו :

ואחר שראיתי בספרי המסרה והתבוננתי בהם, ראיתים מבולבלים בתכלית, ומשובשים עד שאין בהם בית אשר אין שם מת, היינו הפסוקים שהיה מביא בעל המסורת והבלבול הגדול שהיה בהם, כי אותם חספרים שהיה בחם המסרה סביב, לא היתה המסרה כתובה כסדר הפסוקים שהיה בעמוד, דמיון זה אם היו חמשה או ששה פסוקים בעמוד, האחר מחחיל ויאמר, והשני ויגד, והשלישי וזה, והרביעי וישלח, וחחמישי ותשב, המסורת היה מתחיל וישלח כ׳ב,[67] ואחר כך ויגד כ׳ר,[68] ואחר כך ותשב

---

[67] The instances in which וַיִּשְׁלַח is the *Piel*, future, with *Vav* conversive, are the following: Gen. viii. 7, 8, 12; xix. 29; xlv. 24: Exod. xviii. 27: Numb. xxii. 40: Josh. xxiv. 28: Judges ii. 6; iii. 18; xv. 5: 1 Sam. x. 25; xi. 7; xxx. 26: 2 Sam. iii. 21; xviii. 2: 2 Kings v. 24; xvii. 25, 26; xxiv. 2: Psalm cvi. 15. In the Massorah marginalis on Gen. viii. 7, where the instances are enumerated, twenty-one only are given, and there are no more to be found in the Bible, though the Massorah, like Ibn Adonijah, states that there are twenty-two, unless we include in this rubric וְיִשְׁלַח (Exod. vi. 11), with *Vav* conjunctive. It is moreover to be added, that there is evidently a misprint in the Massorah, where we have וישלח לוט, a second time instead of וישלח את היונה (Gen. viii. 12).

[68] The twenty-four instances in which וַיֻּגַּד, *Hophal*, future, with *Vav* conversive, are as follows: Gen. xxii. 20; xxvii. 42; xxxi. 22; xxxviii. 13, 24: Exod. xiv. 5: Josh. x. 17: Judges ix. 25, 47: 1 Sam. xv. 12; xix. 19; xxiii. 7; xxvii. 4: 2 Sam. vi. 12; x. 17: 1 Chron. xix. 17: 2 Sam. xix. 2; xxi. 11: 1 Kings i. 51; ii. 29, 41: 2 Kings vi. 13; viii. 7: Isaiah vii. 2. They are enumerated in the Massorah finalis, under the letter *He*, p. 22 *b*, col. 4.

then *the fifth* verse, "the word וַתֵּשֶׁב occurs fifteen times,"⁶⁹ without any order or plan. Moreover, most of these [Massoretic remarks] are written in a contracted form and with ornaments, so much so that they cannot at all be deciphered, as the desire of the writer was only to embellish his writing, and not to examine or to understand the sense. Thus, for instance, in most of the copies there are four lines [of the Massorah] on the top of the page, and five at the bottom, as the writer would under no circumstances diminish or increase the number. Hence, whenever there happened to be any of the alphabetical lists,⁷⁰ or if the Massoretic remarks were lengthy, he split them up in the middle, or at the beginning, and largely introduced abbreviations, so as to obtain even lines. Now, when I observed

ט"ו,⁶⁹ בלי סדר ותיקון, ורובם ה"ו כתובים בקשרים וציורים, ע"ד שלא היה באפשרות להבין מהן שום דבר, כי כוונת הסופר היתה ליפות כתיבתו ולא לחבין ולעיין בה; ונם ברובם במשל היו בראש הרף כמו ארבע שורות ולמטה כמו חמש, לעולם הסופר לא היה מוסיף ולא גורע, ואם אירע א'ב או לשון מסורת גדול,⁷⁰ היה מפסיק באמצע או בראש, וכן מקצר מהם הרבה כדי להשוות שורותיו; וכשראיתי כל זה הבלבול, נדרתי חצני, בתחלה לשים כל המסורות על סדר הפסוקים, ואח'כ הפשתי בספרי המסרה שהי' לי חבורים לבד זולת מה שהיה כתוב סביב המקרא, ובמקומות שהיה הדלוג מהסופר והקצור כדי להשוות השורות, שיהיו במספר ד' למעלה וה' לממה, אז הייתי מבקש בחבורי המסרה, והייתי מתקנם על נכון, ובמקומות שמצאתי הפרש בין ספרי המסרה זה אומד בכה וזה אומר בכה, הבאתי דעות שניהב, וכן ימצא כתוב סביבות המקרא הזאת⁷¹ שהדפסנו

all this confusion, I bestirred myself in the first place to arrange all the Massoretic notes according to the verses to which they belonged, and then to investigate the Massoretic treatises in my possession, apart from what is written in the margin of the Bibles. Whenever an omission or contraction occurred [in those copies of the Bible which had the Massorah] in order to obtain even lines, or four lines [of Massorah] at the top [of a page in the Bible] and five at the bottom, I at once consulted the Massoretic treatises, and corrected it according to order. And whenever I found that the Massoretic treatises differed from each other, I put down the opinions of both sides, as will be found in the margin of our edition of the Bible published by us, with the Massorah,⁷¹ the word in dispute being marked to indicate that it is not the lan-

---

⁶⁹ The instances in which וַתֵּשֶׁב occurs, are as follows: Gen. xxi. 16 (twice); xxxi. 34; xxxviii. 11, 14; xlix. 24: Josh. vi. 25: 1 Sam. i. 23: 2 Sam. xiii. 20: 1 Kings ii. 19: Ruth ii. 23, 14. They are enumerated in the Massorah marginalis, on Gen. xxxviii. 11, and on 2 Sam. xiii. 20, where it is distinctly stated that there are only twelve instances; and indeed there are no more to be found in the Hebrew Scriptures. The statement, therefore, in the text, that there are *fifteen* such instances, which is to be found in all the editions of Jacob b. Chajim's Introduction, must be a slip of the pen.

⁷⁰ By Alphabetic Massorah is meant, a certain number of exceptions, or peculiar forms of words, which come under the same rubric, and are arranged and enumerated in alphabetical order.

⁷¹ Hence the Massorah thus put in the margin obtained the name *Massorah marginalis*.

guage of the Massorah; and whenever I took exception to the statement of a certain Codex of the Massorah, because its remark did not harmonise with the majority of the copies of the Massorah, whilst the same difficulty was not found in the others, or whenever it contradicted itself, or where there was a mistake, I made a careful search till I discovered the truth, according to my humble knowledge; but sometimes I had to leave it in uncertainty, and for this reason there will be found many such in the margin of the Bible which we printed. The Lord alone knows how much labour I bestowed thereon, as those will testify who saw me working at it. As to the revision of the verses, it would have been impossible for me to do it correctly without knowing the whole Scriptures by heart, and this is far from me. But for a certain book called *Concordance*, the author of which is the learned R. Isaac Nathan,[72] who lived some forty years ago, published in our printing-office at Venice, I could not have corrected the verses. This is a precious work; it embraces all the points of the Holy Bible, and explains all the sacred Scriptures, by stating all nouns and verbs with their analogous forms, and giving at the heading of every noun

במסורה נקוד על הפלונתא, בהיות כי אינו מלשון בעל המסורת; וכן במקומות שהיה קשה לי על לשון ספר אחד מהמסרה, שלא הייתי מוצא כדבריו ברוב הספרים, ובמסרה אחרת באופן אחר ולא היה קשה, ובמקומות שהיה קשה מדירה אדירים, או שהיה טעות, הייתי חוקר עד שהייתי מוצא האמת לעניות דעתי, ובמקומות הנחתי הדבר בספק, וכן כמה מיני קהוון, כאשר ימצא כתוב סביבות עשרים וארבע זה שהדפסנו; והשם יודע כמה טורח עבדתי על זה, וכבר זה מפורסם לכל מי שראה אותי מתעסק בו: ובהגהת הפסוקים לא היה איפשר שהייתי יכול להגיה אלא אם כן שהייתי יודע כל העשרים וארבע על פה, זה נעלם ממני, ואלולי ספר אחד הנקרא שמו קונקורדנסייא, חברו חכם אחד קרוב לזמנינו זה בכמו ארבעים שנה, שמו רבי יצחק נתן, זכר צדיק לברכה,[72] שכבר נדפס פה ויניציא בבית דפוסינו, לא היה באפשר שהייתי יכול להגיה, והוא כלי יקר, מקיף כל קטרי המכתב הקדוש, ומבאר כל המכתב הקדוש בחברו כל שם ופועל עם הדומה לו, ובראש כל שם ופועל מפרש התיבה הזאת פירש כך וכך, או תפרד לכך וכך ראשים, ופירשם כך וכך, ובציינו אותם הציונים בחלוקת כל פרשה ופרשה, וכל נביא ונביא, לכך וכך פרשיות, ובכל תיבה דורש זאת תמצא בסימן פלוני, בפסוק ד', או כ', או ל', שבסבת זה תכף בנקלה ימצא המבוקש; ואם פסוק אחד יש לו ד', או ח' פעלים ושמות, כגון ובצל ידי כסיתיך, תמצא פסוק זה בשרש צל, ובשרש יד, ובשרש כסה, עד שאם אינך

and verb an explanation, saying the meaning of the word is so and so, and branches out in such and such a manner, and comments upon each one separately. It also marks the division of each chapter, and the number of chapters in every prophetical book, and tells in which chapter and verse every word occurs, *i. e.*, verse 4, 20, or 30, thereby any word wanted may easily be found. And if a verse has four or five verbs or nouns, *e. g.*, וּבְצֵל יָדִי כִּסִּיתִיךָ, *in the shadow of mine hand* [Isa. li. 16], you will find it quoted under צֵל, *shadow*; under יָד, *hand*; and under כָּסָה, *to cover*; so that if you only remember one word in the

---

[72] For R. Isaac Nathan, see Kitto's *Cyclopædia, s. v.*

verse, whether verb or noun, you will easily find the required passage under the root of the verb or noun. The advantage to be derived from this book is indescribable; without it there is no way of examining the references of the Massorah, since one who studies the Massorah must look into the verse which the Massorah quotes, and which without a concordance would take a very long time to find, as you might not know in which prophet the passage referred to occurs, and if you knew the prophet, you might still not know the chapter and verse. Besides, all the world is not so learned in the Scriptures. Whosoever has this concordance does not require any more the lexicon of Kimchi, for it contains all the roots, whereunto is added an index of all the verses in the Bible: none of them is wanted. In conclusion, without it I could not have done the work which I have done.

Seeing that the Massorah was too large to be printed entire in the margin, I have not repeated the Massoretic remark after it has been given once. Thus, for instance, וישלח, *and he sent*, occurs twenty-two times: I enumerated the passages in the remark on the words וישלח [Gen. viii. 8], and when I afterwards came again to the word וישלח, in another place, I did not repeat all these references, having given them once before, but simply said the Massoretic remark will be found in section Noah.[73] As the prophetic books are large, every prophet having on an average twenty-five chapters, my labour would have been in vain if I had simply said the word is found in such and such a prophet, since the reference could not be found without great exertion, and the student would soon have grown weary and left it off altogether. I have therefore adopted the division of the chapters which R. Isaac Nathan made, and said it occurs in such and such a prophet,

מסיג או זוכר לידע, כי אם תיבה אחת שהיא פועל או שם מהפסוק, תכף תמצא מבוקשך בשרש הפועל, או השם ההוא; וגדולה מעלה ותועלת זה הספר לאין תכלית, וזולתו ובלעדו אין דרך לעיין במסורת למצוא הפסוק שצריך תכף. כי צריך שהמעיין יבקש הפסוק שמביא המסורת או זולתו שצריך יעבור זמן רב כי יבאו פסוקים שלא ידע באיזה נביא הם, ואפילו ידעו צריך שיבקש כל הנביא, ולאו כל צלמא מקרא גמירי, ומי שהגיע ספר זה לידו, אין צריך לו לשרשי הקמחי, כי יש בו השרשים מוסף עליו המורה מקום מכל פסוקי דמקרא, לא יחסר עד אחד; סוף דבר בלעדיו לא הייתי יכול לעשות מה שעשיתי:

ובהיות כי המסורת היה רב להדפיסו כלו סביב המקרא במקום שכבר הבאתי סימן א', פעם א', לא דשתי להביאו פעם אחרת, דמיון זה וישלח חם כ"ב, כתבתי אותם כולם פעם אחת בסדר נח בפסוק וישלח את היונה, כשהגעתי אחר כך בוישלח אחר, לא רציתי להאריך לכתבו פעם אחרת, כי כבר נכתב ונחתם, אבל כתבתי הוא נמסר בסדר נח; ובנביאים בהיות שהם גדולים וכל נביא יש בו בכמותו בכמו כ"ה פעם, שים בכל פרשה ופרשה, אם הייתי כותב נמסר בנביא פלוני לבד, היה יוצא שכרי בהפסדי, שלא היה באפשרות למצוא כי אם בקושי גדול, והיה המעיין קץ בו, יהיה מניחו מלבקשו, לכן הוצרכתי להשתמש בחלוקת הפרשיות, שהביא בספרו רבי יצחק נתן ספר הקונקורדנצייא.

---

[73] נח is the title of one of the Sabbatic lessons, comprising Gen. vi. 9–xi. 33; *vide supra*, p. 8, § xiv., note 12.

and in such and such a verse. Had I at that time the Massoretic division of the chapters on the whole Bible I would have preferred it, but I did not get it till I had almost finished the work. I have, nevertheless, published it separately, so that it may not be lost to Israel.

To make the Massorah perfect, I was obliged to rearrange the Massorah magna, for it was impossible to print it in the margin of the Bible, for it is too large; I have therein adopted the alphabetical order of the *Aruch*, to facilitate the reader. Moreover, all that we have printed of the Massorah magna in the margin of the Bible, I have also repeated a second time in the Massorah finalis, which I arranged alphabetically according to the example of the *Aruch*, but did not give it again entire; I have only repeated the beginning of the remarks. Thus, for instance, I said "the word וישב occurs fifteen times, as you will find in such and such a prophet and passage;" the same is the case with other observations which I have omitted, and this I have done designedly. Let an illustration suffice. If the student will examine a page of a prophetical or any other book of the Bible, he will find that it has generally ten or eleven verses; that there is not a verse which is without a Massoretic remark on a word or more, and that the Massorah parva notes every word upon which there is any Massorah, and says it occurs four, thirteen, or fifteen times; and that it was impossible to print the whole Massorah which belongs to that page; hence, when there are ten words on it which belongs to the Massorah, I only give four or five at most [in the Massorah marginalis], as the space of the page does not admit of more. Now the student, not knowing whether it is given in another place, or where to look for it, might think that this Bible has not all the Massorah which belongs to it. I have therefore been obliged to indicate in the root of the word in the Massorah magna, in what

וכתבתי נמסר בנביא פלוני, בסימן פלוני, למען ידוץ קורא בו, ואלו הייתי מוצא חלוקת הפרשיות שחלקו בעלי המסרה בכל המקרא, חייתי יותר הפץ להשתמש ממנה מוולחה, ואחר כך הגיעה לידי לאחר שכבר כמעט השלמתי, אמרתי להדפיסה גם היא, לבל תשתכח ותאבד מישראל:

וכדי שיהיה המסורת שלם, הוצרכתי לתקן ולחבר אחר כך המסורת הגדולה, שאין באפשרות להדפיסה סביב שום ספר, כי היא בכמותה הרבה, וסדרתיה כדרך הערוך ממש, למען ידוץ קורא בה: ובן כל מה שהדפסנו מהמסרה סביב העשרים וארבע דהיינו מהמסר׳ האמצעית, לא הגדולה הזרתי והברתי אותה עם המסרה הגדולה שסדרתי כמו הערוך, ולא חשתי לחביא כי אם ראשי פרקים, כגון וישב ט׳ו נמסר בנביא פלוני בסימן פלוני, וכן כל מה שנשמט וזה לסבת ; המשל אם המעיין יעיין בנביא או זולתו, באותו העמוד יש י׳ או י׳א פסוקים, בכל פסוק לא ימנע שלא תחיה בו תיבה ששייך בה מסורת, והמסרה קטנה היא בכל תיבה ששייך בה מסורת, ואומרת ד׳ או ל׳, או ט׳ו, וזה לא היה באפשר לכתוב המסורת כולו שהיה שייך לאותו דף, שאם היו שייכים י׳ תיבות למסורת, הבאתי מהם ד׳ או ה׳ על הרוב, לדוהק רוחב העמוד, והמעיין לא ידע אם הם במקום אחר כבר נדפסם, ובאיזה מקום הם כדי לבקשם במקומם, ויחשוב בלבו שאין כעשרים וארבע זה כל המסורת ששייך בו, לכן הוצרכתי לציין בשרש חתיבה החיא במסרה רבתא, באיזה

part it is printed in such and such a prophet, and with what sign. I have also been obliged to repeat and state in the Massorah finalis many of the Massoretic remarks which the former editors have omitted in sundry places, because the page happened to be just as large as was required for printing the other matter. You therefore find it many a time stated in the margin of the Bible [*i. e.*, Massorah marginalis], *the Massorah on this passage is in the Massorah finalis.* Wherever, also, the Massoretic remarks belonging to a certain page were so numerous as to render it impossible to give them in their proper place, which was too narrow, or wherever there were the alphabetical remarks of the Massorah magna which belonged to the same page, I always noted in the margin, " *This is one of such and such an alphabet, and is noted in the Massorah finalis under such and such a letter,*" so that the student may easily find it. And you must not be astonished to find in the Massorah such language as, " It is noted in *second* or *first* Samuel, or *second* Kings, or *second* Chronicles," or to see Ezra and Nehemiah separated; for the author of the Concordance, who divided the law, prophets, and hagiographa into chapters, also divided Samuel, Kings, and Chronicles respectively into two books, and denominated Ezra the first ten chapters of the book, and the rest of the book he called Nehemiah; and as I have adopted the division of the Concordance, I thought it advisable to append to the end of this introduction a list of all the chapters, with the words with which they begin, and of their number in each book; so that if there crept in any mistakes in printing, they may easily be rectified by this list, printed at the end of the Introduction. We have printed in this Bible the number of every chapter, in order that the student may easily find the passage when the Massorah says, " *It is noted in such a chapter.*"

Behold, I have exerted all my might and strength to collate and arrange the Massorah with all the possible improvements, in order that it may remain pure and bright, and show its splendour to the nations and princes; for, indeed, it is beautiful to look at. This was a labour of love for the benefit of our brethren, the children of Israel, and for the glory of our holy and perfect law, as well as to fulfil as far as possible the desire of Don Daniel Bomberg (may his book protect him!), whose expenses in this matter far exceed my labours. And as regards the Commentaries, I have exerted my powers to the utmost degree to correct in them all the mistakes as far as possible; and whatsoever my humble endeavours could accomplish was done for the glory of the Lord, and for the benefit of our people; and I would not be deterred by the enormous labour, for which cause I did not suffer my eyelids to be closed long, either in the winter or summer, and did not mind rising in the cold of the night, as my aim and desire were to see this holy work finished. Now praised be the Creator, who granted me the privilege to begin and to finish this work. Remember me, O my God, for good! Amen.

לעשות ולרתקן המסרה בכל התיקונים, שאיפשר כדי להשאירה ברה וטהורה, ולהראות העמים והשרים את יפיה, כי טובת מראה היא, וזה לאוהבי תועלת אחינו בני ישראל, ותפארת תורתינו הקדושה והתמימה ולמלאות תאות ושאלת חשר מסי׳ דניאל בומבירגי, ישמרהו צורו, במה שאיפשר אף על פי שכספו היתה גדולה מהשגתי, וכן במפרשים שמתי כל מאמצי כחי לתקן המעוות במה שאפשר, ובמה שהחשינה בו עניות דעתי לשם שמים ולהועיל לבני עמינו, ולא נסוגותי אחור בשביל הטורח הרב, כי שינה לעיני לא נתתי לשובע חן בחורף חן בקיץ, ולא חששתי לקום בלילה לקור, וזולתו כי חפצי וכוונתי היתה לראות תכלית המלאכה מלאכת הקדש, ישתבח הבורא, אשר זיכני להתחיל ולהשלים, זכרה לי אלהי לטובה, אמן:

INDEX I.

PASSAGES OF SCRIPTURE REFERRED TO.

GENESIS.			Chap.	Ver.	Page.	Chap.	Ver.	Page.
Chap.	Ver.	Page.	xliii.	28	65	xxvii.	15	63
i.	1	71, 74, 75	xlv.	24	78	..	27	62
..	1–3	70	xlix.	6	70, 71			
..	2	71	..	24	79	NUMBERS.		
..	4	75				i.	1	69
..	7	75	EXODUS.			v.	13	54
..	26	70	iii.	5	73	..	14	54
..	27	70	..	8	73	vii.	1	59
ii.	2	70, 71	..	17	73	xi.	15	68
..	21–23	70	iv.	19	53	..	32	64
..	22	70	..	20	70, 71	xii.	3	64
v.	2	71	vi.	11	78	..	12	68
vi.	7	70	xii.–xxxv.	3	69	xiii.	29	73
..	9	81	..	40	70, 71	xvi.	15	70, 71
viii.	7	78	..	46	73, 74	xix.	15	76
..	8	78, 81	xiii.	5	30, 73	xxii.	40	78
..	12	78	..	16	61, 62	xxvii.	11	62, 63
xi.	7	70	xiv.	5	78	xxix.	19	60
..	33	81	xv.	7	69	..	31	60
xii.	1	45	xviii.	27	78	..	33	60
xiv.	2	45, 54	xix.	22	58	xxxi.	2	49
..	8	45	xxiii.	13	67	..	22	72
xvii.	19	16	..	19	15			
..	27	45	..	23	73	DEUTERONOMY.		
xviii.	5	49, 67	..	28	78	i.	1	50
..	12	70, 71	xxiv.	5	53, 71	iv.	19	71
..	22	68	..	11	53, 71	v.	31	49
xix.	29	78	xxvii.	11	64	vi.	4	59
xx.	5	54	xxix.	29	31	..	8	61, 62
xxi.	16	79	xxxiii.	2	73	..	9	59
xxii.	20	73	xxxiv.	11	73	vii.	1	73
xxiv.	14	45	xxxix.	12	62	x.	10	72
..	16	45				xi.	13	59
..	28	45	LEVITICUS.			..	18	61, 62
..	55	45, 49	i.	1	30	..	21	59
..	57	45	ii.	15	54	..	30	72
xxv.	6	59	x.	16	15	xiv.	7	70, 71
..	27	62	xi.	6	70	xvii.	3	71
xxvii.	19	15	..	16	71	xx.	17	73
..	29	65	..	39	54	xxii.	15	45
..	42	78	..	42	15	..	16	45
xxxi.	22	78	xii.	5	15	..	19	45
..	34	79	xiii.	10	54	..	20	45
xxxiii.	4	64	..	21	54	..	21	45
xxxiv.	3	45	..	33	15	..	23	45
..	12	45	xiv.	12	31	..	24	45
xxxviii.	11	79	xv.	10	57	..	25	45
..	13	78	xvi.	31	54	..	26	45
..	14	78	xxi.	9	54	..	27	45
..	24	78	xxiii.	42	74	..	28	45
..	25	54	..	43	74	..	29	45

Chap.	Ver.	Page.	Chap.	Ver.	Page.	Chap.	Ver.	Page.
xxiii.	6	. 72	xxi.	14	. 64	1 CHRONICLES.		
xxv.	7	71, 72	xxiii.	5	. 64	xix.	17	. 78
xxviii.	27	45, 51, 63	..	7	. 78	xxv.	1	. 75
..	30	45, 51	xxv.	29	. 11	xxix.	16	. 54
xxxiii.	27	. 53	xxvii.	4	. 78			
xxxiv.	12	. 5	xxx.	26	. 78	2 CHRONICLES.		
xxxviii.	30	. 63	xxxi.	4	. 72	viii.	7	. 73
						x.	16	. 68
JOSHUA.			2 SAMUEL.			xix.	17	. 78
iii.	10	. 73	i.	11	. 64			
vi.	25	. 79	ii..	19	. 79	EZRA.		
viii.	11	. 64	iii.	21	. 78	iii.	2	. 65
ix.	1	72, 73	vi.	12	. 78	iv.	7	. 64
x.	17	. 78	viii.	3	40, 49, 50	ix.	1	. 73
xi.	3	. 73	x.	17	. 78			
xii.	8	. 73	xii.	20	. 64	NEHEMIAH.		
xvi.	3	. 64	xiii,	20	. 79	ii.	6	. 51
xxiv.	11	30, 73	..	21	. 50	iii.	30	. 65
..	28	. 78	..	33	40, 50	..	31	. 65
			xv.	31	. 40	viii.	8	48, 70
JUDGES.			xvi.	12	. 68	ix.	8	. 73
ii.	6	. 78	..	21	. 50	x. 1-10		. 37
iii.	5	. 73	..	23	40, 49			
..	18	. 78	xviii.	2	. 78	ESTHER.		
ix.	25	. 78	..	20	40, 50	ii.	9	. 59
..	47	. 78	xix.	2	. 78	ix.	27	. 65
x.	13	. 40	xxi.	11	. 78			
xi.	17	. 72	xxiv.	14	. 64	JOB.		
xv.	5	. 78	xxx.	33	. 40	vii.	20	. 68
xvi.	31	. 58				xiv.	5	. 64
xx.	13	. 50	1 KINGS.			xv.	15	. 64
xxi.	20	. 65	i.	1	. 65	xx.	11	. 64
			..	51	. 78	xxiv.	1	. 64
RUTH.			ii.	19	. 79	xxvi.	14	. 64
ii.	11	. 49	..	29	. 78	xxix.	19	. 76
..	14	. 79	..	41	. 78	xxxi.	11	. 54
..	23	. 79	ix.	9	. 65	..	20	. 64
iii.	5	40, 49, 50	..	20	. 73	xxxii.	3	. 69
..	12	40, 49, 50	x.	5	. 64	xxxvii.	12	. 64
..	14	. 64	xii.	7	. 65	xxxviii.	41	. 64
..	17	40, 49, 50	..	16	. 68	xxxix.	26	. 64
			xvii.	15	. 54	..	30	. 64
1 SAMUEL.			xviii.	42	. 64	xl.	17	. 64
i.	9	16, 25	xxii.	44	. 67			
..	23	. 79				PSALMS.		
ii.	9	. 64	2 KINGS.			v.	10	. 76
..	24	57, 58, 66	iv.	34	. 64	xxiv.	6	. 64
iii.	13	. 68	v.	9	. 64	xxxvi.	7	49, 67
v.	6	45, 51, 63	..	18	40, 49, 50	xlv.	10	. 34
..	9	45, 51, 63	..	24	. 78	lviii.	8	. 64
..	12	45, 51, 63	vi.	13	. 78	lxviii.	26	49, 67
vi.	4	45, 51, 63	..	25	. 51	lxxiii.	16	. 54
..	5	45, 51, 63	viii.	7	. 78	lxxvii.	38	. 15
..	17	. 63	x.	27	. 51	lxxx.	14	. 15
vii.	9	. 65	xi.	18	. 64	lxxxi.	12	. 72
x.	21	. 64	xvii.	25	. 78	cv.	22	. 64
..	25	. 78	..	26	. 78	..	40	. 64
xi.	7	. 78	xviii.	27	. 51	cvi.	15	. 78
xii.	10	. 65	xix.	31	. 40	..	20	68, 69
xiii.	19	. 65	..	37	40, 50	..	45	. 64
xv.	12	. 78	xx.	18	. 65	cxliv.	2	. 65
xviii.	5	. 64	xxii.	5	. 65	cxlvii.	19	. 64
xix.	19	. 78	xxiv.	2	. 78	cxlviii.	2	. 64

PROVERBS.			JEREMIAH.					Chap.	Ver.	Page.
Chap.	Ver.	Page.	Chap.	Ver.		Page.		xl.	26	64
vi.	13	64	i.	5	.	52		xlvii.	11	64
xxii.	25	34	ii.	11	.	68		xlviii.	16	16, 40, 49
xxiii.	35	77	..	24	.	57				
xxvi.	24	34	iii.	2	45, 51, 63			DANIEL.		
xxx.	10	34	v.	16	.	76		v.	21	65
..	17	34	xv.	8	.	64		xi.	15	65
			xvii.	11	.	64				
ECCLESIASTES.			·xxvi.	1		74, 75		HOSEA.		
ii.	11	64	xxviii.	1		74, 75		iv.	7	68
v.	9	54	xxxi.	38	40, 49, 50					
			xxxviii.	16		40, 50		OBADIAH.		
SONG OF SONGS.			xxxix.	12		40, 50		..	11	64
ii.	11	64	..	14	.	23				
v.	7	77	xlviii.	7	.	65		HABAKKUK.		
			l.	29	40, 49, 50			i.	12	68
ISAIAH.			li.	3		40, 50		iii.	14	64
vii.	2	78								
xiii.	16	45, 51, 63	LAMENTATIONS.					ZECHARIAH.		
xxx.	33	54	iii.	19	.	69		ii.	12	68
xxxvi.	12	51	..	39	.	64		xiv.	2	45, 51
xxxvii.	30	65								
..	32	50	EZEKIEL.					MALACHI.		
xlii.	24	34	iii.	12	.	50		i.	13	68
xlviii.	8	26	vii.	21	.	65				
li.	16	80	viii.	17	.	68				
lii.	5	64	xvii.	21	.	64				
lvi.	10	64	xxxi.	5	.	64				
lvii.	2	36	xl.	22	.	64				

INDEX II.

TOPICS AND NAMES.

A

ABARBANEL, see ABRAVANEL.
ABRAVANEL, his opinion about the origin of the *Keri* and *Kethiv*, 44–47, refuted by Jacob b. Chajim, 50–52, 54.
ABJA, Rabbi, 63, 71.
ABOTH d' Rabbi Nathan, 54.
ACHAH, Rabbi, 58, 71.
ADELKIND, Cornelius, 10.
AIN, the middle letter in the Psalms, 15.
AKIBA, Rabbi, 60.
ALASHKAR, Moses b. Isaac, 2.
ALTON, Chajim, 4, 38.
ANTHROPOMORPHISMS, removed from the text, 68.
ARAMA, 10.
ARUCH, the, 40; different editions of, 41, 49, 51, 67; its definition, *Itur Sopherim*, 67, 82.

B

BEN-ASHER, 7.
BEN-NAPHTALI, 7.
BENJAMIN of Tudela, 41.
BERESHITH, Rabba, see MIDRASH.
BIBLE, the Rabbinic, description of, 6, &c., 21, 40.
BOMBERG, Daniel, establishes a Hebrew printing office at Venice, 4; his great expenses and work connected with the Rabbinic Bible, 8, 9, 41, 77, 78; engages Levita as corrector of the Hebrew works, 9; his publications, 10; suppresses Jacob b. Chajim's name in consequence of his embracing Christianity, 11, 14; parts with Jacob, 13.
BUXTORF, 35.

C

CASSEL, David, 10.
CHARLES V., 9.
CHRISTIANS charging the Jews with wilfully altering the text, 42; refutation of the charge, 66–71.
CODICES, three, of the Temple, and their readings, 52, 53.
CORECY, Moses de, 10.
CROWNS, Book of, 61, 62.

D

DELITZSCH, 24.
DERENBURG, Dr., 25.

E

EGIDIO, de Viterbo, Cardinal, befriends Levita, 9.
ELDERS, 37.
ELIEZER, Rabbi, 53.
EPHODI, his view of the origin of the *Keri* and *Kethiv*, 42, 43; refuted, 55.
ERSCH and Gruber's Encyklopädie, 10.
ETHERIDGE, DR., 41.
EUPHEMISMS, substituted for cacophonous expressions, 51, 63.
EZRA, author of the *Keri* and *Kethiv*, 44–47.

F

FERRER, Vincente, preaches persecution of the Jews, 2.
FERRERAS, 3.
FRANKEL, *Vorstudien zu der Septuaginta*, 71.
FRENSDORFF, Dr., 11; his edition of the *Ochla Ve-Ochla*, 25, 26; declares that the *Ochla Ve-Ochla* is not the same as that used by Jacob b. Chajim, 27, 28.
FUERST calls Jacob b. Chajim *Tunisi*, 1; erroneously asserts that Jacob b. Chajim's Introduction was published in English, by Kennicott, 6; his opinion about the date of the edition of Jacob b. Chajim's Treatise on the Targum, 10; his enumeration of Jacob b. Chajim's works, 10, 14; he regards the *Ochla Ve-Ochla* as lost, 25.

G

GAON, 65.
GEIGER, his opinion on the Commentaries ascribed to Ibn Ezra, 7; his description of the Massorah, 15; his charges against Ibn Adonijah of suppressing the materials, 17; refutation of the charges, 18–23; strictures on Frensdorff's remarks on the *Ochla Ve-Ochla*, 26; his fixing the date of the *Ochla Ve-Ochla*, 34; *Urschrift und Uebersetzungen der Bibel*, 49, 53, 69, 70, 71.
GERSHON b. Jehodah, 24.
GERUNDENSIS, Moses, see NACHMANIDES.
GRAETZ, *Geschichte der Juden*, 24, 57.

H

HALLE MS. of the Massorah, described 28–30; its relation to the printed Massorah of Jacob b. Chajim, 30, 31; to the *Ochla Ve-Ochla*, 31–33; its date, 34.
HANNAEL, Rabbi, 48.
HAPHTARA, see PENTATEUCH.
HERETICS, see CHRISTIANS.
HUNNAH, Joshua, 57, 59.
HUPFELD, his description of the Halle MS. Massorah, 28.
HAVDALAH, 75.

I

IBN Adonijah, see JACOB BEN CHAJIM.
IBN Aknin quotes the *Ochla Ve-Ochla*, 24, 25.
IBN Chabib, Jacob, 10.
IBN Ezra, 6, 7; commentaries ascribed to him, which belong to Moses Kimchi, 7; his rendering of Gen. i. 1–3, 70.
IBN Shemtob, 10.
IDA, Rabbi, 64.
IKA, Rabbi b. Abaja, 48.
ISAAC b. Jehudah quotes the *Ochla Ve-Ochla*, 24, 25.
—— b. Moses Ha-Levi, see EPHODI.
—— b. Asher, 57.
—— Rabbi, 48, 57.
ISHMAEL Rabbi, 39, 53, 60, 61, 69.
ITUR Sopherim, 42, 48, 49, 67, 68.

J

JACOB b. Chajim, also called Ibn Adonijah, and *Tunisi*, probable date and place of his birth, 1, 2; emigrates from Tunis, 4; becomes connected with Bomberg, edits the Babylonian and the Jerusalem Talmuds, 1, 5, 38; the Hebrew Concordance of Nathan, the Jad Ha-Chezaka of Maimonides, 5; publishes the great Rabbinic Bible, 6; his treatise on the Targum, 9, 12, 13; his name suppressed, 11, 36; embraced Christianity, 11, 13, 14, 36; his death, 14; his description of the state of the Massorah, 19; the relation of his recension of the Massorah to the *Ochla Ve-Ochla*, 25–28; his labour connected with the Massorah, 20, 34, 35; refutes Abravanel, 48; his opinion of the origin of the *Keri* and *Kethiv*, 56.
JARCHI, see RASHI.
JEHUDAH b. Nathan, called *Riban*, 57.
—— b. Bethara, 60.
—— Rabbi, 74.
JEWS persecuted in Spain, 2.
JONATHAN b. Uzziel, 6.
JOSEPH the Blind, 7.

K

KABBALAH, the, studied by Christians, 4, 9.
KAHANA, Rabbi, 71, 72.
KENNICOTT, edits a Latin version of Jacob b. Chajim's Introduction, 6.
KERI, the. always followed in reading the Scriptures, 44.
KERI and Kethiv, 40; its origin, 42, 69, 73; number of in each book of the Hebrew Scriptures, 47, 48.
KERI velo Kethiv, 40, 49, 55; number of, 50.
KETHIV velo Keri, 40, 47, 49, 55; number of, 50.
KIMCHI, David, 6, 7; quotes the *Ochla Ve-Ochla*, 24, 25; his opinion about the origin of the *Keri* and *Kethiv*, 43, 44; refuted, 55.
KIMCHI, Moses, author of commentaries ascribed to Ibn Ezra, 7.

L

LEBRECHT regards the *Ochla Ve-Ochla* as lost, 25.
LETTER, the middle in the Psalms, 15.
LEVI b. Gershon, see RALBAG.
LEVITA calls Jacob b. Chajim Ibn Adonijah, 1; teaches Christians, 4; writes an epilogue to the Rabbinic Bible, 9; praises Ibn Adonijah; loses all his property at the sacking of Rome; goes to Venice, 9; his revision of works, 10; abuses Jacob b. Chajim for embracing Christianity, though he praises his literary works, 11, 23; his opinion about the duration of the Massorites, 15; his description of the state of the Massorah, 19, 20; affirms that the present compilation of the Massorah made by Jacob b. Chajim is chiefly from the *Ochla Ve-Ochla*, 23–25, 26–28.
LUZZATTO, 10; his declaration that Jacob b. Chajim did embrace Christianity, 11–13.

M

MAHARAM, see MEIER of Rottenburg.
MAIMONIDES, his legal code called *Jad Ha-Chezaka*, 5, 59; his *More Nebuchim*, 52.
MARTINEZ, Fernando, preaches persecution of the Jews, 2.
MASSORAH, 14; its meaning, 15; origin and import, 15–17; its condition, 7, 8, 19, 41; its utility, 72, &c.
—— finalis, 6, 7, 40, 41, 82, 83.
—— magna, 6, 16, 40; divided into two parts, 32, 83.
—— marginalis, 6, 19, 40, 79, 83.
—— parva, 6, 16, 18, 40.
—— the Great, 24; how treated by the Scribes, 78, 79.
MASSORITES, their duration, 15, 16.
MASSORETIC order of the Books in the Bible. 26; treatises, 16, 17, 78.

MASSORETIC sign explained, 72, 73.
MECHILTA, 10, 69, 71.
MEIER, of Rottenburg, 77.
—— b. Samuel, 57.
—— Rabbi, 59, 60.
MICHAELIS, 35.
MIDRASH Rabboth, 10, 59, 64.
———— Ruth, 37.
———— Tanchuma, 10.
———— Tilim, 10.
MISHRACHI, Elias, 10.
MOORS, crusade against them, 2.
MORDECAI b. Hillel, 76, 77.
MORINUS, 35.
MOSES, the Punctuator, or *Ha-Nakdan*, 7, 18.
—— b. Nachman, see RAMBAN.
MEZUZAH, 59.
MOZARQUIVER captured by the Spaniards, 23.

N

NACHMANIDES, see RAMBAN.
NATHAN, Isaac, 5, 80, 81.
———— b. Jechiel, 41.
NAVARRO, Pedro, conquers Bugia, 4.
NEHEMIAH, Rabbi, 53.
NEUBAUER, 24.
NORZI, Salomon, 24, 25.

O

OCHLA VE-OCHLA, origin of its name, 16, 17, 19; declared by Levita to be the basis of the present Massorah, refuted, 23, 24, 26, 27; whether it is the identical one quoted by Kimchi, Ibn Aknim, Isaac b. Jehudah, Elias Levita, 25; is edited by Dr. Frensdorff, 26; its relation to the Massorah of Jacob b. Chajim, 25-27; to the *Ochla Ve-Ochla* quoted by the mediæval lexicographers, 28; its age, 33, 34; Frensdorff's edition quoted, 45, 49, 50, 51, 64, 65, 69.
ONKELOS, 6.

P

PAPA, Rabbi, 59.
PARIS Massorah, edited under the name of *Ochla Ve-Ochla*, see FRENSDORFF and *Ochla Ve-Ochla*.
PENTATEUCH, the, divided into Sabbatic lessons, the manner in which it is quoted in Jewish writings, 45.
PESICTA Sutrata, 10.
PHYLACTERIES, 61.
PINSKER, 69.
PIZZIGHTONE, David de, 5.
PLATO, 70.
POLYGLOTT, Complutensian, 3, 22.
PRESCOTT, 3.
PROPHIAT Duran, see EPHODI.
PTOLEMY, king, 69.

R

RAB, 48.
RABE, 71, 72.
RABBINIC BIBLE, see BIBLE.
RALBAG, also called Rabbi Levi b. Gershon, 6, 7, 10.
RAMBAM, see MAIMONIDES.
RAMBAN, also called Moses b. Nachman, or Nachmanides, 10, 39, 40, 56.
RASHBA, 55.
RASHBAM, 39, 40, 57.
RASHBAN, also called R. Samuel b. Meier, 39, 40, 57.
RASHI, 6, 7, 24, 34, 49, 50, 51; his interpretation of 1 Samuel ii. 24; differs from the Massoretic text, 57-59, 60, 61, 63, 64, 65, 66, 70.
RAYMOND Martin, 67.
REDAK, see KIMCHI.
REFORMATION, 6.
REIFMANN, his opinion on the commentaries ascribed to Ibn Ezra, 7.
RIBA, see ISAAC B. ASHER.
RIBAN, see JEHUDAH B. NATHAN.
ROSSI, Azzariah de, his date, calls Jacob b. Chajim Ibn Adonijah, 1.
ROTTENBURG, Meier, 76.
RULES, exegetical, 60-63.

S

SAADIA Gaon, 7, 34, 64, 65.
SABBA, Abraham, 10.
SABBATICAL lessons, see PENTATEUCH.
SACCUTTO, Abraham, 2; emigrates from Tunis, 4.
SALOMON, b. Abraham b. Adereth, 10.
———— b. Isaac, see RASHI.
———— b. Jehudah, see NORZI.
SAMARITANS, the, refuse to adopt the revision of the text, 53.
SAMUEL, b. Meier, see RASHBAM.
———— Mar, 59.
———— Rabbi, 57.
SCRIBES, see SOPHERIM.
SEPTUAGINT, the, 69.
SHIMSHON b. Abraham, 12.
SIMEON, Rabbi, 74.
SIMON, the Just, 37.
———— b. Lakish, 52.
SIPHRA, 10.
SIPHRI, 10.
SOAVE, Moses, 12.
SOPHERIM, the origin of their name, 15, 43; members of the Great Synagogue, 37; authors of the *Keri* and *Kethiv*, 43; their emendations of the text, 42, 48, 49, 67-69.
SPAIN, expulsion of the Jews from, 2.
STEINSCHNEIDER, 10, 17, 24, 41.
SYNAGOGUE, the Great, its origin and constitution, 37; the members thereof, the compilers of the Hebrew canon, the Book of Esther, &c, 37, 38; the authors of the *Keri* and *Kethiv*, 42, 43, 70.

T

TAM, 57, 62, 63.
TAGIN, Sepher, see BOOK OF CROWNS.
TALAVERA, Fray Fernando de, 2.
TALMUD, the, *editio princeps* of, 5; its explanation of Nehemiah viii. 8, 48; differences between it and the Massorah, 42, 57, 58, 63, 64, 65; the different Tracts of it quoted:—

Baba Mezia, 54 *b* . . . 62, 63.
Baba Bathra, 111 . . . . 63.
Erechin, 17 *a* . . . . . 74, 75.
Gittin, 86 . . . . 67.
Jebamoth, 106 *b* . . 66, 71, 72.
—————— 13 *b* . . . . . 53.
—————— Jerusalem, i. 6 . 53.
Kethuboth, 104 *a* . . . . . 36.
Kiddushin, 30 *a* . . . . . 15.
Megilla, Jerusalem, i. 11 . . 53.
—————— 9 *a* . . . . 71.
—————— 24 *b* . . . . . . 63.
—————— 25 *b* . . . . . 45, 51.
Menachoth, 34 *a b* . 59, 61, 62.
Maccoth, Jerusalem, ii. 7 . . 39.
Nedarim, 37 *b* . . . 48, 49, 55, 57, 70, 71.
Nidda, 33 *a* . . . . . . 57.
Pessachim, 16 *b* . . . . . 74.
—————— 103 *b*,—104 *a*, 75, 76.
Rosh Ha-Shana, 4 . . . . 32.
Sabbath, 55 *b* . . . . . 57, 59.
—————— 103 *b* . . . . . 60.
Sanhedrin, 4 *b* . . . . . 60.
Shebiith, Jerusalem, v. 1 . . 37.
Sopherim vii. 1 . . . . . 65.
—————— vi. 4 . . 52, 53, 55.
—————— vi. 8 . . . . . 50.
—————— vi. 9 . . . . . 50.
—————— vii. 2 . . . . . 53.
Sopherim viii. 8 . . . . . 45.
—————— ix. 9 . . . . . 51.
Sota, 20 *a* . . . . 39.
Succa, 6 *b* . . . . 74.
—————— 46 *b* . . . . 61.
Taanith, 4 *b* . . . . . . 61.
Taharoth . . . . 12.
Zebachim, 24 *b* . . . . . 62.
—————— 115 *b* . . . . 53.
—————— Mishna, xiv. 4 . 53.
TIKUN Sopherim, 42 . . . 48, 68, 69.
TOSSAFOTH, 57, 58; mentions variations between the readings of the Talmud and the Massorah, argues from the Massorah against the Talmud, 60-63, 71, 72, 74.
TUNIS, the supposed birth-place of Jacob b. Chajim, 2, 3.
TUNISI, see JACOB B. CHAJIM.

V

VAV, the middle in the Pentateuch, 15.
VERSE, the middle in the Pentateuch, 15; in the Psalms, 15.

W

WEISS, his commentary on the Mechilta, 71.
WORD, the middle in the Pentateuch, 15.

X

XIMENES, Cardinal, goes to Granada to convert the Mussulmans, 2; causes the destruction of Arabic MSS, 3; triumphantly enters Cran, 4; does not describe the materials used in the Complutensian Polyglott, 22, 23.

Z

ZUNZ, 24, 41.

THE

MASSORETH HA-MASSORETH

OF

ELIAS LEVITA,

BEING AN EXPOSITION OF THE MASSORETIC NOTES
ON THE HEBREW BIBLE,

OR

THE ANCIENT CRITICAL APPARATUS OF THE OLD TESTAMENT

IN HEBREW, WITH AN ENGLISH TRANSLATION,

AND

CRITICAL AND EXPLANATORY NOTES,

BY

CHRISTIAN D. GINSBURG, LL. D.

ספר

מסורת המסורת

חברו

ר' אליהו המדקדק י"ץ בר אשר הלוי האשכנזי זצ"ל

להבין ולהורות, לאנשי הדורות, דרך בעלי המסורת, בקיצור לשונם, וחידותם וסימנם,
בראשי תבות ובנוטריקון, לכלם עשה תיקון:

נדפס בוויניסיה בשנת רצ"ח בבאזל בשנת רצ"ט ובבזוולצבאך בשנת תקל"א

יצא לאור עוד הפעם עם תרגום בריטני
ומבואר היטיב בבאור מספיק

מאתי

כריסטיאן דוד גינצבורג

TABLE OF CONTENTS

Massoreth Ha-Massoreth

Preface

Life of Elias Levita

Information for the Reader

Preface (of Elias Levita)

Introduction I. A Song of Praise, Simple, and of Four Feet

Introduction II. The Rhythmical Introduction, According to German Rhyme

Introduction III. I Shall Now Turn My Face to the Third Introduction 1

MASSORETH HA-MASSORETH

FIRST PART: 1

SECTION I. treats on *defective* and *plene* in so far as they relate to the *matres lectiones Vav* after *Cholem* and *Shureck*, and *Jod* after *Chirek* and *Tzere*. 1

SECTION II. treats on the passages wherein the *Vav* is absent after the *Cholem* in verbs and nouns, and the difference between them. 1

SECTION III. treats on nouns which are *Milra* and have a *Vav plene* after the *Cholem* on the top, and those which are *Milra* and have not the *Vav*; as well as of all the *Cholems* on the participle *Kal*, which are generally defective, and most of the plurals feminine which have a *Vav* at the end. 1

SECTION IV. treats on the absent *Vav* of the *Shurek*, and on the *Kibutz* being substituted in its place. 1

SECTION V. treats on all the words which have a long *Chirek*, i. e., *Chiruk* with a *Jod*, having mostly *Jod*; and on those words which have *Cholem*, being mostly defective of *Vav*. 1

SECTION VI. treats on the quiescent *Jod* after the *Tzere* and *Segol*, as well as on the quiescent *Jod* after the *Kametz* of the third person. 1

SECTION VII. treats on the *plene* and *defective* of monosyllabic words, being small words. 1

SECTION VIII. treats on the Massoretic marks, or words, which have two or three quiescents, some being *plene* and some *defective*, or all being *plene* or all *defective*. 1

SECTION IX. treats on words which have a quiescent *Aleph*, either expressed or not, and which are called '*with audible Alephs*,' or '*without audible Alephs*.' 1

SECTION X. treats on words, the final *He* of which is either *plene* or *defective*, and are called *Maphkin He*, consisting of four kinds. 1

SECOND PART: 180
   SECTION I. Concerning *Keri* and *Kethiv*, divided into seven classes. 180
   SECTION II. Concerning *Kametz* and *Pattach*. 195
   SECTION III. Concerning *Dagesh, Raphe, Mapik,* and *Sheva*. 197
   SECTION IV. Concerning *Milel, Milra,* and *Pesakim*. 204
   SECTION V. Concerning *Registers, Groups, Resemblances,* and *Parallels*. 210
   SECTION VI. Concerning *Junctions, Severances,* and *Identical*. 212
   SECTION VII. Concerning *the Presence* or *Absence of Prefixes* or *Serviles*. 219
   SECTION VIII. Concerning *Conjectural Readings, Misleadings,* and *Exchanges*. 225
   SECTION IX. Concerning *Letters, Words, Expressions, Short Letters, Accents, Certainties,* and *Transpositions*. 228
   SECTION X. Concerning *Scripture, Book, Form, Connection,* and *Verse*. 234

THIRD PART; OR, THE BROKEN TABLES 244

Now Before I Finish to Speak, I Shall Compose A New Song 267

That You May Know How Many Times Each Letter Occurs in the Bible, Read all the Words in this Poem. 269

Index I. Massoretically Annotated Passages of Scripture Referred to 279

Index II. Massoretic Lists Quoted Entire 298

Index III. Massoretic Terms and Abbreviations Explained 302

Index IV. Massoretic Lists Quoted in this Book, Which Are Also Found in Ochla Ve-Ochla 303

Index V. Topics and Names 304

PREFACE.

THE work now submitted to the public in the original Hebrew, with an English translation, is an explanation of the origin and import of the Massorah. Those who are acquainted with the fact that our Hebrew Bibles abound with marginal and textual glosses, — to which even the Bibles issued by the Bible Society, which boasts that it circulates the pure word of God without note or comment, form no exception — and who know that there is no guide in our language, or in any modern language, to these enigmatical notes, will welcome this Treatise, written by the first, and almost the only, Massoretic expositor. For be it remembered that BUXTORF's Latin Dissertation, entitled, *Commentarius Masorethicus*, published in 1620 and 1665, is to a great extent made up of LEVITA's work, interspersed with notions utterly at variance with those of LEVITA, and without giving his explanation of the plan of the Massorah.

For an account of LEVITA himself, and the extraordinary controversy to which this Treatise gave rise almost all over Europe during the time of the Reformation, we must refer to the Life prefixed to this volume.

The text of the Work is that of the *editio princeps*, 1538, carefully collated with the only two other editions of it, Basel, 1538, and Sulzbach, 1771. The results of the collation have been duly given in the notes.

All that I have ventured to do with the text has been to divide it into paragraphs, and to print in larger type, or to point, those words only which are the subject of Massoretic annotation, so as to enable the student to see which word is selected for discussion; since in the original, where chapter and verse are not specified, several words of a passage had to be quoted to indicate the section from which it was taken.

By comparing every allusion to the Massoretic registers with the Massorah itself, and by giving every such rubric in full, I have not only been enabled to correct many errors in the text of the Treatise, which had arisen either from a slip of the pen on the part of the author, or through misprints, but have supplied the student with the most important part of the Massorah, as will be seen from the extensive Index of the Massoretically annotated passages and the Index of parallels between the Massoretic lists and the *Ochla Ve-Ochla* appended to the work.

The order of the passages of Scripture, in any of the rubrics quoted in the notes, is that of the Massorah, and it is to be hoped that the trouble and labour which I have expended in appending book, chapter, and verse to every expression, in every list, will help the Biblical student to prosecute his Massoretic studies. The edition of the Massorah referred to throughout the work is that contained in FRANKFURTER'S Great Rabbinic Bible, Amsterdam, 1724–27.

I take this opportunity to express my hearty thanks to the learned Dr. STEINSCHNEIDER and the Abbate PIETRO PERREAU, Librarian of the Bibliotheque at Parma, for information duly acknowledged in the proper place.

BROOKLEA, AIGBURTH ROAD,
    LIVERPOOL, *December*, 1866.

LIFE OF ELIAS LEVITA.

THE perpetual expulsions and wanderings to which the Jews have been subjected, ever since their dispersion, have not been favourable to the writing of Biographical Dictionaries. Though they may have had enterprising compilers, who were ready to issue "The Men of the Time," the fact that the children of the same parents were often born and brought up in different countries, wasting their youth in journeys often, in perils of waters, in perils of robbers, in perils by their own countrymen, in perils by the Christians, would have almost precluded the possibility of such an undertaking. Hence it is that the very names, as well as the mere dates and birth-places, of some of the most distinguished Jewish *literati*, are matters of dispute, and that next to nothing is known of their private history and domestic life. But for the Oriental custom of giving some scraps of autobiography in the Introductions and Appendices, in the Prologues and Epilogues, of their works, many of the Jewish authors, to whom political economy, medicine, astronomy, philosophy, philology, exegesis, and poetry owe an immense debt of gratitude, would have been, to the honest historian and grateful student, like Melchisedec, without father, without mother, without descent, having neither beginning of days nor end of life.

The history of the author of the famous *Massoreth Ha-Massoreth*, now published with an English translation, and of many other works, fully illustrates these remarks. The year of his birth, his proper name, and the incidents of his life are only to be gathered by piecing together the autobiographical fragments scattered through his different works. Inattention to this fact has caused the greatest divergence of opinion among scholars on almost every point of his life.

His name among Christians is Elias Levita. Elias, or more correctly Elijahu (אליהו), was the name given to him by his parents on the eighth day of his birth, when he was dedicated to the Lord and made a member of the Jewish community by the sign of the covenant enjoined in Gen. xvii. 10-14; whilst Levita = Ha-Levi (הלוי) simply denotes that he belonged to the tribe of Levi. His name among the Jews, which is given by himself in sundry places of his writings, is

Elijahu Bachur, the German (אלִיהו בחור אשכנזי). Now Landau,[1] Steinschneider,[2] Dr. Holmes,[3] and others, maintain that he obtained the appellation *Bachur* from his Hebrew Grammar, which he designated by this title. But Levita himself tells us the very reverse, that he called the work in question by his own surname, which he had from his youth. Thus, in the Introduction to the *Book Bachur*, he says, "Behold, I have called this book Bachur, for three reasons:—i. Because the book itself is choice and excellent [in allusion to Is. vii. 15, 16], being entirely pure meal without any chaff. ii. Because it has been compiled for every young man to study therein in the days of his youth, so that his heart might be improved in his later days; and, iii. Because it is my surname I have founded it upon the name Bachur."[4] To the same effect is his remark at the end of the book: "To those who ask thee, whose book art thou? say Elijahu's, whose surname is Bachur;"[5] as well as the poem to the second edition: "Because it is useful for the young, as well as excellent, and my own name is Bachur, I called it Bachur."[6] This is moreover corroborated by the fact, that he calls himself Bachur in the Fiction entitled *Baba-Buch*, which he wrote *eleven years before* he published the Grammar in question, (*vide infra*. p. 14).

He was born in 1468, as is evident from the poem which he appended to his edition of R. Isaac Duren's[7] work on the Ceremonial Law, published at Venice, 1548, and which is as follows:—

[1] In his edition of R. Nathan b. Jechiel's *Aramaic Lexicon*, called הערוך, vol. i., p. 38. German Introduction. Prague 1819. For an account of the life of R. Nathan and his celebrated Lexicon, we must refer to Kitto's *Cyclopædia of Biblical Literature*, Alexander's edition, *s. v.* NATHAN.

[2] *Catalogues, Libr. Hebr.*, *in Bibliotheca Bodleiana*, col. 934.

[3] Kitto's *Cyclopædia of Biblical Literature*, *s. v.* ELIAS.

[4] והנה קראתי שם הספר הזה ספר הבחור, וזה לשלוש סבות, האחת בהיות הספר הזה בחור וטוב, וכולו סולת. אין בו מסולת. השנית בעבור היותו מחובר אל כל בחור ללמוד בו בימי בחרותו ויטיב לבו באחריתו. השלישית, בעבור היות כנוי מישונה. ובשם בחור אכונה.

[5] לשואלי ספרי למי אתה. יאמר לאליהו כנוי שמו בחור.

[6] יען לכל בחור הוא טוב וגם בחור ואני שמי בחור בחור קראתיהו.

[7] R. Isaac b. Meier flourished A.D. 1320–1330, at Düren on the Röer, where he was Rabbi of the Jewish community, and whence he derived his surname. His work on the Ceremonial Law he entitled שערים *Gates*, because it discusses the laws of legal and illegal meats (הלכות איסור והיתר) in ninety-six gates or sections. It is, however, commonly called (שערי דורא) *the Gates* of or by *Duren*, which some have erroneously translated *porta habitationis*. It was first published at Cracow, 1534. The edition to which Elias Levita wrote the poems is either the second or third. Comp. Fürst, *Bibliotheca Judaica*, i., 213; Steinschneider, *Catalogus Libr. Hebr. in Bibliotheca Bodleiana*, col. 1104–8.

"An excellent work is the 'Gates of Duren,' by Isaac Rabbi of Duren.

Therein are described all proscribed meats; there is nothing like it in propounding the laws.

Therein, too, are exhibited the laws of purification, with most of the opinions of the learned in the law.

Published *Shebat* 3, 308 [= Decemb. 13, 1548], of the short era of the creation.

The writer of this poem is Elijahu Bachur, aged four-score years by reason of strength."[8]

To understand the dates of this epilogue, it is necessary to remark that the Israelites reckon from the creation of the world, and that their chronology is 230 years shorter than ours. Thus, for instance, whilst this year, *i.e.* 1866 A.D., is with us 5856 A.M., it is with the Jews 5626 A.M. Moreover, it is to be noted that in Hebrew MSS., as well as in printed books, two modes are adopted of expressing the date. The one is by writing the full numbering: that is, 5626 A.M. = 1866 A.D., which is called *the Great* or *Full era* (פרט גדול); and the other is by omitting the thousands, and leaving them to be understood as 626, instead of 5626, which is called *the Short era* (לפרט קטן abbreviated לפ״ק), and which is more generally used for the sake of brevity. Accordingly, 308 stands for 5308 = 1548, and if Elias Levita, as he tells us himself, was eighty years old in 1548, he must have been born in 1468.[9]

[8] ספר נעים ,שערי דורא ,על שם יצחק ,רב מדורא:
בו אסור כל דברי מאכל ,אין כמוהו ,דינים הורה,
בו נצמדה הלכות נדה ,עם רוב דיעות ,לוקדי תורה,
נדפס לפרט גימ״ל משב״ט ,כן מספר קטן של היצירה
המשורר הוא אליהו בחור זקן פ' לגבורה —

[9] With Elias Levita's own statement before us, the reader will be surprised at the following difference of opinion about the date of our author's birth:—

Dr. Holmes (*Kitto's Cyclopædia*, new ed. s. v. ELIAS)	A.D. 1470.
Fürst (*Bibliotheca Judaica*, i., 239)	,, 1471.
Kalisch (*Hebrew Grammar*, ii., 33)	,, 1474.
Ganz (*Zemach David*, i., Anno. 277), Jechiel (*Seder Ha-Doroth* i. 95a, ed. Lemberg 1858), &c., &c.	,, 1477.
Landau (*Nathan's Aruch*. i., 38, German Introd. Prague, 1819)	,, 1509.

We are surprised at Dr. Kalisch's error, since this learned scholar quotes in the foot note on p. 34 of his Hebrew Grammar, the life of Levita, by Buber, in which it is proved to demonstration that Levita was born in 1468, and since Jost, who was also formerly in error upon this subject, has corrected his mistake in his *Geschichte des Judenthums*, (iii., 119, Leipzig 1859,) four years before the appearance of the Hebrew Grammar. (Longman, 1863). Comp. also Graetz, *Geschichte der Juden*, ix., 284, Leipzig 1866.

Exceedingly little is known of Elias Levita's family. From his own signature we learn that his father's name was Asher, and that he was born in Germany. The celebrated Sebastian Münster, in whose house Levita lived for some time, who translated many of his books into Latin, and who ought therefore to be regarded as the highest authority on this subject, distinctly tells us that the place where his parents resided, and where he was born, is Neustadt, on the Aisch, near Nurmburg.[10] Münster's statement is fully borne out by Levita's own remarks in his different works, in which he always includes himself when speaking of the Germans. Thus, in his Exposition of 712 words from Jewish literature, he says, on the expression משקיט "it denotes small writing; that is, when the writing is not in square characters it is מִשְׁקִיט. It is now many years ago that I was told that it is an Arabic expression, signifying *thin, attenuated*; but I afterwards got to know that it is not Arabic at all. I have asked many Jews from Italy, France, Spain, Greece, and Arabia, all of whom pronounce it in this way, but none of them knew its derivation. *We Germans*, however, pronounce it מעשיט, and we too do not know whence it is derived."[11] To the same effect is Levita's remark in the Introduction to his Massoretical work, entitled *the Book of Remembrance*: "I shall put down in the explanation of each word its signification in German, *which is the language of my countrymen*."[12] From the words, "to those who ask thee who made thee, say the hands of Elias made

---

[10] Comp. Wolf, *Bibliotheca Hebræa*, i. 153; iii. 97.

[11] משקיט קורין לכתיבה דקה רוצה לומר שאינה כתיבה מרובעת משקיט: וזה ימים רבים שהוגד לי שהוא לשון ערבי פרוש רזה וכחושה, ואחר כך נודע לי שאינו לשון ערבי כלל: ושאלתי ליחידים רבים לועזים וצרפתים וספרדים ויונים וערביים וכולם קורין לה כן ולא ידעו לפתרו מה הוא ֹ ואנחנו האשכנזים קורין להם מעשיט ולא ידענו מה הוא.

See also *the Tishbi* under the expression פתח, רב קרבץ, תקן and other places, in all of which he classes himself with the Germans, saying אנחנו האשכנזים *we Germans*. The passage quoted from Levita's Epilogue to his מתורגמן, where he says, אלך לי אל ארצי אשר יצאתי משם, היא מדינת וויניציאה ואמות בעירי עם אשתי הזקנה, *I shall now return to my country, which I have left, namely, to the city of Venice, and die in my town with my aged wife*, to prove that he was born at Venice, is both at variance with his other remarks and inconclusive. For it will be seen that he does not call Venice his native place (עיר מולדתי), which he would undoubtedly have done had he been born in it, but simply styles it "*my town*" (עירי), "*the town which I left*" (אשר יצאתי משם), which any one would do who had lived in a town many years, and left there his wife and family.

[12] See גם אכתוב אצל כל ביאור כל מלה ומלה פתרונה בלשון אשכנו שהיא לשון בני עמי. Frankel's *Monatschrift fur Geschichte und Wissenschaft des Judenthums*, xii. 96—108. Breslau, 1863, where the learned Frensdorff has printed the Introduction to this unpublished work.

me, the son of a man who is called Asher Levi, a German, a man of valour and distinction," in the Epilogue to the book now edited with an English translation, the erudite Frensdorff ingeniously conjectures that R. Asher, Levita's father, was a military man, perhaps holding the office of a commissary in the German army, since the phrase איש היל *men of valour* also denotes a military man, and the expression אפרתי is used in later Hebrew for *rank*. Frensdorff moreover submits that this will explain the origin of Levita's surname, Bachur, inasmuch as, the son of a military man, he could legitimately substitute for איש חיל *military man*, and אפרתי *officer*, the word בחור in allusion to Exod. xiv. 7; Judg. x. 15; 1 Sam. xxiv. 3; Jerem. xlix. 19; &c., &c.[13]

From the day of his birth to his thirty-sixth year (1468–1504) we hear nothing either of him or his family. The state of the Jews in Germany was too deplorable to admit of any record being kept about the personal circumstances and doings of private individuals. Indeed, it may well be questioned whether, since the advent of Christ, the destruction of Jerusalem, and the dispersion of the Jews, there was a period in the history of the world pregnant with greater events for the Christian nations, and fraught with more terrible results for the Jewish people, than that in which Levita spent his youth. When he was two years of age, all his brethren were expelled from Mayence and the Rheingau by Adolph of Nassau (October 29, 1470), after being recognised Archbishop of electoral Mayence by the Pope, on the deposition of Diether of Isenburg, the rival Archbishop, who converted the ancient synagogue into a church. When he was seven years of age, his youthful heart was afflicted with the horrible tidings that Bishop Hinderbach had the whole Jewish community at Trent burned (1475), in consequence of a base calumny that they had killed for their Passover a Christian boy named Simon. The infamous calumny about the murder of this boy rapidly spread through Christendom, and everywhere kindled the fires of persecution, so much so that, notwithstanding the prohibition of Pope Sixtus IV. (October 10, 1475) to worship Simon of Trent as saint till the charge had been properly investigated, the Jews in Germany were massacred whenever they quitted their quarters. The Bishop of Nassau nearly exterminated all the Jews under his jurisdiction; and the magnates of Ratisbon, in the very neighbourhood of Levita's birth-place, expelled all the Jewish popula-

---

[13] In Frankel's *Monatschrift*, xiii. p. 99.

tion from their dominions (1477–1480) when he was about twelve years of age.

The awful sufferings which the Jews had to endure in Germany, from those whose Saviour was a Jew, and whose Apostles and Prophets were Jews, strangely contrasted with the kind treatment which they experienced in Turkey, from the infidels, the followers of the false prophet, and must have produced an extraordinary and indelible impression upon so shrewd a mind as that of Levita. When he was about fifteen years of age, Isaac Zarphati (1475–1485), one of the numerous Jews who fled from the fiery persecutions under the Cross to seek safety under the Crescent, addressed the following epistle to his brethren in Germany:—"I have been informed of the calamities, more bitter than death, which have befallen our brethren in Germany; of the tyrannical laws, the compulsory baptisms, and the banishments which take place daily. And if they fly from one place, greater misfortunes befall them in another place. I hear an impudent nation lifting up its raging voice against the faithful, and see its hand swinging over them. There are woes within and woes without; daily edicts and taskmasters to extort money. The spiritual guides and the monks, the false priests, rise up against the unhappy people, and say, 'We will persecute them to destruction, the name of Israel shall no more be remembered.' They imagine that their religion is in danger, because the Jews in Jerusalem may, peradventure, purchase the church of the sepulchre. For this reason, they have issued a decree that every Jew who is found on a Christian ship sailing for the East is to be thrown into the sea. How are the holy German community treated; how are their energies weakened! The Christians not only drive them from place to place, but lurk after their lives, brandish over them the sharpened sword, cast them into the flaming fire, into surging waters, or into stinking swamps. My brethren and teachers, friends and acquaintances, I, Isaac Zarphati, who come from France, was born in Germany, and there sat at the feet of masters, proclaim to you, that Turkey is a land in which nothing is wanted. If ye are willing, it will be well with you. You will be able safely to go from Turkey to the Holy Land. Is it not better to live among Mahommedans than among Christians? Here, we are allowed to dress in the finest materials; here, every one sits under his own fig-tree and vines; whilst in Christian countries, you are not even permitted to dress your children in red or blue without exposing them to be beaten red or blue. Hence you are obliged to walk about like beggars and in rags! All your days are gloomy, even your Sabbaths and festivals; strangers enjoy your possessions, and what use are treasures to a wealthy Jew? He only keeps them to his own misfortune, and they are all lost in one day. You call them yours; no! they are theirs. They invent lying accusations against you; they regard neither age nor knowledge. And when they give you a promise, though sealed with sixty seals, they break it. They always inflict upon you double punishment, the most cruel death, and plunder. They prohibit the instruction in our schools, disturb our prayers forbid the Jews to work on Christian festivals, or to carry on business. And now, O Israel! why sleepest thou? Arise, and quit this cursed land!"[14]

Such lessons of Christian persecution and Mahommedan protection did Levita learn when he was about fifteen years of age; and there can be but little doubt that it was in consequence of the terrible sufferings which the Jews had to endure in Germany, and Isaac Zarphati's thrilling summons to his brethren to quit this hot-bed of suffering, that Levita's family, and as many other Jews as could afford it, emigrated, and sought an asylum wherever it could be found. The fact that Levita had already acquired a very high reputation, and delivered lectures on Grammar, at Padua, in the thirty-sixth year of his age, shews that his family must have settled in this town some years before, to allow sufficient time for the acquisition of his learning and influence in a place which was then the chief seat of Jewish learning in Italy. His flight into Venetia, however, did not place him beyond the reach of the agonising cry of his suffering brethren. Whilst diligently engaged in the study of Grammar and the Massorah, at the age of twenty-four (1492), Levita heard of the harrowing scenes enacted in Spain, where the whole Jewish population, about 300,000 in number, were expelled,—a calamity which, in Jewish history, is only equalled in magnitude by the destruction of the Temple and the dispersion of the Israelites by Titus. Many of these brokenhearted wanderers who sought refuge in Italy, Levita must have seen. But the cup of bitterness was not yet full. In his twenty-eighth year,

[14] This interesting Address to the Jews of Germany by Isaac Zarphati, which is to be found in the Imperial Library of Paris, (*ancien fonds* No. 291), has been published by Dr. Jellinek, in his work entitled קונטרס גזרות תתנ״ו *Contribution to the History of the Crusades*, p. 14, &c. Leipzig, 1854. For a thorough and most masterly critique on the Epistle, we must refer to Graetz, (*Geschichte der Juden*, viii., pp. 288 and 446, &c. Leipzig, 1864,) whose translation we have followed.

he heard of the edict issued (December 20, 1496) by Emanuel, King of Portugal, that all the Jews and Moors of his dominions should submit to Christian baptism, or quit the country by October next (1497) on pain of death. He, moreover, heard that the king, disappointed at so few Jews embracing Christianity, issued a secret command from Estremo Castle (February 4, 1497), forcibly to take all Jewish children of his dominion, both boys and girls, up to fourteen years of age, from their parents, and to baptise them on Easter Sunday; the heart-rending effects of which are described by an eye-witness to the scene in the following terms:—"I have seen," relates Bishop Ferdinando Couthin, of Algarve, who protested against this compulsory baptism, "how multitudes were dragged by the hair to the baptismal font, and how the afflicted fathers, with their veiled heads, and agonising cries, followed their children, and protested at the altar against this inhuman compulsory baptism. I have also seen other inexpressible barbarities which were heaped upon them."[15] And when at last the period fixed for their departure had arrived, and about 20,000 Jews were again driven from their homes into the wide, wide world, to seek a resting-place, Levita again saw many of his wandering brethren, who filled his heart with their afflictions, more bitter than death. We shall hereafter see that it is necessary to bear these things in mind, in order to understand the charges against which Levita defends himself in the second introduction to this work.

These sufferings and repeated expulsions of the Jews, however, were overruled by Him who makes the wrath of man to praise Him, for the advancement of Hebrew literature, for the extension of Biblical knowledge, and for kindling the light of the Reformation, in which Elias Levita played an important part. Though the bulk of the Jewish population in Germany, 300,000 in Spain, and 20,000 in Portugal preferred to quit their homes and everything dear and near unto them; and though many of them submitted to the most cruel deaths rather than embrace the Christianity in the name of which these barbarities were perpetrated; yet an immense number of them, not having a martyr's courage, or being reluctant to lose their children, who were snatched from them, embraced the Christian faith. Many of these Neophytes secretly remained Jews, whilst others sincerely believed the religion which they were at first forced to embrace. Among them were men of most distinguished attainments and extraordinary know-

[15] Graetz, *Geschichte der Juden*, viii., 390, &c. Leipzig, 1864.

ledge of Hebrew and Biblical literature. These soon began to spread the knowledge of the sacred language among Christians, by the aid of the newly invented art of printing. And as many of the Jewish converts were Kabbalists, they also initiated their Gentile disciples into its mysteries, and made almost as large a number of converts among Christians to this esoteric doctrine as Christianity had gained among the Jews.

Foremost in the ranks of Jewish converts who laboured in the department of Biblical literature were Alphonso de Alcala, Paul Coronel, and Alphonso de Zamora, who were employed in editing the celebrated Complutensian Polyglott, the sixth volume of which is almost entirely the work of Zamora. To these are to be added Felix Pratensis, the famous editor of the *editio princeps* of Bomberg's Rabbinic Bible, and Jacob b. Chajim, the editor of the second edition of Bomberg's Rabbinic Bible, who immortalised his name by his elaborate Introduction to this Bible, and by compiling and editing for the first time the critical apparatus of the Old Testament, called the Massorah. As propounders of the Kabbalah, among the Jewish converts, are to be mentioned Paul de Heredia, the author and translator of sundry Kabbalistic works, which he dedicated to Pope Innocent VIII.; Paul Ricio, professor at Pavia, physician to the Emperor Maximilian I., who translated a large portion of Joseph Gikatilla's Kabbalistic work, entitled "The Gates of Light," which he dedicated to Maximilian, and which Reuchlin used very largely; Vidal de Saragossa de Arragon, Davila, &c.[16]

The Jews themselves had a still greater phalanx of literary and scientific men who laboured in the departments of Biblical exegesis, the traditional law, the Kabbalah, philosophy, astronomy, &c. These literati supplied those Christians who impugned the infallible decisions of the Pope and his conclave respecting matters of doctrine, and who appealed to the Word of God as their sole guide, with the means of understanding the original language in which the greater part of the Bible is written. At the head of those who were thus enriching Biblical literature were Don Isaac b. Jehudah Abravanel (1437–1509), the

---

[16] According to a statement by Abraham Farissol, in his MS. work entitled *the Shield of Abraham* (מגן אברהם), twelve distinguished converted Jews formed themselves into a literary society, and conjointly issued works to prove the truth of Christianity from the *Sohar* and other Kabbalistic writings. The passage from Farissol's MS. work, giving this account, has been printed by Graetz, *Geschichte der Juden*, ix. 195.

famous statesman, philosopher, theologian, and commentator, who wrote copious commentaries on nearly the whole of the Hebrew Scriptures; Messer Leon, or Jehudah b. Jechiel, as he is called in Hebrew (1430–1505), Rabbi and physician at Mantua, who wrote a very elaborate Hebrew Grammar, a masterly Treatise on Hebrew Rhetoric, after the manner of Aristotle, Cicero, and Quintilian, and a Treatise on Hebrew Logic, and who was called the Hebrew Cicero; the two Aramas, Isaac, the father (1430–1494), and Meier, the son (1470–1556), both of whom wrote extensive expositions of sundry books of the Scriptures; Abraham Saccuto (1450–1520), the famous historian and lexicographer; Saadia Ibn Danan (1450–1502), poet, lexicographer, and commentator; Abraham de Balmes (1450–1521), physician, philosopher, and grammarian; Jacob Mantino, a distinguished Hebraist and physician; Abraham Farissol (1451–1525), the famous cosmographer and commentator; Levi b. Chabib, Isaac b. Joseph Caro, Jacob Berab Obediah Seforno, Jacob b. Jechiel Loanz, Joseph Ibn Jachja, &c., &c., all of whom contributed materially to the diffusion of Biblical knowledge in its sundry departments. None of these Hebraists, however, who were the contemporaries of Elias Levita, and with many of whom he had personal intercourse, surpassed, or even equalled, our author in his successful efforts, either in mastering the grammatical structure of the Hebrew language, or in diffusing the knowledge of this sacred tongue among Jews, but more especially among Christians, than Levita. And it is not too much to say, that the revival of Hebrew learning and Biblical knowledge in Europe, towards the close of the fifteenth and the commencement of the sixteenth centuries, resulting in the Reformation, which was effected by the immortal Reuchlin, was the result of the tuition which this father of the Reformation received from Jacob b. Jechiel Loanz, physician to the Emperor Frederick III., Obadiah Seforno, and from Levita.

It was not, however, the wish to become more thoroughly acquainted with the import of the Scriptures which kindled the desire in Reuchlin, and in a number of other eminent Christians, to learn Hebrew, which made them seek the tuition of Loanz, Levita, Seforno, and a host of other Hebraists, and which was the means of calling forth the energies and works of Levita. The Kabbalah was the primary cause of the rage among the Christian literati of those days to study Shemitic languages. This esoteric doctrine, which was declared by the celebrated scholastic metaphysician, Raymond Lully (1236–1315), to be a divine science, and a genuine revelation whose light is revealed to a rational soul, captivated the mind of John Pico della Mirandola (1463–1494). Mirandola, the marvellously gifted son of the sovereign of the small principality of Mirandola, in Italy, received his first lessons in Hebrew, as well as in Aristotelian Arabic philosophy, from Elias del Medigo, or Elias Cretensis, as he is sometimes called, who was born of Jewish parents in the same year as his distinguished pupil and faithful friend. But as Elias del Medigo was hostile to the Kabbalah, and could not, therefore, initiate Mirandola into its mysteries, the Count, who was the wonder of his days, had to put himself under the tuition of Jochanon Allemano, a Rabbi from Constantinople, who had settled down in Italy, and who was very profound in this theosophy. With his marvellous retentive faculties, extraordinary intellectual powers, and almost boundless knowledge, Mirandola soon overcame the difficulties and unravelled the secrets of the Kabbalah. To his amazement, he found that there is more Christianity than Judaism in the Kabbalah. For, according to his showing, he discovered therein proofs of the doctrine of the Trinity, the Incarnation, the divinity of Christ, original sin, the expiation thereof by Christ, the heavenly Jerusalem, the fall of the angels, the order of the angels, purgatory, and hell-fire; in fact, the same Gospel which we find in St. Paul, Dionysius, St. Jerome, and St. Augustine.

As the result of his Kabbalistic studies, he published in 1486, when only twenty-four years of age, *nine hundred theses*, which were placarded in Rome, and among which was the following: "*No science yields greater proof of the divinity of Christ than magic and the Kabbalah.*" So delighted was Pope Sixtus IV. with the discovery, that he wished to have Kabbalistic writings translated into Latin, for the use of divinity students; and Mirandola, with the aid of his Jewish teacher, did not delay to gratify the wish of the supreme Pontiff.[17]

The Kabbalah and Hebrew, as well as Aramaic, the clue to this esoteric doctrine, now became the favourite studies, to the neglect of the classics. Popes, cardinals, princes, statesmen, warriors, high and low, old and young, were in search for Jewish teachers. Whilst this Kabbalistic epidemic was raging in Italy, Reuchlin (1455–1521), the reviver of literature in Germany, arrived at Rome with Eberhard the

---

[17] For an account of the import and history of this esoteric doctrine, see *The Kabbalah*, &c., by Ginsburg, Longmans. 1865.

Bearded (1482), in the capacity of private secretary and privy councillor to this prince. From the eternal city he accompanied him to Florence, where he became acquainted with Mirandola, and caught the infection of the esoteric doctrine. The infection, however, proved innocuous for a little time, since, on his return to Germany (1484), he was appointed licentiate and assessor of the supreme court in Stutgard; and, as the Dominicans elected him proctor of their order in the whole of Germany, it precluded the possibility of his entering at once upon the study of Hebrew and Aramaic. But the disease fully developed itself when he returned from his second journey to Rome and Florence (1490), after having come into contact a second time with Mirandola, who told him of the wonderful mysteries concealed in the Kabbalah.

The great influence of Reuchlin soon spread the desire for studying Hebrew and the Kabbalah among Christians in Germany. Every one who had any claim to literary attainments was now in search of a Jewish teacher. Reuchlin put himself under the tuition of R. Jacob b. Jechiel Loanz, physician to Frederick III., and made such extraordinary progress, that, within four years of beginning to study Hebrew, he published his first Kabbalistic Treatise, entitled, "*Concerning the Wonderful Word,*" which he dedicated to Dalberg, Bishop of Worms. It was this intense love for Hebrew and Hebrew literature which made Reuchlin espouse the cause of the Jews, and defend them and their writings against the misguided and malicious assaults of the fanatical Pfefferkorn on his former co-religionists, and which kindled the fire of the Reformation.

In Italy the Kabbalah and Hebrew were studied to a still greater extent. Here Abraham Saba, Jehudah b. Jacob Chajath, Joseph Shraga, Kana or Elkana, Jehudah Ibn Verga were the teachers of this theosophy among the Jews; whilst among the Christians the chief Jewish teachers were R. Jachanon Alleman, who initiated Mirandola into its mysteries, and Samuel Abravanel, in whose house Baruch of Benevent delivered lectures on the Kabbalah to most distinguished Christians. Baruch of Benevent also instructed Egidio de Viterbo (afterwards cardinal) in this esoteric doctrine, and translated the Sohar into Latin for him. It was this Egidio, as we shall see hereafter, who, in consequence of his being seized with the general desire to study the Kabbalah, was the means of calling forth Elias Levita, and of encouraging our author to write most of his works, thus constituting him the chief teacher of Hebrew among Christians.

We have already seen that, up to his thirty-sixth year (1504), Levita delivered lectures on Hebrew grammar in the great Jewish academy at Padua to a large number of Jewish students, who came to be taught by him from far and wide. As the text-book for these lectures he took R. Moses Kimchi's Outlines of Hebrew Grammar, entitled "Journey on the Paths of Knowledge,[18] which most probably commended itself to him because of its conciseness, and because its author was the first who employed therein, as a paradigm of the regular verbs, the word פקד, instead of the less appropriate verb *mediæ gutteralis* פעל, which, in imitation of the Arabic grammarians, had been used in all other grammars. Though Moses Kimchi flourished about 1160–1170, and must have written this short grammar three hundred and fifty years before it was annotated by Levita, yet the manual was still in MS., and the copy which Levita used as the basis for his lectures must have been made by himself. His explanations were so acceptable, that he was requested by his pupils to publish them, together with the text book (1504).

Unhappily, however, the plague broke out at Padua, and as Christians usually believed that the Jews were the cause of every epidemic and calamity, the Jewish quarter was blocked up, and the entrance to the street in which Levita resided was closed. When thus shut up in the house, his amanuensis escaped with the MS. to Pesaro, where he had the work printed without Levita's name, but with an Introduction by Benjamin of Rome, who was, consequently, taken by every body to be the author of the Commentaries to M. Kimchi's Grammar. The plagiarist also interpolated the annotations with excerpts from another work, and in this form Levita's maiden production was most incorrectly printed in another name at Pesaro (1508). In this mutilated form, and under the surreptitious name, M. Kimchi's "*Journey on the Paths of Knowledge*," with Levita's Commentary, became the manual for students of the Hebrew language, both among Jews and Christians. It was speedily reprinted several times at Pesaro (1509–18, 1518–1519); it made its way to Germany and France, where it was reprinted (Hagenau, 1519; Paris, 1520); and became the text book of the early Reformers, who were

---

[18] The full Hebrew title of this concise Grammar is מהלך שבילי הדעת קרבת מליצת חכמה יתרון, the initials of which yield the author's name, משה קמחי. Sometimes it is simply called המהלך or ספר קרוק. For an account of the life and writings of Kimchi, we must refer to Kitto's *Cyclopædia of Biblical Literature*, new ed. *s. v.* MOSES KIMCHI.

studying Hebrew to translate the Scriptures; and was translated into Latin by Sebastian Münster (Basle, 1531; *ibid*, 1536). We shall have to recur to this production when we come to the period of Levita's life when he thought it his duty to claim the paternity of the annotations.

The dry studies of grammar and philology did not deprive him of his humour, for, three years after the publication of the annotations to M. Kimchi's work, Levita amused himself by writing, in German, a fiction, entitled *Baba-Buch* (בבא בוך), purporting to be a history of the Prince of Baba. It was evidently intended to be a song, since he remarks in the rhythmical Preface—"*Aber der* ניגון (= Melody) *der darauf wird gehen, Den kenn ich nit geben zu verstehen, Denn einer kennt musiga oder* (טולפה). *So wollt ich ihm wohl haben geholfen, Aber ich sing' es mit einem welschen Gesang, Kann er drauf machen ein bessern so hab er Dank.*" That he composed it in 1507, he most distinctly declares at the end of the book in the following words—"*Damit hat das Buch ein Enden. Doch will ich nennen vor . . Elia Bachur nennt er sich zwar, Ein ganz Jahr hat er drüber verschrieben, Und hat es gemacht das selbig Jar, Das man zählt* 267 [=1507], *Er hot* [lot = lost?] *es aus in Nisan und hob es an in Ijjar . . . soll uns führen ken Jerusalem hinein, Oder irgend ein Dörfel daneben* חסלת אסטוריא של בבא דאנטונא. Here endeth the history of Baba de Antona." This book was first printed in 1508.[19]

But Levita was not destined long to enjoy his peaceful studies and innocent recreations. Five years after the outbreak of the epidemic, and only twelve months after the publication of this fiction, the army of the league of Cambray took Padua (1509) and sacked it, when Levita lost every thing he possessed, and in a most destitute condition had to leave the place in which he had successfully taught for some years, and where he was held in high estimation, to seek a livelihood in the wide wide world. As the Kabbalah was a classical study at Rome, where the popes and cardinals looked upon it as an important auxiliary to Christianity, Hebrew teachers were in great requisition in the Eternal City. Knowing this, Levita at once betook himself to the capital. It was here that he heard of the scholarly and liberal minded Egidio de Viterbo, general of the Augustine order, and

---

[19] The above extract is made from Steinschneider's *Catalogus Libr. Hebr. in Bibliotheca Bodleiana*, col. 935, where an account is also given of the different editions of the Fiction in question, and the errors of biographers are corrected.

afterwards cardinal, who was engaged in studying Hebrew, and of course the esoteric doctrine. He therefore determined to call upon him.

The first interview between the eminent Christian scholar and the famous Hebrew grammarian is thus described by the latter. "When I heard of his fame, I waited upon him at his palace. On seeing me he enquired after my business; and when I told him that I am the grammarian from Germany, and that I devote my whole life to the study of Hebrew philology and the Scriptures, . . . he at once rose from his seat, came towards me, and embraced me, saying, 'Are you forsooth Elijahu, whose fame has travelled over countries, and whose books are circulated everywhere? Blessed be the Lord of the Universe for bringing you here, and for our meeting. You must now remain with me; you shall be my teacher, and I will be a father to you. I will maintain you and your family,' " &c.[20]

Such a cordial reception could not fail in its effect, and Levita at once accepted the offer of the generous Egidio. As Egidio's chief object in learning Hebrew was to be able to fathom the mysteries of the Kabbalah, Levita had not only to instruct his pupil in the sacred tongue, but to aid him in his endeavours to acquire a knowledge of the esoteric doctrine. Hence we find that as early as 1516—that is before Egidio was elevated to the dignity of Cardinal—Levita copied for him three Kabbalistic works, viz., i. *A Commentary on the Book Jetzira* (פירוש ספר יצירה); ii. *The Mystery of the Angel Raziel* (סוד רזיאל); and iii. *The Book on the Wisdom of the Soul* (ספר חכמת הנפש). It is also supposed that Levita supplied at this time the passages from the Sohar to the work entitled, "*On the Mysteries of the Catholic Truth*," by Petrus Galatinus, which was finished in September, 1516, and published in 1518, since its Gentile authors could not possibly, without the aid of a Jew, have dived into the Sohar. We do not, however, lay much stress on this, though the supposition proceeds from no less an authority than the celebrated historian, Dr. Graetz.[21] We have seen that there were plenty of converted Jews, Kabbalists, to aid Galatinus in a work, the express design of which was to convince the Jews of the truth of the Catholic religion, without being obliged to appeal to Levita for

---

[20] See below, in the Second Introduction, where the whole of the interview is narrated.

[21] *Geschichte der Juden*, ix. 99.

help in such an undertaking, which must have been repugnant to his Jewish feelings.

The intimacy of Levita with Egidio, however, was the means of producing works of far greater importance, and of more permanent utility to Biblical literature, than the *De Arcanis Catholicæ Veritatis* of Galatinus. The very year in which this assault on the Jews and Judaism appeared, Levita published his grammar (1518), entitled, *The Book Bachur* (ספר הבחור). This grammar he wrote at the suggestion, and for the use, of Cardinal Egidio, to whom he dedicated it, as may be seen from the following words in the Introduction to the work in question: "In the year 5277 A.M. [= 1517 A.D.] the Lord stirred up the spirit of a wise man, conversant with all sciences, and of high dignity, Cardinal Egidio—may his glory be exalted! He was anxious to find out the excellent words and the beautiful writing in the books of our sacred language. For this reason he called on me, his servant, Elijahu Levita, the German, the least of the grammarians, and said to me, What art thou doing, Elijahu? Arise now, and make a book which shall pleasantly set forth the grammar of the Hebrew language, since all the Hebrew grammars which I have seen do not satisfy me, nor do they quench my desire for grammar; as some of them are too lengthy, multiplying useless rules, and some are too short in stating what is necessary. Gird up thy loins, therefore, like a man, and adopt the medium between the two extremes, propound the science of grammar in rules not hitherto laid down, but necessary to be exhibited; make them into a book for the benefit of the multitude, so that it may be an ensign for the people, whereunto the Gentiles shall come, and find rest for their souls. When I heard his encouraging words, I at once determined to accede to his request, and compiled this little work on grammar."

Levita, as we have seen, called this grammar *Bachur* (בחור), for three reasons, which are based upon the threefold meaning of the expression, as well as upon the design of the work. As the word בחור denotes both *youth* and *excellent*, and is also his surname, he called it by this name, because, he naïvely tells us, it is designed for the young, it is excellent, and it is his proper name. The treatise is divided into four parts, each one of which is subdivided into thirteen sections, answering to the Thirteen Articles of the Jewish Creed, whilst the total number of all sections, being fifty-two, represents the numerical value of the name אליהו. The first part discusses the nature of the

Hebrew verbs; the second the changes in the vowel-points of the different conjugations; the third the regular nouns; and the fourth the irregular nouns. The simple and beautiful Hebrew in which it is written, as well as the clearness and perspicuity with which it sets forth the structure of the sacred language, at once made the treatise a universal favourite with Hebrew students, both Jewish and Gentile. Not even the very elaborate and masterly Grammar of Abraham de Balmes, which was published five years later (1523), could supersede it. The *Bachur* was the Gesenius of the time, whilst the *Mikne Abraham* (מקנה אברהם), which is the name of De Balmes' Grammar, was the Ewald among Hebrew students. Münster published it, with a Latin translation, for the use of Christians in Germany and elsewhere (1525). The revision of it will be discussed when we arrive at that part of Levita's life when he engaged in it.

In the same year in which Levita carried through the press in Rome (1518) his excellent Grammar, he also published "*Tables of Paradigms*," (לוח בדקדוק הפעלים והבנינים), exhibiting in an elementary form the Hebrew conjugations. The design of these Paradigms, which he compiled from two different sections of the *Bachur*,[22] is to give to the tyro some notion of Hebrew Grammar. These Paradigms are of such extreme rarity, that no Hebrew copy of them has as yet been discovered, and they are only known from Münster's translation. He moreover completed and printed a treatise on the Irregular Words in the Bible, the discussion of which he designedly excluded from his Grammar. This dissertation is entitled "*The Book on Compounds*" (ספר ההרכבה), because it treats on words composed of different words and conjugations. It consists of two hundred and twelve articles, answering to the numerical value of Levita's surname בחור *Bachur*; so that the two numbers together, viz., of the sections in the grammar, and of the articles in this treatise, represent the complete name אליהו בחור *Elijahu Bachur*. The 216 words in this dissertation are not arranged according to their roots, because there is a great difference of opinion among grammarians and lexicographers respecting the etymology of some of them, but they are put down in alphabetical order. The manner in which he treated them

---

[22] אני אליהו דלוי חברתי הלוח הזה לתת לנער דעת בדקדוק - - ויוסף לקח משני המאמרים משונים של ספר הבחור. Comp. Steinschneider, *Catalogus Libr. Heb. in Bibliotheca Bodleiana*, col. 2012, &c., and by the same Author, *Bibliographisches Handbuch*, p. 81, No. 1162.

will be best seen from his own description of the plan of the work: "As my design in this treatise," he says in the Introduction, "is to explain those words only which are anomalous in their grammatical structure, and since the principal grammarians advance different opinions about them, I have stated all their various opinions, and sometimes also contributed my share, according to my limited understanding." This work, too, was translated into Latin by Münster, and published at Basle, 1525. It had such a wide circulation among Christian students, and especially among the early Reformers, that it was reprinted in the Latin version, Basle, 1536, and underwent several editions in the original Hebrew.

His desire to explain every intricacy and anomaly in the Hebrew language, and yet the fear lest hampering his Grammar with too many digressions might preclude it from becoming a manual for the people at large, produced in him the conviction that those points which required lengthy and elaborate explanations would be more acceptable if appended to the book in the form of Dissertations. He therefore promised, in sundry parts of the *Bachur*, to discuss these subjects at the end of the Grammar. But, as is often the case, when he had finished the book, he found that untoward circumstances rendered it impossible for him to compile the promised Appendices, and had to publish it without them. This he tells us is the reason why he was obliged to publish the dissertations separately. As soon as he had carried through the press his "*Treatise on the Compounds,*" he betook himself to the work of these dissertations, and succeeded in publishing them two years after the appearance of the preceding treatise (1520). As the Grammar was the centre around which the sundry treatises clustered, he constituted it the model after which he formed these dissertations. Hence, like the Grammar, he divided them into four parts, consisting respectively of thirteen sections, according to the thirteen articles of the Jewish creed, whilst the sum total of the sections, namely, fifty-two, like that of the Grammar, represents the numerical value of the author's name (אליהו). The first section, or dissertation, which is preceded by a separate Introduction and Table of Contents, discusses, in thirteen stanzas or poems, the laws of the letters, the vowel points, and the accents; and in consequence of its being written in separate poems or stanzas it is denominated "*The Poetical Section or Dissertation*" (פרק שירה). The second section, which is also preceded by a separate Introduction and Table of Contents, discusses, in thirteen chapters, written in prose, the different parts of speech, and hence is called "*The Section on the Different Kinds of Words*" (פרק המינים). The third section, which is preceded by an Introduction only, treats on the numbers and genders of the several parts of speech, seeing that some of them only occur as masculine, some only as feminine, some only in the singular, some only in the plural, some only in the singular and plural feminine, some only in the singular and plural masculine, and some as common genders. These words are here classified according to rules; hence it is styled "*The Section of Rules*" (פרק המדות). The fourth section treats on the seven servile letters (מש״ה וכל״ב), and hence is denominated "*the Section on the Servites*" (פרק השמושים). The four dissertations were first published at Pesaro (1520), under the general title "*the Sections of Elijahu*" (פרקי אליהו). They also soon found their way into Germany, where they were re-published, with a Latin translation by Münster, Basle, 1527.

The four grammatical treatises which he composed at Rome, and his residence for thirteen years at the palace of Cardinal Egidio, where he constantly came into contact with the chief literary men of the day, extended Levita's fame over Europe, and he was appealed to from far and wide for his opinion on matters of Hebrew literature. No allurements of society, however—no worldly pleasures or gain—could tempt him from his work. Whilst in the house of his friend the Cardinal, he not only devoted his time to the instruction of his eminent pupil, and writing the valuable grammatical treatises, but took lessons from Egidio in Greek, and made such rapid progress, that he could read with fluency the Septuagint and the Greek classics.

There can be but little doubt that Levita's writings were intimately connected with the studies of his most distinguished and accomplished pupils. Their rapid progress in Hebrew, their desire to master those portions of the Scriptures which are written in Chaldee, as well as to read the paraphrases, and their diving into Kabbalistic works, necessarily involved more extensive instruction, both in the higher branches of Biblical literature and in the special dialects in which the important documents of the esoteric doctrine are written. Hence it is that we now find him (1520) most industriously engaged upon two particular works: one a most gigantic work on the Massorah, to which we shall have to recur when we arrive at the period of its completion; and the other an Aramaic Grammar. After labouring nine years on a Concordance to the Massorah, and making considerable progress in the Aramaic Grammar, he was again driven from his peaceful studies at the sacking of Rome by the Imperialists under Charles V. (May 6, 1527), when the greater part of his MSS. and property were destroyed.

The plan which he adopted in compiling the Aramaic Grammar will best be gathered from his own words: "Since the time when the Chaldee Paraphrases were made," Levita says, in the Introduction to his Lexicon on the Targumim, "there has not been a wise and intelligent man in Israel who could make a Grammar to them, such as was made by Jehudah, who was the first Hebrew grammarian of blessed memory, and before whom there was no Grammar at all to the sacred language. Having found the twenty-four sacred books pointed, accented, and annotated by the Massorites, he set about to aid the Israelites, and to enlighten the eyes of the exiles in the grammar thereof. After him came R. Jonah, after him R. Saadia Gaon of blessed memory,[23] and after them again grammarians without number. But there was no one engaged in the grammatical study of the Targum to correct its blunders; every one turned his back to it. Hence came to pass the general confusion. I, therefore, submitted that there is a proper way for making a Grammar to the language of the Targum; that the Targum of Daniel and Ezra should be made the basis, and the conjugations should be founded upon it alone, and not upon the Targumim generally; and that the rules of grammar should be deduced therefrom, though they may not all be obtained from such scanty materials. Now, when I was at Rome, my heart was filled

[23] The above piece of literary history fully illustrates our remark on page 1 about the ignorance which prevails respecting even the dates of the most distinguished Jewish literati. Even Levita, with all his learning, describes Jehudah Chajug as the oldest, Jonah Ibn Ganach as the next in age, and Saadia as the third in chronological order. Whereas Saadia was born A.D. 892, Ibn Ganach about 995, and Jehudah Chajug about 1020–1040. For notices of the lives and works of these eminent Hebraists we must refer to Kitto's *Cyclopædia of Biblical Literature*, new ed., and only add here, as supplementary to the article JEHUDAH CHAJUG in the Cyclopædia, that he also wrote a Commentary on the Song of Songs, which is referred to Ibn Aknin, as will be seen under the article IBN AKNIN in the Cyclopædia. He has, moreover, written Commentaries on *the Pentateuch* (quoted by Ibn Ezra on Gen. xli. 48; Exod vii. 5; x. 8; xxi. 8; Numb. x. 36; xxiii. 13; Deut. xxix. 29): on *Isaiah* (quoted by Ibn Ezra on Is. xiv. 20, xxvi. 20, xlix. 8, lxi. 10): on *Habbakuk* (quoted by Ibn Ezra on Habak. ii. 19, iii. 2): on *the Psalms* (quoted by Ibn Ezra on Ps. lxviii. 14, lxxxiv. 7, cii. 28, cxxxvii. 2, cl. 6): on *Job* (quoted by Ibn Ezra on Job xxxviii. 5): on *Ruth* (comp. Ibn Ezra on Ruth i. 20): and on *Ecclesiastes* (comp. Ibn Ezra on Eccl. ix. 12, xii. 5).

with the desire to undertake this work, and I actually finished one part. But the evil days came, and the city was captured, when this portion was either destroyed or taken away, since no one knows what has become of it."

Deprived of his MSS., despoiled of his property, driven from his peaceful studies and from an influential circle of literary friends at Rome, Levita betook himself to Venice in a most destitute and deplorable condition, in 1527. Venice was then the chief seat of Hebrew learning, and had the chief printing establishment for Hebrew books. Here Daniel Bomberg, of Antwerp, established his celebrated printing office in 1516, which created a new epoch in Jewish typography. Within the ten years which intervened between its establishment and the arrival of Levita at Venice (1516-1527), the indefatigable and enterprising Bomberg had already issued from his press the first two editions of the celebrated Rabbinic Bible, the one edited by Felix Pratensis (1516-17), a converted Jew, and the other by Jacob b. Chajim (1524-25), who also embraced christianity; two beautiful editions of the Hebrew Scriptures without the Rabbinic commentaries (1518, 1521); the first complete edition of the Babylon Talmud, which is the model of all succeeding editions; the *editio princeps* of the Jerusalem Talmud (1523); the *editio princeps* of the first Hebrew concordance to the Scriptures, by Isaac Nathan b. Kalonymos (1523); the elaborate Hebrew grammar by De Balmes (1523); and a host of other very important Biblical and Rabbinic works. It was this honourable distinction which Venice obtained as the seat of Hebrew literature, which made Levita decide to make it his future abiding place.

Destitute and deplorable as his condition was on arriving with his wife and children at Venice in 1527, it was not as calamitous as his plight after the sacking of Padua in 1509, when he arrived at Rome. His four works on the grammar and structure of the Old Testament Hebrew, had now obtained for him a world-wide reputation. They had been reprinted, translated into Latin, circulated all over Europe, studied by the most distinguished scholars of Christendom, and were constantly appealed to as the highest authority. Levita himself in the truly Oriental manner, which was also the fashion among Occidental scholars at that time, naïvely recounts the glory of his own productions and success in the following words: "The four works of mine, owing to their wisdom and knowledge, have been published several times, translated into languages of the Christians, and are studied both by Jews and Christians, as their fame has travelled far and their excellence is known all over the world; they send forth an odour like precious ointment, on which account I congratulate myself. Now I speak the truth when I say that there is no author whom God has permitted to see in his lifetime, his works so much referred to and studied, and so many times reprinted as He has permitted me during my lifetime." This Eastern self-laudation is, according to the modern interpretation of some great and good men who have resorted to it in our days, simply giving the opinion of others about ourselves.

With such a world-wide reputation, Levita had no difficulty in finding occupation at Venice. Indeed Bomberg, who was the great centre of Hebrew literature in this city, knew Levita personally, and published a poem of his in the second edition of the Rabbinic Bible (1525), two years before his arrival at Venice. He therefore at once employed him as corrector of the Hebrew Press, and editor of sundry Hebrew works. As the first instalment of his labours in connection with Bomberg's printing office, is to be mentioned the new edition of David Kimchi's (1160–1235) Hebrew Lexicon, commonly called "*The Book of Roots*" (ספר השרשים), which, though corrected by Isaiah b. Eleazar Parnas, was revised by Levita, who also wrote a laudatory poem to it by way of Epilogue (1529). Besides revising the works published by Bomberg, he devoted all his spare time to the elucidation of the Massorah, which, as we have seen, he had already begun when at Rome. The means for supporting his family he chiefly derived from tuition, as the salary which he got from Bomberg must have been exceedingly small.

To the furtherance of Biblical literature, it happened that the erudite and liberally-minded George de Selve, afterwards bishop of Lavour, was then the French Ambassador of Francis I., at Venice. Though occupying a most distinguished position among the statesmen and scholars of the sixteenth century, he placed himself under the tuition of Levita, and made such marvellous progress in Hebrew, that he could express himself with the same facility in it as in Latin and Greek, which constituted the three literary languages of the day. The intimacy which arose between the distinguished pupil and the renowned teacher was the means both of enriching Biblical literature and of promoting the study thereof in France, for De Selve most generously put him in a position to complete his stupendous Massoretic

Concordance. With such princely aid, Levita could devote himself more than ever to his darling work; and after labouring over it more than twenty years, and getting all the help he could obtain in the investigation of MSS., collating, copying, &c., &c., he completed his gigantic "*Book of Remembrance*," as he called it, in 1536, and dedicated it to his friend and liberal patron, George de Selve, Bishop of Lavour. As this important work has never been printed, and moreover as its history and De Selve's connection with it can only be seen from Levita's most simple and most beautiful Hebrew Dedication, we subjoin the following translation of it:[24]

"To his most exalted Eminence, my lord, George de Selve, Bishop of Lavour, peace be multiplied! It is now some years since I began a work which appeared to me important and very useful to those who study the structure of the sacred language. The devastation of Rome, however, which took place shortly after it, was the cause of my not finishing it at that time and leaving it incomplete. And even the incomplete part was taken from me, and became a prey of spoil; it was torn and shattered so that nothing but a small portion was left to me, which I brought with me here to Venice, and I gave up all thought of finishing the work any more. But God, who willed that I should complete it, and that the book should be published, stirred up your spirit, and put it into your heart, to study the sacred language under me, which you learned from me with great ease and in a very short time; so that you are famed for your knowledge of the three classical languages — the sacred Hebrew, the rich Greek, and the elegant Latin tongues; you have now acquired all accomplishments,

---

[24] The only portions of this gigantic work which have been published are the Dedication and the Introduction. These the learned Frensdorff printed in Frankel's *Monatsschrift fur Geschichte und Wissenschaft des Judenthums*, vol. xii., pp. 96–108; Breslau, 1863. Our translation is made from the Hebrew text, which, with a few manifest errors, we also reprint below, as the periodical in which they are published is not possessed by every reader who might wish to be acquainted with Levita's text.

אל רום מעלת השר המאושר אדוני זור'וו דסאל'ווא הנגמון דלאב'ור שלום רב בהיות כי בשנים שעברו התחלתי במלאכה אחת דנראה בעיני היותה טובה ומעולה מועילה מאד לכל הבאים ללמוד ולהבין דרכי לשון הקודש הזה אכן החורבן של רומי הבא סמוך אחר' זאת היה סבה שלא השלמתיה בעת ההיא עובתיה חסרה. ואף אותו חלק הבלתי שלם לוקח ממני והיה לשלל ולבזה מקורע ומטושטש ולא נשארו בידי רק מעט והבאתיו עמי הנה בעיר ויניס'יאה, ולא היתה מחשבתי להשלים הספר הזה עוד. אכן ברצות ה' שהמלאכה הזאת תהיה נגמרת והספר הזה יצא לאורה העיר ה' את רוח אדוני ושם בלבבו ללמוד עמי בלשון הקודש הזה ולמדהו ממני בקלות ובזמן קצר מאד, והרי לך שם בשלושה· לשון עברי הקדושה· ולשון יון הרווחה· ולשון לאטי'נו הצחה· ברי שחתיה שלם בכל השלמיות

and you, my lord, are among the wise like the sun among the stars. You know, my lord, that we one day happened to converse about this work, and that you asked me to show you the disordered portion of it which was still left to me. When you read it you were pleased to think highly of it, and of the advantage which it would be to those who study the Hebrew language. You urged me with all your might to undertake the labour of completing it, and you promised to pay the expenses of the amanuensis, punctuators, and all the rest of them, to bring it to completion, and did it. All this devolved upon you. Thus was I encouraged to undertake this great labour, as well as great honour. I rested neither day nor night till, by the help of God, and by the munificence of you, my lord, I have been permitted to complete it.

"Now, since it is the general custom of the country for everyone who has written a book to dedicate it to one of the great princes of the earth, it is my bounden duty to inscribe this work to no one else but to you. I am, however, far from doing this simply because of the highly exalted position which you occupy, but because of your liberal hand and generous heart, since you, my lord, are the cause of my having completed it, and it is through you that we hope soon to see it printed, published, and fill the earth with its glory. Accept therefore, my lord, this work with the same benign countenance which you have always shown to me; not as if it were mine, sent as a present from me to you, but as from a servant who has laboured for his master, and whose earnings are the earnings of the master. When you read it, you will gather therein some of the fruits of your generosity, and of the silver and gold you have spent on it, which exceeds all the labour and trouble I have spent on it. I cannot sufficiently commend, extol,

והרי אדוני בין החכמים, כמו השמש בין הכוכבים, והנה ידעת אדוני כי יום אחד נפל בינינו הדבור ודברנו מזה החבור, ובקשת ממני אדוני להראותך הקונטרסים הנשברים, אשר בידי נשארים, ובקראך בו, זכרת רב טובו ותועלתו המגיע ממנו לתלמידי הלשון הזה ובקשת ממני בכל עוז שאקבל עלי הטורח להשלימו, והבטחת וקיימת לתת שכר הסופרים והנקדנים וכל אשר יצא עליו לחזק את בדקו ולגדור את פרצו עליך היו כלנה. ובכן התעוררתי ונכנסתי בטורח הגדול ועול הכבד הזה. וביום ובלילה לא שכב לבי עד כי זכיתי להשליכו בעזרת ה' ובעזרת נדבת יד אדוני הטובה עלי. והנה בהיות המנהג הנהוג בארץ שכל מי שיחבר ספר חדש להדפיסו ויחסו לשם אחד מהשרים הגדולים אשר בארץ הזה, היה מן העול והחמס ליחס את הספר הזה כי אם אליך השר, וחלילה לי מעשות כדבר הזה לא בלבד בעבור כבור מעלתך ויקר תפארת גדולתך כי רבה היא, כי גם בעבור נדבות ידך ורחב לבבך באשר אתה אדוני היית סבה להשלימו ולהקימו על רגליו ועל ידך נוכה בלנו במהרה לאורו ולהדפיסו, ותמלא כל הארץ כבודו, על כן תקבל נא אדוני את הספר הזה בסבר פנים יפות כמו שהראית לי תמיד, ולא כאילו הוא שלי ודורון שלוח לך ממני, כי אם כעבד המשועבד לרבו, וכל מה שקונה עבד קונה רבו, ובקראך בו תלקט קצת פרי נדבתך אשר התנדבת וכספך וזהבך אשר הוצאת על ככה, והוא שקול כנגד כל הטורח והעמל אשר אנכי ברדתי ועמלתי ויותר. והנה לא אוכל לשבח ולהלל ולפאר את מלאכת הספר הזה כראוי לו אך יהללוהו

and magnify the book, but its labour will praise it in the gates; and I trust to God that every scholar like you, who reads it, and sees its excellence and usefulness, will be delighted with it, find in it what he wants, praise it, and put it as a crown on his head. Now you, my lord, will be praised in the mouths of all far more than the book and I. To you the highest praise is due, for the virtues which you have displayed in the faithful discharge of your duty, both towards God and man. Every one who sees you reveres you, and every one who hears of you speaks highly of you. Happy the sovereigns who have such learned and wise ambassadors and ministers as you are, and happy the learned and wise who have such masters and princes as you have," &c., &c.

As to the plan, contents, and design of this Massoretic Concordance, these will be gathered from the following translation of the Introduction[25] to it :—

"Thus says Elias Levita. Having determined to compile this great and stupendous work, to put down therein some of the Massoretic annotations wherever required, and to arrange it grammatically, I must acquaint you with what I have done in this my book, and also explain to you the method which I followed, the good hand of the Lord helping me. Notice, in the first place, that this book is arranged according to the order of '*The Book of Roots*,' by David Kimchi of blessed memory; but with this difference, that whilst he only adduces under every root one or two examples of each conjugation and tense, or two examples of each of the different nouns, I give under every root all

בשערים מעשיו. ואקוה לאל שכל חכם לב כמוך היום יקרא בו ויראה את טובו ותועלתו יתענג בו וימצא מרגוע לנפשו וישבחנו. וכתר לראשו יענדנו. ואתה אדוני תשובה בפי כל יותר מהספר וממני כי לך נאה להודות באשר נודעת ונכרת זה שנתים בקרב הארץ ובמקום הזה אשר עמדת פה שליח שלוח ומאת אדונך המלך הגדול מלך צרפת יר"ה אל יקר תפארת גדולת השררה יר"ה אשר בוויני'סיא. ועשית הטוב והישר בעיני אלהים ואדם כל הימים. וכל עין ראתה אותך תעידך ואזן שמעה ותאשרך. ואשרי למלכים אם היו להם משרתים ושריב חכמים ונבונים כמוך. ואשרי לחכמים ונבונים. אם היו להם ארונים ופטרונים כמוך. ובזה הנני אקוד ואשתחוה לאדוני אפים ארצה. ועפר רגליך אלחך. ואהיה עבד נרצע לאהבתך. תמיד מוכן לשירותך. ואעתיר לאל בעד הצלחתך. ובהתמדת בריאותך. כרצון נפשך וכבקשתך ובקשת פה"ות אחד מעבדי אדוני הקטנים. רך בחכמה ואב בשנים.

אליה הלוי אשכנזי.

[25] אמר אליהו הלוי אחרי אשר הסכמתי לחבר את הספר הזה חבור גדול והפלא ולשים בו קצת ענינים מדברי המסורת במקום הצורך ולסדרהו על פי הדקדוק. אודיע נא אתכם את אשר אני עושה לספרי זה, ואורה אתכם את הדרך אשר אלך בה כיד ה' הטובה עלי. ראשונה דעו נא לכם כי הספר הזה יהי מסודר על סדר ס' השרשים של הר"דק ז"ל, אבל הוא לא הביא בכל שרש רק ב' או ג' פסוקים מכל בנין ופעולה או ב' מכל מין ממיני השמות הנמצאים בשרש ההוא אמנם אני אביא בכל שרש כל הפעלים והשמות וחמלות אשר נמצאו

the verbs, nouns, and expressions which are to be found from this root in all the Hebrew Scriptures, and arrange them according to the order of the seven conjugations as classified in the paradigm of the grammar. Thus, for instance, I first give the *Kal*, then *Niphal*, then *Piel*, *Pual*, *Hiphil*, *Hophal*, and *Hithpael*, having already proved in the *Book Bachur* that the quadriliteral conjugation has no real existence. I have then divided each conjugation into its six tenses, viz., Præterite, Participle present, Past participle, Infinitive, Imperative, and Future.

"Having enumerated all the conjugations in this manner, I give the nouns which occur from this root. I give first nouns-adjective, which are again subdivided according to their order; that is, the singular masculine is separate, the plural masculine, the singular and plural feminine, as well as each construct and absolute state, are given separately. I also give separately each word which begins with one of the seven servile letters (מש״ה וכ״לב), always giving first the *Vav*, which is the most frequent prefix, and then stating those with prefix *Beth*, and the rest in their alphabetical order. The same plan I pursue with the other nouns, always giving first those which have no formative additions from the letters האמנ״תי, as well as with the sundry proper names, *ex. gr.* names of men, countries, cities, deserts, pools, rivers, and seas. Of these I only adduce those which are found in the Massorah, and they are very numerous. Last of all follow the conjunctions. Of these, too, I only give those which occur in the Massorah, and which are very numerous.

"Now let that which I have written on the root אכל serve as an illustration. I have put together—i., All the passages of the Scrip-

בשרש ההוא בכל עשרים וארבעה ספרים, ואסדרם על סדר שבעה הבנינים כמו שהם מסודרים בלוח הדקדוק. דהיינו אתחיל בבנין הקל ואח״כ נפעל ופעל ופעל הדנוש ופעל והפעיל והפעל והתפעל, וכבר הוכחתי בספר הבחור כי הבנין המרובע בטל מעיקרו ואין בו ממש, ואחלק כל בנין לשש פעולותיו, דהיינו עבר ובינוני ופעול ומקור וציווי ועתיד, ואחר שהשלמתי כל הבנינים בזה האופן אתחיל בשמות הנמצאים באותו השרש, ובראשונה יסעו שמות התארים ואחלקם ג״כ לפי הסדר דהיינו היחידים לבד והרבים לבד וכן היחידות והרבות, והמוכרחים של כל אחד לבד והסמוכים לבד ועם שבע אותיות המשמשות בראש סימנם מש״ה וכ״לב, ואתחיל תמיד באות הו״יו כי היא תשמש יותר מכולן, ואח״כ אסדר אותם שעם בי״ת השמוש והשאר אסדר לפי סדר הא״לף בי״ת, וכן אעשה בשאר מיני השמות, ובתחלה אשים אותם שחם בלי תוספת אותיות האמנ״תי, ואף שמות העצמים הפרטים כמו שמות בני אדם ושמות ארצות ועיירות ומדברות ונהרות ואגמים וימים, אמנם לא אביא מהם רק שנמצא ומהם במסורת והם רבים מאד, ואחרונה יסעו מלות הטעם וגם מהם אקח כל מה שנמצא ומהם במסורת וגם הם רבו למעלה ראש, והמשל מכל מה שאמרתי מן שרש אכל אכתוב כל אכל הנמצאים בכל כ״ד ספרים יחד ואח״כ כל ואכל ואח״כ כל אכלת ואח״כ כל

tures in which אָכַל Kal pret. 3rd pers. sing. mas. occurs; then all of וְאָכַל Kal pret. 3rd pers. sing. mas. with the conjunct.; then all of אָכַלְתָּ Kal pret. 2nd pers. sing. mas.; then all of וְאָכַלְתָּ Kal pret. 2nd pers. sing. mas. with the conjunct.; and so the whole of the praeterite. Then, ii., The present participle, beginning with אוֹכֵל of which I say there are ten instances of plene, and give them all. I then state all the defectives, then follow all the instances of בְּאֹכֵל וְאֹכֵל הָאֹכֵל, &c., &c. The same method I pursue with all the conjugations, that is, giving all the passages of the Niphal, and of all the other conjugations. Then, iii., I give the nouns, beginning with those instances of אֹכֶל which are *Milel*; then follow those with the formative prefix *Mem*, *ex. gr.* מַאֲכָל, which occurs four times with *Pattach* under the *Caph*, all the others having *Kametz*; then follow all the instances of the forms מַאֲכֶלֶת. מַאֲכֹלֶת and in this manner all the words which are alike in spelling and pronunciation are put together, and the whole of such a class is called a camp or rubric. And if there happens to be any word with Massoretic annotations, I divide the camp into two camps, as I have remarked above under the rubric אוֹכֵל, where I put the ten instances of plene as one class, and the defectives into another, thus making two camps. You are moreover to observe that I give after every class the verbs with the suffixes of the same rubric. Thus, for instance, after the verb אָכַל I give all the instances in which it occurs with the suffix, as אֲכָלוֹ Kal pret. 3rd pers. sing. mas., with suff. 3rd pers. sing. mas., אֲכָלַנִי pret. 3rd pers. sing. mas., suff. 1st. pers. sing.; so also וַאֲכָלָם, and after every rubric. The same is the case with nouns; after אֹכֶל I give all the instances of it with the pronominal suffixes, as אָכְלָהּ, אָכְלָם and so all the ten pro-

ואכלת וכן כל העבר ואח"כ אתחיל בבינוני ואתחיל אוכל י' מלאים ואביא את כלם ואח"כ אביא כל החסרים, ואח"כ ואכל ואח"כ באכל ואח"כ האכל וכן כלם וכן כל הבנין, ואתחיל בבנין נפעל נאכל וכל מה שנמצא ממנו בבנין נפעל וכן בשאר הבנינים אכתוב כל מה שנמצא ממנו, ואח"כ אתחיל בשמות ואתחיל אכל אותם שהם מלעיל, ואח"כ בתוספת מ"ם האמנ"חי, מאכל ד' פתחין והשאר קמוצין ואח"כ משקל אחר מאכלת ואח"כ משקל אחר מאכלת ובזה האופן יהיו כל המלות השוות במכתב ובמבטא מקובצים יחד ואקרא לכל קבוץ מלות כאלה מחנה אחת. ואם יהיה במחנה אחת איזה דבר של מסורת אחיב את המחנה ההיא לשתי מחנות כמו שכתבתי לעיל במחנה אוכל י' ומלאים הדי מחנה אחת והחסרים יהיו למחנה אחרת הרי ב' מחנות, ועוד תדע כי אחר כל מחנה ומחנה אכתוב החנויים הנמצאים במלות של המחנה ההיא, והמשל אחר מחנה אכל אכתוב כל כנוייו כמו הראשון אכלו. אכלני חרב וכן וכאלם, וכן אחר כל מחנה וכן בשמות אחר מחנה אכל אכתוב כינוייו את כל אכלם, לא תתן את אכלך. וכן כל עשרה הכנויים על הסדר נסתר נכח מדבר בעדו וכן הרבים וכן

nominal suffixes in the order of third person, second person, and first person, as well as the plural and feminine.

"Not to increase, however, the size of the book beyond what is necessary, I have taken care to give each noun and verb in one place only, and not to repeat it in two or three different places, as the author of the Concordance[26] has uselessly done. Hence, where two verbs occur in several places, joined together, as לאכול ולשתות, *to eat and to drink*, I cite all the instances under the root אכל, *to eat*, in the section comprising the Infinitive; and when I come to the root שתה, *to drink*, in the section containing the Infinitive, I state 'See the root אכל, *to eat*, under the Infinitive.' The same is the case with the combined words לשמור ולעשות, *to observe and to do*, I give all the passages under the root שמר, *to observe*, and state, under the root עשה, *to do*, 'See under the root שמר, *to observe*;' as well as with nouns joined to verbs, or with verbs joined to nouns, I always adduce them under the root of the verbs, and do not give them again under the root of the nouns, provided the Massoretic annotations do not necessitate their being given a second time under the root of the nouns.

"Before, however, I illustrate this by an example, you must notice that each book of the Hebrew Scriptures is divided into small sections, which the Christians call chapters. The same is the case with the Pentateuch, each book of which has been divided by the Massorites into sections. Thus, for instance, the book of Genesis, they divided into twelve sections, Exodus into eleven sections,

הנקבה, והנה כדי שלא להרבות כמות הספר יותר מדי הסכמתי לחיות נזהר בכל עוז שלא לכתוב שם או פעל אחד רק במקום אחד ולא בשנים או בשלושה מקומות כמו שעשה בעל הספר הקונקרדנצייה[26] ללא תועלת ולכן הסכמתי כשיבאו שני פעלים הנמצאים בהרבה מקומות סמוכים יחד כמו לאכול ולשתות אכתוב את כלם בשרש אכל במחנה לאכול וכשאגיע לשרש שתה במחנה לשתות אכתוב עיין בשרש אכל במחנה לאכול, וכן לשמור ולעשות אכתוב כלם בשרש שמר ובשרש עשה אכתוב עיין בשרש שמר, וכן חשמות הסמוכים אל הפעלים או שהפעלים סמוכים אליחם אכתוב אותם תמיד בשרשי הפעלים ולא אכתבם פעם אחרת בשרשי השמות אם לא תכריחני המסורת לכתוב אותם פעם שני בשרש השמות, וטרם אבאר זה לך במשל צריך שתדע כי כל ספר של העשרים והארבעה נחלק לפרשיות קטנות קראו להם הגוים קאפיטולי וכן בה' חומשי תורה כמו שחכמי המסורת חלקו כל ספר לפרשיות כגון ספר בראשית פרשיותיו י"ב ס' שמות פרשיותיו י"א וכן כלן, הנה הם חלקו ס' בראשית לנ'

---

[26] The author of the above-named first Hebrew Concordance is R. Isaac Nathan b. Kalonymos. He lived at Avignon, Montpellier, in the time of Peter de Luna, or the anti-pope Benedict XIII. R. Nathan devoted eight years of his life (1437-1445) to this Concordance, which was first printed by Bomberg, Venice, 1523. Comp. *Kitto's Cyclopædia of Biblical Literature*, new ed. *s. v.* NATHAN.

&c., &c., whereas the Christians divided Genesis into fifty chapters, Exodus into forty chapters, and so all the books of the Bible, as Joshua into twenty-four chapters, Judges into twenty-one chapters, &c., &c., making many chapters in the large books, and few chapters in the smaller ones. You are, moreover, to observe, that the Christians also divided Samuel and Kings into two books respectively; the second book of Samuel beginning with 'And it came to pass after the death of Saul,' and the second part of Kings with 'Then Moab rebelled.' Hence, wherever you find Samuel or Kings with two over it, it denotes 2 Sam. or 2 Kings. They also divided Chronicles into two books, the first book extending to the words 'And Soloman was strengthened,' whilst from these words onward is the second book. Hence, whenever you find Chronicles with two over it it denotes 2 Chronicles.

"And now for the illustration of what I have written above. The words ויכלו השמים *and the heavens were finished* (Gen. ii. 1), I give under the root כלה *to finish;* האזינו השמים *Give ear, O ye heavens!* (Deut. xxxii. 1,) I give under the root אזן *to be acute.* The same is the case with מוסדות השמים *the foundations of the heavens* (2 Sam. xxii. 8); בסערה השמים *by a whirlwind to the heavens* (2 Kings ii. 1); נפתחו השמים *the heavens were opened* (Ezek. i. 1); ישמחו השמים, *let the heavens rejoice* (Ps. xcvi. 2); ויזעקו השמים *and they cried to the heavens* (2 Chron. xxxii. 20), &c., &c.; which I give under the roots of the respective verbs; and when I come to the root שם, section השמים *the heavens,* I put down all the above phrases

קאפיטולי וס' שמות למ' קאפיטולי וכן כל שאר ספרי המקרא כגון יהושע כ"ד קאפיטולי שופטים כ"א וכן כלם הנגדול לפי גדלו והקטן לפי קטנו . וצריך שתדע עוד כי הם חלקו ס' שמואל לב' חלקים ה' מלכים לב' חלקים, החלק השני משמואל מתחיל ויהי אחרי מות שאול, והספר השני ממלכים מתח"ל ויפשע מואב ולכן בכל מקום שתמצא שמואל עם בי"ת למעלה ד"ל מן ויהי אחרי מות שאול והלאה וכן כשתמצא מלכים עם בי"ת למעלה ד"ל מן ויפשע מואב והלאה, וכן חלקו דברי הימים לב' ספרים הספר הראשון עד ויתחזק שלמה ומשם והאלה נקרא ספר שני ולכן בכל מקום כשתמצא ד"ה עם בי"ת למעלה ר"ל דברי הימים שני . והנה המשל על מה שכתבתי לעיל אכתוב ויכלו השמים (ראשית ב') בשרש כלה, האזינו השמים (דברים ל"ב) בשרש אזן, מוסדות השמים (שמואל כ"ב), בסערה השמים (מלכים ב'), נפתחו השמים (יחזקאל א') ישמחו השמים (תלים צ"ו), ויצעקו השמים (ד"ה ל"ב) ודומיהם, והנה כשאגיע לשרש שם במחנה השמים אכתוב את כלם יחד בלי מראה מקום כגון ויכלו השמים, האזינו השמים, מוסדות השמים, בסערה השמים, נפתחו השמים, ישמחו השמים, ויצעקו השמים ודומיהם כל חד בשרשי חמלות שלפניהם ואקרא

together, without the references, as '*and the heavens were finished,*' '*Give ear, O ye heavens!*' with the remark that each phrase will be found specified under the roots of the respective verbs which precede the noun. This camp or section I call *the mixed multitude*. Hereupon I give those passages in which the word '*heavens*' precedes the verb, *ex. gr.* השמים אעלה *the heavens I shall ascend,* השמים כסאי *the heavens are my throne,* &c.: each of which I give under the root of the respective verbs. The same I do when two or three words are joined together; these I only give in one place, *ex. gr.* the words כסף וזהב *silver and gold,* which frequently occur together, I give all of them under the root זהב *to shine,* with the references and respective passages; and when I come to the root כסף *to become pale,* I say, For כסף וזהב *silver and gold,* see the root זהב *to shine.* Also the phrases דבר וחרב ורעב *pestilence and sword and famine,* I give them all under the root דבר *to destroy*; and when I come to the root חרב *to destroy,* I say, See under the root דבר *to destroy*; the same I do under the root רעב *to be hungry.* This method I pursue with all the nouns which are connected with another noun or verb, either preceding or following them. In all such cases I give in the first mixed multitude, all the words which precede the word good, as דבר טוב *a good thing,* מזבח טוב *a good altar,* ברכת טוב *a good blessing,* &c., &c.; and then I put down in the opposite mixed multitude, those words which are preceded by the expression טוב *good,* as טוב תתי *good to give,* טוב עבוד *good to serve,* &c., &c.; so also with the root לבב; in the first mixed multitude I give the phrases חכם לב *wise of heart,* ערלי לב *circumcised of heart,* &c., &c.; and in the reverse mixed multitude, לב רגז *heart of restlessness,* לב נדכה &c., &c.

למחנה הזאת האספסוף, ואח"כ אכתוב אותם שמלות השמים קודמין אל הפעלים כמו השמים אעלה, השמים כסאי, השמים החדשים, השמים מספרים ודומיהן בשרשי המלות וכן כשיהיו ב' או ג' שמות רצופים לא אכתבם רק במקום אחד והמשל כסף וזהב הנמצא הרבה פעמים כמוכין יחד אכתוב את כלם בשרש זהב עם מראה מקום שלהם וכשאגיע לשרש כסף אכתוב כסף וזהב עיין בשרש זהב, וכן דבר וחרב ורעב אכתוב את כלם בשרש דבר וכשאגיע אל שרש חרב אכתוב עיין בשרש דבר וכן אעשה בשרש רעב, וזה אעשה בכל השמות אשר הם סמוכים לשם או לפעל אחד לפניהם או לאחריהם אכתוב האספסוף כמו דבר טוב, מזבח טוב, ברכת טוב, רודפי טוב, שוחר טוב, מצא טוב ודומיהם רבים במלות הקודמים למלת טוב ואח"כ אכתוב האספסוף ההפך דהיינו המלות אשר טוב קודם אליהם, כמו טוב תתי, טוב עבוד, טוב וסלח, טוב וישר וכאלה רבות אשר טוב קודם להם, וכן בשרש לבב האספסוף חכם לב, חקקי לב, ערלי לב, מננת לב וכו' והאספסוף ההפך, לב רגז, לב נדכה, לב נשבר, לב סורר ודומיהם רבים. ועוד זאת אעשה כדי לקצר ולא להאריך

"Moreover, for the sake of brevity, whenever one, two, or three verbs are joined to a noun, I write at the beginning of the root of the word in question, See such and such a root, *ex. gr.* at the beginning of the root דָּם *blood*, I say, See under the root שפך *to shed*, and under the root נקה *to be clean*, section נקי *pure*; at the beginning of the root קוֹל *voice*, I say, See under the roots שמע *to hear*, and קרא *to call*; at the beginning of the root סוּם *horse*, I remark, See under the root רכב *to ride*; and at the beginning of the root בית *house*, I state, See under the root בנה *to build*; so that there is no necessity to put down in any of these a separate mixed multitude. Also in those roots in which there occur several kinds of nouns, I write at the head of each of them, the root which occurs therein. Thus בשר *flesh*, לחם *bread*, חרב *sword*, אש *fire*, &c., because many of these occur under the root אכל *to eat, to consume*, I say at the beginning of every root of these words, See under the root אכל *to eat*, so that there is no necessity for making of them a separate mixed section. The rule is this, that whatever I could abridge in the nouns I shortened, but I have not shortened the verbs, but put them all down; not a single one of these has been omitted intentionally, except the future with *Vav* conversive as וידבר ויאמר &c., &c.; these have only been given in case there is any Massoretic remark on them.

"It is to be noticed, that all nouns and verbs of which the Massorites have given the number, I have fully enumerated, without making any separate mixed section whatever; as, for instance, the word ראש occurs 151 times; וְרֹאשׁ occurs 11 times; הָרֹאשׁ twice; לְרֹאשׁ 24 times; מֵרֹאשׁ 14 times; ראשון 8 times; הראשון 63 times; &c., &c.; also וראיתי occurs 12 times; ויאמר 91 times. Of these I

כל שם שׁשרש אחד או ב' או ג' מיוחדים לו אכתוב בראש שרש של השם ההוא עיין בשרש פלוני ופלוני והמשל בראש שרש דם אכתוב עיין בשרש שפך ובשרש נקה במחנה נקי, ובראש שרש קול אכתוב עיין בשרש שמע וקרא ובראש שרש סום אכתוב עיין בשרש רכב ובראש שרש בית אכתוב עיין כשרש בנה ואין צריך לכתוב מאחד מכל אלה האספסוף, וכן בשרש שימצאו בו הרבה מיני שמות אכתוב בראש כל אחד מהם השרש אשר ימצא בו, בשר ולחם וחרב ואש בעבור שהרבה מהם נמצאו בשרש אכל אכתוב בראש כל שרש של אלו עיין בשרש אכל ואין צריך לעשות מהם האספסוף, וחכלל ני כל מה שאוכל לקצר בשמות אקצר אבל לא אקצר בפעלים אך אכתוב כלם ולא אניח אף אחד מהם אם לא בשכחה ובשגגה הוץ מפעלי עתתדיים הבאים עם ו' ו החפוך על יו"ד האיתן כגון ויאמר וידבר ויקח ויתן ויעש ויצא וילך וישב ודומיהם לא אביא מדם רק מה שנמצא בהם במסורת ודוק ותמצא. ודע כי בכל שם או פעל שנתנו בעלי המסודת סימן במספרם אכתוב את כלם ולא אעשה מהם אספסוף כלל והמשל ראש קנ"א, וראש י"א, הראש ב', לראש

have not omitted a single one. But the words of which the Massorites have not given the number, I have not had the heart to enumerate, for fear I should give the wrong number. As a rule, whatever I could put into a separate section I did put. Now I called this book the 'Book of Remembrance,' because therein are mentioned all the subjects which are advantageous to the study of the Scriptures, and therein all the words are examined. The use of this work is tenfold.

"i. It is like a Lexicon, explaining all the words which occur in the Hebrew Scriptures, as I give under each root an explanation of all the words in succession which occur in this root. For it sometimes happens that one root has two, three, four, and as many as ten different significations. I moreover give with the explanation of every word its meaning in German, which is the language of my countrymen. ii. It is as a Grammar, because therein is explained the grammatical structure of all the words under their respective roots, so that the things explain themselves. Thus, if one has any difficulty about the grammar of a word, he need only look at the section, and under the part of speech into which I have put it, *ex. gr.* וְאָהֲבָא you will know that its root is חבא, and you will see that I put it under the *Niphal*, future, first pers. The same is the case if it is a noun, you will recognise whether it is a noun-adjective or substantive, or to what form it belongs, from the sections into which it is placed. iii. It is a model for the Codices of the Law, for thereby may be corrected all the Hebrew Scriptures with regard to plene and defective, Milra, Keri

כ"ד, מראש י"ד, ראשון ח' הראשון ס"ג ודומיהון וכן וראיתי י"ב, ויאמר צ"א פתחין לא אניח אף אחד מחם, אבל המלות שלא כתבו חם מנינם לא ימלאני לבי לכתוב מספרם מיראתי פן שניתי במספרם, והכלל כל מה שאוכל לעשות מחם האפפסוף אעשה.

והנה קראתי שם הספר הזה ספר הזכרונות כי זכר כל המעשים המועילים למקרא בתוכו בא והוא דורש את עניני המלות כלם. והנה התועליות המניעות מזה הספר הם עשרה:

התועלת הא' הוא שיחי' הספר הזה כדמות ספר השרשים מבאר כל המלות חנמצאים בכ"ד ספרים, ואכתוב בכל שרש ביאורי כל המלות חנמצאות בשרש ההוא זו אחר זו כי לפעמים יהיו בשרש אחד ב' או ג' או ד' וכו' עד י' ענינים גם אכתוב אצל כל ביאור מלה ומלה פתרונה בלשון אשכנז שהיא לשון בני עמי.

התועלת הב' שיהיה הספר הזה כדמות ספר דקדוק, וזה כי יבוארו בו דקדוק של כל המלות הנמצאות בשרש ההוא וזה כי יבוארו מצד עצמם כי כאשר יקשה לאדם דקדוק של מלה אחת הלא יראה המחנה אשר שמתיה בו באיזה מין ופעולה ודבור, והמשל כי ערום אנכי ואחבא ידעת ששרשו הב"א ותראה כי שמתיה בבנין נפעל בעתיד במחנה המדבר בעדו וכן אם הוא שם יכיר אם הוא תאר או שם דבר או איזה משקל הוא לפי המחנה אשר יחנה שם.

התועלת הג' הוא שיהיה הספר הזה כדמות תקון ספר תורה כי בו יגיה אדם כל כ"ד ספרים

and Kethiv, Tikkun Sopherim, the large and small letters, and as I have stated above in the Introduction. iv. It explains the great and small Massorah, and I am persuaded that whoso consults this book will understand most of the Massoretic remarks and signs which were unknown to him before. v. It serves as a concordance for those who read the Bible, the Mishna, the Talmud, the Kabbalah, Grammar, or Commentaries, and who meet in these works passages of Scripture adduced as evidence which they cannot find in the Bible. Now this book will enable them easily to find the place, and show them the book and chapter in which these passages occur, as I have mentioned in the Introduction above. vi. It will be of use to preachers who, in composing sermons, want to find passages illustrative of their text. Thus, for instance, if one has to preach about *righteousness*, he needs only look into the root צדק, section צדקה, and he will not require to search through all the sections of this root, comprising either verbs or nouns, but simply section צרקה and section לצדקה, הצדקה, בצדקה. So also if he has to preach about *peace* or *joy*, he only needs to look into the roots שלם and שמח. vii. To those who wish to write Hebrew letters, adopting the style of the Bible, they will easily find the passages, as I have illustrated it, with respect to preachers. Thus, for instance, if anyone wishes to write a letter to his friend to buy or to make him some garments, he need only look into the root לבש, and if he does not find under it what he wants, he is to look into the root בגד or

במלוי וחסרון ובמלרע בקדרע בקרײן וכתיבן בתיקון סופרים באותיות גדולות וקטנות כאשר כתבתי לעיל בהקדמה.

התועלת הד' הוא שיהי' הספר הזה כדמות באור למסרה גדולה וקטנה, ומבטיח אני כל המעיין בספר הזה ישכיל ויבין רוב דברי בעלי המסרת וסימניהם אשר לפנים לא ידעם.

התועלת הה' הוא שיהי' הספר הזה כדמות מראה מקום לכל מי שיקרא באחד מהספרים מקרא משנה גמרא קבלה ודקדזק ופירושי' וימצא שם ראיית פסיק ולא ידע מקומו או הלא בזה הספר קל מהרה יבין דרכו וידע את מקומו וימצאהו באיזה ספר ובאיזה פרשה ר״ל קאפיטולו הוא כאשר הראיתיך בהקדמה לעיל.

התעלת הו' הוא שיהי' הספר הזה מבחר וטוב לכל הבא לעשות איזה דרשה וירצה להביא ראיות מהפסוקים לדרוש ההוא, והמשל הרוצה לדרוש בעניני הצדקה הלא יעיין בשרש צדק במהנה צדקה ולא יצטרך לבקש בכל מחנות השרש לא בפעלים ולא בשמות רק במתנה צדקה ובמחנה בצדקה הצדקה לצדקה, וכן אם ידרוש בענין שלום או בענין שמחה יבקש בשרש שלם ושמח.

התועלת הז' מי שירצה לכהוב כתבים בלשון עברי על פי פסוק הלא ימצא הפסוקים כפי הדרוש אשר יחפוץ, לפי המשל שנתתי למעלה בענין הדרוש, והמשל אם רוצה לכתוב כתב לחבירו מענין מלבושים שיקנה לו או יעשה לו יעיין בשרש לבש ואם לא ימצא בו מבוקשו יעיין בשרש בגד או בשרש ככה בענין כסות או בשרש חליץ בענין מחלצות.

F

מחלצות under חלץ, or into the root חלץ under כסות, כסה under כסה. viii. To those who want to write poetry, they will find under every root the words which rhyme. Thus, for instance, if one wants to write a poem, each line of which is to terminate in בָרִים, and he requires אֲבָרִים, שְׁבָדִים, עֲבָרִים, גְבָרִים, חֲבֵרִים, דְבָרִים, גְבָרִים, he is only to look under the roots of these words, and he will find verses containing all these, and will be able to select the most appropriate ones. ix. The book will be of use to those who study the Kabbalah, for they will find in it all the sacred names. Thus, for instance, the Kabbalistic student who wants to know the virtue of the divine names representing judgment or mercy, or what other powers or attributes they have, he will find the divine names divided into classes, as the name אדני occurs 134 times, exclusive of those passages in which it is joined to יהוה, &c., &c. x. It will be useful as a defence of our faith against those who attack our religion; and in two respects. In the first place, those who dispute with us are in the habit of adducing passages according to the signs which the Christians made in the Bible, and which they call chapters, saying, Is it not written in such and such a book, and in such and such a chapter? Now he who uses this book will also be able to do the same thing. Secondly, it is well known that most of the controversies which take place between us and them are about the Messiah — whether he has already come, or whether he is

התועלת הח' הרוצה לעשות חרוז או שיר שקול חלא ימצא בכל שרש המלות הדומות במבטא בסוף התיבה והמשל הרוצה לעשות שיר משובח שיהי' סוף כל חרוזתו ברים וצריך לעשות אברים גברים דברים חברים גברים עברים שברים הלא יעיין בשרשי המלות האלה וימצא פסוקים מכל אלה ויבחר מהם הנאותים למבוקשו, ודוק.

התועלת הט' הוא שיחי' הספר הזה טוב לענין הקבלה כי ימצאו בו כל השמות הקדושים, והמשל המקובל חרוצה לדעת כח השמות של מדת הדין או של מדת הרחמים או שאר הכחות או המדרות שיש לחם הלא ימצא בו השמות נחלקים למיניהם כגון השם של אדנות הנכתב א"לף ד"לת נו"ן יו"ד שהוא אדני הס קל"ד זולת אותם שהם סמוכים לשם י' ה' ו' ה' כמו כה אמר אדני יהוה שהם רבים מאד מאד, וכן אדני אלהים, אלהים אדני, ואלהי שהם מלעיל ואלוה שהם הסרים ואלוחים שהוא מלא אשר לכלם מדות וכחות מיוחדות הנודעות לבעלי הקבלה הלא ימצא כלם בזה הספר איש בשרשו ובמחנהו.

התועלת העשירי הוא שיחי' הספר הזה טוב לספר נצחון ויועיל מאד להתווכח עם המתנגדים אלינו באמונתנו, וזה בשני אופנים, האחד שהם דנילים להתווכח עמנו ומביאים ראי' מן הפסוקים על פי הסימנים שעשו בכל העשרים וארבע וקראו לחם בלשונם קאפיטולי ואומרים הלא כתוב בספר פלוני בכך וכך קאפיטולי, ומי שירגיל את עצמו בספר הזה ידע יבין לעשות כן גם הוא, והאופן השני ידוע הוא כי רוב הוויכוחים אשר בינינו ובינם הוא בענין המשיח אם כבר בא או עתיד לבוא, ועל אריכות הגלות ועל הגאולה ועל חגן עדן וגיהנם.

yet to come; about the duration of our dispersion, about our restoration, about Paradise and Hell. Now, he who wants to enquire into these matters, let him look into the roots משח, *to anoint;* גלה, *to take captive;* גאל *to redeem,* &c., and he will find all the passages treating thereon. Also, as to their opinion about the word שאול, explaining, 'I will go down into *Sheol* unto my son' (Gen. xxxvii. 35) to mean *hell,* if you look under the root שאל you will there find proof that, in most cases, it denotes *the grave,* and not *hell.* The Holy One, blessed be He, save us from its power. Blessed be His glorious name!"

It is greatly to be regretted that this stupendous work has not been published. Levita himself often refers to it as his *chef-d'œuvre*: he laboured over it more than twenty years (1514–1536). Through the intervention of his pupil, patron, and friend, De Selve, he sent the MS. to Paris, to be printed, and in 1538, when Levita wrote the third Introduction to his *Massoreth Ha-Massoreth,* he fully believed that it was actually in the press. "I hope to God, blessed be His name," says he, in this Introduction, "that it will soon see the light, having given it to be printed in the great city of Paris, in the kingdom of France;" and even three years later, he still says, in the Introduction to his Explanation of the 712 words, "*The Book of Remembrance* I am now printing." From some unknown cause, however, the work was not printed, and the MS., consisting of two immense folios, is in the Imperial Library at Paris. The copy is the identical one which Levita sent there to be printed. It has his autograph subscription, and the only defect in it is supposed to be in the absence of an Introduction, to which Levita refers. This Introduction, however, could not have been lost, since the present binding of the MS. is that in which it was put under Henry II., as has been pointed out to Frensdorff by the learned librarian, M. Breal.[27]

Whatever might have been the cause of the non-publication of *The Massoretic Concordance,* and however great his disappointment, Levita, in other respects, had to congratulate himself on the good

ומי שבא להתווכה על זה יעיין בשרש משה ובשרש גלה ובשרש גאל וימצא כל הפסוקים שמדברים מזה, וכן מה שהם מהזיקים דתם עם מלת שאול ומפרשים ארד אל בני אבל שאולה ניהנם והנה המעיין בשרש שׁאל ימצא שם ראיות שרובם נאמרים על הקבר ולא על הגיהנם — הק״בה יצילנו מידי, ברוך שם כבודו :

[27] Comp. Fraukel's *Monatschrift fur Geschichte und Wissenschaft des Judenthums,* vol. xii., p. 101.

effect which his MS., accompanied by the warm and laudatory recommendations of his friend the Bishop of Lavoure, produced at Paris. Paris, for more than a century, had not a single Jewish inhabitant. Ever since the expulsion of the Jews from France, in 1395, in consequence of the decree passed by Charles VI., September 17, 1394; "commanding it, as an unalterable law, that, in future, no Jew is to live, or even temporarily to abide, in any part of France, whether in Languedoil or in Languedoc:" the sovereigns of that country— Charles VII., Louis XI., Charles VIII., Louis XII., and even Francis I. in the earlier part of his reign—would not tolerate any Jews in their dominions. The Kabbalistic epidemic, however, from which the Pope himself was suffering, the rage for studying Hebrew amongst the highest of the land, and the great demand for Jewish teachers, had now changed the aspect of affairs. So marvellous was the change, that Guillaume Haquinet Petit, father-confessor of Louis XII., the very man who, in 1514, effected the condemnation, by the Paris University, of Reuchlin's work, as heretical, because it defended the Jews and the Jewish writings against the infatuated assaults of Pfefferkorn, now appeared as the promoter of Hebrew literature. It was upon his advice that Francis I. invited Augustin Justiniani, bishop of Corsica, to Paris, to become professor of Hebrew in the University. Justiniani, who learned his Hebrew from the celebrated Jewish physician, Jacob Mantin, also conducted the Hebrew studies at the University of Rheims. As a text-book for teaching the Grammar, he reprinted the vitiated edition of Moses Kimchi's *Outlines of Hebrew Grammar*, with Levita's annotations (Paris, 1520).[28] To shew the French Christians at large the value of Hebrew literature, and to point out the great advantage to be derived from studying it, this Dominican, Justiniani, also published in the same year (1520) a Latin translation, from the Hebrew, of Maimonides' clebrated religio-philosophical work, entitled *The Guide of the Perplexed*,[29] the very book which, three centuries ago, the hyper-orthodox Jews, with the

[28] A description of this Grammar has already been given, *vide supra*, p. 13.

[29] Maimonides was born at Cordova, March 30, 1135, and died December 13, 1204. A biographical sketch of this most distinguished Jewish philosopher, as well as an analysis of his remarkable works, will be found in Kitto's *Cyclopædia of Biblical Litarature*. We have only here to add that Justiniani, who was aided by his teacher, Jacob Mantin, in the translation of *The Guide of the Perplexed*, entirely omitted to acknowledge the important help he obtained from this Jewish physician. Comp. Wolf, *Bibliotheca Hebræa*, iii. 780, &c.

assistance of the Dominicans, publicly committed to the flames, as a most heretical and pernicious production.

Great as was the change which had now taken place in France with regard to Hebrew literature (1520), it had not as yet reached its culminating point. It was only on the arrival of Levita's MS. of *The Massoretic Concordance* at Paris, whither De Selve had sent it to be printed at his own expense, that we actually see how love for Hebrew overcame hatred of the Hebrews. Attracted by his fame, and highly recommended by his pupil, the bishop of Lavour, Levita received an invitation from Francis I. to come to France, and accept the chair of Hebrew at the University; the very country which, for a hundred and thirty years, had been shut against the Jews, and where, at the time when he received this invitation, not a single Jew was to be found! But Levita declined the honourable position. Much as he loved to be the first Hebraist in Europe, he did not like to be a unique Hebrew in France. He therefore preferred to remain at Venice, in the midst of his friends and disciples.

He also declined invitations from several cardinals, bishops, and princes, to become Hebrew professor in Christian Colleges.[30] Though he cheerfully gave Hebrew instruction to single Christian pupils, such as cardinal Egidio, Reuchlin, De Selve, and other eminent men, yet his motives for declining to separate himself from his Jewish disciples altogether, and to become entirely a teacher of the Gentiles, may easily be understood. Notwithstanding the express avowal of these eminent Christians, that they learned Hebrew in order to study the Kabbalah, and to convince the Jews from this esoteric doctrine of the truth of Christianity, they imbibed an interest in and love for the Jews with their attachment to the Hebrew language. Reuchlin most nobly pleaded the cause of the Israelites in Germany against the calumnies of Pfefferkorn[31] and the Dominicans.

---

[30] Comp. כי כמה פעמים נקרא נקראתי משרים רבים ונכבדים גם מקרדינאלי גם מהגמונים גם מעיר פרי"ז אשר בצרפת בצואת המלך יר"ה ולא הטיתי אזן in the second Introduction to his explanation of the 712 words in Hebrew literature, entitled *Tishbi*.

[31] The fanatical and misguided Joseph Pfefferkorn was born at Moravia, 1469, only twelve months after the birth of Elias Levita; he embraced Christianity, and was publicly baptised at Cologne, 1505, when thirty-six years old. His works against his former co-religionists and Reuchlin, which obtained such unenviable notoriety, and which were the means of calling forth the Reformation, are—i. *Der Judenspiegel*, Nurmberg, 1507; ii. *Die Judenbeichte*, Cologne, 1508; iii. *Das Osternbuch*, Cologne and Augsburg, 1509 iv. *Der Judenfeind*, ibid, 1509; v. *In Lob und Ehren dem Kaiser Maxi-*

Egidio befriended them at Rome, whilst De Selve, bishop of Lavour, effected such a change in France in favour of the Jews, that Levita, as we have seen, was invited by the king to the professorial chair at the University. Luther too, as long as Reuchlin was living, entertained the highest opinion of the Jews. In his treatise, entitled, "*That Jesus Christ is born a Jew*" (1523), which he published two years after Reuchlin's death, he still exclaimed, "Our fools, the popes, bishops, sophists, and monks, those coarse asses'-heads, have hitherto proceeded with the Jews in such a fashion, that he who was a good Christian might well have desired to become a Jew. And if I had been a Jew, and had seen the Christian faith governed and taught by such blockheads and dolts, I should sooner have become a hog than a Christian; for they have treated the Jews as though they were dogs and not men."[32]

There were, however, circumstances aggravating both to the Jews and Christians. The Jews were exceedingly vexed by the avowal that the object of the Christians in studying Hebrew was to proselytise them; that many eminent Jews had been gained over to the Church; and that at this very period of Levita's life, no less a man than the pious and learned Jacob b. Chajim, to whom the world is indebted for the celebrated Rabbinic Bible, and for editing the Critical Apparatus of the Old Testament, had now also embraced Christianity (1536).[33]

milian, Cologne, 1510; vi. *Ein Brief an Geistliche und Weltliche in Betreff des kaiserlichen Mandats die judischen Schriften zu vertiligen*, given by Graetz, note 2, p. xiii.; vii. *Der Handspiegel*, Mayence, 1511; viii. *Der Brandspiegel*, 1513; ix. *Die Sturmglock*, Cologne, 1414; x. *Streitbüchlein wider Reuchlin und seine Jünger*, Cologne, 1516; xi. *Eine mitleidige Clag' gegen den unglaübigen Reuchlin*, 1521; comp. Graetz, *Geschichte der Juden*, vol. ix. Supplementary Notes, p. x. &c., Leipzig, 1866.

[32] Hengstenberg, Commentary on Ecclesiastes, with other treatises. Clark's Translation, p. 415, Edinburgh, 1860.

[33] This celebrated Hebraist and Massorite was born about 1470, at Tunis, whence he is also sometimes called *Tunisi*. Besides editing the stupendous Rabbinic Bible (1524-5), and publishing the *editio princeps* of the *Jerusalem Talmud* (1523), Biblical literature is indebted to him for a *Dissertation on the Targum*, which is prefixed to the edition of the Pentateuch with the Targum and the Five Megilloth (Bomberg, 1527, 1543-4). His elaborate Introduction to the Rabbinic Bible has recently been re-published, with an English Translation and Notes by Ginsburg (Longmans, 1865). Fürst's assertion, (*Bibli theca Judaica*, iii., 452) that this Introduction had been translated into English by Kennicott, in his work entitled *The state of the printed Hebrew text of the Old Testament*, Oxford, 1758, is incorrect. Kennicott simply published an abridged and incorrect *Latin* version, from a MS. which he found in the Bodleian Library. From the remark of Levita in the second Introduction to the *Massoreth Ha-Massoreth* (comp. *infra*), it would seem that Jacob b. Chajim was already dead in 1538. That he had then

Impatient Christians, again, though now ranged in battle array against each other as Catholics and Protestants, and consigning one another to eternal damnation as heretics, were extremely angry with the Jews for not at once relinquishing their religion and embracing Christianity, which was then torn in pieces and weltering in blood. So wroth were the Christians of that day with the Jews for not filling up with converts from Judaism the ranks in the Church, which the professed followers of the Prince of Peace had decimated in the religious wars, that even Luther, forgetful of his former kindly feelings, and with strange inconsistency, admonished his protestant followers to "burn their synagogues, force them to work, and treat them with all unmercifulness!"[84] Such love and hatred alternately displayed, for the express purpose of gaining converts, had its effect upon the Jews. The orthodox portion of the Hebrew community began to realise that in teaching Christians Hebrew, and in initiating them into the mysteries of the Kabbalah, they were furnishing them with weapons against the Jews. They, therefore, became exceedingly displeased with those members of the synagogue who were engaged in tuition among Christians; and as Levita was the most distinguished teacher of the Christians, the cry of the Jews was loudest against him. His manly, straightforward, and noble defence of himself is contained in the second Introduction of his *Massoreth Ha-Massoreth*, and may be seen below, for which reason we do not reproduce it here.

been a Christian, is not only evident from Levita's vituperations in question, but also from the statement of the editor of the *Mishna*, with Maimonides' commentary, published at Venice, 1546. At the end of Tractate *Taharoth*, the editor remarks ואלה הם דברי המגיה הראשון שהיה שמו לפנים בישראל יעקב בר חיים שהגיה סדר טהרות עם פירוש רבינו שמשון ז״ל, ולפי שאמר החכם קבל האמת מפי שאמרו ראינו להדפיס דבריו פה "these are the words of the first editor, whose name was formerly among the Jews, Jacob b. Chajim, and who revised the Tractate *Taharoth*, with the commentary of R. Shimshon of blessed memory. Now since the sage said, 'Receive the truth by whomsoever it is propounded,' we deemed it proper to print his remarks here." This apology from the second editor for printing, in a work intended for the Jews, opinions propounded by one who had ceased to be a member of the community, puts the question beyond the shadow of a doubt. The learned Frensdorff was so much struck with the remark of Levita upon this subject, and was so unwilling to believe it, that he wrote to Professor Luzzatto for more information about it; and Luzzatto again, who communicates the above extract from the editor of the Mishna, was so afflicted by finding it to be true, that he delayed replying to Frensdorff's letter, because he was unwilling to make it known that so learned a man had embraced Christianity. Comp. *the Hebrew Essays and Reviews*, entitled *Ozar Nechmad*, vol. iii., p. 112, &c., Vienna, 1860.

[84] Hengstenberg; Commentary on Ecclesiastes, with other treatises. Clark's Translation, p. 418. Edinburgh, 1860.

By the extraordinary amount of labour, research, and study which he bestowed, for more than twenty years, on collating and elaborating the materials for the Massoretic Concordance, Levita became one of the most accomplished scholars in this singular department of recondite Biblical learning. His pupils, to whom he had often explained the import of the enigmatical phrases and peculiar signs whereby the Massorites indicate the correct readings, orthography, and exegesis of the Hebrew text, and who were delighted to see the meaning of the Massoretic signs surrounding the margins of Hebrew bibles, at last urged him to write them a Commentary on the Massorah, which they might use as a manual. To this earnest and flattering request of his disciples he could all the more cheerfully accede, since he himself had been contemplating writing such a treatise for twenty years, and was only prevented from carrying out his design by untoward circumstances. Now that he had finished the Massoretic Concordance, and had the leisure, he at once betook himself to the work of supplying his disciples with the desired text-book, and two years after the completion of the gigantic Concordance he published at Venice (1538), by the aid of his friend Bomberg, the celebrated *Massoreth Ha-Massoreth* (מסורת המסורת).

Before entering into the history of this book and the extraordinary controversy it called forth, it will be necessary to give a succinct analysis of its contents. The *Massoreth Ha-Massoreth* consists of three parts, preceded by a Notice to the Reader, a Preface, and three Introductions. The Notice to the Reader explains the references in this book to the then newly introduced division of the Hebrew Scriptures into chapters, and the books of Samuel, Kings, and Chronicles, respectively, into two books, and shews how any original ideas propounded by the author are indicated. The Preface sets forth the plan and contents of the book. The first Introduction consists of a Song of Praise to the Creator, who guided his people in former days, and who vouchsafed wisdom to the Massorites in their work, as well as to the author, in order to explain the Massorah. The second Introduction begins with a piece of autobiography; then states how the author came to compile this book; describes his researches in the Massorah, the state of the Massoretic MSS., the importance of the Massorah, his connection with Cardinal Egidio, and his defence for teaching him Hebrew. The third Introduction explains the meaning of the word *Massorah*; discusses different opinions about the origin of the Massorah, the vowel points, the accents, &c., &c. Then follow the three parts which, according to the Jewish custom of naming things after national events, are respectively denominated the *First Tables*, the *Second Tables*, and the *Broken Tables*, after the events recorded in Exodus xxiv. 12, xxxi. 18, xxxii. 19, xxxiv. 1–4. In harmony with its appellation, the *First Tables*, or the first part, he divided it into ten sections, denominated commandments (עשרת הדברים), answering to the Decalogue on the tables; whilst each of these sections actually begins with the very words which commence the respective commandments of the Decalogue. These ten sections are occupied with the discussion of *plene* and *defective*. The *Second Tables*, or part, also consists of ten commandments, or sections, which discuss respectively the important Massoretic points of—i. The *Keri* and *Kethiv;* ii. *Kametz* and *Pattach;* iii. *Dagesh, Raphe, Mappick,* and *Sheva;* iv. The accents on the tone-syllable, and *Psick;* v. Registers, groups, parallels, and analogous forms; vi. Peculiar conjunctions, disjunctions, and resemblances; vii. Words with prefixes, serviles, and solitary; viii. Conjectural readings, errors, and variations; ix. The terms for letters, written and oral words, small letters, accents, certainties, and transpositions; and, x. The Massoretic expressions for Scriptures, a single Book of the Scriptures, form, dividing spaces, &c. The *Broken Tables*, or the third part, discusses the abbreviations, or broken words, used by the Massorites, whence the part obtained its name. It also describes some of the principal men who have written on the Massorah, as well as some ancient Codices.

This remarkable book was first printed by his friend, M. Bomberg, at Venice, 1538, the text not being pointed. Levita appended to this edition the poem of Saadia, giving the number of times which each letter of the alphabet occurs throughout the Hebrew Scriptures, as well as an explanation of this poem. In less than twelve months it was re-published at Basle, 1539, the text pointed. In this edition Münster translated into Latin the three Introductions, the first and second being in an abridged form, and gives a brief summary of the contents of the three parts. He, however, omitted Saadia's poem, with Levita's explanations. It is very strange that Münster does not mention on the title-page that the book had already appeared at Venice, and that his edition was a reprint.

The third part, or the *Broken Tables* as it is called, was republished separately, in Rabbinical characters, at Venice (ש״כו = 326 =) 1566, some copies being dated (ש״ו = 306 =) 1546, under the title, *A Commentary on the Massorah, called the Gate of the Broken Tables* (פירוש המסורת וקרא שמו שער שברי לוחות). This part of the book was also re-published with additions by Samuel b. Chajim, Prague, 1610. The three introductions were also translated into Latin by Jo. Lud. Mich. Nagel (Altdorf, 1758–71). The third and last edition of the entire Hebrew text was published at Sulzbach, 1771, in Rabbinical characters. This edition is exceedingly defective, whole passages being omitted, as will be seen in the notes to our edition. The editor, Kalmen Dishbek, misled by Münster's silence about the Venice edition, describes the Basle edition (1539) as the *editio princeps*, and hence, necessarily, also omitted Saadia's poem and Levita's explanation of it. Fürst, indeed (*Bibliotheca Judaica*, ii. 240), and others, say that there was also an edition of it at Sulzbach, 1769, two years before the one we have specified. But this must be a mistake, since the editor of the 1771 edition distinctly describes it as *the second*, and the Basle as *the first*.[35]

The only translation extant of this book is the German, which was published at Halle, 1772,[36] and which is generally, but incorrectly, ascribed to the celebrated Joh. Salomo Semler. That Semler himself was not the translator, but that he simply superintended the translation, and made notes to it, is stated on the very title-page of the book.[37] The preface, however, which was written by this scholar, puts the whole question beyond the shadow of a doubt; and the erroneous opinion of bibliographers on this subject can only be accounted for on the supposition that they have either not perused the preface or

---

[35] Thus the editor distinctly says on the title-page נדפס מקדמת דנא בעיר באזיל בשנת רצ״ט לפ״ק; והובא עתה שנית לבית הדפום ע״י הנעלה כמהורר קלמן דישבעק

[36] From a passage quoted by Semler, in his Preface to Meyer's German Translation (p. 9), it indeed appears that the celebrated Reformer, Conrad Pellican (1487–1556), translated the whole book into Latin shortly after the publication of the Hebrew. The passage in question, which is quoted from *the Life of Pellican*, prefixed to the first volume of his *Commentaries*, is as follows: "Adhæc tota biblia *transtuli* e chaldaico in latinum . . . . et utrumque Targum libri Esther, de quo sibi Judæi mire placent. Quin et Targum Hierosolymitanum in quinque libros Mosis. Præter hæc *transtuli* quædam Talmudica opuscula: *librum Massoreth*, quem Hebraicum edidit *Elias* grammaticus." But this Latin version has never been published.

[37] Ueberſetzung des Buchs Maſſoreth Hammaſſoreth. Unter Aufſicht und mit Anmerkungen D. Joh. Salomo Semlers.

not seen the book. In this preface Semler gives the following history of the translation. A respectable young man, named Christian Gottlob Meyer, who had an excellent opportunity, at Berlin, to acquire, under the guidance of an expert teacher, a greater knowledge of Jewish learning than ordinary Jewish youths, became convinced of the truth of Christianity. He therefore left Judaism, and was publicly admitted into the church at Halle. Here, whilst prosecuting his study, Semler became acquainted with him. Convinced of the sincerity of the young man, and being anxious that he should not neglect his Hebrew learning, Semler asked him to translate the *Massoreth Ha-Massoreth* after his college hours, omitting, however, the poetical Introductions, which are somewhat more difficult. The translation thus made by Meyer, Semler sometimes read with the translator, and endeavoured to arrange the German in such a manner as to make it more intelligible. He also did the same with the German translation of the poetical Introductions, which was made by another Jew, named Aaronssohn, a clever *Candidatus Medicinæ* at the University. Semler, moreover, made sundry notes to this German translation.[38] With this plain statement of Semler before us, we

[38] Die Gelegenheit zu dieser deutschen Uebersetzung ist diese. Ein artiger junger Mensch, Christian Gotlob Meyer, der in Berlin ehedem die gute Gelegenheit, in jüdischer Gelersamkeit unter Anfürung eines geschickten Lehrers weiter als andere Judenknaben zu kommen, sehr gut genuzt hatte, ist nach und nach, zumal durch den Gebrauch deutscher moralischer Schriften, in gebundener und ungebundener Rede, zu eignem Nachdenken gekommen, und hat über den Grund und die Art seiner bisherigen jüdischen Religion so lange ernstliche Betrachtungen fortgesetzt, daß er endlich sich entschlosser, von den Grundsätzen der christlichen Religion eine nähere Erkentnis zu suchen. Er kam endlich nach Halle, wo er unter der Anleitung des Magister und Oberdiaconus an der Ulrichskirche, Hrn. Schultze, sehr bald in der Einsicht so weit gekommen, daß er sich von selbst entschlossen, öffentlich zu der christlichen Religion überzutreten.—

Da ich nun gerne auch dazu helfen wolte, daß er seinen guten Anfang hebräischer oder rabbinischer Lectüre nicht etwa wieder vernachläßigen solte; so habe ich ihm dieses Büchelchen gegeben, nach und nach, ohne seinen Schulstudien Eintrag zu thun, eine Uebersetzung davon vorzunehmen; doch mit Auslassung der poetischen Vorreden, welche etwas schwerer seien.—

Diese Uebersetzung habe ich zuweilen mit dem Uebersezer wieder durchgegangen, und habe die deutsche Schreibart etwas verständlicher einzurichten gesucht, obgleich der Charakter eines jüdischen Aufsatzes nicht ganz zu verändern war. Hie und da bemerke ich aber doch einige Stellen, die noch deutlicher hätten ausgedruckt werden können; so auch hie und da von der Uebersetzung der poetischen Vorreden gilt, welche Hr. Aronssohn,

hope that the question as to the authorship of the German version will in future be regarded as settled.

As to the merit of it, considering that it was made by a young man, and the great difficulties he had to encounter, the translation must be pronounced pretty fair. For critical purposes, however, the utility of it is greatly impaired, for the following reasons. Passages are frequently altogether omitted. The elaborate and most difficult second Introduction has not been translated into German at all. And, lastly, young Meyer, remarkable as was his knowledge of Hebrew considering his age, was not familiar with the Massoretic language, which requires special study. Hence it is that many of the passages, though literally translated, are less intelligible in the German than they are in the Hebrew. Hence, too, the many serious blunders and mistranslations which are dispersed throughout the work.

The storm which the original publication of this work raised (1538) was truly marvellous, and, after raging for more than three centuries, cannot be said to have as yet fully subsided. The cause of this storm was the array of most powerful arguments which Levita made in the third introduction, to prove that the vowel-points now to be found in the Hebrew Bibles are not of the same antiquity with the text, but that they were invented and put there by the Massorites about five hundred years after Christ. The authority of the vowel-points had indeed been questioned by some Jewish authorities long before Levita's time. As early as the ninth century, Natronai ii. b. Hilai, who was Gaon or spiritual head of the College in Sora (859–869), in reply to the question whether it is lawful to put the points to the Synagogal Scrolls of the Pentateuch, distinctly declared that "since the Law, as given to Moses on Sinai, had no points, and the points are not Sinaitic [*i. e.* sacred], having been invented by the sages, and put down as signs for the reader; and moreover since it is prohibited to us to make any additions from our own cogitations, lest we transgress the command 'Ye shall not add,' &c. (Deut. iv. 2); hence we must not put the points to the Scrolls of the Law."[89] Three

ein geschickter Candidatus Medicinæ auf hiesiger Universität, gemacht hat. Ich habe hie und da einige Anmerkungen dazu gesezt, welche theils das Nachdenken befördern, theils auf einige andere Bücher weisen; habe aber freilich nicht viel Zeit darauf wenden können.—Seite 12–15.

[89] This fact, which is cited in *the Vitry Machsor*, from the Theological decisions, (תשובת הגאונים) is communicated by Luzzatto in *the Hebrew Essays and Reviews*,

centuries later, no less a scholar than the celebrated Ibn Ezra, in speaking of the two dots over the letter ש, the one on the right indicating that it is *Shin* and the one to the left shewing that it is *Sin*, remarked that "it was the custom of the sages of Tiberias to put down these points to mark the double pronunciation, and that they were the chief authorities, since from them proceeded the Massorites, from whom we obtained the whole system of punctuation."[40]

From Ibn Ezra this opinion was also espoused by some Christian scholars in the middle ages, who, hating the Jews, wished to base upon the late origin of the points the charge against them of having introduced innovations and corruptions into the text of the Bible. Thus, the celebrated Dominican, Raymond Martin, who studied Hebrew, Chaldee, and Arabic, to convert the Jews and the Mahommedans to Christianity, and who had acquired such a knowledge of Rabbinical Literature that he even excelled St. Jerome, boldly, but most incorrectly, asserted that the vowel-points in the text of the Old Testament were put there by Ben Naphtali and Ben Asher, *circa* 900–960, and that the *Emendations of the Scribes* (תקון סופרים) are simply a few of the many wilful corruptions and perversions introduced by the Jews into the sacred text, to obliterate the prophecies about

---

called *Kerem Chemed* (vol. iii., p. 200, Prague, 1838). The *Vitry Machsor*, or Ritual of the Synagogue, of Vitry, in France, was compiled, *circa* 1100, by R. Simcha of Vitry, a disciple of Rashi, and obtained its name from the place in which the compiler lived. It not only comprises the whole *Cycle of the Daily and Festival Services*, but various legal and ritual laws from ancient documents. The passage in question is as follows in the original, וששאלתם אם אסור לנקוד ספר תורה, ספר תורה שניתן למשה בסיני לא שמענו בו ניקוד ולא ניתן ניקוד בסיני, כי החכמים צייגוהו לסימן, ואסור לנו להוסיף מדעתנו פן נעבור בבל תוסיף, לפיכך אין נוקדין ספר תורה. It is also to be remarked that the MS. of this *Machsor*, which is one of the only two copies which have survived the ravages of time, and a description of which was published by Luzzatto in 1838, in the above-named Essays, was formerly the property of the celebrated antiquarian Guiseppe Almanzi, of Padua, and is now in the British Museum (Add. 27200-201). Dr. William Wright has given an account of it in the *Journal of Sacred Literature*, July, 1866, p. 356, &c. See also Fürst, *Geschichte des Karäerthums*, vol. i., pp. 114 and 179, Leipzig, 1862.

[40] Abraham b. Meier Ibn Ezra, was born in Toledo, 1088-9, and died 1176. He was a most distinguished mathematician, astronomer, philosopher, poet, physician, theologian, grammarian, and commentator. A sketch of his life, with a description of his works, will be found in Kitto's *Cyclopædia of Biblical Literature*, new ed. s. v. IBN EZRA. The above quotation is from his Hebrew Grammar, entitled *On the Purity of the Hebrew style*, (צחות) which he wrote at Mantua in 1145. It is as follows in the original, כן מנהג חכמי טבריא והם העקר, כי מהם היו אנשי המסורת ואנחנו מהם קבלנו כל הנקוד Comp. p. 7, *a*, editio Lippmann, Fürth, 1827.

the incarnation of the Deity.⁴¹ As Raymond Martin was the great Rabbinical oracle of the Christians in the middle ages, and moreover as his opinion was confirmed by no less an authority than the celebrated Nicolas de Lyra,⁴² it was regarded as paramount by all succeeding Catholic writers.

⁴¹ This remarkable Spanish Dominican was born about 1220, and died about 1287. He was greatly aided in his Hebrew and Chaldee studies by Pablo Christiani, a celebrated converted Jew, who was also a Dominican, and who held at Barcelona the famous discussion with the learned Nachmanides, about the questions at issue between Judaism and Christianity (July 20, 24, 1263), an account of which is given in Kitto's *Cyclopædia of Biblical Literature*, new ed. *s. v.* NACHMANIDES. Raymond Martin, himself, sat with Pablo Christiani, Arnold de Singarra, and Peter de Janua, in the commission appointed by the Bull of Clement iv. (1264), to examine the charges which Pablo Christiani brought against the Talmud, that it blasphemes Christ and the Virgin Mary. The work which has immortalised Raymond Martin's name is entitled *the Dagger of Faith* (FUGIO FIDEI). He completed it in 1278. He quotes in it extracts from the Talmud, Rashi, Ibn Ezra, Maimonides, Kimchi, and the writings of other Jews, with the greatest ease; showing from them that Jesus is not only foretold in the Hebrew Scriptures as the Messiah, but also in the Rabbinical writings. From its immense erudition, this work became the grand storehouse from which Christians in the middle ages and in modern days derived their Jewish learning, and weapons against the Jews. It was first edited with very elaborate annotations by Jos. de Voisin, Paris, 1651, and then again, with an introduction and the treatise by Hermann, a converted Jew, by Joh. B. Carpzow, Leipzig, 1687. It is to the second edition that our references are made. The passage in question bearing on the vowel-points contains properly his criticism on Hos. ix. 12, and is as follows:—
" Cæterum sciendum, quod nec Moyses punctavit legem, unde Judæi non habent eam cum punctis, *i. e.* cum vocalibus scriptam in rotulis suis; nec aliquis ex prophetis punctavit librum suum; sed duo Judæi, quorum unus dictus est *Nepthali*, alter vero *Ben Ascher*, totum vetus Testamentum punctasse leguntur; quæ quidem puncta cum quibusdam virgulis sunt loco vocalium apud eos: cumquæ venissent ad locum istum, et secundum orthographiam debuissent punctare בשורי *incarnatione mea*, punctaverunt בסורי *in recessu meo*, ut opus incarnationis removerent a Deo." (*Pars* iii., *Dist.* iii. cap. xxi., p. 895.)

⁴² Nicolas de Lyra was born of Jewish parents about 1270, at Lyre, a small town in the diocese of Eurecca, whence he obtained his name *Lyra*. Having embraced Christianity when young, he entered the Church in 1291, and became such an accomplished scholar and lecturer on the Bible that he was styled *the most distinguished doctor*. He died at Paris, October 23, 1340. The work which has immortalised his name is a commentary on the Bible, entitled " *Postillæ perpetuæ in universa Biblia*," in which he advanced the most enlightened views to such an extent that he is justly regarded as the forerunner of the Reformation. The extent to which Luther is indebted to him for his sentiments may be gathered from the couplet of the Reformer's enemies,

Si Lyra non lyrasset,
Lutherus non saltasset.
If Lyra had not harped profanation,
Luther would never have danced the Reformation.

As to the passage bearing on the origin of the vowel-points, after quoting with approval Raymond Martin on Hos. ix. 12 (see the preceding note), he remarks, " Puncta

To invest it with an air of originality, Jacob Perez de Valencia gives the following amusing account of the origin of the vowel-points— " After the conversion of Constantine the Great, the Rabbins perceived that great multitudes of Gentiles embraced Christianity with the greatest devotion all over the globe; that the Church prospered very favourably; and that also of the Jews an immense number became convinced of the truth by experience and miracles, whereby their gains and revenues were lessened. Roused by this wickedness, they assembled in great multitudes at the Babylon of Egypt, which is called Cairo, where they, with as much secresy as possible, falsified and corrupted the Scriptures, and concocted about five or seven points to serve as vowels, these points having been invented by Ravina and Ravashe, two of their doctors. The same Rabbins also concocted the Talmud.[43] Hence De Valencia maintains " that no faith is to be placed in the Holy Scriptures, as the Jews now interpret and punctuate them."[44]

Jewish commentators and grammarians, however, as a rule, when they had not to dispute with the Karaites for rejecting the traditions of the Fathers, maintained that the vowel-points were either given to Adam in Paradise, or communicated to Moses on Sinai, or were fixed by Ezra and the Great Synagogue. This view was deemed all the more

non sunt de substantia littere, nec a principio scripturere fuerunt, unde et rotuli qui in synagogis eorum legentur sunt sine punctis, sed permagnam tempus postea inventa sunt hujus modi punctu ad facilius legundum." *Comment. on Hos.* ix. 12. For a sketch of his life and writings, see Kitto, *Cyclop. of Bib. Lit.*, new ed., *s. v.* LYRA.

[43] Jacob Perez de Valencia, commonly called Bishop of Christopolitanus, was born about 1420, at Valencia, whence he derived his name. He became a hermit of the order of Augustin, and died in 1491. He was a voluminous writer, and the above extract which is from his commentary on the Psalms, is as follows in the original. " Post conversionem Constantini M. videntes Rabbinos omnes gentiles cum tanta devotione ad fidem Christi converti per totum orbem, et Ecclesiam tanto favore prosperari et etiam quod infinita multitudo Judæorum videntes manifestam veritatem per experientiam et miracula, pariter convertebantur, et sic deficiebant quaestus, et reditus, et tributa Rabbinorum, hac iniquitate commotos magna multitudine congregatos fuisse apud Babyloniam Ægypti, quae dicitur Cayre : ibique quanto magis caute potuerunt, conatos fuisse falsifiàcre et perverteré Scripturas a vero sensu e significatione. Inde confinxisse supra 5, vel. 7, puncta loco vocalium. Quorum punctorum inventores fuisse Ravina Ravasse, duos Doctores eorum. Addit, istos Rabbinos confinxisse libros Talmud." *Prolog. in Psalmos Tract. vi.*, Comp. Hody *De Bibliorum Textibus Originalibus*, lib. iii., p. ii., p. 442. Oxford, 1705.

[44] " Ideo nulla fides adhibenda est scripturæ s.; sicut hodie habent (Judæi) sic interpretatam et punctuatam. *Ibid.* Tract. ii., fol. xxiii.

orthodox, since the famous *Sohar*,[45] the sacred code of the Kabbalists, which was believed to be a revelation from God, communicated through R. Simon b. Jochai (*circa* A.D. 70–110), declared that "the letters are the body and the vowel-points the soul, they move with the motion and stand still with the resting of the vowel-points, just as an army moves after its sovereign"[46] (*Sohar* i., 15, *b.*); that "the vowel-points proceeded from the same Holy Spirit which indited the sacred Scriptures, and that far be the thought to say that the scribes made the points, since even if all the prophets had been as great as Moses, who received the law direct from Sinai, they could not have had the authority to alter the smallest point in a single letter, though it be the most insignificant in the whole Bible"[47] (*Sohar on the Song of Solomon*, 57 *b*, ed. Amsterdam, 1701). As the Kabbalah was believed to be a genuine revelation from God, its opinion about the antiquity and divinity of the vowel-points was adopted as final. Great therefore was the consternation which the appearance of the *Massoreth Ha-Massoreth* created. For the chief teacher of the age to deny the divine origin and the antiquity of the vowel-points, and more especially to defend his heterodoxy by unassailable arguments, was a most unpardonable sin.

As Levita's arguments became known to the Christian world, through Münster's Latin translation of the Introductions, as well as through Pellican's unpublished version of the entire Book, within twelve months after the publication of the original work, divided Christendom, though differing on almost all other points, at once agreed to welcome the great grammarian's results, from diametrically opposite motives. The unwary Protestant leaders who were already prepossessed with the notion of the late origin of the vowel-points, from the assertions of Raymond Martin, Nicolas de Lyra, Jacob Perez de Valencia, John Pico della Mirandola, and Reuchlin, rejoiced that their predilections were now confirmed by arguments. Hence Luther, Calvin, Zwingle,

---

[45] For an analysis of the *Sohar*, see Ginsburg, *The Kabbalah*, &c., p. 78, &c. Longmans, 1865.

[46] והמשכילים יהירו כגונא דתנועי וכ״ע דטעמי דמנגני ובנגונא דילהון אזלין אבתרייהו אתוון ונקודי ומתנענען אבתרייהו כחיילין בתר מלכיהון. גופא אתוון ורוחי נקודי כלהו נטלי במטלנין בתר תנועי (ונ״ע טעמי) וקיימי בקיומייהו כד נגונא דטעמי נטיל נטלי אתוון ונקודי אבתרייהו כד איהו פסיק אינון לא נטלין וקיימי בקיומייהו : זוהר חלק א׳ דף ט״ו ב׳.

[47] נקודין אינון נפקין מרוא דמוחא לקיימא אתוון על תיקונייהו ובנקודה חדא אשתני תיבה ואעבר להחיא תיבה מקיימא כגונא אחרא : בוציונא דקרדינותא כד במא ההוא אוירא דכיא במוחא בטש ולא בטש ממא לגביה דההוא מוחא ואסתליק מניה ממא ולא ממא כדין ההוא בטישו נפיק לגביה אתוון כיון מוחא ואתוון אתנקידו ואם חאמר נקודי תקון סופרים הוא חס ושלום דאפילו כל נביא דעלמא יהון כנשמה דקביל אורייתא מטורא דסיני לית לון רשו לחדתא אפילו חדא נקודה זעירא באת חד אפילו את זעירא דאורייתא : זוהר שיר השירים דף נ״ז ב

Mercer,[48] &c., boldly disclaimed the antiquity, divine origin, and authority of the points. Their conviction undoubtedly was, that by liberating themselves from the traditional vowel-point of the Synagogue, after having discarded the traditions of the Church of Rome, they could more easily and independently prosecute their Biblical studies without any trammels whatsoever. Besides having rejected the traditions of the Fathers, the Reformers could not, without exposing themselves to the charge of inconsistency from their antagonists, adhere to the traditions of the Rabbins.

To the Church of Rome, again, which was embittered by the cry of the newly risen protestant leaders, that the Bible, and the Bible alone, without gloss and without tradition, is the rule of faith and practice, Levita's work was like a God-send from another point of view. She eagerly laid hold of the admission made by this great teacher of the age, that the vowel-signs are an uninspired invention of the Jews, made centuries after Christ, in order to confute thereby the claims of her opponents. From the novelty of the points she deduced,

[48] Dr. Kalisch (*Hebrew Grammar*, Part ii., p. 65, note d. Longman, 1863,) is surely incorrect in his statement that "the Reformers, as Luther and Calvin, were of opinion that the vowel-points were at least fixed by Ezra, or the Great Synagogue." Nothing can be more explicit than Luther's remark on Gen. xlvii. 31: "At the time of St. Jerome, the points did not as yet exist, and the whole Bible was read without them. I submit that it is the modern Hebrews who affixed them, in order to give a proper sense and meaning to the Hebrew language. However, since they are not friends but enemies of Holy Writ, I often utter words which strongly oppose these points." In his Comment. on Is. ix. 6, he says "that most dangerous people, the Jews, falsify the words of the prophets with the points and distinctions; and their points, which are nothing but a modern invention, most assuredly are not to be preferred to the simple, correct, and grammatical sense." And again, in his Treatise entitled Schem Hamphoras (1543), he says, mit dieſer Weiſe könnte man der Jüden Verſtand in der Bibel fein ſchwächen, und iſt das Vortheil da, daß Moſe und die Propheten nicht haben mit Puncten geſchrieben; welches ein neu Menſchenfündlein, nach ihrer Zeit aufbracht; darum nicht Noth iſt dieſelben ſo ſteif zu halten, als die Jüden gerne wolten, ſonderlich wo ſie dem neuen Teſtament zuwider gebraucht werden. Eben ſo ſoll man auch mit der æquivocatio und distinctio thun, wo ſie wider das neue Teſtament bienen. Die Jüden haben doch Luſt, alle ihr Ding zweifelhaftig und nichts gewiſſes zu machen.

Equally explicit is the remark of Calvin, in his commentary on Zechariah xi. 7. "Scio, quanta industria veteres scribæ puncta excogitarint, cum jam linguæ non esset tam communis et familiaris usus: qui ergo puncta negligunt, vel prorsus rejiciunt, certe carent omni judicio et ratione: sed tamen habendus est aliquis delectus. Si enim legamus hic, proditores, nullus est sensus : si legamus, funiculos, nulla littera mutatur; interea mutantur duo puncta. Cum ergo id necessario postulet res ipsa, miror cur interpretes ita serviliter passi fuerint se regi, ut non spectarent Prophetæ sensum."

i. That the Bible could only be read in ancient days by the few authorised spiritual teachers, and, ii., That the Scriptures without these points cannot possibly be understood, apart from the traditional interpretation transmitted by the Church of Rome. This opinion soon found its way into England, and when the controversy between the Roman Catholics and Protestants had fairly began, we find Dr. Thomas Harding (1512–1572), who was Professor of Hebrew at Oxford, in the reign of Henry VIII., a staunch Protestant in the reign of Edward VI., who became a zealous papist at the accession of Queen Mary to the throne, and the celebrated antagonist of Bishop Jewel, arguing as follows: — "Among the people of Israel, the seventy elders only could read and understand the mysteries of the holy books, that we call the Bible. For, whereas the letters of the Hebrew tongue have no vocals, they only had the skill to read the Scripture by the consonants; and thereby the vulgar people were kept from reading of it, by special providence of God, as it is thought, that precious stones should not be cast before swine, that is to say, such as be not called thereto, as being, for their unreverend curiosity and impure life, unworthy."[49]

Similar was the language which the Romanists used on the Continent against the Protestants, who appealed to the Scriptures in matters affecting their faith and practice. John Morinus (1591–1659), the distinguished Orientalist, who renounced Protestantism, and entered the congregation of the Oratory in 1618, solemnly declares, in his learned "*Biblical Exercitations on the Hebrew and Greek Texts*," that "the reason why God ordained the Scriptures to be written in this ambiguous manner (*i. e.* without points), is because it was His will that every man should be subject to the *Judgment of the Church*, and not interpret the Bible in his own way. For seeing that the reading of the Bible is so difficult, and so liable to various ambiguities, from the very nature of the thing, it is plain that it is not the will of God that every one should rashly and irreverently take upon himself to explain it; nor to suffer the common people to expound it at their pleasure; but that in those things, as in other matters respecting religion, it is His will that the people should depend upon the priests."[50]

---

[49] The works of John Jewel, Bishop of Salisbury, vol. ii. p. 678. The Parker Society edition.

[50] Comp. Morinus, Exercitationes Biblicæ de Hebraici Græcique textus Sinceritate. Exercitat. iv. cap. ii., s. 8, p. 198. &c. Paris, 1633.

Alarmed at the use made by Catholic controversialists of the avowal that the points are a late human invention, and bitterly smarting under the arguments deduced therefrom, the defenders of Protestantism commenced beating a retreat. Forgetting that the very originators and leaders of the Reformation, partly from a desire to throw off every thing traditional, and partly from undisguised hatred of the Jews, had decried the vowel-points as lustily as the Catholics, Protestant champions changed their tactics, and began to declare that the points were put to the text by the Prophets themselves, and that to say otherwise is nothing more nor less than *heathenism* and popery. Thus, the charge of Gregory Martin (*circa* 1534–1582), in his work, entitled "*A Discovery of the Manifold Corruptions of the Holy Scriptures by the Heretics*" (1582), that Protestants in their versions follow the Hebrew vowels, which are not only a late invention of, but have been wilfully corrupted by, the Jews, was rebutted by the celebrated Fulke, the great champion of Protestantism, with the declaration, that, "seeing our Saviour hath promised that never a prick [= a vowel-point] of the law shall perish, we may understand the same also of the Prophets, who have not received the vowels of the later Jews; but even of the Prophets themselves, however, that heathenish opinion pleaseth you and other papists."[51] Among those who beat a retreat, are also to be found the very eccentric but very distinguished Hebraist, Hugh Broughton (1549–1626), who likewise deduced the antiquity and authority of the points from Matt. v. 18;[52] and the celebrated John Piscator (1546–1626), who remarks, in his Commentary on the passage in question, that "it appears from this that the Holy Bible in the time of Christ had the points, and that the punctuation was approved by our Saviour."

Both Catholics and Protestants, however, chiefly relied upon abusing each other, and upon their common hatred of the Jews, to make good their assertions. To examine Levita's arguments, to test his appeal to the Talmud and other Jewish writings of antiquity, and to corroborate or refute his statements—for this there was not

[51] A defence of the sincere and true translations of the Holy Scriptures into the English tongue, against the manifold cavils, frivolous quarrels, and impudent slanders of Gregory Martin, one of the readers of Popish divinity, in the traitorous seminary of Rheims, by William Fulke, D.D. (1583). Parker Society edition, p. 578, with p. 55.

[52] Broughton's opinion on the vowel-points is to be found in his Commentary on Daniel, chap. ix. 26, published under the title Daniel: his Chaldee visions and his Hebrew; both translated after the original and expounded, &c. London, 1597.

sufficient Talmudical learning and critical tact, either in the Church of Rome or among Protestants. Their Oriental studies were chiefly intended to fathom the mysteries of the Kabbalah and to convert the Jews. The first attempt to meet Levita's book with arguments, derived from ancient Jewish documents, as far as we know, was made by the learned Azzariah de Rossi,[58] in 1574-5, nearly forty years after the appearance of the *Massoreth Ha-Massoreth*. In his celebrated work entitled *The Light of the Eyes* (מאור עינים), De Rossi devotes the fifty-ninth chapter of Part iii. to an examination of the arguments advanced by Levita against the antiquity of the points, and maintains therein that—i. The existence of the vowel-points seems to be indicated in the Talmud *(Nedarim,* 37, 6; the corresponding passage in the *Jerusalem Gemara* and the *Midrash Bereshith Rabba,* cap. xxxvi.) ii. The *Bahir* and *Sohar,* which according to De Rossi were respectively compiled by R. Nechunja b. Cahana and R. Simon b. Jochai, before ever the Mishna was edited, specify the vowel-points by name, and describe them as having a divine origin. iii. The analogy of other languages, and especially the Eastern and cognate tongues, such as the Syriac, Chaldee, Arabic, and Persian, all of which have vowel-signs, shows beyond doubt that the Hebrew too had points from the remotest antiquity. iv. The nature and genius of the Hebrew language absolutely pre-supposes the permanent existence of points, since, in the case of certain expressions, it cannot be told, without these signs, whether they are nouns, verbs, or particles. Thus, for example; without points it is impossible to say what the word שלמה is; whether it is שְׁלֹמֹה *Solomon,* שִׁלְמָה *retribution,* שְׁלֵמָה *whole,* or שַׁלָּמָה *wherefore.* v. The command (Deut. xxvii. 8) to write *very plain and intelligibly* (באר הטיב) unquestionably premises that, under certain circumstances, though not generally, the Law was written with vowel-signs, else it would not have been "very plain and intelligible;" and, vi. He appeals to St. Jerome's

---

[58] De Rossi, also called among the Jews *Azzariah Min Ha-Adomim*, was born at Mantua in 1513, and died in 1577. He was the first and most distinguished Biblical critic among the Jews of the sixteenth century; and his celebrated work, entitled *the Light of the Eyes* (מאור עינים), which consists of three parts, may almost be designated a Cyclopædia of Biblical Literature. It was first printed at Mantua 1574-5, in square characters; a second edition of it was published at Vienna, 1829, in Rabbinical characters. The chapter treating on the vowel-points is p. 178 *b*—181 *a*, ed. Mantua, and, p. 286 *b*—292 *a*, ed. Vienna. For a sketch of De Rossi's life, and an analysis of his works, see Kitto's *Cyclopædia of Biblical Literature*, new ed., *s. v.* ROSSI.

statement in his epistle to Evagrius, where, in speaking of Enon near Salim, he remarks "it matters not whether it be called *Salem* or *Salim*, since the Hebrews very seldom use the vowel letters in the middle: and the same words are pronounced with different sounds and accents, according to the pleasure of readers and the variety of country;"[54] whence De Rossi deduces that *perraro* implies their existence and occasional use.

As to the origin and development of the vowels, he submits that their force and virtue were invented by, or communicated to, Adam, in Paradise; transmitted to and by Moses; that they had been partially forgotten, and their pronunciation vitiated during the Babylonian captivity; that they had been restored by Ezra, but that they had been forgotten again in the wars and struggles during, and after, the destruction of the Second Temple; and that the Massorites, after the close of the Talmud, revised the system, and permanently fixed the pronunciation by the contrivance of the present signs. This accounts for the fact that the present vowel-points are not mentioned in the Talmud. The reason why Moses did not punctuate the copy of the Law, which he wrote, is that its import should not be understood without oral tradition. Besides, as the Law has seventy different meanings, the writing of it, without points, greatly aids to obtain these various interpretations; whereas the affixing of the vowel-signs would preclude all permutations and transpositions, and greatly restrict the sense, by fixing the pronunciation. This is an epitome of the arguments used by De Rossi against Levita.

Being thus supplied with weapons from the Sohar and the Talmud, the hard-pressed Protestants, who were smarting from the onslaughts of the Catholics, and had beaten a retreat, now opened a new campaign. Under the leadership of Buxtorf, the father, they began defending, with a display of Rabbinical bayonets, the antiquity and divinity of the vowel-signs which they had formerly abandoned. Undaunted by the fact that the Catholics had been the undisputed masters of the field for three centuries, and that they had been strengthened in their position by the leaders of the Reformation, yet, to oust their common enemy, the Jews, the Protestant champion,

---

[54] The passage in question is as follows in the original, "Nec refert, utrum *Salem* [שלם], an *Salim* [שלים] nominetur; cum vocalibus in medio litteris perraro utantur Hebræi; et pro voluntate lectorum, atque varietate regionum, eadem verba diversis sonis atque accentibus proferantur." *Ad Evagrium Epist.* cxxvi., Opp. vol. i., p. 1062, ed. Paris.

Buxtorf, made his first appearance on the field in 1620. As the Christian opponents of the vowel-points, whether Catholics or their allies the Protestants, used no arguments, but contented themselves with mere assertions, and as, moreover, Levita was the first who defended his position with appeals to ancient documents, Buxtorf's attack was entirely directed against the renowned teacher of Hebrew, who was the leader of the opinions on this point of the allied Catholic and Protestant armies.

The arguments which were to discomfit Levita, Buxtorf published in his *Commentary on the Massorah*.[55] The ninth chapter of this work, which contains the defence of the antiquity and divine authority of the points against Levita, is chiefly made up of De Rossi's arguments and quotations from Jewish writings, whilst the rest of the book, which is an explanation of the Massorah, is, to a great extent, an elaboration of Levita's *Massoreth Ha-Massoreth*, the very treatise which had caused this controversy. Feeble as the arguments are, they appeared, nevertheless, very plausible and very learned; so that those who earnestly wished the points to be of divine origin at once ranged themselves under the leadership of the justly-renowned Buxtorf.

But Buxtorf was not destined to carry every thing before him in this first battle against Levita. His alliance with the learned De Rossi only produced a counter alliance and a masterly defence, under the leadership of Lewis Cappellus, who elaborated, expanded, and supplemented Levita's arguments against the points with far greater skill than that displayed by Buxtorf in his elaboration of De Rossi's arguments for the points. The treatise thus produced Cappellus sent in MS. to be examined by his opponent Buxtorf, who returned it with the request that it might not be printed. He then sent it to Erpenius, Professor of Oriental languages at Leyden, who was so convinced by its arguments and learning that, with the sanction of the author, he printed it at Leyden, under the title, "*The Mystery of the Points Unveiled.*"[56]

Its immense erudition, conclusive reasoning, and overpowering arguments soon convinced the most learned Biblical scholars that

---

[55] Tiberias sive Commentarius Masorethicus. Basle, 1620.

[56] The *Arcanum punctationis revelatum* was first published anonymously at Leyden, 1624, 4to. It was afterwards republished, with the *Vindiciæ Arcani punctationis* and Cappellus' other works, by his son; Amsterdam, 1689, fol. It is to this edition of the collected works that our references are made.

the vowel-points were centuries later than the Christian era; and Protestants, instead of combating the Roman Catholics on this point, were now fairly divided into two hostile camps, under the respective leadership of Cappellus and Buxtorf. The followers of Buxtorf were for a considerable time doomed to almost fatal inaction. For though Cappellus' work, as we have seen, appeared in 1624, and though Buxtorf had carefully perused it in MS. before this date, yet he made no reply to it for several years, and died (Sept. 13, 1629) without answering it. It was during this time of anxious suspense that Father Morinus published his merciless attack on the vowel-points, already alluded to (*vide supra*, p. 50), in which he compared the Scriptures to a mere nose of wax, to be turned any way, to prove thereby the necessity of one infallible interpretation.

At last, however, after a silence of four and twenty years, Buxtorf, the son, who succeeded his father in the Hebrew chair at Basle, published, in 1648, a reply to Cappellus' work, entitled, "*A Treatise on the Origin, Antiquity, and Authority of the Vowel Points and Accents in the Hebrew Scriptures of the Old Testament, against Lewis Cappellus' Mystery of the Points Unveiled;*" thus assuming the leadership of the vowelist party, whom death had deprived of their great champion. But, though the work occupies upwards of 450 small quarto pages, it contains very little more than an expansion of the arguments used by Buxtorf senior, in his *Tiberius*, with an increased number of quotations from Jewish writings. It was not to be expected that Cappellus would be silenced by this reply, and he at once wrote a rejoinder to it, entitled, "*A Vindication of the Mystery of the Vowels Unveiled;*" but he died (June 18, 1658) before the publication of it, and his son, Jacques Cappellus, to whom the MS. was left, did not publish it till 1689, five and twenty years after the death of Buxtorf junior.

An important point is to be noticed in this controversy, in which Cappellus entirely deviates from the opinion of his master, Elias Levita. Levita, though maintaining the novelty of the vowel-points, firmly believed that the very same pronunciation and sounds, which are now denoted by the vowels and accents, were perfectly known and used by the Jews from the remotest antiquity, long before these arbitrary signs were invented, and that they represent the true and genuine reading as it came from the inspired writers of the respective books; and, consequently, the reading which these points have fixed is as much of divine authority as the letters, the difference between them being, that the letters were written, whilst the points were transmitted by oral tradition. At first Cappellus seems also to have endorsed this view of Levita in a somewhat modified form. Thus he distinctly declares that, "when I say that the points were invented and added to the consonants by the Massorites of Tiberias, I do not mean, as I have stated before, that the reading of the sacred text was invented by them out of their own brain, and that they fixed, according to their own will and fancy, what these points denote and express; but what I mean is, that they express by these marks of their own invention the reading of the sacred text which obtained everywhere among the Jews, which they themselves had been taught by their masters in the scholastic institutions, which they had received by oral tradition from the Fathers, and which reading the Jews believed to be the same ancient and authentic reading of Moses and the prophets. Since, therefore, these Tiberian masters did nothing more than express, with all possible accuracy, the reading which they had been taught, which they had received from their ancestors, by tradition from the Fathers, and which all the Jews believed to be the very ancient and authentic reading of Moses and the prophets, by signs of vowels and accents of their own invention, there is no reason why this reading should not be accepted by all the Jews."[57]

Later on, however, Cappellus changed his mind, or, perhaps, more boldly avowed, what he had hitherto kept back, that, with the changing of the ancient letters in which the Hebrew was originally written, and in adding the points, the *matres lectiones* were eliminated and the Hebrew text was greatly corrupted. His assault on the inte-

---

[57] " Cum dico a Masorethis Tiberiensibus excogitata esse puncta et consonis addita, non hoc volo, uti jam monui, ab iis excogitatam, atque de proprio cerebro pro eorum libitu et arbitrio confictam esse lectionem sacri textus, quam punctis illis signarunt, atque expresserunt; sed hoc duntaxat volo, expressam esse ab iis, notulis a se excogitatis, lectionem sacri textus, quae tum ubique inter Judæos obtinebat, quamque ipsi edocti fuerant a suis magistris scholastica institutione, atque orali, et πατροπαραδότῳ traditione ab iis acceperant, quam lectionem credebant Judæi antiquæ Mosaicæ et Propheticæ authenticæ conformem esse. Cum itaque magistri illi Tiberienses nihil aliud praestiterint, quam ut lectionem quam edocti erant, et a majoribus suis traditione πατροπαραδότῳ acceperant, quamque omnes Judæi propterea eandem esse cum antiqua Mosaica et authentica Prophetica existimabant, vocalium et accentuum figuris a se excogitatis exprimerent quam poterant accuratissime, nihil est quod quis putet, non potuisse ill m lectionem omnibus Judæis probari." *Arcanum punctationis revelatum*, lib. ii., cap. xvii. 5 & 6, Opp. p. 775, ed. Amsterdam, 1689.

grity of the Massoretic text he published at Paris, 1650, under the title of *Critica Sacra*. To this work Buxtorf junior replied within three years of its publication, in a volume containing no less than 1040 quarto pages.[58] But though both these works repeatedly touch the question about the origin of the vowel-points, and though the controversy about the integrity of the text has arisen from, and is in some measure connected with, the dispute about the points, yet the two controversies are totally distinct, and ought not to have been confounded with each other.

The "*Mystery of the Points Unveiled*" created quite as great a revolution among scholars in the seventeenth century as the *Massoreth Ha-Massoreth*, of which it was an exposition. Its author's fame as a critic soon spread over Europe, and his work, as well as the rejoinder to it by Buxtorf junior, divided Protestant Christendom everywhere into two hostile camps—vowelists and anti-vowelists. The controversy was soon transplanted into England, where Cappellus was known, having studied two years at Oxford, and where Biblical and Talmudical studies were at that time zealously prosecuted, under the guidance of Brian Walton, and Lightfoot. In the Prolegomena to the London Polyglott, Levita's original opinion is more strictly followed than that of Cappellus. It is there maintained that the vowel-points were invented by the Massorites about A.D. 500; that these points were not arbitrary inventions of the Massorites, but express the traditional and true reading of the text and the sense of the Holy Ghost; that it is not lawful for any one to reject the Massoretic reading at pleasure; that all Christians are tied to it, unless some error or better reading can be clearly proved; and that the controversy, therefore, "is only about the present points, in regard of their forms, not of their force and signification."[59]

Whilst Levita and Cappellus were represented in England by Walton, De Rossi and Buxtorf had their chief representative here in Lightfoot. This learned Hebraist thought that his dicta would be quite sufficient to silence his opponents, and therefore deigned no more than to deliver himself as follows, after the masterly recapitulation of the arguments against the antiquity of the vowel-points given

[58] Anticritica, seu vindiciæ veritatis Hebraicæ; adversus Ludovici Cappelli Criticam quam vocat sacram. Basle, 1653.

[59] Comp. Prolegom. iii., sect. 38—56, with Walton's *Considerator Considered*, ed. Todd, p. 210, &c. London, 1821.

in Walton's Prolegomena: "There are some who believe the Holy Bible was pointed by wise men of Tiberias. I do not wonder at the impudence of the Jews who invented the story, but I wonder at the credulity of Christians who applaud it. Recollect, I beseech you, the names of the Rabbins of Tiberias, from the first situation of the University there to the time that it expired; and what at length do you find, but a kind of men mad with Pharisaism, bewitching with traditions and bewitched, blind, guileful, doting, they must pardon me if I say, magical and monstrous! Men, how unfit, how unable, how foolish, for the undertaking so divine a work! Read over the Jerusalem Talmud, and see there how R. Judah, R. Chaninah, R. Judan, R. Hoshaia, R. Chija Rabba, R. Chija bar Ba, R. Jochanan, R. Jonathan, and the rest of the grand doctors among the Rabbins of Tiberias, behave themselves, how earnestly they do nothing, how childishly they handle serious disputes! And if you can believe the Bible was pointed in such a school, believe also all that the Talmudists wrote. The pointing of the Bible savours of the work of the Holy Spirit, not the work of lost, blinded, besotted men."[60]

It was this dogmatic and abusive assertion, of one who was deemed the highest authority in matters of Hebrew learning in England, as well as the conviction that those who defend the novelty of the points "not only make doubtful the authority of the Scriptures, but wholly pluck it up by the roots," which stimulated the celebrated Dr. Owen to issue his attack on Walton's Polyglott and the anti-vowelists.[61] With the exception of the endorsement and elaboration of Lightfoot's diatribe, Dr. Owen's work in defence of the vowel-points is simply made up of the De Rossi-Buxtorf arguments greatly diluted. The high esteem, however, in which Dr. Owen was held made it necessary that his book,—in which he declared that he "had rather that this work of the *Biblia Polyglotta*, and all works of the kind, were out of the world, than that this one opinion should be received with the consequences that unavoidably attend it,"—should not be left unnoticed. Within twelve months therefore of the appear-

[60] A Chorographical Century, searching out some more memorable places of the Holy Land of Israel, chiefly by the light of the Talmud. Chap. lxxxi., works, vol. ii., p. 73, &c., ed. 1684.

[61] Of the Integrity and Purity of the Hebrew and Greek Text of the Scriptures; with considerations on the Prolegomena and Appendix to the late Biblia Polyglotta. London, 1659, vol. iv., p. 447, &c., of his collected works, London, 1823, to which the references are made.

ance of the attack, Walton published a reply, which, though greatly defaced by bitter invective and inexcusable abuse, contains additional and valuable contributions to the literature of this controversy.[62]

Although the antiquity of the vowel-points still found advocates in Joseph Cooper,[63] Samuel Clark,[64] Whitfield,[65] and Dr. Gill,[66] who published learned dissertations in defence of Dr. Owen and against Bishop Walton; yet it must be admitted that the *Prolegomena* and "The Considerator Considered" decided the battle in England in favour of the anti-vowelists. Henceforth all Biblical critics, with very few exceptions, regarded the points as modern, useless, and of no authority, though Walton himself, as we have seen, maintained that they, as a rule, represented the ancient and genuine reading. The utter rejection of the points, and the espousal of Cappellus' notions propounded in his *Critica Sacra*, produced lamentable effects in England as far as the criticism of the Old Testament was concerned, from which we are only now recovering. Two different schools of interpreters were erected here upon the ruins of the antiquity of the vowel-points.

The characteristic dogmas of the first school are, that "the Massoretic punctuation is an interpretation of the text made by the Jews, probably not earlier than the eighth century, and that, accordingly, our public translations in modern tongues, for the use of the Church among Protestants, and so likewise the modern Latin translations, are, for the most part, close copies of the Hebrew pointed text, and are in reality only versions at second hand, translations of the Jews' interpretation of the Old Testament;"[67] that the Hebrew text "is

[62] The Considerator Considered, &c. London, 1659. Todd has reprinted this rare book in the second volume of his Memoirs of the life and writings of Bishop Walton. London, 1821.

[63] His Dissertation is entitled Domus Mosaicæ Clavis, sive Legis Septimentum; in quo punctorum Hebraicorum adstruitur antiquitas; eaque omnia, cum accentualia tum vocalia ipsis, literis fuisse coæva, argumentis, undiquie petitis demonstratur. Quæ vero in contrarum ab Elia Levita primipilo, Ludovico Cappello, D. Doctore Waltono, &c., adducuntur, multa cum fidelitate examini subjiciuntur et diluntur, &c. ·London, 1673.

[64] An Exercitation concerning the original of the chapters and verses in the Bible; wherein the divine authority of the points in the Hebrew text is clearly proved by new and intrinsic arguments. London, 1698.

[65] A Dissertation on the Hebrew vowel-points, showing that they are an original and essential part of the Language. Liverpool, 1748.

[66] A Dissertation concerning the antiquity of the Hebrew language, letters, vowel-points, and accents. London, 1767.

[67] Preliminary Dissertation to his translation of Isaiah, new ed., p. xxxviii. London, 1836.

considerably injured, and stands in need of frequent emendation." Hence the disciples of this school resorted to amend the text by the aid of the ancient versions, and had recourse to the most unwarrantable conjectures, thus unsettling the original text and impugning its integrity. The principal disciples of this school are Archbishop Secker, Drs. Durell, Judd, Lowth, Blayney, Newcome, Wintle, Horsley, Good, Boothroyd, and others.

The second school, which is less accomplished, but more lamentable, is the one known by the name Hutchinsonian, after its founder, John Hutchinson (1674–1737). Believing that "Holy Scripture has a language of its own, which does not consist of words, but of signs or figures taken from visible things; so that the world which we now see is a sort of commentary on the mind of God, and explains the world in which we live;" this peculiar philosopher, like his Kabbalistic prototypes, was obliged to discard the vowel-points, and everything else which determined the pronunciation of the words and fixed their meaning. Hutchinson endorsed and reproduced all the base calumnies brought together by Raymond Lully, Wagenseil, &c., against the Jews, whom he always styles *the apostates*, and maintains that the sacred text was designedly corrupted by these apostates through the insertion of the points and letters, which was "their last shift to change their evasions of the truth;" that thereby "they make the words different from what they were, or of another root, or of another signification, than the words would have been without pointing in that context."[68] To this wild school belonged the eminently orthodox and pious Romaine, Bishop Horne, the lexicographer Parkhurst, and others.

It was this unwarrantable liberty taken with the text, first started by Cappellus' *Critica Sacra*, and the resort to all sorts of conjectural

[68] The system and the plan of the work may be gathered from its lengthy title; "The Covenant in the Cherubim, so the Hebrew writings perfect. Alterations by Rabbies forged. Shewing the evidence for the Scriptures; that Christianity was exhibited to Adam, invisibles by visibles; past and to come by types; by Cherubim, Urim, Thumim, Sacrifice, Cloud, &c.; that the Jews and Gentiles understood them; that tradition was of the things typified. That though they understood the tradition even of the covenant before the world, they had perverted the intent of it. That the alterations and stories of the Jews, after they had lost their types and Hebrew, are not traditions, but studied evasions to expositions of inspired Christians, &c., and to support their apostacy. That the grammatical formation of the Hebrew, which is descriptive, so gives proper names, cannot admit vowel-pointing, nor Mr. Masclef's method. By J. H." Collected Works, vol. vi., p. 153. London, 1749.

emendations, in order to deduce from the Scriptures the peculiar and preconceived fancies of the different schools, which converted the controversy about the vowel-points into an article of faith in the Reformed Churches of Switzerland. In Switzerland, where the two Buxtorfs successively occupied the professorial chair of Oriental literature, and where their opinions, in matters of Hebrew and Talmudic lore, was regarded as paramount, the theologians enacted a law in 1678, that no person should be licensed to preach the gospel in their churches unless he publicly declared that he believes in the integrity of the Hebrew text and in the divinity of the vowel-points and accents.[69]

After a controversy raging vehemently for more than three centuries, and notwithstanding that the antiquity of the points had been raised to the sanctity of a dogma, modern research and criticism have confirmed the arguments urged by Levita against the antiquity of the present vowel-signs. It is now established beyond the shadow of a doubt, from the discovery of ancient MSS., that there were two systems of vocalisation contrived almost simultaneously, and that the system hitherto regarded by the vowelists as of divine origin is simply one of the two. Indeed the present system, around which the whole controversy clusters, and which has been canonised, is actually the later of the two in point of age.

The earlier, or first system, was developed by Acha or Achai of Irak (Babylon), about 550, from the few simple signs which represented the traditional pronunciation of the text in the East. The peculiarity of this system consists in having signs of a different shape to represent the vowels, and that these are almost uniformly placed *above* the letters. It is therefore designated *the Superlineary system* (מנוקד למעלה). From the fact that its contriver lived in Babylon, it is also called *the Babylon*, or *the Assyrian system*, (נקוד הבבלי, נקוד אשורי) and *the Eastern system*. It has been preserved in the following MSS., i. A MS. of the Pentateuch, embracing only fifteen fragments of Deuteronomy, with Targum Onkelos after each verse, the Massorah marginalis, and the Haphtaroth with the Massorah; the whole consists of seventy-seven leaves, and was most probably written in

---

[69] "Codicem Hebr. V. T. tum quoad consonas tum quoad vocalia sive puncta ipsa sive punctorum saltem potestatem θεόπνευστον esse." *Formula Consensus*, art. iv., comp. Keil's edition of Hävernick's *Allgemeine Einleitung in das Alte Testament*, vol. i., p. 315.

Persia. ii. An equally ancient MS. of the Haphtaroth, consisting of twelve fragments, and containing the Haphtaroth to Exod., Levit., and Numb., which are wanting in the preceding MS., as well as the Haphtaroth of New Year, the Day of Atonement, and the feasts of Tabernacles and Pentecost, the Targum, and the Massorah. iii. A MS. of the major and minor Prophets, consisting of two hundred and twenty-five parchment leaves, and written about A.D. 916.[70]

The later, or second system, is the one which has been for centuries commonly adopted both by Jews and Christians in the pointed editions of the Hebrew Bibles. It was contrived by Mocha, of Tiberias, about A.D. 570, to denote the traditional pronunciation of the text in the West. Hence it is called the Tiberian system (נקוד טברני), and the Palestinian or Western system (נקוד ארץ ישראל). It is far more complete and extensive, and exhibits more sharply the niceties of the traditional pronunciation and intonation of the text, than the Babylonian system, with which it competed.

As the Babylonian system, with all its imperfections, was the first promulgated, and moreover as it obtained prior to the separation of the Karaites from the Rabbinic Jews, it was staunchly followed by the Jews in Babylon, and more especially by the Karaites. The Rabbinic Jews, however, soon discarded the Babylonian system, when they found that the Tiberian or present system of vocalisation was more perfect, and represented more adequately the traditional pronunciation, whilst the Karaite Jews clung to the first or Babylonian system. It was not till the year 957, when the Jews of Palestine sent Missionaries to the Crimea to reclaim the Karaites to Rabbinism, and when these Missionaries succeeded in converting many of the distinguished families, that the said Missionaries, Ephraim, Elisha, and Chanuka, punctuated the Bible MSS. according to the Tiberian or present system, and induced the Karaites to substitute it for the one

---

[70] For a further account of this system, and of the MSS. which exhibit it, we must refer to Pinner, *Prospectus der der Odessaer Gesellschaft für Geschichte und Alterthümer gehörenden ältesten hebräischen und rabbinischen Manuscripten*. Odessa, 1845; Luzzatto's treatise in Pollak's Dissertations, entitled,, *Halichoth Kedem*, p. 23—231. Amsterdam, 1846; Ewald, *Jahrbücher der biblichen Wissenschaft*, vol. i., p. 160—172, Gottingen, 1849; Geiger, *Urschrift und Ueberzetzungen der Bibel*, p. 167—170. Breslau, 1857; Fürst, *Geschischte des Karäerthums*, vol. i., pp. 19, &c., 134, &c. Leipzig, 1862; Kallisch, *Hebrew Grammar*, vol. ii., p. 63, &c. London, 1863; Pinsker, *Einleitung in das Babylonisch-Hebräische Punktationssystem*, Vienna, 1863; Fürst, in the *Zeitschrift der deutschen morgenländischen Gesellschaft*, vol. xviii., p. 314—323. Leipzig, 1864.

which was previously in vogue, and which has only survived in the most ancient MSS. This discovery of modern research, therefore, fully confirms Levita's arguments against the antiquity of the present vocalisation, and must for ever settle the long and vehement controversy.

Within twelve months of the appearance of the *Massoreth Ha-Massoreth*, which caused this protracted and vehement controversy, Levita published (1538) a treatise on the laws of the accents. The rapid succession of these two works is easily accounted for. The vowel-points and accents are most intimately connected with each other, and proceeded from the same authors. Both R. Acha, and R. Mocha, the compilers of the Babylonian and Tiberian systems of vocalisation, included the accents in their respective systems. Indeed the accents determine the sense of a passage quite as much as the vowel-points. If the points fix the pronunciation and meaning of words, the accents indicate the logical relation of each word to the whole sentence and the close of sentences. Hence those who contrived the vowel-signs, to denote the traditional pronunciation of the words, were also obliged to invent the accents, to represent the traditional construction of the sentences. This accounts for the frequent remark of the celebrated commentator Rashi, in his exposition of the Scriptures—" but for the accents on this verse, I could not have made out its meaning;" and the warning of the famous Ibn Ezra—" an interpretation which is not according to the accents is neither to be received nor listened to, for the author of the accents knew the import much better."

It is this importance of the accents which has invested them with a divine halo, and which has made the defenders of the antiquity and divinity of the vowel-points also maintain their antiquity and divinity. Consistently with his arguments against the points, Levita rejects the divine origin of the accents, maintaining that they proceed from the same Tiberian Massorites who contrived the system of vocalisation. As his arguments against the points are also directed against the accents, he refrains from repeating them, and simply refers the reader to the *Massoreth Ha-Massoreth*.

In harmony with its import, he denominated this treatise *The Book of Good Sense* (ספר טוב טעם), since the accent on each word is called in Hebrew טעם *reason, principle*, because it furnishes principles and rules to deduce the import of each verse. The whole treatise consists of eight sections, and discusses the following points. Section i. discusses the number and names of the accents, and their proper division into three classes, viz., 14 *Kings*, so called, because, like monarchs who restrain their subjects, these accents respectively stand between sentences, keeping them within proper bounds. ii. *Servants*, so called, because they act as servants of the monarch, bringing the sentence without pause to the resting place of the kings; and 5 who are neither kings nor servants, thus making 30 in all. Section ii. explains the names of the accents, their laws, the position of the serviles, &c. Section iii. explains how it is that half the number of royal accents follow each other, and the other half does not follow ; that most of the regal accents are placed above the letters, whilst most of the servile accents are placed under the letters ; as well as the reason why some serviles are above the letters. Section iv. explains the distentives, shewing the smaller kings, which cause a longer pause than the greater kings ; that kings have servants, and how many, and which have no servants, and which servants only serve one or two or more kings. Section v. describes the form and names of all the thirty accents. Section vi. treats on the laws of those words which have the accents on the ultima and penultima. Section vii. discusses the laws of the *Metheg* and *Gaja*; and Section viii. the *Makkeph*.

This Treatise, which is a very valuable contribution to Biblical exegesis, was first published by his friend Bomberg, Venice, 1538. Levita appended to this edition a list of printers' mistakes which have crept into the *Massoreth Ha-Massoreth*, as well as into this book. Within twelve months of its appearance, Münster re-published it, with a Latin summary of its contents (Basle, 1539). It is generally bound up with the *Massoreth Ha-Massoreth*, as these two works were re-published in the same year. Münster's edition is not as correct as the *editio princeps*. Although it is acknowledged, by grammarians and expositors of the highest authority, that the accents are not only marks to indicate the tone-syllable, but to show the logical relation of each word to the whole sentence, thus serving as signs of interpretation, yet this branch of ancient exegesis has been greatly neglected. The grammars, while devoting ample space to the discussion of the vowel-points, rarely ever give more than a paragraph or two to the explanation of the laws of the accents, which are of equal importance to the interpretation of the Old Testament. Hence it is, that, whilst Levita's works on the other departments of Biblical literature and exegesis have been reprinted several times, and elaborated and superseded by succeeding researches, the treatise on the accents has never been published again since 1589, and the system of accentuation in the Old Testament is less understood by the generality of Hebrew students in the present day than it was in the days when Elias Levita's treatise first appeared.[71]

Levita's consummate mastery of Hebrew literature in all its different branches was only equalled by his indefatigable zeal and untiring labours to simplify and promote its study. Though he was now seventy years of age, his energies had not abated. No sooner had he finished the *Treatise on the Accents*, than he commenced a Lexicon, explaining those words in the Talmud, Midrashim, and other works in the Rabbinical literature, which were either entirely omitted in the standard Lexicons of R. Nathan b. Jechiel and R. David Kimchi, or had not been treated in all their sundry meanings. He was all the more induced to undertake this work by the rapid progress of his pupils in Biblical Hebrew, and through the great demand, especially on the part of Christians, for keys to the Kabbalistic and Rabbinical writings. In his entire absorption in this Lexicon, and another which we shall soon mention, he forgot the altered circumstances in which he was then placed, and it was not till he had nearly completed the work, after labouring three years over it, that he began to think of the difficulties of finding a publisher, as his friend and patron, "the great printer, D. Bomberg," he tells us, "had given up his printing-office some time since."

But at the very time when he was in this perplexity, and when

---

[71] The above remark does not imply that no superior Treatise has appeared since the publication of Levita's *Dissertation on the Accents*. The learned Heidenheim published an Essay, entitled *The Laws of the Accents*, (ספר משפטי הטעמים) Rödelheim, 1808; chiefly compiled from the ancients, the Massorites, Ben-Asher, Ibn Balaam, Chajug, &c., which is of superior excellence, and in which he corrects some of Levita's mistakes. But Heidenheim's Essay is very rare; being written in Hebrew, it has therefore little advanced the general knowledge of the accents. Separate Treatises have also been published by J. D. Michaelis, *Anfangs-Gründe der Hebräischen Accentuation*, with an Introduction by C. B. Michaelis, 2nd edition, Halle, 1753; Stern, עין הקורא *Leseauge*, illustrated with 900 examples, Frankfort on the Maine, 1840; and recently by A. B. Davidson, *Outlines of Hebrew Accentuation, Prose and Poetical*, London, 1861; in which the part treating on the prose accents is exceedingly defective, as Mr. Davidson could not avail himself of so able a guide in this department as he had in Baer's masterly Treatise on the Poetical Accents, entitled *Torath Emeth*. Mr. Davidson, moreover, whilst he mentions men who have not written separate Treatises on this subject, does not even allude to Levita's excellent *Dissertation on the Accents*.

his plan for sending the Lexicon to Bologna was defeated by the information that the Hebrew press had stopped there, Levita received a letter from Paul Fagius, inviting him to go to Germany, to undertake the supervision of the Hebrew press and the editorship of sundry Biblical works. To us, in whose country the remains of Fagius were ignominiously exhumed and burned, by the command of Mary, in 1556, and the ashes collected again, and honourably interred, by the order of Elizabeth, July 30, 1560, the connection of this learned Hebraist and eminent Reformer with Levita is of special interest. Fagius, who was born at Rheinzabern, in 1504, received his first instruction in Hebrew from Wolfgang Fabricius Capito (1478–1541), who acquired his Hebrew knowledge from two converted Jews, one unnamed, and the other named Matthew Adrian, the well-known author, or compiler, of the *Libellus Hora*, in Hebrew and Latin (1513), now one of the rarest books in existence.[72] Though Capito himself was no profound Hebrew scholar, as may be seen from his writings,[73] yet he imbued Fagius with an intense love for the language.

When Fagius was appointed Protestant pastor of Isny, in Allgau, in 1537, where he had formerly been rector of the Grammar School, he more than ever devoted himself to his Hebrew studies. He was also exceedingly anxious to diffuse the knowledge of the sacred language by means of good elementary books, which were much wanted at that time. To effect this he not only compiled the required manuals himself, but, with the aid of his friend and patron, counsellor Peter Buffler, he established a Hebrew press in the town of his pastoral labours. Feeling, however, his own inefficiency to conduct the printing of books in a language which, with all his love for it, he had not as yet properly mastered, he at once invited Levita to accept the office of supervisor, and offered also to print at Isny his own books, which were then ready for the press, as well

---

[72] For a description of this literary curiosity, see Steinschneider, *Bibliographisches Handbuch*, p. 2, s. v. ADRIANUS. Leipzig, 1859.

[73] Capito's works on Hebrew literature are, i. *Institutiuncula in Hebr. ling.* together with the Psalms in Hebrew, and an introduction by Pellican, Basel, 1516; Luther's own copy of this work, with his marginal annotations in MS., from the library of De Rossi, is to be found at Parma. This is exceedingly interesting to the student of the history of the early translations of the Bible, inasmuch as it shows the Manual which the great Reformer used to acquire his Hebrew knowledge. ii. *Institutiones Hebraicæ*, libr. ii., Basel, 1518, 1525; and iii. *Enarrationes in Habacuc et Hoseam*, 1537.

as those which had already been published. Levita regarded this invitation as providential, and though he tells us he had refused before "sundry calls from princes, cardinals, and bishops, as well as from the king of France," to professorial chairs, the septuagenarian felt that it was the voice of God, and that he must not disobey it.

In the year 1540, therefore, the aged Levita left his wife, children, and numerous friends in Venice, and departed for Isny, carrying with him the MSS. of his two Lexicons, and of the second edition of the Grammar called the *Bachur*, which were then nearly finished, and which Fagius had promised to publish. When the extreme difficulty and discomfort connected with travelling three centuries ago is borne in mind, we shall be able to appreciate the unquenchable zeal of this veteran, who, at the age of seventy, when men generally cling to their homes most tenaciously, left everything near and dear to him, and willingly braved all fatigue and difficulties, to promote the knowledge of the sacred language. Indeed, in the Epilogue to the *Tishbi*, which was the first book printed by Fagius, Levita tells us that he had to finish it on the road. "When I was on my journey," he says, "travelling over a land of mountains and valleys, exposed to the rain of heaven and to the snow which covered the ground, I often stood still, thought over in my mind sundry of the articles, wrote them down upon the tablet of my heart, and when I reached the inn I opened my bag, took out the MS., and put down the things which God put into my heart." [74]

Such was the journey which Levita made to come to Fagius. Let us now hear from the learned Jew what impression he received of the Christian scholar, when the two met together. "When I arrived here," says Levita, "I tasted his pitcher, and found it full of old wine. Indeed, I had not been told half of his wisdom and knowledge. Many draw from the fountain of his learning; he is a great oracle for his people, a beautiful preacher, and an excellent expositor. He is truly worthy that his people should describe him as we describe our Rabbin Moses Maimonides. For just as we say, 'From Moses the law-giver to Moses [Maimonides] none has arisen like Moses;' so they should say, 'From Paul [the Apostle] to Paul [Fagius] none

---

[74] כי בצאתי מביתי לא היה הספר הזה נשלם ובאמת בהיותי בדרך דולך למסעי ארץ הרים וגבעות למטר השמים ולשלג אשר הוה ארץ עמדתי מרעיד עיינתי דברים בשכלי, יכתבתים על לוח לבי, ובבאי אל המלון פתחתי פי אמתחי והוצאתי פנקסי ורשמתי בו את הדברים אשר נתן אלהים בלבי. *Tishbi*, p. 271.

has arisen like Paul.' "[75] This cordiality Fagius fully reciprocated, as may be seen from his Latin Address to the Reader prefixed to the *Tishbi*. Entertaining the same ardent love for Hebrew, agreed upon making united efforts to diffuse the knowledge of it, and thoroughly appreciating each other's character, Levita and Fagius soon became ardent friends, and conjointly produced works which, at that time, were an honour to their authors, and formed important contributions to Biblical literature.

The first work issued from this newly established Hebrew press was Levita's Lexicon, comprising seven hundred and twelve words used in the ancient Jewish literature. He called it *Tishbi*, for three reasons: i. In allusion to the gentile name of his namesake the prophet (i. Kings xvii. 1), whose appellation Levita assumed in accordance with an ancient conceit; ii. Because the last word in this Lexicon is *Tishbi*; and iii. Because the numerical value of the word *Tishbi* (viz. י 10 + ב 2 + ש 300 + ת 400 = 712) represents the total number of sections in this Lexicon. To perfect himself in Rabbinical Hebrew, under the guidance of so excellent a master, as well as to enable Christian students at large to use it as a guide, Fagius, assisted by Levita, translated the whole *Tishbi* into Latin, with the exception of the poetical and rhythmical introductions, which were translated by James Velocian. The third Introduction, which is in prose, is not translated at all; most probably because, as it contains so flattering an account of Fagius, his sincere humility would not tolerate its being translated into a language commonly understood among Christian scholars. Thus, the Hebrew of Levita on the right page and the Latin of Fagius on the left, the Jew and the Christian published their conjoint work, under the same cover, at Isny, 1541. The *Tishbi* was reprinted with the Latin translation by Fagius at Basel, 1557, and without the Latin, *ibid.* 1601; Grodno, 1805, and Chernowitz, 1856.

In the same year in which the *Tishbi* appeared, Levita also carried through the press another Lexicon, comprising all the words which occur in the Chaldee paraphrases of the Old Testament. The diffi-

---

[75] Compare ובבאי הנה תחיתי בקנקנתו ומצאתיו מלא ישן ׳ולא הוגד לי החצי ׳מחכמתו וידיעתו ורבים שואבים מי תורתו׳ ודורש טוב לעמו׳ נאה דורש ונאה מפרש׳ ונאמת ראוי הוא שבני עמו יקראו עליו כמו שאנו קוראין על רבינו משה בן מיימון ממשה עד משה לא קם כמשה׳ כך יאמרו עליו מפאולוש עד פאולוש לא קם כפאולוש, Introduction iii., to the *Tishbi*, or the Introduction in prose, as it is called, towards the end.

culties which he had to encounter to reduce the language of the Chaldee paraphrases to grammatical and lexical form were enormous. The only Aramaic Lexicon extant was the *Aruch*, by R. Nathan b. Jechiel (*circa* 1030–1106), which was completed A.D. 1101, and of which three different editions appeared before the publication of the Lexicon on the *Targumim*. One of these three editions, *i.e.* the *editio princeps*, was published before 1480; the second appeared at Pesaro, 1517; and the third was edited by Levita himself, and published by his friend Bomberg, Venice, 1531. But, marvellous as is the *Aruch*, and though it is still the only clue to the ancient Jewish writings, it is not designed for students of the Chaldee paraphrases. It does not separate the dialects of the Mishna, Gemara, Midrashim, and Targumim, but mixes them up all in one treatise. In addition to the want of forerunners in the lexicography of the Targumim, there was the great difficulty arising from the confused condition of the texts of these paraphrases. But here we cannot do better than give Levita's own words upon the subject, which are as follows:

"I have been asked whether it is possible to make a grammar on the Targum, to which I replied that, in my opinion, the possibility is very remote, owing to the great variations in the Codices with regard to the words and letters, and more especially the vowel-points, which differ exceedingly. This arises from the fact that the Targumists most unquestionably wrote their paraphrases without points, which had not then been invented, as I have previously shown in the Introduction to the *Massoreth Ha-Massoreth*. In confirmation of this, it is also to be adduced that the most ancient Codices are all without the points; for the Massorites, who pointed the Hebrew Scriptures, did not point the Chaldee paraphrases. These were pointed much later, by one or more individuals, men without a name, who exercised an arbitrary independence of each other. Hence it is that their rules are contradictory, and that no examples can be adduced from them to found thereupon a grammar. Hence, too, the fact that, since the Targum was made, there has not been a wise and intelligent man in Israel who could make a grammar to it.

"Not only, however, has no grammar been written, but no one has compiled a lexicon to explain the words, except, indeed, R. Nathan of Rome, in his *Aruch*, which he made in explanation of the Talmud, and in which he adduces some words from the Targumim. But these are chiefly Greek and Latin expressions, occuring for the most part in the Jerusalem Targum, and even many of these he quotes without explaining them, about which I have already had occasion to complain in the *Massoreth Ha-Massoreth*. After him, however, there has been no one who had the courage to handle either the grammar or the lexicography of the Targumim. Now I have been inclined to think that the reason of it is, because that, in years bygone, *i.e.* before the invention of printing, not one copy of the Targum on the Prophets and Hagiographa was to be found in a town, or two in a province. Hence nobody could be found to study them. The Targum Onkelos, which was always to be found plentifully, because we are obliged to read every week the hebdomadal lesson from the law, twice in Hebrew and once in Chaldee, there have indeed been some who studied it; they have also written something on it, but I have not found it of much use; they have likewise made a *Massorah* to it, which, however, I have not yet succeeded in seeing. But with regard to the Targum on the Prophets and Hagiographa, they have not opened their mouth, nor uttered a syllable about it; being neither studied nor asked for, they say, Let it tarry till Elisha cometh." [76]

It was this neglect of the Chaldee paraphrases, and his determination to supply the desideratum, which induced Levita, in spite of all the difficulties to be encountered, to undertake the compilation of a Chaldee Lexicon. He called it *Methurgeman* (מתורגמן), or *the Interpreter*, "because it interprets the Hebrew in Aramaic, and the Aramaic in Hebrew." It was published by his friend, Paul Fagius, at

---

[76] והנה רבים שאלוני האם אפשר לעשות דקדוק על התרגומים האלה, אמרתי לפי דעתי כי אפשרי רחוק הוא, וזה מפני השתנות הנוסחאות במלות ובאותיות ועל כלם בנקדות הם מתחלפות מאד, וזה לפי שבלי ספק המתרגמים כתבו תרגומם בלי נקוד כי לא היו נמצאות, כמו שהוכחתי היטב בהקדמת ספר מסורת המסורת, והראיה עוד כי הנוסחאות הישנות מאד כלם בלתי נקוד, כי לא נקדום בעלי המסורת, כמו שנקדו כל כ"ד הספרים, אלא אחר כך זמן רב נקדו על יד יחיד או רבים אנשים בלי שם כל אחד כרצונו על כן יצא משפטן מעוקל, ואין להביא מהן ראיה לעשות עליהם דקדוק, ולולי כן התחשוב שמיום שנעשו התרגומים לא היה איש חכם ונבון בישראל שהיה יודע לעשות עליהם הדקדוק · · · ·

ואומר כי לא די שלא היה איש שעשה הדקדוק כי אפילו לעשות חבור לפרש המלות לא היה איש חוץ מהרב רבי נתן איש רומי בספרו הערוך שחבר על מלות התלמוד ואגב גררא הביא קצת מלות מהתרגומים ורובם מלות של יון או רומי הנמצאים לרוב בתרגום ירושלמי וככמה מהם הביא ולא בארם וזאת היתה תלונתי עליו בספר מסורת המסורת ואחריו לא קם איש שהתעורר להחזיק בו לא בדקדוק ולא בביאור המלות וחשבתי שהסבה בזה לפי שבשנים שעברו רוצה לומר קודם שנמצאה מלאכת הדפוס לא היו נמצאים תרגום נביאים וכתובים כי אם אחד במדינה ושנים באיקלים לכן לא היה מי שהשגיחה בהם אבל תרגום אונקלוס תמיד נמצא לרוב וזה מפני שחייבים אנחנו לקרא בכל שבוע הפרשה שנים מקרא ואחד תרגום נמצאים קצת אנשים שהשגיחהו בו וכתבו עליו דבר מה ולא מצאתי בהם תועלת רב גם נעשה עליו מסורת ולא ראיתים עד הנה אבל על נביאים וכתובים לא היה פוצה פה ומצפצך ואין דורש ואין מבקש אלא אמרו יהי מונח עד שיבא אליהו Introduction to the *Methurgeman*.

Isny, in the month of August, 1541. At the end of the volume is Fagius's Colophon, which consists of a book with a tree on it, as Fagius properly denotes *book*; on the right of it is the letter פ, initial of Paul; on the left of it is the letter ב, the initial of *book* = Fagius; whilst underneath it is the Hebrew inscription כל אילן טוב נושא פרי טוב, *Every good tree bringeth forth good fruit.* The Colophon of the *Tishbi*, which as we have seen contains the Latin translation of Fagius, is different. Instead of the letters פ and ב there are on the right and left hand the Latin and the Hebrew of the inscription, and underneath are the Hebrew words תקותי במשיח הנשלח שהיא עתיד לדין חיים ומתים, *My hope is in the Messiah who has come, and who will judge the quick and the dead.* This difference is undoubtedly owing to the fact that Fagius, as the joint editor, claimed to have the expression of his faith on the *Tishbi*; whilst the *Methurgeman*, which is the sole work of Levita, has simply the Hebrew date, and no reference to Christ.

In the Epilogue to the *Methurgeman*, Levita tells us that he laboured over it nearly four years; which is fully confirmed by the fact that he already alludes to his being engaged on it in the third Introduction to the *Massoreth Ha-Massoreth* (1538), whilst in the third Introduction to the *Tishbi*, which was written after he had only been three years at work over it, he says, "I know that many will be astonished at the multitude of words from the Targum which I quote, saying, in different places, this expression does not occur again in the Targum, or this expression only occurs once or twice, or it is thus rendered throughout the Chaldee version, except in Job, Psalms, and Proverbs, &c., &c., and will scarcely be inclined to believe all the remarks which I made therein. But if they only knew the great labour which I spent over the *Methurgeman*, they would not be surprised at it. Forsooth, I have been three years writing it, and during this time I have read through all the Chaldee paraphrases over and over again, as the references will show to anyone who consults it. Others, again, may be astonished at my quoting Greek in many places, knowing that I was not learned in this language. But the fact is, that these people do not know that I have learned it from Cardinal Egidio, with whom I resided thirteen years, and who was exceedingly expert in Greek." [77]

[77] וידעתי כי רבים תמהו על רוב מלות התרגו שהבאתי באמרי בהרבה מקומות זה הלשון לא נמצא עור בתרגום או לא במצא רק במקום אחד או שנים או כך הוא מתחדגם בכל המקרא חוץ מן איוב משלי ותלים וכפו אדה רבום ולא אמינו לי בכל האותות אשר עשיתי בקרבם. אמנם אם ידעי חמורה

But though Levita spent such extraordinary labour over this Lexicon, and though the *Methurgeman* is still the only work in which the whole language of the Chaldee paraphrases is treated separately, it has never been republished. The introduction, was translated into Latin by his friend Paul Fagius, Isny, 1542. The single article comprising the root משח which discusses the question of the Messiah in the Chaldee paraphrases, has also been translated into Latin by Gilb. Genebrard, Paris, 1572.[78] Buxtorf has incorporated most of it in his Rabbinical and Talmudical Lexicon, which, however, is not as convenient for the use of students as Levita's work, inasmuch as it mixes up the dialects of the Talmud and Midrashim with the language of the Chaldee paraphrases. The only Lexicon which will supersede it is the one now in course of publication by Dr. Levy.

With the completion of the Chaldee Lexicon, Levita thought he had finished his active life, having now reached his seventy-fourth year. In most affecting language, therefore, he says in the Epilogue to the work in question, that the time has now arrived when he must relinquish his literary labours, since his advanced age and failing health compel him to retire from the battle field. "Seeing that age has overtaken me, that I am very old, that my eyesight grows dimmer every day, and that my strength is fast leaving me, I must retire from the ranks and serve no more. I shall now return to my country which I left, namely, Venice, and die in my town with my aged wife, and no more move my foot from her. She shall close my eyes, and death alone shall henceforth separate me from her. I shall abide there the remaining days of my life, finish the books which I have begun, and then say to the God who created me, Take now my life, for it is better that I should die."

But, notwithstanding this resolution to return to Venice, his unquenchable love for the work, coupled with the fact that he had still some treatises ready for press, and that his friend Fagius too was actually printing sundry books which required his help, induced the

Introduction iii. to the *Tishbi*. שלש עשרה שנה קבלתי כל אלה בי הוא היה בקי מאד כלשון יון ־ בהרבה מקומות בידעם שאינני מכיר הלשון ההוא אבל לא ידעו שמן הקארדינאל אשר עמדתי עמו עברתי על כל התרגמים כמה ובכמה והנסיון יוכיח למי שיעיין בו גם יתמהו על לשון יון שהבאתי הגדול שטרחתי בחבור ספר המתורגמן גם בעיניהם לא יפלא כי באמת שלש שנים עמדתי בחבורו ואז

[78] Dr. Kalisch (*Hebrew Grammar*, ii., p. 34, note d.) is surely mistaken in his remark that Fagius likewise translated this valuable Chaldee Dictionary in 1542. Fagius translated the Introduction only.

aged Levita to remain a little longer at Isny. With impaired eyesight and failing health, but with an enthusiasm for Biblical literature, and an industry which defied and vanquished bodily infirmities, he not only most vigorously continued his own works, but largely aided Fagius in writing and carrying through the press his productions. Some idea may be formed of the amount of mental and physical labour which Levita was still able to perform, though now seventy-four years of age, from the fact that, within twelve months of the appearance of the stupendous Lexicon on the Chaldee paraphrases, he wrote and carried through the press an *Alphabetical List of the Technical Hebrew Words* or *Nomenclature* (שמות דברים), in four columns. Column i. gives these words in Judaio-German, with Hebrew characters. Column ii., in Hebrew. Column iii., in Latin, by Fagius; and column iv. gives them in German, with German characters, Isny, 1542. It was afterwards republished, with an additional column, by Drusius the son, containing the corresponding Greek words, and enriched with explanations by Drusius the father, Francker, 1652, and *ibid.*, 1581.

Besides the *Nomenclature*, Levita also carried through the press this year (1542), a new and thoroughly revised edition of his Grammar, entitled *Bachur*, which as we have seen he published twenty-four years before (1518), at the suggestion and for the use of his pupil Cardinal Egidio. Münster had already republished it, with a Latin translation (1525), seven years after the appearance of the original work, but Levita had nothing to do with it, and made no alterations in it. As it is the new preface added by Levita to this edition which gave rise to the great divergency of opinion about the date of his birth, we shall give it entire. By so doing, the origin of the errors will best be understood. But before doing this, it is necessary to remark that Levita completed the second edition in 1540, when still at Venice, and that it was one of the three MSS. which he took with him to Isny, the other two being the *Tishbi* and the *Methurgeman*. This is evident, from his remark in the Epilogue to the second edition of the *Bachur*, where he distinctly says, " Whoso wishes to know its date, let him take 22 (ביד׳ו) from 322 (ערב״ים)," [79] thus leaving 300 = 1540, the very year in which he received the invitation

[79] והרוצה לדעת עת פרטו
הלא יקח בי׳דו מן ערב׳׳ים

Bachur, p. 103. 2nd edition, Isny, 1542.

from Fagius, and in which he started for Isny. It was very natural that he should print the three new works (namely, the two Lexicons and the Nomenclature) first, and then the second edition of an old work.

Now, in the Introduction to the *Bachur* in question, which he completed in 1540, but which was not printed till 1542, he gives the following piece of autobiography, which caused the errors already alluded to. " Thus sayeth Elias Levita, the German,[80] I was about forty years of age when fate sent me from Venice, and I came to Rome. Here I was requested to compile this book, and I put down its import according to my knowledge. Now the Lord has spared me thirty years longer, and I am now about seventy years old, and am as able now as I was then to engage in the discussion on matters of Grammar, the Bible, and the Massorah. Yea since then I have acquired different ideas, and formed opinions which I did not know before. Moreover, I have since found that I have omitted some things which ought to have been put down, and that I have stated things which ought not to have been written. I regret that I have done it. Still it is not to be wondered at, since we find that even our Rabbins of blessed memory said things in their youth, which they recalled in their old age. Thus we find, ' Raba changed from this;' ' R. Ashi changed from what he said in the former statement, and the law is according to his second statement,' (comp. *Baba Bathra* 157, *b*.) Now as were their thoughts so are mine, and I am not to be better than my fathers. For this reason I have resolved to publish a second edition of this work, with such additions and diminutions as shall make the last edition better than the first. I shall thus prevent students studying erroneous introductions, inconclusive arguments, and incorrect rules, and those

[80] אמר אליהו הלוי האשכנזי בן ארבעים שנה אנכי בשלוח הזמן אותי מווינסייה ובאתי לרומא ושם נדרשתי לאשר שאלוני בחבור הספר הזה ואשיב בו דבר כאשר עם לבבי והנה הזחיה י״י אותי מאז זה שלשים שנה והרי אני כבן שבעים שנה ועודני היום חזק בכחי אז וכחתי עתה לצאת ולבא למלחמת הדקדוק והפסוק והמסורת כי מאז נתחדשו בי דעות אחרות וסברות חדשות אשר לפנים לא ידעתים מצורף לזה כי מאותו היום והלאה מצאתי שהנחתי קצת דברים שהיו ראויים להכתב ולא כתבתים גם כתבתי דברים הלואי ולא כתבתים נחמתי כי עשיתים ואין לתמוה על נכד כי כן נמצא לרבותינו זכרונם לברכה שאמרו דבר בילדותם וחזרו בו בזקנותם כמו שמצינו הדר ביה רבא מהההיא וכן רב אשי הזר ממה שאמר במהדורא קמא והלכה כמהדורא בתרא כדאיתא בסוף פרק מי שמתו ׳ והנה כמחשבותם מחשבותי ולא טוב אנכי מאבותי לכן הסכמתי עם לבבי להדפיס הספר הזה שנית ולהוסיף עליו ולגרוע ממנו ובזה איטיב חסדי האחרון מן הראשון לבלתי לכת אחרי הבחורים ללמוד הקדמות כוזבות וראיות בלתי צודקות וחקים לא טובים וילמדום התל התלמידים הבאים אחרי ונמצא שם שמים מתחלל חס ושלום ולכן בהעתקה הזאת אתקן המעוות וחדורים אישר והמקלקל אכשר וארים מכשול מדרך עמי ובזה יהיה אלהים עמי

that follow, learning blunders, and thereby peradventure profaning the divine name. For this reason, I correct in this edition that which is erroneous, rectify the mistakes, and remove the stumbling block from the way of my people. To this end may the Lord be with me."

It was David Gans,[81] the eminent historian, who first took Levita's remark—" I was about forty years of age when fate sent me from Venice, and I came to Rome," &c.—also to refer to Levita's period of life when he published the Grammar in question. Accordingly, as the first edition of the *Bachur* was published, Rome, 1518, Gans concluded that Levita was born in 1477, and that the second edition appeared in 1547, since Levita himself states that he compiled it forty years later, when he was seventy years of age. This statement of Gans was adopted by Jechiel,[82] in his historical work, by Semler, and others.

---

[81] David Gans was born in 1541, at Lippstadt, in Westphalia, and died 25th August, 1613, at Prague. He was the first German Jew of his age who was distinguished as a historian, geographer, and astronomer; he was acquainted with John Müller, Kepler, and Tycho de Brahe, with whom he carried on a literary correspondence; for the latter he translated into German, extracts from a Hebrew translation of the Tables of Alphonso, composed in 1260. The works which have immortalised his name are as follows: i. A Compendium of History, from the Creation to A.D. 1592, in the form of annals, entitled *The Sprout of David* (צמח דוד), first published at Prague, 1592, then with a continuation to A.D. 1692, by Reindorf, Frankfort on the Maine and Amsterdam, 1692, Furth 1785, and part iii. improved by Mohr, Lemberg, 1847. This chronicle was translated into Latin by Vorst, Leyden, 1644, the second part being abbreviated; and into Judaio-German, by Hena, Frankfort on the Maine, 1698; and ii. An Introduction to Astronomy, the Calendar, and Mathematical Geography, entitled, *A Pleasant and Agreeable Work* (ספר נחמד ונעים), in twelve parts, subdivided into three hundred and five sections. It was finished by the author in 1613, and continued by Joel b. Jekuthiel, Jesnëtz, 1743. The passage in question, which has been the source of the perpetual error respecting the date of Levita's birth, is as follows in the original: רע״ז : אליהו המ״קדק חבר ספר הבחור ברומי בשנת רע״ז ובן ארבעים שנה וכמהדורתו בשנת ש״ז היה בן שבעים שנה *Anno* 277 [= 1518]; *Elias, the German, composed the Book Bachur, at Rome, in the year* 277 [= 1518], *when he was forty years old; and when he published the second edition, in the year* 307 [= 1547], *he was seventy years of age.* Comp. part i., p. 43, b, ed. Frankfort, 1692. In Vorst's Latin translation of this work, the whole passage is thus erroneously rendered, "Elias Grammaticus composuit librum *Bachur* Romae anno 277; et ista aetate sua anno 307, erat filius 70 annorum." Comp. p. 151.

[82] Jechiel Heilprin, the author of the chronicle of Jewish history and literati, entitled, *The Order of Generations* (סדר הדורות), was Rabbi at Minsk, where he died about 1731. His Chronicle was first published at Carlsrühe, 1769. A new and improved edition, edited by H. Sperling and B. Lorje, appeared in Lemberg, 1858. The passage relating to Levita, which the author transferred into this work from the chronicle of Gans, is erroneously copied. It is here as follows: הבחור ברומי רע״ז ס׳ [read חבר] חסר, בן מ׳ שנה ומסורות המסורות חבר רצ״ח ובמדורתו הי׳ בן ע׳ שנת ש״ז, *He composed the Book Bachur, at Rome, in* 277 [= 1518], *when forty years of age, and the Massoreth*

Levita's remark, however, that he was forty years of age, does not refer to the publication of the first edition of the Bachur, but to his leaving Venice and arriving at Rome in 1509, as is evident from the following facts: i. The second edition of the *Bachur* was not published in 307 [= 1547], as stated by Gans and those who follow him, but in 1542.[88] ii. This revised edition, according to his own explicit statement (*vide supra*, p. 73), he finished in 1540. iii. He tells us himself that he was not then seventy years old, but *about* seventy years of age (והרי אני כבן שבעים שנה), that is a little more than seventy, or seventy-two. iv. As this second edition was published two years after its completion, *i. e.*, in 1542, when he was seventy-four years of age, he most unquestionably was born in 1468; and v. This date of his birth is confirmed by Levita himself, for he tells us distinctly (*vide supra*, p. 3), that he was eighty years old in 1548.

In addition to his own two productions, which he published in 1542, the aged Levita carried through the press, in the same year, no fewer than four works published by his friend Fagius. They are as follows: i. The Book of Tobit, in Hebrew, with a Latin translation by Fagius on the opposite page, Isny, 1542, which has been incorporated in the London Polyglott by Walton. ii. The so-called Alphabet of Ben Sirah, in Chaldee, with a Commentary, and a Latin translation by Fagius, Isny, 1542. iii. Gen. cap. i.—iv., with a Latin translation, as well as with an explanation of every word, and a Latin translation of

---

Ha-Massoreth he wrote in 298 [= 1538], *and at the second edition he was seventy years old, which was in* 307 [= 1547]. Comp. vol. i., p. 95, *a*, ed. Lemberg. It will be seen that the words, "and at the second edition he was seventy years of age, which was in 307," have been incorrectly put after the *Massoreth Ha-Massoreth*.

[88] The second edition is now before us, and the complete title and date are thus given by Levita himself:

דקדוק אליהו הלוי
האשכנזי אשר שמו

טוב מהעתקה ראשונית	ספר בחור הוסד שנית
ולעלויא שנת תבנית	עושהו הארוך בו דעניה
שם בו הגה העיונית	ודברים טובים הוסיף בה
עתה כלו חטי מנית׳	בראשוי היתה בו קטנית

נדפס באיזנא הבירה בשנת
מבריאת עולם ש״ב לפר״ט
קטון בחדש סיוי
תהלה לשם
עליוי

ב   פ

Onkelos' paraphrases of the same chapters, Isny, 1542; and iv. An Ethical Treatise in Judaio-German, Isny, 1542. This book, which was afterwards translated into Hebrew, and published under the title, *The Paths of the Righteous* (אורחות צדיקים), Prague, 1581, no less an authority than Jost asserts was written by Levita.[84] Steinschneider and Cassel, however, who are authorities of equal weight, will have it that Levita simply edited it.[85]

Levita's departure from Isny was at last accelerated by the impending change in the position of his friend Fagius. Capito, who, as we have seen, was Fagius's first Hebrew teacher, and who occupied both the office of evangelical pastor and the professorial chair at Strasburg, died of the plague in December, 1541. The choice of a successor was soon made. The name of Fagius at once suggested itself to the managers of the Protestant interests at Strasburg, and accordingly this pious, amiable, and learned clergyman was asked to succeed Capito in the pastorate and professorship. Fagius, in accepting this invitation, stipulated that he should be allowed to go first to Constance, for two years, to organise and consolidate the Protestant interests, in the place where the celebrated council condemned Huss and Jerome of Prague. But, in going to Constance for this short period, he was determined to infuse into the minds and hearts of the Protestants there, a conviction of the importance, and a love for the study, of the Hebrew language, knowing that the most effectual way to strengthen the cause of Protestantism was to advance the cause of Biblical literature.

In going therefore to Constance in 1542, Fagius felt that he could not as yet dispense with the help of Levita. Levita was too sincerely attached to his friend, and had too great a love for Hebrew, not to comply with the appeal of Fagius in behalf of the cause of Oriental learning in his self-imposed sphere of labour; and accordingly the aged Jew accompanied the Christian pastor to Constance. As Fagius's stay here was very limited, and as Levita was very anxious to get back to his wife and children at Venice, they at once set to work. Their efforts were directed to supply students with appropriate elementary books. The first book, therefore, which Fagius published consisted of Gen. i.—iv. in Hebrew, with a German translation, and an appendix

---

[4] Comp. the article *Judenteutsch*, in Ersch and Gruber's *Encyklopädie*, sect. ii., vol. xxvii., p. 323, note i.

[85] Comp. Ersch and Gruber's *Encyklopädie*, article *Jüdische Typographie*, p. 33.

of such notes as should help the tyro in Hebrew to acquire the language, Constance, 1543.[86] Having supplied them with an elementary book for the study of Biblical Hebrew, Fagius was also anxious to furnish the students with a guide to Rabbinical Hebrew, and hence published within twelve months Psalms i.—x. in Hebrew, accompanied by David Kimchi's Rabbinical commentary, with a Latin translation, Constance, 1544.

Whilst Fagius thus manifested his anxiety to supply, with the aid of his Jewish friend, the Protestant Christians at Constance with manuals, Levita was equally anxious to benefit his Jewish brethren, with the help of his Christian friend. As Protestants and Romanists were now vying with each other to furnish their respective communities in Germany with translations of the Scriptures in the vernacular of the people, Levita saw the importance of supplying the German speaking Jews with a Judaio-German version of that portion of the Bible which is hebdomadally read, both publicly and privately. He accordingly translated the Pentateuch, the Five Megilloth, and the Haphtaroth, or lessons from the Prophets, into that dialect. This translation he got Fagius to publish, and it appeared at Constance, 1544.[87]

It was not till the autumn of 1544, when Fagius's two years' term at Constance had expired, and he went to Strasburg to enter upon his duties there, that Levita arrived at Venice, after an absence of nearly four years. Though he was now seventy-six years of age, his intellect was still very active, and the tenderness of his heart was intense. His delight in meeting again those who were dear and near to him, and from whom a literary mission had temporarily separated him, may be surmised from the following touching prayer in poetry, which he offered up for his wife, at the conclusion of his Chaldee Lexicon: "O Lord, I beseech thee, grant to me and my wife this mercy, that she should not be a widow, and that I should not be a widower! Let

---

[86] Comp. Wolf, *Bibliotheca Hebraea*, ii., 396, 456; iv., 135.

[87] Some bibliographers question whether Levita is the author of this Judaio-German version. Steinschneider (*Catalogus Libr. Hebr. in Bibliotheca Bodleiana*, col. 942), puts it among the *opera supposititia*, whilst Graetz (*Geschichte der Juden*, ix., 229, Leipzig, 1866), the latest historian of the highest authority, positively states that Levita made this translation at Constance, when on his way from Isny to Venice. A specimen of this curious version, comprising the first chapter of Genesis, is given by Wolf, *Bibliotheca Hebraea*, iv., 194—198. Comp. also Buber, *Life of Elias Levita*, in Hebrew, p. 31, note 49, Leipzig, 1856.

us both die together; let me sleep in her bosom till the appointed time, when the end shall be ushered in, and we shall rise again, and together be destined for everlasting life."[88]

No sooner had he arrived at Venice, than he began publishing again. He re-commenced his literary work in his old sphere of labour, by editing a *Rhythmical Exposition of the Book of Job* (פירוש איוב), Venice, 1544. Some indeed will have it that Levita is the author of this production, and appeal to Steinschneider in corroboration of this assertion; but this learned bibliographer has shown that it was written by Sarek Barfat, who flourished in the middle of the fourteenth century.[89] When he had, however, fairly settled down, he continued the translation of the Scriptures which he began at Isny; and in 1545, he published a German version of the Book of Psalms, which, like the portion of his former selection, constitutes an essential part of the Jewish Ritual. This version was afterwards re-published at Zurich, 1558, and in other places.[90] In the same year, he also edited a new edition of the first part of Kimchi's celebrated grammar and Lexicon, entitled, *Perfection* (מכלול). This part, which contains the grammar, and ought properly to be called *the grammatical part* (חלק הדקדוק), but which usually bears the general title of the whole work, namely, *Michlol*, had indeed been published three times before, twice in Constantinople, 1532, 1534, and once with a Latin translation by Guidacerus, Paris, 1540. But as a new edition was called for, the publisher entrusted it to the aged Grammarian and Lexicographer, who enriched it with valuable annotations (נימוקים). Venice, 1545.

How powerless age was, in either quenching his zeal or diminishing his labour, may be seen from the fact that when he was seventy-nine

[88] אנא אלי ל' ולאשתי   החסד גם האמת מן,
שהיא לא תהיה אלמנה   ואני לא אהיה אלמי',
יחד נמות ובגן ערנות   תוך היקה אישן עד לוכן,
יבא הקץ ואז' נקיץ   ולחי עד יחד נודכן.

Epilogue to the *Methurgeman*.

[89] Thus Dr. Holmes, in *Kitto's Cyclopædia of Biblical Literature*, new ed., s. v. ELIAS, says, "that E. Levita was its author, and not editor only (as Wolf, *Bibl.* iii., would have it), is demonstrated by Steinschneider (*Catal*, 939, 940)." Now, on referring to Steinschneider, at the column in question, the reader will see that this bibliographer heads this section, i. e., No. 33, as follows: "פירוש איוב, *Expositio libri Job*, rhythmica [auctore Sarek Barfat], (ff. 17)." If any more evidence should be required, we refer to the same *Catalogue*, col. 2500, where Steinschneider has a separate section for Sarek, and the only published work of his there specified is "Historia Jobi Carmine; *anon.* ed. ab Elia Levita, q. v. op. 33-4."

[90] Comp. Steinschneider, *Catalogus Libr. Hebr. in Bibliotheca Bodleiana*, col. 188.

years old (1546), he carried through the press, with the utmost care, no less than seven different works. The first of these was the stupendous Hebrew Lexicon, by Kimchi, which is commonly called *the Book of Roots* (ספר השרשים), but the more proper name of which is *the Lexicon part* (חלק הענין), being the second part of the general work, entitled, *Michlol*. Of this famous Lexicon, seven editions had been published before this date, namely, before 1480 ; Naples, 1490 ; *ibid.* 1491 ; Constantinople, 1513 ; Venice, 1529 ; Soncino, 1532–3 ; and Venice, 1546 : and Levita himself, as we have already seen (*vide supra*, p. 22), took part in the fifth edition, immediately after he was employed by his friend Bomberg as corrector of the press. To the edition, however, which now appeared, as also to that of the first part of this great work published in the preceding year, Levita added valuable annotations (נימוקים). His second and third publications, this year, were, new and thoroughly revised editions of his *Treatise on the Compounds* (ספר הרכבה), with the text pointed, and *the Poetical Dissertations* on various parts of Hebrew Grammar, entitled, *the Sections of Elijahu* (פרקי אליהו) ; whilst his fourth work was a greatly improved edition of his maiden production, which consists of the commentary on M. Kimchi's *Journey on the Paths of Knowledge*.

The curious history of the last mentioned production deserves to be noticed at greater length. We have already seen that Levita's first literary production was published surreptitiously (*vide supra*, *p*. 13). As he soon after was occupied with more important literary works, which secured for him a world-wide renown, he did not much care to claim the book, which was most negligently printed, and swarmed with blunders. But his friends, who knew that he was its author, were very anxious that he should not depart this life without claiming and correcting it. With this wish he now complied ; and, as the work had so long passed in another person's name, Levita felt obliged to give the following account of it, which is written in poetry, and is appended to the edition revised by him : —

אנכי אליהו הלוי דל באלפי
כאשר הייתי בימי חרפי:
בק״ק פאדואה הבירה   שנת סד״ר ליצירה:

When I, Elias Levita, the least in my family,
   Was, in the days of my manhood.
In the city of Padua, A.M. 264 [= A.D. 1504],

כאשר מתלמידי נתבקשתי:	זה הספר פירשתי
החל הנגף בעם:	ויהי באותו הפעם
ברחוב אשר אנכי בקרבו:	וסוגר כל בית ומבוא
ואז עבדי רמני:	ונסגרתי גם אני
והוא הרחיקהו מעל גבולי:	כי נתתי לו הספר להעתיק לי
ולהדפיסו לו ממון פזר:	והוליכו עמו לעיר פיזר
היתה בעיניו נקלה:	והנה זאת הנבלה
ושמי על הספר לא זכר:	ואת כבודי עכר
מר׳ בנימין מעיר רומא:[91]	אך שם בראשי דקדמה
שהוא הפירוש היה חיבר:	שכל דרואה אותו סובר
קצת עניינים מדעתו:	גם הוסיף בו לפי שעתו
עקודים נקודים וברודים:	גם לקט מלשון למודים[92]

I composed this book according to the request of my disciples.
It came to pass, that the plague broke out among the people,
Whereupon every entrance was blocked up in the street where I lived,
So that I too was closed in; then my messenger deceived me.
For I gave him the book to print it for me, and he took it away;
He took it to Pesaro, and spent money in printing it for himself.
This shameful deed appeared a small thing in his eyes.
Most insultingly, he did not mention my name in the book,
But put at the beginning of the Introduction 'R. Benjamin's of Rome,'[91]
That all who use it may think he was the author of this Exposition.
He also erroneously added some things from his own cogitations,
And inserted from the 'Language of the Learned,'[92] diverse fragments,

[91] It is now established almost to a certainty, that this Benjamin of Rome, the author of the propædeutical treatise prefixed to Levita's commentary on the *Journey on the Paths of Knowledge*, is Benjamin b. Jehudah, called הב״א, who flourished A.D. 1330, and is the well known author of commentaries on the books of Chronicles, Proverbs, and other portions of the Old Testament; and that Levita headed his commentary in question by this treatise, because, like his own commentary, it was designed to simplify the study of Hebrew Grammar. The messenger, whose name Levita does not condescend to give in this poetical description, by putting the name 'R. Benjamin of Rome' at the head of it, and withholding Levita's name altogether, led people to believe that this Benjamin was the author of the commentary itself, as well as of the propædeutics. This is the cause of Levita's complaint. Comp. Wolf, *Bibliotheca Hebraea*, iii., p. 152, No. cccxciii.; Steinschneider, *Catalogus Libr. Hebr. in Bibliotheca* Bodleiana, pp. 790, 1840, 2769; by the same author, *Jewish Literature*, pp. 146, 376, London, 1857; and *Bibliographisches Handbuch*, p. 21, No. 206. Leipzig, 1859.

[92] "*The Language of the Learned*," (לשון לימודים) is an extensive Hebrew Grammar, to which is appended a treatise on Hebrew Poetry and Metre (מאמר קצר במלאכת השיר), entitled, *The Holy Shekel* (שקל הקדש). The author of this Hebrew Grammar is David Ibn Jachja, of the celebrated ancient family, Jachja, who also wrote a commentary on Proverbs, entitled, *Select and Pure* (קב ונקי), which was first printed at Lisbon, 1492; and has since been incorporated in the Rabbinical Bibles published at Venice, 1516-7, and

M

וכל זה עשה בלי ידעיתי	והשאיר בו מה ששניתי:
מצורף לזה למען תדע אתה	כי לא היחה כחי אז ככחי עתה:
ועם כל זה נדפס כמה פעמים	על ידי יהודים ועממים:
ונמכרים עם כל השניאות	עד שלא נשאר מהם במציאות:
ובאמת על הראשונים אנכי מצטער	שהיה להם הקוצים לבער:
ולא די שהניחום כמו שהם	אך שהוסיפו טעיות עליהם:
וגם אנכי לב עליהם לא שמתי	אך כי עשיתים נחמתי:
אבל ספרים אחרים חברתי	והטיבותי את אשר דברתי:
ועתה אחרי אשר ימי פנוי לערב	הפצירו בי אנשים לרוב:
מהם מולים מהם ערלים	אשר בדקדוק לשונינו עמלים:
שאקימהו על מכונו	ואמלא את חסרונו:
ואאיר את חשכו	והאמת יעשה דרכו:
אע״פ שהקטן הוא זה החבור	יש בו צרכי צבור:
וכל העוסקים בו באמונה	תהיה המלאכה בידם נכונה:
כי הוא מסודר בסדר יפה	ללמוד כל הדקדוק על פה:
ובזה אין לי ספק	כי כל איש ממנו יסתפק:
ואף אם הספר כבר בידו המציא	ישן מפני חדש יוציא:

All this he did without my knowledge, and left in it my errors;
For you must know, that I was not so expert then as I am now.
It was thus re-published several times, both by Jews and Christians,
Sold with all its blunders, and nothing is left of the editions.
I greatly regret my first blunders, which ought to have been corrected;
And which have not only been left, but increased by fresh blunders.
I did not notice it, but simply regretted that I had made blunders,
And wrote other books wherein I corrected my former mistakes.
Now that my life is drawing near to its evening, many of my friends,
Both Jews and Christians, who studied the grammar of our language,
Have urged me to place it in its right position, supply its deficiencies,
Enlighten its darkness, and make straight its path.
For, although the book is but small, it is much wanted;
And those who study it properly derive advantage from it,
Since it is so arranged that the rules may easily be learned by heart.
I have no doubt that every student will benefit from it,
And even if he has the former edition, he'll prefer the new to the old;

Amsterdam, 1724–7; he died about A.D. 1504. The Grammar was published in Constantinople, 1506, 1519, and an improved edition, *ibid.* 1542. The treatise on Hebrew Poetry is from the pen of an anonymous writer. It consists of seventeen chapters, of which cap. i.—xiv., appended to Ibn Jachja's Grammar, treats on the grammatical points necessary for writing poetry, whilst cap. xv.—xvii., which treats on the construction and metre of the Hebrew poetry, was appended to Levita's commentary on Kimchi's *Journey on the Paths of Knowledge*, by the person who published it surreptitiously. It is to these excerpts that the words עקודים נקודים refer. Comp. Steinschneider's *Catalogus Hebr.*, p. 864, &c., and *Bibliographisches Handbuch*, p. 9, No. 78.

כי יראח בזה סימן ברכה ׃ ואשרי האיש שלֹא ככה ׃
ובכן אשלם המלאכה ואסיר כל טעות ומבוכה ׃
כדין וכהלהכ בשם היחיד במלוכה ׃

For he will find therein an advantage, and hail the man who follows it.
Herewith I finish the work, having corrected in it all mistakes,
As it is meet and proper, in the name of Him who alone is Sovereign.

The other three works which Levita published in 1546 are bound up with the Exposition of the *Journey of the Paths of Knowledge*, and are as follows: — i. A concise Hebrew Grammar, entitled, *The Beginning of my Words* (פתח דברי), from an anonymous pen, "written many years ago in Spain, and exceedingly adapted to learn briefly the sacred language," first published at Naples, 1492, then at Constantinople, 1515, and now "carefully revised by Elias Levita, the Grammarian." ii. The well-known grammar of Ibn Ezra, entitled *On the Purity of the Hebrew Style* (צחות); and, iii., another grammatical treatise by Ibn Ezra, called *The Balance of the Sacred Language* (ספר מאזני לשון הקדש). The pagination of these four treatises is continuous: the first extends over leaf 1—51, the second over 52—132, the third over 133—194, The fourth over 195—236. Levita published these treatises under the general title of *Grammars* (דקדוקים).

Extraordinary as was his prowess to battle against the infirmities of old age, and determined as he was not to relinquish his literary labours till his arms were paralysed and his eyesight completely extinguished, Levita was at last compelled, by the irresistible and overpowering effects of the seventy-nine years which had now passed since he had seen the light, to confine himself to editing valuable works written by others. We cannot ascertain the number of works which he published this year, but we have before us Ralbag's Commentary on the Pentateuch, which Levita edited in 1547. Some idea may be formed of the labour required to carry it through the press, when it is stated that it consists of four hundred and ninety-six folio pages, closely printed, in square Hebrew characters. Levita appended to it a short poem in Hebrew. Twelve months later, he edited R. Isaac Duren's work on the Ceremonial Law, published at Venice, 1548, and appended to it a poem, which we have already mentioned, stating that he was then eighty years of age (*vide supra*, p. 2). This, as far as we know, is the last effort of the great teacher of cardinals and bishops of the Romish Church, and of the originators and leaders of the reformation, and who may justly be regarded as the reviver of Hebrew learning among Christians at the commencement of the sixteenth century, and as one of the most distinguished promoters of Biblical literature. He died, as he prayed to die, at Venice, aged eighty-one. The following simple epitaph indicated, to those who looked at the tomb-stones of the Jewish cemetery, the grave in which were deposited the remains of Elias Levita :—

הלא אבן מקיר תזעק
ותהמה לכל עובר
עלי זאת הקבורה
עלי רבן אשר נלקח
ועלה בשמים
אל—יה י׳ בסערה
הלא הוא זה אשר האיר
בדקדוק אפלתו
ושם אותו לאורה
שנת ש״ט שבט עלה
בסופו ונפשו בצרור החיים צרורה.

The stone cries from the wall,
And mourns before every passer by
Over this grave—
Over our Rabbi who has departed,
And ascended into heaven.
Elias is gone to the Lord in a whirlwind!
He who has shed light
On the darkness of grammar,
And turned it into light.
He ascended Shebat towards the end,
In the year 309 [=1549],
And his soul is bound up in the bundle of life.

INFORMATION FOR THE READER.[1]

THIS is for the information of every reader of this book. The celebrated printer, M. Daniel Bomberg, a Christian,[2] having resolved to issue the 24 sacred books, both in large and small sizes, is now printing them with the divisions, which are called in their language chapters, according to the order of the Christian books. And as there is a great advantage in it, which I have shown long ago in the introduction to the *Book Bachur*,[3] and as he who made the divisions of chapters also divided the books of Samuel, Kings, and Chronicles, respectively, into two books, I too was obliged to follow this method. You are, therefore, to observe, that wherever you will find the word Samuel with the letter *Beth* above it,[4] *e.g.* שמואל֞, it means 2 *Samuel*, which begins with, "And it come to pass after the death of Saul," &c. The word Kings, too, with *Beth* above it,[4] *e.g.* מלכים֞, means 2 *Kings*, and begins with, "Then Moab rebelled," &c.; and also the word Chronicles, or its initials ד״ה, with *Beth* above it,[4] *e.g.* ד״ה֞, means 2 *Chronicles*, and begins with, "And Solomon, the son of David, was strengthened," &c.

I must moreover inform you, that wherever I have propounded something new[5] in this book, or any important rule in which I have

---

[1] The words אזהרה למעיין, *Information for the Reader*, are omitted in the Sulzbach edition.

[2] The word הנוצרי, *a Christian*, is omitted in the Sulzbach edition.

[3] For a description of the Book Bachur, see above, page 16, &c.

[4] The word למעלה, *above it*, is omitted in all the three instances in the Sulzbach edition.

[5] The Sulzbach edition erroneously has the word דבר, *string*, after שאחדש, *I propound new*, as well as before אזה, *something*.

שפתו בגליון מראה באצבע לאמור כזה ראה
וחדש יחדש לך דבר וזה לך האות ובכן
אתחיל בשם ה׳ צבאות:

not been anticipated by any one,
you will find the form of a hand
in the margin against the remark in
question, pointing with its finger
☞ and saying, as it were, 'see, something new is here told you, and
this is to indicate it to you!' Let me now begin the Preface, in the
name of the Lord of Hosts.

הקדמה.

PREFACE.

אמר אליהו ב״ר אשר הלוי האשכנזי,
הנה אנכי טרם אחל לדבר, וביאור דרכי
המסורת לחבר, אודיע נא אתכם את אשר אני
עושה לספרי זה, ראשונה אחלק עקר הספר
הזה לשני חלקים כדמות⁶ שני לוחות אבנים,
וכתבתי על הלוחות הראשונים, את עשרת
הדברים, ובכל דבור ודבור אתן כללים
מועילים, בעניני החסרים והמלאים:⁷ והלחות
השניות, יהיו בעשרה מאמרים שניות, ובהם
אבאר כל הדברים, אשר הסכימו עליהם אנשי
זאת המלאכה, ר״ל בעלי המסורת לדבר בם,
כגון קריין וכתיבין, וכתיבין ולא חשיבין,
וקמצין ופתחין, ומקפין וזקפין וחטפין
ומוקדמין ומאוחרין, וחרומים לאלה רבים,
ואח״כ אעש ארון אחד ואפתח בו שער, ואשים
בו שברי לוחות, הן הם המלות אשר נהגו בהן
בעלי המסורה הקטנה כאשר יתבאר בהקדמתו,
וטרם הולדו נקרא שמו שער שברי לחות,
והוא יהיה החלק האחרון מן הספר, וסמנך
שברי לוחות מונחום באהרון.

Thus says Elias, son of Asher
the Levite, the German, behold,
before I begin to speak, and compose an explanation of the plans of
the Massorah, I must tell you what
I am going to do in this book. I
shall first divide the chief contents
of the book into two parts, after the
manner⁶ of the two tables of stone,
and write upon the first tables ten
commandments [*i.e.* chapters.] In
each one of these commandments I
shall give useful rules respecting
defectives and *plenes*.⁷ The second
tables will contain ten other injunctions [*i.e.* chapters.] In these
I shall explain all the matters wherein all those who have laboured in
this department are agreed; *i.e.,*
show what the Massorites say about
the Keri and *the Kethiv*, *the Kethivs,* which are disregarded, *the
Kametz, Patach, Makeph, Sakeph, Chateph, Transpositions,* &c., &c.
I shall then make an ark, open the door thereof, and put therein
the broken tables, which are the work wherewith the authors of the
Massorah-porva have occupied themselves, as I shall explain in the
Introduction thereunto: and before it is yet born its name shall be
called "the gate [*i.e.* the section] of the Broken Tables." This will
form the last part of this book, and the sign thereof is, "the broken
tables laid down in the ark."

---

⁶ The Sulzbach edition erroneously has כשמות, *according to the names of,* instead of
כדמות, *after the manner of.*

⁷ The Sulzbach edition incorrectly puts המלאים, *plene,* before החסרים, *defective.*

But since I have seen that it is not good for this book to be alone, I shall make for it a help-mate, in the form of an Introduction, of such things which have not hitherto been propounded. Therein shall I dispel questions, explain difficulties, and remove doubts which fall under this investigation, and which are to be found in the treatises of our Rabbins of blessed memory, the men of the Great Synagogue and of the Massorah. And the eyes of those who will see shall behold that which is upright, for they perceive the truth. Moreover, things and remarks occur in this book which will be difficult of understanding to the students thereof, unless they read first the introductions which I have prefixed, and which are three in number. The first is in poetry (שי־), the second in rhyme (בחרוזה), and the third in ordinary prose.

And if I had the power to exact an oath from an Israelite, I would make every one who is about to study this book swear that he will not peruse it till he has read these introductions. However, I beseech and pray you to take my advice about it, and those who will do it will derive the benefit. Now, I am persuaded that no man[8] will regret the time spent in perusing them, but that it will be a pleasant task to those who read them; for they will find therein things, both new and old, which they did not know and never heard before, not only connected with the Massorah, but with grammar, vowel points, &c., which are not mentioned in the works of ancient or modern writers. I will, also, relate ordinary conversations, the talk of the world, what has befallen me, and what I have seen, as well as my defence against many people who have risen against me, and abused me for teaching the law to disciples that are unworthy thereof.[9] All these things are desirable to make us wise, and are pleasant to the imagination. For, verily, my words are not false; whoso is on the Lord's side let him come to me.

והנה ראה ראיתי כי לא טוב היות ספר הזה לבדו, אעשה לו עזר כנגדו, בהקדמת דברים, עד הנה לא נאמרים, יבחם אישב שאלות, ואתריץ קושיות, ואתיר ספקות, אשר יפלו בדרוש הזה, הן בדברי רז״ל, ובדברי אנשי כנסת הגדולה, ובדברי בעל המכורת, ועיני רואים תחזנה משרים, כי דברי אמת ניכרים, מצורף לזה יבאו דברים וענינים בכפר הזה, שתכבד הבנתם על האנשים המעיינים בו, אם לא יקראו תחלה דברי ההקדמות אשר הקדמתי, והם שלשה, הראשונה בשיר, והשנית בחרוזה, והשל שית בהלצה.

ואלו הייתי כדאי להשביע איש מישראל, הייתי משביע את כל הבא ללמוד הספד הזה, שלא ילמדהו עד שיקרא ההקדמות האלה, אך מפיל אני תהנתי ובקשתי לפניהם על ככה, והעושים כן תבא עליהם ברכה, ומובטח אני כי לא איש[8] יתהרט ובן אדם ויתחם, באבוד זמן בקריאה זו, אך יגיע תענוג נמרץ לקוראיו, כאשר ימצאו בם דברים טבים וחדושים, אשר לפנים לא ידעום, ומאז ומקדם לא שמעום, ולא לבד בעניני המסרה, כי גם בדקדוק ובנקוד ושאר ענינים, שלא נזכרו בספרי הראשונים והאחרונים, ואפילו שיחת חולין ומילי דעלמא, ואת כל אשר קראני ואשר הזיתי ואספדה, וגם דברי התנצולתי, נגד אנשים רבים קמים עלי וחרפוני, על שלמדתי תורה לתלמידים, שאינם הגונים,[9] כל אלה דברים נחמדים להשכיל, והאוה לאזנים כי אמנם לא שקר מלי, מי לה' אלי.

---

[8] & [9] The word איש, *man*, as well as the passage beginning with וגם דברי מתנצולתי, *and also my defence*, and ending with הגונים, *worthy*, is wanting in the Sulzbach edition.

שירת משובחת פשוטה ומרובעת [10]

אֶתֵּן שֶׁבַח גַּם תִּפְאֶרֶת, לָאֵל תִּקֵּן רוּם בְּזֶרֶת;
לֹא לְהֶבֶל בָּרָא תֵבֵל, לָשֶׁבֶת הָיְתָה נִגְמֶרֶת;
יִסַּד אֶרֶץ עַל הַמַּיִם, פָּשַׁט אוֹתָהּ כְּאִגֶּרֶת;
הִבִּיט וַיַּתֵּר גּוֹיִם, לָקַח לוֹ אֻמָּה נִבְחֶרֶת;
וַיּוֹצִיאֵם מֵאֶרֶץ כּוּשׁ, מָהוֹן וּרְכוּשׁ נוּף נִנְעֶרֶת;
הֵנִיף בַּיָּם יָדוֹ עַל׳ יָם, צָרִים צָלְלוּ כְעוֹפֶרֶת;
לָמוֹ אֵשׁ דָּת נָתַן מִתַּת, צוּם לִהְיוֹתָהּ נִשְׁמֶרֶת;
וַיַּנְחִילָם אֶרֶץ חֶמְדָּה, וּרְחָבָה עַד יָם כִּנֶּרֶת;
יַחַד שָׁמְנוּ וַיִּבְעָטוּ, הָיוּ כְּפָרָה סוֹרֶרֶת;
אוֹן חָמְדוּ וְיַצְמְדוּ, אֶל הַבַּעַל וּלְעַשְׁתֹּרֶת;
שָׁמַע דְּהָאֵל וַיִּתְעַבַּר, וַיִּשְׁלַח בָּם הַמְּגֶרֶת;
כִּלָּם בְּדֶבֶר וּבַחֶרֶב, גַּם בְּרָעָב שֶׁל בַּצֹּרֶת;
נָטַשׁ הָעִיר סֵתֶר הֲדָרִיר, הָיְתָה הַצֹּאן צָאן נְפוֹצֶרֶת;
זָרָם מֵעֵבֶר לַנָּהָר, בְּיוֹם אֶל אֶרֶץ אַחֶרֶת;
יוֹרְדֵי שִׁנְעָר עָמְדוּ מִצְעָר, לִמְלֹא הָעֵת הַנִּגְזֶרֶת;
שִׁבְעִים שָׁנָה אֶבֶן שָׁמָּה, הָיְתָה הַתּוֹרָה נֶעְדֶּרֶת;
וּשְׁמוּרוֹתָם שָׁנוּ וּלְשׁוֹנָם, לָבְשׁוּ כַגּוֹיִם אַדֶּרֶת;
אָדָם הָיָה נוֹשֵׂא גְוִיָּה, אוֹ נָכְרִיָּה אוֹ מַמְזֶרֶת;
וּבְנֵיהֶם לֹא הִכִּירוּ רַק, לְשׁוֹן שֶׁאִמָּם דּוֹבֶרֶת;
וּבָעֵת הַקֵּץ רוּחַ כֹּרֶשׁ, מֶלֶךְ פָּרַס מִתְעוֹרֶרֶת;
אָמַר לָאֲסִירִים תֵּצֵאוּ, וּבְנוּ הָעִיר הַמְעֻטֶּרֶת;
עָלָה עֶזְרָא הוּא מַלְאָכִי, דּוֹמֶה אֶל מַלְאָךְ הַשָּׁרֵת;
כֹּהֵן וְרַב וְלַסּוֹפְרִים אָב, אֵם לְמִקְרָא וְלַמָּסֹרֶת;
עָשָׂה אָז בַּכֹּל כִּמְצוּלָה, שֶׁאֵין בָּהּ דָּגָה נִשְׁאֶרֶת;
שׂוּם שֵׂכֶל הֵבִין בַּמִּקְרָא, בִּכְתִיבָה זוֹ הַמְאֻשֶּׁרֶת;
קוֹצִים כֻּלָּהּ מִכָּל מִלָּה, הֶחְזִיר אֶל יוֹשְׁנָהּ הָעֲטֶרֶת;
אַחֲרָיו לַאֲלָפִים וּרְבָבוֹת, עָשׂוּ מִשְׁמָר אֶל מִשְׁמֶרֶת;
רוֹב כַּת אַנְשֵׁי זֶה הַמַּעֲשֶׂה, אָז בְּטַבֶּרְיָא מִתְגּוֹרֶרֶת;
יָדָם הָיְתָה בָרִאשׁוֹנָה, בַּחָכְמָה זוֹ הַמְפֹאֶרֶת;
גַּם הִמְצִיאוּ דָת הַנִּקּוּד, מֵהֶם הִיא לָנוּ נִמְסֶרֶת;
גַּם הַטְּעָמִים הָיוּ שָׁמַיִם, לִהְיוֹת בָּם תּוֹרָה נִפְתֶּרֶת;

---

[10] It will be seen that the commencing letters of the first fifteen lines, are the acrostic of אליהו הלוי אשכנזי, *Elijahu Ha-Levi, the German*. In Münster's edition (1539), this acrostic is entirely obliterated by the peculiar mode in which the editor arranged the lines.

INTRODUCTION I.

A SONG OF PRAISE, SIMPLE, AND OF FOUR FEET

I render praise and glory[10] to the Lord, who made the heaven with His span.
Not in vain did He create the world; for a habitation has He made it.
He founded the earth upon the waters; He unrolled it like a scroll.
He looked and rejected the Gentiles; He took to Himself His chosen people.
He brought them out of Egypt, which was spoiled of its treasure and wealth.
He stretched his mighty hand upon the sea, and the enemy sunk down like lead.
To His people He gave the fiery law as a gift; commanding them to observe it.
He caused them to inherit a goodly land; extending to the sea of Gennesareth.
But they grew fat and kicked; they became like a refractory heifer.
They lusted after vanity, and joined themselves to Baal and Ashtoreth.
The Lord heard it, and was angry, and sent a curse among them.
He destroyed them by pestilence, and by sword, and by famine.
He abandoned the city, destroyed the sheepfold, and scattered the sheep.
He drove them beyond the sea, as at this day; into a foreign land.
They abode in Shinar a little while, according to the time appointed.
Seventy years the temple laid waste; the law was forgotten.
The people changed their names and tongue; they dressed like the Gentiles.
The Jew married a Gentile wife, or a stranger, or a bastard;
And the children knew nothing, except the language which their mother spoke.
At the appointed time, the spirit of Cyrus, the king of Persia, was stirred up.
He said to the Captains, Go forth, and build the glorious city.
Ezra then went, who is the messenger, like a ministering angel;
The priest, the prince, and the father of scribes, the nursing mother of the Scripture and Massorah.
By his departure, Babylon remained like a pond, wherein no fish are left.
He applied wisdom to understand the Scripture, in its present superior characters.
He cut off thorns from every word; he restored the crown to its pristine splendour.
After him, thousands and myriads added fence unto fence.
Most of these indefatigable workers sojourned then in Tiberias;
They were the first in this wonderful science;
They invented the system of punctuation, and transmitted it to us.
They, too, added the accents, whereby the law might be explained;

כי לולי טעמי הפסוק, הבנתו לא נכרת;
כי הם ידעו באור המקרא, מכל גולה הנשארת;
לכן פירוש נגד טעמו, נחשב כסיג או כנעורת;
הורו תיבות איך נכתבות, המלאה או המחוסרת;
גם אם מלה טעמה מעלה, או מקצה בחוברת;
לכללים עשו סימנים, להיות על לב למזכרת;
אך שמו אותותם אותות, חידות עם לשון ברברת;
הרבים לא יחכמו בה, אין מבין מה היא אומרת;
עד כי בא יום אמרו אלי, חברת רעי המהודרת;
נא מה לך פה אליהו, קום ועשה לך שם הפארת;
ולמסרה תאיר אורה, ופתח נא בה המסגרת;
ידענו בך כי זאת עמך, בהיד שכלך היא גוברת;
אז אמרתי שמעי נפשי, למה זה את מתנכרת;
קומי ועשי עת לה׳׳י, פן תהיה תורה מופרת;
מקום הניחו לך אבות, לחיותך בו מתנגדרת;
אז אמרה לי נפשי האח, בזה אנכי בוחרת;
ובכן קמתי לא דוממתי, גם קדמו עיני אשמורת;
עד אוציא לאור תעלומה, היתה עד הנה נסתרת;
אל כל אדם אמתיק סודם, אפקח כל עין עורת;
קצור מלים המועילים, בשני לוחות אהיה תורת;
אתן הלוחות בפומבי, ודלא כמלתא נטמרת;
לעד בנייר יחצבון, עם עט ברזל ובעופרת;
הלוקח לא יחשב, גנב נמצא במחתרת;
לכן אל כל כשופר קול, אריס על גבי רום קרת;
הזריז יקדים למצוה, כי מצוה מצוה גוררת;
לסחורה זאת זרוז יאות, פן תהיה כלה נמכרת;
כי טוב סחרה מכל מסחר, מה לך אל דר או סוחרת;
הא לך אורח למסרה, כי לתורה היא עקרת;
על כן אקרא שם הספר, זה מסורת המסורת;
השיר נשלם אל אל עולם, אתן שבח גם תפארת;

But for the accents, the sense could not be discerned.
They knew the interpretation of the Scriptures better than all the rest of the captivity ;
Therefore, an interpretation contrary to the accents must be regarded as dross or as chaff.
They taught how the words should be written, whether plene or defective ;
Whether a word is to be connected with the preceding, or the following sentence.
They made signs, to serve as rules to aid the memory.
The signs, however, are problems ; riddles taken from foreign languages ;
Many could not understand them ; and did not know what they mean ;
Till the day when it was said to me, by my estimable friends,
"Now, what dost thou here, Elias ? Arise, and make thyself a great name.
Throw light on the Massorah ; and open that which is locked up therein :
We know that this is within thy power ; that thou possessest the mastery over it."
Then said I to myself, 'Hearken, my soul ; Why art thou disquieted?
Arise, it is time to work for the Lord, lest the law become void :
Thy fathers have left a place wherein thou mayest fortify thyself.'
My soul then responded, 'Ah ! This I gladly choose.'
I therefore bestirred myself, and did not rest ; yea, my eyes prevented the night watches,
Till I brought to light the hidden things, which have hitherto been concealed.
Their counsel will be sweet to every man, and the eyes of the blind will be opened.
An abridgment of useful words I will propound, on two tables ;
I will put these tables openly, and not as secret words.
For a witness, they shall be printed on paper with an iron and leaden pen.
The buyer shall not be accountable, if a thief is found breaking in.
Therefore, to all, as with a trumpet, I raise my voice upon the heights of the city.
Let the quick hasten to the good work ; for one good work leads to another.
For such merchandise, quickness is becoming, lest it be all sold ;
As its merchandise is better than all traffic. What are precious stones to thee ?
Behold here an explanation of the Massorah, which is the basis of the law.
Therefore, I call the name of this book, *Massoreth Ha-Massoreth*.
The song is finished, to the God of the universe, I give praise and glory.

INTRODUCTION II.

THE RYTHMICAL INTRODUCTION, ACCORDING TO GERMAN RHYME.

וזאת ההקדמה החרוזית.
על דרך חרוזה אשכנזית:

נאם אליהו הלוי, המוציא והמביא, עצות
מרחוק, לשום לדקדוק חוק, ודרך לחוי
קולות, קטנות עם גדולות, במיעוט דברים,
בחבור ספרים, פרצו עליהם פרץ, ארבעה הם
קטני ארץ, כלם בחכמת הלשון, והספר
הראשון, אשר בהם חברתי, הוא אשר בארתי,
מהלך שבילי הדרך, הועלתו לכל
מודעי, ואחריו ספר הבחור, משיב
מדקדקים אחוד,[11] ואחריו ספר ההרכבה
כל מלה זרה בו נכתבה, ואחריו פרק שירה
עם שאר פרקים עד גמירה, והילדים אלה
ארבעתם, לחכמתם ולדעתם, כמה פעמים
נחקקים, וללשון הגוים מועתקים, ובהם
עמלים, מולים וערלים, ומרחוק נשמע קולם,
וכבודם מלא עולם, וכשמן הטוב נותנים ריח,
ובזה את עצמי אשבח, והיושר אדבר, כי לא
היה מחבר, שזכה אלהים אותו, שראה לפני
מותו, ספריו נזכרים ונעשים, וכמה פעמים
נדפסים, כמו שזכה אותי, בעוד בחיים היותי,
ועוד ידי נטויה, לחנדיל תושיה, ולזכות את
הרבים, ועתה אותי מסבים, תלמידי החגונים,
וכל יודעי לפנים, ומבקשים את פני, לאמר
למען י"י, ולכבוד קדושת התורה, תבאר לנו
המסרה, כי ידענו כי זאת עמך, כי שמענו
ממך, כי ידך גוברת, בכל דברי המסורת, מכל
אנשי דורינו, ומאשר שמענו באזנינו.

Thus saith Elias Levita, who gathered together counsels afar off from innumerable works to compile Treatises on grammar in as few words as possible, and to make a path to the various voices, both small and great. These are my four small productions, all treating on the science of our language. The first volume which I composed is my explanation of the *Journey on the Path of Knowledge;* its utility is known to all. The second is the *Book Bachur*, which animadverts on Grammarians.[11] The third is the *Book on Compounds*, in which all irregular words are explained. The fourth is a *Poetical Section*, together with other Sections appended thereunto. These four productions of mine, owing to their wisdom and knowledge, have been published several times, translated into the languages of the Christians, and are studied both by Jew and Gentile, as their fame has travelled far and their excellence is known all over the world. They send forth an odour like precious ointment, on which account I congratulate myself. Now I speak the truth when I say, that there has been no author, whose works God has permitted him in his lifetime to see so much referred to and studied, and so many times reprinted, as he has permitted me during my lifetime. My hand is still ready to give more help, and to benefit the public. My worthy disciples are around me now, as well as all my old friends; they earnestly entreat me, saying, for God's sake, and for the glory of Holy Writ, explain to us the Massorah; for we know that it is in thy power, as we have heard that thy hand is strong in all Massoretic matters, above all our contemporaries, as well as above all of whom we have heard.

---

[11] The words ואחריו ספר הבחור משיב מדקדקים אחור, *the second is the Book Bachur, which animadverts on Grammarians*, without which Levita's statement is unintelligible, are omitted in the Sulzbach edition.

When I heard their flattering words, I inclined my ear to them and answered, I accede to your entreaty. And indeed their wish fully harmonised with my intention. Now I swear, by the Lord, that this very thing was in my mind before, when I was still in Rome, where I temporarily resided, and composed the above-named works, only that I had not sufficient time, as the evil days came and the city was captured,[12] and I, insignificant one, was compelled by fate to relinquish the contemplated Treatise. Now, after the lapse of years, God having permitted me to settle in this beautiful place, the celebrated Venice, the great city, I comply with their wish, and will perform a work in Israel that whosoever sees it may tell its wonders. I have, therefore, compiled this Treatise on all Massoretic matters, connected with both the Massora *magna* and *parva*, as it is now twenty years that I have been in the way to find out its value, to unfold its import and its laconic style, which is often as obscure as the words of a sealed book.

How I laboured therein, neither resting nor being satisfied, and searched in the correct and excellent books, giving my mind hereunto! Now I swear, by truth and justice, and may God give me riches, that more than once or twice I performed a day or two day's journey to a place, which I either knew myself or of which I had been informed, that there is to be found therein a reliable index of the Massorah. When I examined it, and found it correct, I selected from it the choice and correct articles, as roses from among thorns. Indeed, most of the correct Codices I found to be Spanish, and it is upon these that I relied, and it is their method that I followed. Still, my soul was not as yet satisfied, until I found the *Book Ochla Ve-Ochla*.[13] I got much out of it, and adopted its rules; and, though

---

[12] The capture and sacking of Padua took place in 1509, as described above, *vide supra*, p. 14.

[13] This long lost and most valuable Massoretic work has now been published, with

it is a book of small dimensions, there is nothing like it in the department of the Massorah. It treats upon important matters, and there is no other book which so thoroughly treats on the Massoretic rules, excepting the scattered glosses around the margin in the Codices, which, however, contain numberless errors. For the Scribes have perverted them, as they did not care for the Massorah, but only thought to ornament their writing, and to make even lines so as not to alter the appearance, in order that all the pages should be alike. Moreover, they ornamented them with illuminations of divers kinds of buds, flowers, &c. Hence they were obliged sometimes to narrow and sometimes to widen the margins round the illustrations with words already stated, although they were superfluous and out of place, whilst the Massoretic signs were entirely omitted in their proper place because the space did not suffice ; and hence they had to break off in the middle of a sentence,[14] thus leaving the whole edifice incomplete and greatly defective.[15]

As to the Massorah, in the twenty-four sacred books printed here, I have not seen anything like it, among all the ancient books, for arrangement and correctness, for beauty and excellence, and for good order. They were edited by one of the learned, whose name was formerly Jacob (let his soul be bound up in a bag with holes).[16] But although his edition is exceedingly beautiful, he committed many

---

learned annotations, by Frensdorff, Hanover, 1844. The reader will find all Levita's references to the *Massorah*, contained in the *Massoreth Ha-Massoreth*, compared with the statements in the *Ochla Ve-Ochla*.

[14] The above description of the condition of the Massorah, and of the manner in which it has been treated by the copyists, is almost literally the same as that given by Jacob b. Chajim, the first editor of the Massorah. Comp. Jacob b. Chajim's *Introduction to the Rabbinic Bible*, p. 12 in the Hebrew, and 35 in the English translation, ed. Ginsburg, Longmans, 1865.

[15] The words וחסורי מחסרים are omitted in the Sulzbach edition.

[16] For this celebrated Massorite, and the Bible here alluded to, see above, p. 38. From Levita's vituperation, it is evident that Jacob b. Chajim was now dead, inasmuch as the phrase, "let his soul be bound up in a bag of holes," is a spiteful and unworthy perversion of the beautiful, charitable, and reverential prayer, which the Jews use when speaking of or writing about any one of their brethren who has departed this life, in allusion to 1 Sam. xxv. 29, because he had embraced Christianity.

mistakes, and bore false testimony in many places. This, however, is not to be wondered at, for the work was new, and every beginning is difficult. With great diligence, therefore, with little sloth, and with immense toil, I laboured to separate that which is clear from that which is obscure,—brought the Massoretic materials into order, and put a proper space between each section and every article. You may believe that I have laboured and found what none else has discovered, and discharged my duty in such things in which nobody has preceded me, knowing that the words of the Massorah are completely hidden from our contemporaries. Indeed very few understand the language thereof, which is to them as a dream without an interpretation, and from which they have no advantage; they neither know nor understand, for they dwell in darkness. Yet the Massorah is the fence of the law, and from it are deduced many essential *Halachoth*, reasons and explanations, literal and homiletical meanings, whilst from the defective and plene many laws are deduced; *ex. gr.*, from רב [Exod. xxiii. 2] which is defective;[17] from the first מזזת [Deut. vi. 9][18] which wants the second *Vav*, and many other similar instances from which laws are deduced. It is for this reason that I purpose to explain its import, laws, and rules in this little volume in brevity, and without tediousness, yet in words of great might; propound new things recently brought to light which did not exist before, and they shall be as luminaries in the firmament of the Massorah, so that the wise will understand and prepare their hearts to be wise in the Scriptures; and the name thereof shall be known in

---

[17] Hence it is taken for רב, *chief*, and it is deduced that no one is to speak against its chief, i.e., the King or High Priest, comp. *Sanhedrin* 18, *b.*, and Rashi on Exod. xxiii. 2.

[18] מזוזה, with the Jews, denotes the piece of parchment whereon are written the passages in Deut. vi. 4–9, xi. 13–21, which they regard as containing the injunction to inscribe on the door-posts the words of the Law. The slip of vellum thus written upon is enclosed in a cylindrical tube of lead, cane, or wood, and to the present day is nailed to the right door-post of every door. For a detached description of this institution, we must refer to Kitto's *Cyclopædia of Biblical Literature*, new ed., *s. v.*, *Mezuzah*; and for the law deduced from the word מזוזה, being written definitely in Deut. vi. 9, to which Levita alludes, we must refer to Jacob b. Chajim's *Introduction to the Rabbinic Bible*, p. 9 Hebrew, and p. 21 English translation, ed. Ginsburg.

the mouth of all students, both Jews and Christians,[19] who delight in our Law and profit therefrom.

Now I swear, by my Creator, that a certain Christian encouraged it, and brought me thus far. He was my pupil ten years uninterruptedly,[20] I resided at his house and instructed him, for which there was a great outcry against me, and it was not considered right of me. And several of the Rabbins would not countenance me, and pronounced woe to my soul because I taught the law to a Christian,[21] owing to the interpretation assigned to the words, "And as for my judgments they [i. e. the Gentiles] are not to know them; praise the Lord for it." [Ps. cxlvii. 20). Now my tardiness will not prevent me from making a defence. I shall, therefore, state all that took place. In the year 269 [= 1509], violence rose up into a rod of wickedness, and the arrow was desperate without any fault; for it came to pass, when I was in Padua, that the celebrated city was captured, and sacked, and devastated; the enemies then destroyed my dwelling, together with that of other Jews, and all that I had became a prey, and was like the leaving when the dung is cleared away. Then it fell into my lines to be a roamer at the head of the exiles. I left my place and went to Rome, where resided a very distinguished nobleman, a prince of great dignity, and wise as Solomon, and his name was Cardinal Egidio. When I heard his fame, I paid him a visit.

When he saw me, he asked me about my affairs. I said, Know, my lord, that I am the German grammarian, who possess the sundry secrets connected with the grammar and Scripture, for I have always been

כל התלמידים, גוים[19] כיהודים, אשר לתורותנו חמדו, וממני למדו.

והנני נשבע ביוצרי, כי גוי אחד נוצרי, לוח העירני, ועד הלום הביאני, אשר היה תלמידי, וכעשר שנים תמידי, בביתו עמדתי, [20]ועמו למדתי, ועל זה גדלה עלי הצעקה, ולא נחשב לי לצדקה, וקצת הרבנים, אינם מסבירים לי פנים, ואומרים לנפשי אוי, על שלמדתי תורה לגוי,[21] משום הדרשה הבנויה, על ומשפטום בל ידעום הללויה, והנה לא ישיאני עצלתי, לבלתי עשות התנצלותי, ואגיד כל החויה, ומעשה שהיה כך היה, בשנת מאתים וששים ותשע, החמם קם למטה רשע, ואנוש הצי בלי פשע, ויהי בהיותי, אני בעיר פדואה רבתי, כאשר היא נלכדה, ונשללה ונשדדה, ואויבים את נוי השמו, ככל המון היהודים אשר תמו, והיה כל אשר לי לשלל, כאשר יבער הגלל, ואז נפלו לי חבלים, לגלות בראש גולים, ועזבתי את מקומי, ובאתי עד רומי, ושם שר גדול מאד, חשמן נשא הוד, חכם כידידיה, שמו קארדינאל אינדייה, וכשמעי מהללו, בקרתיו בהיכלו.

וכאשר ראני, על אודותי שאלני, ואמרתי דע אדוני, כי אנכי הפלוני, המדקדק האשכנזי, רזי לי רזי, בדקדוק ובפסוק, כי כל ימי עסוק,

---

[19] The Sulzbach edition substitutes כנכרים, strangers, for גוים, Christians.

[20] The apparent contradiction between the above statements, that he lived in Egidio's house about *ten* years, and the remark in the Introduction to the *Tishbi*, that he had learned from Cardinal Egidio, with whom he was *thirteen* years (הקרדינאל אשר עמדתי עמו שלש עשרה שנה קבלתי כל אלה), is to be accounted for thus: in the *Massoreth Ha-Massoreth*, Levita gives the *round* number, i. e., *about* ten (וכעשר) years; Graetz (*Geschichte der Juden*, ix. 224,) explains it, that as Cardinal Egidio was about several years from Rome (comp. Reuchlin's Letters in Friedländer's *Beiträge zur Reformations Geschichte*, pp. 89, 99), Levita was ten years in his house at Rome, and three years with him away from the Eternal city.

[21] The words ואמרים לנפשי אוי על שלמדתי תורה לגוי, *and they say, Woe to my soul, because I taught a Christian the Law*, are omitted in the Sulzbach edition.

occupied with this work, therefore is no man to be found who is more conversant therewith than I am; as a poet said, that he was never conquered except by a man of one idea. Moreover, I have learned wisdom from my disciples, and they aided me in this knowledge; as a certain Talmudist said, I have learned much from my teachers, more from my fellow students, and most from my learned disciples.[22]

When the prince heard my statement, he came to me and kissed me with the kisses of his mouth, saying, Art thou, my lord, Elias, whose fame has travelled over all countries, and whose books are to be found in every corner?[23] Blessed be the God of the Universe, who brought thee hither, and bade thee come to meet me. Now abide with me and be my teacher, and I shall be to thee as a father, and shall support thee and thy house, and give thee thy corn, thy wine, and thy olives, and fill thy purse, and bear all thy wants. Thus we took sweet counsel together, iron sharpening iron. I imparted my spirit to him, and learned from him excellent and valuable things, which are in accordance with truth. I followed the advice of the sage, who says, "Learn truth, from whomsoever it is propounded."

In conclusion, I fully acknowledge it, as one confesses before a solemn tribunal, and shall not withdraw it, that I have been a teacher to Christians;[24] yea, I have assuredly been; but nevertheless, know that I am a Hebrew, praise the Lord, and revere the Lord, who made heaven and earth; I have not sinned, and am innocent and guiltless. For

---

[22] The above quoted saying is recorded in the Talmud (*Taanith 7 a*), as having been uttered by R. Chanina, and is literally as follows : הרבה למדתי מרבותי ומחברי יותר ומתלמידי יותר מכלן, *much have I learned from my teachers, more from my associates, but most from my disciples*. Levita varied it a little to adapt it to his rhyme. In the *Midrash Jalkut* on Ecclesiastes v. 7, where the same saying is quoted, it is ascribed to R. Berachja. Comp. sect. 973, vol. ii., p. 185 *a*, ed. Frankfort on the Maine, 1687.

[23] This remark is certainly proleptical, since, at the time when Levita had his first interview with Cardinal Egidio, (*circa* 1510), he had not as yet published any books of his own, and even his small maiden production, which appeared in 1508, was published surreptitiously, *vide supra*, pp. 13, 80, &c.

[24] In the Sulzbach edition, נכרים, *foreigners*, is substituted for גוים, *Christians*.

o

the sages only prohibit[25] the communication to a Gentile of the import of the Law,[26] but do not forbid teaching. Their interdict only refers to subjects which contain esoteric doctrines, as the Creation, the Vision of Ezekiel, and the Book Jetzira,[27] which must only be disclosed to the pious, to men of wisdom and intelligence who are of the children of Israel. Thus, also, the passage,

כי חכמים אינם אוסרין,[25] רק שדברי תורה לגוי אין מוסרין, [26] ולא אמרו אין מלמדין, רק עקרי דבריהם עומדין, על דברין ששייך בהן מסידה, כגון [27]מעשה בראשית ומעשה מרכבה וספר יצירה, שאין מגלין אלא לצנועים, אנשים חכמים וידועים, אשר מבני ישראל המה, וכן כצדור אבן במרגמה, אשר על תלמיד שאינו הגון דדשוהו, ולזורק אבן למרקוליס[28] דמוחו, ואמרו כל הלומד תורה לתלמיד

"Like a bag of gems in a heap of stones" [Prov. xxvi. 8], which they interpret of an unworthy disciple, whom they liken to one who cast stones at the statue of Mercurius,[28] saying, Whoso teaches the law to an unworthy disciple shall descend

[25] The Sulzbach edition has substituted שאמרו במה, *in what they say*, for רק ש, *but what*, in consequence of the omission presently to be noticed.

[26] From ולא אמרו, *but they did not say*, to כל הלומד, *whoso teaches*, is omitted in the Sulzbach edition, and the editor substituted, from his own cogitations, the following: אלא בזמנם, שהגוים ההמה בבורא אינם מאמינים, אבל בזמנו זה, לא יעשה כזה, כי אין להם דין גוים הנזכרים בגמרא, וזה פשוט בפוסקים ובסברא, ומה ש—, *it only refers to their time when the Heathen did not believe in the Creator, but in our time, this is not applicable, since they are not like the Gentiles mentioned in the Talmud, as is evident both from the later legislators, and common sense, and what*—. The omission of the lengthy paragraph from the text, as well as the insertion of the concocted passage in question, which was dictated by the censorship of the press, has given rise to the alteration mentioned in the preceding note.

[27] *The work of the Hexahemeron* is technically called, in the Jewish literature, מעשה בראשית, because the first book of Moses, or more especially the history of the cosmogony, begins with the word בראשית, (comp. *Mishna Taanith* iv. 2, *Megilla* iii. 6; *Chullin* v. 5.) *The Vision of Ezekiel*, again, is denominated *the Chariot* (מרכבה), or *the Work of the Chariot* (מעשה מרכבה), in conformity to the former phrase, with which it is generally associated, and comprises Ezekiel, chapters i. and x., which treat on the Divine Throne, resting on wheels, and carried by sacred animals. The Jews, from time immemorial, have attached great mysteries to these sections of the Hebrew Scriptures, which discourse on the cosmogony and theosophy of the Old Testament, and have invested them with the halo of peculiar sanctity. Special directions are given to those who study these biblical questions. Thus the Mishna declares that "the work of the Hexahemeron (מעשה בראשית) must not be expounded in the presence of two persons, and the Chariot (מרכבה), not even in the presence of one person, unless he is a sage, and understands it already from his own cogitations" (*Chagiga* iii. 1). It is to this enactment that Levita evidently refers, since he uses almost the very words of the Mishna.

As to the *Book Jetzira* (ספר יצירה), or *the Book of Creation*, to which reference is made in the text, it purports to be a monologue of the patriarch Abraham, giving the contemplations which led the father of the Hebrews to abandon the worship of the stars, and to embrace the faith of the true God. Its design is to exhibit a system, whereby the universe may be viewed methodically, in connection with the truths given in the Bible, by means of the double value of the twenty-two letters of the Hebrew alphabet, as well as by the ten digits. For an analysis of this famous document, see Ginsburg, *the Kabbalah*, pp. 65–77, Longmans, 1865.

[28] Levita alludes to the ancient mode of worship offered to the heathen deity Hermes, which consisted in mere heaps of stone, called Ἑρμαῖοι λόφοι, ἑρμαῖα or ἕρμακες, being the symbol of Phallus, and thus giving rise to the ithyphalic arrow-form of Hermes. These heaps of stones were more especially collected on the road-sides, and each traveller paid his homage to the deity by throwing a stone to the heap as he passed by, or anointed the heap of stones in which a Hermes was frequently set up, or offered up the firstlings. Comp. Gen. xxviii. 10–22, xxxi. 45–48; *Sanhedrin* 61 a–64 a; *Midrash* on Prov. 26 a, כל מי שחולק כבוד לכסיל כזורק אבן למרקוליס, being the law referred to by Levita. Pauly, *Real Encyclopädie der classischen Alterthumswissenschaft, s. v.* MERCURIUS.

into the grave with sorrow, and his spirit and soul shall be destroyed; as it is written, "a fire not blown shall consume him" [Job xx. 26]; this only refers to an Israelite, but not to a Christian or Mahommedan.

Again,[29] when the Talmud says that the secrets of the law are not to be disclosed except to one who has the five qualifications, viz., advanced age, respectability, and all the rest as they are found in Isaiah," we have sufficient argument in this, that the sages have not enacted a decree that whosoever teaches a Gentile commits a sin. For even according to their words it is permitted to teach Gentiles the Seven Noahic Commandments.[30] Now this argues most powerfully for me. For how can they possibly know these, and fully comprehend the import of the seven precepts, unless they first know the Hebrew language?

שאינו הגון, ירד שאולה ביגון, ורוחו ונשמתו חפח, שנאמר תאכלהו אש לא נפח, לא דברו אלא בישראלי, ולא בארומי או ישמעאלי.

ועוד מה[29] שאמרו בגמרא, אין מוסרין סתרי תורה, אלא מי שיש בו חמישה ענינים, זקן ונשוא פנים, וכולי כדאיתא בישעיה, ודי לני בזו ראיה, שחכמים לא גזרו גזרה, שהתלמוד לנוי יהיה עברה, כי אפילו לפי דבריהם, מותר ללמוד עמהם, שבע מצות בני נח,[30] וזה לי ליפוי כח, כי איך אפשר זה להודיעם, ודין ז' מצות להשמיעם, אם לא ידעו בראשון, להבין את חלשון, וגם יש לי לחתלות, בהרבה אילנות גדולות, אנשים שהיו לפני. אשר קטנם עבה ממתני, ולזכור בשמם ראוי איניני, ולמדו גוים יותר ממני, מהם שהם חיים עדן, ומהם נשמחם בגן עדן, מהם לומדים רבנים, מהם זקנים ונשואי פנים, מהם חכמים ורופאים, מהם עשירים שעל שמריהם קופאים:[31]

Moreover, I should have to hang on many lofty trees men who preceded me, whose little finger is thicker than my thighs, whose name I am not worthy to mention, and who have taught Christians more than I. Of these, some are still living, some are resting in Paradise, some are teachers and Rabbins, some are elders and men of reputation, some are sages and physicians, and some are rich and settled on their lees.[31]

Now what am I that I should be caught in the snares of my sin, poor and low, burdened with sons and daughters, and having nothing in my possession. My field has been so inundated that there is in it neither wheat nor barley, but terror and storm,[32] and they have

ומה גם אני, הנלכד בחבלי עוני, איש שפל ומשופל, בבנים ובבנות מטופל, ומאומה אין בידי, ונסתחפה שדי, ואין בה חטה ושעורה, רק חתה וסערה,[32] נזרעו בה כלאים,

---

[29] The whole passage from ועוד מה שאמרו, *again what they say*, to הנני אמות, *behold am I to die*, consisting of fifty-four lines in the Hebrew, is entirely omitted in the Sulzbach edition.

[30] According to ancient tradition (comp. *Sanhedrin*, 59 a), God enjoined the following seven commandments on Noah, which both he and all his descendants, that is all mankind, were to observe. To abstain, i. from idolatry; ii. from blasphemy; iii. from murder; iv. from incest; v. from plunder; vi. from disobedience to the powers that be; and vii. from eating flesh cut off from a living beast (אבר מן החי). These seven commandments were imposed upon every heathen who wished to settle down among the Jews in Palestine. The foreigners who accepted and submitted to these conditions were denominated *Proselytes of the Gate* (גרי שער). Comp. also *Sanhedrin*, 56 a; Rashi on *Aboda Sara*, 51 a; Maimonides, *Jad Ha-Chezaka, Hilchoth Melachim* ix. 1.

[31] For the cause of this phalanx of Jewish teachers among Christians, as well as for the outcry of the orthodox Jews against Levita, see above, pp. 9, &c., 38, &c.

[32] The words חטה ישעורה, *wheat and barley*, and וסערה חתה, *terror and storm*, are designedly selected by Levita to form a paronomasia, and though they sound somewhat strangely in the translation, they are very beautiful in the original.

sown therein heterogeneous things. Twice has misfortune laid hold of me. In Padua it took away my money [1509], and then it set its evil eye upon my precious things, which it delivered over into the hands of the rebels. This happened in the year 287 (= 1527), when Rome was destined to destruction and desolation like a plain. Not a single farthing was then left to me; and it was a time of great distress, for there was no covering in the frost, no bread or fuel in the house, my wife was nursing her young ones and was about to be confined, while my daughters had reached puberty, and were ripe for marriage according to custom. Now what can a man do who has thus been overtaken by misfortune, and not to offend in such a burning snare? This ye ought to consider, that the law of nature teaches me that nothing is to be allowed to stand in the way of saving life.

Furthermore, I must inform you, that much good has resulted therefrom; for I solemnly declare that all the Christians whom I know, and whom I or others have instructed, are all of them good and upright men, and with all their power have acted kindly towards Israel; so that the very knowledge of our language among Christians has actually been to our advantage. Surely this speaks greatly for me, and must remove the reproach from me. Moreover, the import of my teaching, whether to Christian or Jew, is simply the grammar of the sacred language, as I only explain to them the rules thereof.[83] If, with this view, they read to me a verse in the Scriptures, why should I not explain it? What impropriety then have I committed?

Besides, if I were not to explain it, will they not learn it from my works which they possess, which everyone can understand, and in which they will find help and satisfaction? Even now I have, day

ויעקבני הזמן פעמים, בפדואה ממוני לקח, ועתה עיניו פקח, על כל מחמדי המובים, ונתנם ביד שובים, וזה היה בשנה פז״ר, כאשר על רומי נגזר, חורבן ובליה כפשוטה, לא נשארה בידי פרוטה, והיתה עת צרה, כי אין כסות בקרה, ובבתי אין לחם ואין עצים, והאם רובצת על האפרוחים או על הבצים, והבנות עומדות על פרקן, ראויות לבעל כדרכן, וחנה איש שזח עליו כלא מצא, מה יעשה ולא יחמא, במכשלח נקלה כזאת, וזה לכם האות, הדין הפשוט אותי לומר, שאין דבר בפני פקוח נפש עומד.

ועוד לכם אודיע, רב מוב אשר מזה הגיע, כי חנני נשבעתי, כי כל הגוים שידעתי, אשר למדתי אני ואחרים, כלם אנשים טובים וכשרים, ובכל מה שהיה ידם לאל, המיבו לישראל, הרי לשונינו שהיא לגוים ידועה, גם היא לנו לישועה, וזה פתחון פה אלי, להרחיק תלונה מעלי, ועוד כי עקר למודי, עם גוי כיהודי, אינו אלא בדקדוק לשון הקדש, וכללים אשר להם אחדש,[83] ואם בזה לפני נקרא, פסוק אחד במקרא, למה לא אבארהו, ומה עשיתי הלא דבר הוא.

ועוד אם לא אבארהו אנכי, הלא יבינהו בלאו הכי, מחבורי אשר תחת ידם, שיבינם

---

[83] That Levita did not exactly confine himself to teaching Christians Hebrew, but that he also aided them to fathom the mysteries of the Kabbalah, for which there was such a rage in Europe at that time, is evident, from the fact that he copied *the Book Jetzira*, and two other theosophic treatises, for Cardinal Egidio *(vide supra,* p. 15). These three documents, which were formerly in the possession of Almanzi, of Padua, are now in the British Museum, Add. 27,199. Comp. Dr. William Wright, in the *Journal of Sacred Literature*, July, 1866, p. 356, note.

after day, Christians coming to me asking instruction in Hebrew, and I respond to everyone who wants me. And why should I be condemned for it, and a reproach be fastened upon me? I speak this in defence of myself. Again, if I also have received, and opened my mouth, and tasted excellent instruction and learning [from Christians],—a honeycomb, and delightful words, which distilled from their mouths drop by drop,—and have eaten the inside and thrown away the shell, but have not eaten the insipid and the white of the egg, if I have tasted a little of this honey, am I to die for it?[84]

כל אדם, ובהם ימצאו מרגוע ופריום, ועדין מידי יום יום, אלי גוים ידרשון, וקרבת חלשון יבקשון, ונדרשתי לאשר שאלוני, ולמה בעבור זה תאשימוני, ותחזיקוני לנבזה, וכי בנפשי דברתי את חדבר הזה, וכן אם גם אני קבלתי, ופתחתי את פי ואכלתי, טוב. דעת וטעם, צוף דבש אמרי נעם, אשר נטף מפיחם מפות מפות, ואכלתי התוך וזרקתי הקליפות, ולא אכלתי התפל וריר חלמות, וטעמתי מעט דבש הזה הנני אמות.[84]

לכן קבלו נא חכמים מלי, וחדל תלונותכם מעלי, כי עיניכם הרואות, כי בתום לבבי עשיתי זאת, וחלילה לי להתיר האסור, והדבר הזה ללב מסור, ורחמנא לבא בעי, והנה כדקאי קאי:

Receive, therefore, ye sages, my apology, and let your complaint cease, for your eyes behold that I have done it in the integrity of my heart, not intending to convert wrong into right. I had a clear conscience in this matter, as is known to the Merciful One who searches the heart. Behold, the matter must remain as it stands.

[84] Levita refers to the instruction in the Greek language, which he received from Cardinal Egidio *(vide supra*, p. 71, &c.), and to his knowledge of various departments of secular literature, which he acquired with the aid of his Christian pupils.

INTRODUCTION III.

I SHALL NOW TURN MY FACE TO THE THIRD INTRODUCTION.

After those truthful words, let me discourse more largely on our subject in general. But, first of all, I must explain what is meant by מסרת, and what is its etymology. Indeed this word does not occur more than twice in the whole Scriptures, viz., למסר [Numb. xxxi. 5], and ימסרו [ibid. xxxi. 6], and Kimchi explains it to mean *a gift made with the whole heart*, and put into the possession of another. Thus, also, the Targum renders ויתנהו, *and he gave him up* [Deut. ii. 33], by ומסריה (see the root מסר.)

It is, however, necessary to remark that the word נתן is never rendered by מסר, unless it is construed with the word ביד, *into the hand*, ex. gr. ויתנהו יהוה אלהנו בידינו or אתן בידך [Exod. xxiii. 31; 2 Sam. v. 19; Jerem. xx. 4, 5], &c., &c.[85] We thus obtain the rule that the word מסר denotes *to give*, or *entrust, something into the hands of another person*, that he might retain it in his possession according to his pleasure, as if it were his own. The same is the case with the doctrines and Hagadah; if one teaches or propounds to another any mysteries, or anything which he did not know before, it is described by the word מסר. Thus it is said in the Mishna, *Moses received the Law from Sinai* (ומסרה), *and delivered it to Joshua, &c.* [Mishna, Aboth, i. 1]; and this is the meaning of the word מסר in question; since it was transmitted to sages, from mouth to mouth, till

ועתה פני אשית,
אל ההקדמה השלישית:

אחר הדברים והאמת האלה ארחיב הדבור בהלצה, ללמד על הכלל כלו יצא, וקודם כל אבאר מהו ענין מסורת, ומאיזה לשון הוא, ואמת כי הלשון הזה לא נמצא בכל המקרא רק בפרשת מטות שתי פעמים וַיַּמָסְרוּ, לִמְסֹר. ופרש בו חרד״ק שהוא ענין נתינה בכל לב והרתשומה ברשות אחר וכו', עד ותרגום ויתנהו ח' אלהינו ומסריה וכו' עיין בשורש מסר:

ואומר אני כי לשון נתינה אינו מתורגם בלשון מסירה רק כשהוא סמוך אצל לשון ביד, כמו ויתננהו ה״ אלהנו בידינו, אתן בידך ודומיהם[85] והכלל כ׳ לשון מסירה נופל על דבר שיתן או יפקיד אדם ביד אחר, שיחזיקנו ברשותו, כרצונו כאלו הוא שלו: וכן בענין הלמוד והההגדה שילמד אדם או יגיד לחבורו איזה סוד או ענין שקודם זה לא ידעהו, נופל בו לשון מסירה, כמו שאמרו במשנה משה קבל תורה מסיני ומסרה ליהושע וכו'; וכן ענין המסורת הזאת לפי שנמסרה

---

[85] That נתן, followed by ביד, is not always rendered in the Chaldee by מסר, is evident from Is. xxii. 21. Indeed Levita's whole stricture on Kimchi's explanation is incorrect, inasmuch as in the passage adduced by Kimchi, namely, Deut. ii. 33, ויתנהו is not followed by ביד, but by לפנינו, and yet the Chaldee paraphrases translate it ומסרה and ומסר, and there is no other instance in the whole Hebrew Scriptures, where ויתנהו,—Kal future, third person singular masculine, suffix third person singular masculine, with Vav conversive, of which the subject is יהוה אלהינו,—is followed by ביד. The only instance which *approaches* the one in question, is the phrase ויתנהו יהוה אלהיו ביד, 2 Chron. xxviii. 5, where indeed the Targum translates it ומסריה; but here it is אלהיו, with suffix third person singular masculine, and not אלהינו, suffix first person plural. Besides, the Chaldee paraphrase of Chronicles was not known till the middle of the seventeenth century, and was published for the first time at Augsburg, 1680-3, more than a hundred and thirty years after the death of Elias Levita.

the time of Ezra and his associates, and by them again to the sages of Tiberias, who wrote it down, and called it *Massorah*.

Now, since in this book I impart some rules to decipher the sage remarks, couched in the enigmatical expressions which occur in both the major and minor Massorah, therefore I deemed it proper to call this book *Massoreth Ha-Massoreth*, as this name is suitable for the book, and the book suitable for the name. I shall now proceed to explain the nature, quality, and object of the Massorah; who compiled it, whether one or many; who invented the vowel-points and accents, and when they were attached to the letters; and shall state the opinion of both the ancients and moderns, as well as give my own, upon this subject. I shall then point out to you, according to the good hand of the Lord upon me, the method which the Massorites adopted, and the work which they have done; what their chief aim was; what they wished, and what they did not wish, to say.

לחכמים איש מפי איש עד עזרא וסיעתו, ומהם להכמי טבריא אשר כתבוה וקראו לח מסרה:

ונם אני בזה הספר אמסור כללים להבין אמרי בינה, בדברים הסתומים במסרה גדולה וקטנה, לכן ראיתי לקרא לו ספר מסורת המסורת, ושם זה נאה לו, והוא נאה לשמו: ועתה אבאר כמותה ואיכותה והועלתה, ומי שחבר אותה יחיד או רבים, ומי שהמציא חנקודות והטעמים, ומתי הושמו כם האותיות, ואכתוב דעת הראשונים והאחרונים, ואחוה דעי אף אני, ואחרי כן אורה ארכם כיד ה' הטובה עלי, את חדרך אשר חלכו בעלי המסורת, ואת המעשה אשר עשו. ומה היתח עקר כונתם, ועל מה דברו, וצל מה לא הפקידו לדבר:

ואתחיל ואומר, הנה דעת דוב האנשים שעזרא הסופר וסיעתו, שהם אנשי כנסת הגדולה, עשו המסורת והנקוד והטעמים על כל המקרא, ומביאים ראיה ש־דרשו רז"ל בנדרים ויקראו בספר בתורת אלהים (נחמיה ח') זה מקרא, מפרש זה תרגום, ושום שכל אלו הפסקים, ויבינו במקרא זה פיסוק טעמים, ואמרי ליה אלו מסורת עכ״ל[86] והנה לפי פשוטו של מקרא אין הפסוק

In the first place, let me remark, that, according to the opinion of most men, Ezra the Scribe, and his associates, who were the men of the Great Synagogue, made the Massorah, the vowel-points, and the accents through all the Scriptures. In support of this, they insist that the explanation (in *Nedarim* [37 b,]) which our Rabbins of blessed memory give of Nehem. viii. 8, viz., "And they read in the book, in the Law of God," means *the original text;* "explaining it," means *the Chaldee paraphrase;* "and gave the same," means *the division of the verses;* "and caused them to understand the Scripture," means *the dividing accents;* or, according to others, it signifies *the Massorah*. Thus far are their words.[36] Now, according to the natural meaning of

---

[86] The passage quoted by Levita is from the *Babylonian Talmud*, *Nedarim* 37 b, *Megilla* 3 a. It also occurs with the following variations in the *Jerusalem Talmud*, רבי זעורה בשם רב חננאל ויקראו בספר תורת ה' זה המקרא מפורש זה תרגום ושום שכל אילו הטעמים ויבינו במקרא זה המסורת, יש אומרים אילו ההכריעים, ויש אומרים אילו ראשי הפסוקים: פרק ד' הלכה א'. R. Seзrah propounded, in the name of Hananeel, "they read in the book, in the Law of God," means *the original text;* "explaining it," means *the Chaldee paraphrase;* 'and gave the sense," means *the division according to the sense;* "and caused them to understand the Scripture," signifies *the Massoreth*. Some,

the context, this verse does not at all speak of Ezra, but refers to the statement in the preceding verse: "Also Joshua, and Boni, and Sherebiah,[87] and the Levites caused the people to understand the Law," and it is of them them that he says, "And they read in the book of the Law," &c., and not of Ezra.

This Midrashic explanation, however, can be consistent with the natural meaning of the text, in the following manner: "And they read in the book, in the Law of God" means *the original text*, that is to say, these men first read the text in Hebrew; then "explained it" in *the Chaldee paraphrase;* that is to say, they translated the verse to themselves into Aramaic, because everybody understood that language; "and gave the sense" means *the verses*, that is to say, they made pauses between every verse, in accordance with the tradition which they possessed from our teacher Moses, of blessed memory, as our Rabbins of blessed memory tell us in *Megilla* [3, *a*], and these are the words: "A verse which was not divided by Moses must not be divided by us." Those who refer the verse in question to Ezra, regard וְשׂוֹם as singular, but they do not know that it is *the infinitive*, and is tantamount to וַיְשִׂימוּ because of ☞ the word וַיִּקְרְאוּ by which it is preceded, and the word וַיָּבִינוּ by which it is followed; since the *infinitive* is everywhere rendered in the singular or plural, in the second person or in the third, masculine or feminine, in agreement with the verbs with which it is connected, and which may either precede or follow it. But this is not the place to expatiate upon this subject.

Now, as to the remark, "'and caused them to understand the Scripture,' denotes *the division of the accents;*" this means, that when reading to the people, they [Ezra and his associates] made[38] pauses

מדבר מעזרא, רק הוא שב על המקרא שלמעלה הימנו, וישוע ובני ושרביה וגו' עד [87] והלוים מבינים את העם לתורה, ועליהם הוא אומר ויקראו בספר תורת אלהים וגו' ולא על עזרא:

אך יש ליישב המדרש הזה עלדרך פשט הכתוב ככה, ויקראו בספר תורת אלהים זה מקרא, ר"ל שאלה האנשים קראו הפסוק בראשונה בלשון עברי, ואח"כ מפורש, זה תרגום, פי' שהיו מתרגמים להם הפסוק בלשון ארמי, לפי שאותו לשון היו מבינים הכל, ושום שכל אלו הפסוקים, ר"ל שהיו מפסיקים בין פסוק לפסוק, כמו שחיתה קבלה בידם ממרע"ה, כמו שאמרו רז"ל במסכת מגלה וז"ל, כל פסוק שלא פסקיה ליה משה לא פסקינן ליה, והמפרשין הפסוק על עזרא חושבים כי ושום הוא לשון יחיד ולא ידעו כי הוא מקור, והרי הוא כמו וישימו בעבור מלת ויקראו שלפניו, ומלת ויבינו של אחריו,

☞ כי כן המקור מבואר בכל מקום בלשון יחיד או רבים, נוכח או נסתר, זכר או נקבה, לפי הפעלים הסמוכים לפניו או לאחריו, ואין כאן מקום להאריך:

ומה שאמרו ויבינו במקרא וח פיסוק טעמים, ר"ל כשהיו קוראין לחן עשו[38] הפסקות

---

however, say it denotes the *pauses*, and others *heads of verses* (*Jerusalem Megilla* iv. 1, 67 *b*, ed. Krotoschin). It is necessary to remark, that in all these passages, the expression מסורת, denotes *the traditional pronunciation of the text*, and that it is not to be confounded with the technical meaning "*critical apparatus*," which it was made to signify in after times.

[87] The word עד, *till*, is omitted in the Sulzbach edition.

[38] The Sulzbach edition erroneously repeats להי, *to themselves*, after עשו, *they made*.

in the middle of the verse, according to the sense of the context, in the same manner as our teacher Moses, of blessed memory, read to the elders. Thus, for example, when he [Ezra] read to them "are they not on the other side Jordan, beyond?" he paused a little at the word "beyond," and then read "the way where the sun goeth down" (Deut. xi. 30), as Rashi explains it on this passage (vide in loco).[39] It is this which our Rabbins, of blessed memory, call *pause* or *division according to the sense,* because the pause makes the verse intelligible and perspicuous; not that they had the accents which we now possess, for they had not as yet been invented, as I shall show in the sequel. And as to the other remark, that "and they caused them to understand the Scriptures," means *the Massorah;* the explanation of this is, that they read every word as it was transmitted to them from our teacher Moses, of blessed memory, *ex. gr.* the *Keris,* and the *Kethivs,* as I shall explain afterwards. It must not, however, be supposed that they [Ezra and his associates] read to them [the people] the Massorah from tradition, or that they wrote the Massorah on the Pentateuch, much less on the whole[40] Bible, as we now have it; for there is no doubt that Ezra did not write anything except in the Law of Moses, as it is written, "This Ezra went up from Babylon, and he was a ready scribe in the Law of Moses, which was given by Jehovah, the God of Israel" (Ezra vii. 6), and again [*ibid.* ver. 11], "Ezra, the priest, the scribe of the words of Jehovah's commandments and of His statutes." He is also called in Aramaic, *the scribe of the Law of the Lord of heaven.*

באמצע הפסוק לפי כוונת הענין, כמו שהיה קורא מרע"ה לזקנים; והמשל כשהיה קורא להם הלא המה בעבר הירדין אחרי (דברים י'א), היה מפסיק מעט במלת אחרי, ואחרי כן קרא דרך מבא השמש כמו שפירש רש"י ע"ש :[39] ורז"ל קראו לזה פיסוק טעמים, לפי שהחהפסק נותן טוב טעם ודעת להבנת הפסוק, לא שהיו להם הטעמים אשר בידינו היום, כי עדיין לא נעשו כמו שאוכיח אח"כ, ולמאן דאמר אלו המסורת, פי' שהיו קוראים להם כל המלות כמו שהיתה מסורה בידם ממר"עה, כגון קריין וכתבן, כמו שיתבאר אח"כ, ואין להבין בכלל שהיו קוראים להם המסורת על פה, או שהם כתבו המסורת על התורה, כ"ש על כל[40] המקרא כמו שהיא בידינו היום, כי בלי ספק עזרא לא כתב דבר רק בתורת משה לבד, כי כן כתיב הוא עזרא סופר מהיר בתורת משה אשר נתן יהוה אלהי ישראל (עזרא ז') ופסוק אחר אומר עזרא הכהן הסופר דברי מצות יהוה וחקיו, וכן נקרא בלשון ארמי **ספר דתא די אלה שמיא:**

---

[39] *Rashi,* רש"י, is the acrostic of רבי שלמה יצחקי, *Rabbi Solomon Isaki* or *Itzchaki = R. Solomon ben Isaac,* the renowned Jewish commentator, who was born A.D. 1040, at Troyes, in Champagne, and died 26th July, 1105. For a sketch of his life, see Kitto's *Cyclopædia of Bibl. Literature, s. v.* RASHI. His explanation of אחרי דרך, Deut. xi. 30, to which Levita refers, is as follows: ומעם המקרא מוכיח שהם שני דבורים שנקדו בשני טעמים אחרי נקוד בפשתא ודרך נקוד במשפל והוא דגש ואם היה אחרי דרך דבור אחד היה נקוד אחרי במרחא ודרך בפשטא ורפי, the accents plainly show that they are two separate statements, inasmuch as they are pointed with two separate accents, אחרי being pointed with the distinctive accent Pashta, and דרך, with Jethiv, and having Dagesh. Now if they had been joined together, אחרי would have been pointed with the conjunctive accent *Mercha*, and דרך with Pashta, and would have been without Dagesh in the Daleth. According to this interpretation, therefore, the verse ought to be translated "these [mountains] are situate on the other side Jordan, far beyond it, towards the way where the sun goeth down."

[40] The word כל, *all,* is omitted in the Sulzbach edition.

Accordingly, I find it very difficult to make out what it was that Ezra wrote in the Law. For there are only two alternatives. Either that he possessed a scroll of the Law, and made another copy from it, without adding to it or taking from it anything, in which case he would be nothing more than any other scribe who copies one book from another; but, from this, no distinction could have accrued to him, since any one of the ordinary writers might have done the same thing, as it is difficult to believe that there were no other writers in all Israel except he. Or it may be said that the scroll of the Law which he had before him was not correctly written as regards *plenes* and *defectives*, *open* and *closed sections*, *large* and *small letters*, &c., &c.,[41] and he wrote them correctly. Here, again,[42] it is difficult to believe that there was not a single correct copy of the Law to be found among all the people of Israel. Forsooth this difficulty puzzled me so much for many years, that I mentioned it to the learned, but they could not give me any explanation of it.

ולפי זה קשה לי מאד מחו שכתב עזרא בתורה, כי לא ימנע מחלוקה אם נמצאה בידו ס״ת והוא כתב כן אחרת ולא הוסיף ולא גרע, א״כ לא היה אלא כסופר המעתיק ספר מספר אחר, ומה מעלה היתה זאת לו, והלא כל סופר הדיוט יכול לעשות כן, ואין להאמין שלא היה בכל ישראל סופר אחר כי אם הוא לבדו: ואם נאמר שחס״ת שהיתה לפניו לא היתה כתובה כתקונה, במלאים וחסרים, ובפרשיות פתוחות וסתומות, ואותיות גדולות וקטנות וכדומה לזה[41] והוא כתב אחת כתקונה, גם זה[42] קשה להאמין שלא נמצאה ס״ת כשרה בכל ישראל, ובאמת כמה שנים הוקשה לי זה ואומר אל החכמים ואין מגיד לי:

וכן קשה לי בענין קרי וכתיב, וזה לפי דעת רוב האחרונים שהקרי והכתיב נמצאים כן, כי בגלות ראשונה אבדו רוב הספרים ונטלטלו, והמעטים הנמצאים חשינם הטלטול ויודעי המקרא מתו, ועזרא וסיעתו החזירו העטרה ליושנה, ותקנו הספרים החם, וכאשר מצאו מחלוקת בספרים, הלכו בהם אחר הרוב לפי דעתם, ובמקום שלא השיגה דעתם על הכדור, כתבו האחד מבפנים והאחד בחוץ או כתבו האחד ולא נקדוהו וכו׳, עיין בהקדמת הרד״ק ביהושע, והאפודי בפרק ז׳

I have, also, felt a great difficulty about the import of the *Keri* and the *Kethiv*. Now, according to the opinions of many modern [grammarians], the *Keri* and the *Kethiv* originated in the following manner. During the first captivity, most of the canonical writings were lost, and even the few books which had been found were impaired by being thrown about; and as those who were skilled in the Scriptures were dead, Ezra and his associates restored the crown to its pristine glory; for they corrected these books, and when they found variations in the books, they decided to follow the majority [of Codd.], and wherever they could not decide properly they wrote down one reading in the text and the other in the margin, or put one down without punctuating it, &c. See *Kimchi's Introduction to Joshua*, and *Ephodi's*

---

[41] An explanation of all the Massoretic phrases will be found further on, and as we cannot give the pages, not being as yet made up, we must refer to the Index, which will enable the reader easily to find the requisite information.

[42] The word זה, *this*, is omitted in the Sulzbach edition.

Treatise, cap. vii.⁴³ Abravanel, however, refutes them in his introduction to Jeremiah, and attempts in a very lengthy manner to correct their blunders; but his corrections are his blunders, for most of his arguments are untenable and shallow. I shall, therefore, not enlarge upon them.⁴⁴

Let me, therefore, simply state my own opinion upon this subject, and reply to the afore-mentioned writers. Now, I submit, if their opinions be really true,—that is to say, if the *Keri* and the *Kethiv* are owing to doubts as above mentioned, —what shall we say to the *Keri* and the *Kethiv* which are found in the books written by the captives themselves, such as Haggai, Zechariah, Malachi, Daniel, Ezra, who wrote his own book and the Chronicles; and Mordecai, who wrote the book of Esther? Were not these themselves among the Men of the Great Synagogue?⁴⁵ Take, for ex-

מספרו,⁴³ והאברבינאל השיג עליהם בהקדמתו לספר ירמי׳, והאריך לשון חשב לתקן עוותם, ותקנתו היא קלקלתו, כי רוב דבריו לא לרצון, ובטלין ומבוטלין, ולכן אין לי להאריך בם:⁴⁴

אך אענה חלקי אף אני, ואשיב על דברי האנשים הנזכרים ואומר, אם כדבריהם כן הוא ר״ל שהקרי והכתיב בעבור הספקות הנ״ל, מה יאמרו על הקרי והכתיב הנמצאים בספרי הגולה שהם חגי זכריה מלאכי דניאל ועזרא כתב ספרו וד״ה, ומרדכי כתב המגלה, והלא הם עצמם היו מאנשי כנה״ג,⁴⁵ וחמשל בספר

⁴³ The Kimchi, referred to in the text, or *Redak* (רד״ק), as the Hebrew text has it, which is the acrostic of ר׳ דוד קמחי, *R. David Kimchi*, is the younger brother of M. Kimchi, to whose grammatical treatise, entitled, *the Journey on the Paths of Knowledge*, Levita wrote the commentary already alluded to, (*vide supra*, pp. 13, &c., 80, &c.) D. Kimchi, who was born in Narbonne, 1160, and died about 1235, is the author of the celebrated grammatical and lexical work, entitled *Michlol*, which Levita edited with annotations (*vide supra*, p. 79, &c.), as well as of valuable commentaries on nearly the whole Hebrew Scriptures. Comp. Kitto, *Cyclopædia of Biblical Literature*, new ed., *s. v.* KIMCHI. The passage detailing his opinion on the origin of the *Keri* and *Kethiv*, to which Levita refers, will be found together with an English translation in Jacob b. Chajim's *Introduction to the Rabbinic Bible*, p. 5 in the Hebrew, and 7 in the English.

Ephodi (אפד), is the appellation of R. Isaac b. Moses Ha-Levi, the celebrated grammarian and polemical writer, who flourished A.D. 1360–1412. It is a contraction of אמר, אני פרופיט דורי, *thus sayeth*, or *I Prophiat Duran*, and though it is the name which he especially assumed after 1391, to conceal his real person from the Christians, who, at the peril of his life, compelled him to abjure Judaism and join the benighted Christians of that day, he is also known by the name *Prophiat Duran*. His excellent grammatical treatise, entitled *the Grammar of Ephod* (מעשה אפד), to which Levita refers, has only recently been published for the first time, Vienna, 1865. The passage in question is to be found in cap. vii., p. 40, and with an English translation in Jacob b. Chajim's *Introduction to the Rabbinic Bible*, p. 4, &c., in the Hebrew, and p. 6, &c., in the English, ed. Ginsburg. For the life and writings of Ephodi, see the Introduction to his Grammar, entitled *Maase Ephod*, pp. 2–49, Vienna, 1865; and Kitto, *Cyclopædia of Biblical Literature*, new ed., *s. v.* PROPHIAT DURAN.

⁴⁴ Abravanel's view, which Levita does not even deign to state, and which he so cavalierly rejects, is given at length by Jacob b. Chajim, in his *Introduction to the Rabbinic Bible*, pp. 5, &c., in the Hebrew, and pp. 7–11 in the English. It is to be remarked, that the theory of this celebrated statesman, philosopher, theologian, and commentator, who was born in Lisbon in 1437, and died at Venice in 1508, has a greater amount of truth in it than any other hypothesis on this vexed question. Comp. Kitto's *Cyclopædia, s. v.* KERI AND KETHIV.

⁴⁵ The Great Synagogue (כנסת הגדולה), to which such frequent references are made in this work, denotes the council, or synod, first appointed by Nehemiah, after the return of the Jews from the Babylonish captivity, to reorganise the religious life of the people. It consisted originally of one hundred and twenty members, comprising the representa-

ample, the book of Ezra (iv. 2), where the textual reading is ולא, with *Aleph*, and they [the Men of the Great Synagogue] wrote in the margin, read ולו with *Vav*. Now if they did it because they were in doubt, not knowing whether to read לא or לו; we ask, was not Ezra there present with them? and did he himself not know whether he wrote ולא with *Aleph* or ולו with *Vav?* The same is the case with the other *Keris* and *Kethivs* found in their books. And it cannot be

עזרא כתיב ולא אנהנו זובחים (עזרא ד')
והם כתבו בחוץ ולו קרי בוי"ו, אם עשו זה
בעבור הספק, שלא ידעו אם הוא לא או לו,
יש להקשות והלא עזרא היה שם עמהם, וכי
לא ידע הוא אם כתב ולא באל"ף או ולו
בוי"ו, וכן בשאר קרי וכתיב שבכספריהם,
ואין לומר שאחרי מות המחברים החם כתבו
שירי כנסת הגדולה הקרי מפני הספק, שהרי
לא היה להם טלטול ולא אבדו הספרים
☞ בשנים מועטות החן, כי לא נמשך זמן
אנשי כ"ה רק קרוב לס' שנה, כדסוכה
בסדר עולם⁴⁶ ובקבלת הראב"ד:⁴⁷

answered that it was after the death of the said authors that the remaining members of the Great Synagogue wrote the *Keri* because of doubts, since there was no dispersion, nor were the books lost in
☞ those few years, for the whole period of the Men of the Great Synagogue did not last more than about forty years, as is shown in *Seder Olam*,⁴⁶ and in Ibn Daud's *Seder Ha-Kabbalah*.⁴⁷ Besides, if

tives of the following five classes of the Jewish nation. i. *The Chiefs of the Priestly Divisions* (ראשי בית אב). ii. *The Chiefs of the Levitical Families* (ראשי הלוים). iii. *The Heads of the Israelite Families* (ראשי העם). iv. *Representatives of the Cities* or *the Elders* (זקנים, πρεσβύτεροι), and v. *The Doctors of the Law*, or *the Scribes* (מבינים, סופרים γραμματεῖς). The number of one hundred and twenty members was, however, not adhered to after the death of Nehemiah, and ultimately it was reduced to seventy. The period of its duration extended from the latter days of Nehemiah to the death of Simon the Just, B. C. 410–300; thus embracing about one hundred and ten years. See Kitto's *Cyclopædia of Biblical Literature*, s. v. SYNAGOGUE, THE GREAT.

⁴⁶ The *Seder Olam* (סדר עולם), or *the Succession of the World's History*, is an ancient Jewish Chronicle, written by R. Jose b. Chalafta, of Sephoris, who flourished *circa* A.D. 100–150. It briefly chronicles the events of the world from Adam to the war under Bar-Kochba, the false Messiah. It is also called *Seder Olam Rabba* (סדר עולם רבא), = *the Major Chronicle of the World*, to distinguish it from a later Chronicle, entitled *Seder Olam Sutta* (סדר עולם זוטא), = *the Minor Chronicle of the World*. The best edition of it is that by Meyer, Amsterdam, 1699, which appeared together with the *Seder Olam Sutta*, a Latin translation, and very elaborate annotations. Levita most probably refers to chapters xxix. and xxx.

⁴⁷ The author of the *Sepher*, or *Seder Ha-Kabbalah* (סדר הקבלה or ספר), = *the Succession of Tradition*, Abraham Ibn Daud or *Rabad* (ראב"ד), as he is called by Levita, which is the acrostic of ר' אברהם בן דוד, *R. Abraham b. David*,—was born *circa* 1110, and died as a martyr 1180. The chronicle of this distinguished moral philosopher gives, in the form of annals, the history of the world from Adam to his own time (1161), showing the uninterrupted chain of tradition to his day, against the opinion of the Karaites, who denied all tradition. As supplement to this chronicle, Ibn Daud wrote a succinct history of the Roman Empire, from its foundation by Romulus till the West Gothic King Reccared, entitled, *Memoirs of the Events of Rome* (זכרון דברי רומי), and the *History of the Jewish Kings during the second Temple* (דברי מלכי ישראל בבית שני). Ibn Daud's Histories were first published, together with the *Seder Olam*, Mantua, 1513, then in Venice, 1545, Basel, 1580; the *Sepher Ha-Kabbalah*, by itself, was published with the *Seder Olam Rabba* and *Sutta*, Cracow, 1820; and with a Latin translation by Gilbert Genebrard, Paris, 1572. Levita's allusion will be found 3 *a*–5 *a* of the last mentioned edition. It must be remarked, that neither the *Seder Olam* nor the *Sepher Ha-Kabbalah* says that the Great Synagogue only continued for forty years. Graetz

ועוד אם היה חקרי והכתיב בעבור הספקות הנ"ל, היה ראוי שיבאו הספקות על דרך המקרה, כפי מרלוקת הספרים, והחבדל שנפל בהם אחת הנה ואחת הנה, ועד שם זעד שם, לא על מלה אחת הרבה פעמים, בנון כ"ב פעמים נערה בתורה כתיבין נער וקריין נערה,⁴⁸ וכן ו' כתיבין עפולים וקריין טחורים,⁴⁹ וכן ה' כתיבין עניים וקריין ענוים וב' להיפך,⁵⁰ ודומה לאלה רבים, איך נפל הספק על כל נערה ועל כל עפולים וענײם:

ויותר קשה לי מה שאמרו בפרק הנ"ל וז"ל, אמר רבי יצחק קריין ולא כתבן וכתבן ולא קריין הלכה לטשה מסיני, קריין ולא כתבן פרת דבלכתו, איש, כאשר שאל וכו', כתבן ולא קריין ולא קריין נא דיכלה, אל ידרוך ידרוך הדורך, ידרוך השני כתיב ולא קרי וכו',⁵¹ ומי יתן שומע לי ויבונני, איך יחבן

the *Keri* and *the Kethiv* originated through the above-mentioned doubtful readings, we should expect these doubtful readings to occur accidentally, according to the differences of the books, and the accidents which befel them,—to be one here and one there—here a little and there a little —but not repeatedly to occur in one and the same word. Thus, for example, נערה is written in the Pentateuch twenty-two times נער, without *He*, and read נערה with *He*⁴⁸; עפולים, *tumors*, which occurs in the text six times, and is read טחורים, *the piles*⁴⁹; עניים, *destitutes*, found five times in the text, and read ענוים, *afflicted*, and twice vice versa;⁵⁰ and there are many more the like instances. Now how could the accident always happen to the expressions עניים and עפולים, נערה?

And my difficulty is increased by what is said in the above-mentioned section of the Talmud [*Nedarim* 37, *b*], and these are the words: "R. Isaac said, the words read from the margin but not written in the text, and the words written in the text but not read, are a Law of Moses from Sinai; the words read from the margin, but not written in the text, are פרת, *Euphrates* [2 Sam. viii. 3], and איש, *man* [*ibid*. xvi. 23]; whilst the words written in the text but not read, are נא, *now* [2 Kings v. 18], and ידרוך, *he shall tread* [Jerem. li. 3], &c."⁵¹ Would that

has shown that its existence extended over a period of one hundred and ten years, so that Levita's argument based upon the shorter period is groundless.

⁴⁸ In the present text, we have only twenty-one instances in which the text has נער and the marginal reading נערה, viz., Gen. xxiv. 14, 16, 28, 55, 57; xxxiv. 3 (twice), 12; Deut. xxii. 15 (twice), 16, 20, 21, 23, 24, 25, 26 (twice), 27, 28, 29.

⁴⁹ The six instances in which the marginal reading substitutes טחורים for the textual עפולים are Deut. xxviii. 27; 1 Sam. v. 6, 9, 12; vi. 4, 5. Comp. *Megilla*, 25 *b*; *Sopherim* viii. 8; *Massorah magna* on 1 Sam. v. 6; *Massorah finalis*, *s. v.* מ"ש; *Ochla Ve-Ochla*, section 170, pp. 38, 114; Jacob b. Chajim's *Introduction to the Rabbinic Bible*, p. 9, &c. English translation.

⁵⁰ The five passages in which the *Kethiv* is עניים and the *Keri* has ענוים are as follows: Ps. ix. 13; x. 12; Prov. iii. 34; xiv. 21; xvi. 19. The instances in which the reverse is the case are Ps. ix. 19; Isa. xxxii. 7.

⁵¹ Levita's quotation of R. Isaac's statement is abridged. Jacob b. Chajim gives it entire in his *Introduction to the Rabbinic Bible*, p. 6 in the Hebrew and p. 12 in the English translation. Of words read from the margin and not written in the text, there are ten instances, viz.—

בני, *the sons of* . . . . Judg. xx. 13.	צבאות, *Sabaoth* . . . Isaiah xxxvii. 32.
פרת, *Euphrates* . . . 2 Sam. viii. 3.	באים, *are coming* . . Jerem. xxxi. 38.
איש, *man* . . . . 2 Sam. xvi. 21.	לה, *to her* . . . . Jerem. l. 29.
כן, *thus* . . . . 2 Sam. xviii. 20.	אלי, *to me* . . . . Ruth iii. 5.
בניו, *his sons* . . . 2 Kings xix. 37.	אלי, *to me* . . . . Ruth iii. 17.

any one might listen to me, and explain to me how it can be said of them that they are a Law of Moses from Sinai, when, of all the instances here adduced, not a single one is to be found in the Pentateuch? And even of those marginal readings not written in the text, which the Massorites added (for R. Isaac only[52] gives five, whilst the Massorites give eight), as well as of the words written in the text, but not read (for R. Isaac only[53] gives six, whilst the Massorites give ten),—of either the one or the other, not a single[54] one is to be found in the Pentateuch. And if it be so, how can it be said that it is a Law of Moses from Sinai, which did not, as yet, exist at all?

And as if this trouble were not enough for us, some later writers must needs add that "every *Keri* and *Kethiv*, throughout the whole Bible, is a Law of Moses." But where have they been authorised to say this, since R. Isaac has only said it of the marginal readings not written in the text, and words written in the text but not read, which are the smallest of the seven classes [of *Keris* and *Kethivs*], as I shall show in the Second Part, section one? If it really is a tradition that the former alone [*i.e.* those given in the Talmud, *Nedarim*], are a Law of Moses from Sinai, I must accept it, for our sages are true, and their words are true. But for that, I should have said that the *Keris* and *Kethivs*, which occur in the Pentateuch, are a Law of Moses from Sinai; and that the men of the Great Synagogue, *i.e.* Haggai, Zachariah, Malachi, Daniel, Mishael, Azariah, Ezra, Nehemiah, Mordecai, Zerubbabel, with whom were associated other sages from the craftsmen and artizans, to the number of a

---

Comp. *Massorah magna* on Deut. i. 1; and on Ruth iii. 17; *Sopherim* vi. 8; *Ochla Ve-Ochla*, section xcvii., pp. 28, 96. Of words written in the text but not read, there are eight instances, viz.:—

אם, *if* . . . . . . 2 Sam. xiii. 33.	אם, *if* . . . . . . Jerem. xxxix. 12.
אם, *if* . . . . . . 2 Sam. xv. 21.	ידרך, *he shall tread* . . . Jerem. li. 3.
נא, *now* . . . . . . 2 Kings v 18.	חמש, *five* . . . . . Ezek. xlviii. 16.
את, *accusative* . . Jerem. xxxviii. 16.	אם, *if* . . . . Ruth iii. 12.

Comp. *Massorah magna* on Ruth iii. 12; *Sopherim* vi. 9; *Ochla Ve-Ochla*, section xcviii., pp. 28, 96; Kitto's *Cyclopædia of Biblical Literature*, *s. v.* Keri and Kethiv.

[52] The word גם, *even*, is omitted in the Sulzbach edition.

[53] The Sulzbach edition erroneously substitutes כי אם, *but*, for רק, *only*.

[54] מהן, *of them*, which is important to the sense, is omitted in the Sulzbach edition.

hundred and twenty persons—noted down according to a tradition which they had, informing them that our teacher Moses, peace be upon him, did not read this word as it is written in the text, because of one of the many secrets known unto them; that our teacher Moses, peace be upon him, delivered them[55] to Joshua, Joshua to the sages, the sages to the prophets, &c., &c., who put it down in the margin, as the *Keri* has it, and that Ezra was the writer thereof. This is, therefore, the very thing which he wrote in the Law of Moses.

The same thing they did with all the words in the Prophets and Hagiographa, respecting which they had a tradition from the Prophets and the sages, delivered from mouth to mouth, that they are not to be read as they are written. But as for the post-exile books, they required no tradition, for their authors were themselves present with them. Whenever, therefore, they [the men of the Great Synagogue] found a word in them which appeared to them not in harmony with the design of the context, and the simple meaning of the passage, the author gave them the reason why he had written in so abnormal a manner; hereupon they wrote the normal expression in the margin as the *Keri*. Herewith the question is fully answered, which I asked above about ולא [Ezra iv. 2], since Ezra did assign a reason why he wrote in such a manner. In like manner, when they read in the book of Haggai (i. 8) ו כבד, Haggai himself told them not to read וְאִכָּבֵד but וְאִכָּבְדָה, as if the ה were written out at the end, and told them that it was owing to the five things which were in the first temple, but not in the second temple,[56] that he

שמשה רבינו ע״ה קרא המלה ההיא ככתיבה לסוד אחד מן הסודות הידוע להם, שמשה רבינו ע״ה מסר[55] ליהושע ויהושע לזקנים וזקנים לנביאים וכו' וכתבוהו בחוץ כקריאתה ועזרא היה הסופר, וזה מה שכתב הוא בתורת משה:

וכן עשו גם כן בנביאים וכתובים בכל המלות שהיתה קבלה בידם מפי הנביאים וחכמי הדורות איש מפי איש שלא יחיו נקראין ככתיבתן, אבל בספרי הגולה לא היו צריכין לקבלה, כי המחברים עצמם היו שם עמהם, וכשמצאו מלה אחת שנראה להם שהיא זרה כפי כוונת הענין ופשט הכתוב, אמר להן המחבר הטעם למה כתב כן בזרותה, או כתבו המלה מחוץ כקריאתה, ובזה יהיה מיושב מה שהקשתי לעיל על ולא אנחנו זובחים, כי הוא אמר הטעם למה כתב כן, וכן כשקראו בספר חגי וארצה בו ואכבד (חגי א׳), אמר להם חגי, אל תקראו וְאִכָּבֵד אלא וְאִכָּבְדָה כאלו היתה ה״א כתובה בסוף, ואמר להן הטעם מפני ה' דברים שהיו במקדש ראשון ולא במקדש שני כתבתיו כן,[56] או כ׳תבו בחוץ

---

[55] In the Sulzbach edition, הסוד, *the secret*, is inserted after מסר, *he delivered*.

[56] According to ancient tradition, the following five things, which were in the first Temple, were wanting in the second Temple: i. The Ark, with the lid and the cherubim upon it; ii. The fire from Heaven (comp. 2 Chron. vii. 1); iii. The Shechinah; iv. The Holy Ghost; and v. The Urim and Thummim. The absence of these five, the same ancient tradition declares, was indicated by the absence of the letter ה, which numerically represents *five*, from the word in question. Hence the remark in the Talmud: אמר רב שמואל בר איניא מאי דכתיב וארצה ב' ואכבד וקרינן ואכבדה מאי שנא דמדסר ה'א אלו חמשה דברים שהיו בין מקדש ראשון למקדש שני אלו הן ארון וכפורת וכרובים אש ושכינה ורוח הקודש ואורים ותומים, *R. Samuel b. Enia sayeth, Why has the Kethiv* ואכבד, *and the Keri* ואכבדה? *What is meant by the absence of the* ה? *It is because of the five things which made the difference between the first and second Temple. They are as follows, the Ark, &c.*

wrote so. Whereupon they wrote in the margin "Read ואכברה." The same thing they did with all the other post-exile books.

In short, the men of the Great Synagogue made the *Keri*, in the Pentateuch, in accordance with a tradition from our teacher Moses, peace be upon him; in the Prophets and Hagiographa, in accordance with a tradition from the Prophets and sages of succeeding generations; and in the post-exile books, in accordance with the directions of the authors themselves; but never on account of any doubtful readings, as many have supposed.

☞ Now, when I gave my heart to inquire into, and examine with wisdom, all which has been done in the matter of the *Keri* and *Kethiv*, I discovered that the *Keri* and *Kethiv* are never found on *plene* and *defective*. That is to say, there is not a word to be found in the whole Bible which is written in the text *plene*, and the the marginal reading of which is *defective* or *vice versa*; and the reason is, that the sense of the word is never affected by its being *defective* or *plene*.

ואכברה קרי, וכן עשו בכל האחרים שבספרי הגולה:

והכלל כי אנשי כנסת הגדולה עשו הקרי שבתורה על פי הקבלה ממשה רע״ה, ושבנביאים וכתובים על פי הקבלה מנביאים וחכמי הדורות, ושבספרי הגולה על פי המחברים עצמם, ולא בעבור הספקות כאשר חשבו רבים:

☞ והנה כאשר נתתי את לבי לדרוש ולתור בחכמה, על כל אשר נעשה בענין קרי וכתיב, עוד זה מצאתי, שלא נמצא קרי וכתיב על ענין הסר ומלא לעולם, ר״ל שלא נמצאת מלה בכל המקרא שהכתיב הוא מלא והקרי הוא חסר, או לחפך, והטעם לפי שלא תשתנה הוראת המלה בעבור חסר ומלא לעולם:

☞ ועוד זה מצארי־תי הכר נא ודע לך, שלא נמצא קרי וכתיב על ענין הנקודות והטעמים לעולם, ר״ל שלא נמצאת מלה שהכתיב נקוד באופן אחד והקרי באופן אחר, וכן לא יבא קרי וכתיב על דגש ורפי, ולא על מלעיל ומלרע, ולא על ימין ושמאל, ולא על מפיק או לא מפיק, וכן לא על אחד מהטעמים המפסיקים או בלתי מפסיקים:

והטעם לפי שלא היתה מחלוקת בכל ישראל בקריאת המלות, כי הכל היו קוראין בתורה בלי נקוד, כמו שקבלו ממשה רע״ה,

☞ I have also discovered this, which is important to remember, that the *Keri* and *Kethiv* are never to be found on the vowel-points and accents. That is to say, there is not a word to be found which is pointed in the text in one way, and the marginal reading of which is in another way. Nor do the *Keri* and *Kethiv* occur with respect to *Dagesh* and *Raphe*, nor in *Milel* and *Milra*, nor on *right* and *left* [*i. e.* the point on letter ש], nor on *Mapik* and *no Mapik*, nor on either of the *accents pausal* or *non-pausal*.

And the reason of it is, because there never was any difference of opinion among all Israel about the pronunciation of the words; for all alike read the Law without points, just as they had received it from Moses; and the other sacred books, as they received them from

---

Comp. *Ioma*, 21 *b*. In the *Midrash Rabba*, on the Song of Songs, viii. 8, where the same thing is recorded, *the holy oil* (שמן המשחה), is substituted for the Shechinah, as one of the five things. Comp. p. 26 *a*, ed. Stettin, 1863.

the Prophets.[57] And as the points which were added in after time are simply signs and marks to indicate the pronunciation, therefore, they do not come within the province of the *Keri* and *Kethiv*. The same is the case with the variations between the Easterns and Westerns, not one of which is on the vowels and accents. By the Easterns are meant the Babylonians, and by the Westerns, the Palestinians.[58] We in all these countries are descendants of the latter, and therefore follow their readings and submit to their authority. Now the variations between these two are, respecting words and letters, *Keri* and *Kethiv*, *plene* and *defective*, but not in vowels and accents. And this is a proof that these variations were written down prior to the invention of the vowels and accents. The variations, however, between Ben-Asher and Ben-Naphtali, which simply refer to the points and accents, were unquestionably written down after the invention of the points and accents; and this is easily understood.

☞ As to these two men, they were the heads of two different Massoretic schools, and their respective names were *Jacob b. Naphtali* and *Aaron b. Asher*.[59] Maimonides, of blessed memory, writes in the *Treatise on the Love of God*, cap. viii., as follows: "The copy which

---

[57] The words ובשאר הספרים כמו שקבלו מהנביאים, *and in the other books as they received them from the Prophets*, which are essential to the argument, are omitted in the Sulzbach edition.

[58] From the Babylonian and Jerusalem Talmuds we see that, as early as the third century of the Christian era, there existed differences between the Easterns and Westerns, which affected both the reading and the exegesis of certain words (comp. Geiger, in the Hebrew Essays and Reviews, entitled, *Kerem Chemed*, vol. ix., p. 69. Berlin, 1856); and that many of the deviating renderings of the Septuagint and of the so-called Jonathan Chaldee version of the Prophets arise from their following the more ancient Eastern readings. These two schools produced in the middle of the sixth century the two systems of vocalisation which we have already described (*vide supra* p. 61, &c.), and bequeathed to us a list of their variations (חלופין), which is given in the Rabbinic Bibles, but which is both exceedingly imperfect and incorrect. It is to this list that Levita refers in the text. The indefatigable Pinsker, who created a new era in the history of the Karaites, has greatly enriched and amended this list from two Codices, of A.D. 916 and 1010. Comp. *Einleitung in das Babylonisch-Hebräische Punktationssystem*, pp. 121–132; Vienna, 1863.

[59] Aaron b. Moses b. Asher, or simply *Ben-Asher*, as he is generally called, flourished *circa* A.D. 900, at Tiberias. He was the most accomplished scholar and representative of the Tiberian system of vocalisation and accentuation, and wrote, in the interests of the Westerns, the following works: i. *A Model Codex of the Bible*, (ספר בן אשר), furnished with the points and accents according to the Western school, which became the standard text, and which Maimonides described in such eulogistic terms;

we have followed in these matters is the famous Codex of Egypt, which contains the twenty-four books, and which had been in Jerusalem for many years, in order that other Codices might be corrected by its text; and all followed it, because Ben-Asher had minutely revised it for many years, and corrected it many times. According to this, many copies were made; and I, too, followed it, in the books of the Law which I myself have written, in all its integrity." [60] And we also, throughout all these countries, follow its readings, whilst the Orientals adopt the text of Ben-Naphtali. The variations in the accents between them are confined to the smaller accents, such as *Metheg, Makiph, Munach*, one *Pashta*, or two *Pashtas*. All this will be thoroughly explained in a separate Treatise, called *Good Sense*, which, by the help of the Lord, I intend to write.[61] These variations between them, which also extend to the vowels, only refer to *Cholem, Kemetz-Chateph, Long-Kemetz, Pattach, Sheva, Chateph-Pattach*, as well as to *Dagesh, Raphe, Milel*, and *Milra*.

הרמב"ם זכרנו לברכה בספר אהבה פרק ח' וז"ל, וספר שסמכנו עליו בדברים אלו הוא ספר הידוע במצרים שהוא כולל כ"ד ספרים שהיה בירושלם מכמה שנים להגיה ממנו הספרים, ועליו היו הכל סומכין, לפי שהגיהו בן אשר, ודקדק בו שנים הרבה, והגיהו פעמים רבות כמו שהעתיקו, ועליו סמכתי בספר תורה שכתבתי כהלכתו,[60] וכן אנחנו סומכין על קריאתו בכל הארצות האלה, ואנשי מזרח סומכין על קריאת בין נפתלי, והפלוגתות שביניהם בטעמים אינן אלא בטעמים הקטנים, כגון מתג ומקף ומונח ובפשטא אחד וב' פשטין, וכל זה יחיה מבואר היטב בספר טוב טעם אשר יערתי חבורו בע"ה,[61] גם הפלוגתות שביניחן בנקודות אינן אלא בחולם ובקמץ חטוף, ובקמץ גדול ופתח, ובשוא ובחטוף פתח, וכן בדגשין ורפין, ומלעיל ומלרע:

ii. *A Treatise on the Massorah*, entitled, *the Massoreth of Ben-Asher* (מסורת בן אשר), stating partly the Massoretic remarks on each word in the margin of the text itself (מסרת גליונית, מסרת הפנים), and partly at the end of the Codex (*Massorah finalis*). Comp. Pinsker, *Likute Kabmonijot*, text p. 130; iii. *A Treatise on the Accents* (ספר המ[ו]דרוקי הטעמים), first printed in the Rabbinic Bible, Venice, 1517; and then again by Leopold Dukes, Tübingen, 1846; iv. *A Treatise on the Consonants and Vowels* (ספר דקדוקי האותיות והנקודות), of which fragments only have survived, which are inserted in his treatise on the accents, and against which the celebrated Saadia Gaon wrote a dissertation; and v. *A Treatise on Assonances* (שמונים וזוגין), giving eighty Hebrew words, similar in sound, but differing in sense. Moses b. David b. Naphtali, again, or simply Ben-Asher, as he is generally called, represented the Easterns, and wrote in the interests of the Babylonian school, i. A Model Codex of the Bible, and ii. A Treatise on the system of vocalisation and accentuation. Comp. Fürst, *Introduction to the Hebrew and Chaldee Lexicon*, p. xxi. A list of the variations between these two representatives of the Easterns and Westerns, is given at the end of the Rabbinic Bibles.

[60] The *Treatise on the Love of God* (ספר אהבה), which Levita quotes, is simply one of the component parts of Maimonides' gigantic work on the Biblical and traditional Laws, called *Deuteronomy; Second Law* (משנה תורה), or *Jad Ha-Chezaka* (יד החזקה) = *the Mighty Hand*, in allusion to Deut. xxxiv. 12. The part consists of the following six *Halachoth* (הלכות), or *Tractates*: i. On the reading of Shema; ii. On Prayer and the Priestly Benediction; iii. On Phylacteries, Mezzuza, and the Scroll of the Law; iv. On the Fringed Garment; v. On Benedictions, and vi. On Circumcision. The quotation in question is from Tractate iii., and the portion which treats on the Scroll of the Law, or *Hilchoth Sepher Thora*, viii. 4. The reference in the text is, to say the least, most indefinite.

[61] The treatise on the accents, entitled, *Good Sense* (טוב טעם), to which Levita refers, appeared within twelve months of the publication of this statement. *Vide supra*, p. 63, &c.

☞ Now it is evident, from all I have said, that the *Keri* and *Kethiv* never occur with respect to *plene* and *defective*, nor on a single one of the vowel-points and accents. Let me, therefore, warn and caution every one who reads the folio or quarto editions of the four and twenty books published here, in Venice, in the year 278 (= 1517),[62] to pay no attention to the false remarks printed in the margin, in the form of *Keri* and *Kethiv*, *plene* and *defective*, *Milel* and *Milra*, and *variations in the vowels and accents*, or to any of those things which ought not to have been done, as I have stated above. The author of them did not know how to distinguish between his right hand and his left. Not being a Jew, he knew nothing about the nature of the Massorah, and what he did put down simply arose from the fact, that he sometimes found variations in the copies which he had before him, and, as he did not know which reading was the correct one, he put down one in the margin and another in the text. Sometimes it so happened that he put the correct reading into the text, and the incorrect one into the margin, and sometimes the reverse is the case; thus, he was groping in darkness, like a blind man. Hence, they are not to be heeded, for they are confusion worse confounded.

Now, before quitting the subject of the *Keri* and *Kethiv*, let me remark, that, being anxious to know the number of all the *Keris* and *Kethivs* throughout the Scriptures, I counted them several times, and found them to be 848, and indicated this by the mnemonical sign, "*Karjan Ve-Kathban*."[63] Of these, 65 are in the Pentateuch,[64] 454 in the Prophets, and 329 in the Hagiographa.

---

[62] This refers to the first edition of the great Rabbinic Bible, in folio, published by Bomberg, 1516-17, and the quarto edition, also published by Bomberg, 1517. Comp. Wolf, *Bibliotheca Hebraea* ii. 367; Masch, *Bibliotheca Sacra* i. 17; Steinschneider, *Catalogus Libr. Hebr. in Bibliotheca Bodleiana*, col. 7; Kitto, *Cyclopædia of Biblical Literature*, s. v. RABBINIC BIBLES.

[63] That is to say 848, which is the numerical value of קר״ין וכ״תבן, viz., ק 100, + ר 200, + י 10, + י 10, + ן 50, + ו 6, + כ 20, + ת 400, + ב 2, + ן 50 = 848.

[64] Levita is surely wrong in saying that there are only sixty-five *Keris* and *Kethivs* in the Pentateuch. In again going through the Massoretic notes in the Bible, we have found eighty-two. They are as follows:—Genesis viii. 17; x. 19; xiv. 2, 8; xxiv. 14, 16, 28,

It is astonishing that in the Pentateuch there should only be 65 *Keris* and *Kethivs*, 22 of which relate to נערה, which is written in the text נער, and the marginal reading is נערה; whilst in the book of Joshua, which is only about a tenth the size of the Pentateuch, there occur 32,[65] and in the book of Samuel, which in quantity is about a fourth of the Pentateuch, there are found 133.[66] It is also to be noticed that, of the many Catalogues, Registers, and Alphabetical Lists of the *Keris* and *Kethivs* in the Great Massorah, not a single one is found in the Pentateuch. Thus, of the 62 words in which two letters are transposed;[67] the 12 words

ויש לתמוה למה לא נמצאו בתורה רק ס"ח קרי וכתיב אשר מהן כ"ב דכתיבין נער וקרינן נערה, וספר יהושע שהוא רק בעשירית בכמות התורה ונמצאו בו ל"ב,[65] וספר שמואל שהוא כמעט הרביעית מן התורה ונמצאים בו קל"ג[66] הלא תדאה כי רוב חזוגין וחשיטין ואלפא ביתין מן קריין וכתבן שבמסרה הנדולה, אין גם אחד מהן בתורה, וחמשל ס"ב מלין דמוקדמין ומאוחרין,[67]

33, 55, 57; xxv. 23; xxxvii. 3, 29; xxx. 11; xxxiii. 4; xxxiv. 3 (twice), 12; xxxvi. 5, 14, 15; xxxix. 20, 22; xliii. 28; xlix. 11 (twice): Exod. iv. 2; xiii. 11; xvi. 2, 7, 13; xxi. 8; xxii. 4, 26; xxvii. 11; xxviii. 28; xxxii. 17, 19; xxxv. 11; xxxvii. 8; xxxix. 4, 21, 33: Levit. ix. 22; xi. 21; xvi. 21; xxi. 5; xxiii. 13; xxv. 30: Numb. i. 16; iii. 51; x. 36; xi. 32; xii. 3; xiv. 36; xvi. 11; xxi. 32; xxvi. 9; xxxii. 7; xxxiv. 4; Deuter. ii. 33; v. 10; vii. 9; viii. 2; xxi. 7; xxii. 15 (twice), 16, 20, 21, 23, 24, 25, 26 (twice), 27, 28, 29; xxvii. 10; xxviii. 27, 30; xxix. 22; xxxiii. 9. The numbers, therefore, given in Kitto's *Cyclopædia of Biblical Literature, s. v.* KERI and KETHIV, must be corrected. The instances in which the *Keri* and *Kethiv* are on the word נער, have already been specified. *Vide supra*, p. 109, note 48.

[65] According to our collation of the text, we find *thirty-five Keris* and *Kethivs* in the Book of Joshua expressly so marked, viz., Josh. ii. 13; iii. 4, 16; iv. 18; v. 1; vi. 5, 7, 9, 13, 15; viii. 11, 12, 16; ix. 7; xi. 16; xv. 4, 47, 48, 53, 63; xvi. 3; xviii. 12, 14, 19 (twice), 24; xix. 22, 29; xx. 8; xxi. 10, 27; xxii. 7; xxiv. 3, 8, 15; and at least three, though not designated *Keri*, are nevertheless such, viz., xvi. 5; xviii. 8, 9. Comp. also *ibid*. v. 15; vii. 21; ix. 7; x. 8; xii. 20; xv. 63; xxiv. 19.

[66] Equally wrong is Levita's statement about the number of *Keris* and *Kethivs* in the books of Samuel, inasmuch as a careful perusal of the Massoretic remarks will show that there are 161, and not 133. They occur as follows:—1 Sam. ii. 3, 9, 10 (twice); iii. 2, 18; iv. 13; v. 6, 9, 12; vi. 4, 5; vii. 9; viii. 3; ix. 1, 26; x. 21; xi. 6, 9; xii. 10; xiii. 8, 19; xiv. 27, 32 (twice); xv. 16; xvii. 7, 23, 34; xviii. 1, 6, 7, 9, 14, 22; xix. 18, 19, 22, 23 (twice); xx. 1, 2 (twice), 24, 38; xxi. 12 (twice); xxii. 13, 17, 18 (twice), 22; xxiii. 5; xxiv. 9, 19; xxv. 3, 18 (twice), 34; xxvi. 5, 7 (twice), 11, 16, 22; xxvii. 4, 8; xxviii. 8; xxix. 5 (twice); xxx. 6, 24:—2 Sam. i. 8, 11; ii. 23; iii. 2, 3, 12, 15, 25; v. 2 (thrice), 8, 24; vi. 23; x. 9; xii. 9, 20, 22, 24, 31; xiii. 32, 34, 37; xiv. 7, 11, 21, 22, 30; xv. 8, 20, 28; xvi. 2, 8, 10 (twice), 12 (twice), 18; xvii. 12, 16; xviii. 3, 8, 12, 13, 17, 18; xix. 7, 19, 32, 41; xx. 5, 8, 14, 23, 25; xxi. 4, 6, 9 (twice), 12 (twice), 16, 20, 21; xxii. 8, 15, 23, 33, 34, 51; xxiii. 8 (twice), 9 (thrice), 11, 13, 15, 16, 18, 20 (thrice), 21, 37; xxiv. 14, 16, 18, 22. These, it must be remarked, do not include either the *Keri Ve-lo Kethiv* or the *Kethiv Ve-lo Keri*, which have already been enumerated (*vide supra*, p. 109, n. 51).

[67] The sixty-two words in which two letters following each other are transposed, are as follows:—

הולך	. . . Josh. vi. 13	מבואך	. . 2 Sam. iii. 25	וגורנך	. . Jerem. ii. 25
גלון	. . . Josh. xx. 8	והוציתוה	. . 2 Sam. xiv. 30	במרצותם	. . Jerem. viii. 6
גלון	. . . Josh. xxi. 27	בעברות	. . 2 Sam. xv. 28	שוחם	. . Jerem. ix. 7
והימשני	. . . Judg. xvi. 26	נפצות	. . 2 Sam. xviii. 8	שומע	. . Jerem. xvii. 23
ותראנה	. . . 1 Sam. xiv. 27	ויקלהו	. . 2 Sam. xx. 14	הוידע	. . Jerem. xxix. 23
בגוית	. . . 1 Sam. xiv. 18	האורנה	. . 2 Sam. xxiv. 16	וברורותך	. . Jerem. xxxii. 23
בגוית	. . . 1 Sam. xix. 22	האהל	. . 1 Kings vii. 45	התעתיה	. . Jerem. xlii. 20
בוית	. . . 1 Sam. xix. 23	הממותים	. . 2 Kings xi. 2	אשויתיה	. . Jerem. l. 15
בגוית	. . . 1 Sam. xix. 23	ימות	. . 2 Kings xiv. 6	תכשלי	. . Ezek. xxxvi. 14
והגרוי	. . . 1 Sam. xxvii. 8	ואכול	. . Is. xxxvii. 30	היאתון	. . Ezek. xl. 15

וי״ב מלין החסרין וי״ו בראש חתֿבה וקריין, which have no *Vav* conjunctive in
וי״א מלין בחפך ; ⁶⁸ וי״ח חסרין וי״ו בסוף' the text, and yet are read in the
תיבותא וקריין, וי״א מלין בחפך־ ; ⁶⁹ וכ״ט margin with it, and the 11 words
חסרים ה״א בסוף חתיבה וקריי, וכ׳ מלין in which the reverse is the case ; ⁶⁸
בחפך ; ⁷⁰ ואלפא ביתין מן ע״ה מלין דכתיבין the 18 words which want the
suffix *Vav* in the text, and are
read in the margin with it, and the 11 words in which the reverse is
the case; ⁶⁹ the 29 words which in the text want *He* at the end, and
in the margin are read with it, and the 20 words in which the reverse
is the case; ⁷⁰ the alphabetical list of 75 words, every one of which is

אמות	. .	Ezek. xlii. 16	הילכות	. .	Prov. xxxi. 27	שמלי	. . Ezra ii. 46
ומהאראיל	.	Ezek. xliii. 15	ובתובנתו	. .	Job xxvi. 12	ומבלהים	. . Ezra iv. 4
והאריאל	. .	Ezek. xliii. 16	יבדר	. . .	Eccl. ix. 4	ואוצאה	. . Ezra viii. 17
נטוי	. .	Ps. lxxiii. 2	ובמלואת	. .	Esther i. 5	בצחחיים	. . Nehem. iv. 7
פלאיה	. .	Ps. cxxxix. 6	מומכן	. .	Esther i. 16	למלוכי	. . Nehem. xii. 14
וגדלותיך	.	Ps. cxlv. 6	ידרון	. . .	Dan. iv. 9	עיות	. . 1 Chron. i. 46
כשאוה	. .	Prov. i. 27	והמיגכא	. .	Dan. v. 7	הוריהו	. 1 Chron. iii. 24
הלוך	. .	Prov. xiii. 20	תובל	. . .	Dan. v. 16	שטרי	. 1 Chron. xxvii. 29
יומת	. .	Prov. xix. 16	תוכל	. . .	Dan. v. 16	ושמרימות	2 Chron. xvii. 8
ועיף	. .	Prov. xxiii. 5	והמינכא	. .	Dan. v. 16	לועדה	. 2 Chron. xxix. 8
תרצנה	. .	Prov. xxiii. 26	והמינכא	. .	Dan. v. 29		

The list of these transpositions is given in the Massorah finalis, under letter *Vav*,
and in the *Ochla Ve-Ochla*, section xci., pp. 27, 93, &c.

⁶⁸ The twelve words which are in the text without the *Vav* conjunctive, but are read
with it in the margin, are as follows:—

בניכי	. .	2 Kings iv. 7	עד	. . .	Job ii. 7	אין	. . Lamen. v. 3
תחת	. .	Isa. lv. 13	די	. . .	Dan. ii. 43	זקנים	. . Lamen. iv. 16
דור	. .	Prov. xxvii. 24	לא	. . .	Lamen. ii. 2	אינם	. . Lamen. v. 7
יולד	. .	Prov. xxiii. 24	לא	. . .	Lamen. v. 5	אנחנו	. . Lamen. v. 7

The eleven words which, on the contrary, have *Vav* conjunctive in the text, but not
in the marginal reading, are as follows:—

וכי	. .	2 Sam. xvi. 10	ותקעו	. .	Jerem. iv. 5	והרשענו	. . Dan. ix. 5
ומסגרתיה	.	1 Kings vii. 36	ויורה	. .	Jerem. v. 24	וחסד	. . Nehem. ix. 17
וראתה	. .	2 Kings xi. 1	ויציאו	. .	Jerem. viii. 1	וישמח	. . Prov. xxiii. 24
ואת	. ,.	2 Kings xvi. 17	וכל	. . .	Jerem. xii. 12		

These instances are enumerated in the Massorah marginalis on Dan. ix. 5; Massorah
finalis, under the letter *Vav*; and *Ochla Ve-Ochla*, sections cxvii. and cxviii., pp. 32, 101.

⁶⁹ The eighteen words, which according to the Massorah want the suffix *Vav* in the
text, are as follows:—

וישתחו	. .	Gen. xxvii. 29	וישתחו	. .	1 Kings ix. 9	והללוה	. . . Ezek. vii. 21
וישתחו	. .	Gen. xliii. 28	וידבר	. .	1 Kings xii. 7	שוי	. . . Dan. v. 21
ויצו	. . .	Judg. xxi. 20	יקח	. . .	2 Kings xx. 18	ויעל	. . . Ezra iii. 3
ויעלה	. .	1 Sam. vii. 9	ויתנו	. .	2 Kings xix. 5	אחרי	. . . Nehem. iii. 30
ויאמר	. .	1 Sam. xii. 10	ואכול	. .	Isaiah xxxvii. 30	אחרי	. . . Nehem. iii. 31
אמר	. . .	1 Sam. xiii. 19	יחד	. .	Jerem. xlviii. 7	וקבל	. . . Esther ix. 27

The eleven words which on the contrary terminate with *Vav* in the textual reading,
but have no *Vav* in the marginal reading, are as follows:—

ויאמרו	. .	Josh. vi. 7	ויבאו	. .	1 Kings xii. 3	ויצוהו	. . 2 Kings xvi. 15
ויאמרו	. .	Josh. ix. 7	ויבאו	. .	1 Kings xii. 21	יצאו	. . Ezek. xlvi. 9
ויאמרו	. .	1 Sam. xv. 16	שממותיהו	.	2 Kings ix. 33	ויעמידו	. . Nehem. iii. 15
רגליו	. .	2 Sam. xxii. 34	ויבאו	. .	2 Kings xiv. 13		

These instances are partly enumerated in Tract *Sopherim* vii. 1; and entirely in the
Massorah marginalis on 1 Kings i. 1, xii. 3; Massorah finalis under letter *Vav*; and *Ochla
Ve-Ochla*, sections cxix. and cxx., pp. 32, 102.

⁷⁰ The twenty-nine words which have no *He* in the textual reading, but have it in the
marginal reading, are as follows:—

in the text written with a *Jod* in the יו״ד באמצע תיבותא וקריין וי״ו, ואלפא
middle, and in the margin read with ביתא מן ע' מלין בהפך,[71] אין גם אחד מהן
Vav, and the alphabetical list of
70 words in which the reverse is the case;[71] not one of all these occurs

וארב	. . Josh. xxiv. 3	ותעגב	. . Ezek. xxiii. 16	נטע	. . Prov. xxxi. 16
הגג	. . 1 Sam. ix. 26	עת	. . Ezek. xxiii. 43	בליל	. . Prov. xxxi. 18
ואת	. . 1 Sam. xxiv. 19	חמש	. . Ezek. xlv. 3	את	. . Job i. 10
והמ	. . 2 Sam. xxi. 9	ואכבד	. . Hag. i. 8	וירא	. . Job xlii. 16
יהי	. . 1 Kings i. 37	לכן	. . Ruth i. 12	בליל	. . Lament. ii. 19
והית	. . 2 Kings ix. 37	ואלע	. . Ruth iv. 4	הביש	. . Lament. v. 1
ונרא	. . Isaiah xli. 23	ואת	. . Ps. vi. 4	ונשוב	. . Lament. v. 21
הן	. . Isaiah liv. 16	ועת	. . Ps. lxxiv. 6	את	. . Eccl. vii. 22
ירא	. . Jerem. xvii. 8	שת	. . Ps. xc. 8	את	. . Nehem. ix. 6
תעש	. . Jerem. xl. 16	וארבע	. . Prov. xxx. 18		

The twenty words which on the contrary terminate with *He* in the textual reading, but not in the marginal reading, are—

ואראה	. . Josh. vii. 21	הזאתה	. . Jerem. xxvi. 6	הרבה	. . Ps. li. 4
ואביאה	. . Josh. xxiv. 39	קוה	. . Jerem. xxxi. 39	אהביה	. . Prov. viii. 17
הארי	. . 2 Sam. xxiii. 20	ובאה	. . Jerem. xliii. 11	ורעה	. . Prov. xxvii. 10
וקוה	. . 1 Kings vii. 23	נמצאה	. . Jerem. xlviii. 27	פקדה	. . Dan. ix. 18
ותראה	. . Jerem. iii. 7	רעה	. . Micah iii. 2	אריה	. . Lament. iii. 10
באה	. . Jerem. xv. 9	וקוה	. . Zech. i. 16	אלה	. . Ezra v. 15
דרעה	. . Jerem. xviii. 10	ישעה	. . Ruth i. 3		

These instances are given in the Tract *Sopherim* vii. 2 ; Massorah marginalis on Prov. xxxi. 16 ; Lament. ii. 19, v. 1 ; Eccl. vii. 23 ; Massorah finalis under letter *He*, and *Ochla Ve-Ochla*, sections cxi. and cxii., pp. 31, 99, &c.

[71] The following are the words which in the textual reading have *Jod* in the middle of the word, and are with *Vav* in the marginal reading:—

אזכיר	. . Ps. lxxvii. 12	ובשגיב	. . 1 Kings xvi. 34	מידעת	. . Isaiah xii. 5
ארינה	. . 2 Sam. xxiv. 18	ולשימו	. . Isaiah x. 6	מיסרות	. . Ezek. xli. 8
בחניו	. . Isa. xxiii. 13	וריב	. . Job xxxiii. 19	נסיסים	. . Ezra ii. 50
ברתיקות	. 1 Kings vi. 21	ונציירי	. . Isaiah xlix. 6	שימה	. . 2 Sam. xiii. 32
בכיס	. . Prov. xxiii. 31	והירא	. . Dan. ii. 22	עינתם	. . Hos. x. 10
בגיים	. . Ps. lxxix. 10	וסיפניה	. . Dan. iii. 10	עליה	. . 1 Chron. i. 51
גיים	. . Gen. xxv. 23	ותשיח	. . Lament. iii. 20	פטירים	. . 1 Chron. ix. 33
גדירה	. . 1 Chron. xii. 15	זידה	. . 2 Kings xxiii. 36	ציף	. . 1 Chron. xi. 20
הדרופי	. . 1 Chron. xii. 5	חישה	. . Ps. lxxi. 12	קריא	. . Numb. i. 16
המעינים	. 1 Chron. iv. 41	ישיב	. . 2 Sam. xv. 8	ראית	. . Isaiah xlii. 20
ויישם	. . Gen. xxiv. 33	יניו	. . Ps. lxxii. 17	ראית	. . Eccl. v. 10
וילינו	. . Exod. xvi. 2	יצפינו	. . Ps. lvi. 7	שיש	. . Isaiah xxviii. 15
ויירש	. . Numb. xxi. 32	ימישו	. . Ps. cxl. 11	שיחה	. . Jerem. xviii. 22
ויים	. . Josh. xv. 53	יריםו	. . Ps. lxvi. 7	שביתכם	. Jerem. xxix. 14
וינימו	. . Judg. vii. 21	יקצרון	. . Job xxiv. 6	שובבים	. . Jerem. l. 6
ורעיתי	. . Judg. xi. 37	כמיש	. . Jerem. xlviii. 7	שביתך	. . Lament. ii. 14
וייחל	. . 1 Sam. xiii. 8	לעדיא	. . Nehem. xii. 16	שילל	. . Micah i. 8
וייחר	. . 2 Sam. xx. 5	לעזיר	. . 2 Sam. xviii. 3	שעריריה	. . Hos. vi. 10
ושיא	. . 2 Sam. xxi. 25	מדין	. . 2 Sam. xxi. 20	שדין	. . Job xix. 29
ומניאל	. 1 Chron. viii. 25	מגדיל	. . 2 Sam. xxii. 51	תחיל	. . Ezek. xxx. 16
וצפינך	. . Ps. xvii. 14	מיסך	. . 2 Kings xvi. 18	תמיש	. . Prov. xvii. 13
וצירים	. . Ps. xlix. 15	מיצקת	. . 2 Kings iv. 5	תמריק	. . Prov. xx. 30
וגיש	. . Job vii. 5	מידע	. . Ruth ii. 1	תרים	. . Ps. lxxxix. 18
והיתי	. . Job vi. 2				

The following is the Alphabetical list of words, which, on the contrary have *Vav* in the middle of the word in the textual reading, and have *Jod* in the marginal reading—

אסורי	. . Gen. xxxix. 20	ארצום	. . Jerem. l. 44	גול	. . Prov. xxiii. 24
אבוגיל	. . 1 Sam. xxv. 18	בעוני	. . 2 Sam. xvi. 12	דהוא	. . Ezra iv. 9
אנועך	. . 2 Sam. xv. 20	בור	. . Jerem. vi. 7	הוצא	. . Gen. viii. 17
אושר	. . Isaiah xlv. 2	בהלויחם	. . Nahum ii. 6	החרסות	. Jerem. xix. 2
אולי	. . 2 Kings xxiv. 15	ברוות	. 1 Chron. vii. 31	הלחות	. Jerem. xlviii. 5

in the Pentateuch.[72] There is undoubtedly a reason for all this, but I do not know it. I have now satisfied my desire in explaining that which I deemed necessary about the nature of the *Keri* and the *Kethiv*.

☞ I shall now say something about the nature of *plene* and *defective*. First of all, I say, it appears that, to the words which were found written *plene* or *defective*, nothing new whatsoever was added by the men of the Great Synagogue out of their own understanding; but that Ezra transcribed them, into his copy of the Law, just as he found them in the Codex of the Law which was made from the scroll of the Law of Moses received from Sinai, and which the prophet Jeremiah concealed,[73] according to the opinion of some, without adding anything to it or taking anything from it. The same is the case with the *defective* and *plene* of the Prophets

בתורה;[72] ועל כל פנים טעם יש בדבר, ואנכי לא ידעתי, וכאן נשלם חפצי מה שראיתי לבאר בענין קריין וכתבן:

☞ ועתה אדבר מעט מענין המלאים והחסרים, ואתחיל ואומר, כי המלות שנכתבו חסרים או מלאים נראה כי לא חדשו אנשי כנסת הגדולה בהן דבר מדעתם, רק עזרא כתבם בתורה, כאשר מצאם בטופס ס״ח אשר הועתק מספר תורת משה אשר קבל מסיני שגנז ירמיה הנביא לפי דעת האומרים כבה,[73] ולא הוסיף ולא גרע, וכן החסרים והמלאים שבנביאים ובכתובים, אם נמצאו בידם נופי

הבצור	. . Zech. xi. 2	יעבור	. Ezek. xlviii. 14	עשוות	. 1 Sam. xxv. 18
המבוא	. Ezek. xlii. 9	יעור	. . 1 Chron. xx. 5	עופי	. . Jerem. xl. 8
המבונים	. 2 Chron. xxxv. 3	יחואל	. 2 Chron. xxix. 14	עני	. . Amos viii. 4
הושר	. . Ps. v. 9	ינועון	. . Ps. lix. 16	עפרון	. 2 Chron. xiii. 19
התעוף	. Prov. xxiii. 5	יכסומו	. . Ps. cxl. 10	עתודים	. Esther viii. 13
הנתונים	. Ezra vii. 17	יכשולו	. . Prov. iv. 16	צעוריהם	. Jerem. xiv. 3
הכעוסני	. Jerem. xxv. 7	לוש	. 2 Sam. iii. 15	צעוריה	. Jerem. xlviii. 4
החטשות	. 2 Chron. xxvi. 21	לדוגים	. Jerem. xvi. 16	צפועי	. . Ezek. iv. 15
וילונו	. . Numb. xiv. 36	לרוב	. Judg. xxi. 22	קרואי	. . Numb. xxvi. 9
ושדצומה	. Joshua xix. 22	לשור	. 1 Sam. xviii. 6	שושק	. . 1 Kings xiv. 25
וצנוף	. Isaiah lxii. 3	לסוד	. Ezek. xviii. 18	שרוקה	. Jerem. xviii. 16
ואלול	. Jerem. xiv. 14	למוסדה	. Isaiah xlii. 24	שרותך	. Jerem. xv. 11
ותרמות	. Jerem. xiv. 14	למענותם	. Ps. cxxix. 3	שפרורו	. Jerem. xliii. 10
וסום	. Jerem. viii. 7	מניוח	. 1 Sam. xx. 1	שמור	. 1 Chron. xxv. 24
ואתוקידהא	. Ezek. xli. 15	מופעת	Jerem. xlviii. 21	שבותם	. . Zeph. ii. 7
ותלון	. 1 Chron. iv. 20	נוב	. . Isaiah lvii. 19	שבות	. Ps. lxxxv. 2
ויזואל	. 1 Chron. xii. 3	נובי	. . Nehem. x. 20	שלשום	. Prov. xxii. 20
והכונו	. 2 Chron. xxxv. 4	נמוות	. Isaiah iii. 16	תנואון	. Numb. xxxii. 7
דוקך	. Ps. lxxiv. 11	נפושסים	. Nehem. vii. 52	תרוב	. . Prov. iii. 30
יצוע	. 1 Kings vi. 5	שם	. 2 Sam. xiv. 7	תשוחה	. . Job xxx. 22

It will be seen that the Massorah finalis, under letter *Jod*, where these alphabetical lists are found, only gives seventy-two of the former, whereas of the latter it gives seventy-five. Comp. also *Sopherim* vii. 4; *Ochla Ve-Ochla*, sections lxxx. and lxxxi., pp. 24, 85, &c.

[72] Levita is surely incorrect in his statement that not one of the variations specified in these lists occurs in the Pentateuch. In perusing them it will be seen, that in the list of eighteen words (No. 69), we have Gen. xxvii. 29; xlii. 28; in the list of seventy words (No. 71), we have Gen. xxiv. 33; xxv. 23; Exod. xvi. 2; Numb. i. 16; xxi. 32; and in the next list (also No. 71), Gen. viii. 17; xxxix. 20; Numb. xiv. 36; xxvi. 9; xxxii. 7.

[73] According to the traditional explanation of Deut. xxxi. 26, a copy of the entire Pentateuch was deposited by Moses in the Ark of the Covenant (Comp. *Gittin* 60 *a*; *Baba Bathra* 14–15; *Menachoth* 30 *a*; *Jerusalem Targum* on Deut. xxxi. 26). This Codex Jeremiah concealed when he concealed the Ark, together with the Tabernacle and the Altar of Incense. 2 Maccab. ii. 5.

and Hagiographa. Thus, when they [Ezra and his associates] found the very autographs of the authors themselves, as was the case with the book of Isaiah, which Isaiah himself wrote, the Psalms which David wrote, the Proverbs which Solomon wrote, and with all or part of the books which they possessed, they required no tradition to guide them, but copied exactly as they found it: *plene* wherever there was *plene*, and *defective* wherever there was *defective*. But when they did not find the autograph itself, which seems most likely to have happened, they undoubtedly followed the majority of Codices, which they had collected from different places, one here and one there, as the twenty-four books were then not joined together into one volume. Now they [Ezra and his associates] have joined them together, and divided them into three parts: the Law, the Prophets, and the Hagiographa, and arranged the Prophets and Hagiographa not in the order in which they have been put by our Rabbins of blessed memory, in *Baba Bathra* [14 *a*].

הספרים אשר כתבו המחברים עצמם, כגון ישעיה שכתב הוא בעצמו, וכן תהלים שכתב דוד, ומשלי שכתב שלמה, וכן כלן או מקצתן אשר נמצאו בידם, לא היו צריכים לקבלה אלא הניחום כמו שמצאום, במקום מלא מלא, ובמקום חסר חסר, אבל אם לא נמצאו כמו שהוא קרוב לודאי, הלכו אחר רוב ההעתקות הנמצאות, אחת הנה ואחת הנה, כי לא היו הכ״ד ספרים מחוברים יחד, והם חברום ועשו מהם ג׳ חלקים, תורה נביאים וכתובים, וסדרום נביאים וכתובים‎ זה אחר זה שלא כסדר שסדרום רז״ל בבבא בתרא:

וזהו סדרן של רז״ל סדרן של נביאים, יהושע שופטים שמואל מלכים, ירמיה ישעיה יחזקאל, תרי עשר: וסדרן של כתובין רות תהלים איוב משלי קהלת שיר השירים קינות אסתר ד״ה, ונותנים טעמים וסברות נכונות על סדרן זה, ואין כאן מקומן:

ובעלי המסורת סדרו נבאים בסדר הזה, רק שהקדימו ישעיה לפני ירמיה ויחזקאל, לפי שזמנו היה קודם זמנם, וכן נמצא סדורן בכל ספרי ספרדים המובהקים, אבל בספרי האשכנזים והצרפתים הם סדורים בסדר של רז״ל, אכן בכתובים בעלי המסרה סדרון של רז״ל, וזהו, ד״ה תהלים איוב משלי, רות שיר השירים קהלת קינות אסתר, דניאל עזרא, וכן בספרי הספרדים, אבל בספרי האשכנזים סדרן

The following is the order of our Rabbins, of blessed memory:— The position of the Prophets is—Joshua, Judges, Samuel, Kings, Jeremiah, Isaiah, Ezekiel, and the twelve minor Prophets. The order of the Hagiographa is—Ruth, Psalms, Job, Proverbs, Ecclesiastes, Song of Songs, Lamentations, Esther, and Chronicles, and they [the Rabbins] gave appropriate reasons for this classification, which would be out of place here.

The Massorites too have adopted this order in the Prophets, only that they have put Isaiah before Jeremiah and Ezekiel, because he lived before them. The same order is also found in all the correct Spanish Codices; whilst the German and French Codices adopt the order of the Rabbins, of blessed memory. But in the Hagiographa, the Massorites have altered the order of the Rabbins of blessed memory as follows: Chronicles, Psalms, Job, Proverbs, Ruth, Song of Songs, Ecclesiastes, Lamentations, Esther, Daniel, Ezra, which is followed in the Spanish Codices; whereas the German Codices have the following order:— Psalms, Proverbs, Job, the Five Megilloth, Daniel, Ezra, and Chronicles. It is the custom to put the Five Megilloth in the order in which they are read in the Synagogue, according to their respective seasons, that is, Song of Songs, Ruth, Lamentations, Ecclesiastes, and Esther.[74]

☞ Having now reached the place in which I, at the beginning of this Introduction, promised to state my own opinion about the points and accents, I shall first do battle against those who say that they were given on Sinai, and then state who invented them, and when they were originated and affixed to the letters. But if anyone should prove to me, by clear evidence, that my opinion is opposed to that of our Rabbins of blessed memory, or is contrary to the genuine Kabbalah of the *Sohar*,[75] I will readily give in to him, and declare my opinion as void. Up to this time, however, I have neither found, nor seen, nor heard, any evidence, nor anything approaching to it, that is worthy to be relied upon, that the points and accents were given upon Sinai.

I shall here state what I have found written on this subject in some treatises of later writers, but not in the works[76] of the Rabbins of blessed memory. Kimchi, in his *Michlol*, after citing the statement of the Talmud that it is necessary to make a pause between the conjunctions, remarks thus: "—בְּכָל (Deut. xi. 13) is pointed with *Kametz*, because of the *Makeph*, and if it were read without the *Makeph*, it would be pointed בְּכֹל with *Cholem*, and this, certainly, the Rabbins of blessed

ככה, תהלים משלי איוב, המש מגלות, דניאל עזרא ד"ה, וה' המגילות נוהגים לכתוב סדרן לפי הסדר שקוראים אותן בבית הכנסת בזמנם, דהיינו שיר רות קינות קהלת אסתר:[74]

☜ וְעַתָּה הגעתי עד המקום אשר אמרתי בתחלת ההקדמה הזאת להוות דעי אף אני בענין חנקודות והטעמים, ואערוך מלחמה נגד האומרים שנתנו מסיני, ואודיע מי יסדם, ומתי הוסדו והושמו עם האותיות, ומי שיוכיחני בהוכחה ברורה שדעתי זאת נגד דעת רז"ל, ונגד הקבלה האמתית שבספר הזוהר[75] יבוטל דעתי מפני דערו, אבל עד הנה לא מצאתי ולא ראיתי ולא שמעתי דבר ראיה, או סמך שראוי לסמוך עליו, שהנקודות והטעמים נתנו מסיני:

והנני אכתוב כל מה שמצאתי כתוב על ככה בקצת דברי האחרונים אך לא בדברי[76] רז"ל, כתב הרד"ק במכלול כאשר מביא מאמר רז"ל שצריך ליתן רוח בין הדבקים, וז"ל, הנה בְּכָל־לְבַבְכֶם, נקוד בקמץ מפני המקף, ואם יקרא אותו בלא מקף יהיה נקוד

---

[74] The Five Megilloth are respectively read every year, on five annual festivals, as follows:—i. The Song of Songs on Passover; ii. Ruth on Pentecost; iii. Lamentations on the Ninth of *Ab*; iv. Ecclesiastes on Tabernacles; and v. Esther on Purim. These festivals occur in the succession in which they are enumerated. Hence the present order of the Five Megilloth.

[75] The important passage ונגד הקבלה האמתית שבספר הזוהר, *or against the genuine Kabbalah of the Sohar*, which was first animadverted upon by Azzariah de Rossi (*Meor Enajim* 287, &c., ed. Vienna, *vide supra*, p. 52), and of which the Buxtorfs made such terrible use against Levita *(Commentarius Masoreticus*, cap. ix., p. 74, ed. Basel 1620), is entirely omitted in the Sulzbach edition. That the *Sohar* does mention the vowel-points has already been shown (*vide supra*, p. 48), and Levita's assertion to the contrary is to be accounted for on the supposition advanced by De Rossi, that it arose from his not having read the *Sohar*, which had not then been printed.

[76] The Sulzbach edition erroneously has אך בלא דברי, instead of אך לא בדברי.

memory did not say, in order that the vowel-points should in any way be changed from what they were as given to Moses on Sinai."[77] Thus far his remark. But one must hesitate to accept this statement, inasmuch as it contradicts what he has said before on the *Niphal* conjugation of the regular verb, which is ☞ as follows : [78] "The inventors of the points made a distinction between the singular third person præterite and the participle, as they are pronounced alike, and pointed the past tense with *Pattach*, under the second radical [נִפְקַד], and the participle with *Kametz* [נִפְקָד]." Thus far the substance of his remark. We therefore see, from his own words, that even he believed that there were men who invented the points, namely, ֵ ֶ ָ ַ ְ &c. Hence it is evident that when he remarks, "as they were given to Moses on Sinai," he does not mean to say the form of the points, but the five major and the five minor sounds; and this is the reason why he uses the words "to change the *vowels*," and does not say the *points*. Thus, also, when [79] he said, "*as* they were given," and not "*which* were given," his words are to be understood in the same way, and I have no need to dwell on this point any longer.

R. Levi b. Joseph, author of the book *Semadar*, says, at the beginning of his work, as follows : [80] "If any one should ask, Whence do we know that the points and accents were dictated by the mouth of the Omnipotent? the reply is, It is to be found in the Scriptures, for it is written, 'And thou shalt write upon the stones all the words of this law *very plainly*' (Deut. xxvii. 8). Now, if the points and accents, which

---

[77] Kimchi's remark, to which allusion is made in the text, is to be found on p. 25 *b* of Levita's own edition of the *Michlol*, Venice, 1545, and on p. 81 *a*, ed. Hechim Fürth, 1793.
[78] This quotation is to be found on p. 18 *b*, &c., ed. Venice, 1545, and on p. 61 *a*, ed. Fürth, 1793.
[79] The Sulzbach edition has omitted the word מה, *what*.
[80] Nothing is known of this Grammatical Treatise, entitled *Sepher Ha-Semadar* (ספר הסמדר) = *the Book of the Vine-blossom*, or of its author, beyond the fact that it is also quoted by Azzariah de Rossi (*Meor Enajim*, cap. lix.), who endorses the above-named arguments for the antiquity of the vowel-points, and by Samuel Archevolti, in his Grammatical Treatise, entitled *Arugath Ha-Bosem* (ערוגת הבושם) = *A Trellis for Aromatic Plants*, published at Venice, 1602, and Amsterdam, 1730, who also espouses its sentiments. Comp. Buxtorf, *De Punctatorum Antiquitate*, p. 42, &c., Basel, 1648.

make the words plain did not exist, how could one possibly understand plainly whether שְׁלָמָה means *wherefore*, *retribution*, *Solomon*, *garment*, or *perfect?*" Thus far his remark. I leave it to the reader to judge whether this is reliable proof.

Again, I found another book, which seems to me to be the work called *Instruction for the Reader*, and the author of which I do not know, say as follows:[81] "There are some of the punctuators who, not knowing thoroughly the true nature of the points, ask why we do not find two *Sarkoth* on one word, seeing that there are two *Pashtin?* But had they known that there never existed more than one *Sarka*, and that no more than one *Sarka*, followed by a *Segol*, was revealed to our teacher Moses of blessed memory, they would not have asked such a question." Thus far its remark. Now all this is vain and wrong, since two *Sarkos* are frequently found, as I shall show in my book, entitled *Good Sense*, under the form *Sarka*.

Again, I found in the treatise published here, around the *Massorah finalis*, which some say is *The Book Shimshoni*, but which I say is R. Moses the Punctuator's, as I shall show in part iii., called the *Broken Tables*, as follows:[82] "It is true that the points were given on Sinai,

ואילולי הנקוד וחטעמים שמבארין חתיבורת אין אדם יכול לחבין ביאורם, כנון שְׁלָמָה שְׁלָמָה, שְׁלֹמֹה, שַׁלְמָה, שַׁלְמָה, שְׁלֵמָה, עכ"ל, ראו נא אם זאת ראיה טובה לסמוך עליה:

ועוד מצאתי בספר אחד נראה לי שהוא הספר הנקרא הוריית הקורא, ולא ידעתי מי הוא המחבר ו"ל,[81] ויש מן הנקדנים אשר לא עלה בידם אמתת הנקוד מקשים ואומרים למה לא נעשה ב' זרקות במלה אחת כמו שנעשה ב' פשטין, ואלו ידעו שאין כעולם אלא זרקא אחת ולא חראו לו למשח רע"ה אלא זרקא אחת ואחריו סגול, לא הקשו על זה עכ"ל, והנה כל זה הבל ושקר כי נמצאו ב' זרקאות לרוב, כמו שאבאר בספר טוב טעם בתמונת הזרקא:

ועוד מצאתי במה שנדפפ פה סביב המסרה הגדולה, ואומרים שהוא ספר השמשוני, ואני אומר שהוא של רבי משה הנקדן כמו שיתבאר בשער שברי לוחות, וזה לשונו,[82] אמת הוא שהנקוד נתן מסיני אלא

---

[81] The *Horajoth Ha-Kore* (הריית הקורא) = *Instruction for the Reader*, by Ibn Balaam, (flourished, A.D. 1050-1090), discusses, in twenty-four chapters, the accents and vowel-points of the Hebrew language. From Dukes' publication of the Introduction and Table of Contents, it is evident that cap. i.—xvii. of this Treatise are devoted to the doctrine of the prose accents of the twenty-one sacred books; whilst cap. xviii.—xxiv. are taken up with the metrical accents of the three remaining books, viz., the Psalms, Proverbs, and Job. The seventeen chapters which discuss the prose accents were re-cast by the author himself, and designated טעמי המקרא, *A Treatise on the Accents of the Scriptures*. It was first published by the learned John Mercier, Paris, 1565, and Heidenheim inserted twelve chapters of it in his work ספר משפטי הטעמים, *On the Laws of the Accents*. Rödelheim, 1808. The second part, which assumed the name of טעמי אמ"ת ספר, *A Treatise on the Accents of Job, Proverbs, and the Psalms*, was also published first by John Mercier, Paris, 1556, and recently by G. J. Polak, Amsterdam, 1858. Comp. Fürst, *Zeitschrift der deutschen morgenländischen Gesellschaft*, vol. xx., p. 201, Leipzig, 1866; Steinschneider, *Catalogus Libr. Hebr. in Bibliotheca Bodleiana*, col. 1294, &c.

[82] The *Treatise on the Vowel-points and Accents*, by R. Moses the Punctuator, who lived in London *circa* A.D. 1230, is alternately designated כללי הנקוד, *the Laws of the Points* (*vide infra*, Part iii., *sub* רמ"ה); Wolf, *Bibliotheca Hebraea* i. 822); שערי הנקוד והנגינות, *the Gates to the Vowel-points and Accents* (comp. *Massorah marginalis* on Amos iv. 1; Ps. cxxxvi. 3); דרכי הנצוד והנגינות, *the Method of the Vowel-points and the Accents* (Wolf, *Bibliotheca Hebraea* i. 592); and הוריית הקורא, *Instruction to the Reader*

but they were forgotten again, till Ezra came and revealed them." ☞ Thus far its remark. Now the truth is that I do not understand this truth. But it is undoubtedly true that the law which Moses put before the Children of Israel was a plain Codex, without points and without accents, and even without the division of verses, as we see it to the present day.[83] According to the opinion of the Kabbalists, the whole Law is like one verse, and indeed, some of them say, like one word, from which they combine sundry Divine Names. Thus says Nachmanides of blessed memory, in the Introduction to his Commentary on the Pentateuch, which you may consult.[84]

ששכחחו עד שבא עזרא וגלחו עד כאן לש׳,
☞ ובאמת אינני מבין זה האמת, אך אמת הוא שאין בו ספק שזאת התורה אשר שם משה לפני בני ישראל, היה ספר פשום בלי נקוד ובלי טעמים, ובלי סמני סופי פסוקים, כאשר אנחנו רואים חיום,[88] ולפי דעת בעלי הקבלה כל התורה היא כפסוק אחד, וי״א חיבה אחת, ויוצאין מהן שמות של הק״בה, כמו שכתב הרמ״בן ז״ל בפתיחתו לפירוש התורה ע״ש:[84]

ואני אומר אם אמת הוא שהנקוד נתן מסני לא ימנע מהחלוקה, אם נאמר שהק״בה הראה למשה רבנו ע״ה צורת הנקודות וחטעמים של אש, לאמר כזה ראה הוא ָ קמץ, וכזה הוא ַ פתח, וכזה הוא ֵ צרי, וכזה הוא ֶ סגול, וכזה הוא זרקא, וכזה הוא פזר, וכן כלם, ומר״עה הראה חמונתם לישראל ולא שם אותם עם התיבות, א״כ מח תועלת חיתה

Now, I submit, if it be true that the points were given on Sinai, we cannot escape one of these two alternatives. We must either say that God revealed to Moses, our teacher of blessed memory, the forms of the points and accents in fire, saying, this ָ is the shape of *Kametz*, this ַ the shape of *Pattach*, this ֵ is the form of *Tzere*, this ֶ is the form of *Segol*, this ֯ the shape of *Zarka*, this ֯ the shape of *Pazer*, and so on; and that Moses, our teacher of blessed memory, showed these forms to Israel, and *did not* affix them

---

of the Scriptures (comp. Steinschneider, *Bibliograph. Handbuch*, p. 95, Leipzig, 1865). It was first published by Jacob b. Chajim in the margin of the Massorah finalis, Venice, 1525, to which edition Levita refers. It has since been reprinted in all the editions of the Rabbinic Bibles, and has been republished separately with a short commentary by Zebi b. Menachem, Wilna, 1822, and with corrections and German notes by the learned Frensdorff, Hanover, 1847. Levita's quotation will be found on p. 1 Hebrew text, and animadverted upon p. 1 in the German notes, of the last mentioned edition.

[83] The Synagogal Scrolls of the Law, out of which the hebdomadal lessons are read among the Rabbinic Jews, have to the present day neither the vowel-points nor the accents, nor any of the Massoretic glosses whatsoever, (*vide supra*, p. 44, &c.) It is to this fact that Levita refers.

[84] Ramban רמ״בן is the acrostic of ר׳ משה בן נחמן, *R. Moses b. Nachman* = Nachmanides, the distinguished Talmudist, Commentator, Moral Philosopher, Kabbalist, and Physician, who was born at Gerona, in Catalonia, *circa* A.D. 1195, and died at Acco *circa* 1270. The passage to which Levita refers, is as follows:— עוד יש בידינו קבלה של אמת כי כל התורה כולה שמותיו של הק׳בה שהתיבות מתחלקות לשמות בענין אחד כאלו תחשוב על דרך משל כי פסוק בראשית יחולק לתבות אחרות כגון בראש ייתברא אלהים וכל התורה כן מלבד צירופיחן וגימטריותיחן של שמות, *We possess a faithful tradition that the whole Pentateuch consists of names of the Holy One, blessed be he; for the words may be re-divided into sacred names of a different import, so that it is to be taken as an allegory. Accordingly, the words* ברא אלהים בראשית (Gen. i. 1), *for instance, may be re-divided into the words* בראש יתברא אלהים. *This is the case with the whole Law, which consists of nothing but permutations and numerals of divine names.* For a sketch of the life of Nachmanides, see Kitto's *Cyclopœdia, s. v.*; and for his relation to the Kabbalah, see Ginsburg, *the Kabbalah*, p. 108, &c., Longmans, 1865.

to the words; in which case the Israelites would have derived no benefit from seeing them. Or we must say, that he *did* affix them to the words, and come to the conclusion that he wrote another Codex, besides our Pentateuch, with points and accents, and recited it with them, till they knew it, and that afterwards, each one who wished copied it. In this case the question arises, How could the points and accents be forgotten, unless we say that all these copies were afterwards lost? which is altogether incredible. Even the explanation which the sages give of Neh. viii. 8, quoted above [p. 103, &c.], does not at all mention the points. This is also the opinion of Ibn Ezra, peace be upon him, who says in his Grammar, entitled *Purity*,[85] "There are many commentators who maintain that those who divided the verses committed blunders, but this is not correct. To this class belongs R. Moses Ha-Cohen, &c., but I am perfectly astonished at it, for how could the divider commit blunders if he was Ezra the Scribe? In short, after the divider there were none so wise as he was, since we see that, throughout the whole of the Scriptures, he never made a pause which is not in its proper place." Thus far his remark. The meaning of מפסיק is the one who made the dividing accents.

לחם לישראל בראיה זו, ואם נאמר ששם אותם עם החיבות צריכים אצחנו לומר, שכתב להם ספר זילרת ספר התורה כעין החומשים שלנו עם הנקודור. והטעמים וקרא בו עמהם עד שידעו אותם, וא"כ כח כל מי שרצה העתיק לו חומש אחר כמהו, ואם כן איך שייך בהן שכחה אם לא נאמר שאבדו הספרים החם כלם, וזה רחוק להאמין, ואפילו לפי מדרש חכמים ש־דרשו על פסוק ויקראו בספר תורת אלהים כמו שכתבתי לעיל, לא זכרו בו הנקוד כלל, וכן דעת ר' אברהם א"ע בספר צחות, וז"ל, ⁸⁵ יש מפרשים רבים מטעים את המפסיק ולא דבדו נכינה, ומהם רבי משה הכהן וכו׳. עד ואני אתמה מזה תמהון גדול, איך טעה המפסיק ואף כי אם הוא עזרא הסופר, והכלל כי המפסיק לא היה אחריו חכם כמהו, כי הנה ראינו בכל המקרא לא הפסיק אלא במקום הראוי עכ"ל, ופירוש המפסיק מי ששם הפסקת הטעמים

ותמיה אני עליו איך כנהו כאן בלשון יחיד ואין ספק כי היו אנשים רבים, כמו שאוכיח אח"כ, וכן כנה אותם בעצמו בספר מאזנים בלשון רבים, והנה כאן מובן מדבריו שאין דעתו שהטעמים ניתנו מסיני, וכן מצאתי בספר אחד הנקרא צח שפתים

Now I am astonished at his speaking here of one divider, since there is no doubt that there were many dividers, as I shall show hereafter; and since Ibn Ezra himself speaks of them in the plural, in his grammar called *The Balance*. At any rate, his words here show that he was not of opinion that the accents were given on Sinai. I

---

[85] The passage alluded to is to be found on p. 73 *a*, *b*, ed. Lippmann, Fürth, 1827, and in its entirety is as follows:— יש מפרשים רבים מטעיב את המפסיק, ולא אמרו נכונה, מהם ר"מ הכהן שאמר כי למכביר (איוב ל"ו כ"א) סמוך עם על כפים כסה אור (שב פסוק ל"ב)׳ וכן ברוגז רחום תזכור (חבקוק ג' ב') רבק עם אלה מחמון יבוא (שם ג' ג')׳ ובכר פרשתי שנידם שהם מוכרתים׳ וכל זה אירע בעבור שמצאו בדברי היחיד שיש עשרה פסוקים במקרא שהיו ראויב להיותם דבוקים׳ ואני לפי דעתי . . . לא הפסיק כי אם במקום ראוי. Both Buxtorf (*De Punctatorum Antiquitate*, p. 11, &c.) and Morin (*Lib.* ii., *Exercit.* xii. c. 7) have elaborated upon this passage; the one trying to prove from it that Ibn Ezra maintained the antiquity of the vowel-points, and the other to show that he regarded the Massorites as having lived after the close of the Talmud.

have also found the following words, in a book called *The Purity of the Language*:[86] "We must know that the points were given on Sinai; not that they were put on the Tables of Stone; but when the Lord spake in the holy tongue, those who heard him could distinguish between the vowel-points and syllables,[87] both short and long. Just as the vigour of the human voice utters higher or lower notes according to requirement, so ought we to distinguish from the mouth of readers between אָ with a *Kametz* and אַ with *Pattach*, between אָ with *Tzere* and אֶ with *Segol*, between אוֹ with *Cholem* and אֳ *Chateph-Kametz*, between אוּ with *Vav* and אֻ without the *Vav*, between אִי with *Jod* and אִ without *Jod*."[88] Thus far his remark.

וז"ל,[86] יש לנו לדעת כי חנקוד נתן בסיני ולא שנקדו חלחות, אך כאשר דבר הק"בה לשון הקדש הביגו השומעים כל התנועות וחקולות[87] הקטנות והגדולות כאשר נכון הדבר במוצא פה החזק הוא חרפה, כך יש להכיר מפי הקוראים בין אָ קמץ לאַ פתח, ובין אֵ צרי לאֶ סגול, ובין אוֹ חולם לאֳ חטוף קמץ, ובין אוּ בויו לאֻ בלי ויו, ובין אִ ביוד לאִ בלי יוד[88] עכ"ל:

וגם כתב החכם בעל ספר הכוזר במאמר ג' מספרו וז"ל,[89] אמר החבר בלי ספק שחיח שמור בלבבות בפתחא וחקמץ וחשבר והשבא והטעמים וכו', עד ושמו שבע המלכים והטעמים אותות לתכונות ההם אשר חעתיקום בקבלה ממר"עה, ומה תחשוב על אשר חקנו המקרא בפסוקים תחלה, ואחר כן בנקוד,

The learned author of *The Khosari* also remarks, in section iii. [31,] as follows:[89] "The master replied, Doubtless the *Pattach, Kametz, Sheber, Sheva*, and the accents were committed to memory * * and they put the principal vowels and the accents as marks, to indicate what was received from Moses by tradition. What thinkest thou about it? that they have received the Bible first

---

[86] Wolf (*Bibliotheca Hebraea* i. 80, 160) conjectures that the *Purity of the Language* (צַח שְׂפָתִים), may simply be another name for the well known work of Ibn Ezra, entitled *Purity* (צחות), quoted in the preceding note. After carefully perusing, however, Ibn Ezra's work in question, and not being able to find in it Levita's quotation, we endeavoured to obtain some information on this subject. And accordingly, in addition to the information in a private communication from Dr. Steinschneider, that the *Zachoth Sephasajim* is "still extant in a MS. of De Rossi (Cod. 764)," at Parma; we have received from the learned librarian, the Abate Pietro Perreau, a description of the codex in question, of which the following is the substance. The MS. is a folio on parchment, written in Rabbinical characters, and contains four works: i. The Hebrew Lexicon of Solomon Parchon [an account of which will be found in Kitto's *Cyclopædia*, s. v. PARCHON]; ii. Several Sections (שערים), also by Parchon, being a supplement to the Lexicon; iii. The *Zach Sephasajim*, which only extends over four folios of the MS., and is complete, as is evident from the conclusion צח שפתים סליק, *here endeth the Purity of the Languages*; and iv. The *Instruction to the Reader of the Scriptures* (ספר הוריית הקורא) [a description of which has already been given. *Vide supra*, p. 123, note 81].

[87] The word וחקולות, *and the syllables*, is omitted in the Sulzbach edition, whilst והגדולות, *the long*, is wrongly put before הקטנות, *the short*.

[88] This sentence is erroneously transposed in the Sulzbach edition.

[89] The author of *the Khosari* is R. Jehudah Ha-Levi, a very distinguished Hebraist, Poet, and Moral Philosopher, who was born in Castile *circa* 1086. For the life of this literator, as well as for an analysis of his celebrated work, entitled *Khosari*, to which Levita refers, see Kitto's *Cyclopædia*, s. v. JEHUDAH HA-LEVI. It is to be remarked that Levita's quotation is not literal. Thus the word והנשייה, *and pronunciation*, after והשבר, *and Sheber*, is omitted, &c., &c.

with divisions into verses, then with vowels, then with accents, then with definitions respecting the preservation of *plene* and *defective*, and even the exact number of letters?" Thus far his remark. From this we see that he was not of opinion that Moses wrote them, but that it was only preserved in memory what Moses' pronunciation was, viz., what distinction he made between the pronunciation of *Kametz* and *Pattach*, between *Tzere* and *Segol*, &c. Would that this sage author had explained to us whom he meant by "they put"— whether the men of the Great Synagogue or the Massorites. I think that it refers to the Massorites.[90]

☞ Now this is my opinion upon the subject. The vowel-points and the accents did not exist either before Ezra or in the time of Ezra, or after Ezra till the close of the Talmud. And I shall prove this with clear and conclusive evidence.

First,— in all the writings of our Rabbins of blessed memory, whether the Talmud, or the Hagadah, or the Midrash, there is not to be found any mention whatever of, or any allusion to, the vowel-points or accents. Is it possible that, if they had the vowel-points and accents, they would not even once have mentioned the name *Kametz*, *Pattach*, *Segol*, or *Tzere?* or the *Pashta*, *Darga*, *Tebir*, &c.? Do not reply, that their existence is implied in their remarks respecting certain words: "Do not read so, but so;" *ex. gr.*, Do not read בָּנַיִךְ, but בֹּנָיִךְ (Is. liv. 13); Do not read וְשָׁם, but וְשָׂם (Ps. l. 23); as well as in their declaration, "There is a solid root for the reading of the text, and there is a solid root for the traditional pronunciation:" since, according to my opinion, all this favours my conviction, that they had not the vowel-points, but that they were in the habit of reading without points, and therefore they said, "Do not read so, but so."

ואחר כן בטעמים, ואחר כן במסורת, על שמירת המלא והחסר, עד אשר מנו אותיותיה עכ"ל, הרי שאין דעתו שמשה כתבם רק שהיה שמור בלבבות איך קרא משה ר"ל, איך שקרא הפרש בין קמץ לפתח, ובין צרי לסגול ודומיהן, ומי יתן שפירש לנו החכם על מי שב הכנוי של וִשָׂמוּ אם על אנשי כנסת הגדולה, או על בעלי המסורת, ועל דעתי שהוא שב על בעלי המסורת : [90]

☞ והוא לך דעתי בענין רזה, אחשוב שהנקודות והטעמים לא היו קודם עזרא, ולא בזמן עזרא, ולא אחר עזרא עד חתימת התלמוד, ויש לי להוכיח זה בראיות ברורות ונכוחות :

הראיה הראשונה כי לא נמצא בכל דברי רז"ל בתלמוד ובהגדות ומדרשות לא זכר ולא רמז משום נקודה או טעם לעולם, כי איך אפשר אם היו לחם הנקודות והטעמים שלא היו זוכרים פעם אהת קמץ או פתח או סגול או צרי, וכן פשטא, דרגא, תביר ודומיהן, ואל תשיבני ממה שאמרו על קצת המלות אל תקרי כך אלא כך, כמו וכל בניך למודי יהוה (ישעיה נ"ד) אל תקרי בָּנַיִךְ אלא בֹּנָיִךְ, אל תקרי וְשָׁם דרך (תלים נ) אלא וְשָׂם דרך, וכן מה שאמרו יש אם למקרא ויש אם למסורת, כי לפי דעתי כל אלה לי לישועה שלא היו לחם חנקוד, אלא היו רגילין לקרא כך בלי נקוד, לפיבך אמרו אל תקרי כך אלא

[90] Even those scholars, who like Levita regard the vowel-points as a post-Talmudic invention, most unhesitatingly affirm, that וִשָׂמוּ, *and they put*, is the predicate of אנשי כנסת הגדולה, *the men of the Great Synagogue;* comp. *Khosari* p. 249, note 3., ed. Cassel, Leipzig, 1853.

For if the vowel-points had come from Sinai, and the words in question had been pointed in a certain manner, God forbid that the Rabbins should say, "Do not read so."[91] The intelligent student will understand and admit that it is so.

Secondly,—What is still greater proof, is the following remark in the Talmud *(Baba Bathra*, 21 *b)*, "Joab slew his teacher because he had performed the work of the Lord deceitfully, in reading to him זָכָר instead of זֵכֶר (Deut. xxv. 19)." Now is it credible that he would

כך, כי אם היה חנקוד מסיני וחיתה המלה נקודה כך, חלילה לחם וחם לומר אל תקרי כך,[91] וחמשכיל יבין וישכיל כי כן הוא :

ועוד ראיה אחרת וגדולה היא אלי, מה שאמרו רז״ל בבבא בתרא כי יואב הרג את רבו על שעשה מלאכת י״י רמיה, והקרא לו תמחה את זכר עמלק (דברים כ״ח), חיש לחאמין שאם חיה לחם חנקודות וחיה נקוד זָכָר ב׳ו נקודות שהיה קורא זָכָר ב״ב קמצין, אין זאת חי אני לפי דעתי :[92]

ועוד ראיה ממה שנמצא בפרק קמא דחניגה על פסוק ויעלו עולות ויזבחו זבחים וגומר (שמות כ״ד), מר זוטרא אמר לפיסוק

have attempted to read זָכָר with two *Kametz*, if they had had the points, and the word in question had been pointed זֵכֶר with six points. By the life of me, this could not have been done, according to my opinion.[92]

Thirdly,—In *Chagiga*, where the passage "they brought burnt offerings and killed sacrifices," &c., (Exod. xxiv. 5) is discussed, Mar

---

[91] The Talmudic discussions on this phrase are to be found in *Sanhedrin*, 4 *a*; *Sebachim*, 37 *b*; *Pessachim*, 86 *b*; *Kiddushin*, 18 *b*. Levita's argument, deduced from this fact, has also been espoused and elaborated by Capellus, *Arcanum Punctat.* lib. i. cap. v., sect. 4, &c.; and Morin, *Exercit.* lib.: *ex.* xii., cap. 3–5; *ex.* xv., cap. 3–5. Comp. also Gesenius, *Geschichte der Hebräischen Sprache*, p. 182, &c., Leipzig, 1815; Hupfeld, *Studien und Kritiken*, p. 554, Hamburg, 1830. For the attempts to refute it on the part of the vowelists, see Buxtorf, the father, *Tiberias*, cap. ix., pp. 76–86; Buxtorf, the son, *De Punctatorum Antiquitate*, p. 103, &c.; Gill, *A Dissertation concerning the Antiquity of the Hebrew Language*, p. 153, &c., London, 1767.

[92] To understand Levita's allusion, it is necessary to relate the circumstances which called forth the story quoted in the text. "R. Dime, of Nehardea, maintains that he only is to be appointed as teacher of youths who has a good pronunciation, even if he is not so learned, since it is difficult to unlearn an acquired mistake in pronunciation." To enforce his axiom, the Rabbi narrates the following story, which relates to Joab's slaying the whole male population in Edom (1 Kings xi. 15, 16). כי אתא לקמי דדוד אמר ליה מאי טעמא עבדת הכי אמר ליה דכתיב תמחה את זכר עמלק אמר ליה והא אנן זכר קרינן אמר ליה אנא זכר אקריון אזל שייליה לרביה אמר ליה היאך אקריתן אמר ליה זכר שקל ספסירא למיקטליה אמר ליה אמאי אמר ליה דכתיב ארור עושה מלאכת ה' רמיה אמר ליה שבקיה להחוא גברא דליקום בארור אמר ליה כתיב וארור מונע חרבו מדם איכא דאמרי קטליה ואיכא דאמרי לא קטוליה *When he returned to David, he asked him, What is the reason that thou hast acted thus?* [*i.e.* slain the males only], *whereupon he* [Joab] *replied, Because it is written, Thou shalt blot out the males of Amalek* [Deut. xxv. 19]. *He* [David] *then said to him, We read Secher = the memory, to which he* [Joab] *replied, I have been taught to read Sachar = males, and went to inquire of his Rabbi, asking him, How dost thou teach me to read it? He* [the Rabbi] *replied, Secher = memory. Hereupon, he* [Joab] *seized his sword to slay him* [the Rabbi]. *He* [the Rabbi] *asked why? He* [Joab] *replied to him, Because it is written,* "*Cursed be he that doeth the work of the Lord deceitfully*" [Jerem. xlviii. 10]. *Upon which he* [the Rabbi] *said, Away with him who lays hold of a curse. He* [Joab] *said again, It is written,* "*And cursed be he who keepeth back his sword from blood.*" *Some say he then killed him* [his Rabbi], *and some say he did not kill him* (Comp. *Baba Bathra*, 21 *a-b*). Levita's argument, deduced from this, that the Talmudists must have had an unpointed text—Buxtorf, the father (*Tiberias*, p. 86), Buxtorf, the son (*De Antiquitate Punctat.* p. 108, &c.), Whitfield (*A Dissertation on the Hebrew vowel-points*, p. 259, &c.), and Gill (*Dissertation*, p. 156, &c.) have tried to refute.

Sutra remarks, this discussion is necessary, in order to know where to place the dividing accent (*Chagiga* 6 *b*). From this, too, it is evident that they had no accents (see Rashi *in loco*).

Fourthly,—Almost all the names of both the vowel-points and the accents are not Hebrew, but Aramean and Babylonian; as, for instance, *Tzere, Segol, Cholem, Melaphum;* so also *Mapik, Dagesh, Darga, Tebir,* &c. Now, if it were true that they were given on Sinai, what is the meaning of Aramean names at Mount Sinai? Were not all the commandments given on Sinai in Hebrew?

I therefore submit that it is perfectly evident to me that the vowel-points neither existed nor obtained in the days of the Talmudic sages, and much less in the time of the men of the Great Synagogue. These men did not require them, for they could read without vowel-points and accents, making a pause where the sense required it, and reading on when the sense did not require a pause, just as they had heard and received it from the Prophets; as our Rabbins of blessed memory say, "And the Prophets transmitted it to the men of the Great Synagogue" [*Aboth* i.]; and the sages who were in their days, viz., the great and small Sanhedrim, as well as the priests who served God at the altar, received it from them, generation after generation, till by habit they knew how to read without vowel-points and accents.

Now there are some who might ask, How was it possible, before the invention of the vowel-points, to teach a child the correct reading from a book which was not pointed? But this is no question. For the sacred tongue was the language which all spoke, both young and old, children and women, since they had no other language till they were led captive from their land. When, therefore, a child was being taught to know the letters, his teacher read with him from a book each verse two or three times, till he was familiar with it, and as the child was

---

טעמים וכו', גם משם ראיה שלא היו לחם טעמים, עיין מה שפירש רש"י שם

וְעוֹד אהרת כי השמות מן [93] הנקודות והטעמים רובן אינן לשון עברי רק לשון ארמי ובבלי, כגון צרי, וסגול, חולם מלא פום, וכן מפיק, דגש, דרגא, תביר, ודומיהן, ואם אמת הוא שנתנו מסיני מה ענין לשון ארמי אצל הר סיני, והלא כל המצוות נאמרו בסיני בלשון עברי:

לכן אומר אני כי ברור לי שהנקוד לא היה ולא נברא בימי חכמי התלמוד, וכ"ש בימי אנשי כנסת הגדולה, כי לא היו צריכין להם, כי היו בקיאים לקרא בלי נקוד וטעמים, וקראו במקום העמדת הענין בהפסקה, ובמקום סמיכת הענין בהתמדת הדבור, כאשר שמעו וקבלו מפי הנביאים, כמו שאמרו רז"ל, ונביאים מסרוהו לאנשי כנסת הגדולה וחכמים שהיו בימיהם, כגון סנהדרי גדולה וקטנה, וגם הכהנים הנגשים אל י"י קבלו מהם דור אחר דור, עד שמכח ההרגל ידעו לקרא בלי נקוד וטעמים:

ורבים ישאלו איך היה אפשר קודם שנמצאו הנקודות ללמד לנער הקריאה הנכונה מתוך ספר שאינו נקוד, וזו אינה שאלה, כי לשון הקדש היה הלשון שדברו בו כלם, נער וזקן טף ונשים, כי לא היה לחם לשון אחרת, עד שגלו מעל אדמתם, וכאשר נער אחר למד עד שהכיר האותיה, היה רבו קורא עמו מתוך הספר פסוק אחד ב' או ג'

---

[93] The Sulzbach edition erroneously has כי השמות מן השמות עם הנקודות:

conversant with the language, he could easily remember the words which he read, and whenever he met them again he read them without difficulty. To make this more plain to yòn, listen to what I have seen, and I will relate it.

☞ Now when I was in Rome, I saw three Chaldeans, who arrived from the country of Prester John,[94] having been sent for by Pope Leo X. They were masters of the Syriac language and literature, though their vernacular language was Arabic.[95] The special language, however, wherein the books were written, as well as that of the gospels of the Christians which they brought with them, was Syriac, which is also called Aramean, Babylonian, Assyrian, Chaldee, Tursaea or Targum, being denominated by these ☞ seven names. Pope Leo X. had sent for them, in order to correct by their Codices his exemplar of his New Testament, which was written in Latin. I then saw in their hands the Book of Psalms, written in Syriac characters, as well as translated into Syriac; that is to say, the text was written with Syriac characters, the origin, pronunciation, and form of which greatly resemble the Hebrew. Now I saw them reading this Psalter without points, and asked them, Have you points, or any signs to indicate the vowels? and

פעמים עד שהיה שגור בפיו, ולפי שהנער היה בקי בלשון ההוא היה נקל לו לזכור המלות שקרא, ובכל מקום שמצאם קראם בלי משגה, וכדי להבינך זה יותר אחיך שמע לי וזה חזיתי ואספרה:

☜ בהיותי ברומי ראיתי והנה שלשה אנשים כלדאים באו ממדינת פריטי יואן[94] אשר אפיפ״יור ליאון העשירי שלח אחריהם, והם היו יודעי ספר ולשון כשדים לשונם החכמוני הוא לשון ערבי[95] אבל הלשון המיוחד להם שבו נכתבו ספריהם וכל האוונגיליון הנוצרית הוא להם בלשון הזה, והוא לשון כשדים ☜ הנקרא גם כן ארמי, או בבלי, או אשורי, או כלדאי, או טורסאי, או תרגום, הרי שבע שמות נקראו לו, ולכך שלח האפיפ״יור אחריהם, להגיה מספריהם, ספרי אוונגיליון שלו הכתוב לשון לטין, ואז ראיתי בידם ספר תהלים כתוב ארמית ומתורגם ארמית, ר״ל שהיה כתוב באותיות ארמיות שמוצאם ומבטאם וצורתם קרובים מאוד ללשון העברי: וראיתי שקראו באורתו תהלים בלרתי נקוד, ושאלרתים לאמור היש לכם נקודות או אורתות וסימנים

---

[94] Prester [= Priest] John, is celebrated, both among Latin and Oriental writers, as a Christian sovereign and priest in the far east of Asia. It is said that the information about him was first brought to Pope Eugenius III. in 1145, by two Armenian delegates who visited Rome. And a letter of Pope Alexander III., dated 1177, is still extant, which this Pontiff addressed to the said *Johannes, Rex Indorum*, and in which he is described as a Christian king of Asia, desiring union with the Catholic Church. The story about this romantic monarch was so eagerly seized by the faithful of the middle ages, because his supposed existence counteracted the unfavourable impression which the conquests of the Mohammedans and Heathens achieved in Christian countries. In the fifteenth century, he again appears in the annals of history, as *Presbyter Johannes Rex*, in Africa, and more especially in Æthiopia. Levita's reference is most probably to Nestorians or Maronites, since he describes Syriac as their ecclesiastical language. For the story about Prester John, see Ersch and Gruber's *Allgemeine Encyklopädie*, section ii., vol. xxii., pp. 219–21; Herzog, *Real-Encyklopädie für Protestantische Theologie und Kirche*, vol. v., 313; vol. vi., 765, &c.

[95] The Sulzbach edition erroneously substitutes עברי *Hebrew*, for ערבי *Arabic*. The extract of the above passage in Kitto's *Cyclopedia, s. v.* XIMENES, having been made from the Sulzbach edition, contains the same blunder, and must therefore be corrected.

they answered me, "No! but we have been conversant with that language from our youth till now, and, therefore, know how to read without points." Thus far their remark.[96]

You, therefore, see that it is possible for a man to learn by habit to read without points. The same was the case among us, prior to the invention of the points, and it continued till the time after the close of the Talmud, which took place in 8989 of the creation = 436 after the destruction of the second Temple. Since then, the sacred tongue began gradually to disappear, till the time of the Massorites, who are the men of Tiberias, which is Mouzia. They were great sages, and thoroughly conversant with the Scriptures and the structure of the language, more so than all the other Jews who lived in that generation, and none like them have existed since. This is attested by R. Jona [Ibn Ganach], the Grammarian, in his treatise on the *Quiescent Letters*, which is as follows: "The distinction between the ר with and without the *Dagesh* was well understood by the men of Tiberias, but not by us, for they knew better the purity of the language than all other Jews." Thus, also, says Abraham Ibn Ezra, who writes in the book *Purity* as follows;[97] "This is the manner of the sages of Tiberias, and they are the foundation, for from them were the Massorites, and from them we have received all our vowel-points."

This, however, I observed, that the Massorites did not give names to the points, except to the *Kametz* and the *Pattach*, in which are included the *Tzere* and the *Segol;* that is, they called the *Tzere Kametz* and the *Segol Pattach*. It was not till the rise of the first grammarians that some distinction was made between these names, and that they were thus designated. Thus, for instance, they called this point ָ the long *Kametz*, this ֲ short *Kametz*, this ַ long *Pattach*, and

---

[96] The expression עכ״ל, *thus far their remark*, is omitted in the Sulzbach edition.

[97] Levita's quotation is to be found on p. 7 a of the *Zachoth* (צחות) = *Purity*, ea. Lippmann, Fürth, 1127.

this ־ָ the short *Pattach*. But no mention whatever is made of the rest of the vowels throughout the whole of the Massorah, both *magna* and *parva*, wherin *Chirek* is called אִי, *Cholem* אוֹ, *Shurek* אוּ, *Kibutz* אֻ, and the *Sheva* and the three *Chataphs* are called by quite different names, as I shall explain in Part ii., section 3. For instance, the Massorites remark, "There are twenty-one words which occur twice, once with אוֹ, and once with אוּ, as הָאֱמֹר [Ezek. xxviii. 9], and הָאֱמוּב [Micah i. 7]; and they have no parallel;"[98] but they do not say one with *Cholem* and one with *Shurek*. They also note, "Twenty-seven words are written with אִי, every one of which has no parallel, as לָלִין [Gen. xxiv. 23], יַפִּיל [Exod. xxi. 27];"[99] but they do not say that they are written with *Chirek*. Those Codices of the Massorah, in which the name *Cholem*, *Chirek*, or *Shurek* occurs, do not state the language of the Massorites, but display the wisdom of the transcribers, who wrote so in order to show that they understood the Massorah.

☞ I shall now[100] state to you the reason why they did not give names to the other vowels, just as they named the *Kametz* and the *Pattach*. It is this. The forms of all other vowels have signal letters appended to them. Thus, for instance, since the *Vav* and the *Jod* are the *matres lectiones* of the vowels אִי, אוּ, אוֹ; hence, the Massorites were satisfied with these designations, and did not give them any other names.[101] But the *Kametz* and the *Pattach*, which have no such

שאר הנקודות לאנזכרו בשמם בכל המסרה גדולה וקטנה, רק קראו לחירק אִי, ולחולם אוֹ, ולשורק אוּ, ולקבוץ אֻ, ולשוא ולג׳ חטפין קראו שמות אחרות, כאשר יתבאר בלוחות שניות במאמר ג׳ : והמשל באמרם במסורה כ״א מלין חד אוֹ וחד אוּ כמו הָאֱמֹר תאמר אלהים אני (יחזקאל כ״ח) לית, וחד הָאֱמוּב (מיכה ב׳),[98] ולא אמרו חד חולם וחד שורק, וכן כ״ז מלין דכתיבין אִי וכל חד לית דכוותיה, כגון לָלִין לית, יַפִּיל לית,[99] ולא אמרו דכתיבין חירק, והנוסחאות שנמצא בהן חולם, או חירק, או שורק, אינו מלשון בעלי המסורת, רק התחכמות הסופר שכתב כן כדי להראות שהוא הבין המסורת:

☞ וְעַתָּה[100] אודיעך חטעם למה לא קראו להן שמות כמו שקראו לקמץ ולפתח, וזה לפי צורת הנקודות האחרות יש להן סימן אותיות המשך ר״ל היו״ד והוי״ו אוֹ אוּ אִי, והספיקו בשמות האלו ולא קראו להן שמות אחרים,[101] אבל הקמץ והפתח שאין להן אות

---

[98] Both in the Massorah finalis, under letter *Vav*, and in the *Ochla Ve-Ochla*, section lv., where the list in question is given, it is designated כ״א זוגין, *twenty-one pairs*. The expression מלין, *words*, in the text of Levita, must therefore be a slip of the pen. It is also to be remarked, that in the *Ochla Ve-Ochla* the names of the vowels are given (חד מלא פום וחד קמץ פום), which, according to Levita, shows that it is a later addition, and that the title of this rubric in the Massorah finalis is the genuine old designation.

[99] The list of these twenty-seven instances is given in the Massorah finalis, under the letter *Jod*, and in the *Ochla Ve-Ochla*, section ccxiv., pp. 45, 127, &c. Neither the Massorah finalis, however, nor the *Ochla Ve-Ochla* designates the list in question, כ״ז מלין דכתיבין אי, *twenty-one words which are written with* אי. In the former it is expressly entitled דכתיב׳ בחירק י׳, *which are written with Jod Chirek*, thus giving the very name of the vowel-sign which Levita disputes; whilst in the latter the rubric in question is entitled כ״ז מלין דכל חד לי כתי׳ י׳ במצע תיבות׳ וכל דכות׳ כתב ו׳, *twenty-seven words*, *which only occur once with Jod in the middle of the word, and which in all other passages are written with Vav*.

[100] The Sulzbach edition erroneously insert והנה, *and now*, before עתה, *now*.

[101] The whole sentence והספיקו בשמות האלו ולא קראו להן שמות אחרים, *and they were satisfied with these designations, and did not give them other names*, is omitted in the Sulzbach edition.

matres lectiones, had to be distinctly named. Thus, also, the short *Kametz* and the short *Pattach*, which have mostly no *matres lectiones*, as I have explained it in the "*Poetical Section*," had likewise to be specified by names, that is short *Kametz* and short *Pattach*. Afterwards came some grammarians who changed these names: they called the short *Kametz Tzere* and the short *Pattach Segol*, wherewith all others agree; but they do not agree in the names of the other vowels.

Hence there are some who call the vowel אֹ *Cholem* and others who call it *Melaphum*; thus R. Solomon b. Isaac [Rashi] calls it, in his Commentary on Exod. xv. 5 and Isa. i. 31, which you may consult. We Germans call the vowel אוּ *Melaphum*; but I do not know whence we obtained it, for in none of the works by the grammarians and the punctuators do we find it called so; they designate it *Shurek*. Again, we call the vowel אֻ *Shurek*, whilst the grammarians call it three-points, or *Kibutz*; generally, however, it is called *Kibutz of the Lips*, and some call it *Kibutz of the Mouth*. The vowel אִ is called *Chirek*: there are some who call it *Sheber*; it is so called by Ibn Ezra, in many places, and he states that this is its name in Arabic; whilst the sage author of the *Khozari* calls *Chirek* the long *Sheber* and *Tzere* short *Sheber*; but I am certain that the short *Chirek*, that is, without the *Jod*, was called *Sheber*, and the long one, with the *Jod*, was simply called *Chirek*.

Thus have I expatiated at large upon this subject, till I have made it evident that the vowel-points and the accents were neither given on Sinai, nor were they invented by the men of the Great Synagogue, but that they are the work of the Massorites, who flourished at a later period, as I have stated. In short, they are the self-same who have

---

הִמְשֵׁךְ הוּצְרְכוּ לִקְרֹא לָהֶן שֵׁמוֹת מְיוּחָדִין, וְכֵן הַקָּמֵץ קָטָן וּפַתָּח קָטָן, שֶׁאֵין לָהֶן אִתִּיוֹת הַמֶּשֶׁךְ עַל הָרוֹב כְּמוֹ שֶׁבֵּאַרְתִּי בְּפֶרֶק שִׁירָה, לְפִיכָךְ קְרָאוּ לָהֶן שֵׁמוֹת מְיוּחָדִין שֶׁהֵן קָמֵץ קָטָן וּפַתָּח קָטָן, וְאח"כ קָמוּ מְדַקְדְּקִים אֲחֵרִים וְשִׁנּוּ אֶת שְׁמוֹתָן וְקָרְאוּ לְקָמֵץ קָטָן צֵרִי וּלְפַתָּח קָטָן סֶגוֹל, וּלְדַעַת אֵלֶּה הַסְּכִים דֵּעוֹת כֻּלָּן בְּשָׁוֶה, אֲבָל שְׁמוֹת שֶׁל שְׁאָר הַנְּקוּדוֹת לֹא הַסְּכִים עֲלֵיהֶן דֵּעוֹת כֻּלָּן בְּשָׁוֶה:

יֵשׁ שֶׁקּוֹרֵא לַנְּקוּדוֹת אוֹ חוֹלָם, וְיֵשׁ שֶׁקּוֹרֵא לוֹ מְלֹא פוּם, וְכֵן קְרָא לוֹ רַבֵּנוּ שְׁלֹמֹה יִצְחָק כְּמוֹ בְּמִלַּת יְכַסְיָמוּ וּפָעֲלוּ לְנִיצוֹץ ע"ש: וַאֲנַחְנוּ הָאַשְׁכְּנַזִּים קוֹרְאִין לַנְּקוּדָה אוּ מְלֹא פוּם, וְלֹא יָדַעְתִּי מֵאַיִן הוֹצִיאוֹנוּהוּ, כִּי אֵין בְּכָל סִפְרֵי הַמְדַקְדְּקִים וְהַנַּקְדָּנִים שֶׁקָּרְאוּ לוֹ כֵן, אַךְ קָרְאוּ לוֹ שׁוּרֵק, וַאֲנַחְנוּ קוֹרִין שׁוּרֵק לַנְּקוּדָה אָ, וְהַמְדַקְדְּקִים קוֹרִין לוֹ שְׁלֹשָׁה נְקוּדוֹת אוֹ קִבּוּץ, וְהֵעָקַד שֶׁקָּרְאוּ לוֹ קִבּוּץ שְׂפָתַיִם, וְיֵשׁ קוֹרִין לוֹ קִבּוּץ פּוּם, וּנְקֻדַּת אִי קָרְאוּ לוֹ חִירֵק, וְיֵשׁ שֶׁקּוֹרִין לוֹ שֶׁבֶר, וְכֵן קָרָא לוֹ ראב"ע בְּהַרְבֵּה מְקוֹמוֹת, וְכָתַב שֶׁהוּא נִקְרָא כֵן בִּלְשׁוֹן עֲרָבִי, וְהֶחָכָם הַכּוּזָרִי קָרָא לְחִירֵק שֶׁבֶר גָּדוֹל, וְלְצֵרִי שֶׁבֶר קָטָן,[102] וּבָרוּר לִי, כִּי הַחִירֵק שֶׁל תְּנוּעָה קְטַנָּה, ר"ל שֶׁהִיא בְּלִי יוֹד הוּא שֶׁקָּרְאוּ לוֹ שֶׁבֶר, וְאוֹתוֹ שֶׁהוּא עִם הַיּוֹד קָרְאוּ חִירֵק סְתָם:

וְהִנֵּה הֶאֱרַכְתִּי עַד הִנֵּה בְּיוֹתֵר, עַד שֶׁבֵּאַרְתִּי וּבֵרַרְתִּי שֶׁהַנְּקוּדוֹת וְהַטְּעָמִים לֹא נִתְּנוּ מִסִּינַי, וְגַם אַנְשֵׁי כְּנֶסֶת הַגְּדוֹלָה לֹא הִמְצִיאוּם כְּלָל, וְאֵינָם אֶלָּא מַעֲשֵׂי יְדֵי בַּעֲלֵי הַמָּסוֹרֶת שֶׁקָּמוּ אַחַר כָּךְ כְּמוֹ שֶׁבֵּאַרְתִּי, וְהַכְּלָל כִּי הֵם

---

[102] Levita's allusion is to be found in the *Khosari* ii. 8, p. 191, ed. Cassel.

preserved the Law and the Prophets in their proper state; and there can be no doubt that, if they had not existed, the cake would have been entirely consumed, and the law would have become, as it were, two laws, and there would not have been found two Codices among all the copies of the Scriptures agreeing together, as is the case with the books of other authors.

Look at the many changes and variations which are to be found in the Targum of Onkelos, though a Massorah was made thereon, called[103] *The Massorah on the Targum of the Pentateuch*, because it does not follow the plan of the Massorah on the Bible in numbering the words, letters, &c., but simply enumerates some particular words, the Targum rendering of which differs from what it usually is in all other places. Thus, for instance, יְדַעְתִּי is rendered in eleven passages by יְדַעְנָא,[104] and in all the rest by שְׁבוּ ;יְדָעִית is rendered three times by אוֹרִיכוּ; עֵץ is rendered twice by אָלָן, &c., &c. See the Introduction to my Lexicon, which I wrote on all the Targums; viz., Onkelos on the Pentateuch, Jonathan on the Prophets, and Aquilas on the Hagiographa (some say that the latter is by R. Joseph),[105] and which I have named *Methurgeman*, before it has appeared. I hope to God to publish it soon, and to be permitted to see it before I die.[106]

In their works, however, the Massorites have toiled most diligently, and counted all the verses, words, and letters of every book, for which they are called Numberers = *Sopherim*. Hence, by their diligence, they have so far learned to know that the *Vav* in נחון

העמידו התורה והמקרא על עמדם, ובלי ספק לולי באו כבר כלתה החררה, ונעשית חתורה כשתי תורות, ולא היו שני ספרים בכל ספרי המקרא שחיו מסכימים יחד, כאשר קרה לשאר ספרי המחברים:

הלא תראה כמ השנויים וחילופים נמצאו בתרגום אנקלוס, ואע״פי שנעשה עליו ספר הנקרא[108] מסורת התרגום על התורה, אבל אינו חולך בדרך המסורת של המקרא במספר החיבות והאותיות ודומיחן, רק הוא מונה קצת מלות מיוחדות שהתרנום שנה לשונו בם שלא כמנהג בשאר חבריהם, כגון ידעתי י״א[104] דמתורגמין ידענא וכל שאר ידעית, וכן שבו ג׳ דמתורגמין אוריכו, ועץ ב׳ דמתורגמין אלן, וכן חרבה כאלה, ותמצאם בחקדמתי מספר השרשים אשר חברתי על כל התרנום, דחיינו אונקלוס על התורה, ויונתן על נביאים, ועקילוס על כתובים, ויש אומרים שהוא תרנומו של רב יוסף,[105] ומרם חולרו קראתי שם הספר ההוא מתורגמן, אקוה לאל מהרה אוציא החבור חהוא לאורה בדפוס ואראנו במרם אמות:[106]

אך המעשה אשר עשו בעלי המסורת הוא שהשתדלו בכל מאמצי כחם, ולא נחו ולא שקמו עד שמנו כל הפסוקים והחיבורת והאותיות מכל ספר וספר, לפיכך קראו להם סופרים, חלא תראה שהגיע מהשתדלותם עד שידעו כי וי״ו דגחון (ויקרא י״א) חצי התורה

---

[108] The word הנקרא, *which is called*, is omitted in the Sulzbach edition.

[104] In the Sulzbach edition, the abbreviation י״א, *eleven*, has erroneously been resolved into יש אומרים, *some say*, which has no sense; and דמתורגם is substituted for דמתורגמין.

[105] As the discussion of the authorship of the Chaldee paraphrases is too lengthy to be entered upon here, we must refer to Kitto's *Cyclopædia*, s. v. JONATHAN B. UZZIEL, JOSEPH B. CHIJA, ONKELOS, and TARGUM, where the necessary information is given at length.

[106] Levita did live to see his Chaldee Lexicon published. For a description of it, see above, p. 69, &c.

[Levit, xi. 42] is the middle of all the letters in the Pentateuch; that "Moses diligently sought" [Levit. x. 16] are the middle of all the words, דָּרֹשׁ terminating the first half, and דָּרַשׁ beginning the second; and that "the breast-plate" [Levit. viii. 8] is the middle of all the verses. This they have done in all the 24 sacred books.[107] Moreover, they have counted the verses, words, and letters of each Pericope in the Pentateuch, and made marks accordingly. Thus, the Pericope *Bereshith* has 146 verses, the mnemonical sign being the name Amaziah; *Noah* has 153 verses, the mnemonical sign of which is Bezaleel;[108] thus giving a proper name as a mnemonical sign for each hebdomadal section, to indicate the number of its verses. Again, *Bereshith* has 1915 letters, and the sign is א"ץ טי"ו. But I must also explain to you how it is that א signifies 1000, and final ץ 900.

☞ You must observe that the Kabbalists and Massorites have taken the five final letters into the number of the alphabet, and thus made the entire letters to be 27 in number. They are divisible into

---

[107] Levita evidently refers here to the fact recorded in the Talmud (*Kiddushin* 30 *a*), which is as follows :—לפיכך נקראו הראשונים סופרים שדיו סופרים כל האותיות שבתורה שדיו אומרים וא"ו דגחון חציון של אותיות של ספר תורה דרש דרש של תיבות והתגלח של פסוקים יכרסמנה חזיר מיער עי"ן דיער חציים של תהלים והוא רחום יכפר עון חציו דפסוקים, *therefore were the ancients called* SOPHERIM, *because they numbered the letters of the Scriptures. Thus they say that the* VAV *in* גחון [Levit. xi. 42], *is the middle of all the letters of the Pentateuch; that* דרש דרש [*ibid*. x. 16], *are the middle of all the words; that* והתגלח [*ibid*. xiii. 33], *is the middle of the verses; that the* AIN *in* מיער [Ps. lxxx. 14], *is the middle letter of the Psalms, and that "but he, being full of compassion, forgave their iniquity"* [*ibid*. lxxviii. 38], *is the middle of the verses*. On the same page in the Talmud, we are further told as follows:—ת"ר חמשת אלפים שמונה מאות וטמונים ושמונה פסוקים הוי פסוקי ספר תורה יתר עליו תילים שמונה חסר ממנו דברי הימים שמונה, *the Sages submit that the number of verses of the Pentateuch is 5888, that of the Psalms 8 less, and that of Chronicles 8 more.*

[108] From time immemorial, the Pentateuch has been divided into fifty-four sections, for the purpose of hebdomadal lessons, since some years, according to the Jewish chronology, have fifty-four Sabbaths. Each of these Pericopes, called *Parsha* (פרשה), or *Sidra* (סידרא), has a special name, which it derives from the first or second word wherewith it commences; and Jewish writers, when quoting a passage from the Pentateuch, cite the respective names of the Pericope instead of giving the chapter and verse. *Bereshith*, which Levita quotes, is the name of the first Pericope, embracing Gen. i. 1–vi. 8, and is the first hebdomadal lesson in the first Sabbath of the Jewish year. The name *Amaziah*, which is the mnemonical sign of the number of verses, indicates it by its numerical value, viz., ה 5 + י 10, + צ 90, + מ 40, + א 1 = 146. The hebdomadal lesson, *Noah*, comprises Gen. vi. 9–xi. 32, and the 153 verses of which is consists are indicated by the mnemonical sign *Bezaleel* which is of this numerical value, viz.— ל 30 + א 1 + ל 30 and צ 90 + ב 2 = 153. A full description of the Sabbatic lessons, as well as of the manners and customs connected therewith, is given in Kitto's *Cyclopædia, s. v.* HAPHTARA.

three parts, each part consisting of 9 letters. The first part extends from א to ט, and forms the units; the second part extends from י to צ, and constitutes tens; whilst the third part constitutes the hundreds, and consists of ק ר ש ת ך ם ן ף ץ. In this manner the value of the letters rises to thousands, ת being 400, final ך 500, final ם 600, final ן 700, final ף 800, and final ץ 900. For the number 1000 we have to return to the beginning of the alphabet, and when written out fully אָלֶף it is 1000. Some say that it is on this account called *Aleph*. When another number is added to it, it is only written 'א. This explains what I have said above, that א"ץ signifies 1900. They have also given 1534 as the number of verses in Genesis, the sign of which is א"ך ל"ד; 5842 as the number of verses in the whole Pentateuch; and 600,045 as the number of letters in the whole Pentateuch.

☞ Moreover, we find that the Massorites have also counted each separate letter of the alphabet in the whole twenty-four sacred Scrip-

הראשון מן האלף עד הט' הוא וחלק האחדים, השני מן היוד עד הצדי חלק עשיריות, וחלק השלישי חלק המאיות והוא ק ר ש ת ך ם ן ף ץ, ובאופן זה יעלה מספר האותיות לחשבון האלף, כי התיו היא ד' מאות, וכף פשוטה ת"ק, ומ"ם סתומה ת"ר ונו"ן פשוטה ת"ש, ופ"ה פשוטה ת"ח, וצדי פשוטה תת"ק, ולמנין אלף הוזר הדין לראש האלפא ביתא, וכותבין אלף במלואה, ויש מי שאמר לכך נקראת אלף, וכאשר יצטרף עמה מנין אחר כותבין רק א' לבד, וזהו מה שכתבתי למעלה א"ץ, שהוא אלף ותשע מאות, וכן פסוקים של ספר בראשית אלף וחמש מאות ושלשים וארבעה סימן א"ך ל"ד, וכן מספר הפסוקים של כל התורה כלו חמשת אלפים ושמונה מאות ומ"ב, ומספר אותיות של כל התורה ששים רבוא וארבעים וחמשה:

☞ ועוד מצאנו שמנו מספר כל אות ואות של כל העשרים וארבעה, ומצאו מספר האלפין מ"ב אלפין שע"ז, ומספר הבית ל"ח אלפין וי"ח, ומספר הגימל כ"ט אלפין תקל"ז, וכן כל אות ואות, וכבר נעשה על זה חרוז יפה מתחיל אהל מכון בניני וכו', וקבלתי כי ר' סעדיה גאון הבראותו, ונדאין הדברים, כי נמצאים בו מלות זרות וחמורות, אשר לא מלשון מקרא המה, וכמוהם נמצאים בספר אמונות[109] שחבר, ואולי אדפיסהו

tures, and have ascertained that the letter א occurs 42,377 times, the letter ב 35,218 times, the letter ג 29,837 times, &c. Indeed a beautiful poem was written long ago on this subject, beginning "The Tent, the place of my buildings," and I have heard that Saadia Gaon is the author of it. This statement is confirmed by the fact that there are in it foreign and obscure words, which are not Biblical, such as are to be found in the work, entitled *Faith [and Philosophy]*,[109] which he wrote. I may, perhaps, append it to this treatise,

---

[109] Saadia's philosophical treatise, to which Levita refers, was originally written in Arabic, circa A.D. 933–937, entitled כתאב אלאמאנאת ואלאעתקאדאת. It consists of ten sections, and discusses the following subjects:—Section i. The creation of the world and all things therein. ii. The Unity of the Creator. iii. Law and Revelation. iv. Obedience and Rebellion, Divine Justice and Freedom. v. Merit and Demerit. vi. The Soul and Immortality. vii. The Resurrection. viii. Redemption. ix. Reward and Punishment. And x. The Moral Law. The original Arabic, with the exception of a specimen of the Introduction, has not as yet been published. It is in Ibn Tibbon's Hebrew translation of it, made in 1186, and published in Constantinople 1562, Amsterdam 1648, Berlin 1789; and in Fürst's German translation, published at Leipzig, 1845, that this treatise is accessible to scholars.

with a short explanation, for it is difficult to understand it without a commentary.

Now I return to the former subject, and submit that, after all the work which the Massorites have done, it is impossible for any mistake or alteration whatever to happen to any of the books of the Scriptures. It is, therefore, not in vain that our Rabbins of blessed memory have said, "The Massorah is a fence to the Scriptures," and that they have also explained the words, "Every man's sword was on his thigh, because of the terrors by night" [Song of Songs iii. 8], to refer to "the Massorah, and to the signs designed to preserve the law from being forgotten in the captivity."[110] Indeed, there were hundreds and thousands of Massorites, and they continued generation after generation for many years. No one knows the time when they commenced, nor when they will end in future. For even at the present day, if any one wishes to engage in the work, and make signs and rules whereby to find out the number of words, or other Massoretic subjects, he is quite at liberty to do so; but only under this condition, that he must not add to nor diminish from anything which the men of the Great Synagogue have determined as regards *plene* and *defective*, *Keri* and *Kethiv*, the major and minor letters, the open and closed sections of the Pentateuch, &c., &c. Neither must he gainsay the statements of the Massorites respecting the vowel-points and the accents, the number of words which they have counted, and marked with mnemonical signs.

☛ Indeed I, the author of this book, have myself invented various Massoretic signs and rules, which are not to be found in the treatises of the ancients, and have embodied them in my great work, on which I have laboured more than twenty years, and which I have called *The Book of Remembrance*. I hope to God, blessed be

בסוף החבור חזה עם קצת פירוש, כי קשה הבנתו בלי פירוש:
והנני חוזר על הראשונות, ואומר כי אחר המעשה אשר עשו בעלי המסורה. אי אפשר שנפל או שיפול חלוף או שינוי בשום צד בכל ספרי המקרא, ולא לחנם אמרו דז"ל מסורת סיג לתורה, וכן דרשו על פסוק איש חרבו על ירכו מפחד בלילות (שיר ג'), אלו המסורת והסמנים שלא תשכח תורה בגלות,[110] והאמת כי בעלי המסורת היו למאית ולאלפים דור אחר דור כמה שנים, ולא נודע לנו זמן התחלתם, גם זמן התימתם, אד עוד היום מי שיחפוץ לקרב אל המלאכה ולעשות סמנים וכללים למצא חשבון ממלות או ענינים מםסורת הרשות בידו, אך בתנאי שלא יוסיף ולא יגרע על מה שהסכימו עליהם אנשי כנסת הגדולה במלאים וחסרים, ובקרי בכתיב, ובאותיות גדולות וקטנות, פתוחות וסתומות בתורה וכדומה לאלה: גם לא יכחיש דברי בעלי המסורת בענין הנקודות והטעמים, וסכומי המלות שמנו הם ונתנו בהן סימנים:

☛ **והלא** אנכי המחבר חדשתי כמה ענינים וכללים מעניני המסורת, אשר לא נמצאו בדברי הקדמנים, וכתבתים בספרי הגדול אשר עמלתי בו עשרים שנה ומעלה, וקראתי שמו **ספר הזכרונות** אקוה לאל ית'

---

[110] The saying that the Massorah, or the traditional pronunciation of the text, is a fence to the Scriptures, was propounded by the celebrated R. Akiba, who flourished circa A.D. 80–120; comp. *Aboth* iii. 13. The explanation of Song of Songs iii. 8, as referring to the Massorah, to which Levita alludes, is to be found in Rashi's Commentary *in loco*.

he, that it will soon make its appearance, as I have given it to be printed in the great city of Paris, in the kingdom of France.[111]

☞ Remark now, that the Great Massorah, which is extant, is almost endless. Indeed I believe[112] that if all the words of the Great Massorah which I have seen in the days of my life were written down and bound up in a book, it would exceed in bulk all the twenty-four books of the Bible. I have already stated in the poetical Introduction that it is not to be found collected in any book, except in the treatise *Ochla Ve-Ochla*, which is so called from its beginning words. Even the greatest part of the Massorah which has been printed here in Venice in the Great Bible is taken from this work.[113] Kimchi quotes it under the root קרב (*vide in loco*).

Now that which constitutes the Massorah marginalis is simply an abridgement of the Massorah magna; for, certainly, the Massorites would not write their remarks around the margins, since they were too small, and the space was too narrow, to contain their words. They wrote their remarks in separate treatises, and taught them publicly; hence the works were largely circulated, and the Scribes, who copied the Bible, selected from them what they pleased, each one according to his fancy, and wrote it in the margin, both above and below. Some copied large pieces, and others smaller portions, according to the size of the book into which they were writing it, as I have stated in the poetical Preface (*vide supra*, p. 94).

On the sides of the margins, however, and between the columns of the pages, the Massorites wrote down the suggestions, the mne-

במהרה יצא משפטו לאורה, כאשר נתתיו לחדפיסו בעיר הגדולה פאריז אשר במלכות צרפת: [111]

☞ והנה דע לך כי המסרה הגדולה הנמצאה כמעט אין לה קץ, והאמת ששערתי[112] אני שאם היו כל דברי המסרת הגדולה אשר ראיתי אני בימי כלם כתובים וקשורים יחד על ספר, ירבה כמותו בכמות כל העשרים וארבע, וכבר כתבתי בהקדמה החרוזית כי לא נמצא ספר מחובר ממנו רק ספר אכלה ואכלה הנקרא כן בעבור התחלחו, גם כל המסורה הנדפסרת פה וויני"סייה בעשרים וארבע הגדול, רובו אינו אלא מספר החוא,[113] והר"דק ז"ל הזכירו בשרש קרב ע"ש:

וגם מה שנמצא כתוב בגליונות הספרים אינו אלא קצור מהמסרה הגדולת, כי ודאי בעלי המסודות לא כתבו דבריהם סביב הגליונות, כי קצר חמצע מהשתרע, והיריעה קטנה מהכיל את כל דבריהם, אך כתבו דבריהם קונטרס קונטרס, ולמדום ברבים, ונתפשטו החעתקות ההם הנה והנה, והסופרים כותבי ספרי המקרא, לקטו מהם איש כל חישר בעיניו, וכתבום סביב הגליונות למעלה ולמטה, יש האריך ויש קצר, לפי גדול כרך הספר וקטנוורנו, כמו שכרתבתי בהקדמה החרוזית ע"ש:

אכן בגליונות שבצדדי הספרים ובין העמודים, כתבו הרמזים והסימנים וסכום

---

[111] For the nature and history of this work, see above, p. 28, &c.

[112] The Sulzbach edition erroneously substitutes ששמעתי, *which I have heard*, for ששערתי:

[113] This statement of Levita is contradicted by no less an authority in Massoretic lore than the learned Frensdorff. Frensdorff shows that Jacob b. Chajim, the first editor of the Massorah, which is now printed in the several Rabbinic Bibles, did not derive the greater part of his materials from the *Ochla Ve-Ochla*. . Comp. Introduction to the *Ochla Ve-Ochla*, p. 10.

monical signs, the numbers of the words, and the subjects, with great brevity, indicating them by initial letters and *Notaricons;* and this is called the Massorah *parva*, as I shall explain in Part iii., called *The Broken Tables*. Moreover, on the centre of each word whereon they made any Massoretic gloss, they put a circle, referring to what the Massorah says respecting it. Thus, for instance, on וַיַּבְדֵּל, *and he divided*, which occurs three times in the Bible,[114] the circle on the top thereof refers to the 'ג in the margin, or *the three times*. The same is also the case when a word only occurs once; they put a circle on it, referring to the marginal remark, לית or ל = *no other*, as I shall explain in the above-named Part. When the circle is placed between two words, the marginal remark refers to both words thus joined together. Thus, for instance, the circle between ברא°אלהים, *God created*, refers to the note in the margin, that "*thrice these words occur joined together;*"[115] the circle between פני°תהום, *the face of the abyss*, refers to "*it occurs twice conjointly;*"[116] and between רוח°אלהים, *the Spirit of God*, to "*it occurs eight times conjointly.*"[117] In the better Codices, the word *conjointly* is omitted, since the verse is understood without it, as I shall explain in the *Second Part*, section vi. When three, four, or five words are joined together for some Massoretic remark, the circle is placed between every two words. Thus, the circles between את°השמים ואת°הארץ, *the heavens and the earth*, refer to the marginal remark י"ג, "*it occurs thirteen times;*"[118] and between וידבר°יהוה אל°משה ואל°אהרן, *and Jehovah spake to Moses*

[114] The three instances in which ויבדל occurs, are Gen. i. 4, 7; 1 Chron. xxv. 1.

[115] The three passages in which ברא אלהים occur conjointly, are Gen. i. 1, ii. 3; Deut. iv. 32.

[116] The two instances in which פני תהום occur, are Gen. i. 2; Job xxxviii. 30.

[117] The eight passages in which רוח אלהים occur, are as follows:—Gen. i. 2, xli. 38; Exod. xxxi. 3, xxxv. 31; Numb. xxiv. 2; Ezek. xi. 24; 2 Chron. xv. 1, xxiv. 20. They are enumerated in the Massorah magna on Exod. xxxv. 31, with the remark וכל שמואל דכר, *and every passage in Samuel is like them*, viz., 1 Sam. x. 1, xi. 6, xvi. 15, 16, 23; xviii. 10, xix. 23.

[118] The instances in which את השמים ואת הארץ occur, are Gen. i. 1; Exod. xx. 11; xxxi. 17; Deut. iv. 26; xxx. 19; xxxi. 28; 2 Kings xix. 15; Isa. xxxvii. 16; Jerem. xxiii. 24; xxxii. 17; Hag. ii. 6, 21; 2 Chron. ii. 11.

and Aaron, refer to the marginal remark ב׳", "*it occurs twelve times.*"[119] Sometimes two circles are placed on one word, referring to two separate Massoretic remarks in the margin. Thus, מֵחֲטוֹ, *from sinning*, one circle refers to ג׳, "*it occurs three times,*" and the other to "*it is one of the five words in the Pentateuch wherein* א *is deficient.*"[120]

☞ Notice, also, that when the total number of times that a certain word occurs in the Bible is stated, the words themselves are never quoted, but the beginning of the respective verses in which these words occur are given. Thus, on לאור [Gen. 15], the marginal remark is, "*It occurs seven times, and the sign thereof is* '*God called*' [Gen. i. 5]; '*and I will bring the blind*' [Is. xlii. 16]; '*the just Lord*' [Zeph. iii. 5]; '*therefore it is for*' [Is. lix 9]; '*the indignation of the Lord*' [Micah. vii. 9]; '*with the light He shall rise*' [Job xxiv. 14]; '*He discovereth deep things*'" [Job xii. 22]. All these are the beginnings of the verses in which the expression לאור occurs. Sometimes the Massoretic sign on the text is in Aramaic. Thus, on לאור in question, the sign is in Aramaic, "*the blind man cried, intending to go out by night, and he rose in the movning.*" On comparison, it will be found that this sign refers to each of the seven verses quoted above. When, however, the commencing words of a verse are of frequent occurrence, such as ויהי, *and it came to pass*, והיה, *and it was*, וידבר, *and he spake*, ויאמר, *and he said*, &c., two or three of the principal words in the verse are selected for the sign, and not the very word which commences the verse. But this is easily understood. Sometimes the order of the verses in the Bible is inverted, to construe an attractive mnemonical sign, by combining the

וידבר ֹיהוה אל ֹמשה ואל ֹאהרן י״ב
(שמות ו'),[119] ולפעמים עשו על מלה אחת
ב' ענולים, להורות על ב' ענינים הנרשמים
בחוץ, כגון מֵחֲטוֹ לי (בראשית כ') ג', והוא
חד מן ח' מלין דחסרי אלף בתורה, העגול
האחד מורה על הג', והשני מורה על ה' מלין
החסרים א':[120]

☞ ודע כאשר הביאו סך מנין של מלה
אחת, להודיע כמה פעמים נמצאת במקרא,
לא כתבו חברי המלה החיא ממש, אלא
כתבו ראשי הפסוקים אשר נמצאת בהם המלה
ההיא, והמשל לאור ז', וסמנהון ויקרא אלהים
(בראשית א'), והלכתי עורים (ישעיה מ״ב),
יהוה צדיק, על כן רחק, זעף יהוה, לאור
יקום, מגלה עמוקות, כל אלה הם ראשי
הפסוקים שנמצא בהם לאור, ולפעמים
עשו עליהן סימן בלשון ארמי, כגון על לאור
ז', וסימנהון בלשון ארמי צוח סומיא וסבר
למיפק בליליא וקם בצפרא, דוק ותמצא הסימן
הזה מכוון עם ז' הפסוקים הנ״ל, אבל
כשיש ר״פ מן מלות מורגלות, כגון ויאמר,
וידבר, ויהי, ויהי ודומיהן, לקחו ב' או ג'
מלות שהן עקרי הפסוק ההוא לסימן, ולא
לקחו מלת ראש הפסוק ממש, וזהו קל להבין,
ועוד שנו לפעמים סדר הספרים של המקרא,
כדי לעשות סימן יפה בקשור דברים, דבר

---

[119] The Massorah marginalis on Numb. xix. 1, which also mentions twelve passages wherein וידבר יהוה אל משה ואל אהרן only quotes eleven, viz., Exod. vi. 13; Levit. xi. 1, xiii. 1, xiv. 33, xv. 1; Numb. ii. 1, iv. 1, 17, xiv. 26, xvi. 20, xix. 1.

[120] The three instances in which מחטא occurs, are Gen. xx. 6; 1 Sam. xii. 23; Ps. xxxix. 2. They are stated in the Massorah marginalis on Exod. xx. 6. The five instances in which *Aleph* is wanted, are Gen. xx. 6; Numb. xi. 11, xv. 24; Deut. xi. 12, xxviii. 57.

words in their proper sequence. Thus, on וְטוֹב [Gen. xviii. 7], the marginal remark is, *it occurs five times with Kametz*, and the sign thereof is, in Aramaic, *"an excellent youth ran and found wisdom,"* which is not according to the regular order: since *youth* is taken from *"the youth Samuel"* [1 Sam. ii. 26]; *excellent*, from *"Saul the chosen"* [1 Sam. ix. 2]; *run*, from *"unto the herd he ran"* [Gen. xviii. 7]; *and he found*, from *"and they found pasture"* [1 Chr. iv. 40]; and *wisdom*, from *"they increased wisdom"* [1 Kings x. 7].

☞ As a rule, most of the remarks of the Massorites relate to the words and things which are liable to be mistaken. Thus, on וְרוּחַ אֱלֹהִים, *and the Spirit of God*, the remark is ח׳, *it occurs eight times*,[121] for in all other passages it is רוּחַ יְהוָה, *the Spirit of Jehovah*. The same is the case with the remark on וִיהִי, *and it shall be*, *"it occurs thirty-two times,"*[122] as in all other places it is וַיְהִי, *and it came to pass;* and so in numerous other instances. Thus, also, they did not put down the word לֵית, *not extant*, except in the case of those words which might be mistaken, as on וְתֵרָאֶה, *and it shall be seen*, it is remarked ל׳, *no parallel;* on יֵאָכֵל, *it shall be eaten*, it is remarked, *it occurs twenty-three times;*[123] on וְיָבֹאוּ, *and they shall come*, it is noted, *it occurs seven times.*[124] But in cases of words which are not liable to be mistaken, such as מְרַחֶפֶת, *hovering*, or יִקָּווּ, *let them be gathered*, or וְלִמְשׁוֹל, *and to rule*, or הָרָקִיעַ, *the firmament*, &c., &c., these they have not marked with לֵית. Mostly, however, they noticed the words which in some places have the *Vav* prefix, and in others have

---

[121] For these eight instances, see p. 139, note 117.

[122] The thirty-two instances in which ויהי occurs with *Vav* conjunctive, in all other instances being with *Vav* conversive, are as follows:—Gen. i. 6; ix. 26, 27; Exod. ix. 22; x. 21; xviii. 19; Deut. xxxiii. 6; 1 Sam. x. 5; xx. 13; xxviii. 22; 2 Sam. v. 24; xviii. 22, 23; 1 Kings xiii. 33; xiv. 5; xxi. 2; 2 Kings ii. 9; Jerem. xiii. 10; Hos. xiv. 7; Amos v. 14; Micah i. 2; Malachi iii. 10; Ps. ix. 10; lxxxi. 16; xc. 17; civ. 20; Ruth iii. 4; iv. 12; 1 Chron. xiv. 15; xxii. 16; 2 Chron. xviii. 12; xix. 11. They are enumerated in the Massorah finalis, under the letter *He*, 23 a, col. 2.

[123] The remark in the Basel and Sulzbach editions, that יאכל, Niphal future, 3rd person singular, *"occurs seventeen times* (י״ז)," is surely a mistake, since the word in question occurs twenty-three times, as follows:—Gen. vi. 21; Exod. xii. 16, 46; xiii. 3, 7; xxi. 28; xxix. 34; Levit. vii. 6, 15, 16 (twice), 18, 19, xi. 34, 41; xvii. 13; xix. 6, 7, 23; xxii. 30; Numb. xxviii. 17; Deut. xii. 22; Ezek. xlv. 21. They are thus given in the Massorah finalis under the letter *Aleph*, p. 6 b, col. 2.

[124] The seven instances in which וְיָבֹאוּ occurs with *Shera* under the *Vav*, called *Raphe* in the Massorah, are as follows:—Exod. xiv. 16, 17; Deut. x. 11; Josh. xviii. 4; Is. xiii. 2; Jerem. iii. 18; Ezek. xxxiii. 31. In all other passages the *Vav* has *Pattach*, which in the language of the Massorah is called *Dagesh*.

it not. Upon all this I have treated in my great work, entitled *The Book of Remembrance*, where you can see it.

Some, however, maintain that the Massorah does not notice words which are liable to be mistaken, but that it cites and counts them in order to deduce therefrom some homiletical, exegetical, or legal point. Thus, for instance, when the Massorites remark on בראשית, *in the beginning*, ג׳ ר״פ, "*it occurs three times at the beginning of the verse*," [125] it is because there is a Midrash; so they also remark on ויבדל, *and he divided*, ג׳, "*it occurs three times*,"[126] in harmony with the three *separations* which are recited at the termination of the Sabbath, viz., between light and darkness, &c.; on יעופף, *shall fly*, ב׳, "*it occurs twice*";[127] and in a host of other passages. From all these words some Midrash is to be deduced, and it is for this reason that the Massorites have noted down their number. To this effect a book has been written, which is ascribed to R. Jacob Baal Ha-Turim, of blessed memory.[128]

וחבריהן אינם כן, וכל אלה הביאותים בספר הזכרונות הגדול ומשם תראם:

ויש אומרים שהביאו קצת מלות שלא יש בהן חשש, רק הביאום ומנו אותם כדי ללמוד מהן מדרשים ופשטים, ודינים ומשפטים, כגון בראשית ג׳ ר״פ[125] יש בזה מדרש, וכן ויבדל ג׳ כנגד ג׳ הבדלות שאומרים בליל מוצאי שבת בין אור לחושך וכולי,[126] וכן יעופף ב׳,[127] וכן הרבה והרבה מאד, ועל כלן יש לדרוש איזה דבר, לפיכך כתבו בעלי המסורת מנינם, וכן חובר על זה ספר, ויחסו אותו לר׳ יעקב בעל הטורים ז״ל:[128]

---

[125] The three instances in which בראשית begins a verse are, Gen. i. 1; Jerem. xxvii. 1|; xxviii. 1. Now the Talmud relates the following story:—בקש הקב״ה להחזיר את העולם לתוהו ובוהו בשביל יהויקים כיון שנסתכל בדורו נתיישבה דעתו בקש הקב״ה להחזיר את העולם לתוהו ובוהו מפני דורו של צדקיהו כיון שנסתכל בצדקיהו נתיישבה דעתו, *God wanted to reduce the world again to void and emptiness, because of the wicked Jehojakim; but when He looked at the people of His time, His mind was appeased; God again wanted to reduce the world to void and emptiness, because of the people of Zedekiah's time, but when He looked upon Zedekiah, His mind was appeased* [Erachin, 17 a]. From this it will be seen, that the enumeration by the Massorah of these three passages in question is intimately connected with the story in the Talmud, where Jerem. xxvii. 1 and xxviii. 1 are brought together with Gen. i. 1, shewing that God wished, in those two cases where בראשית occurs, to destroy the work of the first בראשית. Comp. also *Sanhedrin*, 103 a.

[126] The three instances in which ויבדל occurs, are as follows:—Gen. i. 4; 7; 1 Chron. xxv. 7. From this the ecclesiastical legislators deduced, that "*Whoso recites the separations which God effected must not mention less than three . . . . because* ויבדל *occurs three times*" (כל הפורת לא יפחות משלשה הבדלות), *Pessachim*, 103 b—104 a). The reference here is to the prayer which the Jews to this day offer on the Sabbath evening, at the going out of the sacred day and the coming in of the week day, and which is denominated *Havadalah* (הבדלה). In this prayer, which is as follows, are contained the three separations in question:—ברוך אתה י״י אלהינו מלך העולם המבדיל בין, *Blessed art thou, O Lord*; קדש לחל בין אור לחשך בין ישראל לעמים בין יום השביעי לששת ימי המעשה, *Our God, King of the world, who hast made a separation between the holy and the common, a separation between light and darkness, and a separation between Israel and the other nations*. Comp. also Jacob b. Chajim's *Introduction to the Rabbinic Bible*, p. 12 Hebrew and p. 32 English, ed. Ginsburg.

[127] The two instances in which יעופף occurs are, Gen. i. 20; Isa. vi. 2. From the combination of these two passages, in which alone the expression occurs, it is deduced that the angels are included in the winged creatures, created on the fifth day of the hexahemeron. Comp. *Midrasch Rabba* on Genesis, p. 3 a, ed. Stettin, 1863.

[128] Jacob b. Asheri, also called *Baal Ha-Turim*, after his celebrated Ritual Work,

However, I have noticed that he only explains the words which occur two, three, four, or five times, but not more. Now what is to be done with those which occur from ten, twenty, to a hundred times, &c.? As for instance, בְּעֵינֵי, *in the eyes of*, which occurs 139 times; רֹאשׁ, *head*, which occurs 151 times. How is it possible to assign a reason for all these? But the words of the Law are like a hammer, which breaks the rock and divides it into many pieces, since the Law may be interpreted in seventy different ways. Herewith the Introductions are completed, by the help of Him who creates souls, and in whose name I shall commence the Treatise itself, and explain each one of the ten sections on *plene* and *defective*, their laws and regulations; and the contents thereof are as follows:—

והנה ראיתי שאינו מפרש רק המלות הנמצאות ב' או ג' או ד' או ה' פעמים, ולא יותר, ומה נעשה באותן הנמצאות י' או כ' עד מאה פעמים ויותר, כגון בְּעֵינֵי קל״ט, רֹאשׁ קנ״א, איך אפשר לתת טעם על כלן, אך דברי תורה כפטיש יפוצץ סלע מתחלק לכמה נצוצות, ובשבעים פנים התורה נדרשת, ובכן נשלמו ההקדמות, בעזרת יוצר נשמות, ובשמו אתחיל החבור, ואבאר כל דבור ודבור, מן דברות העשר, של כל מלא וחסר, ודינן ומשפטן, וזהו פרטן:

was born in Germany, *circa* A.D. 1280, and died A.D. 1340. The Commentary to which Levita refers is an exposition of the Pentateuch, and interprets the sacred text according to the hermeneutical rules called גימטריא, reducing every letter of a word to its numerical value, and explaining it by another word of the same quantity. The great value of this Commentary consists in its explanations of the Massoretic notes. The portion which treats on the Massorah has been detached from the general Commentary, and published separately in most of the Rabbinic Bibles. Comp. Kitto's *Cyclopædia*, s. v. JACOB B. ASHERI.

FIRST PART.

לוחות ראשונות:

SECTION I. treats on *defective* and *plene* in so far as they relate to the *matres lectiones Vav* after *Cholem* and *Shureck*, and *Jod* after *Chirek* and *Tzere*.

SECTION II. treats on the passages wherein the *Vav* is absent after the *Cholem* in verbs and nouns, and the difference between them.

SECTION III. treats on nouns which are *Milra* and have a *Vav plene* after the *Cholem* on the top, and those which are *Milra* and have not the *Vav;* as well as of all the *Cholems* of the participle *Kal*, which are generally defective, and most of the plurals feminine which have a *Vav* at the end.

SECTION IV. treats on the absent *Vav* of the *Shurek*, and on the *Kibutz* being substituted in its place.

SECTION V. treats on all the words which have a long *Chirek, i. e., Chiruk* with a *Jod*, having mostly *Jod;* and on those words which have *Cholem*, being mostly defective of *Vav*.

SECTION VI. treats on the quiescent *Jod* after the *Tzere* and *Segol*, as well as on the quiescent *Jod* after the *Kametz* of the third person.

SECTION VII. treats on the *plene* and *defective* of monosyllabic words, being small words.

SECTION VIII. treats on the Massoretic marks, or words, which have two or three quiescents, some being *plene* and some *defective*,[1] or all being *plene* or all *defective*.

הדבור הראשון בביאור שעיקר חסר ומלא לא נאמר רק על וי"ו הנחה אחר החולם והשורק, והי"ו ד הנחה אחר החירק והצרי:
הדבור השני בביאור המקומות שחסר בהן הוי"ו אחר ההולם בפעלים ושמות וההפרש שביניהן:
הדבור השלישי בביאור שהשמות שהם מלרע הם מלאים וי"ו אחר החולם שבראשם, ואותם שהם מלעיל הם חסרים וי"ו, וכל החולמים שבבינוני מבנין הקל הם על הרוב חסרים ורוב לשון רבות מלאים וי"ו בסוף:
הדבור הרביעי בביאור הוי"ו השדוקה, מתי היא חסרה ובא תחתיה קבוץ שפתים:
הדבור החמישי בביאור כל תיבה ששייך בה חירק גדול, ר"ל הירק עם יו"ד היא על הרוב מלאה יו"ד, והתיבה ששייך בה חולם היא על הרוב חסרה וי"ו:
הדבור הששי בביאור היו"ד הנחה הבאה אחר הצרי והסגול, וכן יו"ד נחה הבאה אחר קמץ לכינוי הנכתר:
הדבור השביעי בביאור המלות המלאים והחסרים שהם של תנועה אחת, דהיינו מלות זעירות:
הדבור השמיני בביאור איך נמסר על מלה שיש בה ב' או ג' נחים קצתן מלאים וקצתן חסרים,[1] או כולן מלאים או כלן חסרים:

---

[1] The Sulzbach edition rightly inserts וקצתן חסרים, *and some being defective*, which has dropped out from the ed. Basel, 1539.

SECTION IX. treats on words which have a quiescent *Aleph*, either expressed or not, and which are called '*with audible Alephs*,' or '*without audible Alephs*.'

SECTION X. treats on words, the final *He* of which is either *plene* or *defective*, and are called *Maphkin He*, consisting of four kinds.

END OF THE CONTENTS OF THE FIRST PART.

SECTION I.—I, Elias Levita, the author, have already explained, in my *Poetical Dissertation*,[2] the law of the letters יהו״א, which prolong the syllables, and are quiescent; for their nature is to be quiescent in the middle and end of the word, as well as to indicate the five long vowels, respecting which I have given the mnemonical sign, "Good Elijahu."[3] Now, there ought properly to be one of the letters אהו״י after every long vowel. Thus, after *Kametz* in the middle of the word there ought to be a quiescent *Aleph*, and at the end of the word *Aleph* or *He* quiescent; after *Chirek* and *Tzere* there ought to be a quiescent *Jod*; and after *Cholem* and *Shurek* a quiescent *Vav*. But they do not generally occur so in the Scripture, and it is these which the Massorites call *defective*, and whenever they do occur they are denominated *plene*.

☞ Know that the import of most of the *defectives* and *plenes*, which the Massorites have marked as such, is about the quiescent *Vav* and *Jod* in the middle of the word, *Vav* after *Cholem* and *Shurek*, and the *Jod* after *Chirek* and *Tzere;* and that in only few cases did they remark *plene* and *defective* upon *Aleph* and *He*, as I shall explain hereafter. I shall begin with the absence of the *Vav* at the *Cholem*, for this occurs most frequently, and say—

[2] For a description of this grammatical work, see above, p. 13, &c.
[3] It will be seen that in this mnemonical sign, אֵלִי יָהּ הוּא טוֹב, *good Elijahu*, are contained all the five vowels, (viz., a, e, i, o, u,) both in the original Hebrew and in its English equivalent. The discussion of this subject, to which Levita refers, is to be found on p. 36 of the Poetical Dissertation, ed. Prague, 1793.

הדבור התשיעי בביאור המלות שיש בהן אלף נחה כתובה או כשאינה כתובה, וקראו להן מפקין אך או לא מפקין אלף:

הדבור העשירי בביאור המלות שתבוא בהן הה״א בסוף חסר או מלא, וקראו לה מפקין ח״א, והן של ד׳ מינין:

סליקו הסימנים, מהלוחות הראשונים:

הדבור הראשון: אנכי אליהו הלוי המחבר כבר באריתי בפרק שירה[2] דין אותיות יהו״א, שהם אותיות המשך והנוח, כי כן דרכם לנוח באמצע המלה ובסופה, והן מורות על חמש התנועות הגדולות, אשר נתתי סימנם אליהו טוב,[3] והנה היה מן הראוי להיות אחר כל תנועה גדולה אחת מאותיות אהו״י, דהיינו אחר הקמץ שבאמצע המלה היה ראוי אל״ף נחה, ושבסוף המלה אל״ף או ה״א נחה, ואחר החירק והצרי יו״ד נחה, ואחר החולם והשורק וי״ו נחה, והנה על הרוב לא יבאו במסרה, והם שקראו בעלי המסרה חסרים, וכאשר יבאו במכתבת קראו להם מלאים:

☞ ודע כי העקד ורוב החסרים והמלאים שעליהם כתבו בעלי המסרת הם חוי״י והיו״ד הנחים באמצע התיבה, הוי״ו אחר החולם והשורק, והיו״ד אחד החירק והצרי, ועל המעט כתבו מלא או חסר על הא״ף וההא״א, כאשר אבאר אח״כ, אתחיל בחסי״י הוי״ו עם החולם כי הם הרבים ואומר:

☞ Know that most of the words with *Cholem* in the Scriptures want the *mater lectionis Vav*. Still, the Massorites have not marked as *defective* every word with *Cholem* which has not the *Vav*; nor have they marked as *plene* every word with *Cholem* which has the *mater lectionis Vav;* but they have only noted those words as *defective* which generally have *Cholem* with the *Vav*, but which, in a few instances, occur without *Vav;* as I shall explain hereafter. The same is the case with the words which generally have *Cholem* without *Vav*; when these occur with *Vav* the Massorites have marked them *plene*.[4]

☞ The general rule is, that in the case of all the words which occur more as *plene* than *defective*, the Massorites enumerated the *defective;* and whenever the *defectives* are more frequent than the *plenes*, they enumerated the *plenes*, as I shall explain in the following Section. Know, moreover, that the vowel-point is never altered because of its being *defective* or *plene*, except in the case of the *Shurek* with *Vav*, which is changed into *Kibutz of the lips*, as I shall explain in Section iv.

☞ Know, also, that the meaning of the word is never changed because of *defective* and *plene*. Hence it is that there is never *Keri* and *Kethiv* with respect to *defective* and *plene*, as I have already stated in the Introduction. Know, likewise, that there is a difference between the simple word *defective*, marked on a certain word, and the Massorites saying, *and defective*, with the *Vav* conjunctive, as well as between the simple *plene* and *and plene*. This I shall explain in Part ii., Sect. viii. I shall there also explain the import of the phrases, '*entirely plene*,' '*entirely defective*,' as well as the meaning of '*partly plene and partly defective*,' and '*partly defective and partly plene*.'

SECTION II.—There is no noun to be found in the whole Bible, with *Cholem* as the last vowel, which is not written *plene*, with the *mater lectionis Vav*, except in a few instances which deviate from this rule,

☜ דע כי רוב החולמים שבמקרא חסרי וי״ו המשך, אך לא על כל חולם שהוא בלי וי״ו כתבו חסר, גם לא על כל חולם שהוא עם הוי״ו כתבו מלא, רק המלות שדרכן לבא בהן החולם עם הוי״ו על הרוב, כאשר אבאר אח״כ, כשיכואו בלי וי״ו אז נמסר עליהן חסר, וכן המלות שדרכן לבא בהן החולם על הרוב בלי וי״ו, כשיבאו עם הוי״ו, נמסר עליהן מלא:[4]

☜ והכלל כל מלין שחמלאים מרובין על החסרים, הם מונין את החסרין, וכשהחסרין מרובין על המלאים, הם מונין את המלאים, כאשר אבאר בדיבור שאחר זה, ויש לך לדעת שלא תשתנה נקודה מהנקודות בעבור חסר או מלא לעולם, רק חשורק עם הוי״ו ישתנה לקבוץ שפתים, כאשר אבאר בדבור הרביעי:

☜ ודע גם כן שלא תשתנה הוראת המלה בעבור חסר ומלא לעולם, לכן לא יבא קרי וכתיב מעניין חסר ומלא לעולם, כמו שכתברתי בהקדמה, ויש לך לדערע שיש הפרש בין אמרם על מלח אחת חסר, ובין אמרם וחסר עם וי״ו השימוש, וכין בין מלא ומלא, וזה יתבאר לך בלוחות שניות במאמר ח', וגם יתבאר בו עניין מלא דמלא, או חסר דחסר, וכן עניין מלא חסר, או חסר מלא:

הדבור השני: לא יהיה לך שם בכל המקרא שיהיה תנועתו האחרונה חולם שאינו כתוב מלא עם הוי״ו, חוץ ממעטים יוצאים

---

[4] The whole of this sentence is transposed in the Sulzbach edition.

as I shall explain in the following section. Upon these *plenes* there was no necessity to remark that they are *plene* because they are the most frequent, as I have stated in the preceding Section.

☞ Know that just as nouns are generally *plene*, so verbs are generally *defective*. Thus, for example, the word פְּקֹד, *number*, whereon the Massorites remark "it occurs four times—twice *plene* and twice *defective*," viz. : "Number all the first-born" [Numb. iii. 40], and "Number the children of Levi" [*ibid*. iii. 15], both of which are *defective*, because they are verbs; whilst "Against the inhabitants of Pekod" [Jer. l. 21], and "Pekod and Shoa" [Ezek. xxiii. 23], are *plene*, because they are proper names. Thus, also, the future tense, as אֶפְקֹד, *I shall number*, and יִפְקֹד, *he shall number*, &c., which is generally *defective*, the Massorites have not noted as *defective*, because it is mostly so. And even verbs in which the second letter is quiescent, because the middle-stem letter is *Vav*, as, for instance, יָשֹׁב *he shall return*, תָּשֹׁב *thou shalt return*, אָבֹא *I shall come*, יָבֹא *he shall come*, תָּבֹא *thou shalt come*, נָבֹא *we shall come*, since these are generally *defective*, the Massorites counted the *plenes*.

Take, for example, nouns, the last vowel of which is *Cholem*, as גָּדוֹל *great*, כָּבוֹד *honour*, קָדוֹשׁ *holy*, שָׁלוֹם *peace*, רָחוֹק *far*, קָרוֹב *nigh*, צָפוֹן *north*, דָּרוֹם *south*, גִּבּוֹר *strong*, שְׁאוֹל *hades*, חֲמוֹר *an ass*, תְּהוֹם *deep*, as well as nouns which have an additional syllable, either at the beginning or end, as מִזְמוֹר *a song*, אֶשְׁכּוֹל *cluster*, זִכָּרוֹן *remembrance*, שִׁגָּעוֹן *madness*, עִוָּרוֹן *blindness*, תִּמָּהוֹן *terror*, &c., and those in which the *Vav* is the radical, as מָכוֹן *a place*, מָעוֹן *a dwelling*, מָלוֹן *an inn*; on all the above, and the like, the Massorites did not remark *plene*, because they are generally so written, but they counted the *defectives*, as קָדֹשׁ, *holy*, occurs thirteen times *defective*;[5] also when it is in the construct, as קְדֹשׁ occurs three times *defective*;[6] גִּבֹּר *strong of*, three times

---

[5] The thirteen instances in which קדוש, *holy*, occurs as *defective* are as follows:—Exod. xxix. 31; Levit. vi. 9, 19, 20; xxi. 7, 8; xxiv. 9; Numb. vi. 5, 8; Deut. xxvi. 19; Ezek. xlii. 13; Nehem. viii. 9, 11. They are enumerated in the Massorah marginalis on Exod. xxix. 31.

[6] The three instances in which the construct קדוש is without *Vav* are, Ps. xlvi. 5; lxv. 5; Isa. xlix. 7. They are mentioned in the Massorah marginalis on Ps. lxv. 5.

defective;⁷ שָׁלֹם *peace of*, eight times *defective*;⁸ זִכְרֹן *remembrance of*, three times *defective*.⁹ There are, again, a few words which are always *defective*, for which reason the Massorites did not consider it necessary to mark them as *defective*, as קָטֹן *small*, מְאֹד *very*, כֹּחַ *power*. About לֹא *not*, and כָּל *all*, I shall speak¹⁰ in Section viii., if God permit.

As to the *plenes*, about which I treated above, and their like, when they occur with ה feminine, they too generally continue *plene*, as גְּדוֹלָה *great*, קְרוֹבָה *near*, רְחוֹקָה *far*, &c.; but the reverse is the case with plurals, both masculine and feminine, because they are generally *defective*, as גְּדֹלִים *the great*, mas., קְדֹשִׁים *the holy*, mas., גִּבֹּרִים *the strong*, mas., קְרֹבִים *the near*, mas., גְּדֹלוֹת *the great*, fem., קְרֹבוֹת *the near*, fem., רְחֹקוֹת *the far*, fem. This is because there are two quiescents following each other in these words, as I shall explain in its proper place, in Section viii. Thus, also, every *Cholem* which stands before ת in the feminine plural is according to rule *plene*, because it ends the word; as הַפָּרוֹת הָרַקּוֹת וְהָרָעוֹת, *the lean and ill favoured kine* [Gen. xli., 20]; לְרַקָּחוֹת וּלְטַבָּחוֹת וּלְאֹפוֹת, *to perfumers, butchers, and to bakers* [1 Sam. viii. 13]. The same rule obtains in all the plurals and participles, both active and passive; as פּוֹקְדוֹת, and פְּקֻדוֹת, as well as in the participles of all the conjugations, examples of which need not be adduced. All feminine plurals, however, which have no *Vav*, the Massorites marked as *defective*. Thus, for instance, בְּתֻלֹת *virgins*, [Esther ii. 2]; and the participles הֹלְכֹת, *they are coming down* [Exod. ii. 5]; and יֹשְׁבֹת, *they are sitting* [1 Kings iii. 17]. About the participles passive, I shall speak in its proper place, in Section vii., and I shall also discuss all this in the Section on the two quiescents, which is Section viii.

---

⁷ The three instances in which גבור is *defective* are, Gen. x. 8, 9; Deut. x. 17. They are given in the Massorah marginalis on Gen. x. 8.

⁸ The Basel edition states that there are three instances in which שלום is *defective*; but this is evidently a mistake, for there are eight, as follows:—Gen. xxxvii. 4; 1 Sam. xvi. 4; 1 Kings ii. 5, 6; v. 26; Jerem. xv. 5; Ezek. xiii. 16 (twice). They are enumerated in the Massorah marginalis on Gen. xxxvii. 4. The Sulzbach edition omits שלום altogether, and substitutes for it ארן.

⁹ The three passages in which זכרון is *defective* are, Exod. xxviii. 12 (twice), 29.

¹⁰ The Sulzbach edition erroneously inserts מהן *about them*, after אדבר *I shall speak*.

149

SECTION III.—There is no triliteral noun to be found, the first syllable of which has *Cholem* with the *mater lectionis Vav*, except when the accent is on the ultima, since, in those which have the tone on the penultima, the *Cholem* in the first syllable is generally without the *mater lectionis Vav*. *Plenes*, for example, are עוֹלָם *eternity*, כּוֹכָב *star*, גּוֹרָל *lot*, אוֹפָן *a wheel*, אוֹצָר *a store*, תּוֹלָע *a worm*, שׁוֹשָׁן *a lily*. Also, those with *Tzere*; ex. gr., יוֹבֵל *jubilee*, אוֹיֵב *an enemy*, עוֹרֵב *a raven*, שׂוֹרֵק *a vine*. These are generally *plene*; the *defectives* are but few, as לְעֹלָם *for ever*, which occurs 18 times *defective*;[11] גֹּרָל *lot*, 4 times *defective* in this form;[12] חֹתָם *seal*, 7 times *defective* in this form;[13] אֹיֵב *enemy*, three times *defective* in this form.[14] I shall acquaint thee with the meaning of בלישנא, *in this form*, in Part ii., Section ix.

Moreover, nouns derived from irregular verbs, the first radical of which is *Jod*, and which have an additional *Mem* or *Tav*, are generally *plene*; as תּוֹרָה *law*, תּוֹשָׁב *an inhabitant*, מוֹצָא *a going out*, מוֹרָא *fear*, מוֹעֵד *appointment*, מוֹפֵת *a miracle*, &c., &c. The *defectives* are exceedingly few. But the pronouns אוֹתוֹ *him*, אוֹתְךָ *thee*, אוֹתִי *me*, אוֹתָם *them*, אוֹתָהּ *her*, though they have the tone on the ultima, are generally *defective*. Hence, because these are the majority, therefore the *plenes* are enumerated, and not the *defectives*. Thus, on אוֹתוֹ *him*, it is remarked, "it occurs twenty-four times *plene*;"[15] on אוֹתְךָ *thee*, "it

הדבור השלישי: לא תשא את שם של שלש אותיות נעות על שפתיך, כשהתנועה הראשונה חולם עם וי"ו, רק בטעם מלרע, כי אותם שהם בטעם מלעיל, החולם שבראשם חסר וי"ו על הרוב, והמלאים כמו עוֹלָם, כּוֹכָב, גּוֹרָל, אוֹפָן, אוֹצָר, תּוֹלָע, שׁוֹשָׁן; וכן בצדי יוֹבֵל, אוֹיֵב, עוֹרֵב, שׂוֹרֵק, רובן מלאים, והחסרים הם מעטים כמו לְעֹלָם, י"ח חסרים,[11] גֹּרָל ד' חסרים בלישנא,[12] חֹתָם ז' חסרים בלישנא,[13] אֹיֵב ג' חסרים בלישנא,[14] ועוד אודיעך מהו ענין בלישנא בלוחות שניות, במאמר ט':

וכן בשמות נחי פ"י יו"ד הבאים בתוספת מ"ם או תי"ו, רובן מלאים, כמו תּוֹרָה, תּוֹשָׁב, מוֹצָא, מוֹרָא, מוֹעֵד, מוֹפֵת, ודומיהן, והחסרים הם מעטים מאד, אבל אוֹתוֹ, אוֹתְךָ, אוֹתִי, אוֹתָם, אוֹתָהּ, אע"פי שהם בטעם מלרע רובן חסרים, מפני רבויים, לפיכך נמנין המלאים ולא החסרים, כמו אוֹתוֹ כ"ד מלאים,[15] אוֹתְךָ י"ן

---

[11] The eighteen instances in which לעלם occurs *defective* are as follows:—Gen. iii. 22; vi. 3; Exod. iii. 15; xv. 18; xxi. 6; xxxi. 17; xxxii. 13; Levit. xxv. 46; Deut. v. 26; xxxii. 40; 1 Kings i. 31 ii. 33; ix. 5; x. 9; Ps. xlv. 18; lxxv. 10; xcii. 9. Though the word in question is marked in each of these passages as *defective*, we could not find the entire list anywhere enumerated in the Massorah. On Exod. iii. 15, and Ps. xlv. 18, the Massorah marginalis remarks that a list of the eighteen instances is given in the Massorah on Ps. lxxv. (לעלם י"ח נמסר בתהלים סימן ע"ה). On Ps. lxxv., again the Massorah marginalis remarks that the eighteen instances are enumerated in the Massorah finalis, under the letter *Ajin Vav* (לעלם י"ח חסר וסי' במס' רבתא בערך ע"י); and on examining the Massorah finalis, to which we are referred again, we find that it simply states לעלם י"ח וחס' וסמני' נמסר בתלים סימן ע"ה, "The word לעלם occurs eighteen times defective, and the passages are given in the Massorah marginalis on Ps. lxxv." Comp. p. 49, col. 2.

[12] The Massorah marginalis on Levit. xvi. 8 gives the four instances in which גרל is *defective*, as follows:—Levit. xvi. 8; Numb. xxxvi. 3; Judg. i. 3; Dan. xii. 13; including, as it will be seen, the plural גרלות.

[13] The seven instances in which חותם is *defective* are as follows:—Gen. xxxviii. 18, 25; Exod. xxviii. 11, 36; xxxix. 14; 1 Kings xxi. 8 (twice). They are enumerated in the Massorah marginalis on Exod. xxviii. 11.

[14] The three passages in which איב occurs *defective* are, 1 Sam. xviii. 29; Jerem. vi. 25; xv. 11. They are given in the Massorah marginalis on 1 Sam. xviii. 29.

[15] The twenty-four instances in which אותו occurs *plene* are as follows:—Josh. xxiv. 4, 14, 22; 1 Sam. xii. 24; 2 Kings i. 15 (twice); iii. 11, 12, 26; viii. 8; ix. 27; x. 16;

occurs seventeen times *plene;*"[16] on אוֹתָךְ *thee*, fem., "sixteen times *plene;*"[17] on אוֹתִי *me*, "twenty-seven times *plene;*"[18] on אוֹתָם *them*, "thirty-nine times *plene*" in the Pentateuch, and the sign of it is "*for it is full* [= *plene*] *of dew* [טל = 39]."[19] The Massorites have also counted the *plene* of the word אוֹתָם *them*, in each book of the Bible, except Jeremiah and Ezekiel, where they have counted the *defectives*, because they are the fewer; and they likewise tell us that אוֹתָה *her*, occurs twelve times.[20] But the nouns, with the tone on the penultima, are mostly *defective;* as חֹדֶשׁ *the new moon*, קֹדֶשׁ *holiness*, אֹהֶל *tabernacle*, גֹּרֶן *area*, &c., &c. On קֹדֶשׁ *holiness* [Dan. xi. 31], the Massorites remark, "*there is no parallel case of plene.*" The meaning of the expression לית, I shall explain in the Third Part, denominated *The Broken Tables*. The word שׂוֹבֶךְ *thicket* [2 Sam. xviii. 9] is also *plene;* and besides these, there are almost no *plenes* in this form of the noun.

Jerem. xviii. 10; xxxvii. 15; Ezek. xvii. 17; xliii. 20; Hos. x. 6; Mal. i. 12, 13; iii. 22; Ps. xviii. 1; lvi. 1; lxvii. 8; ci. 5. They are confusedly enumerated in the Massorah finalis, p. 13 b, col. 2, with the remark, that throughout the books of Joshua and Judges it is likewise *plene*, with the exception of two passages.

[16] The seventeen instances in which אוֹתְךָ masculine, occurs *plene* are, Gen. xvii. 2; xx. 6; xl. 19; xli. 39; Exod. ix. 15; xxv. 9, 22; xxxii. 10; Deut. ix. 14; 2 Sam. xxiv. 24; Ezek. ii. 3, 4; iii. 27; xxix. 5; xxxviii. 4, 17; Ps. xxv. 5. They are enumerated in the Massorah finalis, p. 13 b, col. 3.

[17] The seventeen instances in which אוֹתָךְ feminine occurs *plene*, are Gen. xxxix. 9; Numb. v. 21; Judg. xiv. 15; Jerem. ii. 35; xi. 17; xxx. 14; Ezek. xvi. 4, 39, 40, 57, 59, 60; xxii. 14, 15; xxiii. 25, 29. They are enumerated in the Massorah finalis, p. 13 b, cols. 3 and 4.

[18] The twenty-seven passages in which אוֹתִי is *plene*, are Deut. xxxii. 51; Judg. x. 13; Isa. xxxvii. 6; liv. 15; lvii. 11 (twice); lviii. 2; Jerem. iv. 22; v. 22; ix. 5, 23; xiii. 5, 25; xvi. 11; xx. 11; xxv. 6; xxxi. 34; xxxvii. 18; Ezek. vi. 9; xxiii. 35 (twice); xl. 3; Ps. xxxi. 6; Esth. v. 12; Lament. iii. 2; Nehem. vi. 14. They are given in the Massorah finalis, p. 13 b, col. 3, with the remark that אותי is also *plene* throughout the books of Joshua and Judges, except in two instances.

[19] The thirty-nine passages in which אותם is *plene* in the Pentateuch are as follows: Gen. xli. 8; xlix. 28, 29; l. 21: Exod. xiv. 9; xxix. 3; Levit. x. 2; xiv. 51; xv. 10, 29; xvii. 5; xxii. 16; xxiii. 43; xxiv. 8; xxv. 55: Numb. iv. 12, 19, 23, 49; v. 4; vi. 20; vii. 3, 5, 6; xxv. 4, 17: Deut. iii. 6, 28; ix. 28; x. 15; xii. 29; xviii. 12, 13; xxvi. 16; xxvii. 26; xxxi. 7, 10. They are most confusedly enumerated in the Massorah finalis, p. 13 b, col. 4, to page 14 a, col. 1. The mnemonical sign שראשי נמלא ט׳ל, *for my head is filled with dew*, from *Song of Songs* v. 2, is exceedingly ingenious and beautiful. The force of it will be understood, when it is remembered that the word ראש *head*, is figuratively used for the *Law*, or the *Pentateuch*, and is so rendered by the Chaldee Paraphrasts on *Song of Songs* v. 11; that the word נמלא, *full*, is exactly the expression for *plene;* and that the numerical value of the word טל, *dew*, is 39.

[20] The twelve passages in which אותה occurs *plene* are, Numb. xxii. 33; xxx. 9: 1 Sam. xiv. 27: 2 Sam. xiii. 18: Isa. xxvii. 11; xxviii. 4,; xxxvii. 26; Jerem. xxxii. 31; xxxiii. 2: Hosea iv. 19: Malachi. i. 13: Ps. xxvii. 4. They are enumerated in the Massorah marginalis on Numb. xxii. 33, with the remark that וכל יהושע שופטים ויחזקאל דכר במ׳ג, "*it is also plene throughout the books of Joshua, Judges, and Ezekiel, with the exception of three passages.*"

Moreover, all those which have *Pattach* before the guttural in this form are generally *defective*, as אֹרַח *way*, תֹּאַר *form*, נֹגַהּ *brightness*, נֹכַח *before*, נֹעַם *sweetness*, נֹעַר *boyhood*, טֹהַר *brightness*, פֹּעַל *work*; and only a few of these are *plene*, as צֹעַר *Zoar*, which occurs three times *plene*;[21] and קוֹבַע, כּוֹבַע *helmet*, are sometimes *Milel*, and sometimes *Milra*; and there is a division of opinion about them. Likewise נְחֹשֶׁת *copper*, כַּפֹּרֶת *a cover*, פָּרֹכֶת *curtain*, קְטֹרֶת *incense*, שִׁבֹּלֶת *an ear*, כֻּתֹּנֶת *a tunic*, are *defective*, because they are *Milel*; תּוֹלַעַת *a worm*, is an exception, for it is always written fully, except in two instances, in which it occurs *defective*.[22] The *Cholems*, too, of the participle *Kal*, are generally without *Vav*, whether in the singular masculine, as פֹּקֵד *remembering*, נֹצֵר *keeping*, נֹשֵׂא *forgiving* [Exod. xxxiv. 7]; or plural masculine, as אֹכְלִים וְשֹׁתִים וְחֹגְגִים, *they are eating, and drinking, and dancing* [1 Sam. xxx. 16]; or plural feminine, as עֹשְׁקוֹת *oppressors*, רֹצְצוֹת *crushers*, אֹמְרוֹת *declarers* [Amos iv. 1].[23] It is the *plenes* of all these which are enumerated in the Massorah, as אוֹכֵל *occurs four times plene*,[24] יוֹדֵעַ *ten times plene*,[25] קוֹרֵא *ten times plene*.[26] The same is the case with the twenty-four instances of *plene* in the singular, which have no parallel in the whole Bible; as פּוֹתֵר [Gen. xli. 8], חוֹלֵם [Deut. xiii. 3], טוֹחֵן [Judges xvi. 21], &c., upon each one of which there is a Massoretic remark.[27] The word יוֹשֵׁב is

---

[21] The three instances in which צוֹעַר is *plene* are, Gen. xix. 22, 30 (twice).
[22] The two exceptions in which תּוֹלַעַת is *defective* are, Exod. xxvi. 1; Deut. xxviii. 39.
[23] The whole of this passage is vitiated in the ed. Basel, 1539.
[24] The four passages in which אוכל occurs *plene* are, Gen. xxxix. 6; Isa. xxix. 8; Nahum iii. 12; Ps. xli. 10. They are enumerated in the Massorah marginalis on Gen. xxxix. 6.
[25] This is one of the passages which shows how difficult it is to understand the Massoretic language, and how easily one may mistake the meaning of Levita. In reading the above remark, one might be led to suppose that there are only ten instances in the Bible in which יודע is *plene*, whereas there are no less than twenty-three. Levita's remark, however, is explained by the Massoretic annotation on 1 Sam. xxvi. 12, where it is stated that יודע is *plene* in ten places, viz., 1 Sam. xxvi. 12: Isa. xxix. 11: Jerem. xxix. 23: Ps. i. 6; xxxvii. 18; lxxiv. 9; xc. 11: Ruth iii. 11: Esther iv. 14: Nehem. x. 29; adding וכל תריסר ד"ה קהלת ומשלי דכו, "*throughout the twelve minor Prophets, Chronicles, Ecclesiastes, and Proverbs, it is likewise* PLENE;" which is omitted by Levita.
[26] The ten instances in which קוֹרֵא is *plene* are, Judges xv. 19: Isa. vi. 4; xl. 3; xlv. 3; lxiv. 6; Amos v. 8; Habak. ii. 2; Ps. xlii. 8; 1 Chron. ix. 19; 2 Chron. xxxi. 14. They are given in the Massorah finalis under the letter *Kaph*, p. 56 a, cols. 3 and 4.
[27] The twenty-four, or rather twenty-five, words written plene, which have no parallel, are as follows :—

an exception to this rule, for in some portions of the Bible the instances in which it is written fully are enumerated, whilst in others the *defectives* are counted. Thus, in the Pentateuch and in the earlier prophets the *plenes* are counted, whilst in the later prophets the *defectives* are enumerated. The same is the case in every book of the Hagiographa; some count the *plenes* and some the *defectives*.

The plural, both masculine and feminine, of the participle, is generally written without *Vav*, and only in few instances is it written fully, as יוֹצְאִים, which occurs three times *plene*;[28] יוֹשְׁבִים, three times *plene*.[29] In every such instance the Massorites remark *plene*. Thus, on the word יוֹרְדָה [Lam. i. 16], the Massoretic remark is "*it has no parallel, and it is plene;*" on הַהוֹלֶכֶת [Nehem. xii. 38], the Massorites remark "*no parallel, and plene;*" on הוֹלְכוֹת [Nehem. vi. 17], "*no parallel, and plene;*" on הַיוֹרְדוֹת [Neh. iii. 15], "*no parallel, and plene.*" I shall treat again on this subject in Section viii. But the verbs which have *Cholem* on the first syllable, and whose *Vav* belongs to the root, are generally written fully, as הַקוֹמִים [2 Kings xvi. 7], כּוֹנֵן [Ps. ix. 8], כּוֹנְנֵהוּ, פּוֹנְנָה [Ps. xl. 17]. Comp. also יְשׁוֹבָב and יְקוֹמֵם. The same is the case with those verbs in which *Vav* stands instead of the first radical letter *Jod*, as in the *Niphal* and *Hiphil*, viz., נוֹדַע, נוֹדַעְתָּ, הוֹדִיעַ מוֹדִיעַ, these are generally written fully.

יוֹשֵׁב יוּצָאת מן הכלל שביש מקומות נמנין המלאים, וביש מקומות נמנין החסרים, כגון בתורה ונביאים ראשונים נמנין המלאים, ובנביאים אחרונים נמנין החסרים, וכן בכל ספר וספר מכתובים בקצתן נמנין המלאים, ובקצתן נמנין החסרים:

ורוב לשון רבים ורבות בבינוני חסרים וי"ו, ומעטים הם המלאים, כמו יוֹצְאִים ג' מלאים,[28] יוֹשְׁבִים ג' מלאים,[29] ובכל מקום נמסר עליהן מלאים, וכן יוֹרְדָה מים, נמסר עליו לית ומלא, וכן הַהוֹלֶכֶת לְמוֹאֵל (נחמיה י"ב) לית ומלא, אגרותיהם הוֹלְכוֹת לית ומלא, הַיוֹרְדוֹת מעיר דויד לית ומלא, ועוד אדבר מהם בדבור ח': אבל בפעלים שהחולם בתנועה ראשונה וחו"ו בהן שרשית, הם על הרוב מלאים, כמו הַקוֹמִים עליך, פּוֹנֵן למשפט כסאו, (תלים ט') פּוֹנֲנָה עלינו ומעשה ידינו פּוֹנְנֵהוּ, וכן יְשׁוֹבָב, יְקוֹמֵם, וכן כשהיו"ד במקום יו"ד פ"א הפעל, כגון בנפעל והפעיל נוֹדַע, נוֹדַעְתָּ, הוֹדִיעַ, הוֹדַעְתָּ, מוֹדִיעַ, כּוֹשִׁיב, על הרוב מלאים:

פותר	. . . Gen. xli. 8	שוכב	. . Ezek. iv. 9	בוקר	. . . Amos vii. 14
חולם	. . . Deut. xiii. 4	אונך	. . Jerem. iv. 14	חורש	. . . Amos ix. 13
טוחן	. . . Judg. xvi. 21	הורג	. . Ezek. xvi. 16	ונוטר	. . . Nahum i. 2
בוצץ	. . . 1 Sam. xiv. 4	חולש	. . Isa. xiv. 12	גוער	. . . Nahum i. 4
שורק	. . . Jerem. ii. 21	בכונה	. . Isa. xxiv. 2	הדולג	. . . Zeph. i. 9
בבוצר	. . . Jerem. vi. 9	חולם	. . Isa. xli. 7	נוכל	. . . Malachi i. 14
קולע	. . . Jerem. x. 18	הוזי	. . Isa. xxx. 18	חוגג	. . . Ps. xlii. 5
פודי	. . Jerem. xlvi. 25	שוחט	. . Isa. lxvi. 3	חובר	. . . Ps. lviii. 6
		אוסף	. . Hos. ix. 15		

They are given both in the Massorah marginalis on Genesis xli. 8, and in the Massorah finalis under the letter *Vav*, p. 27 *b*, cols. 3 and 4.

[28] This must be a slip of the pen, since there are four instances in which יוצאים is *plene*, viz., Ezekiel xiv. 22; xlvii. 8, 12; Zechariah 6, 8. They are enumerated in the Massorah marginalis on Ezekiel xiv. 22.

[29] This surely must likewise be a mistake, since יושבים occurs ten times *plene*, viz., Judg. vi. 10: Isa. x. 13: Jerem. xxxvi. 12; xliv. 13: Ezek. iii. 15; viii. 1: 2 Chron. xviii. 9 (twice); xxx. 25; xxxi. 6. The Massorah finalis enumerates them under the letter *Jod*, p. 37 *a*, col. 3.

SECTION IV.—Notice that those words which have always *Vav* with *Shurek* are never noted by the Massorites as *plene*,[30] since it is understood that *Shurek* cannot be without *Vav*, and it is well known that *Dagesh* cannot follow it. Hence those words wherein *Dagesh* does follow the *Vav*, as הֻכָּה *smitten* [Ps. cii. 5], הַיּוּלַד *who is born* [Judg. xiii. 8], &c., which the grammarians call "*quiescent with Dagesh*," the Massorites marked *plene;* whilst those wherein *Vav* is wanted, according to the Massorah, *Kibbutz* takes its place, and they are marked in the Massorah as *defective*.

☞ It is, however, to be remarked that this *Kibbutz* is not called a short vowel, since a long vowel is never changed into a short vowel because of the absence of the *mater lectionis*, but that there are two kinds of *Kibbutzs*. The one, as I have already said, which takes the place of *Vav* with *Shurek*, which is wanted, and the second is really the short vowel, and is never marked by the Massorites as *defective*. If thou shouldst ask, How is it to be known whether it is the *Kibbutz* of the long vowel that takes the place of *Vav* with *Shurek*, or whether it is the short vowel, and does not stand for *Vav* with *Shurek?* the reply is, It is known from grammar that there is a *Dagesh* or *quiescent Sheva* after every short vowel, as I have explained it in the *Poetical Section*.

☞ Hence, if a *Kibbutz* occurs, followed by *Dagesh*, or a quiescent *Sheva*, it is a really short vowel, and the Massorites do not note it as *defective;* as, for instance, the Pual פֻּקַּד *he was numbered*, פֻּקַּדְתָּ *thou wast numbered*, אֲפֻקַּד *I shall be numbered*, יְפֻקַּד *he shall be numbered*, &c.; and as the participal *Hophal* מֻפְקָד *the appointed*, מֻפְקָדִים *overseers* [2 Chron. xxxiv. 12]. But when it is not followed either by *Dagesh* or quiescent *Sheva*, then it stands for *Vav*, with *Shurek*, and the Massorites mark it as *defective*. Thus, for instance, in מֻשְׁלָכִים *cast out* [Jerem. xiv. 16.], the *Kibbutz* is not marked as *defective*, for it is a short vowel, because there is a quiescent *Sheva* after it, whereas בְּחֻצוֹת

---

[30] The Sulzbach edition substitutes עליו, *on it*, for לעולם, *ever*.

into the streets [Ibid.], is marked as *defective*, because it is neither followed by *Dagesh* nor by a quiescent *Sheva*. Thus, also, עֲקֻדִּים נְקֻדִּים וּבְרֻדִּים, *ringstraked, speckled, and dotted* [Gen. xxxi. 10], are not marked as *defective*, because they have *Dagesh*, whilst עֲטֻפִים *the feeble*, and קְשֻׁרִים *the strong* [Gen. xxx. 42], are marked as *defective*, because they have no *Dagesh*. For the same reason שֻׁלְחָן *table*, טֻמְאָה *uncleanness*, חֻפָּה *covering*, סֻכָּה *tabernacle*, חֻקָּה *law*, &c., are not marked as *defective*, because they have a quiescent *Sheva* or *Dagesh*.

Hence every *Kibbutz* at the end of a word is marked by the Massorites as *defective*, because neither *Dagesh* nor a quiescent *Sheva* can be at the end of a word. Thus, the nouns גְּבֻל *border* [2 Sam. xxi. 5], זְבֻל *habitation* [1 Kings viii. 13], גָּלֻת *division* [Exod. viii. 19], גָּלֻת *captivity* [Obad. i. 20], &c., as well as the verbs, viz.—יַאֲרִיכֻן *ye shall prolong* [Deut. v. 16, vi. 2], תַּשְׁלִיכֻן *ye shall cast* [Exod. xxii. 30], יָקֻם *let him arise* [Gen. xxvii. 31], קֻם *arise* [Joshua vii. 10], שֻׁב *return* [Exod. iv. 19], &c.; all these, and the like, are marked as *defective*. The word נְאֻם *oracle*, however, is an exception, and the Massorites do not mark it as *defective*, because it never occurs *plene;* there is no parallel in the whole Bible of a word occurring so often, and always with *Vav defective*.

Notice, also, that most of the *Kal* participles passive singular, both masculine and femenine, are written fully. In the masculine, as כָּתוּב *it is written*, חָתוּם *sealed*, בָּרוּךְ *blessed*, עָצוּם *strong*, the *defectives* being few, as כָּמֻס *laid up* [Deut. xxxii. 34], לָבֻשׁ *dressed* [Prov. xxxi. 21], זָעֻם *despised* [Prov. xxii. 14], &c.; and feminine, as אֲרוּרָה *cursed* [Gen. iii. 17], עֲרוּכָה, שְׁמוּרָה *kept* [2 Sam. xxiii. 5], &c. The *defectives* in this case too being very few, as שְׁלֻחָה *sent* [Gen. xlix. 21], הָעֲשֻׂיָה *ordained* [Numb. xxviii. 6]. But in the construct state they are mostly *defective*, as בְּעֻלַת *wedded* [Gen. xx. iii.], שְׁכֻרַת *drunk* [Is. li. 21], אֲהֻבַת *beloved* [Hos. iii. 1], &c., there being only a few which are written fully, as עֲצוּבַת *pained* [Is. liv. 6].

(ירמיה י״ד), הנה על קבוץ של משלכים לא נמסר חסר, כי הוא ח״ק, שהרי אחריו שוא נח, ועל קבוץ של בחצורת נמסר חסר, כי אין אחריו דגש או שוא נח; וכן עֲקֻדִּים נְקֻדִּים וּבְרֻדִּים (בראשית ל׳) לא נמסר עליהן חסר, כי הם דגושים, ועל הַעֲטֻפִים ללבן וְהַקְּשֻׁרִים ליעקב נמסר חסר, לפי שאינם דגושים; וכן שֻׁלְחָן, טֻמְאָה, חֻפָּה, סֻכָּה, חֻקָּה, לא נמסר עליהן חסר, כי הם בשוא נח או בדגש:

ולכן על כל קבוץ שהוא בסוף התיבה נמסר חסר, כי לא שייך דגש או שוא נח בסוף התיבה, כמו גְּבֻל ישראל, בית זְבֻל לך, ושמתי פְּדֻת, וְגָלֻת החל וכו'; וכן בפעלים, למען יַאֲרִיכֻן ימיך, לכלב תַּשְׁלִיכֻן, יָקָם נא אבי, קָם לך, שֻׁב לך מצרים, וישימם בעפר לָדֻשׁ, על כל אלה ודומיהם נמסר חסר, ומלת נְאֻם יוצאה מן הכלל, שלא נמסר עליה חסר, לפי שלא באה לעולם מלא, ואין לה דומה בכל המקרא מלה שהיא נמצאת כל כך הרבה, וכלם חסרים וי״ו:

ודע כי רוב לשון יחיד בפעול הקל הוא מלא, כמו כָּתוּב, חָתוּם, בָּרוּךְ, עָצוּם, וחחסרים הם מעטים, כמו פָּמַס עמדי (דברים ל״ב), לָבֻשׁ שנים (משלי ל״א), זָעַם ה׳, וכן לשון נקבה על הדרוב מלא, כמו אֲרוּרָה האדמה, עֲרוּכָה בכל וּשְׁמוּרָה, וחסרים הם מעטים, כמו אילה שְׁלֻחָה, הָעֲשֻׂיָה בהר סיני, אבל בסמוכות רובן חסרים, כמו בְּעֻלַת בעל, וּשְׁכֻרַת ולא מיין, אֲהֻבַת ריע, ומעטים המלאים, כמו עֲצוּבַת רוח:

155

Thus, also, the nouns of this form are generally *plene* in the absolute state, as גְּבוּרָה *strength,* קְבוּרָה *sepulchre,* מְלוּכָה *kingdom,* &c., and *defective* in the construct, as קִבְרַת *sepulchre of* [Gen. xxxv. 20], קִבְצַת *heap of* [Ezek. xxii. 20], &c.; but *plene* are גְּמוּלַת *desert* [Isa. lix. 18], &c. The plurals are very seldom *plene,* as בְּרוּכִים *the blessed* [Ps. cxv. 15], אֲרוּרִים *the cursed* [1 Sam. xxvi. 19], אֲסוּרִים *the chained* [Gen. xl. 5], &c., whilst the *defectives* are by far the most, as שְׁקֻפִים *beams,* אֲטֻמִים *closed* [1 Kings vi. 4], שְׂרֻפִים *burnt* [Numb. xvii. 4], &c. Also, כְּתֻבִים *written,* is always *defective* in the Pentateuch, though it is *plene* in the Prophets and Hagiographa; as well as the plurals feminine, which are almost all *defective,* as נְתֻנוֹת *given* Deut. xxviii. 31], צְרֻרוֹת *bound up* [Exod. xii. 34], שְׂרֻפוֹת *burned* [Isa. i. 7], &c., the *pleres* being but few, as הַכְּתוּבוֹת *the written,* חַלּוֹנוֹת *windows,* אֲטוּמוֹת *closed,* עֲשׂוּיוֹת *the made,* רְאוּיוֹת *the seen.* The nouns, too, which are according to this form, are mostly *defective* in the masculine, as כְּרֻבִים *Cherubim,* which occurs thirteen times *defective;*[81] עֲמֻדִים *pillars,* eleven times *defective;*[82] לֵיל שִׁמֻּרִים *night of celebration* [Exod. xii. 42], and יוֹם כִּפֻּרִים *day of atonement* [Levit. xxiii. 28], are both *defective* in this form. The same is the case with the feminine plurals, as גְּבֻלוֹת *borders* [Job xxiv. 2], מַלְכֻיוֹת *kingdoms* [Dan. viii. 22], חֲנֻיוֹת *vaults* [Jerem. xxxvii. 16], &c. I shall again discuss this subject in Section x. which you will see.

Section V.—Both the prophets and other writers have paid much more attention to the quiescent *Jod* with *Chirek,* than to the quiescent

---

וכן השמות על משקל זה על הרוב מלאים, כמו גְּבוּרָה, קְבוּרָה, מְסִבָּה, ובסמיכות חסרים קִבְרַת רחל, קִבְצַת כסף, והמלאים במו כעל גמול; ובלשון רבים מעטים הם המלאים, כמו בְּרוּכִים אתם לי״י, אֲרוּרִים הם, אֲסוּרִים שם ודומיהם, והחסרים הם רבים מאד כמו שְׁקֻפִים, אֲטֻמִים, שְׂרֻפִים, וכן כל כְּתָבִים דאורייתא חסרים, ובנביאים וכתובים מלאים, וכן הרבות כמעט כלהון חסרים, כמו צְנֻמוֹת, שְׁדֻפוֹת קדים, נְתֻנוֹת להם אחר, צְרֻרוֹת בשמלתם, שְׂרֻפוֹת אש, ודומיהן רבים, וכעטים הם המלאים כמו האלורת הַכְּתוּבוֹת, וחלונורת אֲטוּמוֹת, עֲשׂוּיוֹת, רְאוּיוֹת, וכן השמות הבאים על משקל זה רבים מהן חסרים, כמו כְּרֻבִים י״ג חסרים,[81] עֲמֻדִים י״א חסרים,[82] ליל שִׁמֻּרִים, יום כִּפֻּרִים, כל לישנא חסר, וכן לשון רבות, גְּבֻלות ישינו, ארבע כַּלְיוֹת, אל החניות, ועוד אדבר בם בדבור י׳ כ״ש:

והדבור החמשי: כבד כבדו מאוד הנביאים וכותבי הספרים את היו״ד חנחה עם

---

[81] This is another instance which shows how difficult it is to understand Levita's language without consulting the Massorah. From his remark the reader would naturally conclude that כרבים only occurs thirteen times *defective* in the whole Bible, whereas it is found so nearly thirty times. On referring, however, to the Massorah marginalis on Exod. xxv. 18, we find it remarked הכרבים כל אורית חסר ונביא׳ וכתוב׳ מלאים במ׳׳ג חסר, *"the word* כרובים *is defective throughout the Pentateuch, whereas it is plene throughout the Prophets and Hagiographa, with the exception of thirteen passages;"* which are as follows:—1 Sam. iv. 4: 2 Sam. vi. 2: 1 Kings vi. 25, 27; viii. 7: 2 Kings xix. 15: Ezek. x. 1, 2, 3, 6, 7, 8: Ps. lxxx. 2. There can therefore be no doubt that Levita means these thirteen instances of *defective.*

[82] The eleven instances in which עמודים is *defective* are as follows:—Exod. xxvii. 10, 11; xxxviii. 12, 17: Judges xvi. 26: 1 Kings vii. 6, 21: Jerem. xxvii. 19: Ezek. xl. 49: 2 Chron. iii. 16; iv. 12. They are enumerated in the Massorah marginalis on Exod xxxviii. 12.

Vav with *Cholem*; and this is because they have both removed and omitted the *Vav*, as I have already stated; whereas they have both left and put down the quiescent *Jod* in many places. Hence, the punctuators called the *Chirek*, followed by *Jod*, a long *Chirek*, that is, a long syllable; and *Chirek*, not followed by *Jod*, they denominated short *Chirek*, or short syllable. There are therefore two kinds of *Chireks*, one short and the other long; the short one, according to rule, is without *Jod*, and is called a short syllable; whilst the long one, according to rule, has a *Jod*, and is called a long syllable.

☞ It is for this reason that the *Chirek* of the short syllable is never marked by the Massorites as *defective*, and the *Chirek* of the long syllable is never marked as *plene*. Sometimes, however, the long syllable occurs without *Jod*, then the Massorites mark it as *defective*; as בָּנִתִי, *I have built* [1 Kings viii. 13], רָאִתָה, *thou hast seen* [Ps. x. 14], &c.

☞ The sign whereby the *Chirek* of the short syllable may be distinguished from the *Chirek* of the long syllable, is by the absence of *Jod*. It is the same as the one I stated in the case of the *Kibbutz*. That is, whenever *Chirek* is followed by *Dagesh* or quiescent *Sheva*, it is a short syllable, and when these do not follow it, and yet *Jod* is absent, then it is a long syllable, and is *defective*, according to the Massorah. For instance, on וַהֲקִמֹתִי, *and I shall perform* [Gen. xxvi. 3], the Massorites remark, "*Jod is wanted*," because there is no *Dagesh* after the *Chirek*,[33] and, according to rule, ought therefore to be *plene;* whereas on וַהֲשִׁבֹּתִי, *and I shall cause to cease* [Numb. xvii. 20], they do not remark that the *Jod* is wanting, because it is a short syllable, for there is *Dagesh* after it.

☞ According to rule, every *Chirek* which is not followed by *Dagesh*, or quiescent *Sheva*, ought to be *plene*, and is generally *plene*. That is, when it is followed by an audible letter at the end of the word, as קָצִיר

החירק יותר מחוי"ו הנחה עם החולם, וזה שעל הרוב חסירו והחסידו הוי"ו, כמו שכתבתי, אבל היו"ד הנחה השאירוה וקימוה ברוב המקומות, ובעבורה קראו מניחי הנקוד לחירק שאחריו יו"ד חירק גדול, דהיינו תנועה גדולה, והחירק שאין אחריו יו"ד קראו חירק קטן, דהיינו תנועה קטנה; והכלל כי ב' מיני חירק הם, קטן וגדול שם הוא, הקטון דינו בלי יו"ד, והוא תנועה קטנה, והגדול דינו ביו"ד, והוא תנועה גדולה:

☜ לכן כל חירק של תנועה קטנה, לא נמסר עליו חסר לעולם, ועל חירק של תנועה גדולה, לא נמסר מלא לעולם, אך לפעמים תבוא תנועה גדולה בלי יו"ד, ואז נמסר עליו חסר, כמו בנה בָּנִתִי (מלכים ח'), רָאִתָה כי אתה (תהילים ט'), ורומיהן:

☜ והסימן להכיר החירק של תנועה קטנה מחירק של תנועה גדולה, כשהוא חסר יו"ד, הוא הסימן שנתתי בקבוץ, דהיינו החירק שאחריו דגש או שוא נח, הוא תנועה קטנה, וכשאינם אחריו, וחסר יו"ד, הוא תנועה גדולה, וחסר עלפי המסורת; והמשל הנה על וַהֲקִמֹתִי את השבועה (בראשות כ"ו) נמסר חסר יו"ד, לפי שאין אחר החירק[33] דגש, וחיה דינו להיות מלא, ועל וַהֲשִׁבֹּתִי מעלי, לא נמסר חסר יו"ד, לפי שהוא תנועה קטנה שהרי אחריו דגש:

☜ והכלל כל חירק שאין אחריו דגש או שוא נח, דינו להיות מלא, וכן הוא מלא על הרוב, כגון כשיבא אחריו נח נראה בסוף

---

[33] Instead of שאין אחר החירק, *for there is not after Chirek*, the Sulzbach edition has שאין אחריה, *for there is not after it.*

157

harvest, חָסִיד *pious*, אֹפִיר *Ophir*, בַּבִּיר
great, אֱוִיל *a fool*, כְּסִיל *a fool*, &c.
A few of the proper names are to be
found *defective*, as אֹפִר *Ophir* [Gen.
x. 29], דְּבִר *Debir* [Josh. xiii. 26];
also, the name דָּוִד *David* is always
defective, except in five instances in
which it is *plene*.[34] The *Chirek* is
never followed by a quiescent letter
at the end of the word, except
Aleph, as נָבִיא *prophet*, נָשִׂיא *chief*,
הֵבִיא *he brought*, מֵבִיא *bringing*, אָבִיא
I shall bring, יָבִיא *he shall bring*, תָּקִיא
she shall spue out [Levit. xviii. 28];
but וַתָּקִא *and she vomiteth* [Levit.
xviii. 25], which wants *Jod*, has
very few parallels. But *Chirek*,
before the plural termination ים, is
most generally written fully, as
אֲנָשִׁים חֲכָמִים וִידֻעִים *men*, *wise*, *and
known* [Deut. i. 13], &c. This,
however, is the case where no other
Chirek of a long syllable precedes
it, as in those instances which I have
already stated, and the like cases.

התיבה, כמו קָצִיר, חָסִיד, אֹפִיר, כַּבִּיר אֱוִיל, כְּסִיל
ודומיהם, ונמצאות מעטים חסרים בשם העצם,
כגון ואת אוֹפִר ואת חוילה, ומחשבון עד
לדבר, וכן כל דָּוִד חסר חוץ מן ה' מלאים,[34]
ולא יבא אחריו נח נסתר בסוף התיבה לעולם
רק האל"ף, כמו נָבִיא, נָשִׂיא, הֵבִיא, מֵבִיא, אָבִיא,
יָבִיא וכו', ולא תָקִיא הארץ, אבל וַתָּקִא הארץ
אתכם, חסר יו"ד ודומיהן מעטים; אבל החירק
שלפני יו"ד ומ"ם הרבים רובו דרובו מלא,
כמו אֲנָשִׁים חֲכָמִים וִידֻעִים (דברים א')
ודומיהן, וזה דווקא כשאין לפניו חירק אחר
של תנועה גדולה כמו אלה שכתמתי ודומיהן:

☛ אבל כשיחיו שם ב' חריקים רצופים,
כמו אַדִּירִים, כַּבִּירִים, אַבִּירִים, רְבִיבִים וכל
חדומים לאלה, תחסד יו"ד הרבים על הרוב,
כמו את הַתַּנִּינִם ג' חסר בלישנא,[35] וכן כל
צַדִּיקִם דבאוריתא חסד, חוץ מן אחד,[36] וכן
נְשִׂיאִם ד' כתיבים כן באוריתא וכל נביאים
וכתובים דכותיה חוץ מן ד' נְשִׂיאָם,[37] וכן כל
תְּמִימִם דבעידא חסד פי' הסמוכים לבהמה,
כגון כבשים, אֵילִים, עִזִּים ודומיהן, וכל לשון
נְבִיאִם דשמואל וירמיה חסרים חוץ מן ג'

☛ But when two *Chireks* do follow each other, as in כַּבִּירִים *the
mighty*, אַדִּירִים *the strong*, רְבִיבִים *showers*, אַבִּירִים *the potent*, &c., the
Jod of the plural is frequently omitted. Thus, הַתַּנִּינִם, *the sea mon-
sters*, is three times *defective* in this form.[35] The same is the case with
צַדִּיקִם, *the righteous*, which is always *defective* in the Pentateuch,
except in one place;[36] the same with נְשִׂיאִם *princes*, which is so written
four times in the Pentateuch; and likewise in the Prophets and Hagiographa, except in four instances where it is נְשִׂיאָם.[37] The same is the
case with תְּמִימִם *without blemish*; when it refers to animals it is *defective*; that is, wherever it is the predicate to sheep, rams, goats, &c.
The word נְבִיאִם *prophets*, is always *defective* in the books of Samuel

---

[34] That the proper name "David is always *defective*, except in five instances, in which
it is *plene*" is surely a mistake. The Massorah marginalis, both on 1 Kings xi. 4 and
Ezekiel xxxiv. 23, does indeed remark that "David occurs five times *plene* (דויד ה' מלאים),
and enumerates 1 Kings iii. 14; xi. 4, 36; Song of Songs iv. 4; as
the five instances; but it adds וכל ת"יסר ועורא וד"ה דכור מלאים, *that David is also* PLENE
throughout the twelve minor Prophets, Ezra, and Chronicles, which is not to be
gathered from Levita's statement.

[35] The three instances in which תנינים wants the *Vav* plural are, Gen. i. 21; Exod.
vii. 12; Deut. xxxii. 33.

[36] The single instance in which צדיקים is *plene* in the Pentateuch is in Exod. xxiii. 8,
on which the Massorah parva remarks ל' מל' דמל', *no parallel, it is entirely* PLENE.

[37] The four instances in which נשיאם occurs are, Gen. xvii. 20; xxv. 16; Numb. vii.
10; xxvii. 2. They are enumerated in the Massorah marginalis on Gen. xvii. 20.

and Jeremiah, except in three instances in Samuel and in eight instances in Jeremiah; [88] גְּבִיעָם *goblets*, too, is always *defective*; שְׂעִירִים *goats*, is always *defective*, except in two instances; [89] צְמִידָם *bracelets* [Gen. xxiv. 30), and many others, are likewise *defective*. A few plurals, which are preceded by *Tzere* and *Chirek*, are also *defective*. Thus, אֵילָם, *rams*, has never the *Jod* plural in the Pentateuch, except in four instances; [40] the same is the case with הַיֵּמִם, *the hot springs* [Gen. xxxvi. 24]. Besides the *Tzere*, we find הַיָּמִם *the days* [Numb. vi. 5], *defective*, which has no parallel in the Scripture.

Moreover, the participles *Hiphil*, because they have two *Chireks* following each other, are also wanting in most cases the *Jod* of the plural. Three instances of it are to be found in the Pentateuch, viz., מַעֲבִדָם *making labour* [Exod. vi. 5], מַקְדִּשָׁם *making holy* [Levit. xxii. 2], and מַקְצִיפָם *making angry* [Deut. ix. 22]; and some in the Prophets, as מַשְׁחִיתָם *destroying* [2 Sam. xx. 15], &c. The same occurs with *Chirek* before the termination ת, which is always *plene*, as רֵאשִׁית *beginning*, שְׁאֵרִית *residue*, אַחֲרִית *end*, תַּכְלִית *end*, &c., except in those cases where there are two *Chireks* together, as שְׁלִישִׁת *third*, רְבִיעָת *fourth*, חֲמִישִׁת *fifth*, &c., which are generally *defective*.

The rule is that all the plurals of both participles and nouns, which have not two *Chireks* following each other, are written fully, except in a few instances, as מַדּוּחִם *banished* [Lam. ii. 14], &c. Rashi's remarks on פִּילַגְשִׁים *concubines* [Gen. xxv. 6], that it is *defective*, which is taken from *Bereshith Rabba*, is contrary to the Massorah, for the Massorites mark it "*twice plene*."[41]

---

[88] Though the Massorah parva on 1 Sam. xix. 20, also remarks that נביאים occurs three times *plene* ('ב' מל בליש), yet there seem to be four instances; viz., 1 Sam. x. 11, 12; xix. 20; xxviii. 6. The eight instances of *plene* in Jeremiah to which Levita refers are, Jerem. v. 13; vii. 25; viii. 1; xxvi. 8, 11; xxviii. 8; xxix. 1; xxxv. 15. They are enumerated in the Massorah marginalis on Jerem. xvi. 2.

[89] The two passages in which שעירים is *plene* are, Isa. xiii. 21; 2 Chron. xi. 15.

[40] The four instances in which אילים is entirely *plene* are, Gen. xxxii. 15; Levit. viii. 2; Numb. xxiii. 1; Deut. xxxii. 14.

[41] The Massorah marginalis on Gen. xxv. 6 distinctly remarks that the word פילנשים occurs twice *entirely plene*, that is, with the two *Jods* after the two *Chireks*. The one

☞ We also find the Talmud at variance with the Massorah; it takes כַּלּוֹת *finished* [Numb. vii. 1], as *defective*, and remarks on it that it is not *plene*; so also מְזוּזוֹת *doorposts* [Deut. xi. 20], according to the Talmud is *defective*, whereas according to the Massorah it is *plene*; and מַעֲבִירִים [1 Sam. ii. 24], too, is according to the Talmud *defective*, and according to the Massorah *plene*.⁴²

Notice, also, that in some of the words which have two *Chireks*, the first *Jod* is *defective*. Thus, שָׂרִיגִם *branches* [Genesis xl. 10], wants the second *Jod*, whilst שָׂרִגִים *branches* [Gen. xl. 12], wants the first *Jod*; צַדִּקִים *the righteous* [Hos. xiv. 10], wants the first *Jod*, whilst צַדִּיקִם *the righteous* [Ezek. xxiii. 45], wants the second *Jod*. The same is the case with אֱוִלִים *fools*, which wants the first *Jod* five times; and there are some words wanting both *Jods*, as שָׁלִשִׁם *captains* [Exod. xiv. 7], אַדִּרִם *mighty* [Ezek. xxxii. 13].

The participles *Hiphil*, too, are found wanting the first *Jod*; as מַשְׁמִעִים *making a noise* [1 Chron. xv. 28], מְמִתִים *killing* [Jerem. xxvi. 15], מַחְלְמִים *dreaming* [Jerem. xxix. 8], &c. All the other tenses of *Hiphil*, however, are generally *plene*, and there are but few found *defective*; as הִקְרִב *he offered* [Numb. vii. 19], וַיַּמְצִאוּ *and they presented* [Levit. ix. 12, 18], וָאַבְדִּל *and I have separated* [Levit. xx. 26], &c.

☞ The plurals of the passive participles *Kal*, however, sometimes occur without *Jod*, but this only takes place when the *Vav* is written fully, and it is to prevent two quiescents following each other, as I have already explained in Section ii. For example, the words נְתֻנִם נְתֻנִם *they are given, they are given* [Numb. iii. 9], are both with-

☜ וכן מצינו שהגמרה שלנו, חולקה על המסורת, כגון כי ביום כַּלּוֹת משה (במדבר ז') חסר, ונמסר עליו לית מלא, וכן על מְזוּזוֹת ביתך (דברים ו'), מְזוּזת כתיב, ולפי המסורה הוא מלא, וכן מַעֲבִירִים עם ה' לפי הגמרה חסר, ובמסורה הוא מלא: ⁴²

ודע כי יש מאלו של ב' חריקים שתחסר יו"ד קדמאה, כמו ובגפן שְׁלֹשָׁה שָׂרִיגִם חסר יו"ד תנינא, שלשת הַשָּׂרִגִים חסר יו"ד קדמאה, וְצַדִּקִים ילכו בו, חסר יו"ד קדמאה, ואנשים צַדִּיקִם המה, חסר יו"ד תנינא, וכן אֱוִלִים ה' חסר יו"ד קדמאה,⁴³ ונמצאים חסרי ב' היו"דין וְשָׁלִשִׁם על כלו, ובנות גוים אַדִּרִם:

וכן בבינוני הפעיל נמצאים חסרי יו"ד קדמאה, כמו מַשְׁמִעִים בנבלים, אִם מְמִתִים אתם אותי, אשר אתם מַחְלְמִים ודומיהן, אבל כל שאר פעולות ההפעיל הם מלאים על הרוב, ונמצאים מעטים חסרים, כמו הִקְרִב את קרבנו, וַיַּמְצִאוּ אליו, וָאַבְדִּל אתכם ודומיהן:

☜ אבל בפעיל בנין הקל, באים לפעמים חסרי יו"ד חברים, אבל אין זה רק כשהן מלאים וי"ו, וזה כדי שלא יהיו שם ב' נחים רצופין, כאשר באֵרתי בדבור ב'; והמשל נְתוּנִם נְתוּנִם המה לי, שניהם חסר יו"ד, לפי

---

instance is in Gen. xxv. 6, and the other in Esther ii. 14. Now Rashi, who, in his commentary on Gen. xxv. 6, follows the traditional exposition of the Midrash, remarks, "*The textual reading is* פילגשם *defective* [that is without the plural *Jod*], *because Abraham had only one concubine, namely, Hagar, who was identical with Keturah.*" But this reading, which is contrary to the Massoretic text, has evidently arisen from a pious desire to lessen the number of concubines of the father of the Hebrew nation. The *Bereshith Rabba*, from which Rashi's remark is derived, is the part of the *Midrash Rabba*, or exposition of the Pentateuch, which treats on *Bereshith* = Genesis. For an account of the *Midrash*, see Kitto's *Cyclopædic*, s. v.

⁴² For an explanation of *Mezuzah* see above, p. 95, note 18. The variations between the Talmud and the Massorah, adduced by Levita, are taken from Jacob b. Chajim's *Introduction to the Rabbinic Bible*: comp. p. 19, &c., where they are fully discussed.

out *Jod*, because they have *Vav* fully written, whilst נְתָנִים נְתֻנִים *they are given, they are given* [Numb. viii. 16], are *defective* of *Vav*, because they have *Jod plene;* as you will see on examination.

☞ The general rule is that the *Chirek* of the long syllable has mostly the *Jod* written fully, whilst *Cholem* generally is without *Vav*. There is no necessity for me to explain to you that *Cholem* and *Chirek*, with quiescent *Vav* and *Jod* at the end of a word, are always *plene;* as יָדוֹ *his hand*, רַגְלוֹ *his foot*, יָדִי *my hand*, רַגְלִי *my foot*, &c., since it is evident that *Vav* and *Jod* can never be omitted in such cases, because a vowel-point can never be under the final letter of a word, except under *Kaph*, *Tav*, and final *Nun*. These have sometimes *Kametz* at the end of a word, as I shall explain in Section x.

Section VI.— A quiescent *Jod* does not follow *Tzere*, except when it belongs to the root, or when it indicates the plural. It belongs to the root, as הֵיטִיב *doing good,* אֵיטִיב *I shall do good* [Gen. xxxii. 13], תֵּינִק *she shall nurse* [Exod. ii. 7], אֵילְכָה *I shall go* [Micah i. 1]; and it stands for the radical *He,* as צִוֵּיתִי *I commanded* [Deut. iii. 21], קִוֵּיתִי *I wait* [Isa. v. 4], and in a few more such instances. The same is the case in those nouns in which *Jod* is radical, as בֵּיתָה *house*, עַיִן *eye*, or stands for the radical *Vav*, as in צֵידָה *food*, שֵׂיבָה *old age*, the roots of which are צוד, בוש. I shall recur to this subject in the next Section.

The *Jod* after *Tzere*, to indicate the plural, is the same *Jod* as is used with the suffix in plural nouns of the third and second persons, both masculine and feminine, as בְּנֵיהֶם *their sons*, בְּנֵיכֶם *your sons*, בְּנֵיהֶן *their sons* (feminine), בְּנֵיכֶן *your sons* (feminine), בְּנוֹתֵיהֶם *their daughters*, בְּנוֹתֵיכֶם *your daughters*, &c., and these are never marked in the Massorah as *plene;* and a few of these are found *defective*, as נְשִׂיאֵהֶם *their princes* [Numb. xvii. 17], אֲבוֹתֵכֶם *your fathers* [Deut. i. 11]. The expressions אֲלֵהֶם *to them*, and אֲלֵכֶם *to you*, are also found *defective*

שהם מלאים וי"ו, נְתָנִים נְתֻנִים המה לי שניהן חסרים וי"ו לפי שהן מלאים יו"ד ודוק:

☜ והכלל כי חירק של תנועה גדולה על הרוב הוא מלא יו"ד, והחולם על הרוב הוא חסר וי"ו, והנה אין צריך להודיעך ולומר כי החולם והחירק שבסוף התיבה עם הוי"ו הנחה או היו"ד הנחה, הם תמיד מלאים, דהיינו שתמיד הוי"ו כתובה עם החולם, והיו"ד כתובה עם החיריק, כמו יָדוֹ, רַגְלוֹ, יָדִי, רַגְלִי ודומיהן, כי פשיטא שלא יחסרו הוי"ו והיו"דִין באלה לעולם, כי לא תבא נקדה באות שבסוף המלה לעולם, זולתי התיו והכף והנון שהם קמוצים לפעמים בסוף התיבה, כמו שאודיעך בדבור העשירי:

הדבור הששי: לא תבא יו"ד נחה אחר הצירי רק כשהיא שרשית, או שתורה על לשון רבים, השרשית כמו הֵיטִיב אֵיטִיב עִמָּךְ (בראשית ל"ב), וְתֵינִק לָךְ, אֵילְכָה שׁוֹלָל, וכשהיא במקום ה"א שרשית, כמו יהושע צִוֵּיתִי, מדוע קִוֵּיתִי ודומיהן מעטין, וכן בשמות שהיו"ד שרשית, כמו בֵּית ה' עֵין אדם, וכן כשהיו"ד במקום וי"ו שרשית כמו צֵידָה, שֵׂיבָה, שרשם צוד, שוב, ועוד אדבר מכל אלה בדבור שאחר זה:

והיו"ד הבאה אחר הצירי להורות על לשון רבים, היא היו"ד הבאה בכנוי הנסתרים והנסתרות, והנמצאים והנמצאות, בשמות של לשון רבים ודבות, כמו בְּנֵיהֶם, בְּנֵיכֶם, בְּנֵיהֶן, וּבְנֵיכֶן, בְּנוֹתֵיהֶם וּבְנוֹתֵיכֶם וכו', ולא נמסר עליהן מלא לעולם, ונמצאים מעטים חסרים, כמו מאת כל נְשִׂיאֵהֶם, יוסף י"י אלהי אֲבוֹתֵכֶם, וכן אֲלֵהֶם, אֲלֵכֶם, נמצאים חסרים, בכל ספר

in every book of the Scriptures, and they are counted according to the Massorah. Thus, also, the suffix first persons in nouns, as בִּנְעָרֵינוּ *with our youth*, בְּבָנֵינוּ *with our sons* (Exod. x. 9), are not marked by the Massorites as *plene*. But the nouns which have the pronoun, first person, pointed alike, both in the singular and plural, and in which there is no difference in the points, except that the plural has *Jod*, these are marked by the Massorites as *plene*.

Thus, for instance, יָדֵינוּ *our hands* [Deut. xxi. 7], has the Massoretic mark *plene*, whilst וְיָדֵנוּ *and our hand* (Gen. xxxvii. 27), is marked *defective*, because it is the singular, as is evident from the word תְּהִי *let it be*; so also רַגְלֵינוּ *our feet* (Ps. cxxii. 2), is marked *plene*, whilst רַגְלֵנוּ *our foot* [Ps. lxvi. 9], is marked *defective*, because it is the singular. Whereas דְּבָרֵנוּ *our word* (Josh. ii. 14), which is the singular, as is evident from the word זֶה *this;* and the expressions לְבָנוּ and לְבָבֵנוּ *our heart*, in which *Jod* is wanting, are never marked as *defective*, because they do not occur in the plural. But the words wherein a quiescent *Jod* is expressed after *Tzere*, which *Jod* neither belongs to the root nor indicates the plural, are always marked as *plene;* as פְּלֵיטָה *escape* [Jerem. l. 29,] הַשְׁכֵּים *early* [Prov. xxvii. 14], וְתַגֵּיד *thou shalt say* [Exod. xix. 3], and a few more like these.

Moreover, the quiescent *Jod* is also to be found after *Segol*, but this only occurs in the pronouns, second person masculine and third person feminine of plural nouns, both masculine and feminine; as בָּנֶיךָ *thy sons*, בְּנוֹתֶיךָ *thy daughters*, בָּנֶיהָ *her sons*, בְּנוֹתֶיהָ *her daughters*, and they are never marked *plene*. Many of them are found without *Jod*, especially in the case of the suffix second person masculine; as דְּבָרֶךָ *thy words* [Gen. xlvii. 30], of which there are thirteen *defectives*;[43]

וספר, ונמנין על פ׳ המסורת; וכן בכנוי חמדברים בעדם, כמו בִּנְעָרֵינוּ וּבִזְקֵנֵינוּ, בְּבָנֵינוּ וּבִבְנוֹתֵינוּ (שמות י׳), לא נמסר עליהם מלא, אבל השמות שהם בכנוי המדברים בעדם, שהם שוים בנקודתם ליחיד ולרבים ואין הפרש ביניהם בנקודתם רק שלשון רבים הוא ב ו״ד, אז נמסר עליו מלא:

והמשל יָדֵינוּ לא שפכו נמסר עליו מלא, וַיָּדֵנוּ אל תהי בו (בראשית ל״ז) חסר, שהוא לשון יחיד בראית מלת תהי, וכן עומדות היו רַגְלֵינוּ (תהילים קכ״ב) נמסר עליו מלא, למום רַגְלֵנוּ חסר, שהוא לשון יחיד, וכן אם לא תגידי את דְּבָרֵנוּ זה, לשון יחיד בראית מלת זה, וכן כל לְבָבֵנוּ וְלִבֵּנוּ חסרים יו״ד, ולא נמסר עליהן חסר, כי לא נמצאו בלשון רבים; אבל המלות שיש בהן יו״ד נחה כתובה אחר הצרי ואינה שרשית, ונם לא תורד על לשון רבים, תמיד נמסר עליהם מלא, כמו אל יחי לה פְּלֵיטָה, הַשְׁכֵּים ושלוח, וְתַגֵּיד לבני ישראל, ודומיהן מעמים:

והנה נמצא גם כ׳ יו״ד נחה אחר הסגול, וזה דווקא בכנוי הנוכח זכר והנסתרת לנקבה בשמות שהן לשון רבים ורבות, כמו בָּנֶיךָ וּבְנוֹתֶיךָ, בָּנֶיהָ וּבְנוֹתֶיהָ, ולא נמסר עליהם מלא לעולם, ונמצאים הרבה מהן חסרי יו״ד, ובפרט בכנוי הנוכח לזכר, כמו אנכי אעשה כִּדְבָרֶךָ, והם י״ג חסרים,[43] וכן הכן הודיעני נא את

---

[43] The thirteen instances in which the plural דבריך occurs *defective* are, Gen. xxx. 34; xlvii. 30; Numb. xiv. 20; Ps. cxix. 9, 16, 25, 28, 42, 65, 105, 107, 169. The Massorah marginalis, both on Gen. xxx. 34, and on xlvii. 30, mentions the three instances which occur in the Pentateuch as belonging to the thirteen *defectives*, and refers to the Massorah finalis for the whole list. But we could find no such list in the Massorah.

Y

דְּרָכֶךָ *thy ways* [Exod. xxxiii. 13], of which there are three *defective* instances;⁴⁴ חֲסָדֶךָ *thy mercies* [Ps. cxix. 41], which is always *defective* in the plural, and the *Segol* indicates the absence of *Jod*. And although the singular has also *Segol* when it is in pause, as יָדֶךָ *thine hand,* רַגְלֶךָ *thy foot,* אָזְנֶךָ *thy ear,* &c., the singular may be distinguished from the plural by the words with which it is connected; as יָדְךָ *thy hand* [Ps. xxxii. 4], רַגְלְךָ *thy foot* [Ps. xci. 12], אָזְנְךָ *thine ear* [Isa. xlviii. 8], שֹׁמְרֶךָ *thy keeper* [Ps. cxxi. 3], אֹיִבְךָ *thy enemy* [Deut. xxviii. 53]; all of which are singular, and it cannot be said that they are the plural with *Jod* omitted, because the verbs תִּכְבַּד *it is heavy,* תָּגוֹז *it shall dash,* פָּתְחָה *it is opened,* יָנוּם *he shall sleep,* and יָצִיק *he shall oppress,* with which they are respectively connected, are singular.

Thus, also, in Jerem. xxxviii. 22, רַגְלֶךָ *thy feet,* is plural, and *Jod* is omitted, as is evident from the verb הָטְבְּעוּ *they are sunk,* the plural *Jod* is also omitted in פָּעֳלֶךָ *thy work* [Ps. lxxvii. 13], as is evident from בְּכָל *in every one.* All the feminine plurals, with the suffix second person masculine, are likewise without the *Jod* of the plural; as מִנְחֹתֶךָ *thy gifts* [Ps. xx. 4], מִצְוֹתֶךָ *thy commands* [Ps. cxix. 98], בִּקְרֹבוֹתֶךָ *thine honourable* [Ps. xlv. 10], which have always the *Cholem* before the *Segol*, as I have already explained it in the *Bachur;* and they are distinguished from nouns feminine singular in pause, with pronoun, second person, which have also ת with *Segol*, as בִּרְכָתֶךָ *thy blessing* [Gen. xxvii. 35], צִדְקָתֶךָ *thy righteousness* [Ps. lxxi. 15], by the latter having always *Kametz* before the *Segol*.

The *Jod* of the plural is likewise omitted in the suffix third person feminine, as קִבְרֹתֶהָ *her graves* [Ezek. xxxii. 25], &c. The quiescent *Jod*, indicating the plural, occurs after *Kametz*, but this only happens when it is followed by the pronominal *Vav* of third person masculine; as יָדָיו *his hands,* רַגְלָיו *his feet,* &c.; when it is never omitted, except in the

דְּרָכֶךָ וְהֵם ג' חֲסָרִים,⁴⁴ וְכֵן וִיבֹאוּנִי חֲסָדֶךָ חָסֵר כֻּלָּם לְשׁוֹן רַבִּים, וְהַסֶּגּוֹל מוֹרֶה עַל הֱיוֹ"ד הַחֲסֵרָה, וְאַעַ"פִּי שֶׁלְּשׁוֹן יָחִיד בָּא גַּ"כ בִּסְגוֹל כְּשֶׁהוּא בְּהֶפְסֵק, כְּמוֹ יָדֶךָ, רַגְלֶךָ, אָזְנֶךָ וְדוֹמֵיהֶן, תּוּכַל לְהַכִּיר הַיְחִידִים מִן הָרַבִּים בְּמִלּוֹת הַסְּמוּכוֹת לָהֶם, כְּמוֹ תִּכְבַּד עָלַי יָדְךָ, פֶּן תָּגוֹז ג ,בֶן רַגְלְךָ, לֹא פִתְחָה אָזְנְךָ, אַל יָנוּם שֹׁמְרֶךָ, יָצִיק לְךָ אֹיִבְךָ כֻּלָּם לְשׁוֹן יָחִיד, וְלֹא נוּכַל לוֹמַר שֶׁהֵם לְשׁוֹן רַבִּים וַחֲסֵרִים יוּ"ד בַּעֲבוּר תִּכְבַּד, תָּגוֹז, פִּתְחָה, יָנוּם, יָצִיק דִּסְמוּכִים לָהֶם שֶׁהֵם לְשׁוֹן יָחִיד :

וְכֵן הָטְבְּעוּ בִּבְצוֹעַ רַגְלֶךָ הוּא לְשׁוֹן רַבִּים וְחָסֵר יוּ"ד הָרַבִּים בִּרְאִיַּית הָטָּבְּעוּ, וְכֵן וְהִגִּיתִי בְכָל פָּעֳלֶךָ הוּא חָסֵר יוּ"ד הָרַבִּים, בִּרְאִיַּית בְּכָל, וְכֵן לְשׁוֹן רַבּוּת בְּכִנּוּי הַנּוֹכֵחַ לְזָכָר נִמְצָאִים חֲסֵרֵי יוּ"ד הָרַבִּים, כְּמוֹ יִזְכֹּר כָּל מִנְחֹתֶךָ, תַּחְכְּמֹנִי מִצְוֹתֶךָ, בְּנוֹת מְלָכִים בִּיקְרוֹתֶךָ, תָּמִיד חוֹלֵם לִפְנֵי הַסֶּגּוֹל, כְּמוֹ שֶׁבֵּאַרְתִּי בְסֵפֶר הַבָּחוּר : וּבָזֶה הֵם נִבְדָּלִים מֵהַשֵּׁמוֹת שֶׁל לְשׁוֹן יְחִידָה, כְּשֶׁיָּבֹאוּ בְהֶפְסֵק עִם כִּנּוּי הַנּוֹכֵחַ שֶׁאַף הֵם בַּחֵי"ת בִּסְגוֹל, כְּמוֹ וַיִּקַּח אֶת בִּרְכָתֶךָ, פִּי יִסְפֹּר צִדְקָתֶךָ, תָּמִיד קָמֵץ לִפְנֵי הַסֶּגוֹל :

וְכֵן בְּכִנּוּי הַנִּסְתָּרָה נִמְצָאִים חֲסֵרֵי יוּ"ד הָרַבִּים, כְּמוֹ סְבִיבוֹתַי קִבְרוֹתֶהָ, וְדוֹמֶיהָ, וְנִמְצָא יוּ"ד נָחָה הַמּוֹרָה עַל לְשׁוֹן רַבִּים אַחַר קָמֵץ, וְאֵין זֶה אֶלָּא כְּשֶׁיָּבֹא אַחֲרָיו וָי"ו כִּנּוּי הַנִּסְתָּר, כְּמוֹ יָדָיו, רַגְלָיו וְדוֹמֵיהֶן, וְלֹא תֶחְסַר לְעוֹלָם רַק

---

⁴⁴ The three passages in which דרכיך is *defective* are, Exod. xxxiii. 13; Josh. i. 8; Ps. cxix. 37. They are enumerated in the Massorah marginalis on Exod. xxxiii. 13.

word יַחְדָּו *together*, which is always *defective*, except in Jeremiah, where it is found *plene* three times.⁴⁵ To the same category belong the expressions שְׂלָו *quails* [Ps. cv. 40], סְתָו *winter* [Song of Songs ii. 11], עָנָו *humble* [Numb. xii. 3], &c. We also find that the textual reading is *defective*, whilst the marginal reading is *plene*; as יָדָו *his hands*, in the *Kethiv*, and יָדָיו in the *Keri*, [Levit. ix. 22], צַוָּארוֹ *his neck*, in the *Kethiv*, and צַוָּארָיו in the *Keri* [Gen. xxxiii. 4]. But I shall discuss this subject in the Second Part, Section i.

Section VII.—Hitherto, I have treated on biliteral and triliteral words, in which all the letters are audible. I shall now discuss monosyllabic words, called little words. It is well known that the *plene* and *defective* monosyllabic words are those which have in the middle of the word either *Vav* quiescent, with *Cholem* and *Shurek*, or *Jod* quiescent, with *Chirek* and *Tzere*, and that in regard to words with other vowel-points there cannot be *plene* and *defective*, because no quiescent *Vav* or *Jod* can follow these points. On this subject I shall treat again in Section ix.

Now those pointed with *Cholem* are of two kinds. The first class consists of words, the middle letter of which is a quiescent *Vav*, as אוֹר *light*, יוֹם *day*, טוֹב *good*, מוֹר *myrrh*, קוֹל *a voice*, כּוֹס *a cup*, עוֹר *skin*, שׁוֹר *an ox*, בּוֹר *a pit*, עוֹד *again*, אוֹת *a sign*, &c. These are always *plene*; the expression לֹא *not*, is an exception, being always *defective*, except in thirty-five instances;⁴⁶ and the expression עוֹד *again*, is *defective* in fourteen instances;⁴⁷ so also דּוֹר *generation*, is *defective* when

---

⁴⁵ Both the Basel and the Sulzbach editions have הסרים ג׳, "the word יחדיו is always *defective*, except in Jeremiah, where it is found three times *defective*." But this is evidently a mistake for מלאים, *plene*, since the word in question actually occurs three times in Jeremiah, viz., xlvi. 12, 21; xlix. 3.

⁴⁶ The thirty-five instances in which לוא is *plene* are, Gen. xxxi. 35: Levit. v. 1 1 Sam. ii. 24; xix. 4: 1 Kings xviii. 5; xx. 8; xxii. 18: 2 Kings v. 17; vi. 12: Isa. xvi. 14; xxviii. 15: Jerem. ii. 25, 31; iii. 3, 12; iv. 11; v. 9, 10, 12 (thrice), 24; vi. 9; vii. 28; viii. 6, 2¹; x. 4; xv. 7, 11; xxix. 23; xlviii. 27; xlix. 20: Ezek. xvi 56; xxiv. 16: Lament. i. 12. They are enumerated, in a most confused manner, in the Massorah marginalis on Levit. v. 1.

⁴⁷ The fourteen instances in which עוד is *defective* are, Gen. viii. 22; xix. 12; xl. 13: 2 Sam. xiv. 32: 1 Kings xii. 5: Jerem. ii. 9; xiii. 27; xv. 9; xxxiii. 13: Hos. xii. 1, 10: Micah i. 15: Zech. viii. 20: Ps. xxxix. 2; xxxix. 2. Comp. Massorah marginalis on Gen. viii. 22, with Jerem. xv. 9.

במלת יחדו שהיא הסרה לעולם, חוץ בספר ירמיה נמצאים ג׳ מלאים,⁴⁵ ובכללם שְׂלָו, סְתָו, עָנָו, ונמצאים דכתיבים חסרים וקריין מלא, כמו וישא ידו (ויקרא ט׳) ידיו קרי, על צוארו צואריו קרי, ועוד אדבר בם בלוחות שניות במאמר א׳:

הדבור השביעי: לא דברתי עד הנה רק במלות שיש בהן ב׳ או ג׳ אותיות נעות, ועתה אדבר בכלל על מלורי של תנועה אחת הנקראורת מלות זעירות; וידוע כי המלות הזעירות ששייך בהן מלא או חסר, הן אותן שיש בהן באמצע חמלה וי״ו נחה עם חולם או שורק, או יו״ד נחה עם חרק או צרי; אבל אחר שאר הנקודות לא שייך מלא וחסר, כי לא שייך אחריהן וי״ו או יו״ד נחה, ועוד אדבר בם בדבור ט׳:

והנה הנקודות בחולם הם של ב׳ מינין, המין האחד הם של נחי ע״ן וי״ו, כמו אור, יום, טוב, מור, קול, כוס, עור, שור, בור, עוד, אות ודומיהם, הם תמיד מלאים, ומלא לא יוצאה מן הכלל שהיא תמיד חסרה, חוץ בל״ה מקומות,⁴⁶ ומלרת עוד רבא חסרה בי״ד מקומות,⁴⁷ וכן דור נמצא חסר כשיהיו שנים

it is twice repeated, as לְדֹר דֹּר *from generation to generation* [Exod. iii. 15], לְדֹר וָדֹר *from generation unto generation* [Ps. x. 6], &c., as it is explained in the great Massorah.

The second class consists of those words, the second and third radicals of which are the same letters; as קֹר *cold*, חֹם *heat*, רַק *but*, עַל *upon*. All these are *defective*,[48] and this because of the *Dagesh* which they take when formative additions are made at the end, as חֹק *law*, with suffix is חֻקּוֹ *his law*; רֹק *spittle*, with suffix רֻקּוֹ *his spittle*; עֹל *yoke*, with suffix עֻלּוֹ *his yoke*. Thus, also, the word כֹּל *all*, from כָּלַל, has *Cholem*, with *Vav* omitted when it has the accent, except לִכְלוֹ [Jerem. xxxiii. 8]. The Massorah remarks on it, "The *Vav* is not to be read, but read with *Kametz-Chatuph*, as is the rule with כָּל wherever it has *Makkeph*," as I have explained in the *Poetical Dissertation*.

The infinitive and imperative of verbs ע״ע too, have always *Cholem* and are *defective*; as for instance סֹב *return* [Song of Songs ii. 17], תִּשֹּׁלוּ שֹׁל *falling, ye shall let fall* [Ruth ii. 16], תֹּם *finished* [Deut. ii. 14]. Those which have *Shurek* are all from roots the second radical of which is quiescent, as סוּף *a reed* שׁוּק *a street*, טוּר *a wall*, &c., and are always *plene*, because they never have *Kibbutz*, except the imperative of ע״ו, as קֻם *arise* [Josh. vii. 10], רֻץ *run* [1 Sam. xx. 36], שֻׁב *return* [Exod. iv. 19], &c. Those which have *Chirek* are from roots in which *Jod* is radical, as גִּיד *a nerve*, סִיר *a pot*, סִיר *a thorn*, עִיר *a city*, שִׁיר *a song*, אִישׁ *a man*, צִיץ *a flower*, &c., they are generally *plene;* and *defectives* are but few, as רִב *a cause* [Exod. xxiii. 2], נִר *a light* [Prov. xxi. 4]. In the Massorah אִישׁ *a man*, is noted as being three times *defective*, but there are differences of opinion about it among the Massorites. Thus, also, according to the Massorah, סִין *Sin*, is always *plene*, whilst צִין *Zin*, is always *defective*. There are three words which always occur *defective*, viz., מִן *from*, עִם *with*, and אִם *if*, but בֵּן before *Nun* is simply from בֵּן of the root בָּנָה.

סמוכים, כמו זכרי לְדֹר דֹּר (שמות ג׳), וכן לְדֹר וָדֹר ודומיהן, כמבואר במסרה גדולה:

והמין הב׳ הם מן הכפולים, כמו קֹר, חֹם, חֹק, רֹק, עֹל, כלהון חסרים,[48] וזה בעבור הדגש הבא בהן כאשר יתרבו באות שלשית, כמו מן חֹק חֻקּוֹ, ומן רֹק רֻקּוֹ, ומן עֹל עֻלּוֹ, וכן מלת כֹּל נגזרת מן כָּלַל, כשחיא בטעם היא בחולם וחסר וי״ו לעולם, חוץ מן וסלחתי לכול עונותיכם (ירמיה ל״ג), המסורה עליו לא קרי וי״ו, ונקרא בקמץ חטוף כדין כל כָּל המוקף, כאשר בארדי בפרק שירה:

וכן המקור והצווי מן הכפולים תמיד בחולם וחסר, כמו סֹב דמח לך, שֹׁל תָּשֹׁלּוּ לה (רות ב׳), עַד תֹּם כל הדור (דברים ב׳); והשדוקים כלם מנחי העי״ן, כמו סוּף, טוּר, שׁוּק ודומיהן, והם תמיד מלאים, דחיינו שלא יבאו לעולם בקבוץ, רק בצווי מנחי העי״ן, כמו קֻם לך, רֻץ נא, שֻׁב לך מצרים ודומיחם; והחידוקים הם שהי״וד בחם שרשית, כמו גִּיד, סִיר, סִיר, עִיר, שִׁיר, אִישׁ, צִיץ ודומיחם, על הרוב מלאים, ונמצאים מעטים חסרים, כמו לא תענה על רִב, גֵר רשעים, ובמסרה איש ג׳ חסרים, ויש בחן פלוגתה, וכן במסרה כל סִין מלא וכל צֵן חסר; ונמצאים ג׳ מלות שהם חסרים לעולם, וחם אִם, עִם, מִן, אבל יהושע בֶּן נון הוא מן בֶן שרשו בנה:

---

[48] The words כלהון חסרים, *all these are defective*, without which the passage has no sense, are omitted in the Sulzbach edition.

Those which have *Tzere* consist of four classes. The first class embraces nouns in which the second radical *Jod* is audible, as בַּיִת *house*, עַיִן *a well*, יַיִן *wine*, אַיִן *nothing*, חַיִל *strength*, אַיִל *a ram*, זַיִת *an olive*, צַיִד *hunting*, &c. When these are in the construct state, the *Jod* is quiescent with the *Tzere*, as בֵּית *the house of*, עֵין *the well of*, אֵיל *the ram of*, צֵיד *the hunting of*, אֵין *nothingness of*, חֵיל *the strength of*, &c. These are generally *plene*, and the *defectives* are very few, as חֵל *army* [Obad. 20], on which the Massorites remark it occurs five times *defective*;[49] אֵל *porch* [Ezek. xl. 48], on which the Massorites remark, "This *defective* has no parallel."[50] To this class belong those words in which the *Jod* is not audible; as אֵיךְ *how*, בֵּין *between*; some of these are *defective*, as אֵד *a mist* [Gen. ii. 6], חֵק *bosom* [Prov. v. 20], &c.; but there are very few such instances.

The second class embraces words of ע״י, as גֵּר *stranger*, זֵד *proud*, עֵד *witness*, עֵר *Er*, צֵר *Zer*, מֵת *dead*, כֵּן *thus*, &c.; all these are invariably *defective*. The third class consists of words derived from roots ל״ה, as בֵּן *son*, גֵּו *the back*, זֵר *a crown*, עֵץ *wood*, all these are invariably *defective*. The fourth class consists of those derived from ע״ע, as חֵן *grace*, שֵׁן *a tooth*, חֵץ *an arrow*, לֵב *heart*, &c.; all these are invariably *defective*.

☞ The general rule is, that all those derived from ע״ע, whether having *Cholem* or *Tzere*, are always *defective*; whilst those with *Chirek* and *Cholem*, of ע״י, are generally *plene*, the *defectives* being very few, as I have stated above; but when they take formative additions at the end, they are mostly *defective*. Thus, we have from טוֹב *good*, the forms טֹבִים *the good* (mas.), טֹבָה *good* (fem.), טֹבַת *the good* (fem.), many of which are *defective*. The same is the case with קוֹל *voice*,

---

[49] The five passages in which חיל is *defective* are, 2 Sam. xx. 15; 1 Kings xxi. 23; Isa. xxvi. 1; Obad. 2; Lament. ii. 8. They are enumerated in the Massorah marginalis on 2 Sam. xx. 15.

[50] The reference, both in the Basel and Sulzbach editions, to ויאמר אל הפתח, is a mistake for כמו אל אלם. The note in the Massorah parva on the word in question is simply ל׳ חס יו״ד, *no parallel with Jod defective*; so that Levita's remark that it is לית חסר באילים, *no parallel of defective*, among the words אילים, must be derived from another recension of the Massorah.

which with suffix is קֹלוֹ *his voice*, קֹלִי *my voice*, קֹלֹת *the voices*, most of them being *defective*, and which, even without any suffixal addition, occurs in this form seven times *defective*; as קֹל *voice*, הַקֹּל *the voice* [Gen. xxvii. 22]; לְקֹל *to the voice* [Exod. iv. 8 (twice)], &c.⁵¹ Thus, also, from רֹב *contention*, we have הָרֹב [Job. xi. 2; xl. 2]. Moreover the plurals and suffixes with *Tzere* are sometimes also *defective*; as from אַיִל *a ram*, we have אֵלִים *rams;* and a few more such instances.

SECTION VIII.—Nothing more is left for me to explain with regard to *defective* and *plene Vav* and *Jod*, except to state how the Massorites noted those words which have two or three quiescents, some of which are *plene* and some *defective*, or all of which are either *plene* or *defective*.

☞ Let me illustrate it by the example of the word הֲקִימוֹתִי *I have established*, which occurs in the Scriptures in the four following ways:—i. הֲקִימוֹתִי [Ezek. xvi. 60], which is entirely *plene*. On this the Massorites remark, "this is one of the three instances entirely *plene*.⁵² ii. On הֲקִמֹתִי [Gen. xxvi. 3], which is entirely *defective*, they wrote "one of the eleven instances entirely *defective*."⁵³ iii. On הֲקִימֹתִי [Levit. xxvi. 9], they remark, "one of six instances in which it is both *plene* and *defective*."⁵⁴ And iv. On הֲקִמוֹתִי [1 Sam. xv. 13], they remark, "it has no parallel, being *defective* and *plene*." In some recensions it is marked, "it is one of the six with the accent on the

⁵¹ The other three passages in which קול is *defective* are, Gen xlv. 16 ; Exod. xix. 16 ; Jerem. iii. 9. They are enumerated in the Massorah marginalis on Gen. xxvii. 22.

⁵² The other two instances in which הקימותי is entirely *plene* are, 2 Sam. vii. 12 ; 2 Chron. vii. 18. They are given in the Massorah marginalis on Ezek. xvi. 60, where, however, there is a mistake, inasmuch as it substitutes 1 Chron. xvii. 2 for 2 Chron. vii. 18. In the Massorah parva, on the last mentioned passage, the remark כל דמל *entirely plene*, will be found, to which Levita refers.

⁵³ The eleven passages in which הקימתי is entirely *defective*, that is, has neither *Jod* after the *Chirek* nor *Vav* after the *Cholem*, are, Gen. vi. 18; ix. 11, 17; xvii. 7, 19; xxvi. 3; Exod. vi. 4 : 1 Kings ix. 5 : Jerem. xxiii. 4, 5 ; xxix. 10 : Ezek. xxxiv. 29. We could not find the entire list either in the Massorah marginalis on the respective passages, or in the Massorah finalis.

⁵⁴ The other five passages in which הקימתי has *Jod plene* after the *Chirek* and *Vav defective* after the *Cholem*, are, 1 Sam. xv. 13 : 2 Sam. ii. 35 ; vii. 12 : Isa. xxix. 3 : Ezek. xvi. 62. In the Massorah marginalis on Levit. xxvi. 9, where the passages are given, 2 Sam. ii. 35 is erroneously omitted, and 2 Chron. vii. 18, which is entirely *plene*, is substituted for it.

penultima," whilst in others it is marked as one of the four instances.[55] The Codices vary, as I shall explain in Section ix.

It is also to be noticed, that when a word has two quiescents, both of which are *plene*, and one of them belongs to that class of quiescents which is always *plene*, as I have shown in Section ii., the Massorites did not mark it *entirely plene*, but simply *plene*. And if both quiescents belong to those which are always *plene*, the Massorites did not remark upon it at all.

Thus, for example, הוֹלְכִים *they are coming* [Gen. xxxvii. 25], though *entirely plene*, the Massorites simply marked "*plene;*" that is, *Vav* is written fully, but the *Jod* they did not require to mark as being written fully, for it is there in accordance with the law about the *Jod* of the plural,[56] as I have explained in Section v. On לְהוֹרִיד *to go down* [ibid.], again, though *entirely plene*, the Massorites made no remark whatever, because the two quiescents therein are *plene* according to rule, as I have explained in Section iii., since *Vav*, which stands for *Jod* of the first radical, is *plene* according to law.

The same is the case with *Chirek*. When it is followed by an audible letter at the end of a word, it is generally *plene*, according to law, especially in the *Hiphil*, as I have explained in Section v. (*vide supra*, p. 156, &c.) But when both are defective, though one of them belongs to those which are generally defective, as I have explained in Section iii., the Massorites have always marked it entirely *defective*; as הֹלְכֹת *they are coming* [Exod. ii. 5], יֹשְׁבֹת *they are sitting* [1 Kings iii. 17], &c. *Vide supra*, p. 148, &c.

As to the words in which the first quiescent is *plene* and the second is *defective*, or *vice versa*, as גְּדֹלוֹת וְנוֹרָאֹת *great and wonderful*

חד מן ו' דלעיל, ולפעמים נמסר עליהן ד', ומשונין ואבארם במאמר ט' : [55]

אך צריך שתדע, בשיהיו במלה ב' נחין ושניהן מלאים, ואחד מהן הוא מאותן הנחים שדרכם להיות חמיד מלאים, כמו שבארתי בדבור ב', לא נמסר עליה מלא דמלא רק מלא לבד, ואם שניהן מאותן שדרכן להיות חמיד מלאים, לא נמסר עליהן מאומה:

והמשל הוֹלְכִים להוריד מצרימה, הוֹלְכִים אעפ"י שהוא מלא דמלא, לא נמסר עליו רק מלא לבד, ר"ל מלא וי"ו, ועל היו"ד אין צריך למסור מלא, כי כן דין יו"ד הרבים להיות מלא[56] כמו שכתבתי בדבור ה', ועל להוריד אעפ"י שהוא מלא דמלא, לא נמסר מאומה, כי כן דין ב' הנחים האלה להיות מלא, כמו שכתבתי בדבור ג' שהוי"ו הבא במקום יו"ד פ"א הפעל דינה להיות מלא :

וכן החירק שאחריו נח נראה בסוף המלה דינה על הרוב מלא, ובפרט בבנין הפעיל, כמו שכתבתי בדבור ה' ע"ש ; אבל אם שניהם חסרים, אעפ"י שהאחד מהן מאותן שדרכן להיות חסר, כמו שכתבתי בדבור ג', מכל מקום נמסר עליו חסר דחסר, כמו ונערוחיה הֹלְכֹת (שמות ב') יֹשְׁבֹת בבית אחד, ודומיהן ע"ש:

ובמלה שהראשון מלא והשני חסר או להפך, כמו גְּדֹלוֹת וְנוֹרָאֹת, הנה על גְּדֹלוֹת נמסר

---

[55] In the recensions of the Massorah, printed in the Basel and Amsterdam editions of the Rabbinic Bibles, the remark is that הקמוֹתי 1 Sam. xv. 12, is one of the three instances in which it has the tone of the penultima (מלעיל 'ב), and the Massorah marginalis on Gen. ix. 17, gives the three instances as follows:—Gen. ix. 17; Exod. vi. 4; 1 Sam. xv. 13.

[56] The words להיות מלא *to be plene*, are erroneously omitted in the Sulzbach edition.

[1 Chron. xvii. 21], they only remarked on גְּדֻלֹּת *defective*, but not *defective and plene*, because it is the law for *Cholem* of the plural to be written fully; whilst on נוֹרָאֹת *wonderful*, they simply remarked *defective*, but not *plene and defective*, because the *Vav*, which is written fully, stands for the radical *Jod*, which, according to rule, is *plene*, as I have explained all in Section iii. *Vide supra, p.* 148, &c.

There are some words with one or two quiescents, which are either *defective* or *plene*, and do not belong to those which are usually *plene* or *defective;* and yet the Massorites made no remark on them whatever. This arises from the fact that the rule has already been stated on the words in question in another place. Thus, for instance, the Massorites give the general rule, saying, that "תּוֹלְדֹת *generations*, always wants the second *Vav*, except in two instances, where it is written entirely *plene;* in one instance, where it is entirely *defective;* and in three instances, where it is *defective and plene*."[57] Hence there was no necessity for them to mark תּוֹלְדֹת *plene defective* in every passage where it occurs, since the first general rule is sufficient.

The same is the case with the word אֲבֹתֵיכֶם *your fathers*, on which they remark, "throughout the Pentateuch it is *defective* of *Vav*, and has *Jod* written fully, except in one instance where it is written אֲבוֹתֵיכֶם entirely fully, and in another instance where it is אֲבוֹתְכֶם, with *Vav*

---

[57] There is a great difference of opinion among the Massorites as to the reading of the word in question, in the different passages of the Scriptures. The Massorah marginalis on Gen. ii. 4, remarks as follows:— תולדות ב׳ מלאים דמלאי וסי׳ אלה תולדות השמים והארץ, אלה תולדות פרץ׳ וחד חסר דחס׳ אלה תלדת ישמעאל וג׳ כת׳ תלדות עשו אבי אדו׳ ושל אחריו אלה תלדות יעקב ושאר אורייתא תולדת כתיב. *The word* תולדות *is twice entirely* PLENE, *viz.*, Gen. ii. 4, Ruth. iv. 8; *once entirely* DEFECTIVE, *viz.* Gen. xxv. 12; *and thrice it wants the first* VAV, *viz.*, Gen. xxxvi. 1, 9; xxxvii. 2; *whilst in all other passages throughout the Pentateuch it is written with the first* VAV, *and without the second.* Another recension of the Massorah, given in the Massorah finalis under the letter *Jod*, p. 35 *b*, col. 2, is as follows:— מן זה ספר תלדות אדם עד תולדת יצחק תולדת כתיב במ״א תלדות אדם, ומן תולדת יצחק עד סופא דסיפרא תלדות כתיב במ״ב תלדת כתיב חסר דחסר תלדת עשו תלדת ישמעאל וב׳ כתיב תולדות מל׳ דכמל׳ אלה תולדות השמים ואלה תלדות פרץ, וג׳ כתבי תלדות תולדות עשו הוא אדום ושל אחרו אבי אדום אלה תלדות יעקב, *from* Gen. v. 1 *to* xxv. 19, *it is written without the second* VAV, *except in one place, viz.*, v. 1, *where it has the second* VAV *and not the first; from* Gen. xxv. 19, *to the end of the book, it is written with the second* VAV *and without the first, except in two instances, viz.*, Gen. xxxvi. 1, xxv. 12, *where it is entirely* DEFECTIVE; *in two passages, viz.*, Gen. ii. 4, Ruth iv. 18, *where it is entirely* PLENE, *and three passages, viz.* Gen. xxxvi. 1, 9, xxvi. 19. It will be seen that Gen. xxv. 19 is counted twice.

רק חסר, ולא חסר מלא, כי כן דין חולם של לשון רבות להיות מלא, ועל ונוראת נמסר חסר לבד, ולא מלא חסר, לפי שהוי״ו הכתובה היא במקום יו״ד השרש, ודינה להיות מלא, כמו שבארתי כל זה בדבור ג׳ ע״ש:

ויש מלות שיש בהן נח אחד או שנים וחן חסרים או מלאים, ואינן מאותן שדרכן להיות מלאים או חסרים, ואף על פי כן לא נמסר עליהם מאומה, וזה בעבור כלל אחד שנחנו במלה ההיא במקום אחר; וחמשל נתנו כלל אחד ואמרו כל תּוֹלְדֹת חסר וי״ו בתורה, חוץ מן ב׳ כתיבים תּוֹלְדוֹת מלא דמלא, וא׳ תּוֹלְדֹת חסר דחסר, וג׳ תּוֹלְדוֹת חסר מלא,[57] ולכן כל הכתיבין תּוֹלְדֹת אין צריך למסור עליהן מלא חסר, כי הכלל הראשון מספיק:

וכן כל אֲבֹתֵיכֶם שבתורה חסר וי״ו ומלא יו״ד, חוץ מאחד כתיב אֲבוֹתֵיכֶם מלא דמלא

169

plene and *Jod defective;*"[58] hence there was no more any necessity to mark אֲבֹתֵיכֶם *defective and plene* in every single passage where it occurs in the Pentateuch. Thus, also, they counted the expression אֲבוֹתֵיכֶם *your fathers*, both in *plene* and *defective*, in all the other books of the Scriptures; and on those which do not come within this rubric they made no remark whatever. Moreover, there are some words which are classified in their *defectives* and *plenes* according to each book of the Scriptures; and some are classified according to the Law, the Prophets, and the Hagiographa.

☞ The general rule is, that, when a word occurs with two quiescents, and one of them, or both, are either *defective* or *plene*, and if there is no Massoretic remark whatever thereon, you may then take it for granted that that is because the law connected therewith had already been stated, and you will find it if you seek for it. I shall, however, recur again to this subject in the Second Part, Section ix.

On a word which has three quiescents, some of which are *plene* and some *defective*—as וַהֲטִיבוֹתִי *and I shall do good* [Ezek xxxvi. 11], which wants *Jod* after *Teth*, indicating the *Hiphil*, for it ought to be הֵטִיבוֹתִי—the proper Massoretic remark should have been "the first *Jod* is *plene*, the second *Jod* is *defective*, and the *Vav* is *plene*." But for the sake of brevity the Massorites simply remark, "it has no parallel," "it is thus written," or "it is written thus."

The same is the case with the word מְשׁוּבֹתֵיכֶם *your backslidings*, [Jerem. iii. 22], on which the Massorites neither mentioned *plene* nor *defective*, but say this is the textual reading; and with וַיֹּשִׁיבוּם *and He made them dwell* [1 Sam. xii. 8], on which they simply remark, "it is written so."

Notice, that when a word has three quiescents, and all three are *plene*, the Massorites do not remark on it *entirely plene*, but "*all plene;*" as on וַהֲשִׁיבוֹתִיךָ *and I will turn thee back* [2 Kings xix. 28], וּתְפוּצוֹתֵיכֶם

---

[58] In Exod. iii. 13, אבותיכם is entirely *plene*, and in Deut. i. 11 it has *Vav* but wants *Jod*. Comp. Massorah marginalis on Exod iii. 13.

aud your dispersion [Jerem. xxv. 34], וַהֲבִיאוֹתִים and I will bring them [Isa. lvi. 7], &c.; also when all these three are defective, as וַיֹּרִדֻהוּ and they brought him down [1 Kings i. 53], הֲבֵאָנֻם we have brought them [Numb. xxxii. 17], &c.; the Massorites did not remark on them entirely defective, but "all defective." In some Codices they are marked, "this is the textual reading," but the former is more generally used.

SECTION IX.—Hitherto I have explained the law of the defectives and plenes with regard to the letters Vav and Jod; I shall now explain the rule of the letters Aleph and He. Know, then, that Aleph is frequently either quiescent or wanting in the middle or at the end of some words in certain places, and that there is no parallel for these in other places. Thus, for example, שְׁאֵלָתֵךְ thy petition [1 Sam. i. 17], מָלוּ they filled [Ezek. xxviii. 16], וַתְּאַזְרֵנִי and thou hast girded me [2 Sam. xxii. 40], &c.; there are seventeen such instances, and they only occur in the Prophets and Hagiographa.[59] There are also five instances to be found in the Pentateuch, viz., מֵחֲטוֹ from sinning [Gen. xx. 6], וְנִטְמֵתֶם and ye shall be defiled [Levit. xi. 43], וּקְרָאָהוּ and it shall befall him, in Pericope Va-jigash [Gen. xliv. 29); מָצָאתִי I have found, in Pericope Behaaloscha [Numb. xi. 11]; לְחַטָּאת for a sin offering, in Pericope Shelach [Numb. xv. 24]; מֵרֵאשִׁית from the beginning, in Pericope Ekeb [Deut. xi. 12].[60] Now I wonder why they did not count these with the other

הדבור התשיעי: לא באדתי עד הנה רק דין החסרים והמלאים של וי"ו או יו"ד, ומעתה אבאר דין הא"לף והה"א; ודע כי האל"ף תנוח או תחסר לפעמים באמצע המלה או בסופה, בקצת המלות שאין כן בשאר חברותיהן, כגון את שְׁאֵלָתֵךְ, מָלוּ תובך חמם, וַתְּאַזְרֵנִי חיל והם י"ז במספר ואינם רק בנביאים וכתובים;[59] ועוד נמצאו ה' בתורה ואלו הן מֵחֲטוֹ לי, וְנִטְמֵתֶם בם, וּקְרָאָהוּ אסון דרינג, ואם מָצָאתִי חן רבחעלותך לְחַטָּאת דשלח, מֵרֵאשִׁית השנה דעקב;[60] ותמהתי למה לא כללום עם

וּתְפוּצוֹתֵיכֶם, ונפלתם וַהֲבִיאוֹתִים אל הר קדשי, וכן כשיהיו שלשן חסרים, כמו וַיֹּרִדֻהוּ מעל המזבח, עד אשר הֲבֵאָנֻם ורומיהן, לא נמסר עליהן חסר דחסר, אלא כלו חסר; וביש נוכחאות דכתיב עליחן כן כתיב, והראשון יותר נהוג:

---

[59] The Massorah only gives sixteen words, which respectively occur in one place with silent Aleph or altogether without Aleph, and have no parallel in other places. They are as follows:—

שלחך	. . . 1 Sam. i. 17	פלסר	. . 2 Kings xvi. 17	הסורים	. . Eccl. iv. 14
חמאים	. 1 Sam. xiv. 33	פלנסר	. . 1 Chron. v. 26	השמפות	. Nehem. iii. 13
ותזרני	. . 2 Sam. xxii. 40	מלו	. . Ezek. xxviii. 16	קרוא	. . Esther v. 12
לחשות	. 2 Kings xix. 25	נשו	. . Ps. cxxxix. 20	שרית	. 1 Chron. xii. 38
וירפו	. . . 2 Kings ii. 22	ונשו	. . Ezek. xxxix. 26	קראים	. . . Ps. xcix. 6
		משתו	. . Job xli. 7		

They are enumerated in the Massorah marginalis on 2 Kings xvi. 7. In the Massorah finalis, where under the letter Aleph, p. 1, col. 2, they are also mentioned, it is erroneously stated that there are seventeen instances, which has undoubtedly occasioned the error in our text. These instances are also given in the Ochla Ve-Ochla, section cxcix. pp. 43, 123, where one passage, viz. 1 Chron. v. 26, is wanting.

[60] For the division of the Pentateuch into fifty-four Pericopes, for hebdomadal lessons, see above, p. 135, note 138. Vajigash (ויגש) is the eleventh section, and comprises Gen. xliv. 18—xlvii. 27; Behaaloscha (בהעלותך) is the thirty-sixth section, and comprises Numb. viii. 1—xii. 16; Shelach (שלח), more fully Shelach Lecha (שלח לך), is the thirty-seventh section, and comprises Numb. xiii. 1—xv. 41; whilst Ekeb (עקב) is the forty-sixth section, and comprises Deut. vii. 12—xi. 25.

seventeen; thus registering them all in one list of twenty-two words with *Aleph defective* in the Bible.

Again, there are seventeen words in which the reverse is the case, wherein the *Aleph* is audible, contrary to their normal form in other passages, which the Massorites call *Maphkin Aleph;* as לְצֹנַאֲכֶם *for your sheep* [Numb. xxxii. 24], נָאוָה *comely* [Ps. xciii. 5], כְּמוֹצֵאת *as one finding* [Song of Songs viii. 10], &c.[61] There are also forty-eight words with a silent *Aleph* in the middle of the word; as הָאסַפְסֻף *the mixed multitude* [Numb. xi. 4], וַיֵּאָצֶל *and he separated* [Numb. xi. 25], &c.[62] Now on all these *Alephs* the Massorites never remark, *Aleph omitted*, or *Aleph written fully*, or *the Aleph is audible*, or *the Aleph is silent*, but simply state "*Maphkin Aleph*," or "*Non-Maphkin Aleph*."

חי"ז ויהיו כ"ב דחסר אל"ף בקר־א:

וכן י"ז מלין להפך שתנוע בהן האלף שלא כדין חברותיהן, וקורין להן מפקין אל"ף, כגון וגדרות לְצֹנַאֲכֶם, נָאוָה קדש, כְּמוֹצֵאת שלום;[61] וכן מ"ח מלין דכתיבין אל"ף באמצע התיבה ולא קריין, כמו וְהָאסַפְסֻף, וַיֵּאָצֶל מן הרוח (במדבר י"א) וכו', [62] והנה על כל אלה האלפין לא נמסר חסר אל"ף, או מלא אל"ף, או קרי אלף, או לא קרי אל"ף, רק מפקין אל"ף, או לא מפקין אל"ף:

---

[61] The seventeen words which respectively occur only once with audible *Aleph*, and have no parallel in the other places, are as follows:—

ואביאסף	. . Exod. vi. 24	בלואי	. . Jerem. xxxviii. 12	נאוה	. . . Ps. xciii. 5
הביאו	. . Levit. xxiii. 17	באוש	. . . Amos iv. 10	ואוארעי	. . Job xxxi. 22
לצנאכם	. Numb. xxxii. 24	במלאכות	. . . Hag. i. 13	רבאות	. . . Dan. xi. 12
אדר	. . . 1 Kings xi. 17	ואישי	. . 1 Chron. ii. 13	מנאות	. . . Nehem. xii. 44
אשכים	. . Jerem. xxv. 3	מלאכות	1 Chron. xxviii. 19	כמוצאת	Song of Songs viii. 10
ובאורוע	. Jerem. xxxii. 21	הערביאים	2 Chron. xvii. 11		

They are enumerated in the Massorah finalis under the letter *Aleph*, p. 1, col. 2, and are mentioned in the Massorah marginalis on Exodus xviii. 13, where a reference is given to the Massorah on Ps. xxx., in which place, however, nothing is to be found. They are also given in the *Ochla Ve-Ochla*, section cxcviii. pp. 45, 123.

[62] The words which respectively occur in one place with a silent *Aleph* in the middle of the word, and which have no parallel, are as follows:—

תאספון	. . Exod. v. 7	רפאתי	. . 2 Kings xxi. 9	ירצאתי	. . Ezek. xliii. 27
והאספסף	. . Numb. xi 4	רפאו	. . . Jerem. li. 9	ואענה	. 1 Kings xi. 39
ויאצל	. . Numb. xi. 25	ונרפאו	. Ezek. xlvii. 8	ואעשר	. . Zech. xi. 5
משאת	. Deut. xxiv. 10	בארוך	. 2 Kings xx. 12	וקאם	. . . Hos. x. 14
מראון	. . Josh. xii 20	פארה	. . . Isa. x. 33	ארבאל	. . Hos. x. 14
בארומה	. . Judg. ix. 41	כאביר	. . . Isa. x. 13	ואמאסאך	. . Hos. iv. 6
בלאט	. . Judg. iv 21	הבאיש	. . . Isa. xxx. 5	פארור	. . Joel ii. 6
פלאי	. . Judg. xiii 18	יראת	. . Isa. xli. 25	פארור	. Nahum ii. 11
חטאים	. . 1 Sam. xiv 33	בארות	. . Jerem. ii. 13	דכאת	. Ps. lxxxix. 11
ויאסף	. . 1 Sam. xviii. 29	בארות	. . Jerem. ii. 13	ות־כאונני	. . Job xix. 2
הלאמה	. . 2 Sam. x 17	שאסיך	. Jerem. xxx. 16	מאום	. . Job xxxi. 7
המלאכים	. . 2 Sam. xi 1	פארה	. Ezek. xvi. 57	מאום	. . . Dan. i. 4
ויראו	. . 2 Sam. xi 24	שאמך	. Ezek. xxv. 6	בוראם	. Nehem. vi. 8
המראים	. . 2 Sam. xi 24	השאטים	Ezek. xxviii. 24	נאשים	. Nehem. v. 11
כבאר	. 2 Sam. xxiii 15	השאטים	Ezek. xxviii. 26	למואל	. Nehem. xii. 38
מבאר	. 2 Sam. xxiii 16	ונאשאר	. . Ezek. ix. 8	דאג	. Nehem. xiii. 16
הבאר	. 2 Sam. xxiii 20	וששאתיך	. Ezek. xxxix. 2		

They are enumerated in the Massorah marginalis on Ezekiel i. 1; Job i. 1; and in the Massorah finalis under the letter *Aleph*, p. 1 *a*, cols. 2 and 3. It will be seen that, instead of there being forty-eight, as mentioned in the heading of the Rubric, and by Levita, there are fifty. They are also given with some slight variation in the *Ochla Ve-Ochla*, section ciii. pp. 29, 97, &c.

The meaning of מפקין is *brought out, uttered, pronounced, audible*. So the Chaldee renders מוֹצִיא *uttering, pronouncing* [Prov. x. 18], by מפיק. I have already explained in the *Poetical Dissertations*, Sect iv., that מפיק is only applied to the letters *Vav, Jod*, and *He* when pronounced by the mouth at the end of a word, since the *Aleph* is never pronounced at the end of a word. Hence, when the Massorah uses *Maphkin Aleph*, it denotes that it has the vowel-point, as in the above-named instances. In the *Massorah Parva*, however, they are marked *defective* or *plene*, yet not marked *defective* or *plene* absolutely; but it is distinctly stated, *Aleph defective*, or *Aleph plene*. The same law obtains with regard to *He*, as I shall explain in the following Section.

ופירוש מפקין מוציאין, תרגום של ומוציא דבה דמפיק טיבא, וכבר בארתי בפרק שירה בשיר ד' שמפקין לא נאמר כי אם על אותיות וי"ה כשמוציאים אותם מן הפה בסוף התיבה, אבל האל"ף אין מוציאין אותה מן הפה בסוף התיבה לעולם; אבל כשנמצא במסורת מפקין אל"ף ר"ל שהיא בנקודה כדלעיל, אבל במסרה קטנה נמסר עליהן חסר או מלא, אבל לא חסר, או לא מלא סתם, רק בפירוש חסר אל"ף או מלא אל"ף; וכן דין חח"א כאשר אבאר ברבור שאחד זה:

ויש מלות שתנוח בהן האל"ף בסוף הרתיבה, כגון שימה אחרת מן י"ב מלין דכתיבין אל"ף ולא קרי, כמו ולא אָבוּא שמוע, הָהָלְכוּא אתו,[63] שור וּמריא, דם נָקיא וכולי, ונמסר עליהם יתיר אל"ף, או לא קרי אל"ף; ועוד שימה אחת מן י"ז מלין שיש בהן אל"ף נחה בסוף התיבה והיא במקום ה"א, והיה לכם לוָרָא (במדבר י"א), גָּבְהָא קומתו, לידידו שֵׁנָא וכו',[64] ונמסרן על כל אחת לית כתיב אל"ף:

There are some words in which *Aleph* is quiescent at the end of the word, as in the Register of twelve words, viz., אָבוּא *they willed* [Isa. xxviii. 12], הָהָלְכוּא *who went* [Josh. x. 24], נָקִיא *innocent* [Jonah i. 14], &c;[63] on these the Massoretic mark is either, *Aleph redundant*, or *Aleph not to be read*. There is also another Register of seventeen words, with quiescent *Aleph* at the end of the word standing for *He*; as זָרָא *loathsome* (Numb. xi. 20), גָּבְהָא *it was erected* [Ezek. xxxi. 5], שֵׁנָא *sleep* [Ps. cxxvii. 2],[64] on every one of which the Massorites remark, "*no parallel with Aleph.*"

---

[63] The twelve words which have quiescent *Aleph* at the end are as follows:—

רפוא	. . Numb. xiii. 9	רצוא	. . . Ezek. i. 14	נגוא	. . . Dan. iii. 29
ההלכוא	. . . Josh. x. 24	ואתוקיהא	. . . Ezek. xli. 15	ושיציא	. . . Ezra vi. 15
הקליא	. . 1 Sam. xvii. 17	נקיא	. . . . Jonah i. 14	יפוא	. . Ezra iii. 7
אבוא	. . . Isa. xxviii. 12	נקיא	. . . . Joel iv. 19	ארעא	. . . . Dan. ii. 39

They are enumerated in the Massorah marginalis on Numb. xiii. 9; Ezekiel i. 1; Proverbs i. 1; Ezra i. 1; and in the *Ochla Ve-Ochla*, section civ., pp. 30, 98.

[64] The seventeen words which respectively have in one place a quiescent *Aleph* at the end of the word, and which have no parallel in any other place, are as follows:—

זרא	. . . Numb. xi. 20	שנא	. . . Ps. cxxvii. 2	כלא	. . . Ezek. xxxvi. 5
אלעלא	. . Numb. xxxii. 37	למא	. . . Ezra iv. 22	יורא	. . Prov. xi. 25
ארצא	. . 1 Kings xvi. 9	בדמא	. . . Dan. xi. 44	תבא	. . . Prov. i. 10
אלא	. . 1 Kings iv. 18	כממרא	. . Lament. iii. 12	הרא	. . 1 Chron. v. 26
גבהא	. . Ezek. xxxi. 5	גבעא	. . 1 Chron. ii. 49	כלא	. . Prov. xvi. 30
ופא	. . Job xxxviii. 11	מרא	. . . Ruth i. 20		

They are enumerated in the Massorah finalis under the letter *Aleph*, p. 1 a, cols. 3 and 4. The heading, however, of the Rubric does not give the number, nor does the Massorah marginalis, on Ezekiel xxxi. 5; xxxvi. 5; and Ruth i. 20, where reference is made to them; nor say how many there are belonging to this class.

173

Section X.—The *He* is never quiescent except at the end of a word, in four different ways, which are symbolised by the expression שְׁנָתְךָ *thy sleep*, being the acrostic of, 1. שֹׁרֶשׁ *the root;* 2. נקבה *the feminine;* 3. תוספת *formative addition;* and 4. כנוי *suffix.* i. By radix is meant the radical *He* of verbs ל"ה, as עָשָׂה *to work,* בָּנָה *to build,* &c. ii. By the feminine gender, as פָּקְדָה *she visited,* שָׁמְרָה *she kept,* צְדָקָה *righteousness,* בְּרָכָה *blessing,* &c. About these two classes the Massorites say nothing. iii. By formative addition is meant the *He* added to the end of a word, which consists of two kinds, additions to verbs and additions to nouns. Additions to verbs we have in the imperative singular; as שִׁמְעָה *hear,* סְלָחָה *forgive,* הַקְשִׁיבָה *hearken* [Dan. ix. 19]; in the infinitive פָּשֹׁטָה *to strip,* עָרָה *to make bare,* חֲגֹרָה *to gird* [Isa. xxxii. 11]; and in the future, with *Aleph* and *Nun* of אי"תן; as אֶזְכְּרָה *I shall remember,* אֶשְׁפְּכָה *I shall pour out* [Ps. xlii. 5]; נֵדְעָה *we shall know,* נִרְדְּפָה *we shall pursue* [Hosea vi. 3], &c.; and about these the Massorites say nothing. The additions to the nouns are of two kinds. Of the first are such words as מַעְלָה *upwards,* מַטָּה *downwards,* לַיְלָה *night,* נַחֲלָה *inheritance;* their distinguishing mark is that they are always *Milel;* and about these the Massorites speak but very little. The second class consists of those words which have *He* added to the end instead of *Lamed,* as our Rabbins of blessed memory remarked, "every word which should have *Lamed* at the commencement takes *He* at the end."[65]

הדבור העשירי: לא תנוח הה"א לעולם דק בסוף התיבה לבד והן של ד' מינין, וסימן וערבה שנתך פי' שרש, נקבד, תוספת, כנוי: שרש ר"ל החה"א השרשיר מפעלי נחי למ"ד חח"א, כמו עָשָׂה, בָּנָה ודומיהן; נקבה כמו פָּקְדָה, שָׁמְרָה, צְדָקָה, בְּרָכָה ודומיהן ומן ב' חמינין האלה לא דברו דבר: תוספת ר"ל ה"א הנוספת בסוף, היא של ב' מינין, הנוספת בפעלים, והנוספת בשמות; הנוספת בפעלים כמו בצווי היחיד כמו י"י שִׁמְעָה, י"י הַקְשִׁיבָה; ובמקור כמו פָּשֹׁטָה, עָרָה חֲגֹרָה; ובעתידים עם אל"ף ונו"ן האית"ן כמו אלה אֶזְכְּרָה וְאֶשְׁפְּכָה, נֵדְעָה נִרְדְּפָה ודומיהן, לא דברו מהן דבר; והנוספת בשמות היא של ב' מינין האחד כמו מַעְלָה, מַטָּה, לַיְלָה, נַחֲלָה, וסימנם שהם תמיד מלעיל, ומזה דברו דק מעט, והמן השני הם ההאי"ן הנוספת בסוף התיבה במקום למד, כמו שאמרו רז"ל כל תיבה הצריכה למד בתחילה הטיל לה ה"א בסופה: [65]

---

[65] The grammatical rule to which Levita refers is recorded both in the Babylonian and the Jerusalem Talmuds as having been propounded by R. Nehemiah. In the Babylonian Talmud *(Jebamoth,* 13 *b)* it is as follows:—יי נחמיה אומר כל תיבה שצריכה למ"ד בתחילתה הטיל לה הכתוב ה"א בסופה, *R. Nehemiah sayeth: Every word which requires Lamed at the beginning of the Scripture gives He at the end.* In the Jerusalem Talmud, however *(Jebamoth* i. 6, p. 3 *a,* ed. Graetz), it is תני בשם רבי נחמיה כל דבר שהוא צריך למ"ד מתחילתו ולא ניתן לו ה"א בסופו כגון לחוץ הוצה, לשעיר שעירה, לסוכות סוכותה, *It is propounded, in the name of R. Nehemiah, that every word which ought to have Lamed at the beginning, and has it not, takes He at the end,* as הוצה [Deut. xxv. 5] *instead of* לחוץ; שעירה [Judg. iii. 26] *instead of* לשעיר; סוכותה [Exod. xii. 37] *instead of* סכות. It will be seen that Levita s quotation is from the Babylon Talmud; but since the Jerusalem Talmud, which contains the original rule, as is evident from the whole complexion of the passage, has not the expression תיבה, Levita's animadversions are nugatory. Equally feeble is his stricture on the word לן, since the instances which are adduced in the Talmud itself to illustrate this rule plainly show that R. Nehemiah did not mean to extend it to *every* word, but applied it to those denoting *locality.* For the use of the *local He,* see Gesenius' Grammar, section xc.

174

Now I have to ask two questions about this remark. The first is about their saying תיבה, which embraces nouns, particles, and verbs, whereas the *He* which stands for the *Lamed* at the beginning only occurs in nouns. The second question is about the word *"every,"* the use of which is not justifiable in this place, since all nouns cannot take this *He*, except those which we find in the Bible, and these are not one in a thousand; and since they are chiefly found in names of places, and have been counted by the Massorites, as מִצְרַיְמָה *to Egypt*, which occurs twenty-eight times;[66] בָּבֶלָה *to Babylon*, twenty-nine times;[67] יְרוּשָׁלַיְמָה *to Jerusalem*, five times;[68] חֶבְרוֹנָה *to Hebron*, nine times.[69] There are also to be found a few others; as הָאֹהֱלָה *to the tent*, eight times;[70] הַבַּיְתָה *to the house*, eighteen times;[71] הַמִּזְבֵּחָה *to the altar*, five times;[72] אַרְצָה *to the land*, in connection with בְּנַעַן *Canaan*, eight times *plene*.[73] The Massorites did not count the other

[66] The twenty-eight instances in which מצרימה occurs with *He* at the end are, Gen. xii. 10, 11, 14; xxvi. 2; xxxvii. 25, 28; xxxix. 1; xli. 57; xlv. 4; xlvi. 3, 4, 7, 8, 9, 26, 27; xlviii. 5; l. 14: Exod. i. 1; iv. 21; xiii. 17: Numb. xiv. 3, 4; xx. 15: Deut. x. 22; xvii. 16; xxvi. 5: 2 Chron. xxxvi. 4. They are enumerated in the Massorah marginalis on 2 Chron. xxxvi. 4.

[67] The twenty-nine instances in which בבלה occurs are, Isa. xxxix. 6: 2 Kings xxiv. 15 (twice), 16; xxv. 13: Isa. xliii. 14: Jerem. xx. 4, 5; xxvii. 16, 18, 20, 22; xxviii. 4; xxix. 1, 3, 4, 15, 20; xxxix. 7; xl. 1, 7; lii. 11, 17: Ezek. xii. 13; xvii. 12, 20: 2 Chron. xxxiii. 11; xxvi. 6, 10. They are enumerated in the Massorah finalis, p. 16 *a*, cols 3, 4.

[68] The five passages in which ירושלימה occurs are, 1 Kings x. 2; 2 Kings ix. 28; Isa xxxvi. 2; 2 Chron. xxxii. 9. They are enumerated in the Massorah marginalis on Isa. xxxvi. 2, with the remark that in four of the passages it is *defective*.

[69] The five passages in which חברונה occurs are, Joshua x. 39: 2 Sam. ii. 1; v. 1, 3; xv. 9: 1 Chron. xi. 1, 3; xii. 23, 38. They are enumerated in the Massorah marginalis on Joshua x. 39.

[70] The eight passages in which האהלה occurs are, Gen. xviii. 6; xxiv. 67: Exod. xviii. 7; xxxiii. 8, 9; Numb. xi. 26: Josh. vii. 22: Judges iv. 18. They are enumerated in the Massorah marginalis on Judges iv. 18.

[71] The eighteen instances in which הביתה occurs are, Gen. xix. 10; xxiv. 32; xxxix. 11; xliii. 16, 26 (twice): Exod. ix. 19: Josh. ii. 18: Judg. xix. 15, 18: 1 Sam. vi. 7: 2 Sam. xiii. 7; xiv. 31; xvii. 20: 1 Kings xiii. 7, 15; xvii. 23: 2 Kings iv. 32; ix. 6. They are enumerated in the Massorah marginalis on 1 Kings xiii. 15.

[72] This must surely be a mistake, since there are upwards of thirty instances in which המזבחה occurs, viz.— Exod. xxix. 13, 18, 25: Levit. i. 9, 13, 15, 17; ii. 2, 9; iii. 5, 11, 16; iv. 19, 26, 31, 35; v. 12; vii. 5, 31; viii. 16, 21, 28; ix. 10, 14, 20; xiv. 20; xvi. 25: Numb. v. 26: 2 Chron. xxix. 22 (thrice), 24. The Massorah finalis enumerates them under the letter *Zajin*, p. 30 *a*, col. 1.

[73] The eight passages in which ארצה כנען occur conjointly are, Gen. xi. 31; xii. 5 (twice); xxxi. 18; xlii. 29; xlv. 17; l. 13: Numb. xxxv. 10. The entire list is nowhere given, though the Massorahs marginalis on Numbers xxxv. 10, and finalis, p. 11 *a*, col. 4, refer to each other for it.

instances in which אַרְצָה occurs, because this form is the most frequent. Accordingly, the Rabbins ought simply to have said, "there are some nouns which ought to begin with *Lamed*, but take *He* at the end instead." It may, perhaps, be replied, that the word כל signifies *rule*, since they use it so in another place; "one cannot infer from rules." The additional *He* is also to be found after *Kametz*, under *Tav*, *Kaph*, and *Nun*, at the end of a word, as I shall explain hereafter. I have already shown, in Section v., that a vowel-point does not occur at the end of a word, except under *Tav*, *Kaph*, and *Nun*, which have sometimes *Kametz*, and are not followed by *He*.

Tav is the *Tav* with *Kametz* indicating the singular, which is to be found at the end of the preterite; as דָּרַשְׁתָּ חָקַרְתָּ שָׁאַלְתָּ, *thou hast enquired, thou hast searched, thou hast asked* [Deut. xiii. 15], &c.; by far the greater majority of them are without *He*, and those which have it are but few, as גַּרְתָּה *thou hast sojourned* [Gen. xxi. 23], נֵאַרְתָּה *thou hast made void* [Ps. lxxxix. 40], הִסְכַּנְתָּה *thou art acquainted* [Ps. xxxix. 3], &c. On these the Massorites always remark, *He plene*, but on those which have no *He* they never remark, *He defective*, except on the word נָתַתָּ *thou hast given*, on which the Massorites note "it occurs twenty-nine with *He defective*."[74]

☞ It might be asked, why they give the number of the *defectives* of this word, and not that of other words which have *He defective*, and which are very many. And since the *defectives* are the greater number, ought they not rather to have counted all the instances in which נָתַתָּ *thou hast given*, וְנָתַתָּ *and thou hast given*, occur as *plene*, which are the fewer in number? The reply is, that they have done it, because the *Tav* has *Dagesh forte*, for it is after a short vowel; and it is not normal for *Dagesh forte* to be at the end of a word, without being

---

[74] The twenty-nine instances in which נתח occurs without *He*, are as follows:—Gen. xl. 13; Exod. xxv. 16, 21, 26, 30; xxvi. 34; xxviii. 23, 30; xxix. 3, 6, 17; xxx. 5, 16, 18 (twice); xl. 7 (twice), 8; Levit. ii. 15; xxiv. 7; 1 Kings viii. 34, 39; Judg. xv. 18; Ps. lxi. 6; Dan. x. 12; Nehem. ix. 15, 20, 35 (twice). They are enumerated in the Massorah marginalis on Exodus xxv. 21.

followed by either a silent or vocal letter. Hence the *He* after every *Tav* which has *Dagesh forte* at the end of a word, as you see is the case in the other instances, besides the twenty-nine in question. Thus you will also see it in וְהֵמַתָּה *and if thou shalt kill* [Numb. xiv. 15], וָמַתָּה *and thou shalt die* [Ezek. xxviii. 8], שַׁתָּה *thou hast put* [Ps. xc. 8], &c. This, however, is only the case with irregular verbs, as those mentioned above. Thus, also, in the word אַתָּה *thou,* the *He* is added because of the *Dagesh forte*, for which reason the Massorites did not require ever to make it as having *He plene*. But the regular verbs in which the *Tav* is radical, כָּרַתָּ *to cut off*, שָׁבַתָּ *to rest*, שָׁחַתָּ *to destroy*, &c., these have never *He* after *Tav*, though it has *Dagesh forte*, as וְכָרַתָּ *and thou shalt cut down* [Deut. xx. 20], וְנִכְרַתָּ *and thou shalt be cut off* [Obad. 10], הִשְׁבַּתָּ *thou makest to cease* [Ps. cxix. 119], שִׁחַתָּ *thou hast destroyed* [Is. xiv. 20], and are not marked *defective;* the expression הִצְמַתָּה *thou hast destroyed* [Ps. lxxiii. 27], being an exception to this rule, is marked by the Massorites "*He* written fully."

The final *Kaph*, which has a vowel-point at the end of a word, is the *Kaph* with *Kametz*, indicating the suffix of the second person singular, found in verbs and nouns; in verbs, as מַפְרְךָ וְהִרְבִּתִיךָ וּנְתַתִּיךָ *I will make thee fruitful, and multiply thee, and make thee* [Gen. xlviii. 4]; and in nouns, as שׁוֹרְךָ וַחֲמֹרְךָ וְעַבְדְּךָ וַאֲמָתֶךָ *thine ox and thine ass, thy man servant, thy woman servant* [Deut. v. 14]. There are some, however, with the additional *He*, which the Massorites always mark "*He plene*." Thus, there are in the Massorah twenty-one unique words, *i.e.,* they have no parallel with a quiescent *He* at the end of the word, after כ of the second person singular masculine, as אֲבָרְכֶכָה *I shall bless thee* (Gen. xxvii. 7), יָדְכָה *thy hand* [Exod. xiii. 16], בְּכָה *in thee* [Exod. vii. 29], עִמָּכָה *with thee* [1 Sam. i. 26], &c.; these are called 21 *Vadain* or *Vadja* (see Section ix., Part 2), and you will find that they have pairs or

נח או נע אחריו, ולפיכח באה ה"א אחר כל תי"ו הדנושה בדגש חזק בסוף התיבה, כמו כל שאר נָתַתָּה וְנָתַתָּה חוץ מן כ"ט: וכן וְהֵמַתָּה את העם, לשחת יורדוך רָמַתָּה, שַׁתָּה עונותינו לנגדך ורומיהן, וזה דווקא בפעלים שאינן שלמים, כמו באלה שזכרחי, וכן מלת אַתָּה הה"א נוספת בעבור הדגש החזק, ואין צריך למסור על שום אחד מאלה מלא ה"א, אבל בפעלים השלמים שהתי"ו שרשית, כמו כָּרַתָּ, שָׁבַתָּ, שָׁחַתָּ, הם חמיד בלי ח"א אחריה, אעפ"י שהדרגש חזק, כמו על העיר וְכָרַתָּ, וְנִכְרַתָּ לעולם, סנים חִשְׁבַּתָּ, אֶרֶץ שִׁחַתָּ ורומיחן, ולא נמסר עליחן חסר, ומלת הִצְמַתָּה כל זונה ממך יוצאת מן הכלל, לכן נמסר עליה מלא ה'ח"א:

והכ"ף חבא בסוף התיבה בנקודה היא חכ"ף הקמוצה לכנוי היחיד הנמצא בפעלים ובשמות ובמלות, כמו הנני מַפְרְךָ וְהִרְבִּיתִךָ נְתַתִּיךָ, ובשמות שׁוֹרְךָ וַחֲמוֹרְךָ וְעַבְדְּךָ וַאֲמָתְךָ כָּמוֹךָ, ויש שנכתבו בה"א נוספת וחמיד נמסר עליחן מלא ה"א, וכן במסורת כ"א מלין יחידאין, ר"ל שאין להן דומה דכחיבין בה"א בסוף החיבה כמו וַאֲבָרְכֶכָה לפני י"י (בראשית כ"ז), לאות על יָדְכָה, וּבְכָה ובעמך, הנצבת עִמָּכָה וכו', וקראו לחן כה כ"א ודאין או ודיא, עיין במאמר ט' ונמצאים שיש לחן זוג

---

[75] The whole sentence בלי אות נח או נע אחריו ולפיכך באה ה"א אחר כל תי"ו הדגושה בדגש חזק בסוף התיבה, *without being followed either by a silent or vocal letter, and hence the He after every Tav which has Dagesh forte,* is entirely omitted in the Sulzbach edition.

groups, as בּוֹאֲכָה *as thou comest,* six times; יַכֶּכָּה *he shall smite thee,* three times.[76]

The final *Nun*, with *Kametz* at the end of a word, is the *Nun* of the plural feminine, which normally is followed by *He*, as חֲגֹרְנָה *gird ye,* סְפֹדְנָה *lament ye* [Jerem. xlix. 3], צְאֶנָה *go ye out,* וּרְאֶינָה *and see ye* [Song of Songs iii. 11], וַתָּבֹאנָה *and they came,* וַתִּדְלֶנָה *and they drew* [Exod. ii. 16], &c. There are some words which have *He* omitted; that is, they have final *Nun* with *Kametz,* as לֵכָן *go ye* [Ruth i. 12], וּמְצֶאןָ *and you may find* [Ruth i. 9]; and in the future tense, as תִּהְיֶיןָ *they shall be* [Deut. xxi. 15], תְּחַיֶּיןָ *ye shall let live* [Exod. i. 19], תַּהֲרֶיןָ *they shall become pregnant* [Gen. xix. 36], תִּגַּשְׁןָ *they shall approach* [Gen. xxxiii. 6], &c.

☞ This only occurs in irregular verbs, and there is but one instance of it to be found in the regular verb, viz.—תִּלְבַּשְׁןָ *they shall clothe* [2 Sam. xiii. 18], and the Massorites have marked them all "*He omitted*." The general rule is, that *Tav* and *Kaph*, with *Kametz* at the end of a word, generally want *He*. Hence the Massorites counted the instances in which *He* is *plene*, they being the fewest; whilst in the case of *Nun* with *Kametz* at the end of a word, the *He* being mostly *plene*, they counted the *defectives*.

The *He* suffix is of two kinds. The one is suffix third person feminine, and occurs in three different ways; (*a*), when it is quiescent after *Nun*, with *Kametz* and *Dagesh*, as תַּחְתֶּנָּה *in her place* [Gen. ii. 21]; (*b*), when it has *Kametz*, and is preceded by *Segol*, as וַיִּמְצָאֶהָ *and he*

כמו בואכה ו', יככה ג': [76]

והנה הנו"ן חקמוצה בסוף התיבה היא נו"ן הרבות שדינה לחיות אחריה ה"א, כמו ספודנָה, הגורנָה, צאנָה וראינָה, ותבאנָה ותדלנָה ותמלאנָה ויש שיבאו בחסרון הה"א, ר"ל בנו"ן פשוטה קמוצה, כמו בנותי לכָן, (רות א') ומצאןָ מנוחה; ובעתידים כמו כי תהיֶיןָ לאיש שתי נשים; ותחַיֶיןָ את הילדים, ותהַרֶיןָ שתי בנות לום, ותגשן, השפחות ודומיהן:

☞ וזה דווקא בפעלים שאינן שלמים, ולא נמצא רק אחד בשלמים, והוא כי כן תלבשן, בנות המלך, ועל כלן נמסר חסר ה"א: והכלל התי"ו וחכ"ף הקמוצה בסוף התיבה על הרוב חסרים הה"א לכך נמנין המלאים ה"א, והנו"ן הקמוצה בסוף התיבה, הה"א על הרוב כתובה לכך נמנין החסרים:

וה"א הכנוי היא ב' מינין, האחת היא כנוי הנקבה הפעולה הנסתרת, ובאה בג' אופנים; האחד כשהיא נחה אחר נו"ן קמוצה ורגושה, כמו ויסגור בשר תחתֶנָּה (בראשית ב'); והב' כשהיא נקודה בקמץ וסגול לפניה, כמו ויִמְצָאֶהָ מלאך י"י; והג' כשהיא במפיק אחר

---

[76] The twenty-one words, which have *He* at the end after *Kaph*, of the second person singular masculine, are as follows:—

ואברככה	.	Gen. xxvii 7	בכה	. .	2 Sam. xxii. 30	להלכה	. . . Ps. x. 8
ובכה	. .	Exod. vii. 29	ימצאכה	. .	1 Kings xviii. 12	חלכה	. . . Ps. x. 14
ידכה	. .	Exod. xiii. 16	יעצרכה	. .	1 Kings xviii. 44	כסכה	. . Ps. cxxxix. 5
כמכה	. .	Exod xv. 11	הנכה	. .	2 Kings vii. 2	בכה	. . Ps. cxli. 8
כמכה	. .	Exod. xv. 11	יענוכה	. .	Jerem. vii. 27	יברככה	. . Ps. cxix. 10
אתכה	. .	Numb. xxii. 33	בשמכה	. .	Jerem. xxix. 25	תנצרכה	. . Prov. ii. 11
עמכה	. .	1 Sam. i. 26	הראותכה	. .	Ezek. xl. 4	כחכה	. . Prov. xxiv. 10

They are enumerated in the Massorah marginalis on Exod. vii. 29; in the Massorah finalis under the letter *He*, p. 22 *a*, col. 2; and in the *Ochla Ve-Ochla*, section xcii., pp. 27, 94. The six instances in which בואכה occurs are, Gen. x. 19 (twice); 30; xiii. 10; xxv. 18; 1 Kings xviii. 46. They are given in the Massorah marginalis on Gen. x. 19. The three passages in which יככה occurs are, Isa. x. 24; Jerem. xl. 15; Ps. cxxi. 6.

found her [Gen. xvi. 7]; and (c), when it has *Mappik*, and is preceded by *Kametz*, as וַיִּסְפְּרָהּ *and he declared it*, הֱכִינָהּ *he searched it*, עֲנָתָהּ *he prepared it* [Job xxviii. 27]; כְּסוּתָהּ *her conjugal right*, שְׁאֵרָהּ *her raiment*, *her food* [Exod. xxi. 10]; and רֹאשָׁהּ *her head*, יָדָהּ *her hand*, רַגְלָהּ *her foot;* on all these, and the like, the Massorites do not make any remark. But on those words which have *Mappik* in one place, and are without *Mappik* in another place, they remark, "*no Mappik,*" as בִּזָּהּ *booty* [Ezek. xxix. 19], צֵידָהּ *provision* [Ps. cxxxii. 15], &c. So there are also eleven pairs terminating with *He*, which is once *Mappik* or audible, and once *not-Mappik* or quiescent; as מִכְרָה *sell me* [Gen. xxv. 21], "no parallel, being *Raphe*," whilst the other, מִכְרָהּ *sell me* [Prov. xxxi. 10], has *Mappik.*[77] There are also eleven words which end with a quiescent *He*, and ought to have an audible *He*; as וַתַּחְמְרָה *and they daubed it*, [Exod. ii. 3], הֻיְסָדָה *the foundation thereof* [Exod. ix. 18]; עֲוֺנָה *her sin* [Numb. xv. 31], &c., on each one of these the Massorites remark, "the *He* is not audible," or, "the *He* is feeble."[78]

The second class embraces the *He* which stands for *Vav* masculine, third person, and is preceded by *Cholem;* as בְּרֵעֹה *in its shouting* [Exod. xxxii. 17], שֻׂכֹּה *its hedge* [Lament. ii. 6,] &c. On these the

אות קמוצה, כמו או רָאָהּ וַיִּסְפְּרָהּ, הֱכִינָהּ וגם חֲקָרָהּ; ובשמות שְׁאֵרָהּ כְּסוּתָהּ וְעֹנָתָהּ, וכן ראשָׁהּ, יָדָהּ, רַגְלָהּ, על כל אלה ורומיהן לא נמסר מאומה; אבל על מלה שהיא במפיק וחברותיה בלי מפיק נמסר עליה לית מפיק, כגון ובוז בִּזָּהּ, צֵידָהּ ברך אברך ורומיהן; וכן י"א זוגין חד מפיק וחד לא מפיק, כגון מִכְרָה כיום לית רפה, ואחד במפיק מפנינים מִכְרָהּ וכו', וי"א מלין דלא מפקין ה"א וראויין במפיק כמו וַתַּחְמְרָה בחמר, מיום הֻיְסָדָה, עֲוֺנָה בה וכו', נמסר על כל אחת לא מפיק ה"א, או רפי ה"א: [78]

וְהַמִּין השני הוא הה"א הבאה במקום וי"ו כנוי הזכר הנסתר, ומה שלפניה בחולם, כגון קול העם בְּרֵעֹה, כי פָרֻעַ אהרן, כגן שֻׂכֹּה

---

[77] The eleven pairs, each one of which pair alternately occurs with an audible *He* [=*Mappik*], and with a quiescent *He* [=*Raphe*], are as follows:—

מכרה	. .	Prov. xxxi. 10	מעונה	. .	Deut. xxxiii. 27	לחילה	. .	Ps. xlviii. 14
מכרה	. .	Gen. xxv. 31	נצה	. .	Gen. xl. 14	בבכורה	. .	Isa. xxviii. 4
ושערה	. .	Levit. xiii. 20	נצה	. .	Isa. xviii. 5	בבכורה	. .	Hos. ix. 10
ושערה	. .	Levit. xiii. 4	ואתננה	. .	Isa. xxiii. 18	חכה	. .	Prov. v. 3
לרבעה	. .	Levit. xviii. 23	לאתננה	. .	Isa. xxiii. 17	חכה	. .	Job xxxii. 4
לרבעה	. .	Levit. xx. 16	רכבה	. .	Nahum ii. 14	ערכה	. .	Job xxviii. 13
מעונה	. .	Zeph. iii. 7	לרכבה	. .	Ezek. xxvii. 20	ערכה	. .	Job xxxiii. 5
			חילה	. .	Zech. ix. 4			

They are given in the Massorah finalis under the letter *He*, p. 21 *b*, col. 1, and in the *Ochla Ve-Ochla*, section xliv., pp. 14, 52.

[78] This must be a mistake, since the Massorah gives eighteen words which abnormally have at the end a quiescent *He*. They are as follows:—

ותחמרה	. .	Exod. ii. 3	בבאה	. .	1 Kings xiv. 12	המונה	. .	Ezek. xxxix. 16
הוסדה	. .	Exod. ix. 18	ורחמה	. .	Jerem. xvi. 17	למינה	. .	Ezek. xlvii. 10
עונה	. .	Numb. xv. 31	בה	. .	Ezek. xiv. 4	אנחתה	. .	Isa. xxi. 2
עתה	. .	Josh. xix. 13	כאמה	. .	Ezek. xvi. 44	מוסדה	. .	Isa. xxx. 32
חלבה	. .	Judg. i. 31	הלאתה	. .	Ezek. xxiv. 6	הראשה	. .	Zech. iv. 7
צרה	. .	1 Sam. xx. 20	כלא	. .	Ezek. xxxvi. 5	משכנתה	. .	Job xxxii. 22

Indeed Levita seems also to have mistaken the number of words contained in this rubric, in his annotations on Kimchi's Michlol (32 *b*, ed. Venice), where he says that there are fifteen such words. The list is given in the Massorah finalis under the letter *He*, p. 21 *b*, cols. 1 and 2, and *Ochla Ve-Ochla*, section xliii., pp. 14, 51.

Massorites simply remark, "this is the textual reading," or, "the textual reading is so;" *ex. gr.*, on אָהֳלֹה *his tent* [Gen. ix. 21], they remark, "four times so written;"[79] הֲמוֹנָה *his multitude*, "four times so written."[80] In some Codices, however, we find it remarked on אָהֳלֹה, "Read אָהֳלוֹ;" so also on בְּרֵעֹה, it is remarked "Read בְּרֵעוֹ;" and in a few more. But this is a clerical blunder, for we never find that a word which has in the text *He*, with *Cholem*, has in the marginal reading *Vav*. As to the list of fourteen words which have *He* in textual reading, and *Vav* in the marginal reading, to be found in the Massorah, this refers exclusively to *Vav* with *Shurek*; as יְקָרְחוּ *they shall make bold* [Levit. xxi. 5], where the *Keri* is יִקְרְחוּ; likewise שָׁפְכָה *they have shed* [Deut. xxi. 7], where the *Keri* is שָׁפְכוּ, &c[81] I shall again refer to these in the Second Part, Section i. By the help of Him, who is the last and the first, I have thus finished Part the First; and shall commence Part the Second, by the aid of that One who has no second.

ודומיהן, לא נמסר עליהן רק כן כתיב, או כתיב כן, כמו אָהֳלֹה ד׳ כתיבין כן,[79] הֲמוֹנָה ד׳ כתיבין כן;[80] ויש נוסחאות מצאתי שנמסר על וים אָהֳלֹה אֹהֳלוֹ קרי, וכן קול העם בְּרֵעֹה בְּרֵעוֹ קרי וכן בקצת האחרים, וכולם טעיותי סופרים, כי לא נמצא לעולם מלה דכתיב בסופה ה״א בחולם וקרי בו״ו, ומה שנמצא במסורת י״ד מלין דכתיבין ה״א וקריין וי״ו היינו דווקא וי״ו בשורק, כמו לא יְקָרְחָה קרחה;[81] הוּ קרי, ידינו לא שָׁפְכָה בו קרי ודומיהן, ועוד אדבר בם בלוחות שניות במאמר ראשון, בעזרת אל אחרון וראשון, ובכן נשלם החלק הראשון, ואתחיל החלק שני, בעזרת אחד ואין שני:

---

[79] The four instances in which אָהֳלֹה occurs are, Gen. ix. 21; xii. 8; xiii. 3; xxxv. 21. They are given in the Massorah marginalis on Gen. ix. 21. The Sulzbach edition has erroneously *seven*.

[80] The four passages in which המונה occurs are, Ezek. xxxi. 18; xxxii. 31, 32; xxxix. 11. The Massorah finalis, under the letter *He*, p. 24 *b*, col. 2, refers to Ezek. xxxix. for the enumeration of the passages, but they are not to be found in the Massorah marginalis on the chapter in question.

[81] The fourteen words with *He* at the end, which is read and considered as *Vav*, are as follows:—

יקרחה	. . Levit. xxi 5	נושבה	. . Jerem. xxii. 6	שפכה	. . Ps. lxxiii. 2
שפכה	. . Deut. xxi 7	היה	. . Jerem. l. 6	המורמה	. . Job xvi. 16
נשברה	. . 1 Kings xxii 49	יונה	. . Ezek. xxiii. 43	עדינה	. . Lament. iv. 17
עלה	. . 2 Kings xxiv 10	שממה	. . Ezek. xxxv. 12	שלה	. . Dan. iii. 29
נצתה	. . Jerem. ii 15	היה	. . Ezek. xxxvii. 22		

They are enumerated in the Massorah marginalis on 2 Kings xxiv. 10, and on Lament. iv. 17; and in the *Ochla Ve-Ochla*, section cxiii. pp. 31, 100.

SECOND PART.

Also containing Ten Sections.

THE TABLE OF CONTENTS OF EACH SECTION IS TO BE FOUND AT THE END OF THE BOOK.

SECTION I., concerning the *Keri* and *Kethiv*.—Having stated, at the beginning of Introduction iii., the differences of opinion which obtained among modern writers about the *Keri* and the *Kethiv*, and having given at the end thereof my own opinion respecting it (*vide supra* 106, &c.), I shall now disclose to you the method which the men of the Great Synagogue have therein pursued. First of all, however, you must know that what is written in the margin is the *Keri*, that is, it is thus to be read; and what is in the text, that is, the *Kethiv*, is not to be read at all. Thus, for example, the word הוֹצֵא *bring forth* [Gen. viii. 17], as it is in the *Kethiv*, with *Vav*, and for which *Keri* is הַיְצֵא, with *Jod*. Now, the Massorites put the vowel-points of הַיְצֵא under הוֹצֵא, and it is read הַיְצֵא, being the imperative *Hiphil* of the regular verb, according to the analogy of הַפְקֵד *appoint* [Numb. i. 50]; whilst the textual הוֹצֵא, without the vowels, is the imperative of פ״י, as הוֹצֵא [Levit. xxiv. 13]. The same is the case with הוֹשֵׁר [Ps. v. 9], where the *Keri* is הַיְשֵׁר *make straight*. Hence, the punctuators pointed the textual reading with the points of the word in margin, that is, the points of the text always belong to the *Keri* in the margin; whilst the *Kethiv* is without vowel-points. The same is the case with the accents, which they have always put under the words in the text, according to what it is in the marginal reading. Thus, in 1 Chron. xxii. 7, where the textual reading is בְּנוֹ *his son*, and the marginal reading בְּנִי *my son*, the *Athnach* according to the *Kethiv* ought to be under בְּנוֹ, but because the *Keri* is בְּנִי, the *Athnach* is put under לִשְׁלֹמֹה *to Solomon*. And this is easily understood.

הא לך לוחות שניות,
בעשרה מאמרים שנויות:

ולוח הסמנים של כל מאמר ומאמר,
המצא כאשר הספר נגמר:

המאמר הראשון בקריין וכתבן: הנה
כתבתי בראש חהקדמה השלישית המחלוקת
שבין האחרונים בעניני קריין וכתבן, ובאחרונה
עניתי חלקי אף אני ע״ש; ועתה באתי
להשכילך בינה בדרך אשר הלכו בה אנשי
כנסת הגדולה; וקודם כל דבר צריך שתדע
שכל מה שנכתב בגליון הוא הקרי, ר״ל כן
קורין המלה ההיא, ומה שנכתב מבפנים לא
נקרא כלל; והמשל הוֹצֵא אתך (בראשית
ח'), כך כתיב בוי״ו, והקרי הוא הַיְצֵא ביו״ד,
הנח שמו נקודות של הַיְצֵא תחת הוֹצֵא, אבל
אין קורין אותו רק הַיְצֵא, שהוא צווי מבנין
הפעיל על דרך השלמים על משקל הַפְקֵד את
הלוים, ונשאר בפנים הוֹצֵא בלי נקודות כדין
הצווי מנחי פ״א יו״ד, כמו הוֹצֵא את המקלל;
ובזה הדרך הוֹשֵׁר לפני דרכיך, הַיְשֵׁר קרי,
לכן מתקני הנקוד לא נקרו מלת הכתיב רק
עם נקודת מלת הקרי, דהיינו הנקודות שבפנים
שייכן תמיד תחת הקרי שבגליון, ונשארה
מלת הכתיב בלי נקודות; וכן שמו תמיד
טעם המלה תחת הכתיב לפי משמעות הקרי;
והמשל ויאמר דוד לשלמו בנו אני היה עם
לבבי וגו׳, כתיב בְּנוֹ וקרי בְּנִי, הנה לפי הכתיב
היה ראוי להיות האתנח תחת בנו, ולפי שהקרי
הוא בני שמו האתנח תחת לשלמה, וזה קל
להבין:

☞ It is to be noticed, that wherever the points are more than the letters, [the punctuators] had to put two sorts of points under one letter of the *Kethiv*. Thus, in Jerem. xlii. 6, where the *Kethiv* is אנו *we*, and the *Keri* אנחנו, they had to put two points, namely, *Sheva* and *Shurek* under the *Vav* in אֲנַוּ, to correspond to the points of אֲנַחְנוּ, whilst the word אנו in the text is left without points, and is read אָנוּ, which has no parallel in the Scriptures, except in the Prayer Book, where we find מָה אָנוּ *what are we*.[1] When, however, the word in the text has more letters than are required for the points [of the marginal reading], one letter of the *Kethiv* is left without any vowel-point, as in 2 Kings xix. 23, where, the text has בְּרֶכֶב *with the chariot*, and the marginal reading is בְּרֹב *with the multitude*, the *Kaph* is left without any vowel-point; also in 2 Sam. xxiii. 21, where the *Kethiv* is אשר *which*, and the *Keri* אִישׁ *man*, the *Shin* is without a vowel-point; and in Ezra v. 15, where the *Kethiv* is אלה *these*, and the *Keri* אֵל, the *Lamed* is left without a vowel-point.

When the textual reading has one word, and the marginal reading has two words, they put under the one word of the *Kethiv* all the points of the words in the *Keri*. Thus, in 2 Kings xviii. 27, where the *Kethiv* is שֵׁינֵיהֶם *their urine*, and the *Keri* מֵימֵי רַגְלֵיהֶם *the water of their feet*, the six points of the two words מֵימֵי רַגְלֵיהֶם are put under the one word שֵׁינֵיהֶם. But if, on the contrary, the textual reading has two words, and the marginal reading one word, the last unpointed letter of the first word in the *Kethiv* is omitted altogether in the *Keri*. Thus, in 1 Sam. xxiv. 9, where the textual reading is מִן הַמְּעָרָה *from the cavern*, and the marginal reading מֵהַמְּעָרָה; and Lament. i. 6, where the textual reading is מִן בַּת *from the daughter*, and the marginal מִבַּת; the *Nun* is altogether omitted in both cases. The same is the case with the eight words, which are respectively divided into two words in the textual reading, and which are undivided in the marginal read-

---

[1] The *Prayer Books* (סדורי התפלות), to which Levita refers, are the authorised Liturgies which the Jews use to the present day.

ing. These I have given in the sixth class, for I have thus divided all the *Keris* and the *Kethivs* of the Scriptures into classes, and distributed them under seven classes, corresponding to the seven kinds of fruit for which the land of Israel was famed.²

I.—The first class consists of words which are read from the margin, but not written in the text, and, *vice versa*, which are written in the text but not read. This principally affects the letters *Jod*, *He*, *Vav*, *Aleph*, which thus occur in the beginning, end, or middle of a word. It must, however, be remarked that *Vav* and *Jod* do not occur in this manner when they are quiescent in the middle of a word;

וחנם לפנך במין חשישי, כי בן חלקתי כל קריין וכתבן שבמקרא למינים, והעמדתים על שבעה מינים, זכר לחן שבעה המינים שנשתבחה בהן ארץ ישראל: ²

המין האחד באותיות דקריין ולא כתבן וכתבן ולא קריין, והעקר באותיות יהו״א הנמצאים כן בראש ובסוף ובאמצע חתיבה; אבל יש לך לדעת כי הוי״ו וחיו״ד לא נמצאו כן כשהן נחות באמצע חמלה, ר״ל הוי״ו אחר החולם והשורק, והיו״ד אחר החירק והצרי, כי אלה חם בגדר החסרים והמלאים כאשר בארתי בדבור הראשון; אבל הוי״ו חנמצאת כתיב ולא קרי, היא דוקא אחר קמץ או חטף קמץ, כמו אֶכְרוֹת לכם ברית, אֶשְׁקוֹטָה ואביטה ודומיהן, והן ל״א במספר;³ ולא נמצאת וי״ו קרי ולא כתיב באמצע המלה לעולם, אבל חיו״ד נמצאת קרי ולא כתיב אחר קמץ, כגון צַוָּארָי דעשו, צַוָּארָיו קרי, וכן זה דוד דוֹרְשָׁו שָׁיו

that is to say, *Vav* after the vowel-points *Cholem* and *Shurek*, and *Jod* after *Chirek* and *Tzere*, since such belong to the category of *defective* and *plene*, as I have explained in Part i., Section 1. But the *Vav*, which occurs in the *Kethiv* and not in *Keri*, is only after the vowel-points *Kametz* or *Chateph-Kametz*, as אֶכְרוֹת *I shall covenant*, (Josh. ix. 7), אֶשְׁקוֹטָה *I shall be at rest* (Isa. xviii. 4), &c. There are in all thirty-one such instances.³ *Vav* never occurs as *Keri* in the middle of a word, not being in the textual reading; but *Jod* is found in the *Keri*, and not in the *Kethiv*, after *Kametz*. Thus, for instance, Gen. xxxiii. 4, the *Kethiv* is צַוָּארוֹ *his neck*, and the *Keri* צַוָּארָיו; and in Ps. xxiv. 6, the *Kethiv* is דֹּרְשׁוֹ *his seeker*, and the *Keri* דֹּרְשָׁיו. There

---

² The seven chief productions of Palestine, mentioned in Deut. viii. 8, in praise of the land, are wheat, barley, grapes, figs, pomegranates, olives, and honey. From the fact that these seven kinds are specified in the Pentateuch, Jewish legislation, long before the time of Christ, restricted the offering of the first-fruits to these alone. Comp. *Mishna Bikurim*, i. 3; *Babylon Talmud Berachoth*, 35 *a*; Maimonides, *Jad Ha-Chezaka Hilchoth Bikurim*, ii; Kitto's *Cyclopædia of Biblical Literature*, *s. v.* First-Fruits.

³ The words in which *Vav* occurs after *Kametz* and *Chateph Kametz*, in the textual reading, and from which *Vav* is omitted in the marginal reading, are as follows:—

אֶכְרוֹת . . Joshua ix. 7	בקסים . . Ezek. xxi. 28	אשמור . . Ps. lxxxix. 29
לשאול . . 1 Sam. xxii. 15	במותי . . Deut. xxxii. 13	מלושני . . . Ps. ci. 5
ולשפוך . . 1 Sam. xxv. 31	במותי . . Ps. cxlviii. 4	לגאול . . . Ruth iv. 6
קסומי . . 1 Sam. xxviii. 8	במותי . . Micah i. 3	ואשקולה . . . Ezra viii. 25
אשקוטה . . Isa. xviii. 4	אכתוב . . Hos. viii. 12	אשרודיות . Nehem. xiii. 23
יעבור . . Isa. xxvi. 20	עבור . . Amos vii. 8	עמוניות . Nehem. xiii. 23
אצורך . . Jerem. i. 5	עבור . . Amos viii. 3	ורוהזגה . 1 Chron. vii. 34
לאכול . . Ezek. xliv. 3	וגדול . . Ps. cxlv. 8	תוקהה . 2 Chron. xxxiv. 22
וחובנים . . Ezek. xxvii. 15	וגדול . . Nahum i. 3	למעול . 2 Chron. xxxvi. 14
לכל . . Jerem. xxxiii. 8	לשאול . 1 Chron. xviii. 10	יקצור . . . Prov. xxii. 8
סגור . . Isa. xliv. 17	תדרוש . . . Ps. x. 15	יפול . . . Prov. xxii. 14

They are enumerated in the Massorah finalis, under the letter *Vav*, p. 28 *a*, col. 2.

are fifty-six such instances.⁴ There are also two instances where *Jod* is after *Cholem* in the textual reading, but not in the marginal reading, as רַגְלָיו *his feet* [Ps. cviii. 18], and עֵינָיו *his eyes* [Eccl. iv. 8]; but these belong to the list of six words which have *Jod* in the *Kethiv*, and not in the *Keri*.⁵ Moreover, *Jod* is also found after *Sheva*, as in דְּבָרֶיךָ *thy words*, which occurs eight times with a redundant *Jod*,⁶ מַעַלְלֵיכֶם *your works* [Zech. i. 4], &c. The *Vav* and *Jod* also frequently occur in the beginning and end of words in the marginal reading, and are not in the textual reading, and *vice versa*; and this is also frequently the case with *He*, which I abstain from illustrating by examples, for the sake of brevity.

קרי, והם נ"ו במספר⁴; וב' יודין דכתיבין ולא קריין אחד חולם, ענו בכבל רַגְלָי, נם עֵינָו לא תשבע, והן בכלל ו' דכתיבן יו"ד ולא קרי⁵; ונמצאים יודין אחר שוא, כנון ח' דכתיבין דְּבָרֶיךָ ית"ר יו"ד,⁶ וכן וּמַעַלְלֵיכֶם הרעים ורומיהן; נב נמצאים וי"ן ויוד"ין לרוב בראש התיבה ובסוף התיבה דקריין ולא כתבן או להפך; וכן ההי"ן לרוב, ולבחרי הקיצור לא אביא עליהן ראיות:

---

⁴ The fifty-six words which are in the textual reading without *Jod* (mostly indicating the plural) in the middle, but have *Jod* in the marginal reading, are as follows:—

צוארו	. .	Gen. xxxiii. 4	אלמנתו	. .	Jerem. xv. 8	גבורתו	. . . Job xxvi. 14
ועמודו	. .	Exod. xxvii. 11	ימו	. . .	Jerem. xvii. 11	בתחבולתו	. Job xxxvii. 12
ענו	. . .	Numb. xii. 3	מנרחו	. .	Ezek. xvii. 21	אפרוחו	. . Job xxxix. 30
בינו	. . .	Joshua viii. 11	פארתו	. .	Ezek. xxxi. 5	פחדו	. . . Job xl. 17
חוצאותו	. .	Joshua xvi. 3	עולתו	. .	Ezek. xl. 26	כנפו	. . Job xxxix. 26
מריבו	. .	1 Sam. ii. 9	חלונו	. .	Ezek. xl. 22	חלצו	. . . Job xxxi. 20
עלו	. . .	1 Sam. ii. 9	ותמורו	. .	Ezek. xl. 22	ילדו	. . Job xxxviii. 41
למשפחתו	. .	1 Sam. x. 21	בצאתו	. .	Ezek. xlvii. 11	ברגלו	. . . Prov. vi. 13
ואנשו	. .	1 Sam. xxiii. 5	פרו	. . .	Habak. iii. 14	בשפתו	. . Prov. xxvi. 24
בגדו	. . .	2 Sam. i. 11	שערו	. .	Obad. 11	ארחתו	. . Prov. xxii. 25
שמלתו	. .	2 Sam. xii. 20	דרשו	. .	Ps. xxiv. 6	אדנו	. . Prov. xxx. 10
רחמו	. .	2 Sam. xxiv. 14	חצו	. .	Ps. lviii. 8	מרגלותו	. . Ruth iii. 14
משרתו	. .	1 Kings x. 5	חסדו	. .	Ps. cvi. 45	כנורו	. . . Ezra iv. 7
ברכו	. .	1 Kings xviii. 42	דברו	. .	Ps. cxvii. 19	דמאו	. . Lament. iii. 39
בסוסו	. .	2 Kings v. 9	צבאו	. .	Ps. cxlviii. 2	ויתו	. . 1 Sam. xxi. 14
כפו	. . .	2 Kings iv. 34	חקו	. .	Job xiv. 5	הסכתו	. Song of Songs ii. 11
מזבחתו	. .	2 Kings xi. 18	בקדשו	. .	Job xv. 15	שלו	. . . Ps. cv. 40
צפו	. . .	Isa. lvi. 10	עלומו	. .	Job xx. 11	השלו	. . Numb. xi. 32
משלו	. .	Isa. lii. 5	ויודעו	. .	Job xxiv. 1		

They are enumerated in the Massorah finalis under the letter *Jod*, ב. 34 a, cols. 2 and 3; and in the *Ochla Ve-Ochla*, section cxxviii., pp. 33 and 104. It must be remarked, that this list only registers such words as occur once as *defective*, and therefore excludes many other words which likewise want the *Jod* plural, but which occur more than once.

⁵ The other four which in the textual reading are without the *Jod* plural, but have it in the marginal reading, and which, with the two adduced by Levita, constitute the list of six words, are, ובדמשאתי, 1 Kings xvi. 26; דבריו, Ps. cv. 28; Dan. ix. 12; and שפתיו, Prov. xvi. 27. They are given in the Massorah finalis under the letter *Jod*, p. 34 a, col. 3; and *Ochla Ve-Ochla*, section cxxix., pp. 34 and 105.

⁶ The eight passages in which the textual reading is דברך, with the plural *Jod*, and the marginal reading is without it, are, Judges xiii. 17; 1 Kings viii. 26; xviii. 36; xxii. 13; Jerem. xv. 16; Ps. cxix. 47, 161; Ezra x. 12. They are enumerated in the Massorah finalis under the letter *Daleth*, p. 19 b, col. 2; and *Ochla Ve-Ochla*, section cxxxi., pp. 34 and 105. To supplement our remark on the thirteen instances in which the reverse is the case with the word in question, that is, where the textual reading is דבריך without the plural *Jod*, and the marginal reading is דברך with the plural *Jod* (vide *supra*, p. 161, note 43), we must add that the list is given in the *Ochla Ve-Ochla*, section cxxx., pp. 34, 105, and that Ps. cxix. 17 has inadvertently been omitted.

I have, however, found this, that in all the words which have a letter in the *Keri* and not in the *Kethiv*, the points of the letter in question are put into the text without this letter, whilst the marginal reading has the letter without the point, as is usually the case. Thus, for instance, in Lam. v. 7, the text has אֵינָם֯ *are not*, אֲנַחְנוּ֯ *we*, and the Massoretic remark in the margin is, "Read וְאֵינָם *and are not*," "Read וַאֲנַחְנוּ *and we*." See also the similar instances, of which there are twelve in number.[7] The same method is pursued in the case of *He*. Thus, in 1 Sam. xiv. 32, the text has שָׁלָל֯ *booty*, and the margin has, אך֯ זה לבד מצאתי כי כל המלות שיש בהן אות דקרי ולא כתיב, נקודת אותו האות נקוד בפנים בלי אותה האות, ובקרי נכתב אותו האות בלתי נקוד כמנהג ; והמשל כמו אבותינו חמאו אֵינָם֯ אֲנַחְנוּ֯ עונותיהם סבלנו (איכה ח') נמכר בגליון ואינם קרי, ואנחנו קרי, וכן דומיהן, והם י"ב במספר[7] ; וכן עם חח"א ויעט העם אל שָׁלָל֯ השלל קרי, ודומיהן והן י"ג במספר[8] :

ובמלה שיש בה אות דכתיב ולא קרי, נכתב המלה בפנים עם אותו האות בלי נקוד, כגון מארץ כשדים יֵצְאוּ היו"ד כתיב ולא קרי, אך לא כתבו בגליון צאו קרי רק לא קרי יו"ד ; וכן בעל הכְּנָפַיִם (קהלת י׳) לא קרי ה"א ;[9] וכן באמצע המלה, כגון עם

"Read הַשָּׁלָל *the booty*." See also the similar instances, of which there are thirteen in number.[8]

When, on the contrary, the textual reading has a word with a letter which the marginal reading has not, the word is written in the text with the letter in question unpointed; as יֵצְאוּ *they shall go out* [Jerem. l. 8], which has *Jod* in the *Kethiv*, but not in the *Keri*. In such a case, however, the Massorites do not write in the margin, "Read צְאוּ," but simply remark, "*Jod* is not read." The same is the case with הכנפים *the wings* [Eccl. x. 23], where the marginal remark is, "*He* is not read;"[9] and when the *He* is in the middle of the

---

[7] The twelve words which have no *Vav* conjunctive in the textual reading, and have it in the marginal reading, are as follows:—

בניכי	. . .	2 Kings iv. 7	דור	. . .	Prov. xxvii. 24	אין	. . .	Lament. v. 3
תחת	. . .	Isa. lv. 13	די	. . .	Dan. ii. 43	נקנים	. . .	Lament. iv. 6
עד	. . .	Job ii. 7	לא	. . .	Lament. ii. 2	אינם	. . .	Lament. v. 7
יולד	. . .	Prov. xxiii. 24	לא	. . .	Lament. v. 5	אנחנו	. . .	Lament. v. 7

They are enumerated in the Massorah finalis under the letter *Vav*, p. 27 a, col. 4; and *Ochla Ve-Ochla*, section cxvii., pp. 32 and 101.

[8] The thirteen words which do not begin with *He* in the textual reading, but have *He* at the commencement in the marginal reading, are as follows:—

שלל	. . .	1 Sam. xiv. 32	מלך	. . .	1 Kings xv. 18	דבר	. . .	Jerem. xl. 3
גברים	. . .	2 Sam. xxiii. 9	מלך	. . .	2 Kings xi. 20	מלכים	. . .	Jerem. lii. 32
אחד	. . .	1 Kings iv. 8	מלך	. . .	2 Kings xv. 25	רשע	. . .	Ezek. xviii. 20
שבכה	. . .	1 Kings vii. 20	עם	. . .	Jerem. xvii. 19	עמים	. . .	Lament. i. 18
			ארץ	. . .	Jerem. x. 13			

They are given in the Massorah marginalis on 2 Sam. xxiii. 9; and *Ochla Ve-Ochla*, section clxv., pp. 37 and 112.

[9] There are seven such words, which, on the contrary, have in the *Kethiv He* at the beginning, but not in the *Keri*. Besides the one quoted in the text, the other six are as follows:—

הדחנית	. . .	1 Sam. xxvi. 22	המלא	. . .	2 Kings xiv. 7	הספרים	. . .	1 Kings xxi. 8
ההמון	. . .	2 Kings vii. 13	הסר	. . .	Isa. xxix. 11	הסחבות	. . .	Jerem. xxxviii. 11

They are enumerated in the Massorah finalis under the letter *He*, p. 22 a, col. 2; and *Ochla Ve-Ochla*, section clxvi. pp. 37, 113.

word, as שֶׁהֲתַקִּיף *who is stronger* [Eccl. vi. 10], where the marginal remark is, "*He* is not read."[10] The same, too, is the case in the forty-eight words which have *Aleph* in the middle of the word in the text, and not in the margin; on all of which it is remarked in the margin, "*Aleph* is not read ;" as הָאֲסַפְסוּף *the multitude* [Numb. xi. 4], &c.[11]

☞ Now the rule is, that whenever the letters *Jod*, *He*, *Vav*, and *Aleph* are in the marginal reading, and not written in the text, the Massorites write down the entire word of the *Keri* in the margin; but, on the contrary, when these letters are written in the textual reading, and are not to be read, they simply remark in the margin, "Read not the *Aleph*, *He*, *Jod*, or *Vav*." In one passage, however, both the remarks occur. Thus, Prov. xxiii. 23, where the textual reading is יֹלֵד *he that begetteth*, without *Vav*, and the marginal reading וְיוֹלֵד *and he that begetteth*, with *Vav*, the Massorites give the whole word, remarking, "Read וְיוֹלֵד ;" whilst on וְיִשְׂמַח *and he shall rejoice*, which has *Vav* in the textual reading, but not in the marginal reading, they simply remark, "Read not the *Vav*." Notice, however, that in correct Massorahs, whenever *Vav* and *Jod* occur in the middle of a word in the textual reading, and are not read, the margin has always the remark, "The *Vav* is superfluous," or, "The *Jod* is superfluous;" and this is the proper remark.

☞ As to the other letters, besides *Jod*, *He*, *Vav*, and *Aleph*, there are only a few which are found written in the textual reading, and are not to be read; or *vice versa*. Thus, for instance: i. *Lamed* occurs four times in the middle of words in the text, and is not read; as in וּלְהַלְחֶם *and to the bread* [2 Sam. xvi. 2], עָלְלִין, עָלְלַת *they were, she was, entering* [Dan. iv. 4; v. 8, 10]. In the last three instances the second *Lamed* is not read.[12] ii. *Tzaddi*, as in מְהַצֹּצְרִים *they were*

שֶׁהֲתַקִּיף ממנו כתיב בגליון לא קרי ה"א ;[10] וכן מ"ח מלין דכתיבן אל"ף באמצע התיבה ולא קרי, ועל כלן כתיב בגליון לא קרי אל"ף, כמו וְהָאֲסַפְסֻף אשר בקרבו ודומיהן ;[11]

☞ והכלל כל יהו"א דקריין ולא כתבן נכתב הקרי בחוץ בגליון, וכל דכתבן ולא קריין נכתב בגליון לא קרי יו"ד, או ה"א, או וי"ו, או אל"ף; ובפסוק אחד תמצא שניהם יֹלֵד חכם וְיִשְׂמַח בו (משלי כ"ג), הנה על יֹלֵד שהוי"ו קרי ולא כתיב נמסר וְיוֹלֵד קרי, ועל וְיִשְׂמַח שהוי"ו כתיב ולא קרי נמסר לא קרי וי"ו ; ודע כי במסודות המדויקות על וי"ו ויו"ד דכתיבין באמצע המלה ולא קריין, כתוב בגליון יתיר וי"ו, או יו"ד, ונכון הוא :

☞ ודע כי שאר אותיות שאינם אותיות יהו"א, נמצאים מעט מהן כתיבין ולא קריין וקריין ולא כתיבין, כגון ד' למדין כרתיבין באמצע המלה ולא קריין, כמו וּלְהַלְחֶם והקיץ, והשאר בדניאל באדין עָלְלִין, אדין עָלְלִין לבית משתיא, עָלְלַת, בשלשתן למד השנייה לא נקראת ;[12] וכן הצדי באחד לִמְהַצֹּצְרִים, מְהַצֹּצְרִים

---

[10] This is but one of five instances in which the textual reading has *He* in the middle of the word, and the marginal reading has not. The other four words are בהשדה, בהחפום, 2 Kings vii. 12; 2 Kings vii. 15; כשהסכל, Eccl. x. 3; שהשמם, Lament. v. 18. They are enumerated in the Massorah finalis under the letter *He*, p. 22 a, col. 3.

[11] For the forty-eight instances, see above, p. 171, note 62.

[12] The marginal reading is עָלִין, וְדָלְחֶם (twice), and עַלַּת. They are also given in the Massorah marginalis on Dan. iv. 4; v. 8; and in the *Ochla Ve-Ochla*, section clii. pp. 36, 110.

B B

blowing [2 Chron. xiii. 14, xxix. 28], where the second *Tzaddi* has no vowel-point, and is not read. iii. *Shin*, as יְשָׂשכָר *Issachar*, where the second *Shin* is not read according to Ben Asher's recension, whilst according to Ben Naphtali's it is pointed with *Sheva* as usual. iv. *Kaph*, which is found in the textual reading of בְּרֶכֶב *with the chariot* [2 Kings xxx. 23], whereas the *Keri* is בְּרֹב *with the multitude*, and, *vice versa*, is absent in מִמַּעֲרוֹת *from the caverns* [1 Sam. xvii. 23], in the textual reading, whilst the *Keri* is מִמַּעַרְכוֹת *from the armies*. v. *Ajin* occurs once in the textual reading, and not in the marginal, viz., Amos viii. 8, where the *Kethiv* is נִשְׁקָה *she shall drink*, and the *Keri* נִשְׂקְעָה *it shall rise up.* vi. *Daleth* is twice not in the textual reading, viz. 1 Kings ix. 18, where the *Kethiv* is תָּמָר *Tamor*, and the *Keri* תַּדְמֹר *Tadmor;* and Dan. ii. 9, where the *Kethiv* is *the Aphel* הַזְמִנְתּוּן *ye have agreed together*, and the *Keri* is *the Ithpael* הִזְדַּמִּנְתּוּן.[13] And vii. *Cheth* is four times not in the textual reading, viz. Jerem. ii. 16, where the *Kethiv* is תַּחְפְּנֵם *Tahpenes*, and the *Keri* is תַּחְפַּנְחֵס *Tehaphnehes*, and אָנוּ *we*, which occurs three times in the *Kethiv*, whilst the *Keri* has אֲנַחְנוּ, as stated above.

2.—The second class consists of letters which are interchanged in the *Keri* and the *Kethiv*. In this case, too, it principally takes place with the letters *Jod, He, Vav, Aleph*, as is seen: i. In the twenty-two words which are written in the text with *Jod* in the beginning of the word, and are read in the margin with *Vav;* as יֶחְדָּל *let him cease*, in the textual reading, and in the margin וַחֲדָל *and cease thou* [Job x. 20]; יָשִׁית *let him depart*, of the *Kethiv*, and וְשִׁית *and depart thou*, in the *Keri* [*ibid.*], &c.[14] ii. The ten instances in which the reverse is

[13] Comp. *Ochla Ve-Ochla*, section clxxxi., pp. 40, 117.

[14] The twenty-two words which begin with *Jod* in the text, and are read with *Vav* in the margin, are as follows:—

יבאו	. . . .	Judg. vi. 5	יחזה	.	Jerem. xxxviii. 2	יחדל	. . . Job. x. 20
יחנני	. . .	2 Sam. xii. 22	ישבי	.	Jerem. xlviii. 18	ישית	. . . Job. x. 20
יפצחו	. . .	Isa. xlix. 13	ילבשו	.	Ezek. xlii. 14	יבא	. . . Prov. xviii. 17
יאברו	. .	Jerem. vi. 21	ידיה	.	Ezek. xlv. 5	ישאל	. . . Prov. xx. 4
ישית	. .	Jerem. xiii. 16	יכשלו	.	Nahum iii. 3	ירום	. . . Dan. xi. 12
יסורי	. .	Jerem. xvii. 13	יצהר	.	1 Chron. iv. 7	ירמתה	. . . Ezra x. 29
יחזה	. . .	Jerem. xxi. 9	יחבה	.	1 Chron. vii. 34	יקפאון	. . . Zech. xiv. 6
			יאשר	. . .	Ps. xli. 3		

They are enumerated in the Massorah marginalis on Hosea i. 1; 1 Chron. i. 1: in the Massorah finalis under the letter *Jod*, p. 34a, col. 3: and in the *Ochla Ve-Ochla*, section cxxxiv., pp. 34, 106. All the editions of the *Massoreth Ha-Massoreth*, viz., Venice, 1538, Basel, 1539, and Sulzbach, 1771, erroneously state that there are fifty-two (כ״ב) such instances.

the case, as in the textual reading וְדָכָה *and he is crushed*, for which the *Keri* has יְדַכֶּה *he shall be crushed* [Ps. x. 10], &c.¹⁵ iii. The alphabetical list of words which have *Jod* in the middle of the word in the *Kethiv*, and *Vav* in the *Keri*. These are seventy in number, the *Jod* in all these instances being pointed with *Cholem* or *Shurek;* the *Cholem* is placed upon the letter preceding the *Jod*, as the *Kethiv* אַזְכִּיר *I shall cause to remember*, and the *Keri* אֶזְכּוֹר *I shall remember* [Ps. lxxvii. 12]; גֹּיִם *princes*, the *Kethiv*, and גּוֹיִם *nations*, the *Keri* [Gen. xxv. 23], &c.; whilst the *Shurek* is put into the *Jod*, as in the *Kethiv* וַיְישֶׂם *and he placed*, וַיּוּשַׂם *and there was placed*, in the *Keri* [Gen. xxiv. 33]. The pointing in some Codices of the first *Jod* in וַיְישֶׂם with *Kibbutz* is an egregious mistake, for there is no letter to be found with the point *Kibbutz* before quiescent *Jod;* the *Kethiv* is קְרִיאֵי *the called*, where the *Jod* has *Shurek*, and the *Keri* is קְרוּאֵי [Numb. i. 16], &c.¹⁶ The same is the case where the *Jod* is at the end of the word, as in the *Kethiv* תֵּצְאִי *thou shalt go out*, which is in the *Keri* תֵּצְאוּ *ye shall go out;* the *Kethiv* תֵּלְכִי *thou shalt go*, which is in the *Keri* תֵּלְכוּ *ye shall go* [Jerem. vi. 25]. In all these instances the *Shurek* is in the *Jod*, but no *Kibbutz* before it; and there is no *Kibbutz* before the *Jod*, viz., הַיֹּצְאֵי תֵּלְכִי.¹⁷ In the words, however, which have *He* at

בהפך וְדָכָה וְשׂוֹחַ יִדְכֶּה קרי, יָשׁוֹחַ קרי ;¹⁵
וכן אלפא ביתא דכתיבין יו"ד באמצע
תיבותא וקריין וי"ו, והן ע" במספר, וכל
היו"דין האלח נקודתן חולם או שורק החולם
נקוד על האות שלפני היו"ד, כמו אֶזְכִּיר
מעללי יה, אזכור קרי, שני גיים בבטנך גוים
קרי ודומיהן; אבל חשורק נקוד בתוך
היו"ד, כמו וייֶשֶׂם לפניו לאכול, וַיּוּשַׂם קרי;
ויש ספרים שנקוד בפנים וַיְשֶׂם היו"ד
הראשונה בקבוץ, והוא טעות גמורה, כי לא
נמצא אות נקודה בקבוץ לפני יו"ד נחה;
וכן קְרִיאֵי העדה היו"ד בשורק קְרוּאֵי קרי,¹⁶
וכן בסוף התיבה, כמו אל תֵּצְאִי השדה, ובדרך
תֵּלְכִי, תֵּצְאוּ קרי, תֵּלְכוּ קרי, בכולן חשורק
בתוך חיו"דין ולא בקבוץ לפניהם תֵּצְאֵי
תֵּלְכִי :¹⁷ אבל המלין דכת' ה"א בסוף וקריין

¹⁵ The ten instances in which the reverse is the case, that is which begin with *Vav* in the textual reading, and have *Jod* in the marginal reading, are as follows:—

ושפטדהו	. Ezek. xliv. 24	ודכה	. . . Ps. x. 10	וקר	. . . Prov. xvii. 27
ועשו	. Ezek. xlvi. 15	רצפן	. . . Prov. ii. 7	ועיף	. . . Prov. xxiii. 5
ושאג	. . . Isa. v. 29	וחכם	. . Prov. xiii. 20	ורב	. . 2 Chron. xxiv. 27
		ושרם	. . . Prov. xi. 3		

They are enumerated in the *Massorah marginalis* on Hosea i. 1; 1 Chron. i. 1; Prov. xi. 3; and in the *Ochla Ve-Ochla*, section cxxxv. pp. 34. 106. Here again all the three editions of the *Massoreth Ha-Massoreth* erroneously state that there are *fifty-six* (נ"ו) such instances. It will be seen that וְשׂוּחַ, given by Levita, is not among the number.

¹⁶ The alphabetical list of the words which have *Jod* in the middle in the textual reading, and *Vav* in the marginal reading, has already been given, vide supra, p. 118, note 71.

¹⁷ The two expressions תצאי and תלכי, belong to the following list of twenty-four words with *Jod* at the end in the textual reading, and *Vav* in the marginal reading.

דדי	. . 2 Sam. xxiii. 9	ועקי	. Jerem. xlviii. 20	ושפי	. . Job xxxiii. 21
ילדתני	. . Jerem. ii. 27	תשמחי	. . Jerem. l. 11	נפשי	. . Job xxxiii. 28
תצאי	. . Jerem. vi. 25	תעלזי	. . Jerem. l. 11	והיתי	. . Job xxxiii. 28
תלכי	. . Jerem. vi. 25	תפושי	. . Jerem. l. 11	כלהי	. . . Ezra x. 35
שאי	. . Jerem. xiii. 20	ותגדלי	. . Jerem. l. 11	נשאי	. . . Ezra x. 44
וראי	. . Jerem. xiii. 20	במי	. . Isa. xxv. 10	למלוכי	. Nehem. xii. 14
דברי	. . Jerem. xiii. 18	סבבני	. . Ps. xvii. 11	ידעי	. . 2 Chron. ix. 29
הילילי	. Jerem. xlviii. 20	ושבי	. . . Job. vi. 29	וישבי	. 2 Chron. xxxiv. 9

They are enumerated in the *Massorah marginalis* on Jerem. i. 1.; *Massorah finalis*

the end in the *Kethiv*, and in the *Keri Vav* with *Shurek*, the letter which precedes the *He* is always pointed with *Kibbutz*, as יִקְרְחָה *he shall make bald* [Levit. xxi. 5], שָׁפְכָה *she has shed* [Deut. xxi. 6], &c., of which there are fourteen in number.¹⁸ There are also many other words in which the letters *Jod*, *He*, *Vav*, and *Aleph* are interchanged, but I prefer brevity.

There are also other letters which have interchanged; but this interchange only takes place in the case of those letters which resemble each other in writing, as *Beth* with *Kaph*, *Daleth* with *Resh*, *He* with *Cheth*, *Cheth* with *Tav*, *Daleth* with final *Kaph*, and *Shin* with *Teth*; or of those letters which belong to some organ of speech, as *Beth* with *Mem*, *Mem* with *Pe*, *Aleph* with *Ajin*, *Ajin* with *Cheth*, *Daleth* with *Tav*.

As illustrative of all these, are to be adduced: i. The eleven words which are in the *Kethiv* with *Beth*, and in the *Keri* with *Kaph*, as the *Keri* בְּאָמְרָם *is their saying*, and the *Kethiv* כְּאָמְרָם *as their saying* [Esth. iii. 4], &c.; and the three instances in which the reverse is the case, *ex. gr.* the textual reading יָכִין *he shall prepare*, and the marginal reading יָבִין *he shall understand* [Prov. xx. 24], the *Kethiv* וְזָבּוּד *and Zabbud*, and the *Keri* וְזַכּוּר *and Zaccur* [Ezra viii. 14], &c.¹⁹ ii. The textual reading being *Beth* and *Daleth*, whilst the marginal is *Beth* and *Resh*, constitutes וְזָבוּד one of the two instances which are written with *Daleth* and read *Resh*, the other instances being אֶעֱבוֹד *I shall serve*, in the *Kethiv*, and אֶעֱבוֹר *I shall pass over*, in the *Keri* [Jerem.

וי"ו שרוקה, חמיד נקוד בקבוץ באות שלפני הה"א, כמו לא יִקְרְחָה, ידינו לא שָׁפְכָה ודומיהן, והן י"ד במספר; ¹⁸ ועוד יש הרבה אותיות יהו"א המתחלפים זו בזו ובחרתי בקצור:

☞ ויש שאר אותיות המתחלפות זו בזו, אבל אין זה רק באותיות הדומות במכתב, כנון בי"ת בכ"ף, דלי"ת ברי"ש, ה"א בחי"ת, חי"ת בתי"ו, דלי"ת בכ"ף פשוטה, ושי"ן בטי"ת; או שהם ממוצא אחד, כנון בי"ת במ"ם, מ"ם בפ"א, אל"ף בעי"ן, עי"י בחי"ת, דל"ת בתי"ו:

והמשל על כל אלו כנון י"א מלין דכתיבין בי"ת וקריין כ"ף, כנון ויהי בְּאָמְרָם אליו (אסתר ג') כאמרם קרי וכו', וג' להפך כנון מה יָצִין דרכי יכין קרי, ומבני בגוי עותא וְזָבּוּד, וזכור קרי; ¹⁹ כתיב בפנים בבי"ת ודל"ת וקרי וזכור בכ"ף ורי"ש, ובזה היא אחת מב' מלין דכתיבין דל"ת וקריין

under the letter *Jod*, p. 34 a, cols. 3 and 4; and in the *Ochla Ve-Ochla*, section cxxxvii., pp. 35, 107. It is to be added, that the words תֵּצֵא and תֵּלְכִי, after לפניהם, are omitted in the Sulzbach edition.

¹⁸ For the fourteen instances alluded to in the text, see p. 179, note 81.

¹⁹ The eleven words which have *Beth* in the textual reading, and *Kaph* in the marginal reading, are as follows:—

בשמעכם	. . Josh. vi. 5	בשמעו	. . 1 Sam. xi. 6	באמרם	. . Esther iii. 4
בעלות	. . Josh. iv. 18	בשמעך	. . 2 Sam. v. 23	וזבוד	. . Ezra viii. 14
בעלות	. . Judg. xix. 25	ויבו	. . 2 Kings iii. 24	זבי	. . Nehem. iii. 20
בחם	. . 1 Sam. xi. 9	יבלו	. . Job xxi. 13		

The third of the three instances in which the reverse is the case, that is, the textual words being with *Kaph*, and the marginal reading with *Beth*, is בכלי, 2 Sam. xii. 31. The first list is given in the Massorah marginalis on Hosea i. 1; 1 Chron. i. 1: in the Massorah finalis under the letter *Beth*, p. 15 a, col. 2: and in the *Ochla Ve-Ochla*, section cxlix., pp. 36, 109. The second list is given in the Massorah marginalis on 2 Sam. xii. 31; Hosea i. 1; 1 Chron. i. 1: in the Massorah finalis, under the letter *Beth*, p. 15 a, col. 2: and in the *Ochla Ve-Ochla*, section cl., pp. 36, 110.

ii. 20]; and the four instances in which the reverse is the case, as the *Kethiv* הַשְׂרֵמוֹת *the burned cities,* and the *Keri* הַשְּׂדֵמוֹת *the fields* [Jerem. xxxi. 40], &c.[20] iii. The one instance in which the textual reading is final *Kaph* and the marginal *Daleth*, viz., the *Kethiv* יָךְ and the *Keri* יָד *side* [1 Sam. iv. 13]. iv. The four cases in which the textual reading has *Cheth* and the marginal *He*, as the *Kethiv* רַחִיטֵנוּ *our bower,* and the *Keri* רַהִיטֵנוּ [Song of Songs i. 17], &c.[21] v. The instance in which the *Kethiv* has *Shin* and the *Keri* has *Teth*, viz., וַיַּעַשׂ *and he made,* which is read וַיַּעַט *and he flew* [1 Sam. xiv. 32]. vi. The one case in which the textual reading has *Cheth* and the marginal *Tav*, viz., the *Kethiv* יֵרָחֵק *it shall snap,* and the *Keri* יֵרָתֵק *it shall be bound* [Eccl. xii. 6]. vii. The six words having *Beth* in the textual reading and *Mem* in the marginal, as the *Kethiv* בָּאָדָם *is man,* and the *Keri* מֵאָדָם *from man* [Josh. iii. 16], &c.[22] viii. The one case where the text has *Pe* and the margin *Mem*, viz., the *Kethiv* פָּרָק *broth,* and the *Keri* מָרָק *broth* [Is. lxv. 4]. ix. Where the text has *Cheth* and the margin *Ajin*, viz., the *Kethiv* חֵץ *an arrow,* and the *Keri* עֵץ *wood* [1 Sam. xvii. 7]. x. Where the text has *Ajin* and the margin *Aleph*, viz., the two instances in which the *Kethiv* has twice עַל *upon,* and the *Keri* אֶל *to,* and the *Kethiv* once עַל, whilst the *Keri* is אַל [1 Sam. xx. 24; Is. lxv. 7 Ezek. ix. 5].[23] xi. Where the text has *He* and the margin *Ajin*, viz.,

[20] The two instances of words with *Daleth* at the end in the *Kethiv*, and with *Resh* in the *Keri*, are also given in the Massorah finalis under the letter *Daleth*, p. 19 b, col. 1; and *Ochla Ve-Ochla*, section cxxiii., pp. 33, 103. The other three words which are written in the text with *Resh*, and are read in the margin with *Daleth*, are עמידור, 2 Sam. xiii. 37; וארמים, 2 Kings xvi. 6; and גרל, Prov. xix. 19. They are given in the Massorah marginalis on Jerem. xxxi. 40; and in the *Ochla Ve-Ochla*, section cxxii., pp. 33, 102.

[21] The other three words which have *Cheth* in the textual reading, and *He* in the marginal reading, are, עמיחור, 2 Sam. xiii. 37; מבחלת, Prov. xx. 21; ולחתם, Dan. ix. 24. They are given in the Massorah marginalis on Prov. xx. 21; Song of Songs i. 16; and in the *Ochla Ve-Ochla*, section cxxi. pp. 33, 102.

[22] The other five words which have *Beth* in the textual reading, and *Mem* in the marginal reading, are, בעבר Josh. xxiv. 15; אבנה, 2 Kings v. 12; ביכרן, 2 Kings xii. 10; במלך, 2 Kings xxiii. 33; וישב, Dan. xi. 18. They are given in the Massorah finalis under the letter *Beth*, p. 15 a, col. 2; and in the *Ochla Ve-Ochla*, section cliv. pp. 36, 110.

[23] The two instances in which the textual reading is על, and the marginal reading אל, are, 1 Sam. xx. 24; Isa. lxv. 7; and the one instance in which the textual reading is עַל with *Pattach*, and the marginal reading אל, is in Ezek. ix. 5. The *editio princeps* of the *Massoreth Ha-Massoreth*, and the Basel and Sulzbach reprints read וא׳ כתיב על וקרינן אל, which is manifestly a blunder. We have therefore corrected the text. The instances in question are enumerated in the Massorah finalis under the letter *Aleph*, p. 6 b, col. 3; and in the *Ochla Ve-Ochla*, section clxvii. pp. 37, 113.

הָפָּרָה *Haupha* [2 Sam. xxi. 16, 18], upon which our Rabbis of blessed memory remark, the *Kethiv* is הָרְפָה, and the *Keri* עָרְפָּה *Orpha;* but I could not find it so in all the best Codices.[24] xii. The three instances where the text has *Daleth* and the margin *Tav*, viz., the *Kethiv* אַחַד *one* (masculine), and the *Keri* אַחַת *one* (feminine) [Is. lxvi. 17], &c.;[25] and the two in which the reverse is the case, viz., the *Kethiv* אַחַת (feminine), and the *Keri* אֶחָד (masculine) [2 Sam. xviii. 12; 1 Kings xix. 4]. xiii. The two instances in which the text has *He* and the marginal reading *Kaph*, viz., the *Kethiv* מַעֲלֵיהֶם *their works*, and the *Keri* מַעֲלֵיכֶם *your works* [Jerem. xxi. 13], and the *Kethiv* עֲלֵיהֶם *upon them*, whilst the *Keri* is עֲלֵיכֶם *upon you* [Jerem. xlix. 30].[26] xiv. The one instance where the text has *Resh* and the marginal reading *Beth*, viz., the *Kethiv* וָאֵשֶׁר *and where*, and the *Keri* וָאֵשֵׁב *and I sat* [Ezek. iii. 15], of which I shall speak again below, under the sixth class. And xv. The one instance in which the text has *Gimmel* and the marginal reading *Zajin*, viz., the *Kethiv* לִבְג *for food*, and the *Keri* לְבַז *for a spoil* [Ezek. xxv. 7], which is owing to the interchange of *Gimmel* and *Zajin* in the alphabet denominated *Atbach*.[27] This also accounts for the textual reading גֵּה *valley*, and the marginal reading זֶה *this* [Ezek. xlvii. 13].

---

[24] Levita must surely be mistaken, since the Rabbis do not say that the *Kethiv* is הרפה and the *Keri* ערפה, but simply try to identify the two words by way of *Midrash*, which is frequently the case. Comp. *Sota*, 42 *b*, and Rashi on 2 Sam. xxi. 18.

[25] The other two instances in which the textual reading has *Daleth*, and the marginal reading *Tav*, are 2 Sam. xxiii. 3, and Song of Songs iv. 2.

[26] The two instances in which the textual reading has הָם, suffix third person plural masculine, and the marginal reading כָם, suffix second person plural masculine, are also given in the Massorah finalis under the letter *He*, p. 22 *a*, col. 4, and in the *Ochla Ve-Ochla*, section cli., pp. 36, 110.

[27] In the alphabet denominated *Atbach* (אטבח), the commutation of the letters takes place according to the numerical value as represented by the respective pairs, which is effected in the following manner. The Hebrew alphabet is divided into three classes, consisting respectively of four pairs, or eight letters, and representing *ten, a hundred, and a thousand*. The first class, therefore, comprises the letters *Aleph, Beth, Gimmel, Daleth, Vav, Zajin, Cheth,* and *Teth;* the second class comprises *Jod, Kaph, Lamed, Mem, Samech, Ajin, Pe* and *Tzaddi;* whilst the third class contains *Final Mem, Final Nun, Final Pe, Final Tzaddi, Koph, Resh, Shin,* and *Tav.* When thus divided and paired, according to their numerical value, we obtain the following Table:—

1.— אט, בח, גז, דו, every pair making 10.
2.— יץ, כף, לע, מס, ,, ,, 100.
3.— קץ, רף, שן, תם, ,, ,, 1000.

As the letters *He, Nun,* and *Final Kaph* are, from their unpairable numerical value, necessarily excluded from being coupled with any other member of the alphabet, they

3.—The third class consists of transpositions, that is, of words wherein one letter is placed in the textual reading later than it ought to be, and in the marginal reading is put earlier, as it should be. There are sixty-two such instances, and not one of them occurs in the Pentateuch, for which reason I give the mnemonical sign for them, "No transpositions in the Law, minus one."[28] Fifty-one of these affect the letters *Jod, He, Vav,* and *Aleph*; as the *Kethiv* הוֹלֵךְ *going*, participle, and the *Keri* הָלוֹךְ *to go*, infinitive [Josh. vi. 13]; וַהֲמִישֵׁנִי [from ימש] *that I may feel* [Judg. xvi. 26]; and the *Keri* וַהֲמִישֵׁנִי [from מוש]; the *Kethiv* הָאֱהֶל *the tent* [1 Kings vii. 45], and the *Keri* הָאֵלֶּה *these*, &c.; whilst eleven affect the other letters, as the *Kethiv* וַתָּאֵרְנָה [from ראה] *and they saw*, and the *Keri* יָתָּאֹרְנָה [from אור] *and they became bright* [1 Sam. xiv. 27]; the *Kethiv* תִּרְצֶנָה [from רצה] *they shall delight*, and the *Keri* תִּצֹּרְנָה [from נצר] *they shall observe* [Prov. xxiii. 26]; the *Kethiv* יִבְחַר *he shall be exempt*, and the *Keri* יֵחָבֵר *he shall be joined* [Eccl. ix. 4], &c.[29] The same is the case with proper names, as the *Kethiv* שַׁמְלַי *Shamlai*, and the *Keri* שַׂלְמַי *Shalmai* [Ezra ii. 46]; the *Kethiv* שִׁטְרַי *Shitrai*, and the *Keri* שָׁרְטַי *Shirtai* [1 Chron. xxvii. 29], &c.; which obtained in consequence of each of these persons having two names.

are doubled when required, or they are coupled together among themselves, whereby they also yield 10, 100, and 1000, as follows: הה = 10, נג = 100, ךּ = 1000. Accordingly the commutation takes place between every pair, and the name *Atbach* (אט״בח), by which this anagramic alphabet is designated, is obtained from the first two specimen pairs of the letters which indicate the interchange. Through the application of this alphabet, Prov. xxix. 21 is rendered—"*He who satisfies his desire in this world, against him it will testify at the end;*" נוער being taken to denote *this world*, עבדו *his servant, his desire*, אחרית *the end, the last day;* whilst מנון, according to the alphabet in question, makes סהדה *witness*, the מ being exchanged with the ס, the נ with the ה, the ו with the ד, and נ again with the ה. Hence, also, we obtain לבנ from לבנ, the נ and ז being interchanged; and hence, too, גה from זה, to which Levita refers in the text. It must be remarked, that interpretation by the aid of this alphabet was resorted to from time immemorial, and that the exposition of Prov. xxix. 21 by its aid is already given in the Talmud. Comp. *Succa*, 52 b. For other anagramic alphabets, see Ginsburg, *the Kabbalah*, p. 54, &c., Longmans, 1865.

[28] To understand Levita's mnemonical sign, it is to be borne in mind that the numerical value of the word אין is sixty-one, viz., ן 50 + י 10 + א 1 = 61; that the expression *minus one* (חסר אחר), which is erroneously omitted in the Sulzbach edition, indicates that one is to be added, thus making the required number 62; and that there is also a play upon the words in the whole phrase, since it alludes to a well known hermeneutical rule denominated מוקדם ומאוחר, according to which whole sentences are transposed. Comp. Kitto's *Cyclopædia of Biblical Literature, s. v.* MIDRASH, Rules xxxi. a d xxxii.

[29] The list in question has already been given, *vide supra*, p. 116, note 67.

4.—The fourth class consists of words, the first of which took from the second, that is, of two words placed together, the first word of which took a letter from the second. This, however, only happens with the formative *He*, at the end of the first word, which belongs to the beginning of the next word. For this reason the punctuators pointed it in the textual reading with *Pattach*, whilst in the marginal reading it is made the article of the next word. There are three such instances in the textual reading, viz., the *Kethiv* הָיִיתָה מוֹצִיא *thou art leading out*, and the *Keri* הָיִיתָ הַמּוֹצִיא [2 Sam. v. 2]; the *Kethiv* יְדַעְתָּה שַׁחַר *thou showest down*, and the *Keri* יָדַעְתָּ הַשַּׁחַר [Job. xxxviii. 12]; and the *Kethiv* מִתַּחְתָּה לְשָׁכוֹת *from the chambers*, and the *Keri* מִתַּחַת הַלְּשָׁכוֹת [Ezek. xlii. 9].[30] There are two instances in which the reverse is the case, viz., שָׁם הַפְּלִשְׁתִּים *there the Philistines*, and the *Keri* שָׁמָה פְּלִשְׁתִּים [2 Sam. xxi. 12]; and the *Kethiv* שׁוּרֵי אֲשַׁכְּלִילוּ *they have finished the walls*, and the *Keri* שׁוּרַיָא שַׁכְלִילוּ [Ezra iv. 12].[31]

5.—The fifth class embraces entire words written in the text but not read, of which there are eight instances; as יִדְרֹךְ *he shall tread* [Jerem. li. 3], which is not read; נָא *now* [2 Kings v. 18], which is in the *Kethiv* but not in the *Keri*, &c.;[32] as well as words read from the margin which are not in the text. Of these there are ten in number, viz., אֵלַי *to me*, which is in the margin but not in the text [Ruth iii. 17]; פְּרָת *Euphrates*, found in the margin but not in the text [2 Sam. viii. 3], &c.[33] I have, however, already discussed this subject, in the third Introduction [*vide supra*, p. 109, note 51].

6.—The sixth class embraces expressions which are written in the text as one word, and read in the margin as two words. Of these

---

[30] The words ומתחתה לשכות הלשכות קרי, are omitted in the Sulzbach edition.

[31] These instances are also enumerated in the Massorah marginalis on 2 Sam. v. 2; Ezra iv. 12; and in the *Ochla Ve-Ochla*, sections ci. and cii, pp. 29, 97.

[32] The Sulzbach edition wrongly substitutes נא כתיב ולא קרי for נא לא קרי.

[33] Both lists will be found on p. 109, &c., note 51. All the three editions of the *Massoreth Ha-Massoreth* erroneously state that there are *ten* (י׳ר) words in the textual reading, which are not read in the marginal reading, and *eight* (ח׳) vice versa. We have corrected the text, since it is well known that the reverse is the case.

there are fifteen in number, as, the Kethiv בְּגַד in happiness, and the Keri בָּא גַד happiness is come [Gen. xxx. 11]; the Kethiv מַזֶּה what is it, and the Keri מַה זֶּה [Exod. iv. 2], &c. Also eight words in which the reverse is the case, being in the text two words, and in the margin one; as מִבִּין יָמִין, for which the margin has מִבִּנְיָמִין from Benjamin [1 Sam. ix. 1], the textual reading לָם רַבָּה to them shall be great, and the marginal reading לְמַרְבֵּה for the increase [Isa. ix. 6], &c.[84]

☞ Now I am greatly astonished at the traditional explanation of this word, saying that there is a final Mem in the middle of the word; since, according to the Kethiv, it is not in the middle of the word, as the Kethiv has two words לָם רַבָּה; and since לָם may be taken for לָהֶם to them, just as אֶרְאֶלָּם [Is. xxxiii. 7] stands for אֶרְאֶה לָהֶב I shall appear to them, and בְּשְׁלָם [1 Kings xxi. 21] stands for בָּשַׁל לָהֶם he boiled for them; so also לָם רַבָּה, as the Kethiv has it, is to be explained by לָהֶם רַבָּה to them is great.[85]

To this class, also, belong — i. Those words which are written in the text in one way, and for which the marginal reading has quite a different expression, as the Kethiv הָעִיר the city, for which the Keri is חָצֵר the court [2 Kings xx. 4], the Kethiv וַאֲשֶׁר and where, and the Keri וָאֵשֵׁב and I dwelled [Ezek. iii. 15], &c., which have already been mentioned under the second class, on the interchange of letters. ii. The Kethiv אֲשֶׁר who, for which the Keri is אִישׁ man [2 Sam. xxiii.

מַזֶּה בידך מַה זֶּה קרי וכו׳": וח׳ מלין להפך דכתיבין תרי וקריין חד, כמו ויהי איש מבין ימין מבנימין קרי, כי ענים ענים קרי, לָם רַבָּה המשרה למרבה קרי:[84]

☜ והנני מרמיה רמזהון גדול על הדרושות שנדרשו על המלה הזאת ואומרים כי המ״ם סתומה באמצע המלה, והרי לפי הכתיב אינה באמצע המלה, כי הכתיב הוא ב׳ מלות לָם רַבָּה, ונוכל לפרש לָם כמו לָהֶם כמו אֶרְאֶלָּם צעקו שהוא כמו אֶרְאֶה לָהֶם: וכן בְּשָׁלָם הבשר בשל להם הבשר, וגם לָם רַבָּה לפי הכתיב פי׳ לָהֶם רַבָּה המשרה:[85]

ובכלל המין הזה מלין דכתיב״ן מלה אחת וקריין מלה אחרת, כגון יצא העיר החיכונה חצר קרי, וכגון ואשר שם משמים ואשב קרי: וכבר זכרתי זה במין ב׳ עם חלוף האותיות, וכן הכה את המצדי אשר מראה איש קרי:

---

[84] The fifteen instances in which the textual reading has one word, and the marginal reading two, are as follows:—

בגד . . . Gen. xxx. 11	מהם . . Ezek. viii. 6	מנהסערה . Job xxxviii. 1
מזה . . . Exod. iv. 2	מלכם . . . Isa. iii. 15	מנסערה . . Job xl. 6
אשדח . . Deut. xxxiii. 2	הלכאים . . . Ps. x. 10	המפרוצים . Nehem. ii. 13
מאשדם . . Jerem vi. 29	ישימות . . . Ps. lv. 16	בנימן . . 1 Chron. ix. 4
והנבהו . . Jerem. xviii 3	לגאיונים . Ps. cxxiii. 4	לבנימיני . 1 Chron. xxvii. 12

The eight instances in which the reverse is the case, that is, the text having two words, and the margin one word, are as follows:—

כי טוב . . Judg. xvi. 25	לם רבה . . . Isa. ix. 6	כי ענים . . Lament. iv. 3
מבין ימין . . 1 Sam. ix. 1	מי אתי . . Isa. xliv. 24	בחר בתהם . 2 Chr. xxxiv. 6
מן המעיה . 1 Sam. xxiv. 9	מן בת . . . Lament. i. 6		

The first list is given in the Massorah marginalis on 1 Chron. xxvii. 12; Tractate Sopherim vii. 3; and in the Ochla Ve-Ochla, section xcix., pp. 29, 96, &c. The second list is given in the Massorah marginalis on 2 Chron. xxxiv. 6; Tractate Sopherim vii. 3; and in the Ochla Ve-Ochla, section c. pp. 29, 97.

[85] For the fanciful interpretations and mysterious meanings ascribed to this word, in consequence of its having a final Mem in the middle, see Kitto's Cyclopædia of Biblical Literature, s. v. KERI AND KETHIV.

21, with 1 Chron. xi. 23]. iii. The five groups of three words, each one of which is written in the text in one way, and is entirely different in the marginal reading. These I have already discussed, under the class of words the letters of which are more than the vowel-points. And iv. Those expressions which are written in the text as one word, and for which the marginal reading has two words entirely different to the textual reading, as the *Kethiv* כַּאֲשֶׁר *as that*, and the *Keri* כְּכֹל אֲשֶׁר *according to all that* [Ezek. ix. 11], the *Kethiv* שֵׁינֵיהֶם *their urine*, and the *Keri* מֵימֵי רַגְלֵיהֶם *the water of their feet* [2 Kings xviii. 27], &c. See above, at the beginning of this Section.

7.—The seventh class embraces cacophonic and euphemic expressions. Our Rabbins of blessed memory say, that all the words which are written in the Scriptures cacophonically must be read euphemically, as—i. The *Kethiv* יִשְׁגָּלֶנָּה *he shall ravish her*, and the *Keri* יִשְׁכָּבֶנָּה *he shall lie with her* [Deut. xxviii. 30]. For this cacophonous term מְשַׁגֵּל, which occurs four times in the textual reading, the *Keri* has always the euphemic word מִשְׁכַּב.[36] ii. חַרְאֵיהֶם *their dung*, and שֵׁינֵיהֶם *their urine*, for which, on account of their both being cacophonous terms, the *Keri* has the euphemic words, צוֹאָתָם *their excrement*, and מֵימֵי רַגְלֵיהֶם *the water of their feet*. And iii. עֳפָלִים, which is *a tumour near the pudenda*, denoting in German Feigblattern, and, being a cacophonous expression, is in the *Keri* טְחוֹרִים *the piles* [Deut. xxviii. 27];[87] *vide* ARUCH, *s. v.* טחר.

The rule which obtained is, that every cacophonous expression was changed for a euphemism, so that man might not utter anything indecent. And indeed there are some who maintain that Hebrew is for this reason called the holy language,[88] because it is all holy, and there is

וכן ה׳ זוגין מן ג׳ ג׳ מלים דכל חד כתיב מלה חד וקרי מלה אחרת, וככר כתבתי מהן לעיל בכלל חמלות שהכתב מרובה על הנקודה; וכן דכתיבין מלה חד וקרי ב׳ מלורת אחרות שאינן דומורת למלה הכתובה בפנים, כמו לאמור עשיחי כַּאֲשֶׁר צויתני, כְּכֹל אֲשֶׁר קרי, וכן שֵׁינֵיהֶם מֵימֵי רַגְלֵיהֶם קרי, עיין לעיל בהתחלת המאמר:

המין השביעי במגונה ונאות, אמרו רז"ל כל הדברים הכתובים במקרא לגנאי קורין אותן לשבח, כמו ואיש אחד יִשְׁגָּלֶנָּה יִשְׁכָּבֶנָּה קרי, וכן בד׳ מקומות כתיב לשון משגל שהוא לשון מגונה וקרי לשון משכב שהוא לשון נאות,[86] וכן לאכול את חַרְאֵיהֶם ולשתות את שֵׁינֵיהֶם לפי ששניהן דברים מגונים קריין צוֹאָתָם ומֵימֵי רַגְלֵיהֶם לשבח, וכן וּעֳפָלִים שהם התחתוניות בלשון אשכנן פייגבלאטרין שהוא לשון מגונה קרי טְחוֹרִים,[87] עיין בערוך בשורש טחר:

והכלל העולה כל מה שהוא בלשון גנאי שנו אותו לשבח כדי שלא יוציא האדם דבר מגונה מפיו; ויש מי שאומר שבשביל כך נקרא לשון העברית[88] לשון הקדש לפי שכלה

---

[86] The four instances in which the *Keri* substitutes the words in question are, Deut. xxviii. 30; Jerem. iii. 2; Isa. xiii. 16; Zech. xiv. 2. Comp. Massorah marginalis on Is. xiii. 16, and *Ochla Ve-Ochla*, section clxix., pp. 38, 114.

[87] There are six instances in which the alteration in question is made in the margin, *vide supra*, p. 109, note 49. The rule of the sages, to which Levita refers, and according to which the alterations in question have been made, is given in the Talmud, *Megilla*, 25 *b*. Comp. also Jacob b. Chajim's *Introduction to the Rabbinic Bible*, pp. 13, 25, ed. Ginsburg.

[88] The words לשון העברית, *the Hebrew language*, are omitted in the Sulzbach edition.

not any indecency in it, since it has neither names for the male and female generative organs, nor words for the discharge of the duties of nature, all these things being expressed by some euphemism, as I have already stated. Still, if this were the reason, it would be more appropriate to call it *the pure*, or *the decent language*, but not the holy language. R. Abraham de Balmes again remarks in his Grammar, entitled *The Possession of Abraham*, as follows: "It is called the holy language, because it was given by the Creator, blessed be his name, who is the Holiest of all holy." Thus far his remark.[39]

☞ However, I have already animadverted upon this question, among many other strictures which I made on his book, submitting that, according to his opinion, it ought more properly to be called *the language of the Holy One*, and not *the holy language*.[40] It seems, however, more appropriate to say that it is designated "the holy language," because the words of the Law, the Prophets, and all the holy statements were uttered therein, and because the Creator is therein called by His holy names, as *the Mighty One, the Almighty of Sabaoth*, &c., as well as His angels, *ex. gr. Michael, Gabriel*, &c., and the holy ones upon the earth, as *Abraham, Isaac, Jacob, Solomon*, &c., &c. On this account it is meet and proper to call it the holy language. Herewith the seven classes are ended, and the First Section is finished.

SECTION II., concerning *Kametz* and *Pattach*.—I have already stated, in Introduction III., that the Massorites only mention the vowel-points *Kametz* and *Pattach*, and that they include in them the minor *Kametz* and the minor *Pattach*, which are *Tzere* and *Segol*.

☞ You must, however, observe, that they have never ranged the major *Kametz* with the minor under the one number, or under the same

---

[39] For De Balmes, see above, pp. 10, 17, 21. The quotation is from section i., p. 3 a, of the Grammar.

[40] From Levita's remark, it would appear that he wrote animadversions on De Balmes' Grammar. We have, however, not been able to find any trace of this publication.

rubric. Thus, when they say that such and such a number have *Kametz*, you must know that these words are either all pointed with *Kametz* only, or with *Tzere* only; as, for instance, the alphabetical list of words, which they describe as having *Kametz* with the accent *Sakeph*; as, אֵדָע *I shall know* [1 Kings xviii. 12], בְּאָרֶז *with cedar* [Jerem. xxii. 14].⁴¹ All the words thus alphabetically enumerated are pointed with *Kametz*, and not one of them has *Tzere*. The same designation they give to the list of words which are pointed with *Tzere*; namely, the fifteen words with *Kametz*: as תְּעַנֶּה. *thou shalt afflict* [Exod. xxii. 22], הַזֵּה *sprinkle* [Numb. viii. 7], &c., all of which are pointed with *Tzere*, and not one of them with *Kametz*. The same rule obtains with *Pattach*. All the words thus described have *Pattach* only; as the six words with *Pattach*, viz., בַּמַּחֲזֶה *in the vision* [Gen. xv. 1], קָרְחָה *baldness* [Isa. iii. 24], &c.⁴² Hence you see that they made no distinction between *major* and *minor* in the naming of the vowels. Indeed, in the Massorah parva, they have not even called them by the names *Kametz* and *Pattach*, but the vowel-points are put under the letter which designates the number of instances wherein the word in question thus occurs; *ex. gr.*, the word בָּהֶן *in them*, " occurs fifteen times [ט"ו] with *Tzere* under *He*."⁴³ The same is the case with *Pattach*; as the word מַאֲכַל *eating*, " occurs

וחמשל כאשר אמרו כך וכך מלין קמצין,
תדע שאותן המלות כלן נקורות בקמץ לבד,
או בצדי לבד, כגון אלפא ביתא מן מלות
קמצין בזקף וסמנם אשר לא אֵדָע, וספון
בָּאָרֶז (ירמיה כ״ב) ; ⁴¹ וכן כל האלפא ביתא
כלן נקורות בקמץ ואין אחד מהם בצירי,
וכן אמרו על מלות הנקורורת בצירי כגון
ט״ו מלין קמצין, וסימנם אם ענה תְעַנֶּה אותו,
הַזֵּה עליחם מי חטאת וכו׳,⁴² כלן נקורות בצירי
ואין אחר מהן בקמץ ; והוא הדין בפתחין
אותן המלות כלן בפתח לבד, כגון ו׳ מלין
פתחין וסימנם בַּמַּחֲזֶה לאמור, מקשה קָרְחָה
וכו׳, הרי שבין גרול וקטן לא הבדילו
בקריאת שמותן ; ובמסרת קטנה אפילו בשם
קמצין ופתחין לא קראו להן, רק משימין
הנקודה תחת אות הסימן המורה על מספר
המלה ההיא, כמו בהן ט״ו,⁴³ וכן בפתח

---

⁴¹ The complete alphabetical list is given in the Massorah marginalis, on Levit. i. 1. We deviate from our general practice, and do not give this alphabetical list, both because it is extremely long, and because it does not contain any material changes in the text.

⁴² The Massorah gives twenty-five such instances; they are as follows:—

תענה	. . Exod. xxii. 22	ותקרא	. . Jerem. xxxii. 23	העלה	. . Habak. i. 15
מרבה	. . Levit. xi. 42	תאבה	. . Prov. i. 10	העברת	. . Josh. vii. 7
לסרבה	. . Isa. ix. 6	מלוה	. . Prov. iii. 17	יישר	. . Prov. iii. 6
מקרה	. . Deut. xxiii. 11	מחוסה	. . Isa. xxviii. 17	ילד	. . Prov. xxvii. 1
ונעשה	. . Josh. ix. 24	מרעה	. . Isa. xxxii. 14	כהן	. . Ezek. xviii. 14
הראה	. . 1 Kings xviii. 1	ומצוה	. . Isa. lv. 4	ועד	. . Jerem. xxix. 23
תהיה	. . Jerem xvii. 17	תראה	. . Dan. i. 13	חבל	. . Isa. lxvi. 7
מורה	. . Jerem. xxxi. 10	הזה	. . Numb. viii. 7	פתח	. . Ps. cxix. 130
		משה	. . Deut. xv. 2		

They are enumerated in the Massorah finalis, under the *Koph*, p. 56 *a*, col. 1.

⁴³ The fifteen instances in which בהן occurs with *Tzere* are as follows:—Gen. xix. 29; xxx. 26, 37; Exod. xxv. 29; xxxvii. 16; Levit. x. 1; Numb. x. 3; Deut. xxviii. 52; Jerem. iv. 29; li. 43 (twice); xlviii. 9; Isa. xxxviii. 16; Ezek. xlii. 14; 1 Sam. xxxi. 7. They are enumerated in the Massorah finalis, under the letter *He*, p. 24 *b*, col. 2. It is in the Massorah parva that the vowel-signs to which Levita refers are given.

four times with *Pattach* [רָ] under the *Kaph*,"[44] and with *Segol*, as הֵן *behold* "occurs five times [הֵ] with *Segol* under *He*."[45] Accordingly, by the vowel-point of the signal letter is to be known what the Massorah treats of; and this is easily understood.

☞ It is, however, to be remarked, that in the words with *Pattach of each Book* the Massorites have put together the *Segols* with the *Pattachs*. Let me now explain what is *Pattach of the Book*. It is known, from the laws of the vowel-points, that when *Athnach* and *Soph-pasuk* come under *Pattach* and *Segol*, they convert the latter into a long *Kametz*. Some instances, however, are left in each book of the Bible, which have not been thus converted, and these are denominated *Pattach of the Book = Pattach de Siphra*. They have been counted by the Massorah, and amount to nineteen in Genesis; as, וַיֹּאכַל *and he did eat* [Gen. iii. 6], וָמַשׁ *and Mash* [ibid. x. 23], וְכַלְנֵה *and Calneh* [ibid. x. 10], אֲבָרְכֵם *I shall bless them* [Gen. xlviii. 9]. Twelve of these have *Pattach* with *Athnach*, and seven with *Soph-pasuk*.[46] In all the other sacred books, too, they have counted those with *Athnach* separately, and those with *Soph-pasuk* separately, whilst the *Pattachs* and *Segols* they have mixed up together.

Section III., concerning *Dagesh, Raphe, Mappik,* and some of the laws of the *Sheva*.—It is well known that *Dagesh* is a point put in the

---

[44] The four passages in which מאכל occurs, with *Pattach* under the *Kaph*, are, Gen. xl. 17; 1 Kings x. 5; Job xxxiii. 20; 2 Chron. ix. 4. They are enumerated in the Massorah marginalis on Gen. xl. 17.

[45] The five passages in which הן occurs, with *Segol* under the *He*, are, Numb. xxiii. 9, 24; Job viii. 19; xxxiii. 12; xxxi. 35. They are enumerated in the Massorah marginalis on Numb. xxiii 9.

[46] The list of the words which have *Pattach* with *Athnach* and *Soph-pasuk*, is nowhere given in the Massorah. From the detached remarks in the Massorah parva, however, we gather the following twelve words, which have *Pattach* with *Athnach*:—

ותאכל	. . . Gen. iii. 6	ויגמל	. . . Gen. xxi. 8	נדר	. . . Gen. xxxi. 13
וכלנה	. . . Gen. x. 10	זקנתי	. . . Gen. xxvii. 2	אגשתי	. . . Gen. xxxiii. 8
ותהר	. . . Gen. xvi. 4	שבע	. . . Gen. xxviii. 10	במה	. . . Gen. xxxiv. 25
ויצחק	. . . Gen. xvii. 17	בת	. . . Gen. xxx. 21	עד	. . . Gen. xlix. 27

To these may be added הזמת (Gen. xxi. 15) and משמרכם (ibid. xlii. 19). As to the seven instances in which the words have *Pattach* with *Soph-pasuk*, we could not find any more than those adduced in the text. It must, however, be remarked, that there is a great difference of opinion upon several of the passages given in the list. Comp. the *Mebin Chidoth*, on Gen. xvii. 17. p. 10 b.

bosom of a letter, whilst *Raphe* is a straight line like a *Pattach* [—] put over the letter, especially over the aspirates *Beth, Gimmel, Daleth, Kaph, Pe,* and *Tav,* as I have explained in the *Poetical Dissertation.* The Massorites speak but very little about these, and, since they have already been explained, I need not speak any more about them. You are, however, to observe, that the Massorites also call the letters *Teth, Samech, Shin, Koph, Tzaddi, Nun, Vav, Zajin, Lamed, Jod,* and *Mem* feeble letters, because they ought to have *Dagesh,* but the *Dagesh* has been dropped for the sake of ease. Most of these occur in the *Piel,* where the characteristic *Dagesh* in the middle stem letter is omitted, as in the *Nun* in וַיְקַנְאוּ *and they envied* [Gen. xxxvii. 11], the *Koph* in וַיְבַקְשׁוּ *and they sought* [Josh. ii. 22], the *Lamed* in שָׁלְחוּ *they sent* [Ps. lxxiv. 7], &c.

But in the letters *Beth, Gimmel, Daleth, Kaph, Pe, Tav,* the *Dagesh* is only very rarely omitted, as in מִבְּצִיר *than the vintage* [Judg. viii. 2], מִגְּבוּרָתָם *from their strength* [Ezek. xxxii. 30], and a few more; and even in the letters *Teth, Samech, Shin, Koph, Tzaddi, Nun, Vav, Zajin, Lamed, Jod, Mem,* the *Dagesh,* as I have already said, is only dropped when one of them is pointed with *Sheva,* and especially in *Mem* with *Sheva* following the article, as הַמְדַבֵּר *who speaks* [Gen. xlv. 12], הַמְלַמֵּד *who teaches* [Ps. cxliv. 1], הַמִּסְכֵּן *who is impoverished* [Is. xl. 20], &c.; all these they call feeble letters, though they have not the straight line of *Raphe* over them. Now I submit that they ought to have the *Raphe* line placed over them, to show that the *Dagesh* is dropped, *ex. gr.* יְקַנְאוּ, יְבַקְשׁוּ, שָׁלְחוּ, הַמְדַבֵּר, הַמְשַׁלֵּחַ, lest the reader should think that the Scribe has inadvertently omitted the *Dagesh* and read it with *Dagesh.* I therefore expostulated with the printers of this district for not even putting *Raphe* on the aspirates, *Beth, Gimmel, Daleth, Kaph, Pe,* and *Tav,* because they said that they did not require it, since when they had no *Dagesh* it was known that they were feeble. But this is a mistake. In the case of well known words, as וַיִּשְׂאוּ *and they lifted up*, וַיִּסְעוּ *and they journeyed*, וַיִּקְחוּ *and they took*, וַיְהַלְלוּ *and they praised*, הַלְלוּיָהּ *praise ye the Lord*, &c., &c., from all of which *Dagesh* has been dropped, there is no necessity for placing the *Raphe* line over them, because they are the majority. The Massorites, also, call every *He* feeble which ought to have *Mappik* but has it not, as טָהֳרָהּ *her purity* [Levit. xii.-5], כְּאִמָּהּ *like her mother* [Ezek. xvi. 44], &c. But I have already discussed this point in Part i., Sections ix. and x., on *Mappik Aleph* and *Mappik Jod*, where I have explained which is *Mappik Aleph* and which is not.

As to *Mappik He*, it is a point in the bosom of the *He*, like *Dagesh* at the end of a word. The Germans used this point, as רַגְלָהּ *her foot*, יָדָהּ *her hand*, &c.; they would not put the point under the *He*, because they thought that it might mislead, lest the reader should read it *Chirek*. This, however, is not to be regarded, since there does not occur a point in the last letter of the word, as I have explained in Part i., Section v.

☞ It is moreover known, from the laws of grammar, that the prepositional letters, *Kaph*, *Lamed*, and *Beth*, are pointed according to rule with *Sheva*, except when it cannot be, as I have explained in the Section on the *Serviles*.[47] Now the Massorites call this *Sheva*, *Raphe*, because it can never be followed by *Dagesh*. Thus, they remark בְּבַיִת *in the house*, "occurs six times *Raphe*;"[48] בְּכֶסֶף *for money*, "occurs fifteen times *Raphe*;"[49] לְכִסֵּא *to a throne*, "occurs six times *Raphe*."[50] They are also called *Raphe* when they are not followed by the aspirates

כמו וַיִּשְׂאוּ, וַיִּסְעוּ, וַיִּקְחוּ, וַיְהַלְלוּ, הַלְלוּיָהּ, בכלן חסר הדגש, ואין צורך לשים עליהם הרפי מפני רבויים: וגם קראו ה"א רפויה כל ה"א שדינה במפיק ואינו, כמו ימי טָהֳרָהּ (ויקרא י"ב), כְּאִמָּהּ בתה ודומיהן; וכבר דברתי בם בלוחות הראשונים בדבור ט' וי', בכלל מפיק אל"ף ומפיק יו"ד, ובארתי שם איזה הוא מפיק אל"ף או לאו:

וְהִנֵּה המפיק ה"א היא נקודה בגוף הה"א, כמו דגש בסוף המלה, כן נוהגין מנקרים אשכנזים, כמו יָדָהּ רַגְלָהּ ודומיהן, ואינם משימים הנקודה תחת הה"א באמרם דאיכא למיחש, שמא יקרא הקורא חירק, אבל אין לחוש על זה כי לא נמצא נקודה באות האחרון של התיבה, כמו שבארתי בלוחות הראשונים בדבור ה':

☞ וְהִנֵּה ידוע מדרך הדקדוק כי אותיות כל"ב המשמשים בראש התיבה, דינם להנקד בשוא לולי המבטלים, כאשר בארתי בפרק השמושים;[47] ובעלי המסורת קראו לשוא כזה רפי, וזה לפי שלא יתכן אחריו דגש לעולם, כמו בְּבַיִת ו' רפין,[48] בְּכֶסֶף ט"ו רפין,[49] לְכִסֵּא ו' רפין;[50] וכן שלא על בג"ד כפ"ת כמו בְּלַיְלָה ג'

---

[47] The section is the last of the four dissertations composing the *Poetical Dissertation*, and the rule here referred to is on p. 63, ed. Prague, 1793.

[48] The six instances in which בבית occurs *Raphe* are, Exod. xii. 46: 1 Kings iii. 17: 2 Sam. vii. 6: 1 Chron. xvii. 5: Isa. v. 8: Amos vi. 9. They are enumerated in the Massorah marginalis on 1 Kings iii. 17.

[49] The fifteen passages in which בכסף is *Raphe* are, Gen. xxiii. 9: Josh. xxii. 8: 2 Sam. xxiv. 24, with 1 Chron. xxi. 22, 24: 1 Kings xxi. 6, 15: Isa. xlviii. 10; lii. 3: Jerem. x. 4: Ezek. xxvi. 12: Micah iii. 11: Ps. cv. 37: Lament. v. 4: Ezra i. 4: Dan. xi. 38. They are given in the Massorah marginalis on Josh. xxii. 8.

[50] The six instances in which לכסא is *Raphe* are, Isa. xxii. 23: Jerem. lii. 32: Ps. ix. 5; cxxxii. 11, 12: Nehem. iii. 7. They are given in the Massorah marginalis on Isa. xxii. 23: Nehem. iii. 7.

Beth, Gimmel, Daleth, Kaph, Pe, and Tav; as בְּלַיְלָה, *in the night*, occurs three times *Raphe*;[51] and בְּחֶרֶב *with the sword*, occurs eight times *Raphe*;[52] or when they are pointed with *Chirek*, on account of the *Sheva* by which they are followed; as בִּבְהֵמָה *in cattle*, which is four times *Raphe*;[53] and בְּשָׂדַי *in the field*, five times *Raphe*,[54] &c. It is further known that the prepositional letters *Kaph, Lamed, Beth*, which are pointed with *Pattach*, indicating the contracted article

רפין[51] בְּחֶרֶב ח' רפין: [52] וכן כשהן נקודים בחירק בסיבת השוא הבא אחריהם, כמו בִּבְהֵמָה ד' רפין,[53] בְּשָׂדַי ח' רפין[54] ודומיהן; וידוע ג"כ כי אותיות כל"ב הפתוחים המורים על ה"א הידיעה, תמיד דגש אחריהם, לפיכך קראו לחיבות הפתחין האלה דגושין, כמו בַּכֹּל ז' דגושין,[55] לַטּוֹב ב' דגושין;[56] וכן כשהן קמוצים בעבור אח"עה מנו אותם, כמו לָאָדָם י"א קמוצים,[57] לָאִישׁ ל"ב קמוצים: [58]

והכלל כי תמיד מוני המועטים אם דגושים אם רפין, וכששניהם מועטים חם מונין את שניהן, כמו בְּטוֹב, ד' רפין, בַּטּוֹב

He, are always followed by *Dagesh*. The Massorites, therefore, call those letters *Dageshed*, which have such a *Pattach*; hence they remark on בַּכֹּל *in all*, "seven times *Dageshed*,"[55] and לַטּוֹב *to good*, "twice *Dageshed*."[56] They also counted them when they are pointed with *Kametz*, because of being followed by the gutturals *Aleph, Cheth, Ajin*, and *He*, as " לָאָדָם *to the man*, eleven times with *Kametz*;"[57] "לָאִישׁ *to the man*, thirty-two times with *Kametz*."[58]

Now the rule is, that they always counted those which are fewer in number, whether with *Dagesh* or *Raphe*, and when both happened to be few, they counted both; as בְּטוֹב *in good*; on which they remark,

---

[51] The three passages in which בלילה occurs *Raphe* are, Gen. xl. 5; xli. 11: Nehem. ix. 19. They are enumerated in the Massorah marginalis on Gen. xl. 5.

[52] The eight passages in which בחרב is *Raphe* are, 1 Sam. xvii. 45, 47: 2 Sam. xii. 9: Isa. xxxi. 8: Jerem. xx. 4: Ezek. xxviii. 23: Hag. ii. 22: Dan. xi. 33. They are enumerated in the Massorah marginalis on 1 Sam. xxii. 45.

[53] As בבהמה only occurs four times *Raphe*, viz., Levit. vii. 21; xx. 15; -xxvii. 10, 26— we have corrected the text, which in the three editions states that the word in question is *six* (ו') times *Raphe*. Comp. Massorah marginalis on Levit. vii. 21.

[54] The five passages in which בשדה is *Raphe* are, Numb. xx. 17; xxi. 22: Isa. v. 8: Ruth ii. 8. 22. Comp. the Massorah marginalis on Numb. xx. 17.

[55] The seven passages in which בכל occurs with *Dagesh* in the *Kaph* are, Gen. xvi. 12; xxiv. 1: 2 Sam. xxiii. 5: Ps. ciii. 19: Eccles. v. 8: Ezra x. 17: 1 Chron. xxix. 12. They are given in the Massorah finalis under the letter *Kaph*, p. 39, col. 4.

[56] The two instances in which לטוב is *Raphe*, *i. e. Pattach* under the *Lamed*, are, Numb. xxxvi. 6, and Eccles. ix. 2. They are given in the Massorah marginalis on Numb. xxxvi. 6.

[57] The eleven places in which לאדם has *Kametz* under the *Lamed* are, Exod. iv. 11 : Jerem. x. 23: Zeph. i. 17: Prov. xxvii. 19: Job xxviii. 28: Eccles. i. 2; ii. 18, 22; vi. 12 (twice); viii. 15. Both the Massorah marginalis on Jerem. x. 23, and the *Ochla Ve-Ochla*, section xv., pp. 62, 175, describe this rubric as follows :—"לאדם occurs five times with *Kametz* under the *Lamed*; it is likewise so throughout Ecclesiastes, except in one place where the *Lamed* has *Sheva*, viz., ii. 26."

[58] The thirty-two passages in which לאיש occurs with *Kametz* under the *Lamed* are, Gen. xliii. 6, 11 ; xlv. 22 : Levit. xvii. 4 ; xxv. 27 ; Numb. v. 8 : Deut. xxii. 16 ; xxv. 9 : Judg. xvi. 19 : 1 Sam. ii. 15; ix. 7; xvii. 26, 27; xxvi. 23: 2 Sam. xii. 4; xviii. 11: 1 Kings viii. 39, with 2 Chron. vi. 30 : Jerem. xxvi. 11, 16 : 2 Kings xxii. 15, with 2 Chron. xxxiv. 23: Malachi ii. 12: Prov. xv. 23: xx. 3, 17; xxiv. 29: Job ii. 4: Ruth iii. 3 : Esther vi. 9, 11. They are enumerated in the Massorah finalis under the letter *Aleph*, p. 6 a, cols. 2 and 3.

"four times *Raphe*," [59] בְּטוֹב "nine times *Dageshed*;" כְּנֶשֶׁר like an eagle, "four times *Raphe*," כַּנֶּשֶׁר "seven times *Dageshed*.[60] When they happen to be pairs, that is, two with *Raphe* and two with *Dagesh*, they call them *Milel* and *Milra*, as I shall explain in the following Section; and when both are equally numerous, as בְּדֶרֶךְ בַּדֶּרֶךְ in the way, בְּמִדְבָּר בַּמִּדְבָּר in the desert, בְּעִיר בָּעִיר in the city, they neither counted the *Raphes* nor the *Dageshes*, because they are very numerous. The exclamatory, or interrogative *He*, too, which is pointed with *Chateph-pattach*, is called *Raphe*; as הֲשֹׁמֵר the keeper? [Gen. iv. 9], is marked "not extant, *Raphe*;" הֲשֹׁפֵט the judge? [Gen. xviii. 25], is "not extant, *Raphe*"; but when it has *Pattach*, on account of being followed by the gutturals *Aleph*, *Cheth*, *He*, and *Ajin*, they do not call it *Raphe*, but *Pattached*; as הָאִישׁ a man? [Neh. vi. 11], is "not extant with *Pattach*;" הֶעָבֶד a servant? [Jerem. ii. 14], is "not extant with *Pattach*," &c.

It is also to be remarked that the Massorites likewise call *Raphe* the *Vav* conjunctive which precedes the letters *Aleph*, *Jod*, *Tav*, and *Nun*; as וְאֶשָּׂא and I shall bear, is marked "twice *Raphe*;"[61] וְיֹאמַר and he shall say, "six times *Raphe*;"[62] וְתִשְׁמַע and hear thou, "five times *Raphe*."[63] The same is the case when it is pointed with *Chirek*, because of the *Jod*, belonging to the preformatives *Aleph*, *Jod*, *Tav*, and *Nun* of the future, whereby it is followed, as I have explained in

---

[59] The four instances in which בְּטוֹב is *Raphe* are, Levit. xxvii. 10: Ps. xxv. 13: Eccl. ii. 1; vii. 14: and the nine passages in which it is בַּטוֹב with *Dagesh* in the *Teth* are, Gen. xx. 15: Deut. xxii. 17: Isa. vii. 15, 16: Jerem. xxix. 32: Ps. ciii. 5: Job xxi. 13; xxxvi. 11: 2 Chron. vi. 41. The former are enumerated in the Massorah marginalis on Levit. xxvii. 10; and the latter, in the Massorah marginalis on Isa. vii. 15, and Job xxi. 13.

[60] The four passages in which כנשר is *Raphe*, that is has *Sheva* under the *Kaph*, are Deut. xxxii. 11; Habak. i. 8; Prov. xxiii. 5; Job. ix. 26; and the seven passages in which the *Kaph* has *Pattach* are, Jerem. xlviii. 40; xlix. 16, 22: Hos. viii. 1; Obad. 4: Micah i. 16; Ps. ciii. 5. For the former, see the Massorah marginalis on Deut. xxxii. 11. The list of the latter we could not find any where in the Massorah.

[61] The two instances in which the *Vav* ואשא, Kal future, first person singular masculine of נשא, has *Sheva* are, Ps. lv. 13; cxix. 48.

[62] The six instances in which the *Vav* conjunctive is ויאמר Kal future, third person singular masculine, has *Sheva* are, 2 Kings ix. 17: Isa. xliv. 16, 17; lviii. 9: Habak. ii. 6: Ps. lviii. 12.

[63] This must surely be a mistake, since ותשמע o ly occurs twice with *Sheva* under the *Vav* conjunctive, viz., Deut. xxxii. 1: 2 Chron. xx. 9.

the Section on the Servile Letters, ex. gr. וַיִּשְׁלַח *and he will send*, on which they remarked, "fifteen times *Raphe*;"[64] וִיהִי *and it shall be*, "thirty-two times *Raphe*."[65] Or when the said *Vav* is pointed with *Shurek*, on account of *Tav* and *Nun* with *Sheva*, belonging to the pre-formative letters *Aleph, Jod, Tav*, and *Nun*, whereby it is followed, as וּתְדַבֵּר *and thou shalt speak*, which is marked "twice *Raphe*" [Is. xl. 27]; [66] וּנְסַפְּרָה *and we shall declare* [Jerem. li. 10], "not extant, *Raphe*," &c.[67]

☞ The rule is, that whenever *Vav* preceding the future is pointed with *Sheva, Chirek*, or *Shurek*, they call it *Raphe*, except when it occurs in pairs, one of which has *Sheva* and the other *Pattach*. In such a case they call it *Milel* and *Milra*, as I have stated above. Mark that they always counted the instances in which it is *Raphe*, because they are the fewer, since in most cases in which *Vav* precedes the letters *Aleph, Jod, Tav*, and *Nun* it is conversive, and has *Pattach*, followed by *Dagesh*. This *Vav* conversive they did not count, because it is the most frequent; but when it has *Kametz*, because of the guttural *Aleph* belonging to the preformatives, *Aleph, Jod, Tav*, and *Nun*, they generally counted it, as וָאָשִׂים *and I shall put*, on which they remark "nine times;"[68] וָאֵדַע *and I shall know*, "three times."[69] Notice, also, that there is a kind of *Sheva*, which they call *Dagesh*, namely, *Sheva* quiescent under the gutturals *Aleph, Cheth, He*, and *Ajin*, as in יַחְפֹּץ *he shall covet*, יַחְמֹד *he shall desire*, &c., whilst they call *Raphe*, the *Chateph-pattach* and *Chateph-segol*, because *Dagesh* never follows them. I have already stated in "*the Poetical Dissertation*," poem viii., that in five instances the *Sheva* is called mobile, and not quiescent.

---

[64] Neither can we understand this remark, since וַיִּשְׁלַח only occurs once, viz., Exod. vi. 11.

[65] The thirty-two instances in which ויהי occurs with *Chirek* under *Vav* conjunctive have already been given. *Vide supra*, p. 141, note 122.

[66] The two passages in which ותדבר occurs with *Shurek* are, Isa. xl. 27: Ezek. xxiv. 27.

[67] The single instance in which ונספרה occurs, is Jerem. li. 10.

[68] The nine instances in which ואשים occurs with *Kametz* under the *Vav* are, Gen. xxiv. 47: Deut. x. 5: 1 Sam. xxviii. 21: 1 Kings viii. 21: Isa. li. 16: Jerem. xiii. 2: Malachi i. 3: Job xxxviii. 10: 2 Chron. vi. 11.

[69] The three passages in which ואדע occurs are, Isa. l. 7: Jerem. xxxii. 8: Ezek. x. 10.

☞ Let me now give you the letters *Aleph, Beth, Gimmel, Daleth*, and *He* as a new and appropriate mnemonical sign for it. *Aleph* [= first] means that whenever *Sheva* is under the first letter of a word, it is vocal, as שְׁמַע בְּנִי *hear my son* [Prov. i. 8]; *Beth* [= two] means that when two *Shevas* occur in the middle of a word, the first is silent and the second is vocal, as יִשְׁמְעוּ *they shall hear*, יִלְמְדוּ *they shall learn*, &c.; *Gimmel*, which is the initial of גְדוּלה *long*, means that whenever *Sheva* follows a long syllable it is vocal, as שָׁמְרוּ *they kept*, וַיֵּשְׁבוּ *and they dwelled*, הֹלְכִים *the coming*, &c.; *Daleth*, which is the initial of *Dagesh*, means that whenever *Sheva* is under a letter with *Dagesh* it is vocal, as דִּבְּרוּ *they spoke*, דַּבְּרָה *a word*, &c.; whilst the letter *He*, which is the initial of הדמות *alike* signifies that when two letters which are alike come together, and the first has *Sheva*, it is vocal, as in הַלְלוּיָהּ *Hallelujah*, where, though the first *Lamed* has no *Dagesh*, yet it is called vocal *Sheva* because of the two *Lameds*, and הִנְנִי *behold I*, in which *Sheva* is vocal because of the two *Nuns*. Remember this mnemonical sign, and treasure it up, for it is useful.

I shall return now to my first subject, and give you an example of a *Sheva*, which the Massorites call *Dagesh*. They make the following remark in the Massorah: "the expression עלמה *to conceal*, has always *Dagesh*;" that is, it is always with simple *Sheva*, as הַעְלֵם יַעְלִימוּ *hiding they shall hide* [Levit. xx. 4], &c. They also say the word חסיה *to trust*, has always *Dagesh*, as אֶחֱסֶה *I shall trust* [Ps. lvii. 2], מַחְסִי *my shelter* [Ps. xci. 2], &c., except in six instances, in which it is *Raphe*, that is, with *Chateph-pattach* or *Chateph-segol*, as מַחֲסֶה *refuge* [Joel iv. 16], אֶחֱסֶה *I shall trust* [Ps. xviii. 3], &c.[70] They also remark, מעשר *tithe*, occurs three times with

---

[70] This is surely a mistake, since the Massorah marginalis on Ps. lxii. 9, enumerates *nine* instances in which חסיה is *Raphe*, or has *Chateph-pattach*. They are as follows:—

מחסה	. . . Ps. lxii. 9	מחסי	. . . Ps. lxxi. 7	לחסות	. . . Ps. cxviii. 9
מחסה	. . . Ps. xlvi. 2	מחסי	. . . Jerem. xvii. 17	לחסות	. . . Ruth ii. 12
מחסה	. . . Joel iv. 16	לחסות	. . . Ps. cxviii. 8	חסיה	. . . Ps. lvii. 2

The Massorah, moreover, adds that אחסה וכל אחסה דכור רפי במ"א ובצל כנפיך, *the future* אחסה *is likewise Raphe*, everywhere except in one instance, viz., Ps. lvii. 2. In the Massorah finalis, under the letter *Cheth* 32 a, col. 2, where reference is made to the word in question, it is also distinctly stated that it is *nine* times *Raphe*.

ועתה אחדש לך סימן יפה א׳, ב׳, ג׳, ד׳ ה׳: וא׳ ר״ל כל שוא שבראש התיבה הוא שוא נע, כמו שְׁמַע בְּנִי: ב׳ ר״ל כשהן ב׳ שואין באמצע התיבה, הראשון נח והשני נע, כמו יִשְׁמְעוּ, יִלְמְדוּ; ג׳ ר״ל גדולה, פירוש כל שוא שאחר תנועה גדולה הוא נע, כמו שָׁמְרוּ, וַיֵּשְׁבוּ, הֹלְכִים ודומיהן; ד׳ ר״ל דגש, כל שוא שתחת אות דגושה, כמו דִּבְּרוּ, דַּבְּרָה ודומיהן; ה׳ ר״ל הדמות, פירוש כשיהיו ב׳ אותיות דומות, והראשונה בשוא הוא נע, כמו הַלְלוּיָהּ, שהל״מד הראשונה אינה דגושה, ומ״מ נקרא השוא נע בעבור שני הלמ״דין, וכן הִנְנִי השוא נע בעבור שני הנו״נין; וזכור זה הסימן, ותצפנהו כי טוב הוא:

והנה חזור על הראשונות, ואתן לך משל על חשוא שקראו דנש; אמרו במסורת כל לשון העלמה בדנש, ר״ל בשוא פשוט, כמו וְאִם הַעְלֵם יַעְלִימוּ ודומיהן; וכן כל לשון חסיה דנש, כמו בצל כנפך אֶחֱסֶה, אומר לי״י מַחְסִי ודומיהן, חוץ מן ח׳ דפויין ר״ל בחטף פתח או בחטף סגול, כמו וי״י מַחֲסֶה לעמו, צוּרִי אֶחֱסֶה בו;[70] וכן אמרו מעשר ג׳ דנושים,

Dagesh, as מַעֲשַׂר the tithe of [Levit. xxvii. 30], &c.,⁷¹ and in all other instances it is *Raphe*, that is, with *Chateph-pattach*, as מַעֲשַׂר the tithe of [Deut. xiv. 23], &c. Examine, and you will find it so.

SECTION IV., concerning *Milel*, *Milra*, and *Psik*.—Mark that there is not a single word in the whole Scripture without an accent either at the beginning, middle, or end. Now, the Massorites call the place on which the accent rests by two Aramaic names. The one is מלעיל *Milel*, which is the translation of the Hebrew מלמעלה *from above;* and the other is מלרע *Milra*, and is the translation of the Hebrew מתחת or מטה *from below.* By this is not meant that the accent is either above or below the centre of the letter, but when the accent is either on the first letter of the word, or on the middle, they call it *Milel*, and when it is on the end of the word they denominate it *Milra*. Now there are some words which, according to rule, are always *Milel;* and there are others, again, which, according to rule, are always *Milra;* whilst some, again, are at times *Milel*, and at other times *Milra*. Still there are exceptions to all these. In the book entitled *Good Sense*, which I have determined to compose, all these rules will be explained, together with all the other laws of the accents, if God permit.⁷² It must be added, that the Massorites make but very few desultory remarks on this subject.

As a rule, they do not note every single word, whether it has the accent on the penultima or on the ultima, but only very occasionally mark some words which are anomalous, either in their accents or points. Thus, for instance, they give a register of thirty-eight words, which in one case only have the accent on the penultima, whilst in all other passages they have the accent on the ultima, as וְהִשְׁקִיתָ *and thou*

---

⁷¹ The three instances in which מעשר occurs with *Dagesh* = with *Sheva* under the *Ajin* are, Levit. xxvii. 32: Numb. xviii. 24: Levit. xxvii. 30. They are given in the Massorah finalis under the letter *Ajin*, p. 51 *b*, col. 2.

⁷² The *Dissertation on the Accents*, to which Levita refers, appeared in 1539, within twelve months of the publication of the treatise on the Massorah (*vide supra*, p. 63, &c.). The discussion on the tone accents, or *Milel* and *Milra*, is contained in the sixth chapter of the dissertation in question.

shalt water it [Deut. xi. 10], on which the Massoretic remark is, "not extant, *Milel ;*"[73] and also another register—in which the reverse is the case—of words, which in one instance only are *Milra*, whilst in all other passages they are *Milel*, as הָבָה *come now* Gen. xxix. 21], noted "not extant as *Milra*."[74] They also remark on וַיֹּסֶף *and he added,* "three times, twice *Milel* and once *Milra;*"[75] as well as on תֹּסֵף *she shall add,* "five times, thrice *Milra* and twice *Milel.*"[76] Those which are *Milel* have *Segol*, whilst those which are *Milra* have, according to grammar, *Tzere;* and, in consequence of this change, the Massorites counted them, and have given the marks of the passages; whilst, with regard to those in which the said change does not take place, as יִקְרָא *it shall be called*, which

בדגלך לית מלעיל ; וכן שימה אחת להפך ;[73]
מלרע וכל חברותיה מלעיל, כמו הָבָה אֶת אשתי
לית מלרע, וסימן אשתי למטה ;[74] וכן וְיוֹסֶף ג',
ב' מלעיל וא' מלרע [75] וכן תֹּסֵף ה', ג' לרע
וב' לעיל, [76] אשר הם דלעיל הם בסגול ואשר
הם מלרע הם בצידי על פי הדקדוק, ובעבור
השתנות כזה, הם מנו אותם ונתנו בהן סמנים ;
אבל מלות שאין בדף השתנות כנ"ל, כגון

---

[73] The thirty-eight words which respectively have in one instance only the accent on the penultima are as follows :—

והשקית . . . Deut. xi. 10	קינה . . . Ezek. xix. 14	למה . . . Job vii. 20
לשרת . . . Deut. xvii. 12	וישבה . . . . Isa. vi. 13	מנע . . . Prov. xi. 26
רבה . . . Gen. xviii. 20	שבר . . . 2 Kings vii. 6	יקרה . . . Prov. xvii. 15
יצחק . . . Gen. xxi. 6	מרה . . . 1 Sam. xxx. 6	תחת . . . Prov. xvii. 10
וספר . . . Levit. xv. 13	התחתנה . . . Ezek. xl. 19	ותאמר . . . Prov. vii. 13
קצה . . . Numb. xxi. 5	החיצונה . . 2 Kings xvi. 18	ארבעה . . . Prov. xxx. 24
רחוקה . . . Judg. xviii. 28	רעה . . . Isa. xxiv. 19	חומה . . . Ezek. xlii. 20
טובה . . . Ruth iv. 15	והגרה . . . Isa. xxxii. 11	בצע . . . Prov. i. 19
הקם . . . 2 Sam. xxiii. 1	והרה . . . Ezek. xxiv. 11	הבו . . . Job. vi. 22
יסף . . . Judg. xiii. 21	בוקע . . . Isa. lxiii. 12	אחו . . . Job xxiii. 9
ושברתי . . . Ezek. xiv. 12	יצק . . . 2 Kings iii. 11	שמע . . . Ps. cl. 5
הרם . . . 2 Kings v. 7	זרה . . . Job xix. 17	הרשע . . . Eccl. iii. 16
צרה . . . Isa. xxviii. 20	צרר . . . Job xxvi. 8		

They are given in the Massorah finalis, under the "variations between the Easterns and Westerns," p. 62 *a*, cols. 3 and 4. The *Ochla Ve-Ochla*, section ccclxxii., pp. 61, 171. gives seventeen additional instances, whilst it omits some which are contained in our list.

[74] The list of words which on the contrary occur only once with the accent on the ultima is as follows :—

הבה . . . Gen. xxix. 21	ואפית . . . Levit. xxiv. 5	מרחם . . . Isa. xlix. 15
מתה . . . Gen. xxx. 1	וראיתה . . . Numb. xxvii. 13	בוקר . . . Amos vii. 14
ירא . . . Gen. xli. 33	לחם . . . Judg. v. 8	וחומץ . . . Ps. lxxi. 4
ויישב . . . Gen. xlvii. 1	זרע . . . Judg. vi. 3	שער . . . Prov. xxiii. 7
שתי . . . Exod. x. 1	ארצה . . . 1 Kings xvi. 9	נוכח . . . Job xxiii. 7
והעלית . . . Exod. xl. 4	השמר . . . Isa. vii. 4	שחר . . . Job xxx. 30
והביאה . . . Levit. xv. 29	שרש . . . Isa. xl. 24		

There are also two others, about which there is a difference of opinion, viz., חוצית Numb. xxxi. 27, and וְעָשִׂיר Zech. vi. 11. They are enumerated in the *Ochla Ve-Ochla*, section ccclxxiii., pp. 61, 172.

[75] The two instances in which ויסף is *Milel* are, Prov. i. 5; ix. 2.; and the one instance of *Milra* is in 2 Sam. xxiv. 3. See the Massorah marginalis on 2 Sam. xxiv. 3.

[76] The three passages in which תסף occurs *Milra* are, Gen. iv. 2; Deut. xiii. 1: Ps. civ. 29. It will be seen that in the first two instances it is the Hiphil future of יסף *to add;* whilst in the third passage it is Kal future, second person singular masculine for תאסף from אסף *to gather*. They are enumerated in the Massorah marginalis on Exod. iv. 12, and in the *Ochla Ve-Ochla*, Section iv. of the additions, pp. 62, 178. The two passages in which it is *Milel* are, Exod. x. 28; Deut. iii. 26. Comp. Massorah marginalis on Exod. x. 28.

occurs twenty-one times,[77] and יֵדַע *he shall know*, nineteen times,[78] which according to rule ought all to be *Milra;* and though some of them are *Milel*, because of the proximity of the accents, as יִקְרָא *it shall be called* [Isa. xxxv. 8], יֵדַע *he shall know* [1 Sam. xx. 3], they do not say a single word inasmuch as no change of vowel has taken place in them.

☞ Mark, moreover, that a kind of *Milel* and *Milra* occurs in the Massorah magna, which does not refer to the position of the accents, but to the change of the vowels. This is the case with words which occur twice, and which the Massorites denominate pairs. They are of two kinds.

The first class consists of two words beginning with the serviles *Kaph, Lamed,* and *Beth,* before the preformative *Aleph, Jod, Tav,* and *Nun* of the future, one word of which is pointed with *Sheva*, and the other with *Pattach*, followed by *Dagesh;* as is the case with those words called *Dagesh* and *Raphe*, as I have explained in the preceding section. Normally there is no difference between those called *Dagesh* and *Raphe* and those which they call pairs, except that the latter only are arranged in pairs. Thus, for instance, the eleven pairs, one which is *Milel*, and one *Milra*, beginning with *Beth;* as בְּדִמְעוֹת *in tears, Milel* [Lament. ii. 11], and בְּדִמָעוֹת, *Milra* [Ps. lxxx. 6], &c.;[79] the alphabetical list of double pairs of words beginning with *Kaph,*

יִקְרָא כ"א,[77] יֵדַע י"ט,[78] כלם דינם לרע, אעפ"י שיש מהם מלעיל מפני קרוב הטעמים, כמו ודרך הקדש יִקָּרֵא לה, אל יֵדַע זאת יהונתן, לא דברו מזה דבר, לפי שאין בהן השתנות הנקודה:

☞ ודע כי נמצא במסרה גדולה ענין מלעיל ומלרע שאינו על הנחת הטעמים, רק על השתנות הנקודות, וזה במלות שנמצאו שנים שנים שקראו להן זוגות, והם של ב' מינין:

המין האחד הוא מן ב' מלין שראשן אותיות כל"ב, או הוי"ו שבראש האית"ן ובמלה אחת הן נקודות בשוא ובהברחתה בפתח ודגש אחריה, כגון אותן שקראו להן דגשין ורפין, כאשר כתבתי במאמר הקודם; והכלל אין הפרש בין הדגשין והרפין, ובין אלו שקראו להן זוגות, רק שאל הן זוגות לבד; והמשל כגון י"א זוגין חד מלעיל וחד מלרע ובי"ת בריששון, כלו בְּדִמְעוֹת עֵינִי מלעיל, בְּדִמָעוֹת שליש מלרע;[79] וכן א"ב

---

[77] The twenty-one instances in which יקרא occurs, are as follows: Gen. ii. 23; xvii. 5; xxxv. 10; xxi. 12: Numb. xxiii. 3: Deut. iii. 13; xxii. 6: 1 Sam. ix. 9: Isa. iv. 1; xiv. 20; xxxi. 4; xxxii. 5; lvi. 7; xxxv. 8; liv. 5; i. 26; lxii. 12: Jerem. xix. 6: Isa. lxii. 4; Prov. xvi. 21: Esther iv. 11. They are given in the Massorah marginalis on Jerem. xix. 6. It will be seen that two of the instances, viz., Numb. xxiii. 3; Deut. xxii. 6, are not from קרא, *to call*.

[78] The nineteen passages in which ידע occurs are, Josh. xxii. 22: 1 Sam. xx. 3; xxi. 3: Isa. vii. 16; viii. 4; lii. 6: Jerem. xxxvi. 19; xl. 15; xxxviii. 24: Job xiv. 21: Ps. xxxv. 8; xxxix. 7; xcii. 7: Prov. xxiv. 12; xxviii. 22: Eccl. viii. 5 (twice); ix. 12; x. 14. They are given in the Massorah marginalis on Ps. xcii. 7.

[79] The eleven pairs of words beginning with *Beth*, which respectively occur once *Milra* (i. e., with *Sheva*, or its substitutive feeble vowel) and once *Milel* (i. e., with the real vowel), are as follows:—

ברמעות	. . Ps. lxxx. 6	במצולה	. . Ps. cvii. 24	בנגע	. . Deut. xxiv. 8
ברמעות	. Lament. ii. 11	במצלה	. . Zech. i. 8	בנגע	. . Levit. xiii. 3
בחיין	. . . Dan. vii. 12	בממלכה	. . Isa. xix. 2	בשאת	. . Exod. xxvii. 7
בחיין	. . . Job xxiv. 22	בממלכה	. . Amos ix. 8	בשאת	. . Levit. xiii. 10
בחרם	. . . Isa. viii. 1	בסכך	. . Ps. lxxiv. 5	בתנור	. . Levit. xxvi. 2
בחרם	. . Exod. xxxii. 4	בסכך	. . Gen. xxii. 13	בתנור	. . Levit. vii. 9
במדינות	. Esther ix. 16	בסירות	. . Amos iv. 2		
במדינות	. Lament. i. 1	בסירות	2 Chron. xxxv. 13		

one of which is *Milel*, and the other *Milra*, as פָאֹהֶל as the tent [Isa. xl. 22], *Milel*, and בְּאֹהֶל [Isa. xxxvii. 12], *Milra*;[80] the twenty-two pairs of two words, each beginning with *Vav*, one of which is *Milel*, and the other *Milra*, as וַיִּתְאָו and he desired [1 Chron. xi. 17], *Milel*, and וְיִתְאָו and he shall desire [Ps. xlv. 12], *Milra*, &c.[84]

מן ב׳ ב׳ מלין כ״ף ברישיהן א׳ מלעיל וא׳ מלרע, פָאֹהֶל לשברת מלעיל, פָאֹהֶל דועי מלרע; [80] וכן כ״ב זוגין מן ב׳ ב׳ מלין וי׳ברישיהן א׳ לעיל וא׳ לרע, וַיִּתְאָו דוד לעיל, וְיִתְאָו המלך יפיך לרע [81]:
והמין חב׳ הוא נאמר על שאר הנקודות, ויש מהן אלפא ביתא במסרה גדולה שקראו

The second kind comprises the other vowel-points. Of these, there is an alphabetical list in the Massorah magna giving words

They are given in the Massorah finalis under the letter *Beth*, p. 14*a*, cols. 3 and 4; Massorah marginalis on Isa. viii. 1; and *Ochla Ve-Ochla*, section xlix., pp. 15, 55.

[80] The alphabetical list of words beginning with *Kaph*, which only occur twice, once *Milra*, or with *Sheva* as its substitutive feeble vowel, and once *Milel*, or with the real vowel, is as follows:

כאהל	. . Isa. xxxviii. 12	כהום	Song of Songs iv. 3	כסוחה	. . . Ps. lxxx. 17
כאהל	. . . Isa. xl. 22	כהום	. . Judg. xvi. 12	כסוחה	. . . Isa. v. 25
כארים	. . Numb. xxiv. 6	כחתן	. . Ps. xix. 6	כסופה	. . Prov. i. 27
כארים	. Song of Songs v. 15	כחתן	. . Isa. lxi. 10	כסופה	. . Isa. v. 28
כאבק	. . . Isa. xxix. 5	כהלב	. . Levit. iv. 26	כערב	. Ps. lxxxiii. 12
כאבק	. . . Isa. v. 24	כהלב	. . Ps. cxix. 70	כערוב	Song of Songs v. 11
כברית	. 2 Chron. xxxiv. 32	כבבור	. Isa. xvii. 13	כצר	. . Lament. ii. 4
כברית	. . Jerem. xxxi. 32	כבבור	. . Ezek. iii. 23	כצר	. . . Isa. v. 28
כגמול	. . . Ps. cxxxi. 2	כמת	. . . Ps. xxxi. 13	כרשע	. . Job xxvii. 7
כגמול	. . . Ps. cxxxi. 2	כמת	. Numb. xii. 12	כרשע	. . Gen. xxiv. 25
וכרקב	. . . Prov. xii. 4	כמופת	. . Ps. lxxi. 7	כשואה	. . Prov. i. 27
וכרקב	. . . Hos. v. 12	כמופת	. 1 Kings xiii. 5	כשואה	. Ezek. xxxviii. 9
וככפיר	. . Ps. xvii. 12	כמלונה	. . Isa. i. 8	כשושנה	Song of Songs ii. 2
וככפיר	. . Hos. v. 14	כמלונה	. Isa. xxiv. 20	כשושנה	. Hos. xiv. 6

This catalogue is given in the Massorah finalis under the letter *Kaph*, p. 38*a*, col. 1; and in the *Ochla Ve-Ochla*, section xi. pp. 7, 19, &c. The alphabetical order will be seen after the letter *Kaph*.

[81] The twenty-two words beginning and ending with *Vav*, each one of which occurs twice, once *Milra*, or with *Vav* conjunctive, and once *Milel*, or with *Vav* conversive, are as follows:—

ויתאו	. . . Ps. xlv. 12	ויפרו	. . Isa. xlv. 8	וישכנו	. . Ps. xxxvii. 29
ויתאו	. 1 Chron. xi. 17	ויפרו	. Gen. xlvii. 27	וישכנו	. . Gen. xxv. 18
ויתמהו	. . Job xxvi. 11	ויעדהו	. 1 Kings xxi. 10	ויבשו	. . Job xii. 15
ויתמהו	. . Gen. xliii. 33	ויעדהו	. 1 Kings xxi. 13	ויבשו	. . Isa. xl. 24
וירדו	. . Numb. xiii. 2	וישבעו	. . Ps. xxii. 27	ויצקו	. 1 Kings xviii. 34
וירדו	. . Numb. xiii. 21	וישבעו	. . Hos. xiii. 6	ויצקו	. 2 Kings iv. 40
וידפכו	. . Job xi. 15	וינהגו	. 1 Sam. xxx. 22	ויצעו	. . Ps. lxxii. 16
וידפכו	. 1 Sam. xxv. 12	וינהגו	. 1 Sam. xxx. 2	ויצעו	. . Ps. xcii. 8
ויחיו	. Ezek. xxxvii. 9	וינורו	. . Levit. xxii. 2	ויצאו	. . Jerem. xv. 1
ויחיו	. Ezek. xxxvii. 10	וינורו	. . Hos. ix. 10	ויצאו	. . Gen. xxxiv. 26
ויסגו	. . Ps. cxix. 5	וירעשו	. . Amos ix. 1	ויצברו	. . Gen. xli. 35
ויסגו	. Ps. lxxviii. 57	וירעשו	. Isa. xviii. 9	ויצברו	. Exod. viii. 10
ויאספהו	. . Habak. i. 15	וירכסו	Exod. xxviii. 28	רצליהו	. Jerem. v. 23
ויאספהו	. 1 Sam. xiv. 52	וירכסו	Exod. xxxix. 21	רצליהו	. 2 Chron. xiv. 3
וינתנו	. 2 Chron. xviii. 14	וישמיעו	. Jerem. xviii. 22		
וינתנו	. 1 Chron. v. 20	וישמיעו	. Nehem. xii. 42		

They are given in the Massorah finalis under the letter *Vav*, p. 29*b*, cols. 1 and 2; and in the *Ochla Ve-Ochla*, section xlv., pp. 14, 52, &c. It will be seen that though the Massorah states in the heading of this rubric that there are *twenty-two* such instances, it gives *twenty-three*. This arises from the fact that the word וישבעו (Ps. xxii. 27; Hos. xiii. 6), which is an addition to this rubric, has inadvertently been mixed up with it. In the *Ochla Ve-Ochla* it is rightly separated.

wherein those which have *Cholem*, *Shurek*, or *Kibbutz*, are called *Milel*; whilst those which have *Kametz*, *Kametz-chateph*, *Pattach*, *Tzere*, or *Chirek*, are called *Milra*. This, however, is only the case with groups of pairs. As, for instance, when a word occurs twice, once with *Cholem* and another time with *Kametz*, *Kametz-chateph*, or *Tzere*; the Massorites call the one with *Cholem*, *Milel*, and the rest *Milra*. Thus, אָכַל [Gen. iii. 11] is *Milel*, אֲכָל *eating of* [Deut. xii. 23], is *Milra*; יִדְלָף *it shall drop* [Eccl. x. 18], is *Milel*, יִדְלָף *Jidlaph* [Gen. xxii. 22], is *Milra*; דֹּעֲכוּ *they are quenched* [Ps. cxviii. 12], is *Milel*, דָּעֲכוּ [Isa. xliii. 17], is *Milra*; אֹרְחוֹת, *the travellers* [Isa. xxi. 13], is *Milel*, אֹרְחַת *a company of* [Gen. xxxvii. 25], is *Milra*; הַמְשֹׁל *to rule* [Judg. ix. 2], is *Milel*, הַמְשֵׁל *to rule* [Job xxv. 2], is *Milra*.[82]

המלורע שבהן חולם, או שורק, או קבוץ מלעיל, ואשר בהן קמץ, או קמץ חטף, או פתח, או צרי, או חירק מלרע; וזה לא נאמר רק על זוגות של שנים שנים מלין; והמשל כשיהיו ב' מלות האחת בחולם וחברתה בקמץ, או בחטף קמץ, או בצרי, קראו אותה שבחולם מלעיל והשאר מלרע; כגון לבלתי אֲכָל ממנו מלעיל, לבלתי אֲכֹל הדם מלרע, יִדְלֹף הבית מלעיל, ואת פלדש ואת יִדְלָף מלרע, דֹּעֲכוּ כאש קוצים מלעיל, דָּעֲכוּ כפשתה מלרע, אֹרְחוֹת דורנים מלעיל, אֹרְחַת ישמעאלים מלרע, הַמְשֹׁל בכם מלעיל, הַמְשֵׁל ופחד מלרע:[82]

[82] The alphabetical list to which Levita refers, and which illustrates all his remarks on the second kind, is as follows:—

אָכֹל	. . . . Deut. xii. 23	הוֹדִיעֵנוּ	. . 1 Sam. vi. 2	מִשְׁקְלָה	. . 2 Kings xxi. 13
אָכַל	. . . . Gen. iii. 11	הוֹדִיעֵנוּ	. . Job xxxvii. 19	לְמִשְׁקָלָת	. . Isa. xxviii. 17
אָמַר	. . Ezek. xxv. 8	וְנֶעְתַּר	. . 1 Chron. v. 20	מֶחְלָד	. . Deut. xxxii. 18
אָמַר	. . Prov. xxv. 7	וְנֶעְתַּר	. . Isa. xix. 22	מֵחֶלְדִּי	. . Ezek. xxviii. 9
אֹרְחוֹת	. . Isa. xxi. 13	וְנִדְחוּם	. . Esther viii. 8	מְאִירוֹת	. . Isa. xxvii. 11
אֹרְחַת	. . Gen. xxxvii. 25	וְנִדְחָם	. . Esther iii. 12	מְאִירָה	. . . Ps. xix. 9
אֶדֶן	. . Nehem. vii. 61	וִיקוּם	. . Eccl. iv. 4	נָתַן	. . 2 Kings xxiii. 11
אֶדֶן	. . Ezra ii. 59	וִיקֻם	. . Job xxii. 28	נָתַן	. . Gen. xxxviii. 9
אָגֵס	. . Esther i. 8	וּמַלְּאוּ	. . Jerem. xxx. 21	נָתַן	. . . Judg. vi. 28
אָנַס	. . Dan. iv. 6	וּמַלְּאוּ	. . Zech. ix. 10	נָתַן	. 2 Chron. xxxiii. 3
בַּקְרֵב	. . . Ps. xxvii. 2	זֶרַע	. . Ps. xcvii. 11	נַחַם	. . Hos. xiii. 14
בַּקְרֵב	. . 2 Sam. xv. 5	זֶרַע	. . Levit. xi. 37	נָחַם	. . 1 Chron. iv. 19
בַּמַעַל	. . Nehem. viii. 6	חָנַן	. . Gen. xxxiii. 5	נָפְלוּ	. . 1 Sam. xxix. 3
בַּמַעַל	. . Josh. xxii. 22	חָנוּן	. . Isa. xxx. 19	נָפְלוּ	. . 2 Sam. i. 10
בַּנַּעַר	. . Job xxxvi. 14	מֶהַר	. . Habak. i. 13	עִנִּיתִי	. . . Ps. cxix. 71
בַּנַּעַר	. 2 Sam. xviii. 12	מַהֵר	. . Prov. xxii. 11	עִנִּיתִי	. . Ps. xxxv. 13
גְּוִיָתֵנוּ	. . Nehem. ix. 37	יְחִינוּ	. . 2 Kings viii. 4	צֵאָה	. . . Isa. iv. 4
גְּוִיָתֵנוּ	. . Gen. xlvii. 18	יְחִנוּ	. . Hos. vi. 2	צֹאָה	. . Ezek. iv. 12
דֹּעֲכוּ	. . Ps. cxviii. 12	יִדְלֹף	. . Eccl. x. 18	קֹרְאֵנִי	. . Isa. xlix. 1
דָּעֲכוּ	. . Isa. xliii. 17	יִדְלָף	. . Gen. xxii. 22	קֹרְאֵנִי	. . . Job iv. 14
הָאָמֹר	. . Ezek. lxxviii. 9	כְּתָם	. . Ps. lxxvii. 72	רִמּוֹנִי	. . Lament i. 19
הָאָמֹר	. . Job xxxiv. 31	כֶּתֶם	. . Isa. xviii. 5	רִמֹּנִי	. . 2 Sam. xix. 27
הַקְצוֹר	. . Isa. lv. 2	לְאָמִים	. . Gen. xxv. 16	שִׁכֻּלְתִּי	. . Gen. xliii. 14
הַקְצֹר	. . Micah ii. 7	לְאֻמִּים	. . Lament ii. 1	שִׁכֻּלְתִּי	. . Gen. xliii. 14
הַמְשֹׁל	. . Judg. ix. 2	לִשְׁבֻיִים	. . Isa. lxi. 1	שֻׁפַּטְנוּ	. . . Dan. ix. 12
הַמְשֵׁל	. . Job xxv. 2	לַשְּׁבָיִם	. Joel iv. 8	וּשְׁפָטֻנוּ	. 1 Sam. viii. 20
הַנֶּחָת	. . Dan. v. 20	מִבְצוּר	. 1 Sam. xiv. 6	תֹּאמְרִי	Song of Songs iv. 5
הַנֶּחָת	. . Joel iv. 11	מִבְצָר	. . Prov. xxv. 28	תֹּאמְרִי	Song of Songs vii. 4

The list is given in the Massorah finalis under the letter *Aleph*, p. 2 *a*, col. 4-2 *b*, col. 2; and in the *Ochla Ve-Ochla*, section v., pp. 5, 13, &c. The latter adds כְּצָרוּף (Zech. xiii. 9; Ps. lxvi. 10), as not being included in the Massoretic list (לבד ממסורתא), whilst it deviates in its description of הנחת and נתן.

They call *Shurek*, *Milra*, in opposition to *Kametz*, *Pattach*, and *Tzere;* as שְׁפָטוּנוּ *they judged us* [Dan. ix. 12], is *Milel*, שְׁפָטָנוּ *he judged us* [1 Sam. viii. 20], is *Milel;* רִמּוּנִי *they deceived me* [Lam. i. 19], is *Milra*, רִמָּנִי *he deceived me* [2 Sam. xix. 27], is *Milra;* יְחַיּוּנוּ *they shall let us live* [2 Kings vii. 4], is *Milel*, יְחַיֵּינוּ *he will make us live* [Hos. vi. 2], is *Milra*. The *Kibbutz* again is *Milel*, in opposition to *Tzere* and *Chirek;* as הוֹדִיעֵנוּ *inform us* [1 Sam. vi. 2], is *Milel*, הוֹדִיעֵנוּ *teach us* [Job xxxvii. 19], is *Milra;* לְאֻמֹּתָם *according to their nations* [Gen. xxv. 16], is *Milel*, לְאִמֹּתָם *to their mothers* [Lament. ii. 12], is *Milra*. Now, though *Kametz-Chatuph* in opposition to *Cholem* is *Milra*, as I have already shown, yet in opposition to *Pattach* it is *Milel:* as הֻנְחַת *he was thrust down* [Dan. v. 20], is *Milel*, הַנְחַת *make to come down* [Joel iv. 11], is *Milra;* נָפְלוֹ *his falling* [1 Sam. xxix. 3], is *Milel*, נָפְלוֹ *his falling* [2 Sam. i. 10], is *Milra*. Thus, also, *Kametz*, though *Milra* in opposition to *Shurek*, as I have stated, is *Milel* in opposition to *Tzere;* as זֹרַע *it is sown* [Ps. xcvii. 11], is *Milel*, זְרוּעַ *sown* [Levit. xi. 37], is *Milra*. It is to be borne in mind that all which I have stated about these two kinds is only to be found in the Massorah magna; in the Massorah parva the Massorites have not remarked upon a single one of these instances, either *Milel* or *Milra*, but they simply say, "not extant."

☞ Let me now explain the meaning of *Piskin*. There is one accent called *Psak* or *Psik*, which is a straight line (|) between two words. It consists of two kinds, the one is a *Psik* not followed by the accent *Rebia*, as in וַיִּקְרָא אֱלֹהִים ׀ לָאוֹר יוֹם *and God called the light day* [Gen. i. 4], עָשׂוּ ׀ כָּלָה *they have done it, they have accomplished* [Gen. xviii. 21]. This is called by the Massorites *Psik of the Book*, because it occurs in every book of the Scriptures, and is enumerated in the Massorah as, in Genesis there are twenty-nine *Piskas*, in Exodus nineteen,

---

[83] The instances which illustrate all the remarks of Levita, made in this paragraph, are contained in the alphabetical list of *Milels* and *Milras* given in note 82 of the preceding page.

and so forth in all the books of the Bible.[84] The second is the accent called *Le-garmiah*, which is in form like the real *Psik*, but it is always followed by the accent *Rebia*. You will find it in the treatise *Good Sense*, as well as in the Third Part called the Broken Tables, where I shall speak about it.

SECTION V., concerning Registers, Groups, Parallels, and Analogous Forms.— Our Rabbins of blessed memory frequently use the word *Shita*, saying, "a *Shita* of such and such an one," "another *Shita*," &c. To the same effect is the use of *Shita* in the Talmud, and I do not know from what language it is derived, neither does the author of *Aruch*[85] give it. I, however, find that the Chaldee of the Song of Songs paraphrases "his cheeks are like beds of balsam" [v. 13], by "the two tables of stone which He gave to his people were written in ten rows [*Shittin*], resembling the rows or beds [*Shittin*] in the garden of balsam." Thus, also, the Targum of Joseph translates, "noted it in a book" [Isa. xxx. 8], by "register it on the lines [*Shittin*] of the book." Thus, too, our Rabbins of blessed memory called the lines of a book *Shita*, when they say, "it is necessary to leave four empty lines [= *Shittin*] between each book," "the beginning of a line [= *Shita*]," "the end of a line [= *Shita*]," &c. They also remark on כְּדָרְלָעֹמֶר *Chedorlaomer* [Gen. xiv. 9], that it is to be separated into two words in one line, but it must not be separated into two lines.[86] The Massorites likewise call that *Shita* which our Rabbins of blessed memory called *Shita*, that is, a register of things

---

[84] The number of *Piskin* in each book of the Bible is as follows:—

Genesis	29	Isaiah	30	Song of Songs	10
Exodus	14	Jeremiah	31	Ecclesiastes	3
Leviticus	8	Ezekiel	28	Lamentations	8
Numbers	22	Minor Prophets	10	Esther	5
Deuteronomy	22	1 and 2 Chronicles	63	Daniel	8
Joshua	17	Psalms	40	Ezra-Nehemiah	13
Judges	7	Job	6		
1 and 2 Samuel	48	Proverbs	8		479
1 and 2 Kings	45	Ruth	4		

They are enumerated in the Massorah finalis, p. 53, &c.

[85] For the author of the *Aruch*, i. e., R. Nathan b. Jechiel, see above, p. 2.

[86] The Talmudic discussion on the orthography of the proper name Chedorlaomer, to which Levita refers, is to be found in *Chulin*, 65 a.

of the same import, as a number of verses, pairs, or words which are alike either in vowel-points or letters. Such a number they called *Shita* [= catalogue, register, list, or rubric].

The rule is, that every collection of verses or of words brought together, which is not alphabetically arranged, they called *Shita* [*i. e.*, catalogue or register]; and I have received it that such a *Shita* has not less than ten lines. These registers are of diverse import. There is a register of so many pairs of words, or of so many verses, or of so many words, or of so many letters, which it is not necessary to illustrate by examples.

☞ Let me now explain the meaning of *Sug* and *Sugin*. Mark, that the proper meaning of זוּג is *a pair, two*. Thus, the Chaldee paraphrase renders a pair by זוּג [2 Kings v. 17], with *Cholem*, but זוּג with *Shurek* means *a bell*, and, in the language of our Rabbins of blessed memory, a pair of phylacteries; thus, also, the phrase "to every one thou givest a pair [זוּג], but me thou didst not give a pair." They call the plural, although masculine, זוּגוֹת; as, the phrase שׁקבל מן הזוגות, which means *received from two Sages*. It is well known that the numbers are divided into two parts, namely, even and odd; the uneven are, 1, 3, 5, 7, and 9, whilst the even are, 2, 4, 6, 8, and 10. Now, the Rabbins of blessed memory call every number which is not uneven זוּגוֹת, = *pairs*, *ex. gr.*, "one should not eat even [זוּגוֹת], nor drink even [זוּגוֹת]," always in the plural feminine; whereas the Massorites always use the plural in the masculine gender, and not only call each pair by the name *Sug*, but even things consisting of twice three, twice four, or twice five, up to ten, they denominate *Sugoth*. There are numerous instances of it to be found in the Massorah magna. There are also registers and alphabetical lists of words which have no pairs, that is, which have no parallels.

In some Codices the expression דמיין = *parallel*, is added to זונין

pairs. Thus, for instance, they remark "there are five parallel pairs of words, which respectively occur twice, once the two words have the *Vav* conjunctive, and once not," as the first, וְיִשָּׂשכָר וּזְבֻלוּן *and Issachar and Zebulun*, [Gen. xxxv. 23]; and the second, יִשָּׂשכָר זְבוּלֻן *Issachar, Zebulun*, [Exod. i. 3], &c.[87] Thus, also, they say that such and such verses are parallel [דמיין], as "the two parallel verses [דמיין] in which all the words terminate with the letter *Mem*," viz., Gen. xxxii. 15, and Numb. xxix. 33. The expression דמיין, however, is only used epexegetically, since it would be sufficient without it. As a rule, the Massorites never employ דמיין, except with respect to groups and verses.

☞ I shall now explain the meaning of דכוותיה. The Chaldee paraphrase renders כָּמוֹהוּ *like it* [Joel ii. 2] by דכוותיה; so also כְּמוֹהֶם *like unto them* [Ps. cxxxv. 18] by דכוותהון. It, too, is simply used as an additional explanation in most places; in a few instances, however, it is really wanted, as will be seen in the Tenth Section of this Part, God helping.

Section VI., concerning Junctions, Severances, and Consecutives.— Mark that the expression סמיכה, which the Massorites use, denotes *approaching, belonging together, connected*, &c., as is the meaning of סָמַךְ in Ezek. xxiv. 2, which has no parallel in the Scriptures. It is, however, frequently used by our Rabbins of blessed memory, as in the phrases, *it is close* (סמוך) *upon dark, it will soon be dark*; *this section* (נסמכה) *is contiguous*, &c. Now, when two or more words are associated together through the addition or diminution of a letter or word, or by the interchange of words which are not in the habit of

---

[87] The five pairs of words which respectively occur once with the *Vav* conjunctive, and once without it, are,—

החסידה האנפה	. . . .	Levit. xi. 19	עשר נכסים	. . . . .	2 Chron. i. 11
והחסידה והאנפה	. . . .	Deut. xiv. 18	ועשר ונכסים	. . . . .	2 Chron. i. 12
עין רמון	. . . . .	Josh. xix. 7	יששכר זבולן	. . . . .	Exod. i. 3
ועין רמון	. . . . .	Josh. xv. 32	וישששכר וזבולן	. . . . .	Gen. xxxv. 23
דכדין אמרין	. . . .	Ezra vii. 17			
ודכרין ואמרין	. . . .	Ezra vi. 9			

They are given in the Massorah finalis under the letter *Vav*, p. 28 *b*, col. 1; and in the *Ochla Ve-Ochla*, section ccli., p. 138.

being joined in this manner, and if it only occurs so in one place, the Massorites remark thereon, "not extant so joined." Thus, on וְדָגָן וְתִירֹשׁ *and corn, and wine* [Gen. xxvii. 37], they remark, "not extant so joined," since, in all other places where these two words occur, the word דָּגָן *corn* has not the *Vav* conjunctive;[88] and שָׁמִיר שָׁיִת *briers, thorns* [Is. xxvii. 4], is marked "not extant so joined," since in all other places it is with *Vav* conjunctive.[89] The same is the case with words which are trans-

דרכן לחסמך באותו אופן, אם לא נמצא כזה רק במקום אחד, כתבו עליה לית דסמיך, כגון וְדָגָן וְתִירֹשׁ לית דכמיך, כי כל שאר דגן ותירוש בלי וי"ו החיבור במלת דגן ;[88] וכן שָׁמִיר שָׁיִת במלחמה לית דסמיך, כי כל שאר שמיר ושית עם וי"ו החיבור ;[89] וכן במלות

[88] The Massorah gives a list of sixty-two pairs, both words of which have *Vav* conjunctive, and are without parallel; viz.:—

ודגן ותירוש . . . . . Gen. xxvii. 37		ובה ומנחה . . . . . Jerem. xvii. 26
והצאן והבקר . . . . . Gen. xxxiii. 13		באף ובחמה . . . . . Jerem. xxi. 5
ושמעון ולוי . . . . . Gen. xxxv. 23		והשכם ושלח . . . . . Jerem. xxvi. 5
ויששכר וזבולן . . . . . Gen. xxxv. 23		ועבדך ועמך . . . . . Jerem. xxxi. 2
וחצרון וכרמי . . . . . Gen. xlvi. 9		ונבלה וטרפה . . . . . Ezek. iv. 14
ואני ועמי . . . . . Exod. ix. 27		ועוף ונפש . . . . . Ezek. ix. 6
ואהרן וחור . . . . . Exod. xvii. 12		וברכב ובפרשים . . . . . Ezek. xxvi. 7
ושהם וישפה . . . . . Exod. xxviii. 20		ואלמנה וגרושה . . . . . Ezek. xliv. 22
ועלה ומנחה . . . . . Exod. xxx. 9		ומשפט וצדקה . . . . . Ezek. xlv. 9
והעלה והשלמים . . . . . Levit. ix. 22		ואלמנה יתום . . . . . Zech. vii. 10
ואלף ושבע . . . . . Exod. xxxviii. 25		והם ובניהם . . . . . 1 Chron. ix. 23
ושור ושה . . . . . Levit. xxii. 23		וששום וטש . . . . . 2 Chron. ix. 13
ועבדך ואמתך . . . . . Levit. xxv. 44		ועשר ונכסים . . . . . 2 Chron. i. 12
והעמלקי והכנעני . . . . . Numb. xiv. 25		ובנינו ובנותינו . . . . . 2 Chron. xxix. 9
ואתה ואהרן . . . . . Numb. xvi. 17		וארבעים ושלשה . . . . . Ezra ii. 25
וחשבון ואלעלה . . . . . Numb. xxxii. 3		ושבעים ושנים . . . . . Nehem. vii. 8
והירדן וגבל . . . . . Deut. iii. 17		ושלשים וארבעה . . . . . 1 Chron. vii. 7
האתת והמפתים . . . . . Deut. vii. 19		וארבעים ושנים . . . . . Nehem. vii. 62
ובאתות ובמפתים . . . . . Deut. xxvi. 8		ועשרים ושנים . . . . . Nehem. vii. 31
ויוסף ובנימן . . . . . Deut. xxvii. 12		ועשרים ואחד . . . . . Nehem. vii. 37
ובנתיה וחצריה . . . . . Josh. xv. 45		ובניו ואחיו . . . . . Ezra viii. 18
ומדין ועמלק . . . . . Judg. vii. 12		ומנעליו ובריחיו . . . . . Nehem. iii. 6
וזבח וצלמנע . . . . . Judg. viii. 10		ושדינו וכרמינו . . . . . Nehem. v. 5
ופסל ומצבה . . . . . Levit. xxvi. 1		ולשמר ולעשות . . . . . Nehem. x. 30
ואיש ואשה . . . . . 1 Sam. xv. 3		ובניו ובנותיו . . . . . Job i. 13
וישראל ויהודה . . . . . 2 Sam. xi. 11		ואשיאלך והדריכני . . . . . Job xxxviii. 3
וארבעים ואחת . . . . . 1 Kings xv. 10		ואברהם ושרה . . . . . Gen. xviii. 11
ושלשם ואחת . . . . . 2 Kings xxii. 1		והוא והדר . . . . . Job xl. 10
ידע וראה . . . . . 1 Kings xx. 22		וחסד ואמת . . . . . Prov. xiv. 22
והגלעד וגבול . . . . . Josh. xiii. 11		והמלך והמן . . . . . Esther iii. 15
והכהנים והנביאים . . . . . 2 Kings xxiii. 2		ולהרג ולאבד . . . . . Esther viii. 11
וחזר ורעב . . . . . Jerem. v. 12		ועיר ועיר . . . . . Esther ix. 28
ובקר וצאן . . . . . 1 Chron. xii. 40			

The list is given in the Massorah finalis under the letter *Vav*, p. 28a, cols. 2 and 3; and in the *Ochla Ve-Ochla*, section ccliii., pp. 50, 139, &c. The latter omits six which the Massorah enumerates, and has fifteen instances which are not given in the Massorah.

[89] This is but one out of sixteen pairs, without the *Vav* conjunctive, which have no parallel. They are as follows:—

בעוף ובבהמה . . . . . Gen. ix. 10		מלך שרים . . . . . Hos. viii. 10
יששכר וזבולן . . . . . Exod. i. 3		שמש ירח . . . . . Habak. iii. 10
עין רמון . . . . . Josh. xix. 7		משה אהרן . . . . . Micah vi. 4
עיר עיר . . . . . Josh. xxi. 40		עשר נכסים . . . . . 2 Chron. i. 11
שמיר שית . . . . . Isa. xxvii. 4		דגן תירוש . . . . . 2 Chron. xxxi. 5
אכל שתה . . . . . Isa. xxi. 5		נעריהם בניהם . . . . . Nehem. x. 29
לכהנים ללוים . . . . . Isa. lxvi. 21		השמים שמי . . . . . Nehem. ix. 6
יען ביעץ . . . . . Ezek. xxxvi. 3			

It will be seen that, though the Massorah states in the heading of this rubric that there

posed in a verse, as שַׁבַּת שַׁבָּתוֹן Sabbatism, Sabbath [Exod. xvi. 23], on which they remark, "not extant so joined;" since in all other passages in which these two words are joined, they are inverted.⁹⁰

המוקדמים והמאוחרים בפסוק, כמו שַׁבָּתוֹן שַׁבַּת קדש ליהוה לית דסמיך, כי כל שאר שבת שבתון,⁹⁰ וכן וידבר משה אל יְהוָה לית

are *sixteen* such instances, it only gives *fifteen*, whilst one of the passages adduced is wrong, viz., דגן תירוש 2 Chron. xxxi. 5, inasmuch as it occurs *twice* in Chron. and Deut. xxviii. 51. The *Ochla Ve-Ochla*, section cclii., pp. 50, 138, &c., which also gives this list, rightly supplies the two deficiencies, viz., שם חם Gen. x. 1; and גדולות בצורות Josh. xiv. 12. Properly speaking החסידה האנפה Levit. xi. 19; and דכרין אמרין Ezra vii. 17, belong to this rubric, and it is difficult to divine why the Massorah does not include them in it, seeing that it includes the other instances from the rubric given on p. 212, note 87.

⁹⁰ This is but one of thirty-nine instances enumerated in the Massorah, which occur in this construction, since in all other passages they are inverted. They are as follows:—

			everywhere else		
שבתון שבת	. . . . . Exod. xvi. 23		,, ,,	. . . . שבת שבתון
אשה ליהוה הוא	. . . . . Exod. xxix. 18		,, ,,	. . . אשה הוה ליהוה
ללאת חמשים	. . . . . Exod. xxxvi. 17		,, ,,	. . . חמשים ללאת
אחד לעלה ואחד לחטאת	. . . . . Levit. xii. 8		,, ,,	. . . אחד לחטאת ואחד לעלה
בנבהמה ובעוף	. . . . . Levit. xx. 25		,, ,,	. . . בעוף ובבהמה
לאמו ולאביו	. . . . . Levit. xxi. 2		,, ,,	. . . לאביו לאמו
אמו ואביו	. . . . . Levit. xix. 3		,, ,,	. . . אביו ואמו
הישר והטוב	. . . . . Deut. vi. 18		,, ,,	. . . הטוב והישר
משפט צדק	. . . . . Deut. xvi. 18		,, ,,	. . . צדק ומשפט
בתמים ובאמת	. . . . . Josh. xxiv. 14		,, ,,	. . . באמת ובתמים
המלך אדני	. . . . . 2 Sam. xiv. 15		,, ,,	. . . אדני המלך
הקם ליהוה מזבח	. . . . . 2 Sam. xxiv. 18		,, ,,	. . . הקם מזבה ליהוה
שקלים חמשים	. . . . . 2 Sam. xxiv. 24		,, ,,	. . . חמשים שקלים
לחרבה לשממה	. . . . . Jerem. xliv. 6		,, ,,	. . . לשמה ולחרבה
קדים רוח	. . . . . Hos. xiii. 15		,, ,,	. . . רוח קדים
כירוחי קדם	. . . . . Job xxix. 2		,, ,,	. . . כימי קדם
אבן ועץ	. . . . . 1 Chron. xxii. 15		,, ,,	. . . עץ ואבן
להדות ולהלל	. . . . . 1 Chron. xxiii. 30		,, ,,	. . . להלל ולהדות
ראה עתה	. . . . . 1 Chron. xxviii. 10		,, ,,	. . . עתה ראה
אל אל	. . . . . Job xvi. 11		,, ,,	. . . אל אל
דבש וחמאה	. . . . . Job xx. 17		,, ,,	. . . חמאה ודבש
בזהב ובכסף	. . . . . Dan. xi. 38		,, ,,	. . . בכסף ובזהב
לכליון ולמחלון	. . . . . Ruth iv. 9		,, ,,	. . . מחלון וכליון
רבים עמים	. . . . . Ps. lxxxix. 51		,, ,,	. . . עמים רבים
שנים שלוש	. . . . . Dan. i. 5		,, ,,	. . . שלוש שנים
והארץ נכבשה	. . . . . Josh. xviii. 1		,, ,,	. . . ונכבשה הארץ
ושה ושור	. . . . . Judg. vi. 4		,, ,,	. . . ושור ושה
וראו ודעו	. . . . . 1 Sam. xxiii. 23		,, ,,	. . . ודעו וראו
ובני שלמה	. . . . . 1 Kings i. 21		,, ,,	. . . שלמה בני
ורבו ופרו	. . . . . Ezek. xxxvi. 11		,, ,,	. . . פרו ורבו
ואמות שלוש	. . . . . 2 Chron. vi. 13		,, ,,	. . . שלש אמות
אחד לעלה ואחד לחטאת	. . . . . Levit. xii. 8		,, ,,	. . . אחד לחטאת ואחד לעלה
ורחץ במים את בשרו	. . . . . Levit. xvi. 6		,, ,,	. . . ורחץ בשרו במים
אך את הזהב ואת הכסף	. . . . . Numb. xxii. 22		,, ,,	. . . את הכסף ואת הזהב
בין השמים ובין הארץ	. . . . . 2 Sam. xviii. 9		,, ,,	. . . בין הארץ ובין השמים
אל ישעיהו הנביא בן אמוץ	. . . . . 2 Kings xix. 2		,, ,,	. . . אל ישעיהו בן אמוץ הנביא
ביד נפתויה ובזרוע חזקה	. . . . . Jerem. xxi. 3		,, ,,	. . . ביד הזקה ובזרוע נטויה
בני יהודה ובני ישראל	. . . . . Hos. ii. 2		,, ,,	. . . בני ישראל ובני יהודה
כמה דחנה וכמה ארוכה	. . . . . Zech. ii. 6		,, ,,	. . . כמה ארכה וכמה רחבה
חקת עולם בכל מושבתיכם	. . . . . Levit. xxiii. 21		,, ,,	. . . לדרתיכם בכל מושבתיכם

They are enumerated in that part of the Massorah finalis which is entitled *Various Readings* (חלופי קריאה) p. 62 b, rubric 3. In the heading of this rubric, as well as in the Massorah marginalis on Job xxix. 2, where reference is made to this list, it is erroneously stated that it contains *thirty* (ל) instances, which has evidently arisen from the dropping of the letter ט [= 9]. The *Ochla Ve-Ochla*, section cclxxiii., pp. 53, 147, &c., gives

Also וַיְדַבֵּ֥ר מֹשֶׁ֖ה אֶל־יְהוָ֑ה, *and Moses spake to Jehovah* [Numb. xxvii. 15], is marked "not extant so joined," for in all other passages it is וַיְדַבֵּ֥ר יְהוָ֖ה אֶל־מֹשֶׁ֥ה, *and Jehovah spake to Moses.* When these constructions occur more than once, the Massorites distinctly mention the number of instances, as on וַיְדַבֵּ֥ר אֱלֹהִ֖ים *and the Almighty spake,* they say "three times together;"[91] וַיֹּ֥אמֶר אֱלֹהִ֖ים, *and the Almighty said,* "twenty-five times thus joined together,"[92] since in all other places it is וַיְדַבֵּ֥ר יְהוָ֖ה *and Jehovah spake,* וַיֹּ֥אמֶר יְהוָ֖ה *and Jehovah said.* Indeed, when there are only two words, the correct Codices have not written down the word דסמיכי, since the circle between these two words is sufficient, as בָּרָ֣א ׀ אֱלֹהִ֑ים *the Almighty created,* "occurs three times" [Gen. i. 1],[93] and there is no necessity for saying "three times thus joined together," as I have stated in the Introduction.

☞ Let me now explain the meaning of *Jechidain, Jechidin,* or *Mejuchadin,* for they are all the same. Mark, that wherever words occur joined together, and if a word, or two words, or more, with which they are thus mostly joined, are wanting either before them, or after them, or in the middle, the Massorites remark on them יחידין = *severed.* For example, i. A word wanted at the beginning viz., אֱלֹהֵ֣י יִשְׂרָאֵ֑ל *the Almighty of Israel,* which "occurs twenty-four times alone,"[94]

דסמיך, כי כל שאר וידבר יהוה אל משה; ואם נמצאו כאלה יותר מבמקום אחד, כתבו עליהם כך וכך דסמיכין, כנון וידבר אלהים ג' דסמיכין,[91] ויאמר אלהים כ"ה דסמיכין,[92] כי כל שאר וידבר יהוה, ויאמר יהוה; והאמת כי בנוסחאות המדויקות כשהם ב' מלות לבד, לא כתבו דסמיכין, כי די להם בעגול שבין ב' המלות, כנון בָּרָ֣א ׀ אֱלֹהִ֑ים ג',[93] ואין צריך לומר ג' דסמיכין, כמו שכתבתי בהקדמה:

☞ ועתה אבאר ענין יחידין, או יחידאין, או מיוחדאין, כי הכלאחד הוא; ודע כי בכל מקום שנמצאים מלין סמוכין יחד, ולפניהם או לאחריהן, או באמצע, חסר מלה או מלות שדרכן על הרוב להסמך שם כתבו עליהן יחידין; והמשל בחסרון מלה לפניהן, כנון אלהי ישראל כ"ד יחדאין,[94] כי כל שאר יהוה אלהי ישראל; והחסרים באמצע, כמו פה אמר

---

forty instances, adding בבקר השכים [Prov. xxvii. 14] which otherwise is השכים בבקר. Properly אל חי [Job xxvii. 2], as Dr. Frensdorff, the learned editor of the *Ochla Ve-Ochla,* rightly remarks, whereon the Massorah parva states "not extant" (ל׳), belongs to this rubric, since in all other passages it is אל חי.

[91] The three passages in which וידבר אלהים occur conjointly are, Gen. viii. 15: Exod. vi. 2; xx. 1. They are given in the Massorah marginalis on Gen. viii. 15.

[92] The twenty-five passages in which ויאמר אלהים occurs, are Gen. i. 3, 6, 9, 11, 14, 20, 24, 26, 29; v. 13; ix. 8, 12, 17; xxi. 12; xvii. 15, 19, 9; xlvi. 2; xxxv. 1: Exod. iii. 14: Numb. xxii. 12: 1 Kings iii. 5, 11: Jonah iv. 9: 2 Chron. i. 11. They are given in the Massorah finalis under the letter *Aleph,* p. 8 b, cols. 2 and 3. All the three editions of the *Massoreth Ha-Massoreth* have *twenty-four* (כ׳ד), which we have corrected, as it is a manifest blunder.

[93] For the three passages in which ברא אלהים occurs, see above. p. 139, note 115.

[94] The twenty-four (כ״ד) must be a mistake for *twenty-eight* (כ״ח), since the Massorah marginalis on Exod. xxv. 10 distinctly enumerates twenty-eight instances in which אלהי ישראל occurs without יהוה. They are as follows: Gen. xxxiii. 20: Exod. xxiv. 10: Numb. xvi. 9: 1 Sam. v. 7, 8 (thrice), 11; vi. 5; i. 17; v. 10; vi. 3: 2 Sam. xxiii. 3: 1 Kings viii. 26: Isa. xxix. 23; xli. 17; xlv. 3, 15; xlviii. 2; lii. 12: Ezek. viii. 4; ix. 3; x. 19, 20; xi. 22; xliii. 2: 1 Chron. v. 26: Ps. lxix. 7: Ezra iii. 2; ix. 4.

for in all other instances it is preceded by יהוה *Jehovah.* ii. A word wanted in the middle, viz., כֹּה אָמַר יְהֹוָה אֱלֹהֵי יִשְׂרָאֵל *thus saith Jehovah, the Almighty of Israel,* which "occurs twenty-five times alone,"[95] as in all other instances it is כֹּה אָמַר יְהוָה צְבָאוֹת אֱלֹהֵי יִשְׂרָאֵל *thus saith Jehovah Sabaoth, the Almighty of Israel.* And iii. Without a word at the end, viz., יְבָרֶכְךָ יְהוָה *Jehovah bless thee,* marked "four times alone,"[96] as in all other instances it is יְבָרֶכְךָ יְהוָה אֱלֹהֶיךָ *Jehovah the Almighty bless thee,* except in the Psalms, where it is likewise so. The same is the case with עַד הַיּוֹם *till the day,* which is marked "nine times alone,"[97] since in all other instances it is עַד הַיּוֹם הַזֶּה *till this day.*

Such severances are also to be found in the case of one word, as לָאֹהֶל *to the tent,* which is marked "five times alone;"[98] and עֵדוּת *law,* and מוֹעֵד *assembly,* are like it — that is, not being לְאֹהֶל הָעֵדֻת *to the tabernacle of our testimony,* and לְאֹהֶל הַמּוֹעֵד *to the tabernacle of the congregation,* which are the most in number; thus, also, יִחְיֶה *he shall live,* "occurs eighteen times alone,"[99] and חָיוֹ יִחְיֶה *living, he shall live,* is like it;" also, יְחִי *let him live,* is twice alone,[100] and יְחִי הַמֶּלֶךְ *let the*

---

[95] The twenty-five times in which כה אמר יהוה אלהי ישראל occurs without צבאות are, Exod. v. 1; xxxii. 27: Josh. xxiv. 2: Judg. vi. 8: 1 Sam. x. 18: 2 Sam. xii. 7: 1 Kings xi. 31: 2 Kings xix. 20: Isa. xxxvii. 21: 1 Kings xvii. 14: 2 Kings ix. 6: Jerem. xxi. 4; xxxvii. 7: 2 Kings xxii. 15: 2 Chron. xxxiv. 23: Jerem. xxxiv. 2, 13; xliv. 19; xlv. 2. They are given in the Massorah finalis under the letter *Aleph*, p. 4 *b*, cols. 3 and 4.

[96] The four passages in which יברכך יהוה occurs without אלהך are, Numb. vi. 24; Deut. xv. 4: Jerem. xxxi. 23: Ruth ii. 4. They are enumerated in the Massorah marginalis on Numb. vi. 24.

[97] The nine passages in which עד היום occurs alone, without הזה, are, Gen. xix. 37, 38; xxxv. 20: 2 Sam. xix. 25: 2 Kings x. 27: 2 Chron. viii. 16: Ezek. xx. 31: 2 Chron. xx. 26: xxxv. 25. They are enumerated in the Massorah marginalis on 2 Chron. xx. 26.

[98] The five passages in which לאהל occurs by itself are, Exod. xxvi. 7, 14; xxxvi. 14, 19: 1 Chron. ix. 19. The Massorah marginalis on Exod. xxvi. 7, which treats on this rubric, is hopelessly erroneous. The only correct signal words, whereby it indicates the passages, are the first and second, viz., ועשית יריעות עזים [Exod. xxvi. 7], ויעש יריעות עזים [Exod. xxxvi. 14]. As to the other three, they are as follows: i. ובייום הקים את המשכן, that is Numb. ix. 15, where it is לאהל העדת, which is not to the point. ii. ויעש שלמה, which is equally wrong, inasmuch as of the five verses which commence with these words, viz., 1 Kings vii. 48; viii. 65; xi. 6: 2 Chron. iv. 18, 19, not one has the word לאהל. And iii. ויקרא המלך ליהוידע, *i. e.* 2 Chron. xxiv. 6, where it is לאהל העדות, and is likewise not to the point.

[99] The eighteen passages in which יחי, the future, occurs by itself, that is, without being preceded by חיה, the infinitive absolute, are, Gen. xvii. 18; xxxi. 32: Exod. xix. 13: Numb. xxiv. 23: Deut. viii. 3 (twice): 2 Sam. i. 10: 2 Kings x. 19: Ezek. xviii. 13, 22, 27; xlvii. 9: Ps. lxxxix. 49: Prov. xv. 27: Nehem. ii. 3: Habak. ii. 4: Eccles. vi. 3; xi. 8. They are enumerated in the Massorah finalis under the letter *Cheth*, p. 31 *a*, col. 4.

[100] The two instances in which יחי occurs by itself are, Deut. xxxiii. 6: Ps. xxii. 27. They are given in the Massorah finalis under the letter *Cheth*, p. 31 *b*, col. 1.

king live, is always like it. Moreover, when two words habitually occur in the same verse, the first without *Vav* conjunctive and the second with *Vav* conjunctive, then wherever the one with the *Vav* occurs, and its companion without the *Vav* does not precede it, the Massorites note on the word in question the number of instances in which it is to be found alone. Thus, for instance, on וּלְמַעַן *and in order that*, the Massorites remark, " it occurs nine times alone, as Exod. ix. 16, &c ;[101] and when לְמַעַן is followed by וּלְמַעַן it is the same," that is, in every verse where לְמַעַן occurs, and is followed by וּלְמַעַן, it is like it, as לְמַעַן תִּירָא אֶת יְהֹוָה אֱלֹהֶיךָ וּלְמַעַן יַאֲרִכֻן יָמֶיךָ *that thou mayest fear Jehovah, thy God,—so that thy days may be prolonged* [Deut. vi. 2], &c. Thus, also, וְלִפְנֵי *and before the face of*, " is sixteen times alone," as Numb. xxvii. 21 ; and wherever לִפְנֵי *before*, is followed by וְלִפְנֵי *and before*, it is like it, as לִפְנֵי מֹשֶׁה וְלִפְנֵי אֶלְעָזָר *before Moses and Eliezer* [Numb. xxvii. 2].[102]

There are, moreover, some words which are called *unique*, because of the word with which they are construed, and which construction has no parallel. Thus, אַתָּה זֶה *thou* occurs eighteen times alone, as אַתָּה זֶה *thou this*, " without parallel ;" אַתָּה תִּהְיֶה *thou shalt be*, " has no parallel," &c.[103] Also וְאַתָּה *and thou*, " is eight times alone ; " as וְאַתָּה

---

[101] The nine passages in which ולמען occurs are, Exod. x. 2 ; ix. 16 : Deut. ix. 5 ; iv. 40 ; xi. 9 ; vi. 2 : Ps. xxxi. 4 : 2 Kings xix. 34 : Isa. xxxvii. 35. As these nine instances are distinctly given in the Massorah marginalis on Isa. xxxvii. 35, and as both the Massorah marginalis on the different passages in question, and the Massorah finalis under the *Lamed*, p. 43 b, col. 1, emphatically state that there are *nine* instances, we have corrected the text which had six (ו'), and which has evidently arisen from a misprint.

[102] The sixteen passages in which ולפני occurs with *Vav* conjunctive, without being preceded by לפני, are, Levit. xvi. 14, 15 ; xix. 14 : Numb. xxvii. 21 : 1 Kings vi. 20 : Isa. xlviii. 7 : Ps. lxxii. 5 : Prov. xv. 33 : Ps. cii. 1 : Prov. xvii. 14 ; xviii. 16 : Job viii. 12 : Ezek. xlii. 4 : Job xv. 7 : Jerem. xliv. 10 : Nehem. xiii. 4. They are given in the Massorah marginalis on Numb. xxvii. 21.

[103] The eleven words which are preceded by אתה, and which in this construction occur only once, are as follows:—

אתה תהיה . . Gen. xl. 40	אתה האיש . 2 Sam. xii. 7	אתה אל . . Jerem. xlvi. 28
אתה זה . . Gen. xxvii. 24	אתה קח . 2 Sam. xx. 6	אתה בן . . Ezek. xliii. 10
אתה הדבר . Exod. vii. 2	אתה אמרת . 1 Kings i. 24	אתה מושל . Ps. lxxxix. 10
אתה דבר . 2 Sam. xvii. 6	אתה תשמע . 1 Kings viii. 43	

They are enumerated in the Massorah finalis, under the letter *Aleph*, p. 9 b, cols. 1 and 2, and in the *Ochla Ve-Ochla*, section cclxi., p. 142, &c. As both the Massorah and the *Ochla Ve-Ochla* leave it beyond the shadow of a doubt that there are eleven such instances, we have corrected the text, which in all the three editions has (י"ח) *eighteen*.

תִּהְיֶה and thou shalt be, "without parallel," וְאַתָּה תֶּחֱזֶה and thou shalt see, "is without parallel," &c.[104] The same is the case with many of the particles, as אֶל to, occurs thirty times alone;[105] וְאֶל and to, forty-six times alone;[106] אַל וְאַל, not and not, אִם וְאִם, with and with, כְּן וְכְן from and from, &c., &c.

☞ Let me now explain the word מוּרְדָּפִים, which is a logical term, denoting *connected, resembling, identical*, just as those words are called synonyms which are identical in sense and different in sound; *ex. gr.*, שֶׁמֶשׁ *sun*, חַמָּה *sun*, חֶרֶס *sun*, as I have explained in the Section on the Different Parts of Speech,

כמו וְאַתָּה תִּהְיֶה לִית דכותיה, וְאַתָּה תֶחֱזֶה לירת דכותיה וכולי;[104] וכן הרבה ממלורד הדבק, כמו אֶל לְמִ"ד יחידין,[105] וְאֶל מִ"ו יחידין;[106] וכן כן וכן, אִם וְאִם, אַל וְאַל ורומיהן רבים מאד:

☞ וְעַתָּה אבאר מלת מוּרְדָּפִים, והיא מלה הגיונית, ופידושה רצופים, כמו שקראו שמות נרדפין כל השמות שהם שוים בפתרון ושונים במבטא כמו שֶׁמֶשׁ, חַמָּה, חֶרֶס כמו

---

[104] The eight words which occur only once preceded by וְאַתָּה, are as follows: —

ואתה ואהרן	Numb. xvi. 17	ואתה עשה . . Judg. xi. 27	ואתה נותן . . Ps. cxlv. 15
ואתה שמעת	. Deut. ix. 2	ואתה תעשה . 1 Kings v. 23	ואתה לך . . Dan. xii. 13
ואתה עשיתה	. 1 Sam. xv. 6	ואתה אדני . . 1 Kings i. 20	

They are given in the Massorah finalis under the letter *Aleph*, p. 13 *b*, col. 2. The *Ochla Ve-Ochla*, section cclxii., pp. 51, 142, gives three additional instances, viz., ואתה שלום 1 Sam. xxv. 6; ואתה תשא 1 Kings v. 23; and ואתה נפשך Ezek. xxxiii. 9. It will be seen that the two instances given by Levita in the text are not included in the Massoretic list. Indeed, though ואתה תהיה occurs only once, ואתה is of frequent occurrence (comp. Exod. iv. 16 : Deut. xxxiii. 44 : 2 Sam. v. 2 : 1 Chron. xi. 2). There must therefore be a mistake in the text. The Sulzbach edition omits וכן ואתה ד' יחידין, which renders the text of that edition perfectly unintelligible.

[105] The list of the thirty instances in which אֶל precedes words in an unparalleled manner is so hopelessly confused, that it would require more space to correct it than the limits of a note permit. We must, therefore, refer to it as it stands in the Massorah finalis under the letter *Aleph*, p. 6 *b*, cols. 3 and 4.

[106] The forty-five words which occur only once preceded by וְאֶל, are as follows: —

ואל קין . . . Gen. iv. 5	ואל אבישי . 1 Sam. xxvi. 6	ואל שמעיהו Jerem. xxix. 24
ואל אמה . . Gen. vi. 16	ואל נגב . . 1 Sam. xxvii. 10	ואל יהודה . Jerem. xxx. 4
ואל הבקר . . Gen. xviii. 7	ואל פארתיו . Ezek. xxxi. 13	ואל ירמיהו Jerem. xxxix. 15
ואל אחיו . . Gen. xxxvii. 10	ואל נצרו . . 1 Sam. x. 14	ואל הנבול . Ezek. xliii. 20
ואל יעקב . . Exod. vi. 3	ואל צקלג . . 1 Sam. xxx. 1	ואל השלחנות Ezek. xl. 43
ואל משה . . Exod. xxiv. 1	ואל נביאי . 2 Kings iii. 13	ואל עמי . . . Joel iv. 3
ואל הארץ . Exod. xxvi. 21	ואל אלהינו . . Isa. lv. 7	ואל אלהים . . Job v. 8
ואל שתי . . Exod. xii. 22	ואל האטים . . Isa. xix. 3	ואל יהוה . . Ps. xxx. 9
ואל הזקנים . Exod. xxiv. 14	ואל האבות . . Isa. xix. 3	ואל הארץ . . Ps. l. 4
ואל הלוים . Numb. xviii. 26	ואל שרה . . . Isa. li. 2	ואל אנשים . Ezek. xxiii. 42
ואל רעשו . . Deut. ix. 27	ואל השמים . . Jerem. iv. 23	ואל עונם . . Hos. iv. 8
ואל חטאתו . Deut. ix. 27	ואל החרב . Jerem. xxxiii. 4	ואל חוף . . Jerem. xlvii. 7
ואל פרעה . . Exod. vi. 13	ואל נבוכדרצאר . Jer. xxv. 9	ואל לב . . Ezek. xi. 21
ואל אשת . . Levit. xviii. 20	ואל ארצו . . Jerem. l. 18	ואל ברכת . Nehem. ii. 14
ואל אבנר . . 1 Sam. xxvi. 14	ואל צדקיהו Jerem. xxix. 21	ואל מקומו . . Eccl. i. 5

It will be seen that the Massorah marginalis, p. 6 *b*, col. 4, gives only forty-five such instances. There must therefore be a mistake in the Massorah marginalis on Exod. xxiv. 14, where, in referring to this rubric, it is stated that there are *forty-four* (מ"ד). In the *Ochla Ve-Ochla*, section lxxxv., pp. 26, 89, &c., where this rubric is given, the heading describes it as containing forty-five (מ"ה), and the rubric only gives this number; yet it mentions two instances not contained in the Massorah finalis, viz., ואל ערת (Numb. xxxi. 12) and ואל צדקיהו (Jerem. xxix. 21), whilst it omits two instances, viz., ואל פארתיו (Ezek. xxxi. 13) and ואל חוף (Jerem. xlvii. 7), which are given in the Massorah finalis. There can, therefore, be but little doubt that the מ"ד = forty-four in the Massorah marginalis on Exod. xxiv. 14, the מ"ה = forty-five in the *Ochla Ve-Ochla*, and the מ"ו = forty-six in the text of Levita, are corruptions of the original מ"ז = forty-seven.

which see.[107] The Massorites, too, employ this expression. Thus, three verses are alike (מוֹרָדִפִים), each one having seventy-two letters; viz., Exod. xiv. 19–21,[108] so also the six verses which are alike, each having five biliteral words, as כִּי נָם גַּם לִי נָם זֶה לְךָ בֵּן [Gen. xxxv. 17], לָךְ לֹא [1 Kings iii. 26], &c.;[109] and the six words which are alike, each having a letter repeated thrice, as בְּבָבַת in the apple [Zech. ii. 12], חָנֵּנִי pity me [Ps. ix. 14], &c.[110]

SECTION VII., concerning the *Presence and Absence of Serviles.* — Mark that נסיב denotes *taking.* Thus, in the Targum, לָקַח *he took* [Gen. ii. 22] is rendered by נסיב; likewise לֹקְחֵי *the takers of* [Gen xix. 14], is translated in the Targum נסבי. This is also the case with the word לקחיה, whenever it occurs in the preterite and participle, it is always rendered in the Targum by נסיבה *to take;* whilst the infinitive, imperative, and the future are always rendered by סיב, with the radical *Nun* omitted.

☞ Now the Massorites were in the habit of marking the prefixes with the expression *Nesiba*, and more especially the letters *Beth*, *Vav*, *Kaph*, *Lamed*, and *Mem*. Thus, for instance, they give a list of twenty-nine words which have the prefix *Beth*, and which in all

שׁבארתי בפרק המינים ע"ש [107]; ובעלי המסורה שמשו ג"כ בזאת המלה, כגון ג' פסוקים מורדפים דבכל חד וחד ע"ב אותיות, ויסע, ויבא, ויט;[108] וכן ה' פסוקים בכל חד ה' מלין מורדפין מן ב' ב' אותיות, כמו פי גם זה לך בן, גם לי גם לך לא יהיה וכו';[109] וכן ו' מלות מן ג' אותיות מורדפין, בבבת עינו, חנני יהוה וכולי:[110]

המאמר השביעי בנסיבין א' משמשין וקרחין: ודע כי נסיב הוא לשון לקיחה, בתרגום של אשר לקח מן האדם רי נסיב מאדם; וכן לקחי בנוחדו תרגום נסבי בנתיה; וכן כל לשון לקיחה בעוברים ובבינונים מתורגמין בלשון נסיבה ; אבל המקור והציווי והעתיד, מתורגם בלשון סיב בחסרון נו"ן השורש:

☞ והנה נהגו בעלי המסורת לכתוב לשון נסיבה על אותיות השימוש שבראשי התיבות, ובפרט על אותיות בוכ"לם, כגון כ"ט מלין נסבי בי"ת בריש תיבותא וכל

---

[107] The "Section on the Different Kinds of Words" constitutes the second of the four sections, composing the work entitled "The Sections of Elias" (comp. p. 54, &c., ed Prague, 1793), a description of which has already been given, *vide supra*, p. 18, &c.

[108] From the fact that these three verses have respectively seventy-two letters, great mysteries have been assigned to them from time immemorial. They have been identified with the Divine name, which consists of seventy-two words, or, according to Ibn Ezra, of the number seventy-two, viz., י 10 + ה 15 + יהו 21 + יהוה 26 = 72; or the tetragrammaton, with each letter written out fully, viz., הי 15 + ו"ו 22 + הי 15 + יוד 20 = 72. Comp. Rashi on *Succa*, 45 a; Nachmanides, *Introduction to his Commentary on the Pentateuch;* Ibn Ezra, *Commentary on Exodus* xiv. 19–21; xxxiii. 21; Ginsburg, *the Kabbalah*, p. 50, &c.

[109] The other three verses which respectively have five biliterals following each other are, Gen. vi. 10: 1 Sam. xx. 29: Nehem. ii. 2. They are noted in the Massorah parva on each verse, and the whole list is given in the Massorah marginalis on 1 Kings iii. 26, and Nehem. ii. 2. The text of three editions of the *Massoreth Ha-Massoreth* states that there are *six* (ו) such verses, but as this is contradicted by the explicit declarations of the Massorah, we have no doubt that it is a misprint, and have therefore corrected the text.

[110] The other four words in which the same letters follow three times are, ממלכה (Ps. cv. 13); וממלכה (1 Chron. xvi. 20); ככבי (Nehem. ix. 23); הממם (2 Chron. xv. 6). Comp. *Ochla Ve-Ochla*, section cclxvii. pp. 52, 143.

other instances have *Kaph*, as בְּמִנְחָה *in the offering* [Gen. xxxii. 21], בַּחוֹל *in the sand* [Exod. ii. 12], &c., for in all other instances it is בְּמִנְחָה *as an offering*, and בַּחוֹל *as sand.*[111] On the contrary, again, there is an alphabetical list of words which begin with *Kaph*, and which have no parallel in any other passage, as בַּבֹּקֶר *as in the morning* [Job xi. 17], and כְּיִשְׂרָאֵל *as in Israel* [2 Sam. vii. 23], being in all other instances בַּבֹּקֶר *in the morning*, and בְּיִשְׂרָאֵל *in Israel.*[112] As to the letter ו there are many alphabetical lists, rows, and registers of pairs, of words which have this prefix and which have it not. All of these are enumerated in the beginning of the work entitled *Ochla Ve-Ochla*, which I mentioned in the Poetical Introduction, which see [*supra*, p. 93]; some of them I also cited in the preceding Sections.

Let me now explain the use of the word מִשַׁמְּשִׁין, which is as follows: — When words begin with two of the servile letters, *Beth*, *Vav*, *Kaph*, *Lamed*, and *Mem*, the Massorites do not mark them נסיבין *they have taken*, but מִשַׁמְּשִׁין *they employ*. Thus, for instance: i. The nineteen words which employ two *Lameds* at the beginning, and which have no parallel, as לָלוּט *to Lot* [Gen. xiii. 5], לְלִבְנָה *to Libnah* [Josh. x. 32], &c.[113] ii. The hundred and eighteen words which

---

[111] The twenty-nine words which occur only once with the prefix *Beth*, and which in all other passages have *Kaph*, are as follows:—

במנחה	. . Gen. xxxii. 21	בראשנים	. 2 Sam. xxi. 9	בפעלם	. . Job xxiv. 5
בחול	. . Exod. ii. 12	בטיט	. . Zech. x. 5	בשבתו	. . Prov. xxxi. 23
בשמע	. . Exod. xvi. 8	ובדבריך	. 1 Kings xviii. 36	בחם	. . Isa. xviii. 4
בשמעם	. 2 Chron. xx. 29	ברצונו	. . Ps. xxx. 6	ובמנחת	. . Ezra ix. 5
בארבה	. . Exod. x. 12	ברביבים	. . Ps. lxv. 11	ובמשפטיך	. Nehem. ix. 29
בעבר	. Exod. xxxiii. 22	בעגלי	. . Ps. lxviii. 31	בלבתך	. . Ezek. xliii. 23
במסלה	. . 1 Sam. vi. 12	במחלקותיהם	. 2 Chr. xxxi. 17	בברכת	. . Prov. xi. 11
בשלש	. . Isa. xvi. 14	במחלקות	2 Chron. xxxi. 15	בלה	. . Lament. iii. 4
בקרא	. Jerem. xxxvi. 13	במחלקותם	2 Chron. viii. 14	בחלילים	. . 1 Kings i. 40
בענקים	. . Josh. xiv. 15	ובהוציאם	2 Chron. xxxiv. 14		

They are given in the Massorah finalis under the letter *Beth*, p. 14 *a*, col. 3. The *Ochla Ve-Ochla*, section ccxv., pp. 45, 128, which also gives this list, omits בשמעם (2 Chron. xx. 29), and במחלקותיהם (2 Chron. xxi. 17), whilst it adds ברמות (Gen. v. 1), and במשמרותהם (2 Chron. xxxi. 17).

[112] As the list, of which the above are examples, contains upwards of one hundred and forty words, making it too long to be given here entire, we must refer the reader for it to the Massorah finalis under the letter *Kaph*, p. 38 *a*, cols. 1 and 2, and the *Ochla Ve-Ochla*, section xix., pp. 9, &c., 34, &c.

[113] The Massorah finalis, under the letter *Lamed*, p. 40 *b*, col. 3, gives the following list of words which have two *Lameds* at the beginning, viz.:—

begin with *Vav* and *Lamed*, as וְכֵן ; ¹¹⁴ וְלִמְשֹׁל בַּיָּם, וְלִמְשֹׁל וְשָׁנִים, וּלְיָמִים כְּמוֹ גַל
and *for days* [Gen. i. 14], וְכֵן ; ¹¹⁵ בַּאֲתָ֫י וּמֵאָ֖ז כְּמוֹ וֹ, מְשַׁמְּשִׁין שָׁמָּה וּלְיָמִים
and *to rule* [Gen. i. 18], מְשַׁמְּשִׁין וּבֵן ; ¹¹⁶ בָּרוּךְ וּמְבָרֲכֶיךָ וב, מְשַׁמְּשִׁין וְלִמְשֹׁל
&c.¹¹⁴ iii. The register of words מָלִים ב' וְכֵן ; ¹¹⁷ אֲשׁוּרֵנוּ וּמִגְּבָעוֹת וֹמֵג
which begin with *Vav*, *Mem*, and
Aleph, as וּמֵאָז and *since then* [Exod. v. 23], &c.¹¹⁵ iv. Those which begin
with *Vav*, *Mem*, and *Beth*, as וּמְבָרֲכֶיךָ and *thy blessers* [Gen. xxvii. 29],
&c.¹¹⁶ v. Those which have *Vav*, *Mem*, *Gimmel*, as וּמִגְּבָעוֹת and *from
the hills* [Numb. xxiii. 9], &c.¹¹⁷ vi. The two words which have *Lamed*

לְלוּט	. . .	Gen. xiii. 5	לַיְלָה	. .	Ps. xix. 3	לְבוּשֶׁךָ	. .	Isa. lxiii. 2
לִבְמָה	. .	Judg. xxi. 19	לָבִיא	. .	Job xxxviii. 39	לְבוּשֶׁךָ	. .	Prov. xxvii. 26
לְהָבָה	. . .	Isa. x. 17	לַחְמְךָ	. .	Prov. xxvii. 27	לְלַעֲנָה	. . .	Amos v. 7
לְלֶשֶׁת	. .	Jerem. xxxv. 4	לָלוּשׁ	. .	Josh. xix. 47	לְלַעֲנָה	. . .	Amos vi. 12
לְבָבָם	. . .	Hos. vii. 2	לָלִישׁ	. .	Josh. x. 35	לְלָשֹׁנוּ	. . .	Gen. x. 5

It will be seen that this list contains fifteen words, though the heading of it in the
Massorah states that there are *eleven* (א"י) such instances. Why Buxtorf omits לְלַעֲנָה
Amos v. 7, and how he came to make it fourteen (י"ד), is difficult to divine. The statement in the text of the *Massoreth Ha-Massoreth*, that there are *nineteen* (ט"י) such
words, must be a misprint.

¹¹⁴ For the list of the one hundred and eighteen instances in question, we must refer
to the Massorah finalis under the letter *Lamed*, p. 40*b*, col. 3; p. 41*a*, col. 1, as it is
by far too long to be inserted here.

¹¹⁵ The list (שמה) of words beginning in one instance only with *Vav* and *Mem*, is
as follows :—

וּמֹאוּ	. . .	Exod. v. 23	וּמֵאֲכַל	. .	Ezra iii. 7	וּמֵרָאשָׁה	. .	Ruth i. 5
וּמֵאֹיְבִי	. .	2 Sam. xxii. 4	וּמֵאֱלֹהִים	. .	2 Chron. xxii. 7	וּמֵאֵבֶל	. . .	Esther ix. 22
וּמֵאַחֲרֵי	. .	Jerem. iii. 19	וּמֵאֲצִילֶיהָ	. .	Isa. xli. 9	וּמֵאַכְלֵךְ	. . .	Ezek. iv. 10
וּמֵאֵפֶל	. . .	Isa. xxix. 18	וּמֵאֲשֻׁר	. .	1 Chron. xii. 36	וּמֵאָרִיךְ	. .	Eccles. viii. 12
וּמֵאַדְמָה	. .	Job v. 6	וּמֵאִי	. .	Isa. xi. 11	וּמֵאֲהָבִיט	. .	Jerem. xxii. 22
וּמֵאַרְצוֹת	. .	Ps. cvii. 3	וּמֵאַנְשֵׁי	. .	Ps. lix. 2	וּמֵאֲמַר	. .	Esther ix. 32
וּמֵאֱלֹהַי	. . .	Isa. xl. 27	וּמֵאַכְלוֹ	. .	Habak. i. 16	וּמֵאָהֳתוֹת	. .	Jerem. x. 2
וּמֵאֵלֶה	. . .	Ps. lix. 13	וּמֵאַכְלוֹת	. .	Prov. xxx. 14	וּמֵאָטוֹר	. .	Zech. x. 5
וּמֵאַסְפְּכֶם	. .	Isa. lii. 12	וּמֵאֲשׁוּרָיו	. .	Isa. ix. 15	וּמֵאַרְצוֹ	. .	Ezek. xxxvi. 20

The list is given in the Massorah finalis under the letter *Mem*, p. 44*a*, col. 2. Of these
twenty-seven, the *Ochla Ve-Ochla*, section xviii., pp. 8 and 31, &c., where this list forms
the first part of a lengthy alphabetical register of words beginning with the letters *Vav*
and *Mem*, only gives sixteen, and omits Nos. 2, 3, 9, 10, 11, 17, 19, 20, 22, 24, and 26,
whilst it adds וּמֵאֲמַר [Dan. iv. 14].

¹¹⁶ The list (שמה) of words beginning in one instance only with *Vav*, *Mem*, and
Beth, is as follows :—

וּמְבָרֲכֶיךָ	. .	Gen. xxvii. 29	וּמֵבִין	. . .	Dan. viii. 23	וּמִבָּמוֹת	. .	Numb. xxi. 20
וּמְבָרֵךְ	. .	1 Chron. xvii. 27	וּמְבָרַכְתָּךְ	. .	2 Sam. vii. 29	וּמִבְקְרוֹן	. . .	2 Sam xii. 4
וּמִבְּלִי	. . .	Job xxiv. 8	וּמְבוֹא	. .	Jerem. xvii. 26	וּמִבַּלְעֲדֵי	. .	Isa. xliv. 6
וּמִבֶּטֶן	. . .	Hos. ix. 11	וּמִבְיָאֵה	. .	Dan. xi. 6	וּמִבְשָֹׂרְךָ	. .	Isa. lviii. 7
			וּמִבְטָח	. .	2 Sam. viii. 8			

These instances are given in the Massorah finalis under the letter *Mem*, p. 44*a*, col. 2.
Of these thirteen words, the *Ochla Ve-Ochla*, section xviii., only gives five, omittting
Nos. 5, 6, 7, 8, 9, 10, 11, and 12, whilst it adds וּכְבָנַיִם 2 Chron. xix. 7. It must be
added that וּמִבֶּטֶן is not unique, inasmuch as, besides Hos. ix. 11, quoted in the Massorah finalis, it occurs in Job xxxi. 8.

¹¹⁷ The list (שמה) of words beginning in one instance only with *Vav*, *Mem*, and
Gimmel, is as follows :—

וּמִגְּבָעוֹת	.	Exod. xxviii. 40	וּמְגָרֵשׁ	. .	Numb. xxxv. 2	וּמִגְדַּפְתָם	. . .	Isa. li. 7
וּמִגְבָעוֹת	.	Numb. xxiii. 9	וּמְגָרָשֶׁיהָ	. .	Numb. xxxv. 4	וּמָגְדָּךְ	. . .	Ps. xlix. 17
וּמִגְרַת	. .	Exod. iii. 22	וּמְגֻרָשָׁיו	. .	Josh. xxi. 42	וּמַגִּישׁ	. .	Malachi ii. 12
וּמִגְרָל	. .	Numb. xxxvi. 3	וּמִגוֹ	. .	Job xxxi. 20	וּמִגֵּאַר	. .	Isa. liv. 9

Of these twelve words, which are given in the Massorah finalis under the letter *Mem*, and *He* at the end, viz., וּבַשְׁפֵלָה *and in the valley* [Is. xxxii. 19] &c. vii. Those which employ *He* and *Vav* at the end of the word, as וְאַנְוֵהוּ *and I shall exalt him* [Exod. xv. 2], וַאֲרֹמְמֶנְהוּ *and I shall extol him* [ibid.] &c. [118] And viii. The expressions which terminate with *Kaph Mem*, or *He Mem*, or *Lamed Mem*,—on all these the Massorites remark, משמשין *they employ*, and not נסיבין *they take*.

דמשמשין לה בסוף התיבה, כגון וּבַשְׁפֵלָה תשפל העיר; וכן דמשמשין הו בסוף, כמו וָאֲנַוֵהוּ, וַאֲרֹמְמֶנְהוּ ורומיהן; [118] וכן מלין דמשמשים כם, או הם, או לם בסוף, על כלן כתבו משמשין ולא נסיבין:

☞ זהנה לא על אותיות השימוש לבד כתבו משמשין, כי גם על אותיות שרשיות כתבו כן, כגון אלפא ביתא מן מלים דמשמשין א״ת ב״ש ג״ר וכולי, כגון אֹרְחַת ישמעאלים ל׳, הרי את, בְּיבֹשׁ קצירה ל׳, הרי בש, גְּעַר חית ל׳, הרי גר; [119] וכן אלפא ביתא מן מלין

☞ It is moreover to be noticed, that the Massorites not only mark the servile letters, as *Meshamshin*, but also the radical letters. Thus, for instance, the alphabetical list of words which employ *Aleph Tav*, *Beth Shin*, *Gimmel Resh*, &c., as אֹרְחַת *company of* [Gen. xxxvii. 25] is marked "not extant" where we have *Aleph* and *Tav* at the two ends; בִּיבֹשׁ *in the withering* [Isa. xxvii. 11] is marked "not extant" where we have *Beth* and *Shin* at the two ends; גְּעַר *rebuke* [Ps. lxviii. 31], is marked "not extant" where we have *Gimmel* and *Resh* at the two ends. [119] Or the alphabetical

p. 44 a, col. 3, the *Ochla Ve-Ochla*, section xviii., only gives two, viz., the fourth and eighth.

[118] The words which occur only once with *He* and *Vav* at the end are as follows:—

ואנוהו	. . Exod. xv. 2	ועתליהו	. 2 Chron. xxii. 10	והביאותיהו	. Ezek. xvii. 20
וארממנהו	. Exod. xv. 2	השכירהו	. Jerem. xlviii. 26	גרשתיהו	. Ezek. xxxi. 11
יבוננהו	. Deut. xxxii. 10	והפצתו	. Job xviii. 11	העירותהו	. . Isa. xlv. 13
יצרנהו	. Deut. xxxii. 10	אשביענהו	. . Ps. xci. 16	בקשתיהו	Song of Songs v. 6
משיתהו	. . Exod. ii. 10	ואראהו	. . Ps. xci. 16	ונשאתיהו	. 1 Chron. xvii. 9
ועשיתיהו	. 1 Kings xvii. 12	ילדתיהו	. Numb. xi. 12	והשפילהו	. . . Job xl. 11
יעברנהו	. Jerem. v. 22	ומעלתהו	. Ezek. xliii. 17	שנאתיהו	2 Chron. xviii. 7
אזקרנו	. Job xxix. 16	מאסתיהו	. 1 Sam. xvi. 7	ואשמנהו	. Jerem. xiii. 5
רממתהו	. Ezek. xxxi. 4	שקויהו	. . Lam. ii. 16	אכלהו	. . Ezek. xv. 5
מסהו	. . Nahum i. 13	והגעתיהו	. Ezek. xiii. 14	ותזבחהו	. 1 Sam. xxviii. 24
ושפטהו	. Ezek. xliv. 24	והשמותיהו	. Ezek. xiv. 8		

They are given in the Massorah finalis under the letter *He*, p. 22 b, col. 3.

[119] It has already been remarked (vide supra, p. 190, &c.), that by bending the Hebrew alphabet exactly in the middle, and putting the one half over the other, a variety of anagrammatic alphabets are obtained, which derive their respective names from the first two specimen pairs of letters indicating the interchange. Here we have an alphabetical list of words which occur only once, arranged according to this anagrammatic alphabet, denominated *Athbash* (את׳בש), that is, the first and last letter of each word in question yields this alphabet. They are as follows:—

ארחת	. Gen. xxxvii. 25	דופק	. Song of Songs v. 2	זרע	. . . Ps. xcvii. 11
אתכרית	. . . Dan. vii. 15	דלק	. . . Dan. vii. 9	חנם	. . . Isa. xxx. 4
ביבש	. . Isa. xxvii. 11	דומשק	. 2 Kings xvi. 10	חרחס	. 2 Kings xxii. 14
בשלש	. . . Isa. xl. 12	הפץ	. . . Job xl. 11	טוחן	. . Judg. xvi. 21
גור	. . . Isa. liv. 15	המץ	. . . Isa. xvi. 4	ירחם	. . . Hos. xiv. 4
גר	. . Isa. xxvii. 9	ויך	. . Ezek. xxxi. 7	ככל	. . Job xxiv. 24
גער	. . Ps. lxviii. 31	וירך	. . Exod. iv. 26	כליל	. . Isa. xxx. 29
		זע	. . . Esther v. 9		

This list is given in the Massorah finalis under the letter *Aleph*, p. 1 b, cols. 2 and 3; and in the *Ochla Ve-Ochla*, section xxxviii., pp. 13, 49. The latter adds the word שחון, Deut. ix. 21, whilst the learned Heidenheim remarks that ירחם, Prov. xxviii. 13, and כליל, Isa. xvi. 3, ought properly to be included in this list.

list of words which employ *Aleph* and *Beth*, *Beth* and *Gimmel*, *Gimmel* and *Daleth*, *Daleth* and *He*, &c., as אֲבִינֵר *Abiner* [1 Sam. xiv. 50], marked "not extant" where we have *Aleph* and *Beth* commencing the word; בִּגְוִיַּת *in the carcase of* [Judg. xiv. 8], marked "not extant;" גַּדֵּל *great* [Numb. vi. 5, Prov. xix. 19], marked "not extant;" דָּהֲרוֹת *rapid courses* [Judg. v. 22], marked "not extant," &c.[120] It is therefore evident that in most of these instances the letters are not servile, and that the Massorites mean that they are employed in the pronunciation of the particular word.

דמשמשין א"ב, ב"ג, ג"ד, ד"ה, כמו אֲבִינֵר לית, בִּגְוִיַּת לית, גַּדֵּל לית, דָּהֲרוֹת לית וכו';[120] הלא תראה כי על הרוב אין בהן אות השימוש אלא ר"ל דמשמשי במבטא מלה ההיא; וגם על יתרון וחסרון מלות הדבק נהגו לכתוב משמשין, כגון ו' זוגין מן ב' ב' בעניינא, קדמאה משמש את, ותנינא לא משמש את, כגון קדמאה אֶת אֲשֶׁר הָאֱלֹהִים עוֹשֶׂה, חנינא אֲשֶׁר הָאֱלֹהִים עוֹשֶׂה;[121] וכן ד' זוגין מן ב' ב' בעניינא, קדמאה משמש לא, ותנינא לא משמש לא, כגון קדמאה לֹא אֲדֹנִי שְׁמָעֵנִי, ותנינא אֲדֹנִי שְׁמָעֵנִי:[122]

☜ והכלל כי ההפרש שבין נסיבין ומשמשין הוא שמלת נסיבין לא באה רק על אות אחת מאותיות דשימוש שבראש התיבה

Moreover, the redundance and the absence of the conjunctive particle they likewise mark as *Meshamshin*. Thus, for instance, the six words which respectively occur twice in the same section, the first time with the particle את, and the second without it. The first of such a pair is אֶת אֲשֶׁר *that which*, [Gen. xli. 25], and the second אֲשֶׁר *which*, without the particle אֶת [Gen. xli. 28].[121] The four words which respectively occur twice in the same section, and which have in the first passage the negative particle לֹא, and in the second passage are without it; as the first לֹא אֲדֹנִי שְׁמָעֵנִי *not my lord, hear me* [Gen. xxiii. 11], and the second אֲדֹנִי שְׁמָעֵנִי *my lord, hear me* [Gen. xxiii. 15], &c.[122]

☞ As a rule, the difference between *Nesibin* and *Meshamshin* is, that the term *Nesibin* is only applied to a single letter of the

---

[120] This list of words, occurring only once, represents another of the anagrammatic alphabets obtained by a similar process to the foregoing, and is denominated *Abbag* (אב׳בג). The words ranged under the alphabet to which Levita refers are as follows:—

אבינר	. .	1 Sam. xiv. 50	חטבות	. . . Prov. vii. 16	עפרות	. . .	Prov. viii. 26
בגרות	. .	Jerem. xli. 17	טירה	Song of Songs viii. 9	פצלות	. . .	Gen. xxx. 37
גדל	. .	Numb. vi. 5	יכרו	. . . . Job xl. 30	צקון	. . .	Isa. xxvi. 16
דהרות	. .	Judg. v. 22	כלוא	. . . . Obad. 16	קראן	. . .	Exod. ii. 20
הומה	. .	1 Kings i. 41	למס	. . . . Job vi. 40	רשם	. . .	Dan. vi. 10
וזהמהו	. .	Job xxxiii. 20	מנע	. . . . Prov. i. 15	שתי	. . .	Ps. lxxiii. 28
זחלתי	. .	Job xxxii. 6	נסתר	. . . Gen. xxxi. 49	תתנו	. . .	Exod. xxii. 29
			סעפים	. . . Ps. cxix. 113			

They are given in the Massorah finalis under the letter *Aleph*, p. 1 b, col. 1; and in the *Ochla Ve-Ochla*, section xxxvii. pp. 13, 48, &c.

[121] The six pairs to which Levita refers we could not find either in the Massorah or in the *Ochla Ve-Ochla*.

[122] The four words which occur twice in the same sentence, once with the negative particle לֹא, and once without it, are as follows:—

לא אדני	. . . .	Gen. xxiii. 11	לא עשיתם	. . . . . .	Ezek. v. 7
אדני	. . . .	Gen. xxiii. 15	עשיתם	. . . . . .	Ezek. xi. 12
לא הפך	. . . .	Levit. xiii. 4	לא נחשב	. . . . . .	1 Kings x. 21
הפך לבן	. . . .	Levit. xiii. 20	נחשב	. . . . . .	2 Chron. ix. 20

They are given in the Massorah finalis under the letter *Lamed*, p. 41 b, col. 4, and in the *Ochla Ve-Ochla*, section ccl., p. 138.

224

serviles at the beginning of a word, and especially to the *Vav* conjunctive, whilst the expression *Meshamshin* is employed to describe two letters at the beginning or end of a word, whether they are servile or radical, as well as to denote the absence of one of the conjunctive particles, as I have explained it. In some Codices, indeed, this order is reversed, but they are not correct.

☞ I shall now explain the expression *Karchin = bare*. It is the opposite to the word *Nesibin*, and is only used with regard to the letter *Vav* at the beginning of a word, and then only when there occur in one verse, or in the same section, three or four words or more, some of which have *Vav* at the beginning and some not. In such a case the Massorites mark those words which have *Vav* with *Nesibin = with*, whilst those which have not *Vav* are marked with *Karchin = bare, without*. Thus, for instance:—i. The six verses repeating respectively a word four times, the first two of which are *Karchin* = without *Vav*, and the second two are *Nesibin* = with *Vav*, viz., בֵּין בֵּין וּבֵין וּבֵין *between, between, and between, and between* [Deut. i. 16], &c.[123] ii. The four verses repeating respectively a word four times, the first three of which are *Karchin* = without *Vav*, and the fourth is *Nesib* = with *Vav*, viz., שָׂרֵי שָׂרֵי שָׂרֵי וְשָׂרֵי *rulers of, rulers of, rulers of, and rulers of* [Deut. i. 15], &c.[124] iii. The two verses containing respectively four words, the first of which is *Karchi* = without *Vav*, and the other three are *Nesibin* = with *Vav*, viz., בְּתוֹךְ וּבְתוֹךְ וּבְתוֹךְ וּבְתוֹךְ *in, and in, and in, and in* [Exod. xxxix. 3], &c.[125] iv. The six words in one verse, the first, second, and

ובפרט על הוי"ו, ומלת משמשין באה על ב' אותיות שבראש התיבה, או בסוף התיבה בין שהן משמשיות או שרשיות, או על חסרון אחת ממלת הדבק, כמו שבארתי ; וביש נוסחאות נשתנה בהן זה הסדר, ואינן מובהקין :

☜ זעתה אבאר מלת קרחי, והיא להפך ממלת נסיבין, ולא באה רק על חוי"ו שבראש התיבה, וזה כשיהיו בפסוק אחד, או בענין אחד, ג' או ד' מלות, או יותר, קצתן עם וי"ו בראש, וקצתן בלי וי"ו, כתבו על אותן שעם חוי"ו נסיבין, ועל אותן שבלי וי"ו קרחין ; כגון ו' פסוקים מן ד' ד' מלין, ב' קדמאין קרחין, וב' בתראין נסיבין ו"ו, כמו ואצוה את שופטיכם וגומר, בֵּין בֵּין וּבֵין וּבֵין ורומיהן ;[123] וכן ד' פסוקים דאית בהון ד' מלין דמיין, ג' קדמאין קרחין, ורביעאה נסיב וי"ו, ואקח את ראשי שופטיכם, שָׂרֵי שָׂרֵי שָׂרֵי וְשָׂרֵי ;[124] וכן ב' פסוקים דכל חד ד' מלין קדמאין קרחין, וג' בתראין נסיבין וי"ו, כמו וקצץ פתילים וגומר, בְּתוֹךְ וּבְתוֹךְ וּבְתוֹךְ וּבְתוֹךְ ;[125] וכן ו'

---

[123] The six verses which respectively have the same words four times, twice with *Vav* conjunctive, and twice without it, are,—

בֵּין בֵּין וּבֵין וּבֵין . . . . . Deut. i. 16	מפני מפני ומפני ומפני . . . Isa. xxi. 15
אל אל ואל ואל . . . . . Deut. xx. 3	בערי בערי ובערי ובערי . . Jerem. xxxiii. 13
כי כי וכי וכי . . . . . 1 Kings xviii. 27	לא לא ולא ולא . . . . . Hos. xi. 9

They are given in the Massorah marginalis on Hosea xi. 9.

[124] The four verses which respectively have the same word four times, in the first instance with the *Vav* conjunctive, and in the other three without it, are,—

שׂרי שׂרי שׂרי ושׂרי . . . Exod. xviii. 21	אל אל אל ואל . . . . . Ps. xxvii. 9
שׂרי שׂרי שׂרי ושׂרי . . . Exod. xviii. 25	דרך דרך דרך ודרך . . . Prov. xxx. 19

They are given in the Massorah marginalis on Exod. xviii. 21.

[125] The other passage in which the same word occurs four times, the first three times with *Vav* conjunctive, and the fourth without it, is פני ופני ופני ופני, Ezek. i. 10.

fifth of which are without the *Vav*, whilst the third, fourth, and sixth have *Vav*, viz., רְאוּבֵן גָּד וְאָשֵׁר וּזְבוּלֻן דָּן וְנַפְתָּלִי *Reuben, Gad, and Asher, and Zebulun, Dan, and Naphtali* [Deut. xxvii. 13]. And, v. The verse שָׂדֵהוּ וְעַבְדּוֹ וַאֲמָתוֹ שׁוֹרוֹ וַחֲמֹרוֹ, *his field, and his man servant, and his maid servant, his ox, and his ass,* in Deut. v. 18, the mnemonical sign of which is ש"ש קרחי, indicating that the words beginning with the two *Shins*, viz., שָׂדֵהוּ *his field,* and שׁוֹרוֹ *his ox,* are without *Vav*, whilst the others have it.

מלוֹת דמיין בפסוק חד אב"ה קרחי גד"ו ווי, וסימן ואלה יעמדו לברך ראובן גד ואשר וזבולן דן ונפתלי, ובפסוק לא תתאוה בית רעך שדהו ועבדו ואמתו שורו וחמורו, וסימן ש"ש קרחי, פירוש שדהו שורו הם בלי וי"ו, ושאר עם הוי"ו:

SECTION VIII., concerning *Imaginary Readings, Misleadings,* and *Variations.*—Know that the expression סבירין denotes *incorrect opinion, imagination, fancy, supposition;* that is, when a man thinks or imagines in his heart that it is so and so, but it is not. In German it is Er meint or wähnet. It has the same meaning in the language of the Mishna, as סבור הייתי *I believed,* סבורים היו *they thought;* in the book of Daniel, as וְיִסְבַּר *and he thought* [vii. 25]; and in the Chaldee paraphrase, which renders the phrase, "there is a way which is right in the view of man" [Prov. xiv. 12], by "there is a way which man [דסברין] *imagine,* &c."

המאמר השמיני בסבירין ומטעין וחילופין: דע כי סבירין הוא ענין מחשבה כוזבת, ר"ל שאדם חושב ומדמה בלבו שהוא כן ואינו כן, ובלשון אשכנז ער מיי"נט או וועי"נט: וכן בלשון משנה סבור הייתי, סבורים היו; וכן בדניאל ויסבר להשניא זמנין, וכן יש דרך ישר לפני איש, תרגום אית אורחא דסברין בני נשא וגומר:

כן יש מלים הרבה במקרא שסבירין בני אדם שהם כן ואינם כן, כמו בהמה אשר יקריב מִמֶּנּוּ, נמסר על מִמֶּנּוּ חד מן ו' דסבירין מִמֶּנָּה, כי בהמה לשון נקבה, וכן השאר;[126] וכן ויעלו בנגב וַיָּבֹא עד חברון, נמסר על וַיָּבֹא חד מן ח' דסבירין וַיָּבֹאוּ;[127] וכן וּבְנֵי דן חשים ג' דסבירין בֶּן; ולהפך ה' דכתיבים בֶּן וסבירין בְּנֵי, כמו וּבֶן זרובבל משלם

Thus there are also many words in the Bible which men imagine ought to be so and so, but they are not. As, i The word מִמֶּנּוּ *from it* [Levit. xxvii. 9], on which the Massorites remark, "one of the six instances supposed to be מִמֶּנָּה *from her,*" since the noun בְּהֵמָה *a beast,* is feminine. To the same effect are the other instances.[126] ii. The word וַיָּבֹא *and he came,* on which they remark, "one of the eight instances supposed to be וַיָּבֹאוּ *and they came.*[127] iii. The expression וּבְנֵי *and the sons of* [Gen. xlvi. 12], "one of the three instances supposed to be בֶּן *son of;*" and *vice versa,* the five instances in which the textual reading has בֶּן *son of,* and the conjectural reading is בְּנֵי

---

[126] The six passages in which the conjectural reading in the Massorah proposes ממנה, third person singular feminine, instead of the textual reading ממנו, third person singular masculine, because of the antecedent to which it refers, and which is feminine, are, Levit. vi. 8; xxvii. 9; Josh. i. 7; Judg. xi. 34; 2 Kings iv. 39: 1 Kings xxii. 43. They are given in the Massorah marginalis on Levit. vi. 8; in the Massorah marginalis on Judg. xi. 34, where five instances only are given, there must therefore be a mistake.

[127] The eight places in which the conjectural reading is plural, instead of singular, are, Numb. xiii. 22: Ezek. xiv. 1; xxiii. 44; xxxvi. 20: 2 Sam. iii. 22: Ezek. xx. 38: Isa. xlv. 24: Jerem. li. 48. They are given in the Massorah marginalis on Numb. xiii. 22. It must be noticed that they are not all the future with *Vav* conversive.

sons of, as in 1 Chron. iii. 19, &c.¹²⁸ iv. The word אֲשֶׁר *which*, is in four instances supposed to be כַּאֲשֶׁר *as which*, and the ten instances in which the reverse is the case, the textual reading having כַּאֲשֶׁר and the marginal conjecture being אֲשֶׁר.¹²⁹ v. The words in which the *Vav* conjunctive is wanting, as לֹא *not* [Exod. xxiii. 13], on which it is remarked, "one of those supposed to be וְלֹא *and not.*" vi. The entire absence of a word from a sentence, as the five passages which are supposed to want אִם *if*, and wherein the scribes mislead, *ex. gr.*, Gen. xxiv. 4; 2 Sam. xix. 8, &c.¹³⁰ vii. In the interchange of words, as the three passages in which the text has מִפְּנֵי *from the face of*, and it is supposed to be מִפִּי *from the mouth*, *ex. gr.*, Numb. xxxiii. 8, &c.¹³¹ viii. The nine passages in which the textual reading עַל *upon*, supposed to be עַד *until*, *ex. gr.*, Gen. xlix. 13, &c.;¹³² and ix. The two passages in which the textual reading is עַל *upon*, and the conjectural reading is עִם *with*, viz., Gen. xxx. 40; 1 Sam. xx. 8.

Some, however, explain the word סבירין *to think it proper*, and submit that it means, "*correctly the reading ought to be so and so.*" This interpretation is strengthened by the fact that the expression occurs in the singular. Thus, in the Massorah on Gen. 1. 13, it is remarked לית

---

¹²⁸ The instances in which the conjectural reading substitutes ובן for the marginal reading ובני, are not *three*, as stated in the text of Levita, but *four*, viz., Gen. xlvi. 22: Numb. xxvi. 8: 1 Chron. ii. 8: vii. 17. Neither is the statement that there are *five* instances in which the reverse is the case correct, since there are *six* such conjectural readings, viz., 1 Chron. iii. 19, 21, 23; iv. 17; vii. 35; viii. 34. They are enumerated in the Massorah marginalis on Gen. xlvi. 22.

¹²⁹ The four passages in which the conjectural reading substitutes כאשר for the textual reading אשר, are, Exod. xiv. 13: Levit. vii. 36, 38: Numb. iv. 49. They are given in the Massorah marginalis on Levit. vii. 36. The ten instances in which the reverse is the case are, Deut. xvi. 10; xxiv. 8: Josh. ii. 7; xiii. 8; xiv. 2. Jerem. xxiii. 27: Isa. li. 13: Hos. vii. 12: Jonah i. 14: Hag. i. 12. They are given in the Massorah marginalis on Jonah i. 14.

¹³⁰ The passages in which the conjectural reading supplies the particle אם, are, Gen. xxiv. 4: 1 Sam. xviii. 25: 2 Sam. xix. 8: Jerem. xxii. 12: 2 Chron. vi. 9. They are given in the Massorah marginalis on Gen. xxiv. 4.

¹³¹ The other two passages in which the conjectural reading has מפי for the textual reading מפני, are, 2 Sam. xvi. 19: Amos v. 19. They are given in the Massorah marginalis on Numb. xxxiii. 8.

¹³² The nine passages in which the conjectural reading has עד for the textual reading עַל, are, Gen. xlix. 13: Josh. ii. 7; xiii. 16: Judg. vii. 22: Jerem. xxxi. 39: Dan. ix. 27: Nehem. xii. 22, 39 (twice). They are given in the Massorah marginalis on Gen. xlix. 13, where, however, the heading, as well as the reference to this rubric made in the Massorah finalis under the letter *Ajin*, p. 49 *b*, col. 3, states that there are eleven such instances, though it enumerates only *nine*, which agrees with the text of Levita.

דסביר אשר על פני; that is, there does not exist in the Bible the phrase עַל פְּנֵי *upon the face of*, for which the conjectural reading substitutes אֲשֶׁר עַל פְּנֵי *which upon the face of*. Hence they explain all the expressions סבירין in the Massorah as *correct opinion*, but it does not appear correct to me, since according to this interpretation it ought more correctly to have been written מסתברין.

There are Codices in which the Massoretic remark on some words is, "imaginary readings and misleadings," or, "misleadings and imaginary readings;" but this is nothing more than an additional explanation. The word *misleadings*, however, occurs sometimes without the expression *imaginary reading*, and this is mostly the case when it refers to verses; as, for instance, "the three verses in which the scribes mislead with regard to the end of the verse, one is 'and to thy seed for ever' [Gen. xiii. 15], the second 'and in thy seed for ever' [Deut. xxviii. 46], and the third 'and in thy seed for ever' [2 Kings v. 27]."[133] To the same effect, also, are the four verses which mislead in connection with the priesthoood,[134] and the two ends of verses which are misleading with regard to *Dagesh* and *Raphe*, viz., לְקַלְלֶךָ *to curse thee* [Deut. xxiii. 5], which has *Dagesh*, and מְקַלְלֶךָ *cursing thee* [Eccles. vii. 21], which is *Raphe*, and the mnemonical sign of which is בָּכָה; that is, the first *Kaph* has *Dagesh*, and the second *Kaph* is *Raphe*. As to the verses which mislead with regard to the accents, they are exceedingly numerous, but this is not the place to expatiate upon them.

You must moreover notice, that the word מטעין cannot mean that men err in these words by reading them so and so, for it is the *Hiphil* which is causative. It denotes that the scribes mislead the reader. Hence, I have found it remarked in accurate Codices on עֲוֺנָם *their iniquity* [Numb. xviii. 23], "the scribes mislead thereby in writing אֶת

---

[133] These three instances are given in the Massorah marginalis on Deut. xxviii. 46, and in the *Ochla Ve-Ochla*, section cclxviii., pp. 52, 143.

[134] The four verses in which the expression *Levites* (הלוים) precedes *Priests* (כהנים) are, Jerem. xxxiii. 21: 2 Chron. xix. 8; xxix. 26; xxx. 21. They are given in the Massorah finalis on Jerem. xxxiii. 21; 2 Chron. xxx. 21; and in the *Ochla Ve-Ochla*, section cclxxx., p. 151.

במקרא על פני שהסברה נותנת להיות אֲשֶׁר עַל פְּנֵי; וכן מפרשים כל סבירין שבמסורת לשון סברא, אבל לא סבירא לי, כי לפי זה היה להם לכתוב מסתברין ודוק:

ויש נוכחאות שנמסר על קצת המלות סבירין וממטעין, או ממטעין וסבירין, ואינו אלא תוספת ביאור; אבל נמצא ממטעין בלי סבירין, וזה על הרוב בפסוקים, כגון ג' פסוקים דמטעים בהן בסוף פסוק, חד וּלְזַרְעֲךָ עַד עוֹלָם, וחד וּבְזַרְעֲךָ עַד עוֹלָם, וחד וּבְזַרְעֲךָ לְעוֹלָם;[133] וכן במתנורת כהונה ד' פסוקים דמטעין בהון;[134] וכן ב' סופי פסוקים דמטעין בהון בדגש ורפי, ארם נהרים לְקַלְלֶךָ בדנ״ש, עבדך מְקַלְלֶךָ ברפי וסימן בָּכָה יעשה, רוצה לומר, כ״ף הראשונה דגושה, והשניה רפויה; ופסוקים דמטעים בהון בטעמא הן הרבה מאוד, ואין כאן מקומם:

ויש לך לדעת כי ממטעין אינו רוצה לומר שטועין בהן בני אדם לקריותן כך, כי ממטעים היא מבנין הפעיל שהוא יוצא לשני, ופירושו הסופרים מטעין את הקוראים; וכן מצאתי בנוסחאות מדויקות על והם ישאו עֲוֹנָם, מטעין ביה ספרי למכתב אֶת עֲוֹנָם: וכן ישתו

עֲוֹנָם with the sign of the accusative before it." So also on תָּמִיד *continually* [Obad. 16], the Massorites remark, "the scribes mislead by it in writing סָבִיב *round about;*" and also on עַל יְרוּשָׁלָם *over Jerusalem* [Eccl. i. 16], "they mislead here by writing בִּירוּשָׁלָם *in Jerusalem*." Now I have seen the remarks of those Codices, which very correctly do not write דטועין *which err*.

SECTION IX., concerning the terms *Letters, Words, Expressions, Short Letters, Accents, Certainties*, and *Transpositions*.—It is well known that each one of the twenty-two letters of the alphabet is called אוֹת *sign*, because it is a sign and mark for the utterance of the voice, and in the plural ought properly to be אוֹתוֹת. But to distinguish it from אוֹתוֹת *wonders, miracles*, it is אוֹתִיוֹת. The Massorites, however, call it אָתִין, which is the Chaldee rendering of אוֹתוֹת *signs* [Gen. i. 14]. Thus, as

המאמר התשיעי באתין, ותיבין, ומלין, וקטיעין, ופשטין, וודאין, ומוקדמין ומאוחרים: ידוע כי כ״ב התמונות של האלפא ביתא כל אחת נקראת אות, לפי שהיא אות וסימן על קול מוצאה ומבטאה, ובלשון רבות היו ראויות להקרא אותות; אך להבדיל בינם ובין אותות ומופתים קראו להן אותיות; ובמסורה קראו להן אתין כתרגומו והיו לאותות לאתין; וכן עם הכנוי, כגון ח׳ פסוקים דמיין בשמתהון ומחלפים באתיחון, כגון דאוריתא ויצהר וחברון ועזיאל, ובדברי הימים יצהר חברון ועזיאל;[185] אבל בלשון יחיד קראו להן אות בלשון עברי, כמו ד׳ זוגין מן ב׳ ב׳ בספרא, קדמאה חסר מלה ויתיר אות, ותנין יתיר מלה וחסר אות קדמאה תירא ואתו תעבד ובשמו תשבע (דברים ו׳), ותנינא אתו תעבד וגו תדבק

in the case of the names where they remark, "there are five verses in which the same names occur, differing only (באתיהון) in their letters," viz., in the Pentateuch, *and Izhar, and Hebron, and Uzziel* [Exod. vi. 18]; in 1 Chron. *Izhar, Hebron, and Uzziel* [xxiii. 12], &c;[185] but when it is in the singular, the Massorites call it אוֹת, just as in the Hebrew. Thus they say, "there are four groups of words, each of which occurs twice in the same book, once with a word less and a letter more, and once with a word more and a letter less." The first of such a pair is, "Jehovah, thy God, thou shalt fear, and Him thou shalt serve, and by His name thou shalt swear" [Deut. vi. 13]; the second, "Jehovah, thy God, thou shalt fear, Him thou shalt

---

[185] The meaning of the Massoretic remark which Levita quotes is, that though the four names עזיאל חברון יצהר עמרם *Amram, Izhar, Hebron,* and *Uzziel*, are exactly the same in all the five passages in which they occur, as far as the words themselves are concerned, yet the letter *Vav* or the conjunctive is placed differently in each passage, as will be seen from the following enumeration of them :—

ובני קהת עמרם ויצהר וחברון ועזיאל . . . . . . Exod. vi. 18.
ובני קהת עמרם ויצהר וחברון ועזיאל . . . . . . 1 Chron. vi. 3.
ובני קהת למשפחתם עמרם ויצהר חברון ועזיאל . . . Numb. iii. 19.
ובני קהת עמרם יצהר וחברון ועזיאל . . . . 1 Chron. v. 28.
בני קהת עמרם יצהר חברון ועזיאל . . . . 1 Chron. xxiii. 12.

They are given in the Massorah marginalis on Exod. xvi. 18, where, however, the instance in Numb. iii. 19 is omitted, though the rubric states that there are *five* such passages. The *Ochla Ve-Ochla*, section cclxxxviii., pp. 54, 152, &c., rightly supplies this omission.

serve, *and to Him thou shalt cleave, and by His name thou shalt swear*" [*ibid.* x. 20].[136] This they do not call אֵת, which is the Chaldee translation of אוֹר, in order that it might not be confounded with the expression אֶת.

☞ Let me now explain the term תיבין *words*. Now it is well known that the ancients called every word תיבה, and I have instituted great search to find out the reason for it, but could not discover the meaning of it, seeing that this expression only occurs to denote the ark of Noah [Gen. vi. 14-16], and the ark in which Moses was exposed [Exod. ii. 3, 5], translated by the Chaldee תיבותא. The Massorites make the plural of תיבה to be תיבין, according to the analogy of the Hebrew מלין or מלים *words*, from מלה *word*, which is only found in Job. Many, indeed, are of opinion that there is no difference between the expressions תיבה and מלה.

☞ Now I submit that there is a difference between them, since the expression מלה denotes a word uttered by the mouth when speaking, as it is used in the writings by our Rabbins of blessed memory; *ex. gr.*, "and they repeated after him [מלה] word [במלה] for word,"

ובשמו תשבע ; [136] ולא קראו לה את כתרגום אות או מופת אך מופהא, כדי שלא לטעות בינו ובין מלח את :

☜ ועתה אפרש מלת תיבן ; ידוע כי הקדמונים קראו לכל מלה תיבה, והרבה בקשתי למצא לוה טעם ולא מצאתי מה ענין הלוה, כי לא נמצא זה השם בפסוק כי אם בתיבה נח ותבת משה, ומתורגמים תיבוותא : ובמסורת אמרו מן תיבה תיבין, כמו שבלשון עברי נאמר מן מלה מלין, או מלים, ולא נמצא רק באיוב, ורבים חושבים כי אין הפרש בן תיבה ומלה :

☜ ואומר אני כי יש הפרש ביניהם, כי לשון מלה נופל על דבור שמוציא אדם מפיו בחיתוך הלשון, כמו שנמצא בדברי רז"ל, והם עונין אחריו מלה במלה ודומיהן ; אבל

---

[136] The Massorah differs as to the number of these instances. Thus, on Isa. i. 1, the Massorah marginalis (as Levita in the text before us) remarks that there are *four* such pairs, and enumerates them as follows:—

את יהוה אלהיך תירא ואתו תעבד ובשמו תשבע . . .	Deut. vi. 13.
את יהוה אלהיך תירא אתו תעבד ובו תדבק ובשמו תשבע . .	Deut. x. 20.
על פי שנים עדים או שלשה	Deut. xvii. 6.
על פי שנים עדים או על פי שלשה עדים . . .	Deut. xix. 15.
ולא אבו שמוע	Isa. xxviii. 12.
לא אבו שמוע חרת יהוה	Isa. xxx. 9.
ואפלה על פני ואזעק ואמר	Ezek. ix. 8.
ואפל על פני ואזעק קול גדול ואמר	Ezek. xi. 13.

In the Massorah marginalis on Ezek. xi. 13, however, it is stated that there are *seven* such instances, and the following two pairs are added:—

וזהנשאו ' ' מי זה מלך הכבוד . Ps. xxiv. 7, 8	וירפאו את שבר עמי . Jerem. vi. 14
ושאו ' ' מי הוא זה מלך הכבוד . Ps. xxiv. 9	וירפאו את שבר בת עמי . . Jerem. viii. 11

There can therefore be but little doubt that the remark in the Massorah finalis, under the letter *Vav*, p. 28 *b*, col. 4, that there are *ten* (י) such instances, has arisen from a corruption of the letter *Vav* (ו), than which nothing is more easy and common. In the *Ochla Ve-Ochla*, section ccxxxiv., p. 133, the following two pairs are added, as being found (לבד ממסורתא) apart from those stated in the Massorah:—

הי־ענבים מהארץ . . . 1 Sam. xxviii. 3	רק הדם לא תאכלו . . Deut. xii. 16
הידעני מן הארץ . . . 1 Sam. xxviii. 9	רק את דמו לא תאכל . Deut. xv. 23

It is also to be added that the pair which forms the fifth in the rubric given in the Massorah marginalis on Ezek. xi. 13, is, in the *Ochla Ve-Ochla*, included in those instances to be found "apart from the Massorah."

whereas תיבה, they employ to designate what is written down in a book, as, for instance, when they say, "every word which requires *Lamed* at the beginning, takes *He* at the end,"¹³⁷ "the initials of words," "the end of words," &c.; but not מלות. Yet I have found that some grammarians make no distinction between the two expressions, and call them both מלה, but I have not found it so in the writings of the ancients.

תיבה לא אמרו רק על מלה הכתובה בתוך הספר, כמו שאמרו כל תיבה הצריכה למ׳׳ד בתחלתה הטיל לה ה׳׳א בסופה;¹³⁷ וכן ראשי תיבות, סופי תיבות, ולא נאמר ראשי מלות, סופי מלות; אך מצאתי קצת המדקדקים לא הבדילו ביניהם וקראו לשניהם מלה, ולא נמצא כן בדברי הקדמונים:

ופירוש קטיעין מלשון קציצה וכריתה, כמו וַיְקַצֵּץ פתילים תרגום ירושלמי וקטע יתחון, וכן יְפַלַּח כליותי יקטע כליותי; והנה ידוע כי נמצא א׳׳ב מן אותיות גדולות,¹³⁸

The meaning of קטיעין is *breaking off, cutting off*; so the Jerusalem Targum renders וַיְקַצֵּץ *and he cut* [Exod. xxxix. 3] by וקטע, and יְפַלַּח *he cleaveth* [Job xvi. 13] by יקטע. Now it is well known that there is an alphabetical list of words with large letters, ¹³⁸ and that there is another

---

¹³⁷ The axiom of the Rabbins, to which Levita refers, has already been discussed, *vide supra*, p. 173.

¹³⁸ The alphabetical list of words in the Hebrew Scriptures, written with majuscular letters, is as follows:—

אדם	. . 1 Chron. i. 1	שבטו	. . . Job ix. 34	שמע	. . . Deut. vi. 4
בראשית	. . . Gen. i. 1	ינדל	. . . Numb. xiv. 17	בשפרפרא	. . Dan. vi. 20
והתגלח	. . Levit. xiii. 33	וכנה	. . . Ps. lxxx. 16	ובהעמיף	. . Gen. xxx. 42
אחד	. . . Deut. vi. 4	וישלכם	. . Deut. xxix. 27	צפו	. . . Isa. lvi. 10
הליהוה	. . Deut. xxxii. 6	משלי	. . . Prov. i. 1	קן	. . Ps. lxxxiv. 4
ויחרא	. . . Esther ix. 9	נצר	. . . Exod. xxxiv. 7	אחר	. . . Exod. xxxiv. 14
זכרו	. . . . Mal. iii. 22	ליני	. . . Ruth iii. 13	שיר	. Song of Songs i. 1
חור	. . . Esther i. 6	משפטן	. . Numb. xxvii. 5	ותכתב	. . Esther ix. 29
		סוף	. . . Eccles. xii. 13		

This list is given in the Massorah marginalis on Gen. i. 1; in the Massorah marginalis on 1 Chron. i. 1, however, where the list is repeated, the following alterations are made, גחון (Levit. xi. 42), is substituted for ויחרא (Esther ix. 9); טוב (Eccles. vii. 1) for שבטו (Job ix. 34); both משפטן (Numb. xxvii. 5), and ובהעמיף (Gen. xxx. 42), are omiitted; and תמים (Deut. xviii. 13) is substituted for ותכתב (Esther ix. 29). In the *Ochla Ve-Ochla* again, where the list is also given, section lxxxiii., p. 88, גחון (Levit. xi. 42) is substituted for ויחרא (Esther ix. 9). אלפים (Dan. vii. 10), representing final *Mem*, is added; וכנה (Ps. lxxx. 16) is given instead of נצר (Exod. xxxiv. 7); and ובהעמיף (Gen. xxx. 42) is omitted. The *Ochla Ve-Ochla*, moreover, (section lxxxii., p. 82), gives another alphabetical list of majuscular letters contained in the Pentateuch alone, which is as follows:—

אשרוך	. Deut. xxxiii. 29	ינדל	. . . Numb. xiv. 17	שמע	. . . Deut. vi. 4
בראשית	. . . Gen. i. 1	והתמכרתם	Deut. xxviii. 68	ופתלתל	. Deut. xxxii. 5
והתגלח	. . Levit. xiii. 33	ובך or ונך	. Deut. ii. 33	ובהעמיף	. . Gen. xxx. 42
אחד	. . . Deut. vi. 4	וישלכם	. . Deut. xxix. 27	צא	. . . Exod. xi. 8
הליהוה	. . Deut. xxxii. 6	מה	. . . Numb. xxiv. 5	ציץ	. Exod. xxviii. 36
גחון	. . . Levit. xi. 42	שלשים	. . . Gen. l. 23	קן	. . Deut. xxii. 6
הכזונה	. . Gen. xxxiv. 31	נצר	. . . Exod. xxxiv. 7	אחר	. Exod. xxxiv. 14
חכלילי	. . Gen. xlix. 12	משפטן	. Numb. xxvii. 5	ערש	. . Deut. iii. 11
טוב	. . . Exod. ii. 2	ויהם	. . Numb. xiii. 30	תמים	. . Deut. xviii. 13

This extended list—and be it remembered that even this list does not give all the

alphabetical list of words with small letters.[189] In the Massorah, every one of the large letters is called *majuscular*, and of the small letters *minuscular*, as בְּרֵאשִׁית *in the beginning* [Gen. i. 1] is marked *Beth majuscular*, and וַיִּקְרָא *and he called* [Levit. i. 1] is marked *Aleph minuscular*.[188] In the correct Codices the small *Vav* is not called זְעִירָא = *minuscular*, but קְטִיעָא, that is, *cut off from below*. Thus, שָׁלוֹם *peace* [Numb. xxv. 12] is marked "*Vav* cut off;" נַפְשׁוֹ *his soul* [Ps. xxiv. 4] is marked "*Vav* cut off," &c.

☞ Now I am astonished that all the commentators whom I have consulted should take this word נַפְשׁוֹ *his soul*, as *Kethiv*, and remark that the *Keri* is נַפְשִׁי *my soul*. Indeed I have also seen some Codices of the Massorah which have the same. But there is no doubt that is a blunder committed by transcribers who confounded the word נַפְשׁוֹ in question with נַפְשׁוֹ, in Job xxxiii 28, which is נַפְשִׁי in the *Keri*, and which is included in the list of forty-one words, written in the text with *Vav* and read in the margin

וא"ב מן אותיות קטנות[189] ובמסורד קראו לכל אחת מהגדולות רבתא, והקטנות זעירא, כמו בְּרֵאשִׁית בי"ת רבתא, וַיִּקְרָא אל"ף זעירא; והנה במסורות המדוקות לא קראו הוי"ו הקטנה וי"ו זעירא, אך וי"ו קטיעא, פירוש קצוצה מעם מלמטה, כמו את ברִיתי שָׁלוֹם וי"ו קטיעא; וכן לא נשא לשוא נַפְשׁוֹ וי"ו קטיעא:

☞ ותמהתי אני על כל המפרשים אשר ראיתי שלפי פי' כלם הוא כתיב נַפְשׁוֹ וקרי נַפְשִׁי, וכן ראיתי ברוב נוכחאות המסורת; אין ספק כי הוא טעות סופרים, וסעו בין זה יבין פרח נַפְשׁוֹ מעבר בשחרת, שהוא קרי נַפְשִׁי; וכן היא נמנה עם מ"א מלך דכתיבין

majuscular letters,—would of itself be fatal to the ingenious theory propounded by Mr. W. H. Black, F.S.A., in a paper read before the Chronological Institute of London, (October 4, 1864), that the sum total of the majuscular letters is designed to give the date of the composition of the Pentateuch. We shall, however, show, in our forthcoming "*Manual to the Massorah*," other reasons why the majuscular letters could never have been intended as Chronograms.

[189] The alphabetical list of the minuscular letters, is as follows:—

וַיִּקְרָא	. . . Levit. i. 1	וּמֵהֵרְתָם	. Numb. xxxi. 24	בְּסוּפָה	. . . Nahum i. 3
הָב	. . . Prov. xxx. 15	תֵּשׁ	. . Deut. xxxii. 18	בְּסֻכָּה	. . . Ps. xxvii. 5
וָגוּשׁ	. . . Job vi. 5	וּלְבִכְתָּהּ	. . Gen. xxiii. 2	לָעוּת	. . Lament. iii. 36
אָדָם	. . . Prov. xxvii. 17	לוּא	. . . Lament. i. 12	בְּשַׁפְפָרָא	. . Dan. vi. 20
בְּהִבָּרְאָם	. . . Gen. ii. 4	מֵמְרִים	. . Deut. ix. 24	לְצוֹחַת	. . Jerem. xiv. 2
נַפְשׁוֹ	. . . Ps. xxii. 30	מוּקְדָה	. . . Levit. vi. 2	פָּרַץ	. . Job xvi. 14
שָׁלוֹם	. . Numb. xxv. 12	וּמְטֹהָרִים	. Nehem. xiii. 30	בִּקְמֵיהֶם	. Exod. xxxii. 25
לַשָּׁוְא	. . . Ps. xxiv. 4	נְעוּ	. . . Nahum i. 3	קַצְתִּי	. . Gen. xxvii. 46
וְיָתְרָא	. . . Esth. ix. 9	וְרָגָן	. . Prov. xvi. 28	רֵאשִׁית	. Exod. xxxiv. 26
חֵף	. . . Job xxxii. 9	וּנְבוּשַׁזְבָּן	. Jerem. xxxix. 13	פַּרְסַנְדָּתָא	. . Esth. ix. 7
טָבַעַ	. . Lament. ii. 9	אָרֶךְ	. . . Isa. xliv. 14	פַּרְמַשְׁתָּא	. . Esth. ix. 9

The list is given in the Massorah finalis under the letter *Aleph*, p. 1 a, col. 1, and in the Massorah marginalis on Levit. i. 1. In the *Ochla Ve-Ochla*, section lxxxiv., pp. 25 and 89, which also gives this list, the following variations occur: יִצְפֹּנִי (Ps. xxvii. 5) is put under the *Nun*, as having the second *Nun* smaller, whilst נְעוּ (Nahum i. 3) is omitted. The three instances which represent the final *Nun* are also omitted; but they are, however, given under a separate rubric (comp. section clxxvii., with the Massorah marginalis on Isa. xliv. 14: Prov. xvi. 28: Jerem. xxxix. 14). Neither does the *Ochla Ve-Ochla* give בִּקְמֵיהֶם (Exod. xxxii. 25) under *Koph*, and רֵאשִׁית (Exod. xxxiv. 26) under *Resh*, which are also omitted from the list given in the Massorah marginalis on Levit. i. 1. Like the Massorah marginalis on Levit. i. 1, the *Ochla Ve-Ochla* rightly marks פַּרְמַשְׁתָּא (Esther ix. 9) as having both a smaller *Resh* and *Tav*.

with *Jod*;[140] whereas נַפְשׁוֹ, in Ps. xxiv. 4, is not given in the list, because it has simply "a cut-short *Vav*." As a rule, the Massorites do not apply the term *cut-short* to any letter but *Vav*, and hence, also, they call it in one place *long*. Thus, the *Vav* in וַיְזָתָא *Vajezatha* [Esther ix. 9], is called "elongated," and not *majuscular*; since *Vav majuscular* is the one in גָּחוֹן *belly* [Levit. xi. 42], as you may see in the alphabetical list of the large letters, and the list of the twenty-two verses which have neither a short nor a long letter, that is, neither *Vav* nor *Jod*, as Ps. cv. 11, &c.[141]

וי"ו וקריין יו"ד,[140] ולשוא נַפְשׁוֹ לא נמנה עמהון, הריששיוה אלא וי"ו קטיעא : והכלל כי לא קראו : וזו קטיעא רק חוי"ו לבדה,כי כן קראו לה רו קום אחד אריך, כגון וי"ו ויְזָתָא וי"ו אריכתא ולא רבתא, כי הוי"ו הרבתא היא וי"ו דגָחון עיין בא"ב רבתא וכ"ג פסוקים דלית בהון לא זעך ולא אריך, פירוש לא וי"ו ולא יו"ד, כמו לאמור לך אחן את ארץ כנען חבל נחלחכם ;[141] ועוד שמשו במלת קטיעא במלה שיש בה

The Massorites also employ the expression קטיעא = *cut short*, with regard to a word which has three quiescents, and is spelled differently in three different places, wanting the first quiescent in the first passage, the second in the second passage, and the two quiescents in

---

[140] The words written with *Vav*, prenominal suffix, third person masculine, and read with *Jod*, mostly suffix, first person, are as follows:—

מצותו	. . . Deut. v. 10	התפחדו	. . Isa. lii. 2	ומיציאיו	. 2 Chron. xxxii. 21
תקעו	. . . Josh. vi. 9	עצתו	. . Isa. xlvi. 11	נדו	. . . . Ps. xi. 1
אזנו	. . . 1 Sam. xxii. 17	מטעו	. . Isa. lx. 21	חסדו	. . . Ps. lix. 11
כלבו	. . . 1 Sam. xxv. 3	תקראו	. . Jerem. iii. 19	וענגו	. . . Ps. cviii. 7
שנאו	. . . 2 Sam. v. 8	תשובו	. . Jerem. li. 34	כדו	. . . Ps. cii. 24
בנפשו	. . 2 Sam. xviii. 13	אכלנו	. . Jerem. li. 34	וידעו	. . . Ps. cxix. 79
בעינו	. . 2 Sam. xii. 9	הממנו	. . Jerem. li. 34	הראיתנו	. . Ps. lxxi. 20
וישבו	. . 2 Sam. xxii. 16	הציגנו	. . Jerem. li. 34	תחינו	. . Ps. lxxi. 20
דרכו	. . 2 Sam. xxii. 33	בלענו	. . Jerem. li. 34	יתרו	. . . Job xxx. 11
העצנו	. . 2 Sam. xxiii. 8	הריחנו	. . Jerem. li. 34	במו	. . . Job ix. 30
הצרו	. . 2 Sam. xxiii. 35	ידו	. . . Ezek. i. 8	או	. . . Prov. xxxi. 2
רגלו	. . . 1 Kings v. 17	התיתו	. . Ezek. xxxii. 32	אשתנו	. . Dan. iii. 19
וקדשו	. . . 1 Kings xv. 15	רבו	. . Hos. viii. 12	לשרשו	. . Ezra vii. 26
נביאו	. . 2 Kings xvii. 13	ישבו	. . 1 Chron. ii. 55	ויעשו	. . . Ezra x. 37
דבאו	. . . Isa. xvi. 3	בנו	. . 1 Chron. ix. 11	יד	. . . Ezra x. 43
הברו	. . . Isa. xlvii. 13	בנו	. . 1 Chron. xxii. 7	וענו	. . Nehem. xii. 9

From this list, which is given in the Massorah marginalis on 1 Sam. i. 1, it will be seen that there are forty-eight such instances, and not forty-one, as is stated by Levita. It is howeyer to be remarked, that in both the Massorah marginalis on 1 Sam. i. 1, and the Massorah finalis under the letter *Vav*, p. 27 *b*, col. 1, where reference is made to this rubric, it is also stated that there are only forty-one such instances; whilst in the Massorah marginalis on Jerem. i. 1, where the list is repeated, it is simply headed by "these are the words" (אלין מלין), &c., without specifying the number. The *Ochla Ve-Ochla*, section cxxxvi., pp. 34, 106, &c., where the list is also given, states that there are forty-seven instances, and the whole number is duly given.

[141] The twenty-three verses which have neither *Vav* nor *Jod* are as follows:— Exod. xx. 13, 15 : Ps. cv. 11 : 1 Chron. xvi. 18 : Numb. vii. 14, 20, 26, 32, 38, 44, 50, 56, 62, 68, 74, 80 : Lament. iii. 65 : Josh. xii. 13, 14, 15 : 1 Chron. i. 24 : Ps. xix. 12 : 1 Chron. xxiv. 14. They are given in the Massorah marginalis on Numb. vii. 14, where, however, the heading of the rubric, as well as the Massorah parva, states that there are only (כ"ב) twenty-two such verses; whilst the Massorah marginalis on Psalm cv. 11, which simply gives the heading, like Levita, most distinctly remarks that there are twenty-three (כ"ג) such verses. The apparent discrepancy is to be accounted for by the fact, that the four commandments, which form in our Bibles four distinct verses (viz., Exod. xx. 13–16), are alternately counted in the Massorah as one verse, and as two verses, according to the two different systems of accentuation.

the third passage. Thus on the words יַאֲרִיכוּן *they shall prolong*, which is once written יַאֲרִכוּן [Exod. xx. 11], once יַאֲרִיכֻן [Deut. v. 16], and once יַאֲרִכֻן [Deut. vi. 2]; the Massorites remark, "it has once its hand [= *Jod*] cut off, once its foot [= *Vav*] cut off, and once it has both its hand and foot cut off." I have already mentioned, in the First Part, Section viii., other phrases whereby the Massorites are in the habit of describing such anomalous words, *vide supra*, p. 166.

☞ As to the meaning of פשטין, it is well known that *Pashta* is the name of one of the accents. Now two such *Pashtas* are sometimes placed on one word, it is then called "two *Pashtin*," as I shall explain in the Treatise, entitled, "Good Sense," with the help of the Lord. Now the Massorites call *Pashtin* some words which in a few places are pointed with *Pattach*, whilst in all other instances they have *Segol*. Thus אַעֲלֶה *I shall bring up*, is marked "eight times Pashtin" [i. e. Hiphil],[142] since in all other passages it is אַעֲלֶה with *Segol* [i. e. Kal]; also וַיַּאַסְפוּ *and they gathered*, is marked "ten times Pashtin" [i. e. Kal], for in all other instances it is וַיֵּאָסְפוּ [i. e. Niphal].[143]

As to the meaning of וּדַאי, it is well known that it is the opposite to *doubtful*, and that the German for it is *gewiß*. The Massorites only use it in three places; one with respect to the sacred name of the Lord, which is written אֲדֹנָי, and on which they remark "one hundred and thirty-four times וַדָיָא or וְדָאִין." The reason of this is, that the name יהוה, being the tetragrammaton, must not be read as it is written, for it must not be pronounced with the lips, but is to be read under the appellation אֲדֹנָי. This reading we have traditionally received from Moses our teacher, peace be upon him. Hence it has the vowel-points of אֲדֹנָי, as follows יְהֹוָה. The reading of it

ג' נחים, ונמצאת בג' מקומות, האחד חסר הנח הראשון, והשני חסר הנח השני, והשלישי הסרים שניהם, כמו יַאֲרִיכוּן א' כהיב יַאֲרִכוּן, וא' כתיב יַאֲרִיכֻן, וא' כתיב יַאֲרִכֻן, נמסר עליהן חד קטיעא ידיה, וחד קטיעא רגליה, וחד קטיעא ידיה ורגליה; וכבר כתבתי בלוחות הראשונות בדבור ח' אופנים אחרים שנוהגים לכתוב על מלות כיוצא בזאת ע"ש:

☞ ופירוש פשטין, הנה ידוע כי פשטא הוא שם אחד מן הטעמים המפסיקים, ולפעמים משימין שנים על תיבה אחת, וקודין לה ב' פשטין, כאשר יתבאר בספר טוב טעם בע"ה; והנה הם קראו פשטין לקצת מלות הנקודות בפתח וכל חברותיהן בסגול, כמו אַעֲלֶה ח' פשטין, כי כל שאר אַעֲלֶה בסגול,[142] וכן וַיַּאַסְפוּ י' פשטין, כי כל שאר וַיֵּאָסְפוּ:[143]

ופירוש ודאי הנה ידוע כי ודאי הוא ההפך מן ספק, ובלשון אשכנז גיוויס, ובמסורת שמשו בה בב' מקומות לבד, הא' על השם הקדוש של אדנות הנכתב א' ד' נ' י', נמסר קל"ד ודאין או ודייא; וזה לפי ששם של הויה, שהוא שם של ד' אותיות אינו נקרא ככתבו כי אין לבטא אותו בפה, אך קודאין אותו בכנוי אדני, וכן קבלנו קריאתו ממר"עה, לכן הוא נקוד בנקודת אֲדֹנָי כך יְהֹוָה, אבל

---

[142] The eight passages in which אעלה is *Hiphil* future are, Exod. iii. 17: Judg. ii. 1: 1 Sam. xxviii. 11: 2 Sam. xxiv. 24: Jerem. xxx. 17; xlvi. 8: Ps. lxvi. 15; cxxxvii. 6. They are enumerated in the Massorah marginalis on Exod. iii. 17.

[143] The ten passages in which ויאספו is *Kal* are, Exod. iv. 29: Numb. xi. 32: 1 Sam. v. 8, 11; xvii. 1: 2 Sam. xxi. 13: 2 Kings xxiii. 1: 2 Chron. xxix. 15; xxiv. 11: Jerem. xl. 12. They are given in the Massorah marginalis on Exod. iv. 29, where, however, they are not designated *Pashtin*, as is stated by Levita, but (פתחין) *Psachin*.

is not certain, whilst *Adonai* is read as it is written, and its vowel-points are certain, whence it is called the *certain* name (plural ודאין); and of which there are one hundred and thirty-four instances. The Massorites say that every אדני יהוה *the Lord Jehovah*, is likewise so, that is, except those to which is joined the tetragrammaton, pointed with the vowel signs of אֱלֹהִים; as אֲדֹנָי יֱהֹוִה, [Gen. xv. 2; Isa. xlix. 22]. I have found two hundred and twenty-two such instances, the mnemonical sign thereof being "the *chariot of* [רכב = 222] the Lord, &c., [Ps. lxviii. 18].[144]

The second place in which the Massorites employ the expression ודאין, is with respect to words ending with *He*, after *Kaph*, the suffix second person singular masculine, of which there are twenty-one in number; as וַאֲבָרְכְכָה *and I shall bless thee* [Gen. xxvii. 7], יָדְכָה *thy hand* [Exod. xiii. 16], &c.,[145] since in all other instances the suffix second person is final *Kaph* with *Kametz*, as יָדֶךָ, רַגְלֶךָ. They dropped the *He* because of their large number, for which reason they are not certain, since they may have *Sheva*, as I have explained under the suffixes of the verbs and nouns; whilst those *Kaphs* which are followed by *He* are certain, and there can be no mistake about them. The meaning of "transpositions" I have explained in Section i., class 3, of Part ii., *vide supra*, p. 191.

Section X., concerning *Scripture, Book, Form, Connection,* and *Verse*.—The Massorites call all the twenty-four sacred books קְרָיָא, just as they are called by the Talmudists מקרא. Thus, for instance, they say, "we have run through the whole [מקרא] scripture," "a man should always divide his time into three, devoting one third to [מקרא] the Scriptures," &c.[146] They also call each separate verse *Mikra*, =

---

[144] Though the Massorah finalis, under the letter *Aleph*, p. 3 *a*, &c., only gives one hundred and thirty-four, yet there can be no doubt that there are many more than those enumerated under this rubric.

[145] The twenty-one words which have *He* at the end, after *Kaph*, of the second person singular masculine, have already been given (*vide supra*, p. 177).

[146] The maxim to which Levita refers was propounded by R. Tamhum b. Hanilai, and is to be found in *Aboda Sara*, 19 *b*. In its entirety it is as follows:—א"ר תנחום בר

scripture, saying, "no scripture oversteps its simple meaning,"[147] "this scripture is anteplaced," &c.

☞ I wonder how it is that most people give this name to the writings of the prophets alone; for I cannot find a reason for it in any of the works which I have seen. But my own opinion is that it arose from the fact that most of the prophets read what they had to say, as we find, "Go and *read* in the ears of the people" [Jerem. ii. 2], "and *read* unto her the *reading* which I speak to you" [Jonah iii. 2], and *read* there [Jerem. xix. 2], &c. It is for this reason that their books are called Scripture [מקרא].

It is, however, to be noticed that the Massorites do not always write the word *Scripture*, or *in Scripture*, whenever they give the import and number. Thus, for instance, on a word which occurs only once, they simply remark, "not extant," and not "not extant in the Scripture." The same is the case when it occurs twice, thrice, or more times; they do not remark on it, "twice in the Scripture," or "thrice in the Scripture," &c. In those Codices where you do find it written so, it has either been done to make it more explicit, or to ornament the writing by filling out the line, as I have already stated in the Poetical Introduction, which see.[148] In the Massorah parva it is never found, whilst the Massorah magna only uses it in a few places. Thus, when a certain word occurs many times in one book, and is only found once in the other books, they remark upon it, "not extant in the other Scriptures, but throughout such and such a book there are instances like it," as in the register of sixteen words, viz., וַיִּתְקַע *and he smote* [Gen. xxxii. 26], on which the Massorites remark, "it does not occur in the Scripture, but throughout Ezekiel, there are

קראו לכל פסוק לבד מקרא, באמרם אין מקרא יוצא מידי פשוטו,[147] מקרא מסורס הוא, וחולחם דבים:

☞ אך תמהתי מה שההמון קוראים שם זה לספרי הנביאים ביחוד, ולא כצאתי מעם כתוב על זה בכל הספרים שראיתי, אך לבי אומר לי לפי שרוב מה שאמרי הנביאים אמרו בקריאה, כמו הלוך וקראת, וקרא אליה את הקריאה, וקראת שם ודומידם, על כן נקראו ספריהם מקרא:

ודע כי לא על כל ענין ועל כל מנין כתבו קריא או בקריא; והמשל על מכה הנמצאה רק פעם אחת כתבו עליה לית. ולא לית בקריא; וכן כשנמצאה ב' או ג' פעמים וכו', לא כתבו ב' בקריא, או ג' בקריא וכו'; ובספרים שנמצא כתוב כן, אינו אלא לתוספת ביאור, או ליפות כתיבתן כדי למלא השורה, כמו שכתבתי בהקדמה החרוזית ע"ש;[148] ובמסרה קטנה לא נמצא לעולם, אכן בקצת מקומות הוצרכו לו במסרה גדולה, כגון כשיש מלה אחת בספר אחד הרבה פעמים ובשאר הספרים לא נמצא רק פעם אחת, כתבו עליה לית בקריא וכל ספר פלוני דכותיה, כגון שמה אחת מן י"ו מל', וַיִּתְקַע כף ירך (בראשית ל"ב), לית בקריא וכל יחזקאל

חנילאי לעולם ישלש אדם שנותיו שליש במקרא שליש במשנה שליש בתלמוד, *R. Tamhum b. Hanilai propounded that man should always divide his time into three parts: one-third he should devote to the study of the Scripture, one-third to the study of the Mishna, and one-third to the study of the Talmud.*

[147] The exegetical rule, that "no Scripture oversteps its simple meaning," to which Levita refers, is to be found in *Sabbath* 63 a, and in many other parts of the Talmud.

[148] For the description of the manner in which the Massoretic notes were treated, to which Levita refers, see above, p. 94.

instances like it;" בַּנָּשִׁים *in the female gender* [Numb. xxxi. 18], "not in the Scriptures, but throughout the Song of Songs, there are instances like it," &c., &c.[149]

דכותיה; וכל הטפ בנשים לית בקריא וכל שיר השרים דכותיה;[149]
וכן שמח אחת מן כ"א דכל חד וחד לית בספרא דכותיה, וכל קריא דכותיה בר מן חד, כגון כל ספר בראשית וילדו בר מן חד ויֻלְּדוּ לו בנים אחד הטבול, וכל קריא וַיֵּלְדוּ בר מן הד וילדו לו בנים וכולי;[150] וכן כל

The same is the case with the register of twenty-one words which respectively occur only once in one book, whilst in all the other Scriptures they are always so, except in one instance. Thus throughout the whole Book of Genesis the word וְיָלְדוּ *and they begat*, is used, and it is only in one instance that וַיֵּלְדוּ *and there were born* [Gen. x. 1] is found; whilst in all the Scriptures it is וַיֵּלְדוּ, and it is only in one place that וְיָלְדוּ is used [Deut. xxi. 15].[150]

---

[149] The sixteen words which have no parallel in the whole Scriptures, except in one book only, where they have respectively a parallel, are as follows:—

למלאכה	. . Levit. xiii. 51	רועה	. Ezek. xxxvii. 24	מזוזות	. . 1 Sam. i. 9
בנשים	. Numb. xxxi. 18	ירעם	. . . Ps. xlix. 15	לצבי	. . . Isa. iv. 2
ואת עשרת	. 1 Sam. xvii. 18	ויאסרהו	2 Chron. xxxiii. 11	ועדתיו	. . Deut. vi. 17
התפקדו	. . 1 Kings xx. 27	לא ימות	. . Prov. xxiii. 13	לפני אלהים	1 Chron. xiii. 10
וצבא	. . . Job x. 17	ותקע	. . Gen. xxxii. 26	השיבנו	. . Lament. v. 21
		תהלה	. . Ps. cxlv. 21		

The list is given in the Massorah marginalis on Levit. xiii. 51, where, however, nine instances only are enumerated, as well as at the end of the Massorah finalis, in that portion which is denominated *Various Readings* [חלופי קריאה], p. 62 *a*, col. 4; and in the *Ochla Ve-Ochla*, section cclxx., p. 144, where all the instances are duly specified.

[150] The twenty-one words which respectively occur only once in a particular book, whilst in all other books of the Scriptures they occur always so, except in one instance only, are as follows:—

וַיֵּלְדוּ	only once in Gen. x. 1, always so in all other	וְיָלְדוּ	. Deut. xxi. 15
וְרָם	,, Deut. viii. 14	Scriptures except	וְרָם	. . Isa. ii. 12
בַּסֵּתֶר	,, Deut. xiii. 7	,, ,,	בַּסֵּתֶר	. 2 Sam. xii. 12
וּמִגְרְשֵׁיהֶם	,, Josh. xiv. 4	,, ,,	מִגְרְשֵׁיהֶן	Numb. xxxv. 7
אָחִיךָ	,, 2 Sam ii. 22	,, ,,	לְאָחִיךָ	. Gen. xx. 16
מָשִׁיחַ	,, 2 Sam. i. 21	,, ,,	מְשִׁיחַ	. Lament. iv. 20
מִקְנֶה	,, Jerem. ix. 9	,, ,,	לְמִקְנֵה	. Gen. xxiii. 18
וּמַיִם	,, 1 Kings xxii. 27	,, ,,	וָמַיִם	. Ezek. iv. 17
חֲפָשִׁי	,, Jerem. xxxiv. 14	,, ,,	חָפְשִׁי	. Isa. lviii. 6
עַל דָּרְכָּהּ	,, Jerem. xviii. 8	,, ,,	אֶל דָּרְכָּהּ	2 Sam. xxiv. 16
מְזֻבְּחוֹתֵיהֶם	,, Ezek. vi. 13	,, ,,	מִזְבְּחוֹתֵיכֶם	Jerem. xvii. 1
תִּקְרָאוּ	,, Zech. iii. 10	,, ,,	תִּקְרָאוּ	. Jerem. iii. 19
רַיְצוּ	,, Jerem. xxxix. 11	,, ,,	וַיְצַוֵּהוּ	2 Kings xvi. 15
זִכְרוּ	,, Malachi iii. 22	,, ,,	זִכְרוּ	. Job xviii. 17
וַיִּשְׂמְחוּ	,, Ps. cvii. 30	,, ,,	וְיִשְׂמְחוּ	. Job xxi. 12
תַּעֲרֹךְ	,, Ps. xxiii. 5	,, ,,	תַּעֲרוֹג	. Joel i. 20
וַפָּרוֹן	,, Eccles. i. 1	,, ,,	זִכְרוֹן	. Levit. xxiii. 24
בְּחָכְמָה	,, Eccles. ii. 21	,, ,,	בְּחָכְמָה	1 Chron. xxviii. 21
וְהוֹשֵׁעַ	,, Eccles. vii. 26	,, ,,	וְהוֹשֵׁעַ	. Isa. lxv. 20
שָׁמְרָה	,, Ps. cxix. 167	,, ,,	שָׁמְרָה	1 Chron. xxix. 18
שָׁיִ	,, Ps. lxxii. 20	,, ,,	שַׁי	. . Isa. xviii. 7

The list is given in that part of the Massorah denominated *Various Readings* (חלופי קריאה), p. 62 *b*, section i., and in the *Ochla Ve-Ochla*, section

We also find that certain words ספרא חד מלה וכל קריא חלוף לה, כגון כל
always occur in one book in the בראשית הַנִּרְאָה וכל קריא הַנִּרְאָה.[151] וכן כל
one form, whilst in all the other
books they occur in a different form; as, for instance, הַנִּרְאָה *who
appeared* [Gen. xii. 7], whilst in all the other Scripture it is הַנִּרְאָה.[151]

cclxxi., pp. 52, 145, &c. The text of the *Massoreth Ha-Massoreth*
describes this rubric as follows: שמה אחת מן כ"א דכל ספרא דכוותה בר מן חד וכל
קריא לית הכוותיה בר מן חד, a register of twenty-one words, *which have parallels
throughout the book, with the exception of one instance;* whilst they have
no parallel throughout the Bible, with the exception of one instance. The
Sulzbach edition omits the second בר מן חד. But that the whole passage
is corrupted is evident, from the reference to this rubric in the Massorah
parva on Gen. x. 1, from its heading both in the Massorah finalis and in
the *Ochla Ve-Ochla,* as well as from the whole context. We have therefore
corrected the text.

[151] The words which always occur in a certain form in one book, but
which in all other books of the Scriptures occur in a different form, are as
follows:—

הַנִּרְאָה	Gen. xii. 7	in all the other books	הַנִּרְאָה
חִירָה	Gen. xxxviii. 1	,,	חִירָם
וַאֲשַׁלְּחָה	Exod. viii. 5	,,	וַאֲשַׁלְּחָה
פֹּרְשֵׂי פְנָפַיִם	Exod. xxv. 20	,,	פֹּרְשִׂם כְּנָפַיִם
וְאַמָּה וָחֵצִי הָאַמָּה	Exod. xxvi. 16	,,	אַמָּה וָחֵצִי הָאַמָּה
מַרְאֶה	Levit. xiii. 20	,,	מַרְאֵה
אִתְּכֶם	Numb. xv. 14	,,	אִתָּךְ
בְּפוּנֹן	Numb. xxxiii. 42	,,	פּוּנֹן
וַיִּפֶּן וַיִּסַּע	Deut. ii. 1	,,	וַיִּפֶן וַיִּסַּע
וַתִּקְרְבוּן וַתַּעַמְדוּן	Deut. iv. 11	,,	וַתִּקְרְבוּ וַתַּעַמְדוּ
אֵלֶּה הָעֵדֹת	Deut. iv. 45	,,	אֵלֶּה הָעֵדוּת
כִּי הַמְּעָרָה	Josh. x. 23	,,	מֵהַמְּעָרָה
יָחֵל	Judg. xiii. 5	,,	יָחֵל
כִּבְשָׂה	2 Sam. xii. 3	,,	כִּשְׂבָּה
נֹבַה	1 Sam. xxi. 2	,,	נבה
בֵּית שֵׁן	2 Sam. xxi. 12	,,	בֵּית שְׁאָן
וַיְשִׁיבֻם	1 Sam. xii. 8	,,	וַיְשִׁיבֵם
אִתִּי	2 Sam. xv. 19	,,	אִתִּי
מִבְּחוּר	2 Kings iii. 19	,,	כִּבְחָר
נִבְנָה	1 Kings iii. 2	,,	נִבְנָה
פְּלֵיתִי	Isa. xlix. 4	,,	פְּלֵיתִי
וְקֵוִיתִי	Isa. viii. 17	,,	קִוִּיתִי
אוּרִיָּהוּ	Jerem. xxvi. 23	,,	אוּרִיָּה
הָאָח	Jerem. xxxvi. 22	,,	הָאָח
עַל לִבִּי	Jerem. vii. 31	,,	אֶל לִבִּי
הַסְּרִינוֹת	Jerem. xlvi. 4	,,	הַסִּרְיֹנוֹת
לַנָּשִׂיא	Ezekiel	,,	לְנָשִׂיא
לְחֹל	Ezek. xlv. 23	,,	לָחֹל
נְהַר כְּבָר	Ezek. i. 1	,,	נְהַר פְּרָת
יְחִזְקִיָּה	Minor Prophets	,,	יְחִזְקִיָּהוּ
רֻחָמָה	Hos. i. 6	,,	רֻחָמָה
חוּרָם	2 Chron.	,,	חִירָם
אֲמַרְתָּה	Psalms	,,	אָמַר
בֵּית אַהֲרֹן	Ps. cxv. 10	,,	בְּנֵי אַהֲרֹן

Or they occur in a certain order in the whole Scripture, except in one book, as, for instance, in all the Scripture we have the construction שַׁבַּת שַׁבָּתוֹן *Sabbath, of Sabbatism*, except in one instance, where it is inverted שַׁבָּתוֹן שַׁבַּת *Sabbatism, Sabbath* [Exod. xvi. 23]; so, also, it is in all the Scripture, we have אָבִיו וְאִמּוֹ *his father and his mother*, except in one instance, where it is אִמּוֹ וְאָבִיו *his mother and his father* [Levit. xix. 3], and there are many instances like it.¹⁵²

קריא שַׁבַּת שַׁבָּתוֹן חד מן בר שַׁבָּתוֹן שַׁבַּת דפרש׳ המן; וכן כל קריא אָבִיו וְאִמּוֹ בר מן חד, איש אִמּוֹ וְאָבִיו תיראו וכאלה רבים: ¹⁵²

והנה כזה מבוארת גם כן מלת ספרא, ר״ל הספר שכתוב בו המלה ההיא; אך צריך שתדע כי כאשר נמסר על מלה אחת אשר בתרי עשר והם הושע, יואל, עמום וכו׳ לית בספרא או כל ספרא דכותיה הוא משמע כל ספר תרי עשר; והמשל כגון בזכריה וְאִם משפחת מצרים לא תעלה, נמסר עליו ג׳

Herewith is also explained the expression ספרא, which accordingly means the particular book wherein the word in question is to be found. It must, however, be borne in mind, that when the Massorites make the remark on a word in the twelve minor Prophets, which are Hosea, Joel, Amos, &c., "it is not in the book," or "throughout the book it is to be found like it," they mean the book containing all the twelve Prophets. Thus, when it is remarked, on וְאִם *and if*, in Zech. xiv. 18, "it occurs three times at the beginning of a verse in the book," it does not

אָמֵן וְאָמֵן	. . . Ps. lxxii. 19	in all the other books .	אָמֵן אָמֵן
רֵים .	. . . Job xxxix. 10	,,	רְאֵם
וְלֹא יֵדָע	. . . Job xv. 9	,,	לֹא יֵדָע
מִשְׁלֵי שְׁלֹמֹה	. . . Prov. i. 1	,,	דִּבְרֵי שְׁלֹמֹה
לַצַּדִּיק	. . . Prov. ix. 9	,,	לַצַּדִּיק
יִקְרָא	. . . Eccles. ix. 11	,,	יִקְרָא
חוֹלָה	. . . Eccles. v. 12	,,	חוֹלָה
עֵדָת	. . . Dan. iii. 27	,,	עֵדָת
קָל	. . . Dan. iii. 5	,,	קָל
כְּבָר	. . . Dan. vii. 13	,,	כְּבָר
בְּאַרְצוֹת	. . . Dan. xi. 42	,,	בְּאַרְצוֹת
יְהוֹיָקִים יְהוֹיָרִיב יוֹיָדָע יוֹצֵרִיב יֵשׁוּעַ	. Ezra	יְהוֹיָקִים יְהוֹיָרִיב יְהוֹיָדָע יְהוֹצָדָק יְהוֹשׁוּעַ
תִּדְבָּקִין	. . . Ruth	,,	תִּדְבָּקוּן
הֲרֵאִינִי הַשְּׁמִיעֵנִי	Song of Songs	,,	הַרְאִינִי הַשְׁמִיעֵנִי
רַבָּתִי בַגּוֹיִם	. . Lament. i. 1	,,	רַבַּת
וְעֶשְׂרִים וּמֵאָה	. . . Esther	,,	מֵאָה וְעֶשְׂרִים
לְחֹדֶשׁ	. . . . Esther	,,	לַחֹדֶשׁ

The list is given in that part of the Massorah finalis called *Various Readings* (חלופי קריאה), p. 62 *b*, col. 1, sec. ii., and in *Ochla Ve-Ochla*, sec. cclxxii., pp. 52, 146, &c. The latter adds יָוְכָן (Ezek. i. 2), which in all other books of the Scripture is יְהוֹיָכִין, and לַהּ (Dan. vii. 7), which is elsewhere לָהּ, whilst it omits חוּרָם (2 Chron.). It moreover rightly has לְחָכָם (Prov. ix. 9) instead of לַצַּדִּיק, in the same verse, since it is the former which is everywhere else לְחָכָם, with *Segol* under the *Lamed*, whilst לַצַּדִּיק also occurs in Proverbs.

---

¹⁵² The list which embraces thirty-nine such instances has already been given, *vide supra*, p. 214.

239

mean that it refers to Zechariah alone, but to all the minor Prophets;[153] or, when it is remarked, on חַפָּאת *sin offering,* in Micah i. 13, "it is not in the book," it means the twelve Prophets. The same is the case with the book of Ezra, which also includes the book of Nehemiah. Thus, for instance, when it is remarked, "וְאַף *and even,* occurs nine times at the beginning of a verse, and throughout Ezra it is likewise so,"[154] it also includes Nehemiah. As to the "*Pattach of the book,*" I have already explained its nature in Section ii., see p. 197. The "*Piska of the book,*" too, has already been explained in Section iv., see p. 209.

Let me now explain the word לשנא. Notice that the Massorites

ד״פ בספרא, אינו ר״ל בזכריה לבד, רק בכל
ת״ע; [153] וכן במיכה ראשית חַפָּאת לית
בספרא ר״ל בכל ת״ע; וכן בספר עזרא
נכלל ג״כ ספר נחמיה, כמו וְאַף גם זאת מ׳
ר״פ וכל עזרא דכותיה ר״ל גם ספר נחמיה;
[154] ופתח דכפרא באדרתי דינו במאמר ב׳
ע״ש; ופסקא דספרא באדרתי דינו במאמר
ד׳ ע״ש:

ועתה אבאר מלת לשנא; דע כי שמשו
בו בב׳ אופנים, הא׳ באמרם בלשנא, וחב׳
באמרם בכל לשנא; וזה מלה אחת שיש לה
דומות באותו לשון בנקוד, או ביתרון, או
בחסרון אות, או בנין אחד, צרפו את כל
המלות ההן יחד, אף אל פי שהן נבדלות
בשאר האותיות והנקודות:

☞ והמשל וַיַּנִּחֵהוּ בגן עדן נמסר עליו
לית וחסר ז׳ חסרים בלשנא, ר״ל בעתיד
הפעיל, אחד מהן וַיַּנִּחֵהוּ, ואחד וַיַּנִחוּם, וא׳
תַּנִּחֵנוּ וכו׳,[155] לפי שבכלן חסר יו״ד ההפעיל

use it in two ways: the one when they say בלשנא, and the other when they remark בכל לשנא. If words are alike in form, having either some of the same vowel-points, or the same addition or omission of a letter, or if they belong to the same conjugation, they (the Massorites) ranged these words together under one rubric, though they differ with regard to the other letters and vowel-signs.

☞ Thus, for instance, on וַיַּנִּחֵהוּ [Gen. ii. 15], the Massorites remark, "not extant, and defective, seven times defective in this form," that is, *the future Hiphil.* One of these instances is, וַיַּנִּחֵהוּ *and he put him* [Gen. ii. 15], וַיַּנִחוּם *and he put them* [Josh. iv. 8], תַּנִּחֵנוּ *thou shalt leave us* [Jerem. xiv. 9], &c.[155] Now, because the *Jod* in all these, which

---

[153] The other two instances in which ואף occurs at the beginning of a verse in the minor Prophets are, Amos ix. 3, 4. We could not find them specified any where in the Massorah.

[154] The nine instances in which ואף begins the verse are, Levit. xxvi. 44: Ezek. xxiii. 40: Habak. ii. 5: Ps. lxxviii. 31: Job xix. 4; xxxvi. 16: Ezra v. 10, 14; vi. 5. They are given in the Massorah marginalis on Job xix. 4; xxxvi. 16: Ezra v. 10. In the Massorah parva, on Ezek. xxiii. 40, and Ps. lxxviii. 31, where reference is made to this fact, it is erroneously stated that there are six [ו] such instances, whilst on Job xix. 4; xxxvi. 16, the Massorah parva remarks that there are ten [י] such passages: and there can be but little doubt that though this, too, is an error, the former is a corruption of the latter, since we have already seen that nothing is more easy than the corruption of Vav into Jod, and vice versa. The remark וכל עזרא דכותיה, is only to be found in the Massorah parva on Ezek. xxiii. 40. It has to be added that the Sulzbach edition omits ואף גם זאת מ׳ ר״פ וכל עזרא דכותיה ר״ל גם ספר נחמיה, *i. e.,* ואף, AND EVEN, *occurs nine times at the beginning of a verse, and throughout Ezra it is likewise so, including therein the book of Nehemiah;* whilst the other two editions omit [מ׳] *nine,* which we have supplied.

[155] The other instances in which the *Hiphil* is defective of the *Jod* are, Gen. xix. 16: Levit. xxiv. 12: 2 Sam. xvi. 11: 1 Kings viii. 9; xiii. 29. They are given in the

is the distinguishing mark of the *Hiphil*, is absent, the Massorites put them together under one rubric. When two words are written and pronounced alike, but differ in sense, they remark on them, "two of two significations." In the Third Part, entitled *The Broken Tables*, I shall again discuss this subject under the initials ת״ל, with the help of God.

Moreover, the expression בלישנא is also used for a root, with all the forms which belong to the same. Thus, it is remarked, with regard to the root רהב, "twelve instances of this root."[156]

כללו אותם בלישנא אחד ; וכשיהיו ב' מלות שווֹת במכתב ובמבטא ושונים בפתרון, נמסר עליהן ב' מב״ לישנא, ובשער שברי לוחות אדבר בם במלת ת״ל בע״ה :

גם יש בלישנא שכולל כל מלות השרש החוא, כגון בשרש רחב י״ב בלישנא ;[156] ויש בלשנא שכולל בשרש אחד רק ענין אחד שבאותו השרש, כמו בשרש עור כתבו על ויהי ערך ז' בלישנא דבבו, כי כל שאר לשוניות שבשרש זה יש להן הוראות אחרות עיין בשרשו ;[157] וכן בשרש שער נמסר על מאה שְׁעָרִים ליח בלישנא, כי כל שאר לשון שער יש לו הוראה אחרת ; אמנם כל לישנא לא כתבו

The term בלישנא is also used for a rubric containing those words only of a root which have the same signification. For example, in the root עור, they remark on עֹרְךָ *thine enemy* [1 Sam. xxviii. 16], "seven times in the signification of *enemy;*" for all the other expressions of this root have another signification (*vide Lex., s. v.*).[157] Thus, also, in the root שער, they remarked on שְׁעָרִים *measures* [Gen. xxvi. 12], "not extant in this signification;" for all the other expressions derived from שער have another meaning. The expression כל לישנא, however, the Massorites only use when a word is construed with

---

Massorah marginalis on Levit. xxiv. 12, and 1 Kings xiii. 29. In both these passages the Massorah gives ויניחהו [Levit. xxiv. 12], which is *plene* in the best Codices, as one of the seven *defectives;* whilst it omits וינחום [Josh. iv. 8], which is really *defective*, and is quoted as such by Levita. There can therefore be but little doubt that the former has been substituted for the latter, through a clerical blunder.

[156] The twelve words which belong to the same root with *He*, since in all other instances this form occurs with *Cheth*, are as follows:—

רחב	. . .	Ps. lxxxix. 11	ורהבם	. . . .	Ps. xc. 10	הרהיבני	Song of Songs vi. 5
רחב	. . .	Ps. lxxxvii. 4	והב	. . . .	Prov. iii. 3	יהרבו	. . . . Isa. iii. 5
תרהבני	. Ps. cxxxviii. 3	רהב	. . . .	Job. xxvi. 12	רהב	. . . . Isa. xxx. 7
רהבים	. . .	Ps. xl. 5	רהב	. . . .	Job ix. 13	רהב	. . . . Isa. li. 9

They are given in the Massorah marginalis on Isa. xxx. 7; Ps. lxxxix. 11; Job ix. 13. On Isa. xxx. 7, and Ps. lxxxix. 11, Jacob b. Chajim, the editor of the Massorah, adds ואֹ. כ״ל ופחד ורהב לבבך, "and it appears to me that רהב [Isa. lx. 5], is one of these." But though this reading is to be found in Jehudah Chajug's *Treatise on the Vowel-points and Accents* [ספר הנקוד, p. 183, ed. Dukes], yet all the best Codices, as well as most of the ancient grammarians and commentators, read the word in question with *Cheth*. Besides, the *Ochla Ve-Ochla*, section ccv. pp. 44, 124, &c., which also gives this rubric, does not include it in the list. Comp. also the remarks of Dr. Frensdorff, the learned editor of the *Ochla Ve-Ochla*, p. 44.

[157] The Massorah marginalis on Micah v. 13, gives *eight* such passages, viz., 1 Sam. xxviii. 16: Micah v. 13, 10: Isa. xiv. 21: Ps. ix. 7; cxxxix. 20: Dan. iv. 16: Jerem. v. 8. The Massorah marginalis on 1 Sam. xxviii. 16, though omitting Dan iv. 16, and Jerem. v. 8; and the Massorah parva on Micah v. 13, and Ps. cxxxix. 20, also state most explicitly that there are [ח׳ בליש׳ דבבו] *eight* passages in which עור denotes enemy. It is only the Massorah parva on Isa. xiv. 21, which, like Levita, says that there are [ז׳] *seven* such instances. The full enumeration of them, however, by the Massorah marginalis, shows that the *seven* must be a clerical error.

another, contrary to its uniform position. Thus, for instance, they remark, "all the expressions of the root שָׁמַע *to hear*, are construed with אֶל, except twelve in this form, which take עַל;"[158] or, "all the expressions of שְׁחִיטָה *to slaughter*, are construed with אֵת, except four, which are without אֵת;"[159] or, "in all phrases אָב *father* precedes אֵם *mother*, except in four instances;"[160] or, "all phrases have חֻקִּים *statutes*, before מִשְׁפָּטִים *laws*, except in eight passages;"[161] and many more like them.

☞ I shall now explain the word עִנְיָנָא. Notice that the expression עִנְיָן is only to be found in the book of Ecclesiastes, where it occurs eight times, and always in the singular. But our Rabbins of blessed memory used it very frequently, and even in the plural. It denotes *business, transaction*, in German Geschäft. Now in the Massorah it is used in the Chaldee sense of transaction, whereas in the Chaldee on Ecclesiastes it is simply rendered by גָּוֵן *colour, form*. Hence when you find in the Massorah בְּעִנְיָנָא, it denotes *in this narrative of the transaction, section, chapter*; as בְּנַפּוֹ alone [Exod. xxi. 3], on which the Massorites remark, "three times, and in the section;" so also the remarks, "not *defective* in the connection," "not *plene* in the connection."

---

[158] The twelve passages in which the verb שמע is construed with the preposition על are, Gen. xli. 15 : Isa. xxxvii. 9 : 2 Kings xx. 13 : Jerem. iv. 16 ; vi. 7 ; xxiii. 16 ; xxvi. 5 ; xxxv. 18 ; li. 27 : Ezek. xxvii. 30 : Amos iii. 9 : Nehem. ix. 9. They are given in the Massorah marginalis on 2 Kings xx. 13, and Ezekiel xxvii. 30. In both instances the Massorah gives a reference, דרשו מעל ספר יהוה (*i.e.* to Isa. xxxiv. 16), which does not contain any such construction, and which must therefore have been inserted by mistake. Indeed Buxtorf, in his edition of the Rabbinic Bible, who only gives the Massoretic rubric once, viz., on Ezek. xxvii. 30, has omitted this reference.

[159] The four instances in which the verb שחט has not את, the sign of the accusative, are, Levit. vi. 18 (twice) : Isa. lxvi. 3 : 2 Chron. xxix. 22. They are given in the Massorah finalis under the letter *Shin*, p. 58 b, col. 4.

[160] This must be a mistake, since both the Massorah parva and the Massorah marginalis, on Gen. xliv. 20 and Levit. xix. 3, distinctly state that there are only three instances in which אם precedes אב, viz., Gen. xliv. 20 : Levit. xix. 3 ; xxi. 2. The last two instances are included in the Massoretic list of thirty passages, in which normal constructions are abnormally inverted, and which we have already given (*vide supra*, p. 214). Why Gen. xliv. 20 is excluded from that list we cannot divine.

[161] The eight passages in which משפטי precedes חקתי, contrary to its usual construction, are, Levit. xviii. 4 ; xxvi. 43 : Ezek. v. 6 (twice) ; xviii. 17 ; xx. 16, 24 ; xxxvii. 24. The Massorah also gives Ezek. xliv. 24 as a ninth instance. But since תורתי intervenes in this passage between the two words in question, there can be little doubt that it is an addition by a later hand, and is therefore rightly excluded from this list in the *Ochla Ve-Ochla*, section cclxxviii., pp. 54, 131.

☞ Let me now explain the word פסוק. Mark that the expression פסוק is not Hebrew, but Aramaic, and many words are rendered by it, that is, by the expression פסקה, which is in German aufhören. Thus, חָדַל it ceased [Gen. xviii. 11] is rendered in the Chaldee by פָּסָק; וַיִּשְׁבֹּת and it discontinued [Josh. v. 12], by וּפְסָק; וַיִּכְלָא and he left off [Exod. xxxvi. 6], by וּפְסָק; וְלֹא יָסָף and he did not add [Deut. v. 19], by פָּסָק; יִכָּרֵת it shall be consumed by פסק [Numb. xi. 33]. Hence, a verse is called פסוק. Hence, also, the dividing space between the sections פיסקא, as in the remark, "there are two sections in the Pentateuch which have no Piska at the beginning, i. e., the Pericopes

ועתה אפרש מלת פסוק; דע כי לשון פסוק אינו לשון עברי אך לשון ארמי, והרבה לשונות מתורגמין כן, ר"ל בלשון הפסקה, בלשון אשכנז אויפהורן, כמו חָדַל להיות לשרה תרגומו פסק, וכן וַיִּשְׁבֹּת המן ופסק, וַיִּכְלָא העם ופסק, וְלֹא יָסָף ולא פסק, טרם יָכָרֵת עד לא פסק; על כן נקרא הפסוק פסוק, ומזה קראו ג"כ למקום חלוק שבין פרשה לפרשה פיסקא, כמו שאמרו ב' פרשיות בתורה דלית בהון פסקא ברישא, והם ויצא ויחי;[162] וב' פרשיות בתורה דלית בהון פסקא באמצע הפרשה, והם ויצא ומקץ;[163] וכן יש פסקא באמצע הפסוק, ד' מנחות בתורה, כנון ויאמר קין אל הבל אחיו ויהי בהיותם בשדה ודוק;[164] ויש קורין פיסקא זו פרינמא, ועוד אזכרנה בשער שברי לוחות; והטעם הנקרא פסק או פסיק כבר זכרתיו במאמר ד' ע"ש; סליק:

Va-Jetze and Va-Jechi;[162] and other two sections in the Pentateuch which have no Piska in the middle of the section, i. e., Va-Jetze and Miketz.[163] There is also a Piska in the middle of the verse; four instances of it are to be found in the Pentateuch, as Gen. iv. 8.[164] Some call this Piska by the name of פרינמא [= πράγμα], but I shall again speak about it in the Third Part, entitled "The Broken Tables." About the accents called Psak, or P'sik, I have already spoken in Section iv. [vide supra p. 209]. End.

[162] For the division of the Pentateuch into hebdomadal lessons, see above, p. 135. Va-Jetze (ויצא) is the seventh of the fifty-four divisions, and embraces Gen. xxviii. 10-xxxii. 3; and Va-Jechi (ויחי) is the twelfth Pericope, extending over Gen. xlvii. 28—l. 26.

[163] The Pericope Miketz (מקץ) is the tenth of the fifty-four sections or weekly lessons, and embraces Gen. xli. 1—xliv. 17.

[164] The other three instances in which there is a Piska or pause in the middle of a verse in the Pentateuch are, Gen. xxxv. 22: Numb. xxv. 19: Deut. ii. 8.

HERE IS THE TABLE OF CONTENTS OF THE TEN SECTIONS IN PART II.[165]	הא לך השמנים כהמלות המצויות, בעשרה מאמרים בלוחות השניות:[165]
SECTION I.—Concerning *Keri* and *Kethiv*, divided into seven classes.	המאמר הראשון בקריין וכתבן ונחלקין לשבעה מינים :
SECTION II.—Concerning *Kametz* and *Pattach*.	המאמר השני בקמצין ופתחין :
SECTION III.—Concerning *Dagesh, Raphe, Mapik*, and *Sheva*.	המאמר השלישי בדגשין ורפין ומקפין ובקצת דיני השוא :
SECTION IV.—Concerning *Milel, Milra*, and *Pesakim*.	המאמר הרביעי במלעיל ומלרע ובפסקים :
SECTION V.—Concerning *Registers, Groups, Resemblances*, and *Parallels*.	המאמר החמישי בשיטין וזוגין ודמיין ודכוותהון :
SECTION VI.—Concerning *Junctions, Severances*, and *Identical*.	המאמר הששי בסמיכים ויחידין ומודרפים :
SECTION VII.—Concerning *the Presence* or *Absence of Prefixes* or *Serviles*.	המאמר השביעי בנהיבין או משמשין וקרחין :
SECTION VIII.—Concerning *Conjectural Readings, Misleadings*, and *Exchanges*.	המאמר השמיני בסבירין ומטעין וחילופין :
SECTION IX.—Concerning *Letters, Words, Expressions, Short Letters, Accents, Certainties*, and *Transpositions*.	המאמר התשיעי באתין ותיבין ומלין וקטיעין ופשטין וודאי ומוקדמין ומאוחרין :
SECTION X.—Concerning *Scripture, Book, Form, Connection*, and *Verse*.	המאמר העשירי בקריא בספרא בלישנא בעינא בפסוק ;
The Second Tables are now ended, In the name of the Creator of heaven and earth ; And in the name of the Lord, the God of Spirits, I begin the Section of the Broken Tables.	סליקו הלוחות האחרונים, בשם בורא עליונים ותחתונים, ובשם אל אלהי הרוחות, אפתח שער שברי לוחות :

[165] These two lines are entirely omitted in the Sulzbach edition.

THIRD PART;
OR, THE BROKEN TABLES.

Thus, says the author already mentioned, the man known by his writings, who works for honour and not for shame, I now render praise to the Lord, who has preserved me, and sustained me, and helped me hitherto, so that I have written the First Tables, and then the Second Tables, each consisting of ten sections. In the one Section which I now add, I shall be able to explain whatever occurs both in the First and Second Parts of this book to the end thereof.

And now my soul rejoices in the thought, and in the name of Him who ordaineth true wisdom, I call its name *The Section of the Broken Tables*, because I shall therein explain the import of the broken and abbreviated words, and of those expressions which are written in *notaricon*, and in initials, in signs, in enigmas, and in diverse phrases, both in the Massorah magna and parva. Now since there are not many who are learned in these matters, and who take it to heart to understand their utility, as I have already mentioned in the Poetical Introduction, which you may there see, I shall explain these things; and, in order to save the public trouble, I shall not lengthen my Treatise, thus acting in accordance with the following saying of our Rabbins of blessed memory in the Talmud : " one should always teach his disciples by a short method." Hence I now commence with cheerfulness to point out the reason for each thing, by the help of heaven. May the Great Name be praised, world without end.

First of all, I must give you a rule whereby to distinguish a word which is described by initials from a word which is simply abbreviated. It is as follows :—When you find two, three, or four letters together, and each one has a mark on the top, they are invariably to be taken as

שער שברי לוחות:

אמר המחבר הנזכר, האיש אשר בכתבו נכר, ודורש לשבח ולא לגנאי, הפעם אודה את י"י, שהחייני וקיימני, ועד הנה עזרני, וכתבתי על הלוחות הראשינים, את עשרת הדברים חמרוכנים, ואחריהן הלוחות האחרונות באו, ובעשרה מאמרות נבראו, וחלא במאמר אחד אשר אוסיף עתה, יוכל לחבראות כל מה שלמעלה ולמטה, בכל דברי הספר הזה עד תומם:

ועתה יעש לבי כאשר זמם, ובשם אשר שת חכמה בטוחות, ואקרא את שמו *שער שברי לוחות*, יען כי אבאר בו הדברים הקצרים והנשברים, והמלורי הנכתבורת, בנוטריקון ובראשי תבות, ובדרך רמיזה וקריצה, כמין חיבה פרוצה, וכל לשון שנשתנה, במסרה גדולה וקטנה, ובם לא רבים יחכמו, ועל לבם לא שמו, להבין מה טבה, וכבר כתבתי הסבה, בהקדמה החרוזית, כאשר שם חזית, ואעשה בהם חבור, ומפני טורח הציבור, לא אאריך הדבור, ואקיים מה שאמרו רז"ל בגמרא, לעולם ישנה אדם לתלמידיו בדרך קצרה, ובכן אחחיל בשובה ונחת, למצוא חשבון אחת לאחת, בסייעתא דשמיא, יהא שמיה רבא מברך לעלם ולעלמי עלמיא:

וקודם כל קודם אחן לך כלל וסימן להכיר חמלה שחי נדרשת בראשי תבות מן המלה שהיא בלתי שלמה וחסר החלק האחרון ממנה; וזה כאשר תמצא ב' או ג' או ד' אותיות יחד, ועל אחת נקודה למעלה ודאי

initials of words; but when they have not all marks, and it is only the last letter which has one mark, it is invariably an abbreviation, and the word in question wants one or two letters at the end; as you will find explained in this Section.

Now I shall begin by explaining the word לית *not extant*, since the Massorites use it more than any other expression. It is the Aramaic compound of לא *not*, and אית *is*, denoting that the word or sentence on which it is remarked has no parallel. This is also its meaning in the Targum, which renders לא יש *there is not* [Job ix. 33], by לא אית, and which frequently translates the Hebrew word אֵין *not, not extant*, by לית (comp. Numb. xxi. 5), and only rarely translates it לא (comp. Exod. xii. 30). In the Massorah parva, instead of לית, the Massorites write a single *Lamed* with a mark over it, as follows: ל׳. And there is no other single letter in the Massorah parva but what indicates some number, except this one. Hence, when a word occurs thirty times, the Massorites do not remark on it ל׳, lest there should be a confusion between it and לית *not*, but they note it by writing out fully the word *Lamed*. Thus, for instance, "the word וַיּוֹסֶף occurs [למ״ד] thirty times;"[1] "the particle אֶל occurs [למ״ד] thirty times alone." In some Codices I have seen כ״י [= 20 and 10] instead of ל׳ [= 30], but the first is more general and more correct.

היא נדרשת לראשי תבות, וכשאין עליהן נקודה, רק על אות האחרון נקודה אחת, ודאי היא מלה בלתי שלמה וחסר אוה אחת, או יותר בסוף התיבה ודוק ותמצא במלורה שאכתוב לך בשער ז:

והנה אחחיל לבאר מלת לית, כי שמשו בה בעלי המסרת יותר מבכל שאר המלות, והיא מלה ארמית, מורכבת מן לא ומן אית פירוש לא יש, רוצה לומר אותה מלה או אותו ענין, שנמסר עליח לית, לא יש אחרת כמוהו; וכן תרגום של לא יֵשׁ בידינו מוכיח (איוב ט׳), לא אית בידנא מכסין: וכן רוב אין מתורגמין לית, כמו אין לחם ואין מים לית לחמא ולית מיא; ומעטים מתורגמים לא, כמו אין בית אשר אין שם מת, לית ביתא דילא הוה תמן מיתא; ובמסרה קטנה כתבו במקום לית למ״ד אחת בנקודה למעלה כזה ל׳, ולא נמצא אות במסרה קפנה העומד יחידי שאינו מורה על מספר מה רק זאת לבדה, לפיכך מלה הנמצאה שלש״ם פעמים, אין כותבין עליה ל׳ שלא למעות בינה ובין לית, אלא כותבין למ״ד במלואה, כמו וַיּוֹסֶף למ״ד,[1] אֶל למ״ד יחידאין; וביש נוסחאות מצאתי כ״י במקום ל׳, אבל הרבשון עקר, וכן עמא דבר:

---

[1] Of the thirty instances in which ויסף occurs, seven are *plene* (i.e. ויוסף), and twenty-three *defective* (i.e. ויסף). The *plenes* are, Numb xxii. 26: Judg. xi. 14: 1 Sam. xx. 17; xxiii. 4: Isa. vii. 10: 2 Chron. xxviii. 22: 1 Sam. xviii. 29. They are given in the Massorah marginalis on Numb. xxii. 2, and 1 Kings xvi. 33. The twenty-three instances in which it is *defective* are, Gen. viii. 10; xviii. 29; xxv. 1: Exod. ix. 34. Numb. 15, 25: Judg. ix. 37: 1 Sam. iii. 6, 8, 21; ix. 21: 2 Sam. ii. 22; vi. 1; xviii. 22; xxiv. 1: Isa. viii. 5. Job xxvi. 1; xxix. 1; xxxvi. 1; xlii. 10: Dan. x. 18. The list of these is no where given in the Massorah. As an illustration of the various ways in which the Massorah annotates the words belonging to the same rubric, we shall specify the thirty instances before us. The Massorah parva annotates twelve passages out of the thirty. In the first instance alone, viz., Gen. xviii. 29, occurs the למ״ד = 30, to which Levita refers; on Gen. xxv. 1, it remarks כל חס במ׳ זי "always *defective*, except seven times;" on Numb. xxii. 15, it states "it occurs twenty-nine (וכ״ט) times;" on Numb. xxii. 25, 1 Kings xvi. 33, Isa. vii. 10, 2 Chron. xxviii. 22, "it occurs (ז׳ מל) seven times *plene*:" whilst on 2 Sam. vi. 1, it remarks, "it occurs (י״ב בסיפ) twelve times in this book." The Massorah marginalis, again, does not notice this rubric more than twice, and then only the seven instances of *plene*, which it gives on Numb. xxii. 2, 1 Kings xvi. 33, simply adding, that in all other instances it is *defective*.

אנ״ך are the initials of **אורייתא** **נביאים, כתובים** the Law, the Prophets, and the Hagiographa; and they are noted on every word which occurs three times, once in the Law, once in the Prophets, and once in the Hagiographa; as **בָּחֲרוּ** they chose, occurs three times, the sign being אנ״ך.[2] In some Codices these instances are marked א״ב א״ב א״ב which are the initials of **אחד בתורה אחד בנביאים אחד בכתובים** once in the Law, once in the Prophets, and once in the Hagiographa. When a word only occurs in the Prophets and Hagiographa, it is marked נביאים כתובים = נ״ב the Prophets, and the Hagiographa; as **הָאָרוֹן** the ark, which is defective in the Pentateuch, whilst in נ״ב = the Prophets and Hagiographa, it is plene. Thus, also, לְעוֹלָם for ever, is marked "eight times defective בנ״כ = in the Prophets and Hagiographa."[3]

אפ״ס are the initials of **אחד פסוק סימן** one verse is the sign, that is, when there are two or three parallel things in one section, or in the same narrative, or in the same book, or even in two sections, or two books, and they only differ in one word, the Massorites note the difference between them, and give them a verse as a mnemonical sign, as in the Section on Eliezer, the servant of Abraham. Here the first statement is בְּקִרְבּוֹ in the midst thereof [Gen. xxiv. 3], and the second is בְּאַרְצוֹ in the land thereof [ibid. xxiv. 37], whilst the mnemonical sign is "I, Jehovah, in the midst of the land" [Exod. viii. 18].[4] Thus, also, Ps. lvi., where in verse 5 it is בָּשָׂר לִי flesh, to me, whilst in verse 12 it is אָדָם לִי man, to me, and the mnemonical verse [אפ״ס] is "upon

---

[2] The three passages in which בחרו has Kametz under the Cheth, being in pause, are, Gen. vi. 2: Isa. lxvi. 4: Prov. i. 29. In all other passages it has Chateph-pattach under the Cheth. The words כן כתבו על כל מלה או לשון הנמצא ג׳ פעמים א׳ בתורה א׳ בנביאים א׳ בכתובים, are omitted in the Sulzbach edition.

[3] The instances in which לעולם is defective have already been given, vide supra, p. 149. The Massoretic remark to which Levita refers is not to be found in the printed editions of the Massorah in the Rabbinic Bibles.

[4] The meaning of the passage and the mnemonical sign is as follows:—In the first passage (Gen. xxiv. 3), giving Abraham's own words, the expression בקרבו in the midst thereof is used; whilst in the second passage (ibid. xxiv. 37), which gives Eleazer's repetitions of what his master had said, the word in question is dropped, and בארצו in the land thereof is substituted. To indicate this change in the words, the Massorites selected the passage in Exod. viii. 18 as a mnemonical sign, showing that just as in this sign בקרב occurs first and הארץ second, so in the two passages for which it is the mnemonical sign, and where the two words are interchanged, בקרבו occurs first and בארצו second.

the flesh of man it shall not be poured" [Exod. xxx. 32].[5] Likewise in 1 Chron. xvi. 16, where it is וּשְׁבוּעָתוֹ לְיִצְחָק and his oath to Isaac, whilst in Psalm cv. 9 it is וּשְׁבוּעָתוֹ לְיִשְׂחָק written with a Sin, and the mnemonical sign is "and Sarah laughed" [Gen. xviii. 12]; that is, the Tzaddi is before the Sin, since Chronicles is before Psalms, as I have explained in the Third Introduction.

When the difference between two words consists in the points, they give for a sign a word which contains the two letters with the two in question. Thus, we have first לָלִין to stay over night [Gen. xxiv. 23], and then לָלוּן [ibid. ver. 25], and the mnemonical word for this difference is הֵלִילוּ howl [Isa. xxiii. 1].[3] Compare also the first לִצְמִתֻת until extinction [Levit. xxv. 23], and the second לִצְמִיתֻת [ibid. ver. 30], where the mnemonical word is חָלִילָה far be it; and although the second Lamed in חָלִילָה has Kametz and not Pattach, they made no distinction between Kametz and Pattach; also, the first הֶחָי the living [Levit. xvi. 20], and the second הַחַי [ibid. ver. 21], and the signal word הֱהָשֵׁב [Gen. xxiv. 5].[7] Thus, also, in verses in which three or four words are alike, but in which only one word has a different servile letter, the Massorites indicate it by a mnemonical verse containing the two words in question; ex. gr., in Deut. xi. 24 it is הַמָּקוֹם the place, with the article, whilst in Josh. i. 3 it is מָקוֹם place, without the He, and the signal verse is וְהִנֵּה הַמָּקוֹם מְקוֹם מִקְנֶה and behold, the place is a place of cattle [Numb. xxxii. 1]. So, also, the first passage כִּי when [Levit. xxv. 25], the second וְכִי and when [ibid. ver. 35], and the third וְכִי and when [ibid. v. 39], are indicated by the signal verse; "and she said unto the men, I know THAT [כִּי], AND THAT [וְכִי] . . AND THAT [וְכִי] Josh. ii. 9.

---

[5] Here again the mnemonical sign על בשר אדם, which contains both words, בשר flesh and אדם man, shows by the position of the two words that בשר is used in the first passage and אדם in the second.

[6] That is, since in the word הלילו, we have first לִי and then לוּ; hence the first syllable indicates לִין with Chirek, which occurs first, whilst the second syllable represents לוּן with Shurek, which occurs second in the section.

[7] The change of the vowel-points in the word החי, having in the first place Segol under the He, and in the second place Pattach, is shown by the mnemonical expression ההשב, which has twice He,—the first with Segol, corresponding to the Segol under the He in החי, in the first passage, and the second with Pattach, corresponding to the Pattach under the He in החי, in the second passage.

אָסָ״ף consists of the initials of *Ethnach*, and *Soph Passuk*. It is only put down on a word which has *Kametz*, on account of *Zakeph*, *Rebii*, or any other pause accent, and which has no parallel, except in the said *Ethnach* and *Soph Passuk*. Thus, הַפָּסַח *the passover* [Numb. ix. 2], is marked, "not extant with *Kametz*, and every instance with *Ethnach* or *Soph Passuk* [אָסָ״ף] is like it." The same is the case when the word occurs more than once, as אָבָד *he perished* [Isa. lvii. 1; Micah iv. 9], which is marked, "it occurs twice, and every instance with *Ethnach* or *Soph Passuk* [אָסָ״ף] is like it." In some Codices, instead of אָסָ״ף, they have written the form of *Ethnach* and *Soph Passuk*, as follows : ׀ ֑, and they say, "every ׀ ֑ is like it." Many have been misled thereby, thinking that it stood for *Cheth* and *Nun*, and read it חֵן *peace, rest;* whereas they are nothing but the forms of *Ethnach* and *Soph Passuk*.

אֱמָ״ת is the acrostic of אִיוֹב מִשְׁלֵי תְלִים *Job, Proverbs*, and *Psalms.* The Massorites assign this sign to these books, though they do not occur in this order, as I have stated in the Third Introduction, for their proper order is as follows: Psalms, Job, and Proverbs; and in accordance therewith I have also found in some Codices the sign תָּא״ם. But they usually write אֱמָ״ת, because this mnemonical sign is more beautiful, since our Rabbins of blessed memory said, "always use an elevating phrase" [*Pessachim*, 3 *a*]. Now on the word עָשָׂה, with *Tzere*, the Massorites remark, "it occurs eight times with *Kametz*, and throughout אֱמָ״ת דת״קע is like it." In this case אֱמָ״ת does not stand for Job, Proverbs, and Psalms, but the whole of it consists of the acrostic of Deuteronomy [אלה הדברים], Proverbs [משלי], the twelve minor Prophets [תרי עשר], Chronicles [ד״ת], Psalms [תהלים], Proverbs [קהלת], and Ezra [עזרא].

שׁב״נ is the acrostic of שׁוֹם בַּר נָשׁ *name of the son of man*, or *proper name*. Thus on אֲחֻזַּת *Ahuzzath* [Gen. xxvi. 26], "not extant, and every proper names [שב״ן] are like it."[8] It is a phrase used in the

---

[8] In the printed editions of the Massorah parva, on Gen. xxvi. 26, the remark is not ליה וכל שב״נ דכותיה *not extant, and every proper name is like it*, as is stated by Levita,

אָסָ״ף ראשי תיבות אתנח וסוף פסוק ולא כתבו זה רק על מלה שהיא קמוצה בעבור זקף, או רביע, או טעם אחד מפסיק, ואין דומה לה רק באתנח וסוף פסוק, כגון ויעשו בני ישראל את הַפָּסַח וכל אָסָ״ף דכותיה; וכן כשיש לה דמיין, כמו אָבַד ב' וכל אָס׳׳ף דכותיה, וכמו אלה רבים; וביש נוסחאות עשו במקום אָסָ״ף חמונת האתנח וס״פ כזה ׀ ֑, ואמרו וכל ׀ ֑ דכוותיה; ורבים טועים בהם וחושבין שהם חי״ת ונו״ן וקורין חֵן לשון חנינה ומנוחה, ואינן אלא צורת האתנח וס״פ:

אֱמָ״ת ראשי תיבות איוב משלי תלים, נתנו בהן זה הסימן אע״פ שאין כדורן כן, כמו שכתבתי בהקדמה השלישית, כי סדורן תלים איוב משלי; וכן מצאתי בקצת נוסחאות סימנם תָּא״ם, אלא נוהגין לכתוב אֱמָ״ת לפי שהוא סימן יפה כמאמר רז״ל לשון מעלייתא נקט: והנה נמסר על מלת עָשָׂה בצידי ח׳ קמצין וכל אֱמָ״ת דת״קע דכותיה, ואיננו איוב משלי תהלים, אלא אלה הדברים, משלי תרי עשר, ד״ה, תהלים, קהלת, עזרא:

שׁב״נ ראשי תיבות שׁוֹם בַּר נָשׁ, פירוש שום בן אדם, כמו שנמסר על וַאֲחֻזַּת מרעהו לית וכל שב״נ דכותיה, פירוש שום בן אדם לשון תרגום ירושלמי אֱנוֹשׁ המה סלה תרגום

Jerusalem Targum which renders אֱנוֹשׁ *man* [Ps. ix. 21], by בַּר נָשׁ *son of man*, בֶּן אָדָם *son of man* [Job. xxxv. 8]; whilst בֶּן אָדָם, which so frequently occurs in Ezekiel, the Chaldee translates בר אדם. On אָחַז *to seize*, too, the Massorites remark, "it occurs three times with *Kametz*, and all [שב״נ] proper names are like it."[9] Also the four pairs, one of each pair being a proper name [שבנ], and the other being different, as קוֹץ *a thorn* [Gen. iii. 18], and קוֹץ *Koz* [1 Chron. iv. 8], proper name; שֹׁהַם *a species of gem* [Ezek. xxviii. 13], and שֹׁהָם *proper name of a Levite* [1 Chron. xxiv. 27], &c. On a feminine proper name, however, the Massorites remark שום איתתא *name of a woman*, as שָׂרַי *the princess of* [Judges v. 15], "not extant, and whenever it occurs as the name of a woman it is like it."

בר נש הינון לעלמי, וכן וּלְבֶן אָדָם צדקתך וּבר נש דכיא; אבל בֵּן אָדָם דיחזקאל מתורגמין בר אדם, וכן אָחַז נ׳ כמצין וכל שב״נ רכותיה[9]; וכן ר׳ זוגין חד שב״נ וחד לשון אחר, כמו וְקוֹץ ודרדר, וְקוֹץ הוליד; וכן וְשֹׁהַם וישפה, וְשֹׁהָם וזכור וכו׳; אבל על שם נקבה כתבו שום איתתא, כמו וְשָׂרַי בישכר לית, וכל שום איתתא דכוותיה:

מס״ה רוצה לומר מסרה הגדולה, כמו שנמסר על אֲסוּרֵי המלך אֲסִירֵי קרי, והוא א״ב במס״ה דכתיבין וי״ו וקרי י״ד[10]; ויש שקורין למסרה גדולה מסו״ה ולמסרה קטנה מס״ה, וכן ראיתי בספר עֵין הקורא ז״ל, ואלה הספרים אשר נתן לי אלהים בזה, מס״ה ומסו״ה ושאר מסורת מקצת כפרים טובים עכ״ל[11]; וביש נוכחאות מצאתי שקראו למסרה גדולה מס״ג ולמסרה קטנה מס״ק, כמו שוהגין לקרא כפד מצות גדול סמ״ג והקטן סמ״ק[12]:

מס״ה means מסרה הגדולה *the Massorah magna*. Thus on אֲסוּרֵי *the chained* [Gen. xxxix. 20], it is remarked, "read אֲסִירֵי, and it is one of the words in the alphabetical list in the Great Massorah [במס״ה], written in the text with *Vav*, and read in the margin with *Jod*."[10] There are some, however, who call the Great Massorah מסו״ה, and the Small Massorah מס״ה. Thus I have seen in the book called "*The Eye of the Reader*," as follows: "These are the books which the Lord has given me, the Small Massorah [מס״ה], the Great Massorah [מסו״ה], and other Massorahs from some good Codices." Thus far his words.[11] I have found that in some Codices the Great Massorah is called *Mesag* [מס״ג], and the Small Massorah, *Mesak* [מס״ק], just as the "*Great Book of the Commandments*" is called *Semag* [ספר מצות גדול = סמ״ג], and the "*Smaller Book of the Commandments*" is called *Semak* [ספר מצות קטן = סמ״ק].[12]

---

but simply ליח שב״נ *not extant*, *proper names*. The Sulzbach edition omits the word כל before שב״נ, which renders the sentence unintelligible.

[9] The three instances in which אָחַז occurs with *Kametz* and *Pattach* under the first and second radicals are, Exod. xv. 14: 1 Kings i. 51: Job xxiii. 9. They are given in the Massorah marginalis on 1 Kings i. 51 and Job xxiii. 9, and in both these passages the Massoretic remark is וכל שום גבר קמץ ומלרע, *but wherever it is a proper name it has Kametz* [under the second radical], *and is Milra*, and not as Levita states in the text.

[10] The alphabetical list referred to by Levita has already been given, vide supra, p. 118, &c.

[11] For the work entitled *The Eye of the Reader* (עיי הקרא), as well as for its author, see below, p. 257, under the initials יה״בי = *Jekuthiel b. Jehudah Cohen*.

[12] The author of *The Major Book of the Commandments* (ספר מצות גדול, called סמ״ג *Semag* from its initials) is R. Moses, the celebrated Jewish preacher of the middle ages

K K

ימ״ה are the initials of יוצא מן הכלל *departing from the rule.* These initials are generally used in Treatises on the Laws of the Accents. When one of the rules of the accents is described, and there are some exceptions to it, they remark on them, " such and such are ימ״ה," = exceptions to the rule. Thus, for instance, before *Sarka* there ought properly to be *Munach,* but " there are thirteen [ימ״ה] exceptions to this rule, having *Mercha* before it;" as, with the help of the Lord, I shall explain in my book, entitled, *Good Sense.*

א״מ א״ח are the initials of אחד מלא אחד חסר *once defective, once plene.* I have already stated in Part i., Section i., that *plene* and *defective* only obtain with quiescent *Vav* and *Jod* in the middle of a word [*vide supra,* p. 145, &c]. Moreover, on words which occur *plene* or *defective* in two, three, or four places, the Massorites remark ב״מ ב״ח = " twice plene, twice defective," or ג״מ ג״ח = " thrice plene, thrice defective," &c., up to ten instances. But from ten and upwards they write the word *plene* or *defective* separately, and the letters denoting the number separately, as on וַיּוֹצֵא *and he brought out,* " it occurs twenty-four times, twelve times *plene* [י״ב במלאים] and twelve times *defective* [י״ב חסרים],"[13] but they never write יב״מ or יב״ח on one word.

ימ״ה ראשי תיבות יוצא מן הכלל נוהגים לכתוב זה בדיני הטעמים, פי׳ לפעמים כשנותנים כלל אחד בטעמים, ויש היוצאים מן הכלל, כורבין עליהן כך וכך ימ״ה, כגון לפני הזרקא ראוי להיות מונח, רק י״ג ימ״ה שלפניהן מרכא, כמו שיתבאר בספר טוב טעם בע״ה:

א״מ א״ח ראשי תיבות אחד מלא אחד חסר, וכבר הודעתיך ברבור ראשון מלוחות הראשונות, כי מלא וחסר סתם לא נאמר רק על ו״י ויו״ד הנחים באמצא המלה ע״ש; וכן על מלות הנמצאות מלאות או חסרות בב׳ או בג׳, או׳ בד׳ מקימות וכו׳, נוהגין לכתוב כן ב״מ ב״ח, או ג״מ ג״ח וכולי עד חיו״ד; אבל מן היו״ד ואילך כתבו מלא או חסר לבד, ותיבת המנין לבד, והמשל וַיּוֹצֵא כ״ד, י״ב מלאים וי״ב חסרים, ולא כתבו יב״מ ויב״ח: [13]

---

he was born at Coucy, not far from Soissons, circa A.D. 1200, and died 1260. The work on the Commandments and Prohibitions consists of sermons which R. Moses de Coucy delivered on his journeys through the South of France and Spain (1235–1245), in the different Synagogues the design of which was to confirm his brethren in the ancient faith, since the orthodox religion of the Jews was at that time being undermined by the philosophy of Maimonides. The work which propounds the six hundred and thirteen precepts was first printed before 1480; then in Soncino, 1488; and in Venice, 1522, 1547, &c. Comp. Fürst, *Bibliotheca Judaica,* i. 189, &c.; Steinschneider, *Catalogus Libr. Hebr. in Bibliotheca Bodleiana,* col. 1795-1798; Graetz, *Geschichte der Juden,* vol. vii., pp. 61, 70, 72, 115, 130, Leipzig, 1863. *The Minor Book of the Commandments* (ספר מצות קטן), called סמ״ק *Semay,* from the initials of its title) is simply an abridgment of the greater work, made by Isaac de Corbeil, A.D. 1277, and is divided into seven parts, for the seven days of the week. It was first published at Constantinople, 1510; then at Cremona, 1556, with glosses, &c.; and at Cracow, 1596, &c. See Fürst, *Bibliotheca Judaica,* i. 186; Steinschneider, *Catalogus Libr. Hebr. in Bibliotheca Bodleiana,* col. 1103.

[13] The twelve passages in which ויוצא is *plene* are, Gen. xv. 5; xxiv. 53; xliii. 23; xlviii. 12: Exod. xix. 17: Judg. vi. 19: 2 Kings xxiv. 13: 2 Chron. xxiii. 14: Ps. cxxxvi. 11: Jerem. x. 13; 1. 25; li. 16; and the thirteen instances in which it is *defective* are, Numb. xvii. 23, 24: Judg. xix. 25: 2 Sam. x. 16; xiii. 18; xxii. 20: 2 Kings xv. 20; xxiii. 6; x. 22: Jerem. xx. 3; lii. 31: 2 Chron. xvi. 2: Job xii. 22. The former are given in the Massorah marginalis on Judg. vi. 19, and the latter in the Massorah

וְעוֹד תדע שלא כתבו ה' דק על מלות שקצתן מלאים וקצתן חסרים, כגון וַתּוֹרֶד ג', א"מ וב"ח; וכן פָּקוֹד ד', ב"מ וב"ח;[14] אבל במלות שלא נמנו רק המלאים לבד או החסרים לבד, כתבו ג"כ המלאים או החסרים לבד, והמנין לבר, כגון אֲבוֹתֶיךָ ג' מלאים, ולא כתבו ג"מ, וכן גָּדְלָה ה' חסרים, ולא כתבו ה"ח:[15] ודע עוד כשתבצא הבי"ת והמ"ם יחד, עם ב' נקודות למעלה, ונסמך אליהן אות אחת מן האל"ף עד היו"ד, כגון בָּמ"א, בָּמ"ב, בָּמ"ג, בָּמ"ד וכולי. הוא ראשי תיבות בר מן אחד, בר מן שנים, בר מן שלשה וכולי; ופירוש בר חוץ מתני תרגומו בר מיני, כגון כל קריאה בָּעוֹף במ' א' וּבָעוֹף,[16] וכן אֲבוֹתֵיכֶם כל אוריתא חסר במ"א מלא, וכן עד עשרה; אבל מן עשרה ואילך עשו ממנו ב' מלין, כגון אֲבוֹתֵיכֶם כל כתובים מלא ב"מ י"א,[17] וכן ב"מ י"א, ב"מ י"ב, ב"מ י"ג

It is, moreover, to be remarked, that they do not write this except on words which are sometimes *plene* and sometimes *defective*, as וַתּוֹרֶד *and she let down*, "occurs three times, once *plene* and twice *defective*," פָּקוֹד "occurs four times, twice *plene* and twice *defective*," &c., &c.[14] But in those words of which either the *plenes* alone or the *defectives* alone are counted, the Massorites also only put down either the *plenes* or the *defectives*, and the respective number, as אֲבוֹתֶיךָ *thy forefathers*, "occurs three times *plene*," and do not give the initials ג"מ;[15] so also גָּדְלָה *great*, "occurs five times *defective*," and they do not write the initials ה"ח. It is also to be noticed, that when the letters *Beth* and *Mem* occur together with two marks above, and one of the letters from *Aleph* to *Jod* is joined to them, as בָּמ"א, or בָּמ"ב, or בָּמ"ג, &c., they are the initials of בר מן אחד *except one*, בר מן ב' *except two*, בר מן שלשה *except three*, &c. The meaning of בר is *except*; so the Chaldee renders חוּץ מִמֶּנִּי, [Eccl. ii. 25], by בַּר מִנִּי *except I*. Thus the Massorites remark on בָּעוֹף *in the fowls*, "it is so in all the Scriptures except once [במ"א], where it is וּבָעוֹף AND *in the fowls*;[16]" also אֲבֹתֵיכֶם *your fathers* [Gen. xlviii. 21], on which the Massorites remark, "it is *defective* throughout the Pentateuch, except once where it is *plene*" [viz., Exod. iii. 13], and so on up to ten instances. But, from ten upwards, the Massorites make this remark in two words, as אֲבוֹתֵיכֶם is "*plene* throughout the Hagiographa, except in sixteen instances;"[17] so also ב"מ י"א = except eleven, ב"מ י"ב = except twelve, ב"מ י"ג = except thirteen,

---

marginalis on Numb. xvii. 23. It will be seen that the Massorah gives thirteen instances of *defective*, including Judg. xix. 25, whilst Levita only mentions twelve. If the text does not contain a clerical error, Levita most probably excludes Judg. xix. 25, because the *Tzaddi* has *Chirek*, and not *Tzere*, as is the case in all the other instances.

[14] The three instances in which ותורד occurs are, Gen. xxiv. 18: 1 Sam. xix. 12 (both *defective*): Gen. xxiv. 46 (*plene*). The Massoretic remark to which Levita refers is to be found both in the Massorah parva and the Massorah marginalis on Gen. xxiv. 18. For the instances in which פקוד occurs, see above, p. 147.

[15] The three passages in which אבותיך is *plene*, that is, has *Vav* quiescent with the *Cholem*, are, Gen. xxxi. 3: Jerem. xxxiv. 5: Prov. xxii. 28. They are given in the Massorah marginalis on Gen. xxxi. 3.

[16] The instances in the Bible where בעוף occurs are only three, viz., Gen. vii. 21; viii. 17; ix. 10; and the one passage in which it is ובעוף with *Vav* conjunctive is in Levit. xx. 25. On none of these passages, however, could we find in the printed Massorahs the remark to which Levita refers.

[17] For the orthography of אבותיכם, see above, p. 168, &c.

&c., all of which are the initials of בר מן = except, as you will find upon examination.

ל״ק are the initials of לא קרי *read not;* they are only found in connection with one of the letters *Aleph, He, Vav,* and *Jod,* as לק״א = *Aleph, is not read,* לק״ה = *He, is not read,* לק״ו = *Vav, is not read,* לק״י = *Jod, is not read.* Comp. what I have said on this subject in Part ii., Section i., class 1 [*vide supra,* p. 182, &c.], and see also Part i., Section ix., [*vide supra,* p. 170, &c.]

כ״כ are the initials of כתיב כן *written thus,* or כן כתיב *thus written,* they are marked on those words which have two or three quiescents, some of which are *plene* and some *defective,* as I have explained in Part i., Section viii. [*vide supra,* p. 169, &c.] I have also discussed it in Part ii., Section ix. It is to be noticed that on the vowel signs and the accents the Massorites never remark כ״כ, but they write it כ״ה, which are the initials of כן הוא *it is so,* as וַתְּכַחֵשׁ *and she denied* [Gen. xviii. 15] "it is so [כ״ה] with *Kametz;*" [18] and תַּדְשֵׁא *let her sprout* [Gen. i. 11], "it is so [כ״ה] with *Marich*" [= a long line under *Tav*], &c. Moreover כ״ה stands also for the number twenty-five. Thus the Massorites remark on וַיָּשֶׁב *and he restored,* "it occurs [כ״ה] twenty-five times;" [19] on אֶחָד *one of,* "it occurs [כ״ה] twenty-five times," [20] and it is always known from the context.

כל׳ with a mark over the *Lamed* stands for כלהון *all,* as כל כ״כ, that is כלהון כתיבין כן *all are written so,* and כל חסרים *all are defective,* or כל מל׳ *all are plene.* But when they have two marks above, they are the initials of כל לישנא, *all the forms,* and I have already explained the

---

[18] That is with *Tzere* under the *Cheth,* since the *Tzere,* as has already been explained, is also called *Kametz.*

[19] The twenty-five instances in which וישב occurs are, Gen. xiv. 16; xx. 14; xl. 21: Exod. iv. 7; xv. 19; xix. 8: Judg. ix. 56; xvii. 3, 4: 1 Sam. xiv. 27; xxv. 21: 2 Sam. xv. 29; xxii. 25: 1 Kings ii. 30: 2 Kings xiii. 25; xvii. 3; xx. 11; xxii. 9: 1 Chron. xxi. 27; 2 Chron. xxxiv. 16: Job xxxiii. 26; Ps. xviii. 25; xciv. 23: Prov. xx. 26: Ezek. xliv. 1. They are given in the Massorah finalis under the letter *Jod,* p. 37 a, col. 1.

[20] The twenty-five instances in which אחד occurs are, Gen. xxi. 15; xxii. 2; xxvi. 10; xxxii. 23; xlviii. 22: Levit. xiii. 2: Numb. xvi. 15: Deut. i. 2; xxv. 5: Judg. xvii. 5: 1 Sam. ix. 3; xxvi. 15; 2 Sam. vi. 20; vii. 7; xix. 22: 1 Kings xix. 2; xxii. 13: 2 Kings vi. 12; xviii. 24: 1 Chron. xvii. 6: Isa. xxxvi. 9; lxvi. 17: Ezek. xxxiii. 30; xlv. 7: Dan. x. 13. They are given in the Massorah marginalis on 2 Kings vi. 12.

meaning of לישנא in Section x. [*vide supra*, p. 240, &c.] In some Codices, instead of כ״ל they write ת״ל, which are the initials of תרי לשנא *two forms*, as the alphabetical list of words which occur twice in the same form, but in a different sense; *ex. gr.*, אֹרֶה *I will teach* [Job xxvii. 11], and אוֹרֶה *I will shoot* [1 Sam. xx. 20], &c.; they are in alphabetical order, and number about a hundred pairs, all of them with two meanings.[21] But, forsooth, among many of them there seems to be no difference whatever, and I shall only mention the most difficult of all, כְּאֲרִי [Isa. xxxviii. 13], and כָּאֲרִי [Ps. xxii. 17]. Would that I knew the difference between them!

כ״ק are the initials of כל קריא *all the Scripture*. I have already explained, in Section x., that קריא is the designation of the twenty-four sacred books, and given the reason why they are so called. I have also explained there that the Massorites always write it out fully, that is, they write it down כל קריאה and not the initials כ״ק [*vide supra*, p. 234, &c.] But when they range many of them together, and make of them one Register, they write on each one of the words thus rubricated כ״ק, as you will see on examination.

פ״ד are the initials of פסח דספרא *Pattach of the Book*. I have already explained its import in Section ii. [*vide supra*, 197, &c]. In correct Codices it is noted in the margin against every *Pattach of the Book* פ״ד, to indicate that it is one of the number rubricated in the Massorah magna. Moreover, פ״ד are also the initials of פסקא דספרא *Piska of the Book*, the import of which I have explained in Section iv. [*vide supra*, p. 209]. This is also the case with the accent called *Legarme*, which I have likewise discussed in Section iv. [*vide supra*, p. 210];[22] and which I shall explain still further in my book called

יש נוסחאות נמסר במקום כ״ל ת״ל ראשי תיבות תרי לישנא; וכן במסרה גדולה אלפא ביתא מן תרין תרין מלין ותרויהון בתרי לישנא, כמו אורה אתכם ביד אל (איוב כ״ז), החצים צדה אורה, וכן כלם על סדר הא״ב, והם כנגד מאה זוגות, כלם בתרי לישנא;[21] והאמת יש בהן הרבה נראה שאין הפרש ביניהן, והנה אזכיר החמור שבכלן, והוא כָּאֲרִי כן ישבר, כָּאֲרִי ידי ורגלי, ומי יתן ואבין ההפרש שביניהן:

כ״ק ראשי תיבות כל קריא, וכבר כתבתי במאמר י', כי קריא ר״ל כל העשרים וארבע, וכתבתי הטעם למה נקרא כן; גם בארתי שם כי לא שמשו בו במסרת דק במלואן, דהיינו שכתבו כל קריאה, ולא בראשי תבות כ״ק; אכן כשצרפו הרבה מהן יחד, ועשו מהן שמה, כתבו אצל כל אחת ואחת מהמלוה ההן כ״ק, דוק ותמצא:

פ״ד ראשי תיבות פתח דספרא, וכבר בארתי דינו במאמר ב'; ובספרים מדויקים נכתב בחוץ בנליון נגד כל פתח דספרא פ״ד, להורות שהוא אחר מן המנויין במסרה גדולה; ונמצא גם כן פ״ד רוצה לומר פסקא דספרא, אשר בארתי דינו במאמר ד'; וכן על הטעם הנקרא לגרמיה, אשר בארתי במאמר ד';[22] ועוד יתבאר בספר טוב

---

[21] As this alphabetical list is by far too long to be given here, we must refer for it to the Massorah finalis under the letter *Aleph*, p. 1 *b*, col. 4—p. 2 *a*, col. 3; and the *Ochla Ve-Ochla*, section lix., p. 62, &c. Dr. Frensdorff has made some very important remarks on this rubric, p. 17, &c.

[22] The Sulzbach edition erroneously omits אשר בארתי במאמר ד, *which I have explained in Section iv*.

Good Sense. Wherever *Legarme* occurs in a verse, the Massorites write against it in the margin לג׳, with one mark over the *Gimmel*, which signifies *Legarme*. Some have mistaken it, and thought that the word in question, on which the Massorites remarked לג׳, occurs thirty-three times in the Bible. But, according to the rule which I have stated at the beginning of this Part, there can be no mistake about it; for, if it had referred to the number, it would have two marks, one on the *Lamed* and one on the *Gimmel*. Now, as the *Gimmel* alone has a mark, it is evident that the word is not written out fully, and that it is the abbreviation of *Legarme*.²³ I shall, however, discuss it again, in its proper place, in my book entitled *Good Sense*.

ל״ד are the initials of לית דכותיה which I have already explained in Section v. Indeed I have not found in the Massorah ל״ד instead of לית דכותיה, but in some grammatical works which treat on the Massorah; *ex. gr.*, the *Book Semadar*, the Treatise called *The Stylus of the Scribe*,²⁴ and a few others.

ר״פ are the initials of ראש פסוק *the beginning of the verse*. This abbreviation, too, has been mistaken, for some have read it רפי *Raphe*, or רפין *Raphin*. But the difference between these two is, that when it has two marks over it it is the acrostic of ראש פסוק *the beginning of the verse*, as I have already stated, and when it has one point over the *Pe* it denotes רפין *Raphes*. Thus, it is remarked, the word וְיֹאמְרוּ *and they shall say*, "occurs nine times (רפ) *Raphe*;"²⁵ וְיָבֹאוּ *and they shall come*, "occurs (רפ) seven times *Raphe*."²⁶ I have already explained, in Section iii. [*vide supra*, p. 198], the reason why it is called *Raphe*.

טעם; בכל מקום שנמצא בפסוק לגרמיה כתבו בגליון נגדו לג׳ בנקודה אחת על הגי״מל רוצה לומר לגרמיה; ויש שטועין בזה, וחושבין כי המלה ההיא אשר נמסר עליה לג׳ היא נמצאת ל״ג פעמים במקרא, אבל לפי הכלל שנתתי בפתיחת השער הזה אין לטעות בה, כי אם היה מורה על המספר היה עליה ב׳ נקודות, אחד על חלמ״ד, ואחד על הגימ״ל, עכשיו שהגימ״ל לבדה היא נקודה הוא ראיה שהמלה אינה נשלמת, ורוצה לומר לגרמיה;²³ ועוד אזכרנו במקומו בספר טוב טעם:

ל״ד ראשי תיבות לית דכותיה, וכבר בארתיו במאמר ה׳, והאמת כי במכרה לא מצאתי ל״ד במקום לית דכותיה, רק בספרי קצת המדקדקים בדברם בעניני מסורת, כגון ספר סדמדר וספר עט סופר,²⁴ ובזולתם מעטים:

ר״פ ראשי תיבות ראש פסוק, וגם בזה יש מקום לטעות, כי יש שקוראין אותו רפי או רפין, וההפרש שביניהן הוא כאשר עליו ב׳ נקודות הוא ראשי תיבות ראש פסוק, כמו שכתבתי, וכשהוא בנקודה אחת על הפ״א רוצה לומר רפין, כגון וְיֹאמְרוּ ט׳ רפ׳,²⁵ וכן וְיָבֹאוּ ז׳ רפ׳,²⁶ וכבר בארתי במאמר ג׳ למה נקראין רפין:

---

²³ Here the Sulzbach edition inserts the words אשר בארתי במאמר ד״, which were omitted from the former part of the paragraph.

²⁴ The *Sepher He-Semadar* is as yet unknown (*vide supra*, p. 122); the *Stylus of the Scribe* will be noticed hereafter under *Kimhi*.

²⁵ The nine passages in which ויאמרו is *Raphe*, that is, has *Sheva* under the *Vav* conjunctive, are, Deut. xxxii. 7: Jerem. xvi. 19: Joel ii. 17: Isa. xiv. 10; xliii. 9: Ps. lxx. 5; xxxv. 27: 1 Chron. xiv. 31: Job xxxviii. 35. They are given in the Massorah marginalis on Isa. xvi. 10.

²⁶ The seven passages in which ויבאו is *Raphe*, that is, has *Sheva* under the *Vav*

ס״פ are the initials both of סוּף פסוק the end of the verse, and of ס׳פי פסוקים ends of verses; as אֲנִי יְהוָֹה I, Jehovah, "occurs twenty times at the end of verses [כ׳ ס״פ] in one book." In some Codices it is remarked on each one of these כם״ף, being the initials of כ׳ סוּפי פסוקים, "one of the twenty at the end of the verses." Thus, also, אֲנִי יְהוָֹה אֱלֹהֵיכֶם I, Jehovah, your God, which "occurs twenty-two times at the end of verses [כ״ב ס״פ];" the Massorites remark, on each of them, כבם״ף.[27]

מ״פ are the initials of מצעה פסוק, that is, "the middle of the verse." מצע is a word by which the Jerusalem Targum renders the Hebrew תוֹך and קֶרֶב. Thus, בְּתוֹך in the midst of [Job xx. 13] is translated במצע; so also בְּקֶרֶב in the midst of [Ps. lxxxii. 1] is rendered by במצע. The word חוּץ except, in the Pentateuch and the Prophets, however, is translated מצעות or מציעותא, or מציעא; and because the language of the Massorites is mostly that of the Jerusalem Targum, they write מצע פסיק, as וְכָל יִשְׂרָאֵל and all Israel, "occurs thirty-five times in the middle of the verse [לה מ״פ], and whenever it occurs in the beginning of a verse it is like it;"[28] so, also, וַנִּשְׁמַע and it was heard "occurs three times, once at the beginning of a verse [ר״פ], once at the end of a verse [ס״פ], and once in the middle of a verse [מ״פ]."[29] In some Massorahs I have found, instead of

conjunctive are, Exod. xiv. 16, 17; Deut. x. 11; Josh. xviii. 4; Isa. xiii. 2; Jerem. iii. 18; Ezek. xxxiii. 31. They are given in the Massorah marginalis on Isa. xiii. 2.

[27] The twenty passages in which אני יהוה occurs at the end of a verse are, Levit. xviii. 5, 6, 21; xix. 12, 14, 15, 18, 28, 30, 32, 37; xxi. 12; xxii. 2, 3, 8, 30, 31, 33; xxvi. 2, 45; and the twenty-one instances in which אני יהוה אלהיכם terminates the verse are, Exod. xvi. 12: Levit. xviii. 2, 4, 30; xix. 2, 3, 4, 10, 25, 31, 34; xx. 7; xxiii. 22, 43; xxiv. 22; xxv. 17, 55; xxvi. 1: Numb. x. 10; xv. 41: Deut. xxix. 5: Ezek. xx. 20. The former are given in the Massorah marginalis on Levit. xviii. 1, and the latter are enumerated in the Massorah finalis under the letter *Aleph*, p. 4 ᴧ, col 4; where those which are כי אני יהוה אלהיכם, are given in one rubric, and those which are אני יהוה אלהיכם, without כי, are given in another rubric. Under the first rubric, which professes to give *ten* (י׳) instances, are mentioned Levit. xi. 44, and Joel iv. 17, neither of which is the beginning of a verse, in the present editions of the Bible. Equally erroneous is the heading of the second rubric, which professes to give *seventeen* (י״ז) instances, in which אני יהוה אלהיכם occur at the end of the verse, and only mentions fourteen.

[28] The thirty-five instances in which וכל ישראל occurs in the middle of the verse are, Deut. xxi. 21: Josh. ii. 17; vii. 24; viii. 21, 15; x. 29, 31, 34, 36. 38, 43: 1 Sam. xvii. 11: 2 Sam. iv 1; xvii. 17: 1 Kings viii. 62, 65: 1 Chron. xiii. 8; 1 Kings xi. 16; xv. 27; xvi. 17: 2 Kings ix. 14: 1 Chron. xiii. 6: 2 Chron. vii. 6; xii. 1; x. 3; xiii. 4, 15 Ezra ii. 70; Nehem. vii. 73: Ezra x. 5: 2 Chron. vii. 6: 1 Chron. xi. 4: Ezra viii. 25. They are given in the Massorah finalis under the letter *Jod*, p. 37 b, cols. 1 and 2.

[29] The three passages in which ונשמע occurs with *Pattach* under the *Vav*, and *Dagesh* in the *Nun* conjunctive, are, Josh ii. 11; Jerem. xxxv. 8, 10. They are given in the

מצע, the word מיסון [= μέσον], but I have not been able to discover the like of it anywhere else.

נ״א are the initials of נוסחא אחרינא *another Recension* or *Codex*. This expression is of frequent occurrence in the writings of our sages of blessed memory; as נוסח הגט *to transfer a bill of divorce,* נוסח הברכה *to transfer a blessing,* &c.; and it appears to me to denote *to transcribe, to write,* like יְסָחוּ [Prov. ii. 22], which denotes *to remove, to transfer.* Hence those words which have been transferred and copied from a book are called נוסחאות *transfers, copies, Codices.* Hence, also, the word יִתְנְסַח [Ezra vi. 11], is *to transfer, to remove.* I therefore submit that נוסחא and העתקה are almost identical.

Let me now mention the names of some of the punctuators and prælectors, which occur in some of the margins of the correct Codices of the Pentateuch. Most of these Codices are German, and I have only seldom found them in the Portuguese Pentateuchs. I shall also describe some of the titles of the books which have been written upon the subject.

רמ״ה, I have been told, is the acrostic of ר' משה חזן *Rabbi Moses Chasan*, who was one of the most correct prælectors, but I do not know who he is. It may be that this is the Moses who wrote the Treatise on the Laws of the Vowel-points, which is printed in the Great Bible round the margin of the Massorah, and begins with, "Thus saith the author, for a truth the vowel-points were given on Sinai," &c. I have already mentioned it in the Introduction to this Massoreth Ha-Massoreth [*vide supra*, p. 123]. Many think that it is the *Book of Shimshon*, but they are mistaken, for we find therein the name Moses signed in many places, as in the beginning of the Treatise, when speaking concerning the vowel-points *Tzere* and *Segol*, which commences מ׳מכון ש׳בתו ה׳שגיח *from the place of his habitation he looketh* [Ps. xxxiii. 14]; and in another place, again, מ׳שפט ש׳מוש ה׳הלם

Massorah finalis under the letter *Shin*, p. 60 a, col. 1. The Massoretic remark to which Levita refers is not to be found in the printed editions of the Massorah.

the Laws respecting the use of the Cholem, &c. Whereas the book *Shimshoni* is nothing but the book called *Chibur Ha-Konim*, beginning with "Know that the fundamental things discussed by the Hebrews are ten," &c.³⁰

מ"ש, In the above-named Codex I found a proof cited from a correct Pentateuch, saying, I found it so in the Pentateuch of R. Meier Spira, which is מ"מ = מאיר שפירע.³¹

יהב"י are the initials of יקותיאל הכהן בר יהודה *Jekuthiel Ha-Cohen b. Jehudah*, the author of the book entitled *the Eye of the Reader*, whose surname in German is Salmen Ha-Nakdan. He thus signs his name in the second poem of the book here alluded to. I have heard that he was from the the city of Prague, in the country of Bohemia; and I said, in a play upon the words, that from the walls [= lines] of the house [= in the stanzas] of his poems, he is recognised to be a Bohemian.³² He composed a very excellent treatise, discussing the vowel-points, and the words, the accents of which are *Milel* or *Milra*,

החולם, והדומים לזה; וספר השמשוני הוא הספר הנקרא חבור הקונים מתחיל, דע כי עקרי הדברים אשר ידברו בהם העברים הם עשרה וכולי:³⁰

מ"ש, מצאתי בספר הנ"ל שהיא מביא ראיה מחומש אחד מוגה, ואומר כן מצאתי בחומש של מאיר שפירע, וזהו מ"ש:³¹

יהב"י ראשי תיבות יקותיאל הכהן בר יהודה, והוא בעל ספר עין הקורא, וכנויו בלשון אשכנז זלמן הנקדן, וכן חתם שמו בשיר השני של ספרו ע"ש; וקבלתי שהוא היה בק"ק פראג שבמדינת פי'הם, ואני אמרתי על דרך הלצת השיר שבכותלי בתי שיריו נכר כי פהמי הוא;³² ועשה חבור נאה מאוד בענין הנקדות והתמלות שטעמן מלעיל או מלרע, ובענין המקפין ובלתי מקפין,

³⁰ R. Shimshon, the grammarian (ור' שמשון הנקדן), flourished about 1240. The treatise which discusses the vowel-points and accents, and to which Levita refers, has not as yet appeared. Excerpts of it, however, have been published in Abicht's *Accentus Hebr. ex antiquissimo usu lectorio vel musico explicati*, &c.; Acced. *Porta accentuum Lat. conversa et notis illustr.*, Leipz. 1713; Delitzsch, in *Jesurun*, pp. 16, 86, 92, 192, 249, 252. Comp. Wolf, *Bibliotheca Hebræa*, vol i. 1152, iii. 1160, iv. 1003; Geiger, *Wissenschaftiche Zeitschrift für Jüdische Theologie*, vol. v., p. 423, &c., Leipzig, 1844; Fürst, *Bibliotheca Judaica*, iii. 16.

³¹ All our endeavours to obtain some information about this Meier Spira have proved abortive. Wolf (*Bibliotheca Hebræa*, i. 756) simply says that Levita quotes him, whilst Fürst, the latest Hebrew bibliographer, remarks (*Bibliotheca Judaica*, iii. 372) that Spira wrote these works: i. A Treatise on Arithmetic; ii. A Commentary on Immanuel b. Jacob's Astronomical Work; and iii. A Pentateuch with the Massorah. Fürst, however, omits his usual references to some works for particulars about the author.

³² To understand this pun, which cannot be reproduced in a translation, it is to be remarked, that Levita refers to an incident in R. Gamaliel's life, recorded in the Talmud, which is as follows:—R. Gamaliel, whilst in the house of study, was asked by Jehudah, a proselyte of Ammonitish descent, whether he might come into the house of study. Gamaliel answered him in the negative, submitting that the Law [Deut. xxiii. 4] prohibited it. R. Jehoshuah was of the contrary opinion, and adduced in support of his view the declaration made in Isa. x. 13, that God had abolished the boundaries of all nations, and thus obliterated the territory of Ammon. He carried his point against Gamaliel, and the latter went to the house of his antagonist to be reconciled with him, since the altercation had assumed an angry tone. "On entering his house, R. Gamaliel perceived that the beams were black, and said to R. Jehoshuah, מכותלי ביתך אהה ניכר שפחמי אתה *from the walls of thy house thou art recognised to be a blacksmith*," for which incautious remark he had again to apologise (*Berachoth*, 28 b). It will be seen that Levita refers to this remark of Gamaliel, and that the pun consists not only in the fact that בית means both *house* and *stanza*, but that פחמי *blacksmith*, with the slight alteration of the ח into ה, denotes *Bohemian*.

L L

as well as those which have *Mappik*, and which are without *Mappik*; and he called this book *the Eye of the Reader*. Hence you find, in the margins of some Codices of the Pentateuch, עֵי"ן, that is עין הקורא; and sometimes it is remarked יהב"י, which is the name of the author, as I have stated.[33]

ע"ס are the initials of עט סופר *Stylus of the Scribe*, which is the name of a book written by Redak,[33] and which is a compendium of the contents of the Massorah and the accents. I have found it quoted in the margins of the Spanish Codices of the Pentateuch, but not in the German Pentateuchs.[34]

רי"ן are the initials of ר' יעקב נקדן *R. Jacob, the Punctuator*. He is often quoted by the above-mentioned R. Shimshon, in his work, but I do not know who he is.[35]

מפ' is the name of a book called מַפְתֵּחַ *The Key*, as וְהַצְּמִידִים *and the bracelets* [Gen. xxiv. 47], it is remarked "in *The Key* [במפ'] is without the second *Jod;*" so also בְּעֵבֶר *on the side* [Judges xi. 18], "in *The Key* is מֵעֵבֶר *beyond*." Also on *defective* and *plene*, we find it quoted in many places, and I do not know its author. I have, however, seen that Ibn Ezra makes the following remark, in his Introduction to the book called *The Balances:*—"R. Levi, the Spaniard,

---

[33] Jekuthiel b. Jehudah Cohen flourished circa A.D. 1250–1300, at Prague. The work entitled *The Eye of the Reader*, to which Levita refers, consists of Massoretic criticisms on the Pentateuch and the Book of Esther, and has been published by the learned Heidenheim, Rödelheim, 1818–1825. Jekuthiel has also written a grammatical treatise called *The Laws of the Vowel-points* (כללי הנקוד, דרכי הנקור), the Introduction and practical part of which were also published by Heidenheim, Rödelheim, 1818–1821. Comp. Kitto's *Cyclopædia of Biblical Literature, s. v.* JEKUTHIEL.

[34] רד"ק are the initials of ר' דוד קמחי *R. David Kimchi*, the distinguished grammarian, lexicographer, and expositor, who has already been noticed (*vide supra*, p. 107). His celebrated grammatical and lexical work, entitled *Perfection* (מכלול), which was edited by Levita, has been described on p. 79, &c. To the article KIMCHI, in Kitto's *Cyclop.*, it is to be added, that Kimchi's Massoretic Treatise, entitled *The Stylus of the Scribe* (עט סופר), to which Levita refers, has recently been published for the first time, Lyck, 1864.

[35] There can be but little doubt that this R. Jacob is the celebrated Hebrew grammarian and poet called Jacob b. Eleazar, who flourished *circa* A.D. 1130, at Toledo. He was a distinguished writer on the vowel-points (whence he obtained the name of *Ha-Nakdan*) and on the etymology of proper names. He moreover formed a correct Recension of the text of the Hebrew Scriptures, after the model of the Codex Hilali, and it is owing to these contributions to Biblical literature that he is so often quoted by Shimshon, Kimchi, and other lexicographers and critics. Comp. Kitto's *Cyclopædia of Biblical Literature, s. v.* JACOB B. ELEAZAR.

from the city of Saragossa, is the author of the book called *The Key."* Thus far his language ;³⁶ but I have not as yet been able to see it.³⁷

מחזורתא *Machsortha* is the name of a work, the author of which I do not know. It is quoted in the margin of the Pentateuch, as "לָסֹבֹב *to compass* [Numb. xxi. 4] has *Beth* with *Dagesh*, but in the *Machsortha* it is *Raphe*." ³⁸

סיני *Sinai*, is the name of a correct Pentateuch which treats on the variations of the accents; as וַיִּשְׁמַע *and he heard* [Exod. xviii. 1], has the accent *Gershaim*, but in Sinai it has *Rebia* ; again, הַמִּדְבָּר *the desert* [Exod. xviii. 5], has *Sakeph*, whilst in Sinai it has *Sakeph-gadol*. But I do not know who the author of it is.³⁹

חומש יריחו the *Pentateuch of Jericho*, is doubtless a correct Codex

פרקוסטה חבר ספר המפתח עכ"ל :³⁶ ואנכי לא ראתיו עד הנה : ³⁷

מחזורתא שם ספר ולא ידעתי מי ילדו, ונמצא בגליונות החומשים, כגון לָסֹבֹב את ארץ אדום הבי"ת דגושה, ובמחזורתא לְסֹבֹב ברפי : ³⁸

סיני שם חומש מדוייק מדבר ממחלוקת הטעמים, כגון וַיִּשְׁמַע יתרו בגרשים, ובסיני הוא ברביע ; ועוד שם אל משה אל הַמִּדְבָּר בזקף, ובסיני בזקף גדול, ולא ידעתי מי הוא המחבר : ³⁹

חומש יריחו מכהמא הוא חומש אחד

---

³⁶ Levita's quotation is not literal. Even in his own edition of Ibn Ezra's *Balances*, the passage is as follows:—ורבי לוי הנקרא בן אל חבאן ספרדי במדינת סרקסטה תקן ספר המפתח, and *R. Levi, who is called Ibn Al-Tabben*, &c., vide p. 197 b, ed. Levita ; Venice, 1546.

³⁷ This R. Levi, the Spaniard, or Abulfihm Levi b. Joseph Ibn Al-Tabben, as is his full name, flourished A.D. 1120. He was a friend of R. Jehudah Ha-Levi, the celebrated poet and philosopher. Besides composing poetry himself, he wrote the Hebrew Grammar called *The Key* (מפתח), to which Levita refers, but which has not as yet been published. Comp. Graetz, *Geschichte der Juden*, vol. vi., p. 131 ; Leipzig, 1861.

³⁸ *Machsortha* (מחזורתא) is the common name of the Jewish Ritual, comprising the whole annual cycle of the Daily and Festival Services. The *cycle*, as is the literal meaning of *Machsortha* (from חזר *to go round*), was generally written by the most distinguished scholars of the respective communities in the various parts of the world, embodying the local usages, and hence obtained the name of the special place where it was written, and the practice which it depicted. The *cycle*, according to the practice of the Synagogue of Vitry, has already been mentioned (*vide supra*, p. 45), and we have to add here that these Rituals not only contained Prayers and Hymns, but gave the text of the whole Bible, so that they became models, after which copies were made. It is owing to this fact that the Bible Codex itself was called *Machsor* (מחזור), as is the case with the Codex made after Ben-Asher.

³⁹ Levita's quotations are not from the Massorah marginalis on these passages, but from the outer margin. The Massoretic glosses in question are not reproduced literally by Levita, as will be seen from the following statements :—On Exod. xviii. 1, the gloss is וישמע ב' בטע שני גרשיין ר"פ בתורה סיני רביע, *the word* וישמע *occurs twice with the accent Gershaim at the beginning of a verse in the Pentateuch, Sinai has Rebia ;* and on Exod. xviii. 5, סיני המדבר בזקף גדול *Sinai has* המדבר *with Sakeph-gadol*. Now according to Levita's reading בסיני *in Sinai*, we are obliged to assume with him that it is the name of a Codex ; but according to the proper reading, we may adopt the opinion of Joseph Eshve, the expositor of the Massorah, which is enunciated on Exod. xviii. 1— ומה שאמר סיני רביע דע כי בעלי מהקני הנקוד והטעמים רבים היו מאוני חכמי טבריא ואחד מהם היה שמו סיני והוא פליג על המסורת דאמר שני מלות וישמע הנז' המה בטעם גרשיים ואמר הוא שהם בטעם רביע *as to the remark, Sinai has Rebia, know that the inventors of the vowel-points and accents were mostly from the spiritual heads and the sages of Tiberias. Now the name of one of these was Sinai, and he differed from the Massorah, which remarks, that* וישמע *in the two passages in question has Gershaim, and said that it has the accent Rebia*. From this it will be seen, that this great Massoretic authority does not take סיני as *Codex Sinaiticus*, but regards it as a proper name of one of the inventors of the vowel-points and accents.

of the Pentateuch, derived from Jericho. It discusses the *plenes* and *defectives*, as הַתּוֹעֵבֹת *the abominations* [Levit. xviii. 27], is in this Pentateuch of Jericho, without the second *Jod*. So also יְלִידֵי *the children of*, which occurs twice in the same chapter [Numb. xiii. 22, 28], the first is *plene* in the Pentateuch of Jericho, and the second is *defective*.

ספר הללי *Codex Hilali*, is quoted by Kimchi in his grammar called *Perfection*, and in his Lexicon, in the following language:—"In the *Codex Hilali*, which is at Toledo, תִּדְּרוּ *ye shall vow* [Deut. xii. 11], is found with *Daleth Raphe*." Thus far his remark. I at first thought that the Codex is so called after its author, whose name was Hillel; but I soon found that in some recensions it is spelt הלאלי, with *Aleph* between two *Lameds* (comp. the root שׁוּם in Kimchi's Lexicon). Moreover, I found that in the Constantinople edition of the *Michlol* it is pointed הֵלָלִי, with *Tzere* under *He*, so that I do not know what it is.[40]

ירושלמי *Jerusalem Codex*, is the book on which R. Jona, the Grammarian, relied, as is attested by Kimchi. It is perhaps the Codex which Ben-Asher corrected,[41] and which remained at Jerusalem for a long time, as I stated in the third Introduction, in the name of Maimonides of blessed memory.

ספר אספמיא *Spanish Codex*, is the general name for the Spanish Codices, for they are more correct than all other exemplars, as I have already stated in the Poetical Introduction. As to אספמיא, it denotes Spain, for thus the Targum renders ספרד [Obad. 20], by ספמיא, and it is also called Hispania in Italian, and Spanien in German.

נפתלי *Naphtali*; I have already mentioned in the third Introduction the variations between Ben-Asher and Ben-Naphtali, and that we

---

מוגה, בא מיריחו, מדבר מענין חסר ומלא, כגון כי כל הַתּוֹעֵבֹת האל בחומש יריחו חסר וי"ו השניה, וכן יְלִידֵי הענק ב' בעניו, ובחומש יריחו הראשון מלא והשני חסר:

ספר הללי מביאו הרד"ק במכלול ובשרשים וז"ל, בספר הללי אשר בטוליטולא נמצא אשר תִּדְּרוּ ליהוה הדל"ת רפויה עכ"ל, ואני חשבתי כי הספר נקרא כן על שם מחברו הנקרא הילל, אך מצאתי בקצת נוסחאות כתיב הלאלי באל"ף בין ב' הלמדי"ן עיין בשרש שום; גם ראיתי במכלול הנדפס בקונשטאנטינו נקדו הֵלָלִי בצידי ההי"א, ולא ידעתי מה הוא:[40]

ירושלמי הוא הספר אשר סמך עליו רבי יונה המדקדק, כמו שהעיד עליו הרד"ק, ואולי הוא הספר שהגיה בן אשר שהיה בירושלים ימים רבים,[41] כמו שכתבתי בהקדמה השלישית בשם הרמב"ם ז"ל:

ספר אספמיא הוא שם כלל לספרי ספרד, כי הם מוהגים מכל שאר הספרים, כאשר כתבתי בהקדמה החרוזית; ואספמיא רוצה לומר ספרד, כי כן תרגום של גלות ירושלים אשר בִּסְפָרַד דבספמיא, וכן נקרא בלעז אספניא, ובלשון אשכנז שפנייא:

נפתלי, כבר כתבתי בהקדמה השלישית המחלוקת שבין בן אשר ובן בן נפתלי, ואיך

---

[40] It is now generally acknowledged among scholars that the *Codex Hilali* derives its name from the fact, that it was written at Hilla, a town built near the ruins of ancient Babel. This Codex, which was completed *circa* A.D. 600, had not only the then newly invented vowel-points and accents, but was furnished with Massoretic glosses. It was brought to Toledo about A.D. 1100, where the grammarian Jacob b. Eleazar used it for his works, and a portion of it was purchased by the Jewish community in Africa, about A.D. 1500. Comp. Kitto's *Cyclopædia*, *s. v.* HILALI CODEX.

[41] For Ben-Asher, and his celebrated Codex, *vide supra*, p. 113, &c.

follow the readings of Ben-Asher.[42] Hence we find in some Codices the opinion of Ben-Naphtali noted in the margin; as וְחָצִיתָ *and thou shalt divide* [Numb. xxxi. 27], which, according to the reading of Ben-Asher, is so written with two *Pashtas*, whilst, according to the reading of Ben-Naphtali, it is וְחָצִיתָ, with one *Pashta*. Hence the remark in the margin נפ׳, that is, נפתלי *Naphtali*, and in some Codices ב״נ, that is בן נפתלי *Ben-Naphtali*. Those Codices in which the reading of Ben-Naphtali is in the text, and the reading of Ben-Asher in the margin, are incorrect, since it is a principle with us to follow Ben-Asher. Hence it is the principle which should be expressed in the text, and not in the margin.

מדינחא׳, that is, מדינחאי *Eastern*. I have already stated, in the above-named Introduction, the variations between the East and the West, and that we follow the Western readings [*vide supra*, p. 113]. Hence it is only necessary to note in the margin the Eastern reading, as on על *upon* [Judg. ix. 3], "the Eastern [מדינחאי] reading is אֶל *to*." Those Codices which have in the margin the Western reading על are incorrect. Moreover, I have also stated already, in the above-named Introduction, that the variations between the Eastern and Western Codices only extend to the Prophets and Hagiographa, and that there is not a single one in the Pentateuch [*vide supra*, p. 114].

אשלמתא *completion, perfection*. The Massorites call the earlier Prophets אשלמתא קדמיתא, and the later Prophets אשלמתא תנינא. Thus "throughout the Pentateuch and the earlier Prophets [ואשלמתא קדמיתא] it is שָׁלַחְתִּי *I have sent*, and וְשָׁלַחְתִּי, with *Kametz* under the *Shin*, except in one instance, where it is וְשִׁלַּחְתִּי [Levit. xxvi. 25], with *Chirek* under the *Shin*; and throughout all the later Prophets [אשלמתא תנינא] it is the same, שָׁלַחְתִּי and וְשָׁלַחְתִּי, with *Chirek* under the *Shin*, except in two instances, where it is שִׁלַּחְתִּי [Jerem. xxiii. 21; xxix. 19]." See the Massorah magna. But I do not know why they are called אשלמתא.

---

[42] For Ben-Asher and Ben-Naphtali, *vide supra*, p. 113, &c.

פריגמא is the name given by the Massorites to a pause, or *hiatus*, in the middle of the verse. Thus, on "And Cain said to his brother Abel o, and it came to pass they were in the fields" [Gen. iv. 8], the Massorites remark, "one of the twenty-five *hiati* [פריגמות] in the middle of the verse:" four of these are in the Pentateuch.[43] I do not know from what language it is derived, and even the author of the *Aruch* does not quote it. The Italians, however, call all the *hiati* between the section, whether open or closed, פריגמא, with *Tzere* under *Pe*; and I have enquired of their sages about it, but they could not tell.[44]

Now the import of open or closed sections is explained by the *Poskim*, who, however, entertain a great difference of opinion about it. Generally the open section consists of two kinds,—one is in the middle of the line, where a vacant space of about nine letters is left, and the second has a whole line left vacant, and the writing commences on the third line. In the case of a closed section, a vacant space of about three letters is left in the middle of the line, and after it the line is finished; and if the closed section terminates at the end of a line, the second line is begun in the middle. The rule is, that the open section is always at the beginning of the line, whilst the closed section is always in the middle of the line.

מיסון [= μεσον] is the *middle*. I have already discussed it under the word מ״פ [*vide supra*, p. 256].

נוסחא is *Codex, recension*. I have already described it under the word נ״א [*vide supra*, p. 256].

I shall now explain some of the mnemonical signs of the Massorah

---

[43] For the four *Piskas* in the Pentateuch, see above, p. 242. The other twenty-one are, Josh. iv. 1; viii. 24: Judg. ii. 1: 1 Sam x. 22; xiv. 13, 19, 36; xvi. 2, 12; xix. 21; xxiii. 2, 11: 2 Sam. v. 2, 19; vii. 4; xxiv. 11: 1 Kings xiii. 20: 2 Kings i. 17: Isa. viii. 3: Ezek. iii. 16; xliv. 15. Fürst (*Hebrew Concordance*, p. 1369, cols. 1 and 2) enumerates no less than thirty-one such *Piskas*. Besides those we have given, he has 1 Sam. xvii. 37: 2 Sam. iv. 20; xii. 13; xvi. 23; xvii. 14; xv ii. 2; xxi. 1, 6; xxiv. 10, 23: Jerem. xxxviii. 28; whilst he omits Gen. iv. 8: 1 Sam. xiv. 13; xix. 21: 2 Kings i. 17: Ezek. xliv. 15. Indeed there is a great difference of opinion among critics as to the number and places of these *Piskas*.

[44] There can be but little doubt that פריגמא is the Greek πρῆγμα, πρᾶγμα.

on the Pentateuch and Prophets, since several of them are difficult to understand.

The mnemonical sign in Pericope Noah.—In Gen. x. 3, it is רִיפַת *Riphath*, with *Resh*, and in 1 Chron. i. 6 it is דִּיפַת *Diphath*, with *Daleth;* and the sign thereof is "*The initials of the names of their respective books*," that is, in Genesis, which is called רֵאשִׁית with *Resh*, it is written *Riphath* with *Resh*; whilst in Chronicles it is written *Diphath* with *Daleth*, according to the name of the book which is called דברי with *Daleth*.

The mnemonical sign in Pericope Va-Jerah.—In the description of Abraham, it is written "and his two young men [אִתּוֹ] *with him*" [Gen. xxii. 3], whilst in connection with Balaam it is "and his two young men [עִמּוֹ] *with him*" [Numb. xxii. 22], and the sign is, "*each man according to his language;*" that is, by Abraham, who was a Hebrew, it is written אִתּוֹ, which is Hebrew; whilst in the narrative of Balaam, who was an Aramæan, as it is said, "from Aram has Balak brought me" [Numb. xxiii. 7], it is written עִמּוֹ, which is Aramæan, as the Chaldee renders אִתּוֹ by עֲמֵיהּ. Another sign for this passage is, "*as is his name, so he is;*" that is, Abraham, which is with *Aleph*, has אִתּוֹ with *Aleph*, and Balaam, which is with *Ajin*, has it written עִמּוֹ with *Ajin*. A third sign is "*Aleph Aleph, Ajin Ajin,*" i. e., Abraham with *Aleph* has *Aleph*, and Balaam with *Ajin* has *Ajin*. Another sign for it, again, is "*their letters are the signs*," that is, the different letters in their names are the signs of the respective expressions in question.

The sign in Pericope Va-Ishlach.—The sign on דִּישָׁן *Dishan* with *Kametz*, and דִּישֹׁן *Dishon* with *Cholem* [Gen. xxxvi. 30], is, "every day wherein the Scroll of the Law is used it is דִּישָׁן *Dishan*, with *Kametz* under the *Shin*, and it begins with the first day of the week," and the order is as follows, *Dishon, Dishan, Dishon, Dishon, Dishan, Dishon, Dishan*. This is the explanation of the Spaniards. The French differ on this subject, saying that the order is *Dishon, Dishan, Dishon, Dishan, Dishon, Dishon, Dishan*, the sign with them being "every day on which the Scroll is read, it is דִּישֹׁן *Dishon*, and beginning with Sabbath." The latter is the correct one, and the proof of it is, that what is holy is placed first, and not last.⁴⁵ Another sign is, "the rich are with *Kametz*," that is, when it is rich in letters, it has *Kametz* and is *plene*, that is it is written דִּישָׁן *Dishan*, with *Jod*; whilst דִּשֹׁן *Dishon*, with *Cholem*, is not rich, for it is *defective*.

כל יומי ספר דְּשָׁן ומתחיל ביום השבת, וזהו העקר, וסימן מעלין בקודש ולא מורידין; ⁴⁵ וסימן אחר עשירים מקמצין, פירוש כל שהוא עשיר באותיות הוא בקמץ מל', רוצה לומר שנכתב ביו"ד הוא דִּישָׁן, וכל דִּשֹׁן בחולם אינו עשיר כי הוא חסר:

The mnemonical sign in Pericope *Shemoth.*—On וָחָיָה *and she shall live*, with *Kametz* under the *Vav* [Exod. i. 16], the Massorites remark, "not extant, once it is וָחָיָה [Esth. iv. 11], with *Sheva* under the *Vav*, and the sign thereof is מלכת שבא, that is, by queen Esther, it is with *Sheva*."

סימן בפרשת שמות, ואם בת הוא וְחָיָה ל', וא' שרביט הזהב וְחָיָה, וסימן מלכת שבא, פירוש גבי אסתר נקוד וְחָיָה בשבא:

The mnemonical sign is Pericope *Boh.*—On "And he went out from Pharaoh" [Exod. x. 18], in connection with the plague of the locusts, the sign is, "*the king is not by the locusts*," that is, by most of the other plagues it is said, "and MOSES went out from Pharaoh," whilst at the place of locusts the name of Moses is not mentioned, because he is king, as it is written, "and he was king in Jeshurun" [Deut. xxxiii. 5]. Hence the sign.

סימן פרשת בא, ויצא מעם פרעה במכת הארבה, סימן מלך אין לארבה ויצא פירוש ברוב שאר המכות כתיב ויצא משה מעם פרעה, אבל בארבה לא נזכר משה שהוא מלך, שנאמר ויהי בישורון מלך, וזהו סימן מלך אין לארבה::

The mnemonical sign in Pericope *Thazriah.*—In the first טָהֳרָה *purity*, construed with בִּדְמֵי *in the blood of* [Levit. xii. 4], the *He* is *Raphe*, or quiescent; whilst the *He* of the second טָהֳרָה, connected with יְמֵי in the same verse, is with *Mappik*, and the sign thereof is יְהוּדָה *Jehudah*; that is, just as the first *He* after the *Jod* is יְהוּדָה vocal, and the

סימן בפרשת תזריע, דמי טָהֳרָה הה"א נחה, ימי טָהֳרָה הה"א במפיק, וסימן יהודה, פירוש הה"א שאחר יו"ד של יהודה היא נעה,

---

⁴⁵ As the above explanation of the mnemonical sign is not very clear, and as it pre-supposes a knowledge of Jewish manners and customs, it requires some further elucidation. It will be seen that the word דישן occurs *seven* times in the same paragraph (Gen. xxxvi. 20-30),—three times with *Cholem* on the *Shin* (*i.e.* דִּשֹׁן Gen. xxxvi. 21, 25, 30), and four times with *Kametz* under the *Shin* (*i. e.* דִּישָׁן verses 26, 28, 30). Now, as the week has seven days, corresponding to these seven instances, and, moreover, as on three of these days an appointed lesson from the Law is read (*i.e.* Saturday, Monday, and Thursday), and the other four days (*i. e.* Sunday, Tuesday, Wednesday, and Friday) are without such lessons, thus corresponding again to the three instances of the *Shin* with *Cholem* and the four without it, the seven days are made the symbol of the seven times דישן; whilst the order of the three days with and the four days without the lesson from the Law is made to symbolise the order in which דישן is read, three times with *Cholem* and four times without (*i.e.* with *Kametz*), beginning with the Sabbath. Accordingly, the first דישן with *Cholem* answers to Sabbath, the first day, with a lesson; the second דישן without *Cholem* answers to Sunday, which is without a lesson; the third דישן with *Cholem* answers to Monday, with a lesson; the fourth דישן without *Cholem* answers to Tuesday, without a lesson; the fifth דישן without a *Cholem* answers to Wednesday, without a lesson; the sixth דישן with a *Cholem* answers to Thursday, with a lesson; whilst the seventh דישן without a *Cholem* answers to Friday, without a lesson.

265

second *He* after the *Daleth* is quiescent, so the *He* in טָהֳרָה connected with יְמֵי is vocal [*i. e.*, beginning with *Jod*], and the one connected with דְּמֵי [beginning with *Daleth*] is quiescent. Another sign is, "*her days are revealed, her blood is concealed;*" and another, "*and we conceal her blood.*" But these are easily understood.[46]

ותח"א שאחר הדל"ת נחה, כן ח"א של טָהֳרָה שסמוך אל יְמֵי נעה, והסמוך אל דְּמֵי היא נחה; וסימן אחר ימיה מגולים דמיה מכוסים; וסימן אחר וכסינו את דמו, וזה קל להבין:[46]

The mnemonical sign in Pericope *Phineas*.—The sign here is בו"ז מי"ם, that is, in the whole of this section it is written וְנִסְכָּהּ *and his drink offering*, and כַּמִּשְׁפָּט *after the manner*, except in the order for the second day, where it is written וְנִסְכֵּיהֶם *and their drink offerings* [Numb. xxix. 19]; for the sixth day, where it is וּנְסָכֶיהָ *and her drink offerings* [ver. 31]; and for the seventh day, where it is כְּמִשְׁפָּטָם *after their manner* [ver. 33]. Hence the letters indicating the days in which these variations occur, viz., ב = second day, ו = sixth day, and ז = seventh day; together with the letters constituting the variations, viz., מ in ונסכיהם [ver. 19], י in ונסכיה [ver. 31], and ם in כמשפטם [ver. 33], yield the sign בו"ז מי"ם *pouring out water;* thus pointing out that the ceremony of pouring out the water is contained in the Law, as is propounded in the Talmud tractate *Taanith*.[47]

סימן בפרשת פנחס, בו"ז מי"ם פירוש כל ענינא כתיב וְנִסְכָּהּ כַּמִּשְׁפָּט בר מן יום ב' כתיב וְנִסְכֵּיהֶם, וביום ו' וּנְסָכֶיהָ, וביום ז' כְּמִשְׁפָּטָם, הרי בו"ז מי"ם, מכאן רמז לניסוך מים מן התורה, כדאיתא במסכת תענית:[47]

סימן בשמואל ב' בסימן כ"א, וחהי עוד מִלְחָמָה ב' בענין, וב' בענין וחהי עוד הַמִּלְחָמָה, וסימן בתוך המלחמה, פירוש הראשון והרביעי מִלְחָמָה וב' אמצעיים הַמִּלְחָמָה:

סימן במלכים ב סימן כ"א, באמת וּבְלֵבָב שלם, ובישעיה סימן ל"ח באמת וּבְלֵב

The sign on 2 Sam. xxi. 15–20. In this section the phrase *and there was still* [מִלְחָמָה] *war*, without the article, occurs twice [verses 15, 20]; "*and there was still* [הַמִּלְחָמָה] THE *war*," with the article, occurs twice [verses 18, 19], and the sign is "*in the centre it is* המלחמה," with the article, that is, the first and fourth, which are the outsides, are מִלְחָמָה, without the article, and the two central ones are הַמִּלְחָמָה, with the article.

The sign in 2 Kings xx. 3.—In 2 Kings xx. 3 we find "in truth and with a perfect [וּבְלֵבָב] heart," whilst in Isa. xxxviii. 3 it is "in

---

[46] The first and third mnemonical signs are not given in the printed editions of the Massorah.

[47] The Talmudic explanation of these variations in the words, and the law deduced therefrom, are to be found in *Taanith*, 2 *b*–3 *a*, as well as in *Sabbath*, 103 *b*. To understand the reference to the traditional enactment, it is necessary to remark, that these words also occur in connection with the other days of the Feast, but without the letters in question. As, according to the Talmudic laws of exegesis, no superfluous letter is ever used in the Bible without its having some recondite meaning (comp. Ginsburg's *Commentary on Ecclesiastes*, p. 30, &c.; Longmans, 1861), the three redundant letters have been combined into מים *water*. This exegetical rule is called גורעין ומוסיפין ודורשין *letters taken from one word and joined to another, or formed into new words*. Comp. Kitto's *Cyclopædia of Biblical Literature*, s. v. MIDRASH, p. 172. rule iii. See also Jacob b. Chajim's *Introduction to the Rabbinic Bible*, p. 22, &c., ed. Ginsburg.

truth and with a perfect [וּבְלֵב] heart," and the sign thereof is "*the beginning of their respective books*," that is, the book of Kings, beginning with וְהַמֶּלֶךְ *and the King*, which has five letters, it is written וּבְלֵבָב, which also contains five letters; whilst in the book of Isaiah, which begins with חָזוֹן, *a vision*, consisting of four letters, it is וּ֗לֵב, also of four letters.

The sign in 2 Kings xxv. 11.—In 2 Kings xxv. 11 we have "the remnant of הֶהָמוֹן *the multitude*," and in Jerem. lii. 15, "the rest of [הָאָמוֹן] *the multitude*," and the sign thereof is "*here* [הֵא] *is seed for you*," the meaning of which is well known. Moreover, in 2 Kings xxv. 12 we have וּמִדַּלַּת *and of the poor one*, whilst in Jeremiah [lii. 15] it is וּמִדַּלּוֹת *of the poor ones*, and the sign thereof is, "*poverty follows upon poverty;*" that is, Jeremiah, who speaks of the sundry desolations of the Temple, has מִדַּלּוֹת in the plural, whilst the Kings, who are rich, have מִדַּלַּת in the singular.

The sign in Isa. xxxv. 10.—In Isa. xxxv. 10 we have יַשִּׂיגוּ וְנָסוּ *they shall obtain and rejoice*, whilst in Isa. li. 11 it is יַשִּׂיגוּן נָסוּ *they shall obtain, they shall rejoice*, and the sign thereof is "*Two Vavs, two Nuns*," that is, in the first instance there are two *Vavs* together [*i. e.*, the last letter is יַשִּׂיגוּ, and the first וְנָסוּ], and in the second instance two *Nuns* meet together [*i.e.*, the last letter of יַשִּׂיגוּן, which is *Nun*, and and the first of נָסוּ which is also *Nun*].

The sign in Ezek. xviii. 6.—In the whole of this section אָכָל *he ate*, is entirely with *Kametz* [viz., Ezek. xviii. 6, 15], except in verse 11, where it is אָכַל, half with *Kametz* and half with *Pattach*, and the sign thereof is, "*he who does not eat* [דלא אכל קמץ], *shuts his mouth;*" that is, whenever אכל is connected with לא, it is with *Kametz*.[48] In the twenty-four sacred books which have here been printed, this Massoretic remark is put into the book of Genesis on the words "in the sweat of thy brow thou shalt eat," [iii. 19], but this is an egregious blunder, and the editor did not understand it.

[48] It is to be remarked, that this mnemonical sign is based upon the double meaning of קמץ, which denotes both the vowel-sign *Kametz* and *to shut*, as well as upon the fact, that when אכל *to eat* is connected with לא *not* it has *Kametz*. Hence the play upon the words דלא אכל קמץ פומיה, *when* אכל *and* לא *are together it is Kametz, or, whoso does not eat, shuts his mouth.*

267

These are the signs which I deemed desirable to explain here, and the enquirer will doubtless discover many more; but I am tired of looking any more for them, and herewith concludes this book. Praised be He, above all, who is able to do all things!	אלה הם הסימנים שראיתי לכתבם פה, ובלי ספק המחפש ימצא יותר מאלה, ואני נלאתי לבקש עוד; ובזה נשלם הספר מכל וכל, ישתבח אשר כל יכול:

והנה טרם אכלה לדבר,	שירה חדשה אחבר:
אתן לאלי יה הלל והודיה,[49]	יען אשר היה אתי בעזרתי;
הואל והורני דעה הבינני,	עד כי למסרה באור הכינותי;
מה הוא בחנם לי גם כן אני חנם,	אורה לכל אדם מיעוט ידיעתי;
תרתי בכל לבי למצא דבר חפץ,	תאמין אמת כי יגעתי ומצאתי;
מפי ספרים קבלתי ולא מפי,	סופרים ולא חבר היה בחברתי;
חשכת אפלתה לאור הפכתיה,	נוע כברה אותה הניעותי;
דברי חכמיה סודם וחידותם,	מי ימצאם אם לא יחרוש בעגלתי;

NOW BEFORE I FINISH TO SPEAK, I SHALL COMPOSE A NEW SONG.

I give to my God praise and thanks,[49] because he was with me as my help.

He deigned to teach me knowledge; so much so, that I composed an explanation of the Massorah.

As He gave it to me freely; I also freely teach every man my scanty knowledge.

I have searched with all my heart to discover the right thing. Thou mayest believe that having laboured I found the truth.

I have received assistance from books, but not orally; nor had I any fellow labourer in my work.

I converted the obscurity [of the Massorah] into light; I have shaken it as in a sieve.

The words of the wise [in the Massorah], their secrets, and enigmas; who can find them unless he ploughs with my heifer?

---

[49] It will be seen, that the initials of the first line in the Hebrew are the acrostic of אליהו *Elias*, the author's name.

אמנם השגיתי כי אין אנוש שלא, יחטא הלא אתי תלין משוגתי;
אחלי שגיאות מי יבין וידעם, יתקון לפי שכלו עוות שניאותי;
האל אלהים הוא ידע וישראל, ידע אשר לא עשיתי בגאותי;
אף לא להראות את יקר גדולתי, כי אם לבקשת אנשי סגולתי;
גם בעונותי בני יצאוני, אין מי שמי יזכור עוד אחרי מותי;
די לי אשר ספרי יחיה ולא ימות, ידביב שפתי עת אישן בקברתי;
לכן לכה ספרי ופשוט בתוך תבל, הראה לכל משכיל מעשה גבורתי;
ולושואלים אותך יד מי הכינתך, תאמר ידי אליה כוננו אותי;
בן איש אשר לוי שמו נקרא, הוא אשכנזי איש חיל ואפרתי;
נגמר שנת יפר״ח תוך פרשת קרח, פה עיר ווינסיה רבתי ושרתי:

נשלמה השירה   וכל הספר עד גמירא:

Forsooth I have committed errors, for there is no man who does not err, so that my error cleaves to me.

I pray, therefore, that whoever understands and knows them, may correct my errors according to his wisdom.

The Lord God knows, and also Israel may know, that I have not done this proudly;

Nor to show thereby my greatness, but simply yielded to the request of my special friends.

Moreover, on account of my sin, I lost my sons: there is none left to perpetuate my house after my death.

It is enough for me that my book will live and not die; it will speak when I sleep in the grave.

Therefore go forth, my book, circulate thyself through the world; show to every wise man the work of my strength.

To those who ask who made thee, say, The hand of Elias made me.

The son of a man who is called Asher Levi, a German, a man of valour and distinction.

It was finished in the year 298 [= 1538], in the week of the Pericope Korah, here in this city, the great and celebrated Venice.

THUS THE SONG IS BROUGHT TO AN END, AND THE BOOK TO ITS COMPLETION.

THAT YOU MAY KNOW HOW MANY TIMES EACH LETTER OCCURS IN THE BIBLE, READ ALL THE WORDS IN THIS POEM.

לדעת מנין כל אות ואות,
אשר בכל המקרא נמצאות,
תקרא את כל דברי השירה הזאת:

I have now come to fulfil my promise which I made in the Third Introduction, towards the end of it [*vide supra*, p. 136]. I there stated that, at the end of this book, I would give and explain the Poem which was written, to show the number of all the letters, as well as the number of each individual letter; that is, how many *Alephs*, how many *Beths*, how many *Gimmels*, &c., are to be found throughout the Bible. It is said that R. Saadia Gaon is the author of it; and this statement seems to be correct, since we find therein very difficult and foreign words, which are not of Hebrew origin, and the like of which are also to be found in the Treatise,

עתה באתי לקיים את דברי אשר דברתי
בהקדמה שלישית קרוב לסופה, ושם הבטחתי
לכתוב ולבאר בסוף הספר הזה החרוז
הנעשה לדעת מספר כל האותיות פרט כל אות
ואות, רוצה לומר כמה אלפי״ן, וכמה ביתי״ן,
וכמה גימלי״ן וכולי, נמצאים בכל המקרא;
ואומרים כי ר' סעדיה הגאון חברהו, ונראין
הדברים אמת, כי כן נמצאים בו מלות
חמורות וזרות מאוד, אשר לא מבני ישראל
המה, וכדמותן נמצאים ג״כ בספר אמונות
שחבר ז״ל:[1]

והנה מספר הבתים שבחרוז הזה, כמספר
אותיות הא״ב, דהיינו שבכל בית ובית הוא
מבאר מנין אות אחת, ונעשה כדמות שיר
מחולק, דהיינו שכל בית נחלק לארבע הרוזות,
אבל אינו נעשה במשקל שיר שקול; ועתה
אבאר:

entitled, *Faith and Philosophy*, which he of blessed memory wrote.[1]

Now the number of the stanzas in this Poem corresponds to the number of the letters in the alphabet. Thus, each stanza propounds the number of one letter, and is made in the form of a complete poem, each stanza being divided into four lines, but it is not written in even metres. Let me now explain it.

---

[1] Saadia's philosophical work, to which Levita refers, has already been described (*vide supra*, p. 136). That Levita most emphatically believed Saadia to have been the author of this poem, is not only evident from the above remark, but is placed beyond the shadow of a doubt, by his epilogue to it (*vide infra*, p. 278). We are, therefore, surprised at the remark of the learned Dukes, that "Elias Levita does not say expressly that R. Saadia was the author of it, but merely quotes it as a common opinion, with which he agrees" (*Berträge zur Geschichte der aeltesten Auslegung und Spracherklärung des Alten Testamentes*, vol. ii., p. 101, &c.; Stuttgart, 1844). It is now, however, almost certain that Saadia b. Joseph Bechor Shor, who flourished in France towards the end of the twelfth century, was the author of this poem, which was first published by Levita in the *editio princeps* of the *Massoreth Ha-Massoreth*, Venice, 1538. It is omitted both in the Basel (1539) and the Sulzbach (1771) editions. It was reprinted in the *Theological Decisions of the Gaonim* (שאלות ותשובות הגאונים), Prague, *circa* 1590; by our countryman Hugh Broughton, in his work, entitled, *Daniel, his Chaldee Vision, and his Hebrew*, &c., at the end of chap. ix., London, 1597; by Buxtorf, in his *Tiberias*, cap. xviii., p. 183, &c., Basel, 1620; in the Compilation, entitled, *Taalamoth Chochma* (תעלומות חכמה), Basel, 1629–1631; by Anshel Worms, in his *Sejag La-Thora* (סיג לתורה), Frankfort-on-the-Maine, 1766; in *Likute Ha-Shas* (לקוטי הש״ס), Koretz, 1784; by Jehudah b. Jacob, Dyherenforth, 1821; and by Fürst, in his *Hebrew Concordance*, p. 1379, Leipzig, 1840.

Mark that the number of each letter is indicated by the initials of the first two lines. Those in the first line signify thousands, and those in the second line denote the remaining numerals—that is, hundreds, tens, and units; and in the third line he quotes one word, which indicates the verse he places under this line; and so, also, in the fourth line he quotes one word from another verse, which he places again under this line, in such a manner, that he brings two verses under each stanza. Now in adding up the number of the two verses, you will thus obtain the number of the letter in question with which the stanza commences. You must not, however, include in this sum the numerical value of the first letter, for this simply indicates the letter under consideration, whether it be *Aleph*, *Beth*, or *Gimmel*, &c.

Thus, for example, in the first stanza commencing אהל מכון בניני *the Tabernacle, my established edifice*, the *Aleph* in אהל indicates the letter *Aleph*, whilst the initials of מכון בניני yield מ״ב = 42, which denote 42,000. In the second line, again, beginning ששם עלו זקני *whither my elders resort*, the initials are שע״ז = 377, and thus we obtain the number of the *Alephs* as 42,377. The same is the case with all the letters. As to the third line, beginning with הקהל *the congregation*, the fourth line, beginning with ולזבח *and for a sacrifice*, &c., they indicate the thirty-two verses, which are respectively placed under each stanza in smaller characters and without points, and in which the number in question occurs. Thus, the first, "all the congregation together was forty thousand," &c. [Ezra ii. 6]; and the second, "and for a sacrifice of peace-offering, two oxen," &c. [Numb. vii. 17]; when the number of these two verses is added up, we obtain the sum total of 42,377. The same is the case with each letter.

Moreover, it is necessary to notice, that whenever you find in a stanza two words ranged together, the initials of which denote tens, and the first of the letters is *Mem*, *Nun*, *Tzaddi*, *Pe*, or *Kaph*, it is used in

על דרך שישמש מנצ״פך, כמו שבארתי מספרם בהקדמה הנ״ל, דהיינו ך משמש ת״ק, ם ר״ד, ן ח״ש, ף ה״ת, ץ תת״ק; והמשל בחרוז הד' המרחיל דהר וכולי, תמצא "כתשועתם" "לעילם" תידעכי כ"ף "כתשועתם" תשמש על דרך מנצ״פך, והיא ח״ק, ולמ״ד לעילם תשמש שלשים כמשפטה; וכן בחרוז הה' המתחיל הלום וכולי, יש בו ב' נוני"ן רצופין, והן "נקצבו" "נטעי", הראשונה תשמש ת"ש, והשניה חמשים כמשפטה, וכן כלם בזה הדרך; לכן בכל מקום שאחת מהן תשמש השמוש הזה, תמצא באמצע בגליון אחת מאותיות מנצ״פך הפשוטות עם עיגול אחד עליה כזה ךְ׳ םְ ןְ ףְ ץְ, דוק ותמצא:

ובכן אתחיל החרוזה.
בעניגים אלה רמוזה:

the manner in which the final *Mem*,
Nun, *Tzaddi*, *Pe*, and *Kaph* are
employed, and the value of which
I have already explained in the
above-named Introduction [*vide
supra*, 136]; that is, final *Kaph* denotes 500, final *Mem* 600, final *Nun*
700, final *Pe* 800, final *Tzaddi* 900.
Thus, for instance, in the fourth
stanza, commencing דהר *powerful*,
&c., where you find כתשועתם
לעילם *like the salvation at Elam*,
you must observe that the *Kaph*
in כתשועתם is employed, according
to the value of final *Mem*, *Nun*,
Tzaddi, *Pe*, and *Kaph*, and denotes
500; whilst the *Lamed* in לעילם
signified 30, as usual. The same
is the case with the fifth stanza,
beginning הלום *hither*, &c., where there are two *Nuns* following each
other, viz., נקצבו נטעי; the first denotes 700, and the second signifies
50, as usual. This method obtains throughout. Hence, wherever one of
these letters is used in this signification, you find in the middle margin
one of the final letters *Mem*, *Nun*, *Tzaddi*, *Pe*, and *Kaph* with a circle
over it, as follows:— ךְ םְ ןְ ףְ ץְ. Examine, and you will find it so.

And now I shall begin the Poem [2]
Which propounds these things.

אֹהֶל מָכוֹן בְּנֵינִי [3]　　　שִׁשִׁם עָלוּ זְקֵנִי
הַקָּהָל עָשׂוּ קְרָבָנִי　　　וּלְזֶבַח הַתּוֹדָה בָּאוּ בָּנִי

כל הקהל כאחד ארבע רבוא אלפים שלש　　ולזבח השלמים בקר שנים אילם חמשה
מאות וששים (נחמי' ז' ס"ו)　　עתודים חמשה כבשים בני שנה חמשה
　　　　　　　　　(במדבר ז' י"ז)

[2] We at first intended to give, with the Hebrew original, an English version of this
poem; but, after translating half of it, we found that the peculiar construction of it, the
way in which the Biblical words are therein used, and, in fact, the whole plan adopted
by the writer to make it at all intelligible to the reader, would require a commentary at
least three times the size of the poem itself. We have, therefore, abandoned our original
intention, and simply subjoin an explanation of each stanza.

[3] א *Aleph*, occurs 42,377 times in the Hebrew Scriptures. The *Aleph* in אהל, the first
word of this stanza, gives the letter the number of which is here discussed, and the
letters מבטש = 42,377, being the initials of the remaining words in the first and
second lines, give the number of times the letter in question occurs in the Bible. The
same fact is also indicated by the passages adduced from Nehem. vii. 66, and Numb.
vii. 17: as in the former the number 42,360 occurs, and in the latter 17; thus yielding
together 42,377.

272

⁴ בָּנֵי לֹא חוֹבְרִים | רִגְמָתָם יֵאַסְפוּ חֲבֵרִים
בִּנְיָמִין וּסְגָנִים דּוֹבְרִים | פַּחַת הַשֵּׁנִי גְבָרִים

פקודיהם למטה בנימין חמשה ושלשים | בני פהת מואב לבני ישוע יואב אלפים
אלף וארבע מאות (במדבר א' ל"ו) | ושמנה מאות ושמנה עשר (נחמי' ז' י"א)

⁵ גְּבָרִים בְּעֶצֶם טֹהַר | ד בֶּן לֶחֶם זֹהַר
כָּל־פְּקוּדֵי הַיִּצְהָר | מִלְּבַד הָרִאשׁוֹן דֹּהַר

כל פקודי הלוים אשר פקד משה ואהרן על | מלבד עבדיהם ואמהתיחם אלה שבעת
פי יהוה למשפחתם כל זכר מבן חדש ומעלה | אלפים שלש מאות שלשים ושבע משוררים
שנים ועשרים אלף (במדבר ג' ל"מ) | ומשוררות מאתים (עזרא ב' ס"ח)

⁶ דֹּהַר לָבוֹא בְּשָׁלוֹם | ד בִּתְשׁוּעָתָם לְעֵילוֹם
וּמִן הַדָּנִי בַּבָּשָׁן וַהֲלוֹם | סְנָאָה יָשׁוּב עַמּוֹ הֲלוֹם

ומן הדני עורכי מלחמה עשרים ושמנה | בני סנאה שלשת אלפים תשע מאות
אלף ושש מאות (ד"ה א' י"ב, לה) | ושלשים (נחמי' ז' ל"ח)

⁷ הֲלוֹם מִבַּעַל־זְוָיוֹת | ז נִקְבְּצוּ נִטְעֵי דָלִיּוֹת
רְאוּבֵן יִטְרֹף אֲרָיוֹת | עֵילָם וְאַשּׁוּר וּמַלְכִיּוֹת

פקודיהם למטה ראובן ששה וארבעים | בני עילם אלף ומאתים חמשים וארבעה
אלף ושש מאות (במדבר א' כ"א) | (נחמי' ז' ל"ד)

⁸ וּמַלְכִיּוֹת עֶצֶר נָפַחַת | ץ צוּרֵנוּ בַּעֲשׂוֹתוֹ בַּחַת
יְהוּדָה נָא אַל תַּשְׁחֵת | עֹזֵר שֵׁנִי וּבֶן זוֹחַת

פקודיהם למטה יהודה ארבעה ושבעים | בני עזגד אלפים ושלש מאות עשרים
אלף ושש מאות (במדבר א' כ"ז) | ושנים (נחמי' ז' י"ז)

⁴ ב *Beth*, occurs 38218 times. The *Beth* in בני, the first word in the stanza, indicates the letter under discussion, and the remaining initials of the first and second lines לח'ריח = 38,218, give the number of times the letter occurs in the Bible, which is also given in the two passages quoted under this stanza, viz., Numb. i. 37, and Nehem. vii. 11; since in the former the number 35,400 occurs, and in the latter 2,818 = 38,218.

⁵ ג *Gimmel*, occurs 29,537 times. The *Gimmel* in גברים gives the letter in question, and the remaining initials of the first two lines, viz., כמך'לו = 29,537, indicate the sum total, which is stated still more explicitly in the numbers to be found in the two passages adduced, viz., Numb. iii. 39, and Ezra ii. 65, in which occur the numbers 22,000 and 7,337 = 29,537. It will be seen that the *Kaph* at the beginning of the second line is used in its final value, as explained above, *vide* p. 136, 270, &c.

⁶ ד *Daleth*, occurs 32,530 times. The *Daleth* in דהר, the first word in this stanza, shows the letter under discussion, and the initials of the remaining words of the two lines, viz., לב ד'ל = 32,530, give the sum total, which is also given in the numbers found in the two passages adduced, viz., 1 Chron. xii. 35, and Nehem. vii. 38, wherein are the numbers 28,600 and 3,930 = 32,530.

⁷ ה *He*, occurs 47,754 times. The *He* under discussion is indicated in הלום, the first word in this stanza, and the number is given in the initials of the remaining words of the first two lines viz., מזן'נד = 47,754, which is also given in the numbers found in the two passages quoted, viz., Numb. i. 21, and Nehem. vii. 37, wherein are the numbers 46,500 and 1,254 = 47,754.

⁸ ו *Vav*, occurs 76922 times. The *Vav* itself is indicated in ומלכיות, the first word

⁹ זֹחַת בְּנֶפֶן בָּקוּק
וּמִן בְּנֵי אֶפְרַיִם בַּחֲבַקּוּק
וּמִן בני אפרים עשׂרים אלף ושׁמונה מאוה
גבורי חיל (ד"ה א' י"ב, ל')

פְּרִי סָרְ־נָיו זָקוּק
בְּנֵי הַשַּׁנִי חָקוּק
בני בנוי אלפִים ששׁים ושׁבעה (נחמי'
ז' י"ט)

¹⁰ הָקוּק בִּתְבוּאַת גֶּרֶשׁ
שִׁמְעוֹן שֵׁנִי זָךְ שׁוֹרֶשׁ
אלה משׁפחות השׁמעוני שׁנים ועשׂרים
אלף ומאתים (במדבר כו', י"ד)

תְּבוּסַת מַלְטֵי זָרֶשׁ
פְּשָׁחוּר לַעֲבוֹד טָרֶשׁ
בני פשׁחור אלף ומאתים ארבעה ושׁבעים
(עזרא ב' ל"ח)

¹¹ טָרֶשׁ יְמָלְאוּ אֲסָמָיו
חַיִּים לְמָסוֹךְ נְעִימָיו
ועשׂרת אלפים חיים שׁבו בני יהודה (דברי
הימים ב' כ"ה, י"ב)

נְטִישׁוֹתָיו בְּתַחֲנוּמָיו
אָמֵר לְהַרְבּוֹת יָמָי.
בני אמר אלף המשׁים ושׁנים (נחמי'
ז' מ')

¹² יָמָיו שִׂמְחָה וְשָׂשׂוֹן
בְּכֹחָם הָאַלּוֹן חָסוֹן
זהב דדכמונים שׁשׁ בבדאות ואלף וסף
מנים חמשׁת אלפים וכתנות כהנים מאָה
(עזרא ב', ס"ט)

תּוֹלְלֵיהֶם בְּקִמְּשׁוֹן
חָרֻם הָרִאשׁוֹן כְּמָסוֹן
בני חרם שׁלשׁ מאות ועשׂרים (נחמי'
ז' ל"ה)

of this stanza, and the number of times it occurs is given in the initials of the remaining words in the first two lines, viz., עוּ"רבב = 76,922, which is also contained in the two passages from Numb. i. 27, and Nehem. vii. 17, viz., 47,600 and 2,322 = 76,922.

9 ז *Zain*, occurs 22367 times. The *Zain* itself is indicated in וזחת, the first word of this stanza, and the sum total is contained in the initials of the remaining letters of the first two lines, viz., כבפ"סו = 22,867, as well as in the two passages from 1 Chron. xii. 30, and Nehem. vii. 19, viz., 20,803 and 2,067 = 22,867.

10 ח *Cheth*, occurs 23,447 times. The letter itself is indicated in הקוק, the first word of this stanza, whilst the number of times it occurs in the Bible is shown by the initials of the remaining letters of the first two lines, viz., כת"מו = 23,447. This is also stated in the two passages of Scripture adduced, viz., Numb. xxvi. 14, and Ezra ii. 38; in the first of which the number 22,200 occurs, and in the second 1247, = 23447.

11 ט *Teth*, occurs 11,052 times. The letter itself is indicated in טרשׁ, the first word in this stanza which begins with *Teth*, and the initials of the remaining letters in the first two lines, viz., אי"נב = 11,052, give the number of times the letter in question occurs in the Bible. The number is also given in the passages of Scripture, 2 Chron. xxv. 12. and Nehem. vii. 40, adduced under this stanza, in the first of which we have 10,000, and in the second 1,052, = 11,052.

12 י *Jod*, occurs 66,420 times. The *Jod* is indicated by the first letter of ימיו, the first word in this stanza, and the number of times is given in the initials of the remaining words in the first two lines, viz., שׁו"חכ = 66,420. This is also given in the two passages quoted under this stanza, viz., Ezra ii. 69, which contains the number 61,000 + 5,000 + 100 = 66,100, and Nehem. vii. 35, which contains the number 320, making in all 66,420.

רָבְצוּ עֲדָרִים בְּתוֹכָהּ כַּרְמִי נָם לָאֵל אֵין כָּמוֹכָה: כרמי שלי לפני האלף לך שלמה ומאתים לנטרים את פריו (שיר השירים ח' י"ב)	13 בְּמַסּוֹן לֹא זָעוּכָה וְהַבָּקָר לְעוֹלָה לְסַמִּיכָה והבקר ששה ושלשים אלף ומכסם ליהוה שנים ושבעים (במדבר ל"א, ל"ח)
ךְ צוּרַת פֶּסֶל אוּמְלָלוּן סוּסֵיהֶם נָטָה לָלוּן: סוסיהם שבע מאות ושלשים ושש פרדיהם מאתים ארבעים וחמשה (עזרא ב' ס"ו)	14 כָּמוֹךְ יָחְדָּלוּן חַיִּים כַּמֵּתִים יִדְּלוּן ועשרת אלפים חיים שבו בני יהודה (ד"ה ב', כ"ה, י"ב)
ךָ בַּבֹּקֶר יָאִיר זָרַח חָרַם שֵׁנִי לוֹ לְהָסִיר מְטוֹרָח: בני חרם אלף שבעה עשר (נחמי' ז' מ"ב)	15 לָלוּן מָלוֹן אוֹרַח אֶפְרַיִם דּוֹר אֹרַח פקודיהם למטה אפרים ארבעים אלף וחמש מאות (במדבר א' ל"ג)
ף פֵּירוֹתָם הִתְמַהְמַהוּנְתָם גְּמַלֵּיהֶם לָבוֹא מִשְׁכְּנוֹתָם: גמליהם ארבע מאות שלשים וחמשה חמורים ששת אלפים שבע מאות ועשרים (עזרא ב' ס"ז)	16 מְטוּרָח נָשְׂאוּ בֵיתָם גָּד נִצָּבִים לַנְחוֹתָם פקודיהם למטה גד חמשה וארבעים אלף ושש מאות וחמשים (במדבר א', כ"ה)

13 כ *Kaph*, occurs 37,272 times. The *Kaph* in במסון, the first word of this stanza, gives the letter in question, and the remaining initials of the first two lines, viz., לו״עב = 37,272, give the number of times the letter occurs in the Bible, which is also stated in the two passages of Scripture adduced under this stanza, viz., Numb. xxxi. 38, containing the number 36,000 + 72 = 36,072, and Song of Songs viii. 12, containing the number 1,200, = 37,272.

14 ך *Final Kaph*, occurs 10,981 times. This is not only indicated by the first, but more especially the last letter in כמוך, the first word in this stanza, whilst the initials of the remaining words in the first two lines, viz., יצ״פא = 10,981, give the number of times the letter in question occurs in the Bible. This is also shown by the numbers occurring in the two passages quoted under this stanza, viz., 2 Chron. xxv. 12, where 10,000 occur, and Ezra ii. 66, where we have 736 + 245 = 981, yielding the sum total of 10,981.

15 ל *Lamed*, occurs 41,517 times. The *Lamed* is indicated by the first letter of ללון, the first word in this stanza, whilst the number is given in the initials of the remaining words in the first two lines, viz., מאך״ז = 41,517. This is also shown in the numbers of the two passages quoted under this stanza, viz., Numb. i. 33, where the number 40,500 occurs, and Nehem. vii. 42, where we have 1,017 = 41,517.

16 מ *Mem*, occurs 52,805 times. The *Mem* is indicated by the first letter of מטורח, the first word of this stanza, and the number of times it occurs in the Bible is shown by the initials of the remaining words of the first two lines, viz., נכף״ה = 52,805. This is also indicated by the numbers occurring in two passages of Scripture adduced under this stanza, viz., Numb. i. 25, and Ezra ii. 67, wherein occur the numbers 45,650 and 435 + 6,720 = 52,805.

¹⁷ מִֽשְׁכְּנוֹתָם כְּמוֹ דָשָׁאוּ
הַמֵּתִים לְפִֽינְחָס נִבְרָאוּ

ויהיו המתים במגפה ארבעה ועשרים אלף
(במדבר כ"ה, מ')

ץ צוֹפֵיהֶם עוֹד נָאוּ
לְבֵית יֵשׁוּעַ כִּי נִבְאוּ:

הכהנים בני ידעיה לבית ישוע תשע מאות
שבעים ושלשה (עז"א ב' ל"ו)

¹⁸ נָבֽאוּ לִבְרָכוֹת בְּחֶשְׁבּוֹן
מְנַשֶּׁה יָשָׁה עִצָּבוֹן

פקודיהם למטה מנשה שנים ושלשים אלף
ומאתים (במדבר א' ל"ה)

ץ צָמְחִיָּה עֲלֵי זֵרְבוֹן
לֶךְ בִּנְחִימָיו נָבוֹן:

ויהי כל ימי לֶמֶךְ שבע ושבעים שנה
ושבע מאות שנה (בראשית ה' ל"א)

¹⁹ נָבוֹן חָכְמוֹתָיו
וַיִּהְיוּ עַל־פִּי דְבָרוֹתָיו

ויהי פקדיהם שמנת אלפים וחמש מאות
ושמנים (במדבר ד' מ"ח)

ן נָטוּ יוֹשֶׁר טִירֹתָיו
הַשְּׁעָרִים חָנוּ סְבִיבֹתָיו:

בני השערים בני שלום בני אטר בני
טלמון בני עקוב בני חטיטא בני שבי הכל
מאה שלשים ותשעה (עזרא ב' מ"ב)

²⁰ סְבִיבֹתָיו יָבֽאוּ גְדוּדִים
בְּהַצּוֹתוֹ אֶת הַבּוֹגְדִים

בהצותו את ארם נהרים ואת ארם צובה
וישב יואב ויך את אדום בגיא מלח שנים
עשר אלף (תהלים ס' ב')

ך כְּמֶרְכְּבוֹת פָּרוּדִים
וּמִקְצָת לְפָנָיו עוֹמְדִים:

ומקצת ראשי האבות נתנו למלאכה וגו'
זהב דרכמנים אלף מזרקות חמשים כתנות
כהנים שלשים וחמש מאות (נחמי' ז', ע')

¹⁷ מ *Final Mem*, occurs 24,973 times. The *Final Mem* is not only indicated by the first, but more especially by the last letter in משכנותם, the first word in this stanza which terminates in *Final Mem*. The initials of the remaining words in the first two lines, viz., כדץ״עג = 24,973, state the number of times the latter occurs in the Bible, which is indicated still more explicitly in the numbers occurring in the two passages of Scripture adduced under this stanza, viz., Numb. xxv. 9, where we have the number 24,000, and Ezra ii. 36, where the number is 973 = 24,973.

¹⁸ נ *Nun*, occurs 32,977 times. The letter itself is indicated by נבאו, the first word in this stanza which begins with *Nun*, and the number of times it occurs in the Bible is shown by the initials of the remaining words of the first two lines, viz., לב״ץ עצ = 32,977. This is also shown by the numbers in the two passages quoted under this stanza, viz., Numb. i. 35, where we have 32,200, and Gen. v. 31, where we have 777 = 32,977.

¹⁹ ן *Final Nun* occurs 8,719 times. The letter in question is not only indicated by the first letter in נבון, the first word in this stanza, but more especially by the last letter of the word, which is *Final Nun*. The initials of the remaining words in the first two lines, viz., חן״יש = 8,719, as usual indicate the number of times the letter in question occurs in the Bible, which is also shown by the numbers to be found in the two passages of Scripture adduced under this stanza, viz., Numb. iv. 48, where the number 8,580 occurs, and Ezra ii. 42, where we have 139 = 8,719.

²⁰ ס *Samech*, occurs 13,580 times. As usual, the letter in question is indicated by the first letter in סביבותיו, the first word in this stanza, whilst the initials of the remaining words in the first two lines, viz., ס״ינך = 13,580, show the number of times it occurs in the Bible, which is indicated more plainly by the numbers in the two passages of Scripture cited under this stanza, viz., Ps. lx. 2, where we have 12,000, and Nehem. vii. 70, where we have 1,000 + 50 + 530 = 1580, making in all 13,580.

276

עוֹמְדִים בְּמַחְלְקוֹתֵיהֶֽם ²¹
בָּאֹרֶךְ וְרֹחַב לָהֶֽם
קִצֵּינִי עֵדָה הֵֽם
אַבְרָהָם לְזִכָּרוֹן בְּפִיהֶֽם׃

והנותר בארך לעמת תרומת הקדש עשרת אלפים קדימה ועשרה אלפים ימה (יחזקאל מ״ח, י״ח)

ואלה ימי שני חיי אברהם אשר חי ושבעים שנה וחמש שנים מאת שנה (בראשית כ״ה, ז)

פִּיהֶם בָּעֹרֶף ²²
סָבִיב נִפְשְׁטָה וְנִטְרָֽף
ן נִיבוֹ נִצְרָֽף
תַּחַת יְרִיעֹתָיו פָּרָֽף׃

סביב שמנה עשר אלף (יחזקאל מ״ח ל״ה)

ויהיו פקודיהם למשפחתם אלפים שבע מאות וחמשים (במדבר ד׳, ל״ו)

פָּרָף אֲרִיגֵֽנוּ ²³
הָאֶלֶף וְצֶלַע נִיהוּגֵֽנוּ
ף צֶדֶק עָנָה הֲגִיגֵֽנוּ
לְעִתִּים יְדָרְכוּ צִיגֵֽנוּ׃

ואת האלף ושבע המאות וחמשה ושבעים עשה ווים לעמודים (שמות ל״ח, כ״ח)

ומבני יששכר יודעי בינה לעתים לדעת מה יעשה ישראל ראשיהם מאתים וכל אחיהם על פיהם (ד״ה א׳ יב, ל״ב)

צִיּגֵֽנוּ יִצְנֹף וְיָצֵץ ²⁴
וְנֶפֶשׁ עוֹד לֹא יַקַּץ
ץ צוֹרְרֵנוּ נְרַצֵּֽץ
נַח סוּפוֹ וָיָצֵץ צִיץ׃

ונפש אדם ששה עשר אלף (במדבר ל״א, מ׳)

ויהיו כל ימי נח תשע מאות שנה וחמשים שנה וימת (בראשית ט׳ כ״ט)

²¹ ע *Ajin*, occurs 20,175 times. The letter itself is indicated by the *Ajin* in עומדים, the first word of this stanza, whilst the initials of the remaining words in the first two lines, viz., בקע״ה = 20,175, show the number of times the letter in question occurs in the Bible. This is moreover shown by the numbers to be found in the two passages of Scripture adduced under this stanza, viz., Ezek. xlviii. 18, where we have 10,000 and 10,000, and Gen. xxv. 7, where the number is 175 = 20,175.

²² פ *Pe*, occurs 20,750 times. As usual, the letter in question is indicated by the *Pe*, the first letter in פיהם, the word with which the stanza begins, whilst the number of times the letter in question occurs is shown by the initials of the remaining words in the first two lines, viz., בכנ = 20,750. This number is also contained in the two passages of Scripture adduced under this stanza, viz., Ezek. xlviii. 35 and Numb. iv. 36, in the former of which the number is 18,000, and in the latter 2,750 = 20,750.

²³ ף *Final Pe*, occurs 1,975 times. The letter itself is not only indicated by the first letter in פוף, the word with which the stanza begins, but more especially by the last letter of this word, which is *Final Pe*. The initials of the remaining words in the first two lines, viz., אץה״ע = 1,975, give the number of times the letter in question occurs in the Bible, whilst the numbers in the two passages of Scripture, adduced under this stanza, show this still more explicitly, viz., Exod. xxxviii. 28, where the number 1,775 occurs, and 2 Chron. xii. 32, where the number is 200 = 1,975.

²⁴ צ *Tzaddi*, occurs 16,950 times. The letter itself is indicated by the *Tzaddi* in ציננו, the word with which the stanza begins; the initials of the remaining words in the first two lines, viz., יץנ׳ = 16,950, show the number of times the word in question occurs in the Bible; and the two passages of Scripture adduced under this stanza, viz., Numb. xxxi. 40 and Gen. ix. 29, are made to state the same fact, inasmuch as the number 16,000 occurs in the first passage, and 950 occurs in the second, yielding together 16,950.

פָּז עָבַר בְּרַתּוֹקָיו ף שׁוֹפְטֶיךָ נָטָה קָו:	²⁵ צִיץ דֵּי פְּרָקָיו תּוֹצָאוֹת חֻקָּיו
בני שפטיה שלש מאות שבעים ושנים (עזרא ב׳, ד׳)	ואלה תוצאת העיר מפאת צפון דמש מאות וארבעת אלפים מדה (יחזקאל מ"ח, ל,)
צְבִי עֶרֶךְ בְּנֶגֶד ע פַּרְעֹשׁ בָּנָיו רוֹדֵף:	²⁶ קַן כּוֹנֵן בְּעֶדְרֶף וּמִן בְּנֵי אֶפְרַיִם צַר רוֹדֵף
בני פרעוש אלפים מאה שבעים ושנים (עזרא ב׳ ג׳)	ומן בני אפרים עשרים אלף ושמונה מאות (דברי הימים א׳, י"ב, ל,)
קוֹל מַשְׁמִיעַ זִמְרָה יַעֲקֹב בֶּן יֵטִיב שִׁירָה:	²⁷ רוֹדֵף בְּרוּחַ בִּגְבוּרָה שְׁנָאָן הַגַּלְגַּל קָרָא
ויחי עקב בארץ מצרים שבע עשרה שנה ויהי ימי יעקב שני חייו שבע שנים וארבעים ומאת שנה (בראשית מ"ז, כ"ח)	רכב אלהים רבותים אלפי שנאן אדני בם סיני בקדש (תהלים ס"ח, י"ח)
קִנְיָה סֹ תִּשְׁעָה חֹלוֹת הַמְשׁוֹרְרִים עוֹז תְּהִלּוֹת:	²⁸ שִׁירָה לַנַצֵּחַ בִּמְחוֹלוֹת מִן הַנָּשִׁים נִתְעַלּוֹת
המשודרים בני אסף מאה ארבעים ושמנה (נחמי׳ ז׳ מ"ד)	מן הנשים אשר לא ידעו משכב זכר כל נפש שנים ושלשים אלף במדבר ל"א, ל"ה)

²⁵ צ *Final Tzaddi*, occurs 4,872 times. The letter is indicated both by the first, and especially by the last, letter in צִיץ, with which this stanza begins. The initials of the remaining words of the first two lines, viz., דפ׳עב = 4,872, indicate the number of times this letter occurs in the Bible; which is also shown by the numbers occurring in the two passages of Scripture adduced under this stanza, viz., Ezek. xlviii. 30 and Ezra ii. 4, in the former of which we have 4,500, and in the latter 372 = 4,872.

²⁶ ק *Koph*, occurs 22,972 times. The mnemonical sign for the letter in question is the *Koph* in the word קַן, with which this stanza begins, and the signs for the number of times it occurs in the Bible are both the initials of the remaining words in the first two lines, viz., כבץ׳עב = 22,972, and the sum total of the numbers contained in the two passages of Scripture adduced under this stanza, viz., 1 Chron. xii. 30, where we have 20,800, and Ezra ii. 3, where we have 2,172 = 22,972.

²⁷ ר *Resh*, occurs 22,147 times. The letter itself is indicated by the *Resh* in רוֹדֵף, with which the stanza begins, and the number of times it occurs is shown both by the initials of the remaining words of the first two lines, viz., כבכ׳מו = 22,147, and by the numbers in the two passages of Scripture adduced under this stanza, viz., Ps. lxviii. 18, in which the number is 22,000, and Gen. xlvii. 28, where we find 147 = 22,147.

²⁸ ש *Shin*, occurs 32,148 times. The *Shin* itself is indicated by the first letter of שִׁירָה, which begins this stanza, and the number of times it occurs in the Bible is shown by the initials of the remaining words in the first two lines, viz., לנ׳קמח = 32,148, as well as by the numbers in the two passages of Scripture adduced under this stanza, viz., Numb. xxxi. 35, where we find 32,000, and Nehem. vii. 44, where it is 148 = 32,148.

²⁹ תְּהִלָּה לִשְׁמוֹ וְתִתְפָּאָרֶת
וּבָקָר פָּלִיל מְקֻטָּרֶת

קָמָה מְשׁוֹרֶרֶת
אִיּוֹב תַּמָּתוֹ תוֹתָרֶת:

וּבקר ששה ושלשים אלף (במדבר ל"א, מ"ד,)

ויחי איוב אחרי זאת מאה וארבעים שנה וירא את בניו ואת בני בניו ארבעה דורות (איוב מ"ב, ט"ז)

³⁰ תּוֹתֶרֶת בָּבְדָה נָשָׁה
זָכָר הִמְלִיטָה כִּי חָשָׁה

רַעֲנַנִיָּה גֹּרְשָׁה
אָדָם הָאֶבֶן הָרֹאשָׁה:

ויהי כל בכור זכר במספר שמות מבן חדש ומעלה לפקדיהם שנים ועשרים אלף שלשה ושבעים ומאתים (במדבר ג' מ"ג)

ויהיו כל ימי אדם אשר חי תשע מאות שנה ושלשים שנה וימת (בראשית ה' ה')

סליק וסימנך כי זה כל האדם:

סליק

השיר נגמר אותו חבר,
אך הנהו גם ביארהו,
בה בשנה סימן לפרט,

הגאון מהר"ר סעדיה:
האיש הלוי אליה:
קטן הלוי אליה:

בנ"ך

²⁹ ת Tav, occurs 36,140 times. The Tav itself is indicated by the first letter of תהלה, with which the stanza begins, and the number of times it occurs is shown by the initials of the remaining words in the first two lines, viz., לו'קמ = 36,140, as well as by the numbers occurring in the two passages of Scripture quoted under this stanza, viz., Numb. xxxi. 44, where we have 36,000, and Job xlii. 16, where it is 140 = 36,140.

³⁰ ת Tav without *Dagesh*, occurs 23,203 times. The letter in question is not only indicated by the first letter of תותרת, with which this stanza begins, but more especially by the last letter which is without *Dagesh*. The number of times it occurs in the Bible is shown by the initials of the remaining words in the first two lines, viz., כג'רנ = 23,203, as well as by the numbers contained in the two passages of Scripture adduced under this stanza, viz., Numb. iii. 43, where we have 22,277, and Gen. v. 5, where we have 930 = 23,203.

INDEX I.

MASSORETICALLY ANNOTATED PASSAGES OF SCRIPTURE REFERRED TO.

GENESIS.

Chap.	Ver.	Page.
i.	1	124, 139, 142, 215, 230, 231
..	2	139
..	3	215
..	4	139, 142, 209
..	5	140
..	6	141, 215
..	7	139, 142
..	9	215
..	11	215, 252
..	14	215, 221, 228
..	15	140
..	18	221
..	20	142, 215
..	21	157
..	24	215
..	26	215
..	29	215
ii.	3	139
..	4	168, 231
..	6	165
..	15	239
..	21	177
..	22	219
..	23	206
iii.	6	197
..	11	208
..	17	154
..	18	249
..	22	149
iv.	2	205
..	5	218
..	8	262
..	9	201
..	29	233
v.	1	168, 220
..	5	278
..	31	275
vi.	2	246
..	3	149
..	10	219
..	13	215
..	14–16	229
..	16	218
..	18	166
..	21	111
vii.	21	251

Chap.	Ver.	Page.
viii.	10	245
..	15	215
..	17	115, 118, 180, 251
..	22	163
ix.	8	215
..	10	213, 25
..	11	166
..	12	215
..	17	166, 167, 215
..	21	179
..	26	141
..	27	141
..	29	276
x.	1	214, 236, 237
..	3	263
..	8	148
..	9	148
..	10	197
..	19	115, 177
..	23	197
..	29	157
..	30	177
xi.	31	174
xii.	5	174
..	7	237
..	8	179
..	10	174
..	11	174
..	14	174
xiii.	3	179
..	5	220, 221
..	10	177
..	15	227
xiv.	2	115
..	8	115
..	16	252
xv.	1	196
..	2	234
..	5	250
xvi.	4	197
..	7	178
..	12	200
xvii.	2	150
..	5	206
..	7	166
..	9	215
..	15	215

Chap.	Ver.	Page
xvii.	17	197
..	18	216
..	19	166, 215
..	20	157
xviii.	6	174
..	7	141, 218
..	11	242
..	12	247
..	15	252
..	20	205
..	21	209
..	25	201, 207
..	29	245
xix.	10	174
..	12	163
..	14	219
..	16	239
..	22	151
..	29	196
..	30	151
..	36	177
..	37	216
..	38	216
xx.	3	154
..	6	140, 150, 170
..	14	252
..	15	201
..	16	236
xxi.	6	205
..	8	197
..	12	206, 215
..	15	197, 252
..	23	175
xxii.	2	252
..	13	206
..	22	208
xxiii.	2	231
..	9	199
..	11	223
..	15	223
..	18	236
xxiv.	3	246
..	4	226
..	5	247
..	14	109, 115
..	16	109, 115
..	18	251
..	23	132, 247

Chap.	Ver.	Page.	Chap.	Ver.	Page.	Chap.	Ver.	Page.
GENESIS.			xxxiii.	8	197	xliii.	11	200
xxiv.	25	247	..	13	213	..	14	208
..	28	109, 115	..	20	215	..	16	174
..	30	158	xxxiv.	3	109, 116	..	23	250
..	32	174	..	12	109, 116	..	26	174
..	33	116, 118, 187	..	25	197	..	28	116, 117
..	46	251	..	26	207	..	33	207
..	47	258	..	31	230	xliv.	17	242
..	53	250	xxxv.	1	215	..	18	170
..	55	109, 116	..	10	206	..	20	241
..	57	109, 116	..	17	219	..	29	170
..	67	174	..	20	155, 216	xlv.	4	174
xxv.	1	245	..	21	179	..	17	174
..	6	158	..	22	242	..	12	198
..	7	276	..	23	116, 212, 213	..	16	166
..	12	168	xxxvi.	1	168	..	22	200
..	16	157, 208, 209	..	5	116	xlvi.	2	215
..	18	177, 207	..	9	168	..	3	174
..	19	168	..	14	116	..	4	174
..	21	178	..	15	116	..	7	174
..	23	118, 187	..	21	264	..	8	174
..	31	178	..	24	158	..	9	174, 213
xxvi.	2	174	..	30	263	..	12	225
..	3	156, 166	xxxvii.	2	168	..	22	226
..	10	252	..	4	148	..	26	174
..	12	240	..	10	218	..	27	174
..	19	168	..	11	198	xlvii.	11	205
..	26	248	..	25	167, 174	..	18	208
xxvii.	2	197			208, 222	..	27	170, 207
..	3	116	..	27	161	..	28	242, 277
..	7	176, 234	..	28	174	..	30	161
..	22	166	xxxviii.	1	237	xlviii.	4	176
..	24	217	..	9	208	..	5	174
..	29	116, 117, 221	..	18	149	..	9	197
..	31	154	..	25	149	..	21	251
..	35	162	xxxix.	1	174	..	22	252
..	37	213	..	6	151	xlix.	11	116
..	46	231	..	9	150	..	12	230
xxviii.	10	197, 242	..	11	174	..	13	226
xxix.	21	205	..	20	116, 118, 249	..	21	154
xxx.	1	205	..	22	116	..	27	197
..	11	116, 193	xl.	5	200	..	28	150
..	21	197	..	10	159	..	29	150
..	26	196	..	12	159	l.	13	174, 226
..	34	161	..	13	163, 175	..	14	174
..	37	196, 223	..	14	178	..	21	150
..	40	226	..	17	197	..	23	230
..	42	154, 230	..	19	150			
xxxi.	3	251	..	21	252	**EXODUS.**		
..	10	154	xli.	1	242	i.	1	174
..	13	197	..	8	150, 151, 152	..	3	212, 213
..	18	174	..	11	200	..	16	264
..	32	216	..	15	241	..	19	177
..	35	163	..	20	148	ii.	2	230
..	49	223	..	25	223	..	3	178, 229
xxxii.	13	160	..	28	223	..	5	148, 167, 229
..	15	158, 212	..	33	205	..	7	160
..	21	220	..	35	207	..	10	222
..	23	252	..	38	139	..	12	220
..	26	235, 236	..	39	150	..	16	177
xxxiii.	4	116, 163	..	40	217	..	20	223
		182, 183	..	57	174	iii.	13	169
..	5	208	xlii.	29	174	..	14	215
..	6	177	xliii.	6	200	..	15	149, 164

Chap.	Ver.	Page.	Chap.	Ver.	Page.	Chap.	Ver.	Page.
iii.	17	233	xv.	2	222	xxviii.	12	148
..	22	221	..	11	177	..	20	213
iv.	2	116, 193	..	14	249	..	23	175
..	7	252	..	18	149	..	28	116, 207
..	8	166	..	19	252	..	29	148
..	11	200	xvi.	2	116, 118	..	30	175
..	12	205	..	7	116	..	36	149, 230
..	15	218	..	8	220	..	40	221
..	19	154, 164	..	12	255	xxix.	3	150, 175
..	21	174	..	13	116	..	6	175
..	26	222	..	23	214, 238	..	13	174
..	29	233	xvii.	12	213	..	17	175
v.	1	216	xviii.	1	259	..	18	174, 214
..	7	171	..	5	259	..	25	174
..	23	221	..	7	174	..	31	147
vi.	2	215	..	19	141	..	34	141
..	3	218	..	21	224	xxx.	9	213
..	4	166, 167	..	25	224	..	16	175
..	5	158	xix.	8	252	..	18	175
..	11	202	..	13	216	..	32	247
..	13	140, 218	..	16	166	xxxi.	3	139
..	18	228	..	17	250	..	17	139, 149
..	24	171	xx.	1	215	xxxii.	4	206
vii.	2	217	..	6	140	..	10	150
..	12	157	..	11	139, 233	..	13	149
..	29	176, 177	..	13	232	..	17	116, 178
viii.	5	237	..	15	232	..	19	116
..	10	207	..	16	232	..	25	231
..	18	246	xxi.	3	241	..	27	216
..	19	154	..	6	149	xxxiii.	8	174
ix.	15	150	..	8	116	..	9	174
..	16	217	..	10	178	..	13	162
..	18	178	..	27	132	..	22	220
..	19	174	..	28	141	xxxiv.	7	151, 230
..	22	141	xxii.	4	116	..	14	230
..	27	213	..	22	196	..	26	231
..	34	245	..	26	116	xxxv.	11	116
x.	1	205	..	29	223	..	31	139
..	2	217	..	30	154	xxxvi.	6	242
..	9	161	xxiii.	2	95, 164	..	14	216
..	12	220	..	8	157	..	17	214
..	18	264	..	13	226	..	19	216
..	21	151	xxiv.	1	218	xxxvii.	8	116
..	28	205	..	5	128	..	16	196
xi.	8	230	..	10	215	xxxviii.	12	155
xii.	16	141	..	14	218	..	17	155
..	22	218	xxv.	9	150	..	25	213
..	30	245	..	16	175	..	28	276
..	34	155	..	18	155	xxxix.	3	224, 230
..	37	173	..	20	237	..	4	116
..	42	155	..	21	175, 218	..	14	149
..	46	141	..	22	150	..	21	116, 207
..	46	199	..	26	175	..	33	116
xiii.	5	141	..	29	196	xl.	4	205
..	7	141	..	30	175	..	7	175
..	11	116	xxvi.	1	151	..	8	175
..	16	176, 177, 234	..	7	216			
..	17	174	..	14	216	LEVITICUS.		
xiv.	7	159	..	16	237	i.	1	196, 231
..	9	150	..	34	175	..	9	174
..	13	226	xxvii.	7	206	..	13	174
..	16	141, 255	..	10	155	..	15	174
..	17	141, 255	..	11	116, 155, 183	..	17	174
..	19-21	219	xxviii.	11	149	ii.	2	174

282

LEVITICUS.			Chap.	Ver.	Page.	Chap.	Ver.	Page.
Chap.	Ver.	Page.	xiv.	20	. 174	xxii.	23	. 213
ii.	9	. 174	..	33	. 140	..	30	141, 255
..	15	. 175	..	51	. 150	..	31	. 255
iii.	5	. 174	xv.	1	. 140	..	33	. 255
..	11	. 174	..	10	. 150	xxiii.	13	. 116
..	16	. 174	..	13	. 205	..	17	. 171
iv.	19	. 174	..	29	150, 205	..	21	. 214
..	26	174, 207	xvi.	6	. 214	..	22	. 255
..	31	. 174	..	8	. 149	..	24	. 236
..	35	. 174	..	14	. 217	..	28	. 155
v.	1	. 163	..	15	. 217	..	43	150, 255
..	12	. 174	..	20	. 247	xxiv.	5	. 205
vi.	2	. 231	..	21	116, 247	..	6	. 150
..	8	. 225	..	25	. 174	..	7	. 175
..	9	. 147	xvii.	4	. 200	..	9	. 147
..	18	. 241	..	5	. 150	..	12	239, 240
..	19	. 147	..	13	. 141	..	13	. 180
..	20	. 147	xviii.	1	. 255	xxv.	17	. 255
vii.	5	. 174	..	2	. 255	..	22	. 255
..	6	. 141	..	4	241, 255	..	23	. 247
..	9	. 206	..	5	. 255	..	25	. 247
..	15	. 141	..	6	. 255	..	27	. 200
..	16	. 141	..	20	. 218	..	30	116, 247
..	18	. 141	..	21	. 255	..	35	. 247
..	19	. 141	..	23	. 178	..	39	. 247
..	21	. 200	..	25	. 157	..	44	. 213
..	31	. 174	..	27	. 260	..	46	. 149
..	36	. 226	..	28	. 157	..	55	150, 255
..	38	. 226	..	30	. 255	xxvi.	1	213, 255
viii.	2	. 158	xix.	2	. 255	..	2	206, 255
..	8	. 135	..	3	214, 238	..	9	. 166
..	16	. 174			241, 255	..	25	. 261
..	21	. 174	..	4	. 255	..	43	. 241
..	28	. 174	..	6	. 141	..	44	. 239
ix.	10	. 174	..	7	. 141	..	45	. 255
..	12	. 159	..	10	. 255	xxvii.	9	. 225
..	14	. 174	..	12	. 255	..	10	200, 201
..	18	. 159	..	14	217, 255	..	26	. 200
..	20	. 174	..	15	. 255	..	30	. 204
..	22	116, 163, 213	..	18	. 255	..	32	. 204
x.	1	. 196	..	23	. 141			
..	2	. 150	..	25	. 255	NUMBERS.		
..	16	. 135	..	28	. 255	i.	16	116, 118, 187
xi.	1	. 140	..	30	. 255	..	21	. 272
..	19	212, 214	..	31	. 255	..	25	. 274
..	21	. 116	..	32	. 255	..	27	. 273
..	34	. 141	..	32	. 255	..	33	. 274
..	37	208, 209	..	34	. 255	..	37	. 272
..	41	. 141	..	37	. 255	..	39	. 272
..	42	135, 196, 230, 232	xx.	4	. 203	..	50	. 180
..			..	7	. 255	ii.	1	. 140
..	43	. 170	..	15	. 200	iii.	9	. 159
..	44	. 255	..	16	. 178	..	15	. 147
xii.	4	. 264	..	25	214, 251	..	19	. 228
..	5	. 199	..	26	. 159	..	40	. 147
..	8	. 214	xxi.	2	214, 241	..	51	. 116
xiii.	1	. 140	..	5	116, 179, 188	iv.	1	. 140
..	2	. 252	..	7	. 147	..	12	. 150
..	3	. 206	..	8	. 147	..	17	. 140
..	4	178, 223	..	12	. 255	..	19	. 150
..	10	. 206	xxii.	2	158, 207, 255	..	23	. 150
..	20	178, 223, 237	..	3	. 255	..	28	. 275
..	33	135, 230	..	8	. 255	..	36	. 276
..	51	. 236	..	16	. 150	..	43	. 278

283

Chap.	Ver.	Page.	Chap.	Ver.	Page.	Chap.	Ver.	Page.
iv.	49	150, 226	xv.	41	255	xxxi.	38	274
v.	4	150	..	31	178	..	40	276
..	8	200	..	41	170	..	44	278
..	21	150	xvi.	9	215	xxxii.	1	247
..	26	174	..	11	116	..	3	213
vi.	5	147, 158, 223	..	15	252	..	7	116, 119
..	8	147	..	17	213, 218	..	17	170
..	20	150	..	20	140	..	24	171
..	24	216	xvii.	4	155	..	37	172
vii.	1	159	..	17	160	xxxiii.	8	226
..	3	150	..	20	156	..	42	237
..	5	150	..	23	250, 251	xxxiv.	4	116
..	6	150	..	24	250	xxxv.	2	221
..	10	157	xviii.	24	204	..	4	221
..	14	232	..	23	227	..	9	275
..	17	271	..	26	213	..	10	174
..	19	159	xix.	1	140	..	7	236
..	20	232	xx.	15	174	xxxvi.	3	149, 221
..	26	232	..	17	200	..	6	200
..	32	232	xxi.	4	259			
..	38	232	..	5	205, 245	DEUTERONOMY.		
..	44	232	..	20	221	i.	2	252
..	50	232	..	22	200	..	11	160, 169
..	56	232	..	32	116, 118	..	13	157
..	62	232	xxii.	2	245	..	15	224
..	68	232	..	12	215	..	16	224
..	74	232	..	15	245	ii.	1	237
..	80	232	..	22	263	..	8	242
viii.	1	170	..	25	245	..	14	164
..	7	196	..	26	245	..	33	116, 230
..	16	160	..	33	150, 177	iii.	6	150
ix.	2	248	xxiii.	1	158	..	11	230
..	15	216	..	3	206	..	13	206
x.	3	196	..	7	263	..	17	213
..	10	255	..	9	197, 221	..	21	160
..	36	116	..	24	197	..	26	205
xi.	4	171, 185	xxiv.	2	139	..	28	150
..	11	140, 170	..	5	230	iv.	11	237
..	12	222	..	6	207	..	26	139
..	20	172	..	23	216	..	32	139
..	25	171	xxv.	4	150	..	40	217
..	26	174	..	12	231	..	45	237
..	32	116, 233	..	17	150	v.	10	116, 232
..	33	242	..	19	242	..	14	176
xii.	3	116, 163, 183	xxvi.	8	226	..	16	154, 233
..	12	207	..	9	116, 119	..	18	225
..	16	170	..	14	273	..	19	242
xiii.	1	170	xxvii.	2	157, 217	..	26	149
..	2	207	..	5	230	vi.	2	154, 217, 233
..	9	172	..	13	205	..	4	230
..	21	207	..	15	215	..	9	95
..	22	225, 260	..	21	217	..	13	228, 229
..	28	260	xxviii.	6	154	..	17	236
..	30	230	..	17	141	..	18	214
xiv.	3	174	xxix.	19	265	vii.	9	116
..	4	174	..	31	265	..	12	170
..	15	176	..	33	212, 265	..	19	213
..	17	230	xxx.	9	150	viii.	2	116
..	20	161	xxxi.	12	218	..	3	216
..	25	213	..	18	236	..	8	182
..	26	140	..	22	214	..	14	236
..	36	116, 119	..	24	231	ix.	2	218
xv.	14	237	..	27	205, 261	..	5	217
..	24	140, 170	..	35	277	..	14	150

284

Deuteronomy.			Chap.	Ver.	Page.	Chap.	Ver.	Page.
Chap.	Ver.	Page.	xxiv.	10	171	iii.	16	116, 189
ix.	22	158	xxv.	5	173, 252	..	17	255
..	24	231	..	9	200	iv.	1	262
..	27	218	..	19	128	..	8	239, 240
..	28	150	xxvi.	5	174	..	18	116, 188
x.	5	202	..	8	213	v.	1	116
..	11	141, 255	..	16	150	..	12	242
..	15	150	..	19	147	..	15	116
..	17	148	xxvii.	8	122	vi.	5	188, 116
..	20	229	..	10	116	..	7	116, 117
..	22	174	..	12	213	..	9	116, 232
xi.	9	217	..	13	225	..	13	116, 191
..	10	205	..	26	150	..	15	116
..	12	140, 170	xxviii.	27	109, 116, 194	vii.	7	196
..	13	121	..	30	116, 194	..	10	154, 164
..	13–21	95	..	31	155	..	21	116, 118
..	20	159	..	39	151	..	22	174
..	24	247	..	46	227	..	24	255
..	25	170	..	51	214	viii.	11	183, 116
xii.	4	152	..	52	196	..	12	116
..	16	229	..	53	162	..	15	255
..	22	141	..	57	140	..	16	116
..	23	208	..	68	230	..	21	255
..	29	150	xxix.	5	255	..	24	262
xiii.	1	205	..	22	116	ix.	7	116, 117, 182
..	3	151	..	27	230	..	24	196
..	15	175	xxx.	19	139	x.	8	116
17	..	236	xxxi.	7	150	..	24	172
xiv.	18	212	..	10	150	..	23	237
..	23	204	..	26	119	..	29	255
xv.	2	196	..	28	139	..	31	255
..	4	216	xxxii.	1	201	..	34	255
..	23	229	..	5	230	..	32	220
xvi.	10	226	..	6	230	..	35	221
..	18	214	..	7	254	..	36	255
xvii.	6	229	..	10	222	..	38	255
..	12	205	..	11	201	..	39	174
..	16	174	..	13	182	..	43	255
xviii.	12	150	..	14	158	xi.	16	116
..	13	150, 230	..	18	208, 231	xii.	13	232
xix.	15	229	..	29	230	..	14	232
xx.	3	224	..	33	157	..	15	232
..	8	176	..	34	154	..	20	116
xxi.	6	188	..	40	149	..	40	171
..	7	116, 161, 179	..	51	150	xiii.	8	226
..	15	177	xxxiii.	2	193	..	11	213
..	21	255	..	5	264	..	16	226
xxii.	6	206, 230	..	6	141, 216	xiv.	2	226
..	15	109, 116	..	9	116	..	4	236
..	16	109, 116, 200	..	27	178	..	12	214
..	20	109, 116	..	44	218	..	15	220
..	21	109, 116				xv.	4	116
..	23	109, 116	Joshua.			..	22	212
..	24	109, 116	i.	3	247	..	45	213
..	25	109, 116	..	7	225	..	47	116
..	26	109, 116	..	8	162	..	48	116
..	27	109, 116	ii.	7	226	..	53	116, 118
..	28	109, 116	..	9	247	..	63	116
..	29	109, 116	..	11	255	xvi.	3	116, 183
xxiii.	4	257	..	13	116	..	5	116
..	5	227	..	14	161	xviii.	1	214
..	11	196	..	18	174	..	4	141, 255
..	17	201	..	22	198	..	8	116
xxiv.	8	206, 226	iii.	4	116	..	9	116

Chap.	Ver.	Page.	Chap.	Ver.	Page.	Chap.	Ver.	Page.
xviii.	12	. 116	xiv.	15	. 150	iv.	13	116, 189
..	14	. 116	xv.	18	. 175	v.	6	109, 116
..	19	. 116	..	19	. 151	..	7	. 215
..	24	. 116	xvi.	12	. 207	..	8	215, 233
xix.	7	212, 213	..	19	. 200	..	9	109, 116
..	13	. 178	..	21	151, 152, 222	..	10	. 215
..	22	116, 119	..	25	. 193	..	11	215, 233
..	29	. 116	..	26	116, 155, 191	..	12	109, 116
..	47	. 221	xvii.	3	. 252	vi.	2	208, 209
xx.	8	. 116	..	4	. 252	..	3	. 215
xxi.	10	. 116	..	5	. 252	..	4	109, 116
..	27	. 116	xviii.	28	. 205	..	5	100, 116, 215
..	40	. 213	xix.	15	. 174	..	7	. 174
xxii.	7	. 116	..	18	. 174	..	12	. 230
..	8	. 199	..	25	188, 251	vii.	9	116, 117
..	22	206, 208	xx.	13	. 109	viii.	3	. 116
xxiv.	2	. 216	xxi.	19	. 221	..	13	. 148
..	3	116, 118	..	20	. 117	..	20	208, 209
..	4	. 149	..	22	. 119	ix.	1	116, 193
..	8	116, 118				..	2	. 141
..	14	149, 214		RUTH.		..	3	. 252
..	15	116, 189	i.	3	. 118	..	7	. 200
..	19	. 116	..	5	. 221	..	8	. 245
..	22	. 149	..	9	177, 236	..	9	. 206
			..	12	118, 177	..	26	116, 118
	JUDGES.		..	20	. 172	x.	5	. 141
i.	8	. 149	ii.	1	. 118	..	10	. 139
..	31	. 178	..	4	. 216	..	11	. 158
ii.	1	233, 262	..	8	. 200	..	12	. 158
iii.	26	. 173	..	12	. 203	..	14	. 218
iv.	18	. 174	..	16	. 164	..	18	. 216
..	21	. 171	..	22	. 200	..	21	116, 118
v.	8	. 205	iii.	3	. 200	..	22	. 262
..	15	. 249	..	4	. 141	xi.	6	116, 139, 188
..	22	. 223	..	5	. 109	..	9	116, 188
vi.	3	. 205	..	11	. 151	xii.	8	169, 237
..	4	. 214	..	12	. 110	..	10	116, 117
..	5	. 186	..	13	. 230	..	23	. 140
..	8	. 216	..	17	109, 192	..	24	. 149
..	10	. 152	iv.	4	. 118	xiii.	8	116, 118
..	19	. 250	..	6	. 182	..	19	116, 117
..	28	. 208	..	8	. 168	xiv.	4	. 152
vii.	12	. 213	..	9	. 214	..	6	. 208
..	21	. 118	..	12	. 141	..	13	. 262
..	22	. 226	..	15	. 205	..	19	. 262
viii.	2	. 198	..	18	. 168	..	27	116, 150, 191, 252
..	10	. 213				..	32	116, 184, 189
ix.	2	. 208		1 SAMUEL.		..	33	170, 171
..	3	. 261	i.	1	. 232	..	36	. 262
..	37	. 245	..	9	. 236	..	52	. 207
..	41	. 171	..	17	170, 215	xv.	6	. 218
..	56	. 252	..	26	176, 177	..	13	166, 167
x.	13	. 150	ii.	3	. 116	..	16	116, 117
xi.	14	. 245	..	9	116, 183	xvi.	2	. 262
..	18	. 258	..	10	. 116	..	4	. 148
..	27	. 218	..	15	. 200	..	7	. 222
..	34	. 225	..	24	159, 163	..	12	. 262
..	37	. 118	..	26	. 141	..	15	. 139
xii.	5	. 237	iii.	2	. 116	..	16	. 139
xiii.	8	. 153	..	6	. 245	..	23	. 139
..	17	. 183	..	8	. 245	..	24	. 116
..	18	. 171	..	18	. 116	xvii.	1	. 233
..	21	. 205	..	21	. 245	..	7	116, 189
xiv.	8	. 223	iv.	4	. 155			

1 SAMUEL.			Chap.	Ver.	Page.	Chap.	Ver.	Page
Chap.	Ver.	Page.	xxvi.	6	218	vii.	12	166
xvii.	17	172	..	7	216	..	23	220
..	18	236	..	11	216	..	29	221
..	23	116, 186	..	12	151	viii.	3	109, 192
..	26	200	..	14	218	..	8	221
..	27	200	..	15	216	x.	9	116
..	29	245	..	16	216	..	17	171
..	34	116	..	19	151	xi.	1	171
..	37	262	..	22	184, 216	..	13	213
..	45	200	..	23	200	..	24	171
..	47	200	xxvii.	4	116	xii.	3	237
xviii.	1	116, 233	..	8	116	..	4	200, 221
..	6	116, 119	..	10	218	..	7	216, 217
..	7	116	..	11	213	..	9	116, 200, 232
..	9	116	xxviii.	3	229	..	12	236
..	14	116	..	6	158	..	13	262
..	20	139	..	8	116, 182	..	20	116, 183
..	22	116	..	9	229	..	22	116, 186
..	25	226	..	16	240	..	24	116
..	29	149, 171, 245	..	21	202	..	31	116, 188
xix.	4	163	..	22	141	xiii.	7	174
..	12	251	..	24	222	..	18	150, 177, 250
..	18	116	xxix.	3	208, 209	..	32	116, 116
..	19	116	..	5	116	..	33	110
..	20	158	xxx.	1	218	..	34	116
..	21	245, 262	..	2	207	..	37	116, 189
..	22	116	..	6	116	xiv.	7	116, 119
..	23	116, 139	..	16	151	..	11	116
xx.	1	116, 119	..	22	207	..	15	214
..	2	116	..	24	116	..	21	116
..	3	206	xxxi.	7	196	..	22	116
..	8	226				..	30	116
..	13	141	2 SAMUEL.			..	31	174
..	17	245	i.	2	183	..	32	163
..	20	178, 253	..	8	116	..	50	223
..	24	116, 189	..	10	209, 216	xv.	5	208
..	29	219	..	11	116	..	8	116, 118
..	36	164	..	20	208	..	9	174
..	38	116	..	21	236	..	19	237
xxi.	2	237	ii.	1	174	..	20	116, 118
..	3	206	..	22	236, 245	..	21	119
..	12	116	..	23	116	..	28	116
..	14	183	..	35	166	..	29	252
xxii.	13	116	iii.	2	116	xvi.	2	116, 185
..	15	182	..	3	116	..	8	116
..	17	116, 232	..	12	116	..	10	116, 117
..	18	113	..	15	116, 119	..	11	239
..	22	116	..	22	225	..	12	116, 118
..	45	200	..	25	116	..	18	116
xxiii.	2	262	iv.	1	255	..	19	226
..	4	245	v.	1	174	..	21	109
..	5	116, 183	..	2	116, 192, 218	..	23	262
..	11	262	..	3	174	xvii.	6	217
..	20	118	..	8	116, 232	..	12	116
..	21	194	..	19	262	..	14	262
..	33	214	..	23	188	..	16	116
xxiv.	9	116, 181, 193	..	24	116, 141	..	20	174
..	19	116, 118	vi.	1	245	..	22	252
xxv.	3	116, 232	..	2	155	xviii.	2	212
..	6	218	..	20	255, 262	..	3	116, 118
..	12	207	..	23	116	..	8	116
..	18	116	vii.	4	262	..	9	150, 214
..	21	252	..	6	199	..	11	200
xxvi.	5	116	..	7	252	..	12	116, 190, 208

Chap.	Ver.	Page.
xviii.	13	116, 232
..	17	116, 255
..	18	116
..	20	109
..	22	141, 245
..	23	141
xix.	7	116
..	8	226
..	19	116
..	25	216
..	27	208, 209
..	32	116
..	41	116
xx.	5	116, 118
..	6	217
..	8	116
..	14	116
..	15	158, 165
..	23	116
..	25	116, 118
xix.	1	262
..	4	116
..	5	154
..	6	116, 262
..	9	116, 118, 220
..	12	116, 192
..	16	116, 190, 232
..	18	190
..	20	116, 118
..	21	116
xxii.	4	221
..	8	116
..	15	116
..	23	116, 232
..	25	252
..	30	177
..	33	116
..	34	116, 117
..	40	170
..	51	116, 218
xxiii.	1	205
..	3	190, 215
..	5	154, 200
..	8	116, 232
..	9	116, 184, 187
..	11	116
..	13	116
..	15	116, 171
..	16	116, 171
..	18	116
..	20	116, 171
..	21	116, 181
..	35	222
..	37	116
xxiv.	1	245
..	3	215
..	10	262
..	11	252
..	14	116, 183
..	16	113
..	18	116, 118, 2 4
..	22	116, 262
..	23	262
..	24	199, 150, 214

1 KINGS.

Chap.	Ver.	Page.
i.	1	117
..	20	218
..	21	214
..	24	217
..	31	149
..	37	118
..	40	220
..	41	223
..	51	249
..	53	170
ii.	5	148
..	6	148
..	30	252
..	33	189
iii.	2	287
..	5	215
..	11	215
..	14	187
..	17	167, 169
..	26	219
iv.	8	184
..	18	172
v.	17	232
..	23	218
..	26	148
vi.	4	155
..	5	119
..	20	217
..	21	113
..	25	155
..	27	155
vii.	6	155
..	13	156
..	21	155
..	20	184
..	23	118
..	36	117
..	45	116, 191
..	48	216
viii.	7	155
..	9	239
..	13	154
..	21	202
..	26	183, 215
..	34	175
..	39	175, 200
..	43	217
..	62	255
..	65	216, 255
ix.	5	149, 166
..	9	117
..	18	186
x.	2	174
..	5	183, 197
..	7	141
..	9	149
..	21	223
xi.	4	157
..	6	216
..	15	128
..	16	128, 255
..	17	171
..	31	216

Chap.	Ver.	Page.
xi.	36	157
..	39	171
xii.	3	117
..	5	163
..	7	117
..	21	117
xiii.	5	207
..	7	174
..	15	174
..	20	262
..	29	239, 240
..	33	141
xiv.	5	141
..	12	178
..	25	119
xv.	10	213
..	15	232
..	17	255
..	18	184
..	27	255
..	33	245
xvi.	9	172, 205
..	26	183
..	34	118
xvii.	12	202
..	13	232
..	14	216
..	23	117
xviii.	1	196
..	5	163
..	12	177, 196
..	24	207
..	27	224
..	36	183, 220
..	42	183
..	44	177
..	46	177
xix.	2	252
..	4	190
xx.	8	163
..	22	213
..	27	236
xxi.	2	141
..	6	199
..	8	149, 184
..	10	207
..	13	207
..	15	199
..	21	193
..	23	165
xxii.	13	183, 252
..	18	163
..	37	236
..	43	225
..	49	179

2 KINGS.

Chap.	Ver.	Page.
i.	15	149
..	17	262
ii.	9	141
..	21	171
..	22	170
iii.	11	149, 205
..	12	149

2 KINGS.			Chap.	Ver.	Page.	Chap.	Ver.	Page.
Chap.	Ver.	Page.	xix.	28	. 169	ix.	19	151, 216
iii.	13	. 218	..	34	. 217	..	23	. 213
...	19	. 237	..	37	. 109	..	33	. 118
..	24	. 188	xx.	3	. 265	x.	3	. 255
..	26	. 149	..	4	. 193	xi.	1	. 174
iv.	5	. 118	..	11	. 252	..	2	. 218
..	7	117, 184	..	12	. 171	..	3	. 174
..	32	. 174	..	13	. 241	..	17	. 207
..	34	. 183	..	18	. 117	..	23	. 194
..	39	. 225	xxi.	13	. 208	xii.	1	. 255
..	40	. 207	xxii.	1	. 213	..	3	. 119
v.	9	. 183	..	5	. 117	..	5	. 118
..	12	. 189	..	9	. 252	..	15	. 118
..	17	163, 211	..	14	. 222	..	23	. 174
..	18	109, 192	..	15	200, 216	..	30	273, 277
..	27	. 227	xxiii.	1	. 233	..	35	. 272
vi.	7	. 205	..	2	. 213	..	36	. 221
..	12	163, 252	..	6	. 250	..	38	170, 174
vii.	4	. 208	..	11	. 208	..	40	. 213
..	6	. 205	..	33	. 109	xiii.	4	. 255
..	12	177, 185	..	36	. 118	..	15	. 255
..	13	. 184	xxiv.	10	. 179	xiv.	15	. 141
..	14	. 209	..	13	. 250	xv.	28	. 159
..	15	. 185	..	15	118, 174	xvi.	2	. 250
viii.	8	. 149	..	16	. 174	..	18	. 232
ix.	4	. 197	xxv.	13	. 174	..	20	. 219
..	6	174, 216	xxix.	16	. 238	xvii.	2	. 266
..	14	. 252				..	5	. 199
..	17	. 201	1 CHRONICLES.			..	9	. 222
..	27	. 119	i.	1	186, 187,	..	21	. 168
..	28	. 174			188, 230	..	27	. 221
..	33	. 117	..	24	. 232	xviii.	10	. 182
..	37	. 118	..	46	. 117	xx.	5	. 119
x.	16	. 149	..	51	. 118	xxi.	22	. 199
..	19	. 216	ii.	8	. 226	..	24	. 199
..	22	. 250	..	13	. 117	xxii.	7	180, 232
..	27	. 216	..	49	. 127	..	15	. 214
xi.	1	. 117	..	55	. 232	..	16	. 141
..	2	. 116	iii.	19	. 226	xxiii.	12	. 228
..	18	. 183	..	21	. 226	..	14	. 250
..	20	. 184	..	23	. 226	..	30	. 214
xii.	10	. 189	..	24	. 117	xxiv.	11	. 233
xiii.	25	. 252	iv.	7	. 186	..	14	. 232
xiv.	6	. 116	..	17	. 226	..	24	. 119
..	7	. 184	..	19	. 208	xxv.	1	. 139
..	13	. 117	..	20	. 119	..	7	. 142
xv.	11	. 266	..	40	. 141	xxvii.	12	. 193
..	12	. 266	..	41	. 118	..	29	117, 119
..	20	. 250	v.	20	207, 208	xxviii.	10	. 214
..	25	. 184	..	26	170, 172, 215	..	19	. 171
xvi.	6	. 189	..	28	. 228	..	22	. 245
..	7	. 152	vi.	3	. 228	xxix	12	. 200
..	10	. 222	..	11	. 232	..	15	. 233
..	15	117, 236	..	20	. 118	..	22	. 241
..	17	117, 170	vii.	6	. 255	xxxiii.	11	. 236
..	18	118, 205	..	7	. 213	xxxiv.	16	. 252
xvii.	3	. 252	..	8	. 255			
xviii.	24	. 252	..	11	. 226	2 CHRONICLES.		
..	27	181, 194	..	31	. 118	i.	2	. 213
xix.	2	. 214	..	34	182, 186	..	11	212, 213, 215
..	15	139, 155	..	35	. 226	..	12	. 212
..	20	. 216	viii.	25	. 118	ii.	11	. 239
..	23	. 181	..	34	. 226	iii.	16	. 155
..	25	. 170	ix.	4	. 193	iv.	6	. 207

Chap.	Ver.	Page.	Chap.	Ver.	Page.	Chap.	Ver.	Page.
v.	12	155	xxxiii.	11	174	ii.	3	216
..	18	216	xxxiv.	6	193	..	14	218
..	19	216	..	9	187	iii.	6	213
vi.	9	226	..	12	153	..	7	199
..	11	202	..	14	220	..	13	170
..	18	214	..	22	182	..	15	117, 152
..	30	200	..	23	200	..	20	188
..	41	201	..	33	207	..	30	117
vii.	18	166	xxxv.	4	119	..	31	117
viii.	14	220	..	13	206	iv.	17	151
..	16	216	..	25	216	v.	5	213
ix.	13	213	xxxvi.	4	174	..	11	171
..	20	223	..	14	182	vi.	8	171
..	29	187				..	11	201
xi.	15	158	EZRA.			..	14	150
xii.	30	277	i.	1	172	..	17	152
..	32	276	..	4	199	vii.	8	213
xiii.	14	186	ii.	25	213	..	11	272
..	19	119	..	36	275	..	17	272, 273
xv.	1	139	..	38	273	..	31	213
..	6	219	..	42	275	..	37	213, 272
xvi.	7	170	..	46	117, 191	..	38	272
xvii.	8	117	..	50	118	..	42	274
..	11	117	..	59	208	..	44	277
xviii.	7	222	..	65	272	..	52	119
..	12	141	..	67	274	..	61	208
..	14	207	..	69	273	..	62	213
xix.	7	221	..	70	225	..	66	271
..	8	227	iii.	2	215	..	70	275
..	11	141	..	3	117	..	73	255
xx.	9	201	..	7	172, 221	viii.	6	208
..	26	216	iv.	2	108, 111	..	9	147
..	29	220	..	4	117	..	11	147
xxi.	17	220	..	7	183	ix.	6	118
xxii.	7	221	..	9	118	..	9	213, 241
..	10	222	..	12	192	..	17	117
xxiv.	6	216	..	22	172	..	15	175
..	20	139	v.	10	239	..	19	200
..	23	216	..	14	239	..	20	175
..	27	187	..	15	118, 181	..	23	219
xxv.	3	119	vi.	5	239	..	29	220
..	12	274	..	9	212	..	35	175
..	25	273	..	11	256	..	37	108
xxvi.	6	174	..	15	172	x.	20	119
..	10	174	vii.	17	212, 214	..	29	151, 213
..	21	119	..	25	255	..	30	213
xxvii.	9	152	..	26	232	xii.	9	232
xxix.	8	117	viii.	14	188	..	14	117, 187
..	9	213	..	17	117, 119	..	16	118
..	14	119	..	18	213	..	38	152, 171
..	22	174	..	25	182	..	42	207
..	24	174	ix.	4	215	..	44	171
..	26	227	..	5	220	xiii.	4	217
..	28	188	x.	5	255	..	16	171
xxx.	21	227	..	12	183	..	23	182
..	25	152	..	17	200	..	30	231
xxxi.	5	213, 214	..	29	186			
..	6	152	..	35	187	ESTHER.		
..	14	151	..	37	232	i.	5	117
..	15	220	..	43	232	..	6	230
..	17	220	..	44	187	..	8	208
xxxii.	9	174				..	16	117
..	21	232	NEHEMIAH.			ii.	2	148
xxxiii.	3	208	ii.	2	219	..	14	159

Chap.	Esther. Ver.	Page.	Chap.	Ver.	Page.	Chap.	Ver.	Page.
iii.	4	. 188	xviii.	28	. 200	xxxviii.	10	. 202
..	12	. 208	xix.	2	. 171	..	11	. 272
..	15	. 233	..	4	. 239	..	12	. 292
iv.	11	206, 264	..	17	. 205	..	19	. 209
..	14	. 151	..	29	. 118	..	30	. 239
v.	9	. 222	xx.	11	. 183	..	35	. 254
..	12	150, 170	..	13	. 255	..	39	. 221
vi.	9	. 200	..	17	. 214	..	41	. 183
..	11	. 200	xxi.	12	. 236	xxxix.	10	. 238
viii.	8	. 208	..	13	188, 201	..	26	. 183
..	11	. 213	..	42	. 221	..	30	. 183
..	13	. 119	xxii.	28	. 208	xl.	6	. 193
ix.	7	. 231	xxiii.	7	. 205	..	10	. 213
..	9	230, 231, 232	..	9	205, 249	..	11	. 222
..	16	. 206	xxiv.	1	. 183	..	17	. 183
..	22	. 221	..	2	. 155	..	30	. 223
..	27	. 117	..	5	. 220	xli.	7	. 170
..	28	. 213	..	6	. 118	xlii.	10	. 245
..	29	. 230	..	8	. 221	..	16	118, 278
..	32	. 221	..	14	. 240			
			..	22	. 206		Psalms.	
			..	24	. 222	i.	6	. 151
	Job.		xxv.	2	. 208	v.	9	119, 180
i.	1	. 171	xxvi.	8	. 205	vi.	4	. 118
..	10	. 118	..	12	117, 240	ix.	5	. 199
..	13	. 213	..	14	. 183	..	7	. 240
ii.	4	. 200	xxvii.	1	. 245	..	8	. 152
..	7	117, 184	..	2	. 215	..	10	. 141
iv.	14	. 208	..	7	. 207	..	13	. 109
v.	4	. 160	..	11	. 253	..	14	. 219
..	5	. 221	xxviii.	13	. 178	..	21	. 249
..	8	. 218	..	15	. 163	x.	6	. 164
vi.	2	. 118	..	27	. 178	..	8	. 177
..	22	. 205	xxix.	1	. 245	..	10	187, 193
..	29	. 187	..	2	. 214	..	12	. 109
..	13	. 230	..	16	. 222	..	14	. 156
..	40	. 223	xxx.	11	. 232	..	15	. 182
vii.	5	118, 231	..	22	. 119	xi.	1	. 232
..	20	. 205	..	30	. 205	xvii.	11	. 187
viii.	12	. 217	xxxi.	7	. 171	..	12	. 207
..	19	. 197	..	8	. 221	..	14	. 118
ix.	13	. 240	..	20	221, 283	..	25	. 252
..	26	. 201	..	22	171, 178	xviii.	1	. 150
..	30	. 232	..	35	. 197	..	3	. 203
..	33	. 245	xxxii.	4	. 178	xix.	3	. 221
..	34	. 230	..	6	. 223	..	6	. 207
x.	13	. 152	xxxiii.	5	. 178	..	9	. 208
..	17	. 236	..	9	. 231	..	12	. 232
..	20	. 186	..	12	. 197	xx.	4	. 162
xi.	2	. 166	..	19	. 118	xxii.	17	. 253
..	17	. 220	..	20	197, 223	..	27	207, 216
..	42	. 166	..	21	. 187	..	30	. 231
xii.	15	. 207	..	26	. 252	xxiii.	5	. 236
..	22	140, 250	..	28	187, 231	xxiv.	4	231, 232
xiv.	5	. 183	xxxiv.	31	. 208	..	6	182, 183
..	21	. 206	xxxv.	8	. 249	..	7	. 229
xv.	9	. 238	xxxvi.	1	. 245	..	8	. 229
..	15	. 183	..	11	. 201	..	9	. 229
..	27	. 217	..	14	. 208	xxv.	5	. 150
xvi.	11	207, 214	..	16	. 239	..	13	. 203
..	14	163, 231	xxxvii.	12	. 183	xxvii.	2	. 208
..	16	. 179	..	19	. 208	..	4	. 150
xviii.	11	. 222	xxxviii.	1	. 193	..	5	. 231
..	17	. 226	..	3	. 213	xxx.	6	. 220

Chap.	Ver.	Page.	Chap.	Ver.	Page.	Chap.	Ver.	Page.
xxx.	9	. 218	lxxii.	16	. 207	cvi.	45	. 183
xxxi.	4	. 217	..	17	. 118	cvii.	3	. 221
..	6	. 150	..	19	. 238	..	20	. 236
..	13	. 207	..	20	. 236	..	24	. 206
xxxii.	4	. 162	lxxiii.	2	117, 179	cviii.	7	. 232
xxxiii.	14	. 256	..	27	. 175	..	15	. 183
xxxiv.	8	. 206	..	28	. 223	cxv.	10	. 237
..	13	. 208	lxxiv.	5	. 206	..	15	. 155
..	27	. 254	..	6	. 118	cxviii.	8	. 203
xxxvii.	18	. 151	..	7	. 198	..	9	. 203
..	29	. 207	..	9	. 151	..	12	. 208
xxxix.	2	140. 163	..	11	. 119	cxix.	9	. 161
..	7	. 206	lxxv.	10	. 149	..	16	. 161
xl.	5	. 240	lxxvii.	12	118, 187	..	17	161, 183
..	17	. 252	..	13	. 162	..	28	. 161
xli.	3	. 186	lxxviii.	31	. 239	..	37	. 162
..	10	. 151	..	38	. 135	..	41	. 162
xlii.	5	152, 173	..	57	. 207	..	42	. 161
..	8	. 151	..	72	. 208	..	47	. 183
xliv.	17	. 221	lxxix.	10	. 118	..	48	. 201
xlv.	10	. 162	lxxx.	2	. 155	..	65	. 161
..	12	. 207	..	6	. 207	..	70	. 207
..	18	. 149	..	14	. 135	..	71	. 208
xlvi.	2	. 203	..	16	. 230	..	79	. 232
..	5	. 147	..	17	. 207	..	98	. 162
xlviii.	14	. 178	lxxxi.	16	. 141	..	105	. 161
xlix.	15	118. 236	lxxxiii.	12	. 207	..	107	. 161
l.	4	. 218	lxxxiv.	4	. 230	..	113	. 223
..	23	. 127	lxxxv.	2	. 119	..	119	. 175
li.	2	. 223	lxxxvii.	4	. 240	..	130	. 196
..	4	. 118	lxxxix.	10	. 217	..	161	. 183
lv.	13	. 201	..	11	171, 240	..	167	. 236
..	16	. 193	..	18	. 118	..	169	. 161
lvi.	1	. 150	..	29	. 152	cxxi.	3	. 162
..	5	. 246	..	40	. 175	..	6	. 177
..	7	. 118	..	49	. 216	cxxii.	2	. 161
..	12	. 246	..	51	. 214	cxxiii.	2	. 172
lvii.	2	. 203	xc.	8	118, 176	..	4	. 193
lviii.	6	. 152	..	10	. 240	cxxix.	3	. 119
..	8	. 183	..	11	. 151	..	5	. 207
..	12	. 201	..	17	. 141	cxxxi.	2	. 207
..	18	. 277	xci.	2	. 203	cxxxii.	11	. 199
lix.	3	. 221	..	12	. 162	..	12	. 199
..	13	. 221	..	16	. 222	..	15	. 178
..	16	. 119	xcii.	1	. 217	cxxxv.	18	. 212
lxi.	6	. 175	..	7	. 206	cxxxvi.	6	. 233
lxii.	9	. 203	..	8	. 207	..	11	. 250
lxv.	5	. 147	..	9	. 149	..	20	170, 240
..	11	. 220	..	20	. 232	cxxxviii.	3	. 240
lxvi.	7	. 118	xciii.	5	. 170	cxxxix.	5	. 177
..	9	. 116	xciv.	25	. 252	..	6	. 117
..	10	. 208	xcvii.	11	. 208	cxl.	10	. 119
..	15	233, 234	xcix.	6	. 170	cxli.	8	. 177
lxvii.	8	. 150	ci.	5	150, 182	..	11	. 118
lxviii.	31	220, 222	cii.	5	. 153	cxliv.	1	. 198
lxix.	7	. 215	ciii.	5	. 201	cxlv.	6	. 117
lxx.	5	. 254	..	19	. 200	..	8	. 182
lxxi.	4	. 205	civ.	29	. 205	..	10	. 177
..	7	203, 207	cv.	9	. 247	..	15	. 218
..	12	. 118	..	11	. 232	..	21	. 236
..	15	. 162	..	13	. 219	cxlvii.	19	. 183
..	20	. 232	..	28	. 183	cxlviii.	2	. 183
lxxii.	1	. 255	..	37	. 199	..	4	. 182
..	5	. 217	..	40	163, 183	cl.	5	. 205

PROVERBS.								
Chap.	Ver.	Page.	Chap.	Ver.	Page.	Chap.	Ver.	Page.
			xxii.	14	154, 182	vii.	23	118
i.	1	172, 230, 238	..	20	119	..	37	236
..	5	205	..	25	183	viii.	5	206
..	8	203	xxiii.	5	117, 119,	..	12	221
..	10	196			187, 201	..	15	200
..	15	223	..	7	205	ix.	2	200
..	19	205	..	13	236	..	4	117, 191
..	20	172	..	23	185	..	11	238
..	27	117, 207	..	24	117, 118, 184	..	12	206
..	29	246	..	26	117, 191	x.	3	185
ii.	7	187	xxiv.	10	177	..	14	206
..	11	177	..	12	206	..	18	208
..	22	256	..	29	200	..	23	184
iii.	6	196	xxv.	7	208	xi.	8	216
..	15	205	..	28	208	xii.	4	208
..	30	119	xxvi.	24	183	..	6	189
..	34	109	xxvii.	1	196	..	13	230
iv.	16	119	..	9	224			
v.	3	178	..	10	118	SONG OF SONGS.		
..	20	165	..	14	161, 214	i.	1	230
vi.	3	240	..	19	200	..	17	189
..	13	183	..	24	117, 184	ii.	2	207
vii.	13	205	..	26	221	..	11	163, 183
..	16	223	..	27	221	..	17	164
viii.	17	118	xxviii.	13	222	iii.	8	137
..	26	223	..	17	231	..	11	177
ix.	2	205	..	22	206	iv.	2	190
..	9	238	xxix.	21	191	..	3	207
x.	18	172	xxx.	10	183	..	4	157
xi.	3	187	..	14	221	..	5	208
..	11	220	..	15	231	v.	2	150, 222
..	25	172	..	18	118	..	6	222
..	26	205	..	24	205	..	11	150, 207
xiii.	20	117, 187	xxxi.	2	232	..	13	210
xiv.	12	225	..	10	178	..	15	207
..	21	102	..	16	118	vi.	5	240
..	22	213	..	18	118	vii.	4	208
xv.	23	206	..	21	154	viii.	9	232
..	27	216	..	23	220	..	10	171
..	33	217	..	27	117	..	12	274
xvi.	19	109						
..	21	206	ECCLESIASTES.			ISAIAH.		
..	27	183	i.	1	200, 236	i.	7	155
..	28	231	..	2	200	..	8	207
..	30	172	..	5	218	ii.	12	236
xvii.	10	205	..	16	228	iii.	5	240
..	13	118	ii.	1	201	..	15	193
..	14	217	..	18	200	..	16	119
..	27	187	..	22	200	..	24	196
xviii.	16	217	..	25	251	iv.	1	206
..	17	186	..	26	236	..	2	236
xix.	16	117	iii.	16	205	..	4	208
..	17	196	iv.	8	183	v.	8	199, 200
..	19	189, 223	..	14	170	..	24	207
xx.	3	200	v.	8	200	..	25	209
..	4	186	..	10	118	..	28	209
..	17	200	..	12	238	..	29	187
..	21	189	vi.	3	216	vi.	2	142
..	24	188	..	10	185	..	4	151
..	26	252	..	12	200	..	13	205
..	30	118	vii.	1	230	vii.	4	205
xxi.	4	164	..	19	201	..	10	245
xxii.	8	182, 251	..	21	227	..	15	201
..	11	208	..	22	118	..	16	201, 206

Chap.	Ver.	Page.	Chap.	Ver.	Page.	Chap.	Ver.	Page.
viii.	1	207	xxx.	5	171	xlix.	4	237
..	3	262	..	7	240, 241	..	6	118
..	4	206	..	9	229, 241	..	7	147
..	5	245	..	18	152	..	9	149
..	17	237	..	19	208	..	13	186
ix.	6	193, 196	..	29	222	..	15	205
..	15	221	..	32	178	..	22	234
x.	6	118	xxxi.	8	200	l.	7	202
..	13	171, 257	xxxii.	11	173, 205	li.	2	218
..	17	221	..	14	196	..	7	221
..	24	177	..	19	222	..	9	240
..	33	171	xxxiii.	7	193	..	13	226
xi.	11	221	..	12	172	..	16	202
xii.	5	118	xxxiv.	16	231	..	21	154
xiii.	2	141, 255	xxxv.	8	206	lii.	2	232
..	16	194	..	10	266	..	3	199
..	21	158	xxxvi.	9	252	..	5	183
xiv.	10	254	xxxvii.	6	150	..	6	206
..	12	152	..	16	139	..	12	215, 221
..	20	175	..	21	216	liv.	6	154
..	21	240	..	26	150	..	9	221
xvi.	3	222, 232	..	30	116, 117	..	13	227
..	4	222	..	32	139	..	15	150, 222
..	14	220	..	35	217	lv.	2	208
xvii.	13	207	xxxviii.	12	207	..	4	196
xviii.	1	206	..	16	196	..	7	218
..	4	182, 220	..	13	253	..	13	117, 184
..	5	178, 208	xxxix.	6	174	..	20	236
xix.	2	206	xl.	3	151	lvi.	10	230
..	3	218	..	12	222	lvii.	1	248
..	22	208	..	20	198	..	11	150
xxi.	2	178	..	22	207	..	19	119
..	5	213	..	24	205, 207	lviii.	2	150
..	13	208	..	27	202, 221	..	6	236
..	15	224	xli.	7	152	..	7	221
xxii.	23	199	..	9	221	..	9	201
xxiii.	1	247	..	17	215	lix.	18	154
..	13	118	..	23	118	lx.	5	240
..	17	178	..	25	171	..	21	232
..	11	178	xlii.	16	140	lxi.	1	208
xxiv.	2	152	..	20	118	..	10	207
..	10	207	..	24	119	lxii.	3	119
..	18	207	xliii.	9	254	..	4	206
..	19	205	..	14	174	lxiii.	2	221
xxv.	10	187	..	17	208	..	12	205
xxvi.	1	165	xliv.	6	221	lxiv.	6	151
..	2	174	..	14	231	lxv.	4	189
..	16	223	..	16	118, 201	..	7	189
..	20	182	..	17	182, 201	lxvi.	3	152, 241
xxvii.	4	213	..	24	193	..	4	246
..	9	222	xlv.	2	118	..	7	170, 196
..	11	150, 208, 222	..	3	151, 215	..	10	183
xxviii.	4	150, 178	..	8	207	..	17	190
..	12	172, 229	..	13	222	..	21	213
..	15	118	..	15	215			
..	17	196, 208	..	24	225	JEREMIAH.		
..	20	205	xlvi.	11	232	i.	1	187
xxix.	3	166	..	17	252	..	5	182
..	5	207	xlvii.	13	232	ii.	2	235
..	8	151	xlviii.	2	215	..	9	163
..	11	151, 184	..	7	217	..	13	171
..	18	221	..	8	162	..	14	201
..	23	215	..	10	199	..	15	197
xxx.	4	222	xlix.	1	208	..	16	186

JEREMIAH.

Chap.	Ver.	Page.	Chap.	Ver.	Page.	Chap.	Ver.	Page.
ii.	20	189	xiv.	9	239	xxvii.	1	142
..	21	152	..	10	141	..	16	174
..	25	116, 163	..	14	119	..	18	174
..	27	187	..	16	153	..	19	155
..	31	163	xv.	1	207	..	20	174
..	35	150	..	5	148	..	22	174
..	62	261	..	7	163	xxviii.	4	174
iii.	2	194	..	8	183	..	8	158
..	5	168	..	9	118, 163	xxix.	1	158, 174
..	7	118	..	11	119, 149, 163	..	3	174
..	9	166	..	16	183	..	4	174
..	12	163	xvi.	2	158	..	8	159
..	18	141, 255	..	9	254	..	10	166
..	19	221, 236	..	11	150	..	14	118
..	22	169	..	16	119	..	15	174
iv.	5	117	xvii.	1	236	..	20	174
..	11	163	..	7	196, 203	..	21	218
..	14	152	..	8	118	..	23	116, 151, 163, 196
..	16	241	..	11	183	..	24	218
..	22	150	..	13	186	..	25	177
..	23	218	..	19	184	..	32	201
..	29	169	..	23	116	xxx.	4	218
v.	8	240	..	26	213, 221	..	14	150
..	9	163	xviii.	3	193	..	16	171, 233
..	10	163	..	8	236	..	21	208
..	12	213	..	10	118, 150	xxxi.	10	196
..	13	158	..	16	119	..	23	216
..	22	150, 222	..	22	118	..	32	207
..	24	117	xix.	2	118, 235	..	34	150
..	28	207	xx.	3	250	..	38	109
vi.	7	118, 241	..	4	174, 200	..	39	226, 118
..	9	152, 163	..	5	174	..	40	189
..	14	229	..	11	150	xxxii.	8	202
..	21	186	..	17	178	..	17	139
..	25	147, 187	xxi.	3	214	..	21	171
..	29	193	..	4	216	..	23	116, 196
vii.	25	158	..	5	213	..	31	150
..	27	177	..	9	186	xxxiii.	2	150
..	28	163	..	13	190	..	4	218
..	31	237	xxii.	2	213	..	8	164, 182
viii.	1	117, 158	..	6	179	..	13	163, 222
..	6	116, 163	..	12	226	..	21	227
..	7	119	..	14	196	xxxiv.	2	216
..	11	229	..	22	221	..	5	251
..	20	163	xxiii.	4	116	..	13	216
ix.	5	150	..	5	116	..	14	236
..	7	116	..	16	241	xxxv.	4	221
..	9	236	..	18	187	..	8	255
..	23	150	..	21	216	..	10	255
x.	2	163, 199, 221	..	22	207	xxxv.	15	158
..	13	184, 250	..	24	139	..	18	241
..	18	152	..	27	226	xxxvi.	10	206
..	23	200	xxv.	3	171	..	12	152
xi.	17	150	..	6	150	..	13	220
xiii.	2	202	..	7	119	..	22	237
..	5	150, 222	..	9	218	xxxvii.	7	216
..	16	186	..	34	213	..	15	150
..	20	187	xxvi.	5	241	..	16	155
..	25	150	..	6	118	..	18	150
..	27	163	..	8	158	xxxviii.	2	186
xiv.	2	221	..	11	158, 200	..	11	184
..	3	119	..	15	159	..	12	171
..	8	240	..	16	200	..	16	110
			..	23	237			

Chap.	Ver.	Page.	Chap.	Ver.	Page.	Chap.	Ver.	Page.
xxxviii.	24	206	li.	48	255	v.	7	223
..	28	252	lii.	11	174	vi.	9	150
..	52	162	..	17	174	..	13	236
xxxix.	7	174	..	31	250	vii.	21	117
..	11	236	..	32	184, 199	viii.	1	152
..	12	110				..	4	215
..	13	231	LAMENTATIONS.			..	6	193
..	14	231	i.	1	193, 206, 238	ix.	3	215
..	15	213	..	6	181, 193	..	5	189
..	19	261	..	12	163, 231	..	6	213
xl.	1	174	..	16	152	..	8	171, 229
..	3	184	..	18	184	..	11	194
..	7	174	..	19	208, 209	x.	1	155
..	8	119	ii.	2	117, 184	..	2	155
..	12	233	..	4	207	..	3	155
..	15	177, 206	..	6	178	..	6	155
..	16	118	..	8	165	..	7	155
xli.	17	223	..	9	231	..	8	155
xlii.	9	216	..	11	206	..	10	202
..	20	116	..	12	208, 209	..	19	215
xliii.	10	119	..	14	118, 158	..	20	215
..	11	118	..	16	222	xi.	12	223
xliv.	6	214	..	19	118	..	13	229
..	10	217	iii.	2	150	..	22	215
..	13	182	..	4	220	..	24	139
xlv.	2	216	..	10	118	xii.	13	274
xlvi.	4	287	..	12	172	xiii.	14	222
..	8	253	..	20	118	..	16	148
..	12	163	..	36	231	xiv.	1	222
..	21	163	..	39	183	..	4	178
..	25	152	..	65	232	..	8	222
..	28	217	iv.	3	193	..	12	205
xlvii.	7	218	..	6	184	..	22	152
xlviii.	4	119	..	12	117	xv.	5	222
..	5	118	..	16	117	xvi.	4	150
..	7	117	..	17	197	..	39	150
..	9	196	..	20	236	..	40	150
..	18	186	v.	1	118	..	44	178
..	20	187	..	3	117, 184	..	56	163
..	21	119	..	4	199	..	57	150, 171
..	26	222	..	5	117, 184	..	59	150
..	27	118	..	7	117, 184	..	60	150, 166
..	40	201	..	18	185	..	62	166
xlix.	3	163, 177	..	21	118, 236	xvii.	12	174
..	16	201				..	17	150
..	20	168	EZEKIEL.			..	20	174, 222
..	22	201	i.	1	171, 172, 237	..	21	184
..	30	190	..	2	238	xviii.	6	266
l.	1	115	..	8	232	..	13	216
..	6	118, 173	..	10	224	..	14	196
..	8	184	..	14	172	..	17	241
..	11	187	ii.	3	150	..	20	184
..	15	115	..	4	150	..	22	216
..	18	213	iii.	15	152, 190, 193	..	27	216
..	21	147	..	16	262	xix.	14	205
..	25	250	..	23	207	xx.	16	241
..	29	109, 161	..	27	150	..	20	255
li.	3	110, 192	iv.	9	152	..	24	241
..	9	171	..	10	221	..	31	216
..	10	202	..	12	208	..	38	225
..	16	250	..	14	213	xxi.	16	152
..	27	241	..	15	119	..	28	182
..	34	232	..	17	236	xxii.	14	150
..	43	196	v.	6	241	..	15	150

Chap.	Ver.	Page.	Chap.	Ver.	Page.	Chap.	Ver.	Page.
xxii.	18	. 119	xxxix.	11	. 179	iv.	4	185, 221
..	20	. 155	..	16	. 178	..	6	. 208
xxiii.	16	. 118	..	26	. 170	..	9	. 117
..	23	. 147	xl.	3	. 150	..	16	. 240
..	25	. 150	..	4	. 177	v.	7	. 117
..	29	. 150	..	15	. 116	..	8	. 185
..	35	. 150	..	19	. 205	..	10	. 185
..	40	. 239	..	22	. 183	..	20	. 209
..	42	. 218	..	26	. 183	..	21	. 117
..	43	118, 179	..	43	. 218	..	29	. 117
..	44	. 225	..	48	. 165	vi.	10	. 223
xxiv.	2	. 212	..	49	. 155	..	20	. 230
..	6	. 178	xli.	8	. 118	..	21	. 231
..	11	. 205	..	15	119, 172	vii.	7	. 238
..	16	. 163	xlii.	4	. 217	..	9	. 222
..	27	. 202	..	9	119, 192	..	10	. 230
xxv.	6	. 171	..	13	. 147	..	12	. 206
..	7	. 190	..	14	186, 196	..	13	. 238
..	8	. 208	..	16	. 117	viii.	22	. 155
xxvi.	7	. 213	..	20	. 205	..	23	. 221
xxvii.	12	. 199	..	24	. 222	ix.	5	. 117
..	15	. 182	xliii.	2	. 215	..	12	183, 208, 209
..	20	. 178	..	10	. 217	..	18	. 118
..	30	. 241	..	15	. 117	..	19	. 173
xxviii.	8	. 176	..	16	. 117	..	21	. 222
..	9	132, 208	..	17	. 222	..	24	. 189
..	13	. 249	..	20	150, 218	x.	12	. 175
..	16	. 170	..	23	. 220	..	13	. 252
..	23	. 200	..	27	. 171	..	18	. 245
..	24	. 171	xliv.	1	. 252	xi.	6	. 221
..	26	. 171	..	3	. 182	..	12	171, 189
xxix.	5	. 150	..	5	. 186	..	18	. 189
..	19	. 178	..	15	. 262	..	31	. 150
xxx.	16	. 118	..	22	. 213	..	33	. 200
xxxi.	4	. 222	..	24	187, 222, 241	..	38	. 214
..	5	172, 183	xlv.	3	. 118	..	44	172, 238
..	7	. 222	..	7	. 252	xii.	13	149, 218
..	11	. 222	..	21	. 141			
..	13	. 218	..	23	. 237	**Hosea.**		
..	18	. 179	xlvi.	9	. 117	i.	1	186, 187, 188
xxxii.	13	. 159	..	15	. 187	..	6	. 237
..	25	. 162	xlvii.	8	. 152	ii.	2	. 214
..	30	. 198	..	9	. 216	iii.	1	. 154
..	31	. 179	..	10	. 178	iv.	6	. 171
..	32	179, 232	..	11	. 183	..	8	. 218
xxxiii.	9	. 218	..	12	. 152	..	19	. 150
..	30	. 252	..	13	. 190	v.	12	. 207
..	31	141, 255	..	14	. 118	..	14	. 207
xxxiv.	23	. 157	xlviii.	16	. 110	vi.	2	208, 209
..	29	. 166	..	35	. 276	..	3	. 173
xxxvi.	3	. 213				..	10	. 118
..	5	172, 178	**Daniel.**			vii.	2	. 221
..	11	169, 214	i.	4	. 171	..	12	. 226
..	12	. 179	..	5	. 214	viii.	1	. 201
..	14	. 116	..	13	. 196	..	10	. 213
..	20	222, 225	ii.	9	. 186	..	12	182, 232
xxxvii.	9	. 207	..	22	. 118	ix.	10	178, 207
..	10	. 207	..	39	. 172	..	11	. 221
..	22	. 179	..	43	117, 179	..	15	. 152
..	24	236, 241	iii.	5	. 238	x.	6	. 150
xxxviii.	4	. 150	..	10	. 118	..	10	. 118
..	9	. 207	..	19	. 232	..	14	. 171
..	17	. 150	..	27	. 238	xi.	9	. 224
xxxix.	2	. 171	..	29	172, 179	xii.	1	. 163

297

Chap.	Ver.	Page.
\multicolumn{3}{c}{HOSEA.}		
xii.	10	163
xiii.	6	207
..	14	208
..	15	214
xiv.	4	222
..	6	207
..	7	141
..	10	159

JOEL.

Chap.	Ver.	Page.
i.	20	236
ii.	2	212
..	6	171
..	17	254
iv.	3	218
..	8	208
..	11	208, 209
..	16	203
..	17	255
..	19	172

AMOS.

Chap.	Ver.	Page.
iii.	9	241
iv.	1	151
..	2	206
..	10	171
v.	7	221
..	8	151
..	14	141
..	19	226
vi.	9	199
..	12	221
vii.	8	182
..	14	152, 205
viii.	3	182
..	4	119
..	8	186
ix.	1	207
..	3	239
..	4	239
..	8	206
..	13	152

OBADIAH.

Chap.	Ver.	Page.
i.	4	201
..	10	176
..	11	183

Chap.	Ver.	Page.
i.	16	223, 228
..	20	154, 165, 260

JONAH.

Chap.	Ver.	Page.
i.	14	172, 226
iii.	2	235
iv.	9	215
vi.	13	236

MICAH.

Chap.	Ver.	Page.
i.	2	141, 160
..	3	182
..	7	132
..	8	118
..	13	239
..	15	163
..	16	201
ii.	7	208
iii.	2	118
..	11	199
iv.	9	248
v.	10	240
..	13	240
vi.	4	213
vii.	9	140

NAHUM.

Chap.	Ver.	Page.
i.	2	152
..	3	182, 231
..	4	152
..	13	222
ii.	6	118
..	11	171
..	14	178
iii.	3	186
..	12	151

HABAKKUK.

Chap.	Ver.	Page.
i.	8	201
..	13	208
..	15	196, 207
..	16	221
ii.	2	151
..	4	216
..	6	201
iii.	10	213
..	14	183

ZEPHANIAH.

Chap.	Ver.	Page.
i.	9	152
..	17	200
ii.	7	119
iii.	5	140
..	7	178

HAGGAI.

Chap.	Ver.	Page.
i.	8	111, 118
..	12	226
..	13	171
ii.	6	139
..	21	139
..	22	200

ZECHARIAH.

Chap.	Ver.	Page.
i.	4	183
..	8	206
..	16	118
ii.	6	212
..	12	219
iii.	10	236
iv.	7	178
vi.	8	152
..	11	205
vii.	10	213
viii.	20	163
ix.	4	178
..	10	208
x.	5	220
..	10	221
xi.	2	119
..	5	171
xiii.	9	208
xiv.	2	194
..	6	186
..	18	237

MALACHI.

Chap.	Ver.	Page.
i.	3	202
..	12	150
..	13	150
..	14	152
ii.	12	206, 221
iii.	10	141
..	22	150, 230, 236

2 MACCABEES.

ii	5	119

INDEX II.

MASSORETIC LISTS QUOTED ENTIRE.

א

א how many times found in the Bible, 271.
Sixteen words with silent Aleph, or altogether without Aleph, 170.
Seventeen words which occur only once with audible Aleph, 171.
Fifty words which have only once silent Aleph in the middle, 171, 185.
Twelve words which have only once quiescent Aleph at the end, 172.
Seventeen words with quiescent Aleph at the end, which have no parallel, 172.
אבנב, Alphabetical list, according to, 223.
אבותך three times, 251.
אהלה occurs four times, 179.
איוב three times definite, 149.
אותה twelve times plene, 150.
אותו twenty-four times plene, 149, 150.
אותי twenty-seven times plene, 150.
אותיות גדולות, Alphabetical lists of, 230.
אותיות קטנות, Alphabetical lists of, 231.
אותך masculine, seventeen times plene, 150.
אותך feminine, seventeen times plene, 150.
אותם thirty-nine times plene, 150.
אחד twenty-five times, 252.
אחו three times with Kametz and Pattach, 249.
אל thirty times construed with other words in an unparalleled manner, 218.
אלהי ישראל twenty-eight times, 215.
אם five times, supposed to be wanting in the text, 226.
אם three times before אב, 241.
אני יהוה twenty times at the end of a verse, 255.
אני יהוה אלהיכם twenty-one times at the end of a verse, 255.
אעלה Hiphil future eight times, 233.
ארצה כנען eight times, 174.
אשר in four times, supposed to be כאשר, 226.
את השמים ואת הארץ occurs thirteen times, 139.
אתבש, Alphabetical list of words, according to, 222.
אתה eleven times in an unique construction, 217.

ב

ב how many times found in the Bible, 272.
Twenty-six words which occur only once with Beth, and which in all other instances have Kaph, 220.

Eleven words with Beth in the textual reading, and Kaph in the marginal reading, 188.
Six words with Beth in the textual reading, and Mem in the marginal reading, 189.
בבית six times Raphe, 199.
בגלה twenty-nine times, 174.
בבהמה four times Raphe, 200.
בהן fifteen times with Tzere, 195.
בואכה six times, 177.
בחרב eight times Raphe, 200.
בחרו three times with Kametz under the Cheth, 246.
בטוב four times Raphe and nine times with Dagesh in the Teth, 201.
בכל seven times with Dagesh in the Kaph, 200.
בכסף fifteen times Raphe, 200.
בליליה three times Raphe, 200.
בן in four instances, supposed to be בני, 225, 226.
בעוף three times, 251.
ברא אלהים three times, 139, 215.
בראשית begins a verse three times, 142.
בשדה five times Raphe, 200.

ג

ג how many times found in the Bible, 272.
גבור three times defective, 148.
גורל four times defective, 149.

ד

ד how many times found in the Bible, 272.
Two words with Daleth at the end in the textual reading, and Resh in the marginal reading, 189.
Two words with Daleth in the marginal reading, and with Tav in the textual reading, 196.
דבריך plural, thirteen times defective, 161.
דבריך eight times with Jod plural in the textual reading, but without it in the marginal reading, 183.
דרכיך three times defective, 162.

ה

ה how many times it occurs in the Bible, 274.
ה in twenty-nine instances, is wanted in the textual reading, but is supplied in the marginal reading, 117, 118.

ה in twenty instances is in the textual reading, but not in the marginal reading, 118.

Thirteen words without He at the beginning in the textual reading, but with it in the marginal reading, 184.

Seven words with He at the beginning in the textual reading, but not in the marginal reading, 184.

Five words with He in the middle in the textual reading, and without it in the marginal reading, 185.

Twelve words with He second radical, whilst in all other instances it is Cheth, 240.

Thirty-two words ending in He and Vav, 222.

Fourteen words terminating with He in the textual reading, and with Vav in the marginal reading.

Twenty-one words with He at the end after Kaph, second person singular masculine, 177.

Eleven words which respectively occur twice, once with audible, and once with quiescent He, 178.

Eighteen words which abnormally terminate with quiescent He, 178.

Two instances in which the textual reading has הם suffix, third person plural masculine, and the marginal reading כם suffix, second person plural masculine, 190.

האהלה eight times, 174.
הביתה eighteen times, 174.
המונה four times, 179.
המובחה thirty times, 174.
הקימותי twice entirely plene, eleven times entirely defective, and six times Jod plene, and Vav defective, 166.
ה׳ five times with Segol, 197.

ו

ו how many times it occurs in the Bible, 272, 273.

Twenty-three verses which have neither Vav nor Jod, 282.

ו conjunctive in eleven instances in the Kethiv, but not in the Keri, 117.

ו suffix, not in the Kethiv in eighteen instances, but in the Keri, 117.

ו suffix in eleven instances in the textual reading, but not in the marginal, 117.

ו in seventy-five instances, to be found in the middle of, or in, the textual reading for which the marginal reading has Vav.

Ten words beginning with Vav in the marginal reading, and with Jod in the textual reading, 187.

Twenty-five words with Vav plene, without parallel, 151, 152.

List of thirty-three words with Vav after Kametz and Chateph-Kametz in the textual reading, and without Vav in the marginal reading, 182.

Forty-eight words terminating in Vav in the textual reading, and in Jod in the marginal reading, 232.

Twenty-two words beginning and ending with Vav, which occurs twice, once Milel, and once Milra, 207.

Five pairs of words which respectively occur twice, once with Vav conjunctive, and once without, 212.

Sixty-two pairs of words in which both numbers have Vav conjunctive, 213.

Sixteen pairs without Vav conjunctive, 213, 214.

Twenty-seven words beginning with Vav and Mem, 221.

Thirteen words beginning with Vav, Mem, and Beth, 221.

Twelve words beginning with Vav, Mem. and Gimmel, 221, 222.

Four proper names occurring five times in the same order, but with the Vav conjunctive differently placed in each passage, 228.

Six verses having the same words four times twice with Vav conjunctive, and twice without it, 224.

Four verses having respectively the same word four times, the first with Vav, and the other three without it, 215.

Forty-eight words in the textual reading with Vav at the end, and in the margin with Jod, 282.

ואדע three times, 202.
ואל forty-five times in an unparallelled construction, 218.
ואם three times at the beginning of a verse, 238, 239.
ואת nine times at the beginning of a verse, 239.
ואשא twice with Sheva under the Vav, 201.
ואשים nine times with Kametz under the Vav, 202.
ואתה eight times in an unique construction, 218.
ויאמר six times with Sheva under the Vav, 201.
ויאמר אלהים twenty-five times, 215.
ויאמרו nine times with Sheva under the Vav, 254.
ויאספו Kal ten times, 233.
ויבא in eight instances, supposed to be ויבאו, 225.
ויבאו with Sheva under the Vav, occurs seven times, 141, 254, 255.
ויבדל occurs three times, 139, 142.
וידבר אלהים three times, 215.
וידבר יהוה אל משה ואל אהרן occurs twelve times, 139, 140.
ויהי occurs thirty-two times, 141, 202
ויוסף thirty times, 245.

ויוסף twice Milel, 205.
ויוצא twelve times plene, 250.
וינחהו Hiphil defective, seven times defective, 239, 240.
וישב twenty-five times, 252.
וכל ישראל thirty-five times in the middle of the verse, 255.
ולמען nine times, 217.
ולפני sixteen times, 217.
ונשמע three times with Pattach under the Vav, and Dagesh in the Mem, 255, 256.
והדבר twice with Shurek, 202.
ותורד three times, 251.
ותשמע twice with Sheva under the Vav, 201.

ז
ז how many times found in the Bible, 273.
זכרון three times definite, 148.

ח
ח how many times found in the Bible, 273.
Four words with Cheth in the textual reading, and with He in the marginal reading, 189.
חברונה five times, 174.
חותם seven times definite, 149.
חיל five times definite, 165.
חלופין, 113.
חסיה nine times with Chateph-pattach, 203.

ט
ט how many times found in the Bible, 273.
טהורים see עפולים.

י
י how many times it occurs in the Bible, 273.
Twenty-two words with Jod at the beginning in the textual reading, and with Vav in the marginal reading, 186.
Fifty-five words with Jod in the middle in the textual reading, and without Jod in the marginal reading, 183.
Twenty-four words with Jod at the end in the textual reading, and Vav in the marginal reading, 187.
י in seventy instances in the middle of a word in the textual reading, for which Vav is to be found in its marginal reading.
יאכל occurs seventy-three times, 141.
יברכך יהוה four times, 216.
ידע nineteen times, 206.
יודע twenty-three times plene, 151.
יהיה eighteen times, 216.
יהי twice, 216.
יוצאים four times plene, 152.
יושבים ten times plene, 152.
יעטף occurs twice, 142.
יקרא twenty-one times, 206.
ירושלימה five times, 174.
ישגלנה four times, altered into ישכבנה, 194.

כ
כ how many times found in the Bible, 274.
Those words beginning with Kaph in the textual reading, and Beth in the marginal reading, 188.
Twenty-one words beginning with Kaph, which occur twice, once Milel and once Milra.
כה אמר יהוה אלהי ישראל twenty-five times, 216.
כנשר four times Raphe, 201.
כרובים thirteen times defective, 155.
כתיב in fifteen instances one word, and the Keri two words; and in eight instances two words, and the Keri one word, 198.
כתיב ולא קרי eight instances, 110, 192.

ל
ל how many times found in the Bible, 274.
Fifteen words beginning with two Lameds, 220, 221.
לא once in four phrases, and once not, 223.
לאדם eleven times with Kametz under the Lamed, 200.
לאהל five times, 216.
לאור occurs seven times, 140.
לוא thirty-five times plene, 163.
למוב twice Raphe, 200.
לאיש thirty-two times with Kametz under the Lamed, 200.
לכסא six times Raphe, 199.
לעולם eighteen times defective, 149.

מ
מ how many times found in the Bible, 275.
מאכל four times with Pattach, 197.
מוקדמין ומאוחרין sixty-two instances of, 116, 117, 191.
מורדפין six verses, 219.
מורדפין six words, 219.
מחמא occurs three times, 140.
מלין, sixteen words without parallel, 236.
מלין, twenty-one, which respectively occur only once in a particular book, 236, 237.
מלין, fifty-one, which always occur in a certain form in one book, but which in all other books of the Scriptures occur in a different form, 237, 238.
מלעיל thirty-eight words only once Milel, 205.
מלרע twenty-two words only once so, 205.
מלעיל ומלרע an alphabetical list of words, 208.
ממנו in six instances supposed to be ממנח, 225.
מעשר three times with Sheva under the Ajin, 204.
מפני three times supposed to be מפי, 226.
מצרימה twenty-eight times, 174.
משפטי precedes חקתי eight times, 241.

נ

נ how many times found in the Bible, 275.
נער written so twenty-one times in the text, and in the marginal reading נערה, 109.
נשיאם four times, 157.
נחה twenty-nine times, 175.

ס

ס how many times found in the Bible, 275.
סמיך thirty-nine instances in which the construction is inverted, 214, 215.

ע

ע how many times found in the Bible, 276.
עד היום nine times, 216.
עור fourteen times defective, 163.
עור eight times in the sense of enemy, 240.
על nine times, supposed to be עד, 226.
על twice in the textual reading, but אל in the marginal reading, 189.
עמודים eleven times defective, 155.
עניים five times in the Kethiv, and in the Keri עניום, 109.
עפולים six times in the Kethiv, and in the Keri מחורים, 109, 194.

פ

פ how many times found in the Bible, 276.
Pattach with Athnach, list of instances, 197.
פני תהום occurs twice, 199.

צ

צ how many times found in the Bible, 276, 277.
צוער three times plene, 151.

ק

ק how many times found in the Bible, 277
קדוש thirteen times defective, 147.
קדוש the construct, three times defective, 147.
קורא ten times plene, 151.
קרי ולא כתיב ten instances, 109.

ר

ר how many times found in the Bible, 277
רוח אלהים occurs eight times, 139, 141.

ש

ש how many times found in the Bible, 277.
Four words with Resh in the textual reading, and Daleth in the marginal reading, 189.
שדם four times without את, 241.
שלום eight times defective, 148.
שמע twelve times construed with על, 241.

ת

ת how many times found in the Bible, 278.
תולעת twice defective, 151.
תנינים three times withe Jod plural, 157.
תסף three times Milra, 205.

INDEX III.

MASSORETIC TERMS AND ABBREVIATIONS EXPLAINED.

	Page.		Page.		Page.
אבבג	223	ירושלמי	260	סמיכין	212–214
אותיות גדולות	230	כ״כ	252	ס״פ	255
אותיות קטנות	231	כל״י	252	ספרא	236–239
אמצה	190, 191	כ״ק	254	ספר הללי	260
א״מ א״ח	250	כתיב ולא קרי	110, 192	פתח	195, 196
אמ׳ת	248	ל׳	245	ענינא	241
אנ־ך	246	לית	245	ע״ס	258
אס׳ח	248	ל׳ד	254	פ״ד	253
אספמיא	260	ל׳ק	252	פסוק	242
אפ״ס	246	לשנא	239–241	פסקא	209, 210
אשלמתא	261	מדינחא	261	פסקא דספרא	209, 210
אחבש	222	מוקדמין ומואחרין	191	פריגמא	262
אתין	228, 229	מורדפין	218, 219	פשטין	233
ב״ח	250	מזוורתא	259	פתח דספרא	197
ב״מ	250	ממעין	227, 228	קטיעא	232, 233
במ״א	250	מיסון	262	קטיעין	230
במ״ב	250	מלא	145–148	קמץ	195, 196
ג״ח	250	מלא דמלא	167	קרחי	224, 225
ג״מ	250	מס״ה	249	קרי	180, &c.
דגש	197, 198	מ״פ	255	קריא	234–238
דכותיה	212	מלעיל	204, &c.	קרי ולא כתיב	109, 198
דמין	211, 212	מלרע	204, &c.	רבתא	231
ודאין	232–234	מפיק	199	רי״ן	258
זוגין	211	מ״ש	257	רמ״ח	256
זעירא	231	מישמשין	220–224	ר״פ	254
הומש יריחו	259, 260	נ״א	256	רפה	197, &c.
חסר	145–148	נוסחא	262	שב״נ	248
חסר דחסר	116	נסיבין	219, 220	שוא	202, &c.
יהב״י	257	נפתלי	260	שימא	210, 211
יחידאין	215–218	סבירין	225–227	תא״ם	248
ימ׳ה	250	סיני	259	היבין	229

INDEX IV

MASSORETIC LISTS QUOTED IN THIS BOOK, WHICH ARE ALSO FOUND IN THE OCHLA VE-OCHLA.

OCHLA VE-OCHLA. Section.	LEVITA. Page.	OCHLA VE-OCHLR. Section.	LEVITA. Page.	OCHLA VE-OCHLA. Section.	LEVITA. Page.
v.	208	cxi.	118	clii.	185
xi.	207	cxii.	113	cliv.	189
xv.	200	cxiii.	179	clxvii.	189
xviii.	221, 222	cxvii.	117	clxix.	194
xxxvii.	223	cxviii.	117	clxx.	109
xxxviii.	222	cxix.	117	clxxxi.	186
xliii.	178	cxx.	117	ccv.	240
xliv.	178	cxxi.	189	ccxv.	220
xlv.	207	cxxii.	189	ccxxi.	236, 237
lxxx.	118	cxxiii.	189	ccxxii.	238
lxxxi.	119	cxxviii.	183	ccxxiv.	229
lxxxii.	230	cxxx.	161, 183	ccl.	223
lxxxiii.	250	cxxxi.	183	ccli.	212
lxxxiv.	231	cxxxiv.	186	cclii.	214
lxxxv.	218	cxxxv.	187	ccliii.	213
xci.	117	cxxxvi.	232	cclxi.	217
xcii.	177	cxxxvii.	188	cclxii.	218
xcvii.	110	cxliv.	109	cclxx.	236
xcviii.	110	cxlv.	184	cclxxiii.	214, 215
xcix.	193	cxlvi.	184	cclxxviii.	241
c.	193	cxlviii.	171	cclxxxviii.	228
cii.	195	cxlix.	170, 188	ccclxxii.	205
ciii.	171	cl.	188	ccclxxiii.	205
civ.	172	cli.	190	iv. additions	205

INDEX V.

TOPICS AND NAMES.

A

ABBAG, alphabet denominated, 223.
ABRAVANEL, Isaac, 9, 10; his view of the Keri and Kethiv, 107.
——— Samuel, 12.
ACHA of Irak, his system of vowel-points, 61, 63.
ADRIAN, Matthew, 66.
ALCALA, Alphonso de, his contributions to the Complutensian Polyglott, 9.
ALLEMANO, Jochanan, 11, 12.
ALMANZI, Guespo, 45.
ARAMA, Isaac, 10.
——— Moses, 10.
ATHBACH, alphabet denominated, 190, 191.
ATHBASH, alphabet denominated, 222.

B

BABA Buch, see LEVITA.
BACHUR, see LEVITA.
BAEHR, on the Poetical Accents, 65.
BALMES, Abraham de, 10; his Hebrew Grammar, 17, 21, 195.
BARUCH of Benevent, 12.
BEN-ASHER, 45, 65, 113, 114.
BENJAMIN of Rome, 81.
BEN-NAPHTALI, 45, 114.
BERAB, Jacob, 10.
BIBLE, the, by whom arranged and divided, 120.
BIBLES, Rabbinic, 9.
BLACK, W. H., his opinion about the design of the majuscular letters, 231.
BLAYNEY, 60.
BOMBERG, Daniel, his Hebrew publications, 21; his connection with Levita, 22.
BOOTHROYD, Dr., 60.
BROUGHTON, Hugh, his opinion of the vowel-points, 51.
BUBER, Life of Levita, 3, 78.
BUXTORF, the father, his defence of the antiquity of the vowel-points, 53, 54, 55–57.

C

CALVIN, 48, 49.
CAPITO, W. F., his date, contributions to Hebrew literature, &c., 66.
CAPPELLUS, Lewis, his controversy with the Buxtorfs about the antiquity of the vowel-points, 54–57.

CARO, Isaac b. Joseph, 10.
CHAJATH, Jehudah b. Jacob, 12.
CHAJUG Jehudah, 20.
CHRONOLOGY, Jewish, 3.
CLARK, Samuel, on the antiquity of the vowel-points, 59.
COMPOUNDS, book on the, see LEVITA.
CONJECTURAL Readings, 225–227.
COOPER, Joseph, on the antiquity of the vowel-points, 59.
CORBEIL, Isaac de, the author of the Compendium of R. Moses' work on the Commandments and Prohibitions, 250.
CORONEL, Paul, his connection with the Complutensian Polyglott, 9.
COUTHIN, Ferdinand, Bishop of Algarve, his description of the heart-rending scenes at the compulsory baptisms of Jewish children, 8.
CRETENSIS, see MEGIDO.

D

DAVIDSON, A. B., Outlines of Hebrew Accentuation, 65.
DAVILA, 9.
DEFECTIVES, 145–148.
DUREN, Isaac, 2.

E

EGIDIO, Cardinal, his interview with Levita, 14, 15; instigates Levita to write the Hebrew Grammar, 16; his connection with Levita, 96, &c.
EPHODI, his view of the origin of the Keri and Kethiv, 206; Grammatical work, 107.
EWALD, Jahrbücher, 62.
EZEKIEL, the Vision of, 98.

F

FAGIUS, Paul, his date, 66; connection with Levita, 67; printing establishment and contributions to Hebrew literature, 68–78.
FARISSOL, Abraham, his account of the labours of converted Jews to demonstrate the truth of Christianity from Kabbalistic works, 9; his cosmography, 10.
FRENSDORFF, Dr., 4, 23, 35, 39, 94.
FULKE, William, 51.

305

FURST, Dr. Julius, Geschichte des Karäerthums, 62.

G

GALATINUS, Petrus, his work entitled On the Mysteries of the Catholic Truth, 15.
GANS, David, his historical work called *Seder Olam*, 3; his date, and opinion about the edition of Levita's Grammatical work, 75.
GEIGER, Dr. Urschrift, 62.
GILL, Dr. John, on the antiquity of the vowel-points, 59.
GOOD Sense, book of, see LEVITA.
GRAETZ, his critique on Isaac Zarphati's Epistle, 7.

H

HARDING, Dr. Thomas, his controversy with Bishop Jewel, 50.
HEBREW, called Sacred, language, 195.
HEIDENHEIM, the Laws of the Accents, 65.
HEILPRIN, Jechiel, his historical work called *Seder Ha-Doroth*, 3; opinion about the date of Levita's publications, 75, 76.
HEREDIA, Paul de, Kabbalist, 9.
HERMES, the worship of, 98.
HEXAHEMERON, the work of, 98.
HILALI, Codex, 260.
HOLMES, Dr., his article, *Levita*, in Kitto's Cyclopædia, 2, 3, 79.
HUTCHINSON, John, his view of the Hebrew verity and the vowel-points, 60; his school, *ibid*.

I

IBN Aknin, 20.
IBN Al-Tabben, his date, and Grammar, called the Key, 259.
IBN Baalam, his date, and works, 123; his opinion about the antiquity of the accents, 123.
IBN Danan, Saadia, 10.
IBN Daud, Abraham, called Rabad, author of the Chronicle Seder Ha-Kabbalah, 108.
IBN Ezra, his date, and Grammar, 45, 125.
IBN Ganach, Jonah, 20, 131.
IBN Jachja, David, his contributions to Biblical literature, 81, 82.
IBN Jachja, Joseph, 10.
IBN Verga, Jehudah, 12.
ISAAC b. Meier, 2.

J

JACOB b. Asheri, called Baal Ha-Turim, his Massoretic commentary, 142, 143.
JACOB b. Chajim, editor of the Massorah, 9, 21; his date and works, 38, 39; his connection with the Ochla Ve-Ochla, 94; his Introduction to the Rabbinic Bible, 107, 109, 194.
JACOB b. Eleazar, his date, and Recension of the Bible, 258.
JEHOVAH, the mysteries connected with the name, 219.
JEHUDAH Ha-Levi, his work entitled Khozari, 126, 133; opinion about the antiquity of the vowel-points, 126, 127.
JEKUTHIEL Ha-Cohen, his date and Massoretic work, 257, 258.
JEREMIAH the prophet conceals a copy of the Law, 119.
JELLINEK, Dr. Adolph, his contributions to the History of the Crusades, 7.
JEROME, St., quoted in support of the antiquity of the vowel-points, 52, 53.
JETZIRA, the book, 98.
JERUSALEM, Codex, 260.
JEWEL, John, Bishop of Salisbury, his controversy with Dr. Harding, 50.
JEWISH CONVERTS diffuse Biblical knowledge, 9.
JOSE, b. Chalaphta, reputed author of the Chronicle *Seder Olam*, 108.
JEWS, persecuted at Mayence, 6; at Trent, *ibid*. Earnestly solicited by Isaac Zarphati to quit Germany, and seek shelter under the Crescent, 6, 7; expelled from Spain, 7; from Portugal, 8; their children forcibly baptised, *ibid*.
JUSTINIANI, translator of the More Nebuchim, 36.

K

KABBALAH, the, studied by Christians, 10, 12, 15, 39.
KALISCH, Dr., his notice of Levita in the Hebrew Grammar, 3; of Luther's and Calvin s opinions about the antiquity of the vowel-points, 49.
KERI and Kethiv, various opinions about the origin thereof, 103-112; numbers of in the Bibles, 115, 116.
KHOSARI, see Jehudah Ha-Levi.
KIMCHI, David, his Grammatical and Lexical works, 79, 107, 258; his opinion about the antiquity of the vowel-points, 121, 122.
KIMCHI, Moses, the time he flourished, 13; his Hebrew Grammar, 13, 36.

L

LAW, Synagogal Scrolls of the, 124; division of, for hebdomadal lessons, 135, 170.
LEVITA, surnamed Bachur, its signification, 2; the date of his birth, *ibid*; his removal from Germany to Padua, 7; his contributions to the revival of Hebrew learning, 10; his flight to Rome and interview with Cardinal Egidio, 14, 15; his journey to Fagius, 66; works, in chronological order:—

Commentary on M. Kimchi's Hebrew Grammar, 13, 14, 36, 80–83, 92.
Baba Buch, 14.
Bachur, 16, 73–76, 92.
Tables of Paradigms, 17.
A Treatise on Compounds, 17, 18, 80, 92.
Poetical Dissertations, 18, 19, 80, 92, 145, 199, 202, 219.
Concordance to the Massorah, 20, 23–35, 137.
Aramaic Grammar, 20.
Massoreth Ha-Massoreth, 40–44.
Treatise on the Accents, called *Good Sense*, 63–65, 114, 123, 204.
Tishbi, 68.
Methurgeman, 69–72.
Nomenclature, 73.
German translation of the Pentateuch, Five Megilloth, and Haphtaroth, 78.
German version of the Psalms, 79.
Annotations on Kimchi's Grammatical and Lexical works, 79.
LANDAU, 2.
LEVI, b. Chabib, 10.
LEVI, b. Joseph, his Grammar entitled the Vine-blossom, 122.
LIGHTFOOT, Dr., his view of the antiquity and authority of the vowel-points, 57, 58.
LETTERS, majuscular and minuscular, alphabetical lists of, 230, 231.
LOANZ, Jacob b. Jechiel, 10; teaches Reuchlin Hebrew, 12.
LOWTH, Bishop, his view about the vowel-points, 59.
LULLY, Raymond, his connection with the Kabbalah, 11.
LUZZATTO, Treatise on the vowel-points in Halichoth Kedem, 62.
LUTHER, Martin, his sentiments about the Jews, 38, 39; his view of the origin and antiquity of the vowel-points, 49.
LYRA, Nicolas de, his date, forerunner of the Reformation, his opinion about the vowel-points, 16, 17.

M

MAIMONIDES, his date and great philosophical work, 36; work on Biblical and Traditional Law, called Jad Ha-Chezaka, 114, 182.
MANTINO, Jacob, 10, 36.
MARTIN, Gregory, his opinion about the Hebrew vowel-points, controversy with William Fulke, &c., 51.
MASSORAH, how treated by copyists, 94; signification of the word, 102, 104; its order of the Bible, 120, 121; magna, and marginalis, 138, 139.
MEDIGO, Elias del, or Elias Cretensis, teacher of Mirandola, 11.
MESSER, Lion, his works, 10.
METHURGEMAN, see LEVITA.
MEZUZAH, the, 95.

MICHAELIS, J. D., Anfangs-Gründe der Hebräischen Accentuation, 65.
MIRANDOLA, John Pico della, his connection with the Kabbalah, 11.
MORINUS, John, his opinion about the Hebrew verity and the vowel-points, 50.
MOSES, Ha-Darshan, his date, and work on the Commandments and Prohibitions, 249, 250.
MOSES, the Punctuator, his date and works, 123, 124; his opinion about the antiquity of the accents, *ibid.*

N

NACHMANIDES, Moses, his date, opinion about the mystic import of the Law, 124.
NATHAN, Isaac, author of the first Hebrew Concordance, 21.
NATHAN b. Jechiel, 2.
NAPHTALI, see Ben Naphtali.
NATRONI II., b. Hilai, his opinion about the antiquity and authority of the Hebrew vowel-points, 44.
NOAH, the seven commandments of, 99.
NOMENCLATURE, see LEVITA.
NUMERALS, how expressed, 135, 136.

O

OCHLA Ve-Ochla, described by Levita, 93, 94, 138.
OWEN, Dr. John, his controversy with Bishop Walton about the antiquity and authority of the vowel-points, 58, 59.

P

PRATENSIS, Felix, editor of the first Rabbinic Bible, 9, 21.
PRESTER JOHN, 130.
PALESTINE, the seven productions of, 182.
PENTATEUCH, the, a copy of deposited by Moses in the Ark of the Covenant, 119.
PERREAU, Abate Pietro, 126.
PFEFFERKORN, his malignity against the Jews, 12; his date and works, 37, 38.
PINSKER, Einleitung in das Babylonisch-Hebräische Punktationssystem, 62.
PINNER, Dr., Prospectus, 62.
PISCATOR, John, his opinion of the vowel-points, 51.
PLENE, 145–148.
PROPHIAT Duran, see EPHODI.
PURITY of Language, an anonymous grammatical treatise, 126.

R

RASHI, 105.
RAYMOND Martin, his opinion about the Hebrew verity and vowel-points, 45, 46.
RICIO, Paul, his Kabbalistic labours, 9.
REMEMBRANCE, book of, see LEVITA.

REUCHLIN, his connection with the Kabbalah, 11, 12.
ROSSI, Azariah de, his date, refutation of Levita's arguments for the novelty of the vowel-points, &c., 52, 53; his Meor Enajim quoted, 122.

S

SABA, Abraham, 12.
SAADIA, Gaon, 20; his date, and philosophical treatise, 156, 269.
SACCUTO, Abraham, 10.
SCRIBES, their name and connection with the Massorah, 135.
SEDER Ha-Kabbalah, 108.
SEDER Olam, the Chronicle, 108.
SEMLER, J. S., his connection with the German translation of the *Massoreth Ha-Massoreth*, 42, 44.
SEFORNO, Obadiah, 10.
SELVE, George de, Bishop of Lavour, his literary connection with Levita, 22; encourages him to undertake the Massoretic Concordance, 23–25, 37.
SHRAJA, Joseph, 12.
SIMON b. Jochai, reputed author of the Sohar, 48.
SIXTUS IV., patronises the Kabbalah, 11.
SHIMSHON, the Grammarian, his date, and treatise on the vowel-points and accents, 257.
SOHAR, the, its view of the antiquity and authority of the vowel-points, 48, 121.
SPIRA, Meier, 257.

STEINSCHNEIDER, Dr., 2, 14, 17, 126.
STERN, Leseauge, 65.
SYNAGOGUE, the Great, its constitution, 107, 108.

T

TEMPLE, the Second, five articles wanted in it which were in the first Temple, 111.
TRANSPOSITION of letters, sixty-two instances of, 116.

V

VALENCIA, Jacob Perez de, his date, opinion about the vowel-points, &c., 47.
VOWEL-POINTS, the, controversy about their antiquity and authority, 44–63; becomes a dogma in Switzerland, 64; superlineary system of, 61; interlineary system of, 61, 62; Levita's opinion about their antiquity, 121, &c.

W

WALTON, Brian, his view of the antiquity of the vowel-points, 57.
WHITFIELD, P., on the antiquity of the vowel-points, 59.
WRIGHT, Dr. William, 100.

Z

ZAMORA, Alphonso de, his contributions to the Complutensian Polyglott, 9.

www.ingramcontent.com/pod-product-compliance
Lightning Source LLC
Chambersburg PA
CBHW071437300426
44114CB00013B/1466